A Far Away Place

Bear River

Mary Marvin McLeod

Edited by John McLeod

Copyright © John McLeod, 2013

All rights reserved

Library and Archives Canada Cataloguing in Publication

McLeod, Mary Marvin, 1920-2003

A Far Away Place, Bear River : a memoir / Mary Marvin McLeod ; edited by John A. McLeod.

ISBN 978-0-9918336-0-3

1. McLeod, Mary Marvin, 1920-2003. 2. McLeod, Mary Marvin, 1920-2003—Family. 3. Bear River (N.S.)—Biography. I. McLeod, John A., 1958- II. Title.

FC2349.B41Z49 2013 971.6'3204 C2013-900147-6

Layout and design by John McLeod

Cover and title page images from the John McLeod collection.

www.marymarvin.com

No names have been changed and all events have been rendered as accurately as possible.

Available 2014, 500 pages

Available 2015, 500 pages

Mary Marvin McLeod was born in Bear River, Nova Scotia, in 1920, the second of ten children, the eldest daughter. She grew up in Bear River and Kentville, Nova Scotia, and worked in Ottawa and Montreal during the war. In 1950, she married Duncan McLeod, a freelance writer, and they moved to Niagara Falls, the town of his birth. There, she had six children: three girls followed by three boys. After a dozen precarious years in 'The Shack' (on McLeod Road, no less), Duncan took steady work at McGill University, and the family decamped to Montreal. Mary began writing *A Far Away Place* in 1980 and worked on it until her passing in January, 2003 in Toronto. She is buried in Kentville with her brother Douglas and her mother. Since 2001, her son, John, has been editing the work and preparing it for publication.

A Far Away Place is a memoir in three parts covering Mary's life until she is 29. The first volume, *Bear River*, takes place in a small farming community in the 1920s. The second volume takes place in the small town of Kentville, Nova Scotia during the 1930s. *Ottawa* covers the war years and ends the trilogy in 1948.

Following *A Far Away Place* will be a collection of Mary's fiction, non-fiction, poetry and letters to her life-long friend, Mary Rochon, whom we meet in book 3 of *A Far Away Place*.

Images from the John McLeod collection

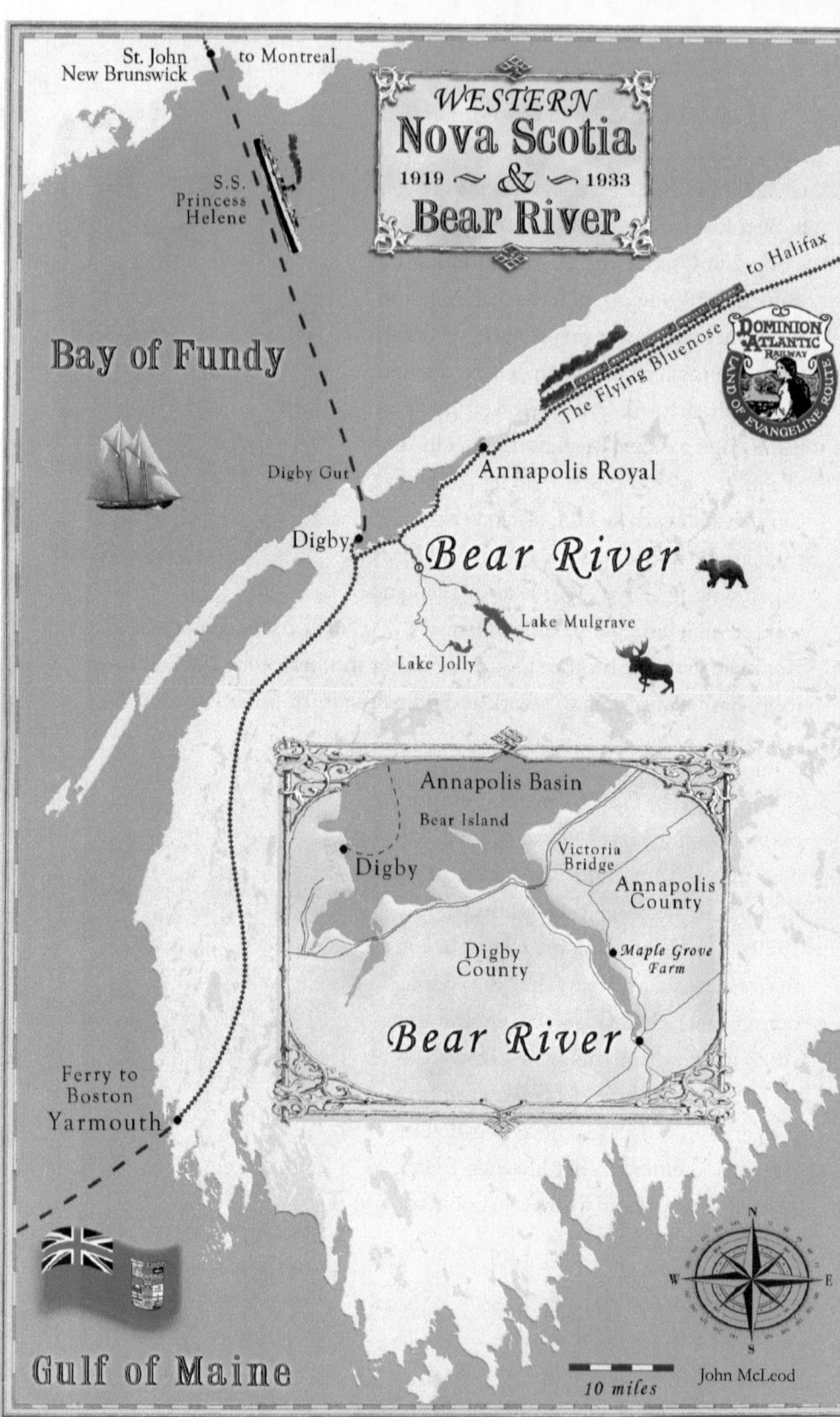

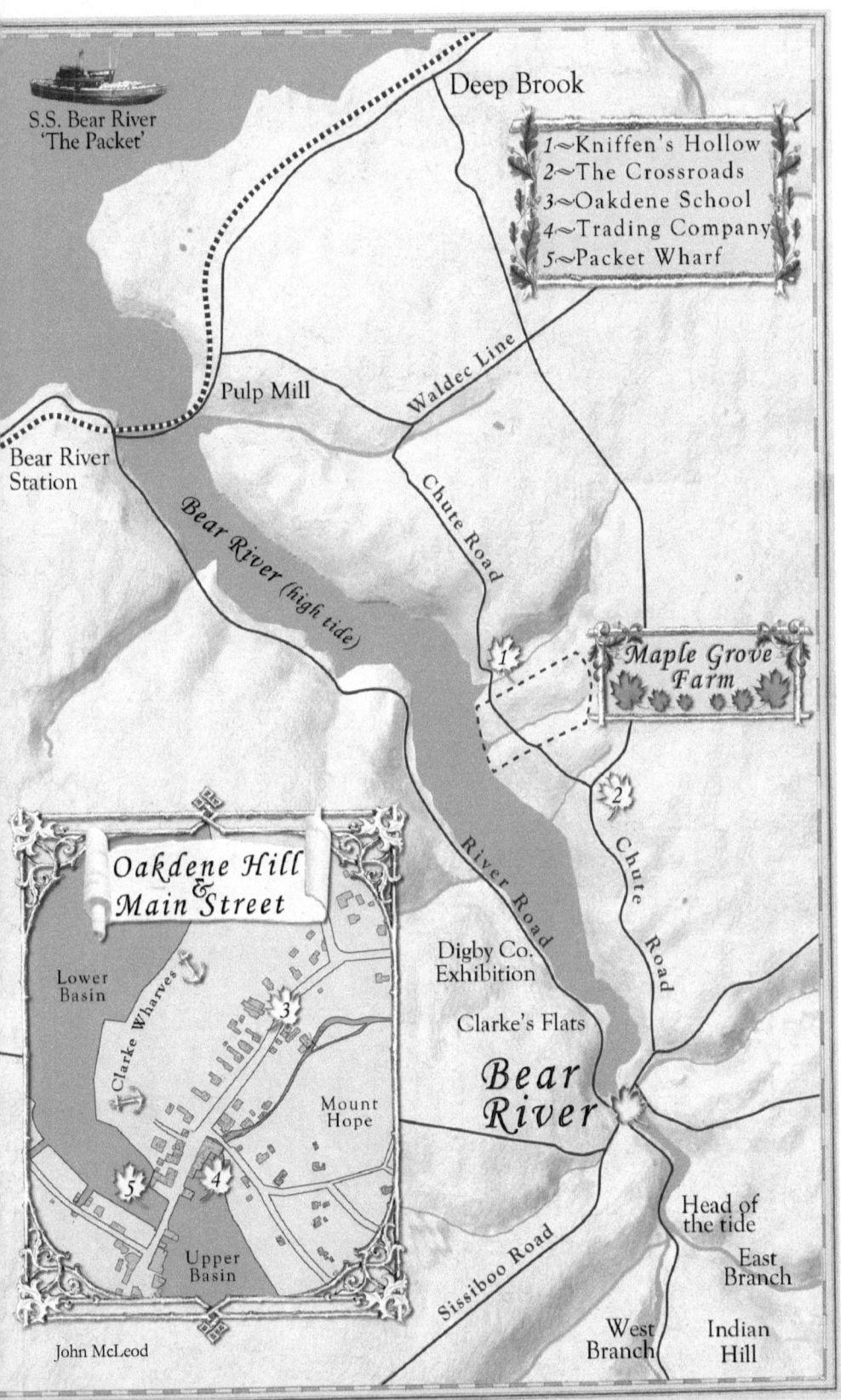

John McLeod collection

Bear River

Courtesy of
The Bear River Historical Society

And the dead shall return to live again

Mary Marvin

John McLeod collection

Daniel James Marvin and Mary Agatha MacGregor
wedding portrait, Helensburgh, Scotland, January, 1918.

***M**y **V**ery **D**ear **J**ohn:*

You have asked me to open my memory box, and though I never thought anyone would want to share my slice of life, which oftentimes I wanted to give away, still, it is my slice and I shall share it with you. Now that I have aged, I am satisfied that my life has followed a certain course set by the stars, and I thank them for it. Why should I do anything else? I am a Libra and I weigh the balance; it is an honest weight. At night when I go to bed, I look out my window, and the stars are always there, winking about the game of chess they have played with me. It is a humour after all.

Should I begin at the beginning, as Alice recommended, and go on to the end? That's all very well if you can find the beginning, but my beginning reaches beyond myself if I am to tell you all I know. No doubt I will pick up some dust along the way, but I shall stumble back and forth through traps and rabbit holes and eventually reawaken, not from a dream, as Alice did, but from the reality of my life, itself as sinuous as a dream. I shall drift like the tides of the Bear River, flowing through the village of Bear River, Nova Scotia, where I was born in 1920.

It would seem strange that a career naval man, as my father was, who had sailed the seven seas with the U.S. Merchant Marine, the U.S. Navy, the Canadian Navy and the British Navy, and had seen all the beautiful cities of the world, would bring his bride to a lonely, long-deserted farm amid the sleepy hills of Bear River. The bustling energy of the wooden ship building days was long since gone when my father arrived. The shambling, white-washed house was as old as the history of the village, one of the oldest in Annapolis County.

However, as a young boy he had sailed with his father to Bear River from their thriving tobacco farm near Charleston, North Carolina, and over time it had evolved into the place of his dreams to which the haunting pulled him back. Perhaps he had visited in the full flush of summer when the little village, which had pompously dubbed itself the Switzerland of Nova Scotia, was celebrating its annual Cherry Carnival–youth and midsummer being the gossamer web-spinners of nascent dreams.

By the time my father had grown up, the village had grown old and settled into the sunset of its golden years. Nor could succeeding generations revive the old heartbeat, because the main artery had ceased to function when the last wooden ship was launched and sailed out to the Bay of Fundy. Even so, the charm of the good old days remained. You can see it still, albeit muted and faded. My father was satisfied with the reflection of what was long gone and would say what a beautiful sight it was when, as a boy, he first saw all the sleek schooners plying up and down the river. As a child, as if I had inherited his dream, those ships plied in my mind too. It must have been a lovely sight.

Young lovers promise to die rather than abandon, so my mother willingly left her talents in Helensburgh, Scotland, where she was born, to eventually have them lost forever in the rough embrace of that demanding farm. But if talent cannot thrive, it can still survive, so the gardens, fields and hills of our farm echoed with Mother's truly beautiful voice. On bright, high summer days, it would seem she was singing its praises, but the farm was merely another stage for the one she had forfeited. Maple Grove farm was the stage on which her stars had plunged her.

Out of the shifting mists of my early Sunday afternoons, even before my brothers and sisters and I went to school, I recall how my father would dutifully read us the Bible, boring our little minds blank. We would escape the torture and run out screaming 'mene mene tekel', and other silly things that tickled our funny bones. And the great word 'begat', "If you don't give me a lick of your lollypop, I'm going to begat you till you're dead!" 'Smote' was another good word, after the deed, and 'smite' in the deadly present. We did a lot of whining about smoting and smiting. They all stuck, all misunderstood.

I haven't gotten around to reading the Bible much since then, other than picking and plucking at Ecclesiastics, but I do remember the caution to 'work by the sweat of thy brow.' It was here, at the beginning of their marriage and in the words of the Good Book, that my parents worked by the sweat of their brows and their very souls. Why did they persist in this struggle, for what dream? The vagaries of nature alone would destroy the dreams of rugged individuals, never mind sensitive artists with sensitive health. The farm was a death wish and they seemed not to know it.

Life could have been so simple and good had the family moved to Montreal, near Dad's workshop on St. Catherine Street, an hour away from St. Anne de Bellevue Military Hospital. It is amazing to me how two clever, intelligent people had such blind eyes. They spent most of their marriage apart, each struggling separately for the same madness, distancing themselves from each other in a way that they could never survive, and they would lose it all in the end–talents, health, farm and family.

Mother was too often alone bearing ten children and running the farm. Dad was just as often in Montreal, working out of a military hospital and maintaining his art work near a viable market, supporting the family and all the needs of the farm. Yearly, new equipment would arrive: a hay mower, a harrow, a whiffletree, a buggy, all paid for in beautiful brass work. If every field that was ever furrowed and planted, if every cove and hill could exhibit like a museum or a concert hall, they would show Dad's hammered brass and ring with the sweet, velvety sounds of Mother's voice. Every seed that was ever planted was hammered and sung to birth, over and over again for twelve years until souls were lost in the soil and barely survived the parting.

I didn't grasp that my father was a sick man, nor did I understand that he had to be away from home because of his health, and he had to make brass work to finance the farm. I had no idea of his division of time between hospitals, work and the farm, only a dumb awareness that it was necessary. It was an accepted way of life, and understanding came only when it was all over.

From my first moments of memory, I was aware that in some way our lives revolved around certain names: Camp Hill Hospital, St. Anne de Bellevue Hospital, Birks Jewellers, Mappin & Webb, The Handicraft Guild. On winter days, Mother would sit at the large oak dining table poring over Dupuy & Ferguson's and Burpee's seed catalogues, regularly dipping her pen to fill out the forms that would, in turn, fill our many gardens and fields. On the couch by the dining room window, we would studiously turn the pages of the flower catalogues, searching for our favourites. In the springtime of our lives we longed for spring, and it was on that couch that we would stand and observe the forbidding winter, licking peep-holes on the frosted window pane to check its progress.

Although she never complained, Mother could not have liked her life on the farm. But I do remember many, many times when she seemed sad and remote. She would stand at the dining room window, leaning on the sash just singing away as if she were really deep down crying, looking up over McCormick's hill, the only opening out of the farm, so compactly cupped by the hills and woods in its little valley. She didn't always know when Dad was coming home. Sometimes he would just appear in the doorway and there would be cries of surprise and tears. The happiness was always short-lived, welcomed with tears and ended with tears, but never a word of complaint.

Hired men would come to plow, spread manure, harrow and do the heavier chores until Dad arrived, but it was normal for Mother to carry pails of slops and middlings out to the pigs, her shoulders sloping with the weight. She would pitch hay down from the loft, ration out Harry's oats and wipe his coat dry of rain and snow, then curry and comb him and cover him with a blanket as she did her children. She would shovel manure from the stalls and pitch it out the trap door to the manure pile for the eventual fertilization of our gardens. At the chicken house, she would be met with baleful eyes and reproachful clucking that escalated into a crescendo as those frenetic creatures rudely trammelled each other to peck at their meal and grain. And the careful plucking of eggs from their nests while their backs were turned, or the outright theft of their fruit from beneath warm bodies when doughty hens refused to budge. Then she would send Ruff, our huge black and tan Airedale scampering over the pasture to round up the cows for milking. Daniel and I would sit in the hay and watch, following behind to watch again as Mother poured the warm milk into the whirring separator. It was a miracle–milk and cream. All the excess went into the butter churn to be rocked back and forth like a baby till every last creamy globule surfaced as if by magic from some secret hiding place in the milk. The realities of the farm could hardly have been what Mother expected. Never again would she find the solid, middle-class security of her parents' home. She would miss that certain gentility, surrounded by close-knit family and friends, involved in activities she loved.

John McLeod collection

Mother on Maple Grove farm in 1919. The inscription on the back reads: "Very fond of Canada, no pride and no hunger, no wonder."

Mother at 16, Helensburgh, 1911

MOTHER ALWAYS SPOKE FONDLY of her life growing up in Helensburgh, Scotland. Her memories seemed idyllic, and when she spoke of home, her enthusiasm bubbled over into her intense brown eyes. She was basically a happy person, and she clung to her memories of home, her life filled with pursuits she loved, the town peopled with aunts, uncles, nephews and cousins. The MacGregors were a vigorous lot who could step to their Morris dances all night, and some of them saw a century out.

Helensburgh was a neat little resort town fronting the Firth of Clyde and set against a hill that overlooked the broader expanse of Gare Loch. To the south was Glasgow and the river Clyde, the greatest shipbuilding region in the world, where the *Cutty Sark*, *Lusitania* and *Aquitania* saw birth and sailed into the history books. To my child's mind, nothing was more thrilling than seeing the little Packet plying up and down the Bear River. We would race to the top of the hay field for a last phantom glance, and I lived on that excitement until the next time. Mother's youth was filled with this excitement, and the childish wonder stayed in her soft voice as she described the magnificent Cunard ocean liners sailing past Helensburgh on their maiden voyages. From the home at 95 East Clyde Street, she only had to look out the front window.

Peter MacGregor married Elizabeth McCullach of Antrim County, Ireland, and together they raised ten children, of whom Mother was the eldest daughter, baptized Mary Agatha MacGregor. Her father called her Polly, and Mother claimed she was the apple of his eye, but then other children claimed the same. Elsie felt that she was the favoured one, because on the night their father died, he had given her the coveted halfpenny piece, a Sunday evening ritual. He was a gentle, well-loved father, and no man could have been a more devoted husband. In Peter MacGregor's eyes, his Lizzie could do no wrong, and she returned his devotion through a long widowhood of love that never waned. Elizabeth McCullach MacGregor (Grandmother) lived to be ninety-six years old, the last 50 years spent mourning her beloved Peter. Her early years pushed aside her old age as Peter MacGregor's placid blue eyes and delicate features gazed at her always from the brass picture frame Dad made for her.

Grandmother had a special pride that her Peter was head gardener at Ardencaple Castle, seat of the Clan MacAulay, onetime allies of the fighting MacGregors. This pride filtered down to the children, and Mother said that Ardencaple gardens were the most beautiful in Helensburgh. Peter MacGregor was piper for the laird, and after special occasions he would walk Mother through the gardens and tell her all about the many flowers and trees. He once said the grapes on the vines were counted. Grandfather passed his love of gardening on to Mother, or perhaps she was born with it, but in any case, a framed picture of Ardencaple castle hung on our parlor wall, and Mother's garden was the most beautiful in Bear River. She knew every type of flower, and in time, necessity extended her competence to the multitude of fruits, vegetables and grains that we grew on the farm.

The gardens of Ardencaple castle, Helensburgh

Mother's best friend growing up was her cousin, Ruby Friel, noted in the family for her impudence. They strode the school hallways arm in arm and attended the same classes. In art class, Ruby would draw humorous sketches of the drawing master and smuggle them across the room to Mother, who gave the works amusing titles. One day the teacher discovered Mother with a drawing but was puzzled by the perspective from the other side of the room. He wandered over, drawing in hand and quickly zeroed in on Ruby, her head cocked and one eyebrow arched defiantly. Assured of her guilt, he ordered Ruby to join Mother at the front of the class, using her last name only.

Lock Shiel near Glenfinnan

Ruby, hands on her hips, reminded the drawing master, "I have a handle to my jug as well as you!" Such cheek! Together, Mother and Ruby enjoyed the hurrying, scurrying lives of teenagers: train trips to Glasgow and Edinburgh for Mother's concerts, weekends in Dumbarton and Balloch to visit relatives, hikes to Argyll Forest and The Trossachs to revel in nature. At Loch Lomond, they peeked inside Rob Roy MacGregor's cave. At Ben Nevis, they climbed as high as was appropriate for energetic young ladies of the day. They spent weekends in the Highlands visiting Grandfather John and Grandmother Joanna (Stewart) MacGregor. The Highland train took them through Scotland's most beautiful scenery, past Fort William and up to Glenfinnan. There, they buggied along the shores of Loch Shiel to Grandfather's stone cottage, wedged against a remote windy hill. Grandfather John was into his active nineties and still worked as a shepherd. Grandmother Joanna was very frail and sat by the fireplace in her rocking chair, covered with a blanket and shawl. For her benefit, Mother and Ruby chatted in Gaelic, relaying all the family news from Helensburgh, while Grandfather sat poised with his chanter, anxious to accompany Mother and Ruby as they sang Scottish ballads. After dinner, he tended the kettle at the fireplace and made scones on the iron grill, a prelude to an evening of bracing Scottish history. Mother would laugh in remembering how she and Ruby sipped tea and nibbled scones while Grandfather regaled them with MacGregor war lore.

The howling wind would rattle the windows like restless souls as the outlawed MacGregor clan, their name abolished, were hunted down and killed like dogs by the dastardly Campbells. The feud took a turn in Bear River, where Dr. Campbell tended to all the family's aches and pains.

Years later on the farm, I heard the aunts and uncles laughing and reminiscing about Grandfather MacGregor's once-a-year forays to Glasgow to stone the Orangemen's parade. He walked the distance, stopping overnight at a graveyard to sleep on a fallen tombstone before thundering on, gathering stones along the way to throw at unsuspecting Orangemen. They said he was well over six feet tall, so he must have put on a frightening performance. Grandfather John MacGregor lived to be 104, still on his feet, having walked miles the night he died.

Painting by John Carlaw, steps from 95 East Clyde Street.

There is no doubt that the MacGregors had a musical gene. All of them sang and played beautifully, and family gatherings often graduated by degrees from occasional song into all-out caleigh.[1] It was a busy, happy home, filled with music as Peter MacGregor taught the five boys the bagpipes and the thin, flute-like chanter, while Grandmother, with her light, sweet voice, taught the five girls to sing. Almost from the first lesson on the first day, Mother surpassed her teacher, and by the age of twelve, her voice was fully developed. When I was much older and visited

---

1 Or Céilidh: singing, dancing and stories, repeated as often as necessary.

Uncle Douglas and Aunt Theresa in Helensburgh, they introduced me to friends and relatives who quickly recalled Mother by her voice: 'none other like it', 'the best I ever heard.' Mother's voice truly was exquisite. She soloed in school and church choirs and then performed recitals of her own. At one concert, a French Countess heard her and begged Grandmother to take her to France to have her voice properly trained. Grandmother said no. Touring the continent with a French Countess was no life for her daughter. The Countess pleaded, and to prove her character, she gave Mother a gold locket of religious significance and a book called *Fabiola or The Church of The Catacombs*, a novel meant to bolster the spirits of embattled Catholics in England. Grandmother wouldn't budge–a pious French Countess was still a Countess, and no girl of hers would be carrying on with that crowd. Mother had to content herself with concerts in Glasgow, Edinburgh, Dundee, and points in between. The Catholic cathedral in Edinburgh asked her to sing at Easter, when they had only ever had a male choir. Then Grandmother attended a rowdy music hall in Glasgow where Mother sang upon request "The Wearin' O' The Green," which just about sizzled Grandmother's liver. That was the dirge that ended Mother's music hall career.

At this point, I should mention the one insulting fact of Grandmother's life: that she was born in Ireland. When Elizabeth McCullach of Antrim County married Peter MacGregor, she sloughed off any and all attachments to her Irish heritage and didn't look back. She embraced Scotland and Scottish history and never again spoke of Parnell, St. Patrick or the Potato Famine. To her, it was a star-crossed calamity that she had been born there. The only time I ever heard her mention home was to convince me that the clouds over Ireland looked like potatoes. I suppose her inquiring, incisive nature helped her reject pixies and pots of gold and all those rainbows leading the Irish astray. She preferred the here and now, and actively involved herself in all the issues of the day. She rattled on about the trade unions, she ranted and raved about religion, and politically, she was a powder keg. As a result, all the MacGregor women held strong political views, though they didn't chain themselves to fences like the fashionable ladies of Glasgow and Edinburgh. Nor did they attack Winston Churchill or starve themselves on hunger strikes and get hauled off to jail.

Suffrage was the subject out on the streets, and Grandmother refused to 'go home and be still,' as advised by men in the know. At the dinner table, she briefed her daughters on the scene and structure of the patriarchy, the heroism of Emmeline Pankhurst, and the hegemony of the greybeards. Properly motivated, Mother and Ruby stomped through the streets chanting for the vote, not quite ready to hurl cobblestones, satisfied with being a nuisance factor in men's lives. The struggle for the vote politically activated Mother, though she only ever dabbled from a distance, reading the Hansard religiously and fuming over House of Parliament shenanigans.

With the vote secured, at least for women of sense over 30, Mother was sent off for a stint at the Poor Clare Convent in Edinburgh. In those days, young ladies were expected to know how to manage every aspect of the home. At the Poor Clare, Mother cooked, cleaned and sewed until she excelled in all the household arts. The curriculum also included accounting and purchasing, which led to Mother's first job at Thorburn's Cooperative on Prince's Street, five minutes from home. There, she found the business milieu as rewarding as music, and it wasn't long before Mr. Thorburn promoted her to manageress. It was at Thorburn's that my parents first saw each other. The war was on and Uncle Peter, Mother's younger brother, was working at a dry dock on the Clyde. He met my father, whose ship was being refitted, and after striking up a casual acquaintance, invited him home for lunch. On the way home, they stopped at Thorburn's, but Mother was too busy for an introduction, only noticing that my father was very handsome. She rushed home for lunch, first stopping at the coat tree in the hallway to take down Dad's officer's cap and read his name stamped on the inside band. When she stepped into the dining room, it was love at first sight. If Mother ever had any other boyfriends, I never heard them mentioned, not even when her sisters were raking their has-beens over the coals. Before Dad sailed, they were engaged. After Mother's death, I read the first letter she wrote him, thanking Dad for the beautiful engagement ring, never anything so beautiful, etc., addressing him, Dear Mr. Marvin, signing the letter abstemiously, Sincerely, with her full name, Mary Agatha MacGregor, as if he might forget. That funny little letter survived the war and both their deaths, the only one. Perhaps it was a private joke when Mother occasionally addressed my father as Mr. Marvin.

On Dad's next visit, they were married by Father Brown at St Joseph's church in Helensburgh. They honeymooned in Edinburgh, and Mother said that when they dined in the restaurant, she hoped no one would notice that they were newlyweds. But when the time came to pay the bill, my father reached into his pocket and pulled out a handful of confetti. The kindly proprietor offered to take the confetti if Dad would keep his money.

As if presaging, there was a surprising codicil to the marriage certificate. Grandfather asked Dad if he would take care of his family should anything happen to him, a tall order since there were ten MacGregors. Dad agreed and later kept his word, when in 1927, Grandmother and the rest of the clan blew in like a sirocco.

As it turned out, the marriage began unhappily. Dad sailed off to war and Mother heard nothing for many months. She thought him lost at sea, and her heart was broken, like those of so many young women. She prayed and prayed, and finally received word that he had been wounded, suffered temporary amnesia, and was recuperating in a hospital in Corfu. When he was transferred to Netley hospital in Southampton, Mother rushed down to be with him and learned that he had miraculously survived an explosion with only a small cut behind his ear, but the wound had developed an infection, and a subsequent operation in Malta made things much worse. Dad was suffering constant headaches, and the doctors didn't know what was causing them. It was only years later, when Dad was living on the farm, that the doctors discovered a tiny piece of shrapnel lodged in his brain.

Helensburgh, Clyde Street, 1920s

Daniel Marvin

*A*T A POINT WHEN I was very young, I realized that the subject of my father's family was closed, and there was no question about it–it was to remain closed. There was also no question that it was a bitter subject. I was curious to know all I could, but I sensed an unspoken anger as Dad quickly changed the subject or brushed it aside. I realized I could not ask any more questions. The few details I did learn were probably considered harmless for children's ears, and since they were so few, I hoarded them in my mind, memorizing names just to know and claim them as mine. After all these years, those names only emerge as underbrush barring the way to an open vista.

There is a strange parallel between my father's life and the life of his farm. Many years have passed since we left the farm in 1931, and nature has come into its own so thoroughly that it has covered our tracks as if we had never been there. Nothing is left of a single building, nothing is left of the gardens and fields. Nature has used them as a pedestrian walk of entanglement, and the dense growth reaches up over your head. Some enterprising woodsman, realizing the prize of the two dozen ancient sugar maples that lined our driveway, levelled every one. If you tried, you couldn't find the driveway that led to our house. Only one remnant lingers, but you must look closely, and that is the shy retreat of Mother's raspberry, blackberry, gooseberry, and black and red currant bushes. But there is a penalty as you try to pluck their stunted summer fruit: you get scratched as you reach, and the defending branches snap back in punishment like barbed wire. At the road leading to the farm, a sign is nailed to a tree–'No Trespassing.'

When my youngest brother, Robert, was out of Queen's University and teaching, he asked me to tell him about our father. Robert wasn't yet in school when Dad died. In cradling Dad's memory, I thought I knew him very well, but I realized that because of his frequent absences from home and his death when I was fourteen, I knew very little, and his memory was more or less the memory of my emotions, the pull and tug at the heart from departures and returns, like a tide washing in and out. Did I really remember him, or was it like pictures of ancestors hanging on the wall. I didn't know them, but I could see them, and my father's picture hung there too.

Had my memory of him filtered into that rotogravure portrait? His blue eyes, not the brown in the portrait, not dark, not light. His reddish-tinged hair. His wide and ready smile, his square teeth with the slight gap in the middle. Could I remember his southern accent, just so, and the way he looked on in absolute dismay at the mischievous originality of his children, hands on his hips, shaking his head and saying, 'Mah, oh mah! Wha yew littah bounders, barbarians, rascals, villains. Wha, ah'll eat mah shirt, Ah'll saw ma leg off, Ah'll be gumsquizzled!' His laugh, with that funny little hitch at the end of it, like a sigh of pleasure. His teaching me to make pastry, to roll it out, to beat up egg whites, and his reasoned reprimand when I didn't want to finish the job and wash up, all when I was eleven. And his many gentle reproaches that I have not forgotten, 'Sweetlady! Yew ah above that. Nevah answer an insult. Turn the other cheek.' All those things were nothing more than brief snatches. In the intimacy of family, having been the object of such love and care, I realized that is all my parents were in the end–brief snatches of memory. A minute past is memory, but Robert was asking for years. All was surface, all faded. I wondered if I knew them at all; there were so many blanks. They were indeed islands.

When we children were very young and all stuffed into double beds, we used to play guessing games before falling asleep and often tried to remember our first memories. Despite the ridicule, I always stuck to my story that I remembered Mother bundling me up on the kitchen table and I cried because I couldn't free my hands. "Oh no," they said, "that's a lie." Still, all my life I have had nightmares that I am desperately trying to free my hands. I found it strange that Robert's memory began with his first year of school. The only thing he could remember before going to school was playing in the sand pit by the Sanatorium woods in Kentville–significantly shifting sand. He remembered nothing of how Dad would pull him and David in the express wagon down to the post office and wait for us to get out of school. Dad would sit reading his papers while they both hung onto his neck screaming, "Dad, love me," and slobbering all over him, much to my embarrassment when I came around the corner and spotted this lavish display of affection. How could Robert's mind have lost hold of hot summer days when it seemed we did nothing but stuff ourselves full of ice cream filled with every known fruit, each child given his choice in turn.

The ice wagon would come along and the big block of ice would leave its perishing mark on the verandah and the back of children's pants as they sat on it to cool off. Dad and I would make the custard while the boys hovered impatiently or rushed over to Oakdene Square to summon little friends. Not even a cool splinter of ice refreshed Robert's memory. And the long walks we loved, Dad pulling the express wagon, his children following like a gaggle of geese. Or Sundays when we straggled up to St. Joseph's, sitting in sheer agony through mass, the two little ones on either side of Dad, the rest of us embarrassed, yawning or suppressing sniggers. Robert remembered nothing. Not even a kiss in perpetuity.

When I tried to sound out details I knew, the tones fell flat, so Robert probed by searching Naval records. For me, having known Dad, I had little interest in his Naval service. What did names like Havana, Vera Cruz, Corfu, Dardanelles, London, Pancho Villa, Pershing and World War I mean to me when I remembered him in Bear River and Kentville. They seemed almost unrelated to him. It was the more intimate details of family I would have searched for, but they were not to be found. Then Robert sent me a letter, and the printed word became more in focus than the picture on the wall. Robert' wrote the letter to me over twenty-five years ago, on May 31, 1960. This is Dad's information:

- Date of birth–August 10, 1890.
- Worked at the Great Lakes Shipbuilding Company, Detroit as a sheet metal worker (1906-1910).
- Worked with The American Steamship Co., Havana, Cuba, as a Marine Engineer (1910-11).
- Joined the American Navy (Marine Corps) May 25, 1911 under the alias of David Marx Barden.
- Gave as his next-of-kin Sarah Benton (his mother).
- Honourably discharged on 11 July, 1914.
- An investigation proved that David Marx Barden and Daniel Marvin were one and the same person.
- Came to Canada (date unknown).
- Joined the Canadian Navy in 1916.

Information on his Canadian Navy enrolment documents:
- Trade–sheet metal worker.
- Height–5'7"
- Chest–32-34-37
- Hair–dark.
- Eyes–brown.
- Weight–130 lbs.
- Personal marks–appendicitis scar.
- Next-of-kin–Mrs. Lewis Farris (cousin), Kentville, N.S.
- Transferred to the British Navy.
- Wounded in the Mediterranean.
- Convalesced at Corfu Hospital and in England.
- Honourably discharged.
- Died in Quebec City on March 7, 1935.

So ends Robert's letter, a trite collection of cryptic details that could never bring to life even a faint shadow of the man who was my father. When Robert sent me the letter, I skimmed over it, but as I look at it now, I realize I ignored significant questions and am surprised that I did. Troubling details surfaced, indelible in the printer's ink. Dad's year of birth is given, but no place of birth, which he said was Forest Gate, London, England. That distant place intrigued me, so I never forgot it. Nor did the letter offer any mention of his residence in Newport News or on the family tobacco farm in North Carolina, where he had lived from the age of seven months. In fact, there is no mention that he was an American citizen or even a Canadian. Under 'personal marks,' an appendicitis scar is noted, but he had a much more obvious one on his face, a long scar that followed his chin line very neatly. Dad said it was caused by a stiletto thrown by a Mexican bandit while he was stationed with the American Navy in Vera Cruz, where Pancho Villa was acting up. It could hardly be overlooked. I ran my finger along it many times when he held me. And his eyes were not brown; they were unmistakably blue. Next-of-kin was recorded as his mother, Sarah Benton, not Mrs. James Marvin. And why her maiden name? Nor was there any mention of his father.

Another mystery was the reference to Mrs. Lewis Ferris of Kentville, Nova Scotia, plainly designated as a cousin. When we moved to Kentville, I heard the name of Mrs. Ferris mentioned just once, when a lady passed our house and I asked Ruth Bowen who she was, since Ruth had been walking with her. Ruth said it was Mrs. Farris and she lived nearby. I never saw Mrs. Farris again. It seems strange that Dad would use her name as a relative, but make no attempt to introduce her to the family or even acknowledge her existence. She simply passed by.

The few details I know of Dad's upbringing I ferreted out on our long walks home from school, when we children had two miles to chatter. But many times when I thought I was getting answers, the boys would turn the tide of conversation to the war. They never tired of the same old stories and loved to repeat names like Mediterranean, Gallipoli, Dardanelles, Gibraltar and Bosphorus. They were fascinated without remorse or pity that Dad had been wounded as he stood on his corvette holding on to a brass stanchion. I don't think the continuous suffering of his head wound, even as he spoke, ever entered their minds. Dad had several sketch books filled with illustrations by war artists, and in the winter, the boys would pull those books off the shelf and lie on their stomachs on the shaggy, red wool rug in front of the Franklin fireplace, reading and commenting as they turned the pages. The depictions were quite graphic: dead soldiers on a ruptured landscape, splayed as they fell, wounded horses, barbed wire, raggedy men peering out of underground holes like furtive animals, vicious skies over stumbling, bandaged survivors. The boys laughed over and over at Bruce Bairnsfeather's puckish private who, it would seem, thought war a happy event. War was the only heritage they were interested in. Little else of Dad's former life escaped.

Dad spoke of his father, when he spoke of him, as if he were a prankster. He had worked as a cartoonist for a nameless London newspaper, and perhaps one must be a prankster to be a cartoonist. It could not have been very rewarding, because he left for Canada to fight in the Riel Rebellion, which was no more rewarding than cartooning and considerably more dangerous. He was wounded and fled across the border to the States. A question arises here as to his dedication to the cause. But in the end there was a reward, because as he recovered in hospital, he was tended by

Miss Sarah Benton, and she tended to him so well that they were married and repaired to her family tobacco farm in North Carolina. Since the tobacco farm had come to Sarah Benton's possession, perhaps she was an only child, but the question arises as to why such a favoured young lady would be nursing in a hospital up north.

The Marvins had five children, and I memorized their names from the first time I heard them: John, Hazel, Ruth, Margaret, and Daniel, who arrived on the scene when his siblings were grown. Of this sizeable family, Dad had not one single picture, nor one word of description other than that he liked Margaret the best. When I asked why he was named Daniel, thinking he was named after Daniel in the lions' den, he explained that his father was drinking and playing poker with friends and lost, and with the game went a bottle of rum and the naming of his soon-to-be-born son after the winner. If that seems far-fetched, that's what he told me. I was not impressed. I once asked Dad why the ministers in Bear River wore their collars backwards, and he said, "Sweetlady, that's because theah don't know any betta." He told us that his mother's family in North Carolina was full of 'bible pounders,' as he called them, and not one of them could preach or utter a sensible word unless drunk, "and then yew couldn't understand a word theah said." His father sounded like one of the bunch and not much better.

Dad seemed amused telling us about how furious his mother would get when his father drew unflattering cartoons of dinner guests. If his father was a prankster with a certain sense of humour, perhaps pompous, maybe shiftless and aimless, it would also appear that he was cruel and lacked any degree of Christian charity. Dad told of an incident when, as a boy, he was walking down the street with his father. A Negro approached, and when he didn't step onto the road, Dad's father took his walking stick and caned him off the sidewalk. Dad said, "Ah'll nevah forget the caning that Nigra took! It nevah should have happened."

Dad told of being punished by his mother for playing behind the barn with the pickaninnies, as he called them, his little Negro friends. They sang and danced to the mouth organ or Jew's harp and taught Dad the knack of clicking bones, which he demonstrated when the appropriate bones were left on our plates. He would click out a complicated rhythm and sing southern tunes about going home or times gone by. This was his only real sentimentality about home. Another time, he helped himself to the punch bowl before one of his mother's parties. Hearing her coming, he hid under the table, later to be hauled out dead drunk and given a sound thrashing.

At the appropriate time, Dad was sent off to the Naval Academy in Norfolk, Virginia, of which I know nothing other than that he learned to ride a horse expertly. He would leave Harry saddled at the barn and give a loud, shrill whistle through his teeth. Harry would thunder through the maple grove at full gallop and Dad would mount him with the ease of a stunt man. We loved it.

When Dad was in his early teens, his father put him on a ship as an apprentice engineer, and with that, he was out of the house for good. For several years, he sailed back and forth to Europe and around the Mediterranean before taking a job with the Great Lakes Shipbuilding Company. I don't think he ever saw home again. There couldn't have been anything waiting for him there. His home life seemed sporadic and stilted, a child among adults, shuffled out of their lives at their earliest convenience. Dad took nothing with him, no pictures, no possessions. He never offered a physical description of his parents, speaking only of his mother's discipline and his father's waywardness. Nor did he give any description of the house, the plantation, the household staff or the daily rounds in a family of five. He made no mention of school or childhood friends or early pursuits. He hadn't a word to say about Newport News, Charleston or Norfolk, and he never mentioned holidays or travel, except for the one trip to Bear River with his father. Nothing of his upbringing surfaced other than his obvious love of art, music and his observance of perfect table manners, which he visited upon his children.

Dad's name change to David Marx Barden when he joined the US Navy in 1911 is a mystery, and as I grope back for an answer using the slim details of his early life, I realize it will remain a mystery. Sailing around the world can keep anyone lost for years, even with identity, so I can only imagine what a young man of twenty would be escaping from with a name change. As for the 'Marx', I suppose it was a rebellious flirtation, because I heard Dad discussing politics many times, and his views never veered from simple common sense.

Daniel Marvin, second from left, with unidentified shipmates.

Enlisting in the US Navy allowed Dad to attend the prestigious Charleston Engineering College, after which he sailed on various battleships. The *USS Louisiana* comes to mind during his Mexican adventure. When Dad came to Canada in 1916, he joined the Canadian Navy as an ordinary seaman and immediately took the engineering exams to regain his officer's rank. The Canadian Navy operated close to home, so the British Navy exercised colonial privilege by snapping Dad up and shipping him to the war zone. Until he was wounded in 1918, Dad jumped from one ship to another, repairing and rebuilding damaged engines. It was dangerous work with the ship sitting helpless and the crew holding their breath as U-boats prowled. Dad would hammer and pound away, fashioning new parts and doing whatever it took to get the ship moving again.

Dad's father died during the war, and his brother John claimed his share of the inheritance, saying the family had been notified that Dad was killed in action. He refused to return it. I once asked Dad if he would ever go home, and he said no, he never would. The only time he attempted to visit the States was on a trip to Boston for an operation to have the shrapnel removed from his head. He was stopped at either Yarmouth or Boston, and Mother later explained that there was fine print about going to the States for an operation. I remember that trip well, the fall rain, Mother standing distraught as Murray Harris' taxi drove off. Perhaps she thought he would never come back, but he did the next day and things went on as before. Then Dad opened the Digby Courier and discovered that his trip and the reason for it were reported in the social column. I never saw him so angry, and I couldn't understand all the fuss just because his name was in the paper. He said, "I don't want my name in the paper." Dr. Campbell was the only person who could have divulged the information.

During Dad's convalescence in England, the doctors remained puzzled by his condition. He showed no visible symptoms other than excruciating headaches, but who can see a headache? They were at a loss to treat him with anything other than rest in a dark room, which seemed to help. When the war ended, everyone anticipated their return to civilian life, Dad had a wife waiting, and the doctors had a backlog of patients, so at the first sign of improvement, all agreed that recovery had occurred. Before leaving Netley, Dad was offered a full disability pension, but he declined, feeling it would be dishonest to take it while he still felt capable of work. Instead, he insisted that should his health fail, he would then accept it. This arrangement proved regrettable.

The British then returned Dad to the Canadian Navy, and he was shipped back to Halifax for demobilization. Upon his honourable discharge, Dad's plans were well laid. His dream was to have a farm of his own, and he wanted to know how to run it properly. His veteran's benefits offered vocational training, so he enrolled in the Agricultural College in Truro, Nova Scotia. Mother came to Canada three months later, the ship passing icebergs in June and Dad meeting her on the dock at Quebec City. She would always fondly remember that summer, both of them young and together for the first time. They boarded in a house on Robie Street, and she often talked of re-visiting Truro but never did. Those were likely her happiest memories of marriage.

In September of 1919, my brother Daniel was born, and shortly afterwards, Dad completed his studies. He had long ago decided where he wanted to live, so without delay, he purchased Maple Grove farm through the Soldier's Settlement Board, 160 acres on the gently sloping hills of the Bear River. The stately grove of two dozen sugar maples would welcome Mother with their oozing sweetness to the rambling, white-shingled home where she would begin a punishing life. After furnishing the house with necessities, depositing a horse and cow in the barn, and filling the chicken house with hens and a rooster, they were more or less destitute. Dad's stipend for attending school had ended, and many months of back pay had been lost on his discharge from Netly, and then lost again on his transfer back to the Canadian Navy. In addition, Mother's Separation Allowance, a monthly payment to the wives of active servicemen, had still not been paid after well over a year. Penniless and woeful, they hunkered down for their first Canadian winter, staring out the window at blizzards until the snow piled up to the eaves and they could stare no more. They ate quiet, candlelit dinners of chickens and their eggs and preserved peaches as many times a day as was necessary. Mother became so sick of peaches that she didn't serve them at our table again until I was fourteen. Then she conquered her emotions and opened a can of Australian peaches, which I went mad over. I couldn't understand her aversion, but it lasted all her life.

For Maple Grove to become the farm he imagined, Dad had to refit and repair it like a ship. He had decided upon early market gardening, and the overhaul must have taken several years, because one of my earliest memories is of watching from the kitchen window as Harry heaved and pulled out raggedy stumps from the apple orchards. That first spring, after the clearing, levelling, and planting, Dad's headaches flared up with a vengeance and continued into the summer. Soon he could only work a few days in a row before taking to his bed. Dad was a wreck and Mother was a nervous wreck with an eight month old baby, another one on the way (me), and no money coming in. Dad appealed to the military for treatment and asked for his pension, but the Canadian Navy knew nothing about a pension, not one granted by the British, and besides, his paperwork was still lost. But they offered to bring him in for examination, and if he qualified for a disability pension, then he would certainly get one. Dad went to Camp Hill Hospital in Halifax, and again the doctors found nothing wrong. They sent him home, his headaches flared up, and again he appealed for help. Back and forth he went for almost two years, trying to convince the doctors he was sick, but never visibly ill. In the meantime, he somehow established the farm and secured accounts to sell everything he grew. The Pines Hotel in Digby and the River View Lodge in Bear River were the best accounts to be had, and they took all he could supply them with. But Dad's health worsened until a serious bout gave Camp Hill no choice but to admit him. The doctors remained puzzled by his condition, and even when they discovered the shrapnel in his head, they still didn't consider it serious, because many men were carrying shrapnel and living normal lives. Yet that tiny piece of metal, so perfectly set, became the tenuous pivot around which our lives revolved. After being admitted to Camp Hill, Dad was transferred to St. Anne de Bellevue Hospital, just outside of Montreal, where he spent the winter. While Dad was an in-patient, Pensions granted him a stipend, which paid for hired men to help Mother in the winter. They would prime the gardens in the spring so that when Dad returned, everything would be ready for him to take over. Then in the fall with the fields set for winter, he would pack his club bag and leave for Montreal, always with a kiss on my forehead, his unspoken promise to return. Thus began the merry-go-round existence that patterned my young years.

Bear River. Unknown artist, circa 1910

THE GENESIS OF THE village of Bear River evolved from the river and the magnificent forest. The river was born of the twin glacial pools of Lake Jolly and Lake Mulgrave, initially trickling down, no more than twin brooks, the east and west arms eventually joining hands at what is known as the Head of the Tide. At this reinforced juncture, it flowed to find the sea, being effortlessly accommodated by twice-daily tides from the Bay of Fundy. On its journey, the river gently turned and widened and then deepened enough to allow schooners and barques to travel up the four miles from the Bay of Fundy and anchor at the village wharf to spill out their cargoes.

The forest was born out of centuries of rest on what was once a glacial bed. Still scattered among the trees are many giant boulders, and one can only assume that time itself was playing a game of marbles while pondering its evolution. As the ice melted, the giant, mittened hand of Nova Scotia grasped for air and light and warmth, pulling itself up to its present level, pushing back the ocean that once held it captive. It would seem that the dying pangs of the ice age gave birth, not only to the river and the forest, but also to its first inhabitants, the Micmac Indians. In time, the French and English aimed muskets at each other, so the Micmacs buried their hatchets and retreated peacefully to Indian Hill, where they hold lookout still.

The French had taken note of the Bear River, and on Champlain's map it bore the name of Riviere St. Antoine. John Cabot renamed it Riviere de Hebert, after a prominent apothecary whose medical prominence is lost, but is cartographically maintained by Bear River historians. The English fractured Dr. Hebert's name and the river became, in plain English, Bear River. It had nothing to do with bears, a common misconception, and this was carried further still by the naming of the small island at the mouth of the river, Bear Island. The Micmacs disagreed on this point and claimed credit with their own legend. One day, three squaws were cooking by the river's edge when three hungry bears stopped by for a bite. With no other thought than the safety of their three babies, the squaws attacked the bears and were promptly swallowed whole. Happily, the bears choked to death. When the braves returned from the hunt, they found three hungry babies and three dead bears, which they promptly tossed into the newly named river. The tale remains open to embellishment.

The first wave of settlers in Bear River, who obviously impinged on the preserve of the Micmacs, were Prussian soldiers exiting the U.S. after their failed mercenary efforts in the American Revolutionary melee. Perhaps the British appreciated their efforts, or perhaps they hesitated over seasoned soldiers returning to Germany, where Frederick the Great would hire them out once again. In either case or both, the British offered the Prussians 400 acres in pristine Nova Scotia, plus a little something to get started. The soldiers, with no better offer on the table from miserly Frederick, and perhaps getting a little tired of his Prussian syndrome, misinterpreted his orders to return to the land. Perhaps they could claim misunderstanding since Frederick refused to speak his native language, preferring French, though he hated the people and was continually cooking up things to do to them. The soldiers could feel quite safe in Nova Scotia, since Frederick saved money by not having a navy and was therefore unable to retrieve his wayward subjects. He squandered Rix dollars on many things, but was penny wise for appearance's sake, wearing his one dress coat stained with food and snuff all his life. So Frederick the Great, who rarely did a good deed or even an insignificant kindness except by accident, was in a way responsible for building up Bear River, as opposed to tearing down Europe. Speculative, you might say, but history is as speculative as the stock market. And it doesn't hurt to speculate that this pretty little village originated because of the deviousness of Frederick's troops, abandoning his mingy paternalism, well beyond his reach, and exhibiting good sense in establishing a creditable ancestry. This preamble explains the German names I remember, like Heisler, Henniger, Zinck, Oickle, Vroom, Albrecht, Rosenkrantz, Snell, Schmidt and others. And then there is the Waldec Line, and somewhere nearby is a stone monument to those settlers, an old and almost forgotten echo.

After the Germans came the Loyalists, fleeing the U.S. to remain British subjects, followed by the ever-present pioneering Scots. Each wave of settlers snipped and clipped the magnificent trees, floating them down river in booms to bring to life a thriving era of ship building at wharves and landings strung along the length of the river. For a hundred years or more, the ring of hammers played tattoo over bird song.

Boats slipped from wharves like sleek sailfish, crowding the river and running out with the tide. The magnificent oak and maple of Bear River sailed the world. Local merchants built their own ships and sent them as far away as China to fill the shelves of their stores.

The major heart-beat of the village died when the last wooden ship was built and sailed out to the Bay. Gradually, wharves positioned along the banks of the river rotted and slumped, leaving their skeletal remains. Fallen pilings were lodged against the shore by the daily tides, and over the years were bleached white like stacked ghosts, pale reminders of Bear River's world-renowned sailing sloops. When Dad walked us home from school, we could look down to the opposite bank, and he would point out with his walking stick the remains of old wharves.

It has been claimed that the shipbuilding era ended in the early 1900s, but that is not true. The very last ship was launched in September of 1925 on my first day of school, an event I couldn't possibly forget. As Dad walked us down Oakdene Hill, shouts, whistles and fanfare filled the air and followed the ship's wake that sunny morning, marking the demise of an era with a flourish and firmly establishing in my mind my first day of school. Dad said it was the last wooden ship to be built in Bear River. It slipped into the water shortly before nine o'clock from the wharf beside Mrs. Schmidt's store.

There were many elderly people in the village who had savoured the tail end of the good old days, and when memories revived, they eagerly launched into the telling when Dad met them along the way. The large and lovely old homes proved that the good old days had been very good. Dad liked to discuss the history of the village and made us feel a special pride in it. And I did. I never liked the farm, the dirt and manure piles, the barns and outhouses, but living in the heart of the village in one of those stately homes with no other disturbance than the Sunday church bells seemed like the most wonderful of dreams.

The beauty of the village was emphasized when I made my first trip to Digby to see my first circus and beheld the strange sight of miles of racks of cod fish drying in the sun and scenting the air. Digby held no charm. For many years until I was eleven and visited Halifax, the village of Bear River remained an orderly, contemplative still-life.

In their pride, the early residents dubbed the village 'The Switzerland of Nova Scotia' and the misnomer adheres to this day. It is true that the hills rise steeply from the riverbanks, but they are no Alpine peaks. Dad called it 'The Venice of Nova Scotia,' a flattery I only ever heard from his lips, but you must remember that he loved Bear River as much as Frederick the Great's absentee Prussians. Before I went to school, my brothers and I would sift through a cardboard box full of postcards that my father had collected from every port of the world. Over the years, cracks and dog-ears made by careless children added to the ancient ruins. My favourites were the great cities of Italy. I once asked Dad why people said 'See Naples and die', and he replied, "Ah say, see Naples and live." The smouldering, conic hill of Vesuvius was all very nice, but the architecture along the wondrous canals of Venice gave me pause. Even to my child's eye, Dad's comparison with Bear River was blatant exaggeration. Personally, I thought it could be nothing less than '*The Moldau* of Nova Scotia.'[1]

In the village proper, the banks on either side had been extended and plumped up with boulders in order to provide a platform for the half-dozen or so stores along Main Street, whose business was in effect conducted in the middle of the river. They scarcely had room for their entrances to cling to the sidewalks, and their back doors swung open to the river. The buildings sat perched on pilings anchored in the mud flats, and the twice daily rise of the tides lapped at their undersides.

---

[1] From Smetana's famous *Ma Vlast* (My Homeland) tone poem. The Vltava originates from two streams, which unite to course majestically, just like the Bear River.

Nova Scotia Archives and Records Management

It didn't matter that the facades of the village stores lacked artistry even by modest standards, and were makeshift on their pinions anchored in the river bed. There were no Roman numerals on cornerstones to lend the patina of glorious age, dignity and history. They were not necessary to make a declarative statement—a century and a half has passed and they still stand, clinging to the sidewalk the same as ever, and not a single building has collapsed into the river. And that is a wonder. After all, it would be an easy thing for the river to reclaim its territory, but it has done no such thing. It has gently acceded, except for one or two buoyant occasions in the rush of spring when it lifted the moorings of the bridge and left the town divided. The river, in fact, gave the village a split personality, because one side of the bridge rests in Annapolis County and the other side rests in Digby County; one half once called Hillsburgh, the other half once called Bridgeport. The charm of the village lay not with its architecture, but with the river and its banks, which rise without preamble to the hills. There was one other flattering deception in praise of the river's beauty: it was once called the Rhine of Nova Scotia, all five miles of it. It is plain to see that the settlers loved Bear River from the beginning: the Micmacs overlooking from Indian Hill, the French, English, Scotch, Americans and Prussians, whose names and flattery remain. And Shakespeare said 'what's in a name'! The homogeneity of the little village was fused by many races and creeds, two municipal bodies and two county bodies, all laced up by the scalloping hills and the peacefully flowing river.

Mary with Donald

THE INCIDENCE OF MY birth on September 29, 1920 places me in the midst of this preamble, two miles from the sleepy little village of Bear River on Maple Grove farm, edging the Chute Road before it dipped down to Kniffen's Hollow and ambled along a few miles to the Waldec Line. Daniel preceded me by a year on September 24, 1919. Eight siblings followed at yearly intervals: Jim, Douglas, Lorna, Joan, Donald, David, Robert and Ian.

A very significant thing happened when I was two, and it left a mark for me to carry to this day. Mother recounted it many times as one of her worst nightmares, always repeated in a tone of voice edging on horror that kept revisiting itself with repetition. Daniel had taken me down to the wood pile and decided to test his strength by lifting a crowbar, which he then let drop on my head. He came home alone, and when Mother asked where I was, Daniel said he thought I was dead because I wouldn't wake up. Mother had premeditated every possible accident on the farm except for that one. She ran down to the wood pile and her scream could be heard across Annapolis County. Dad ran in from the gardens and carried me non compos mentis to the house before galloping in to the village for Dr. Campbell. I regained consciousness with a noticeable dent in my forehead, which I still have, and, as I was led to believe, a noticeable dent in my intelligence.

Before this happened, Mother said I could recite all my nursery rhymes, especially Dokker Fosser went to Gosser, (Dr. Foster went to Gloucester), my all-time favourite. Immediately afterwards, I lost interest in the muse and began to stutter, saving all my intelligent conversation for my dolls. Mother had always been worried about my climbing up to strange out-of-the-way places, but I stopped that too. She had once left me in the kitchen with the doors closed so she could get meat from Eugene Croscup and not worry about my darting near the horse. When she returned, I was sitting on the breakfast table with jam in my hair, sucking on a piece of bread I had dipped in the teapot, having buttered the clock as well as myself. Then one rainy day, she locked me in the upstairs bedroom so she could pick some vegetables in the garden. I was determined to go with her, so I climbed on a chair, crawled over Dad's drafting table and jumped out the window.

Mother said she froze as she watched me float down, land on the grassy embankment and slide down before running up to her. It seems that by the time I was two I had done my worst, and after being hit on the head with a crowbar, I lost my zest for adventure. I became a very quiet child who sat on couches and talked to my dolls. My father would say, "Sweetlady, what do yew have to say to your old Dad?" I would say, "Nothing." He would say, "What are yew thinking about?" And I would say, "I'm not thinking." This went on for years. He was trying to find out if I was mentally retarded. He would sit me on his knee and probe the dent in my forehead, asking if I was sure it didn't hurt. Of course I remember nothing of these early incidents, and perhaps Daniel would not have remembered what he did, had it not been brought up so often, and had there not been such concern about my head and the contents within. This concern trickled all the way down the grapevine to the youngest child and lingered until I left home. When the seed of an idea is planted in little minds before the age of reason, it can germinate and never lose hold; it just flowers and flowers, watered by reminders. The dent in my forehead was like the mark of Cain, and I was never allowed to forget. Sibling voices echoed at opportune moments, 'She got hit on the head with a crowbar.'

 I think I can pinpoint almost to the moment when I was made aware that I was no genius and Daniel was. I was three-and-a-half and Daniel was four-and-a-half. Dad came home from Montreal for spring planting and brought with him a blackboard, a box of chalk and an eraser. We got slates with stylos every Christmas, and while I doodled, Daniel was printing out significant words and reading from large books. All in all, he lived up to my parents' grand expectations. With the blackboard, Dad got busy on the next stage of his learning, arithmetic. Before the summer ended, Daniel was counting up to unknown quantities, backwards and forwards. Mother and Dad beamed with pride, and their praise issued forth. Without a doubt, Daniel was ready for school in September. The pride and excitement rubbed off on me, and I wanted to be part of this cabalistic world of numbers, so I pestered Dad to show me. When he came in before dinner and sat on the dining room couch to teach Daniel, I would watch from the side, told to keep quiet. Then one day I got my turn. Dad patiently tried to explain that one plus one is two, but the way I saw it, one was one and individual ones didn't lose their identity by becoming twos and threes. Having bogged down in philosophy, I more or less cancelled out the applied sciences. Dad made no further headway and finally conceded to Mother, "Dearie, she just can't grasp." Daniel was good at catch-words, and I might have forgotten the whole incident if he didn't have a memory like an elephant and often reminded me that I couldn't grasp, not just one and one, but many other things as well. At four-and-a-half, he had blossomed into an arrogant male egotist, a prime example of a little knowledge being a dangerous thing.

Daniel never let me forget his superiority, but even at that young age, we were devoted to each other. We openly shared all our thoughts, all our dreams. Daniel always honestly confided in me even when he lied outright to Mother and Dad. We respected confidences and never betrayed them. Ours was a holy alliance of sacred trusts, the foundation built pebble by pebble. These childish things structured our faith in each other, a faith established long before we toddled together with our arms around each other's necks on the way to school, he carrying my books. Daniel was my rock, my dearest and most faithful friend.

There was always a sense of loneliness on the farm, a wanting to get away, to be somewhere else. It could have started when Daniel and I were allowed to climb to the top of the steep hay field in front of our house and sit on the large flat rock where Mother could see us. The flat rock had once been the front step of a house that had burned down. Up there, you had a sense of worldliness, of having seen the world, at least another world. You could look out over the hills to the countryside beyond. You could follow the river from the Exhibition buildings all the way out to Bear Island, and then gaze past the Annapolis Basin to the Bay of Fundy. Trains would rattle across Victoria Bridge, whistling an open invitation. In the distance we'd see the Princess Helene steaming out of Digby for St. John, sailing as majestically as any ocean liner. Daniel said it could sail around the world and I believed him. There was always that timeless allure wrapped up in the sea, the promise of something more, just over there. At the top of the hay field, you could feel the ebb and flow of the endless tides, the tugging and pulling of clouds drifting on the breeze as thoughts reached out to some formless dream.

Daniel and Uncle Peter

One Sunday morning, we climbed the hill through an unusually thick fog, calling out to each other to keep our bearings. Our voices echoed all around us like past, present and future as we groped our way up, lost in a dream sequence. Daniel found the flat rock and we sat staring into nothingness waiting for the fog to lift. On days like this, we knew it would mysteriously roll up the hill to reveal a sunny day. A fog horn with its bovine call pulsed restlessly through the mists as if it were climbing up from the bottom of the river. It was a lovely sound drumming on ears on dark nights, as comforting as a lullaby, a reminder that you were not alone. Then the bells of all the village churches began chiming down the river, ringing like an army of angels. As we sat in heaven's anteroom, we heard the Kniffen's horse clip-clopping through the mist like a ticking clock. Every Sunday, the Kniffens and Mr. Bishop would drive by on their way to church, neatly posed in their buggy. We called down, and Mr. Bishop answered from miles away.

On sunny days when Dad delivered vegetables to the Pines Hotel, Daniel and I would race up the hill and sit there waiting until Harry had driven into the village, crossed the bridge and turned up the River Road on the Digby side. When we spotted Harry clopping along, his hooves echoing across the river, we would shout across and wave excitedly. Harry always responded by breaking into a trot, though I was never sure if he heard us, or if Dad encouraged him with a slap of the reins.

Daniel was my early mentor and I learned a lot from him on the flat rock. One day as we lay in the sun, he had me close my eyes and focus intently to see the blood coursing through my eyelids. Another time he said he knew all about the ozone and would teach me how to hear it. Suspecting it was another of his horror stories, I refused, but he dragged me up the hay field and made me lie flat on my back. First I had to breathe deeply to clear my mind, so I started a big argument about that wild idea. Deep breathing was an exercise Dad forced on us when we sat around the house too long in the winter. He would make us stand up and take deep breaths to clear our minds and get our blood circulating. In the summer, he would line us up on the grass by the Bartlett pear tree and put us through our stretches and deep knee bends. Toddlers would roll over backwards like rubber balls and Mother would laugh and say she had never seen anything so ridiculous.

Jim

But Dad did it the navy way. When the boys shinnied up the swing rope like monkeys, Dad would smile and say that one day they would make 'fahn sailahs' (fine sailors).

After arguing about deep breathing and cleared minds, Daniel was absolutely determined and forced me back down on the rock. He thought that listening to the ozone was something wonderful, and he wanted me to experience it. I was to stop listening to the birds chirping, the dogs barking, the horses on the road, and even the wind. I was to listen to the air. For a while we both lay at the top of the hay field breathing deeply, and then he told me to literally leap above the clouds until I heard a humming like hydro lines. There we lay, trying to find depth in our consciousness, waiting for the ozone to appear, and then I heard it, a distant, distinct hum, way up there, lifting me into the upper stratum, high above the miseries of the moment and the earthiness of the farm. Daniel said the best time not only to hear the ozone, but also to sniff it was after a thunderstorm, so after every thunderstorm, I would smell the ozone, and whether it was true or not, the air did smell delicately sweet. Several times that summer, we climbed to the top of the hay field and lay on our backs communing with the ozone. One day Mother called and interrupted Daniel's deep breathing; he had left some chore undone. He stood up and yelled down that he was listening to the ozone. Mother was emphatic, "You get down here in two shakes of a lamb's tail you little villain or I'll ozone you. You'll get more ozone than you ever dreamed of!" Down he flew, but not for long.

Jim and I were a good example of family genes rubbing the wrong way, almost from his cradle days. When Jim started crawling and toddling about, Mother had me watch over him because he simply couldn't be contained. Jim had things to do, and I stood in his way. He quickly broke free. I remember once when Dad returned from the village with sugar candies for all of us. I chose my favourite, maple, and it was so good that I decided to save half for the next day. Jim, a toddler, ate his and then wanted mine as well, crying in outrage when I refused. He caused such a fuss that Mother, busy and frustrated, made me hand it over. I was furious that I couldn't keep what was mine. Jim, so young, learned his lesson. He saw me with Daniel and claimed his territory. What can one say about sibling rivalry?

I suppose I was jealous when Daniel and Jim bonded rolling balls across the floor and playing rubber ducks in the copper bathtub. From then on, they teamed up like two sides of the same coin, putting a different stamp on the same efforts. Daniel brazenly defied Mother and Dad, while Jim tested boundaries with a mischievous flair, masterminding bouts of creative destruction that left Dad shaking his head, "Dearie, ah see it, but ah don't believe it." Both excelled in school, with Daniel playing in the orchestra and Jim sidetracked by sports. Looking back, Jim is something of a blur: running off to the woods with Daniel and Douglas, clutching Harry's mane as he galloped across the pasture, tearing across the mud flats at Kniffen's beach. Jim was a busy boy, a boy's boy with no time for girls who read poetry and talked to their dolls. He was as irrepressible as Daniel, his feet not quite on the ground, always in motion. There was a casual courage to Jim, a readiness to take risks, and it served him well, when after years of skating up and down the hockey rink and racing around the basepaths, he finally took flight and buzzed through the worst air battles of World War II.

Daniel and Jim were more casual observers of nature, more interested in marketing vegetables to the Pines Hotel and wandering about the Digby docks, comparing boats and chatting with the fishermen. Industry and commerce activated them, but Douglas was different, he was a true child of nature, like an Indian who early on understood its mysterious connection to his own life. The moment he crawled out of his cradle, he dropped his rattle and headed for the woods. He needed no toys, though truth to tell, once Christmas was over, so were the toys. Douglas loved to wander alone, and before he started school he knew the woods from front to back. Early in the morning, he would slip off by himself and stay out all day, exploring like a pioneer, even through downpours and thunderstorms. He swore that trout nibbled best when it rained.

I remember sitting on a blanket under the pear tree tending the baby while Douglas, who was very young, kneeled patiently with a sprig of grass prodding bugs. Mother was sitting at the back porch bunching vegetables and asked, "What are you doing, Douglas?" Staring intently in the grass, he said, "I'm tickling bugs." Dad would see him on all fours with his nose in the grass and ask, "Duggy Don, what ah yew doing?" Douglas would say, "I'm looking."

He looked a lot. He sat for hours, staring with studied fascination at his jar of frog's eggs, and then he sat for hours more, closely examining the tadpoles until their final evolution. In the bedroom, a lineup of jars held spiders, centipedes, beetles, crickets, and other bugs I couldn't even look at. He had shoeboxes filled with woodland treasures: leaves, bird feathers, snake skins, anything at all. In his pockets, he kept his latest conversation piece, a fossilled rock or a tiny animal skull. His prized butterfly collection sat on a shelf, a plain piece of cardboard dabbed like a painter's palette, the delicate bodies stabbed through with common pins. I would look out the window and see him racing across the hay field with his butterfly net held high, chasing the beautiful monarch, the most favoured.

To me, life was a bore with nothing going on but babies; occasional interests suddenly waned, but Douglas was enthralled by everything and never stopped bubbling about the wonder of it all. After a day in the woods, he would sit at the dining room table and rattle on about foxes, deer, porcupine, skunk, birds that never came out of the woods, brooks with the biggest trout. Mother and Dad kept him supplied with books and magazines about flora and fauna, which he read and re-read. One day he found an orange fungus, all fingered and scalloped. He thought it beautiful, so he gave it to Mother. She accepted all his little tokens, but this one she threw in the stove, saying, "Oh the nasty thing! It's full of poison." Douglas disagreed, explaining like a botanist all the danger signs. Despite Douglas' assurances, we always stood off when looking at mushrooms, as if we could be poisoned by a glance. Schoolyard stories told of people who fell dead over their plates after one bite.

Another day, Douglas returned with a handful of newborn field mice that he had found in the tall grasses by the river road leading down to our beach. He held out his cupped hands as we crowded around to observe the tiny mice, no bigger than fingernails, their pale blue veins pencilled through pink tissue skin, closed eyelids much too large. They barely looked alive but for the visible beating of their hearts. Douglas wanted to raise them, but Mother made him return them to their nest, where the marauding cats would take up the issue. Those were the only mice I ever saw on the farm.

Douglas knew where all the bird's nests were and kept his collection of bird shells in a shoebox, the robin's egg blue flamboyant against the whites,

Douglas

John McLeod collection

beiges and speckled browns. He imitated every bird, and I don't think there was one he was not on calling terms with. On our way to school, he would break off from the group and whistle to a friend nesting nearby. We were amazed when he caught a crow and taught it to say its name, Jimmy. He kept it caged in the apple packing house until one day, Dad was startled out of his concentration at the work bench by a strange voice. He thought he was hearing things until he moved some crates and found little Jimmy, who then introduced himself. Dad marched Douglas into the apple packing house and made him release it, along with several captive squirrels.

Douglas was of a different mold, but of a mold that Mother understood. They were early soul mates. He was the only child who responded to her love of flowers and birds. She had several bird books, including a beautiful Audubon that Douglas often borrowed to identify a newcomer to the field. Mother had so much to do, but when Douglas started talking birds, they would sit down with their heads together and flip through pages. When he brought her flowers from the woods, he always looked for something new, and Mother would sit and listen as he pointed out subtle differences. Woodland flowers were so tiny and delicate that some could barely be called flowers, but Mother always put them on the kitchen window sill in a chipped tea cup, keeping them until they dried into withered stems.

Daniel, Jim and Douglas had several hundred acres to run ragged and barefoot over, and they knew every inch. On summer nights, they would go to sleep mumbling about getting up at the crack of dawn and fleeing to the woods. The moment they opened their eyes in the morning, they would spring out of bed, and I'd hear them whispering, "Let's build another tree house, let's look for partridge, let's trap squirrels, let's snare rabbits." They would quietly rustle about in the kitchen for bread, potatoes and a frying pan, and off they would splash through the grass with the compulsion of runaway horses. Dawn would break with a hushed pink haze and dry their tracks in the heavy summer dew. Shortly, Dad would come in rattling a pot and singing his hymn to the morning, "Rise and shine, shake a leg, shake a leg, the sun is melting the trees," but no sound would come from empty beds. He would stand with his hands on his hips and say, "Ah will eat mah shirt. Those littah bounders! Dearie, they've given us the slip."

With the late-afternoon shadows, they would return like homing pigeons, but often Daniel and Jim came back without Douglas. Nothing disturbed Mother more. When the boys were off in the woods together, that was different, but one missing child at the end of the day left an ominous gap. If no one knew where he was and it was getting late, Mother would stand at the back door, cup her hands and call up towards the pasture. Then she would send Scotty, our Scottish sheep dog, and if he couldn't find him, the rest of us would soon follow. Our searches started at Kniffen's Brook and moved upstream as our voices chorused over the hills. Many times, Dad said to Mother, "Dearie, calm yourself. That littah boy has the nose of a bloodhound." Douglas had explained that you could never get lost in the woods if you followed the brook. I can still see Mother sitting at the back door worrying about Douglas, bunching carrots for delivery and noting everything in her account book. It was a job that had to be done no matter what, while everyone searched and called.

One day when Douglas failed to appear, Mother called and called before sending Daniel and Jim off in all directions, saying, "That little villain. He's just asking for a tingler." Meanwhile, Douglas sat perched in the quince tree a few yards away. He had spent hours sitting absolutely still, observing a nest of baby robins and waiting for the mother to feed worms to her fledglings. Mother had called at the crucial moment, and though she could be disturbed, the robins could not. When feeding time ended, Douglas slithered down the tree as silently as an Indian and walked up to Mother, enthusing about all he had seen. Mother hadn't the heart to be anything but relieved, and before she could send him to the lilac bush for a tingler, Douglas' curiosity and wonder had her sitting and listening intently.

The tingler held no fear for Douglas, but somehow, despite the confusion and even alarm he caused, he always avoided it. Several times, Daniel and Jim went up Kniffen's brook and found him sitting in quiet anticipation, making one last try for the biggest trout, having ignored their calls echoing through the woods. He would come back with his handful of flowers for Mother, while Dad would stand with his hands on his hips, looking down at him and saying, "Well, yew littah bounder, what is your excuse this time?" That was all the encouragement Douglas needed, and off he would go on a long recitation.. After listening to Douglas' excited explanation,

Dad would throw his hands up in the air and say, as he said many times, "Dearie, this is the only chald who evah gives a sensible excuse."

Douglas loved fishing and often promised to take me along, but Daniel, Jim and Mother always objected. Then one rainy day when Douglas was in a mood to drop a line and no one would go with him, Mother conceded. Off we went in our raincoats and rubber boots, tramping through miles of misty woods with our fishing poles. We followed Kniffen's brook, climbing past sheer cliffs and tumbling waterfalls until we reached Douglas' favourite spot, a deep pool ringed by fir trees. We sat down on pine needles under a canopy of branches, and Douglas happily assured me that there was no better time or place to catch a trout. He then took a sharp rock and cold-heartedly sliced a fat worm in two, one half for him, one half for me, both halves wiggling. Douglas baited my hook and showed me how to hold the pole, suggesting that I stay alert because these trout were smarter than most. As the rain dripped generously through the trees and steadily plinked on my slicker, I hunkered down to the business of fishing. I stared at the tip of my pole; I sat mesmerized by the speckling water; I gazed into the mist beyond the perimeter of trees. Every once in a while, Douglas would wake me from my reverie by pulling a trout up on the bank and smartly bashing its head on a rock. When he suggested that I check my line, I pulled it up to find that the trout had pilfered my worm. When this happened a second time, Douglas explained that I had to have a feel for the line, to notice tiny movements, that I had to outwit the trout, they were very clever, you know. What a disappointment! I had begged to go fishing, to have the same freedom as the boys, but there I sat under a dripping tree, cold and miserable and crying that I wanted to go home. Douglas said all I had to do was leave, but he would be fishing all afternoon. So I left, and in minutes I was lost, standing among the trees and the mist trying to establish a direction. Having read all my fairy tales, *Hansel and Gretel, Little Red Riding Hood*, et al, I realized the fix I was in and started screaming for Douglas. My 6-year-old brother emerged from the trees and led me back to the pool. Douglas was such a patient, gentle soul. He put me to work scratching under the fir trees for bits and pieces to start a fire. Then he twirled a stick between his palms until a feeble plume of smoke wisped up from a glowing ember.

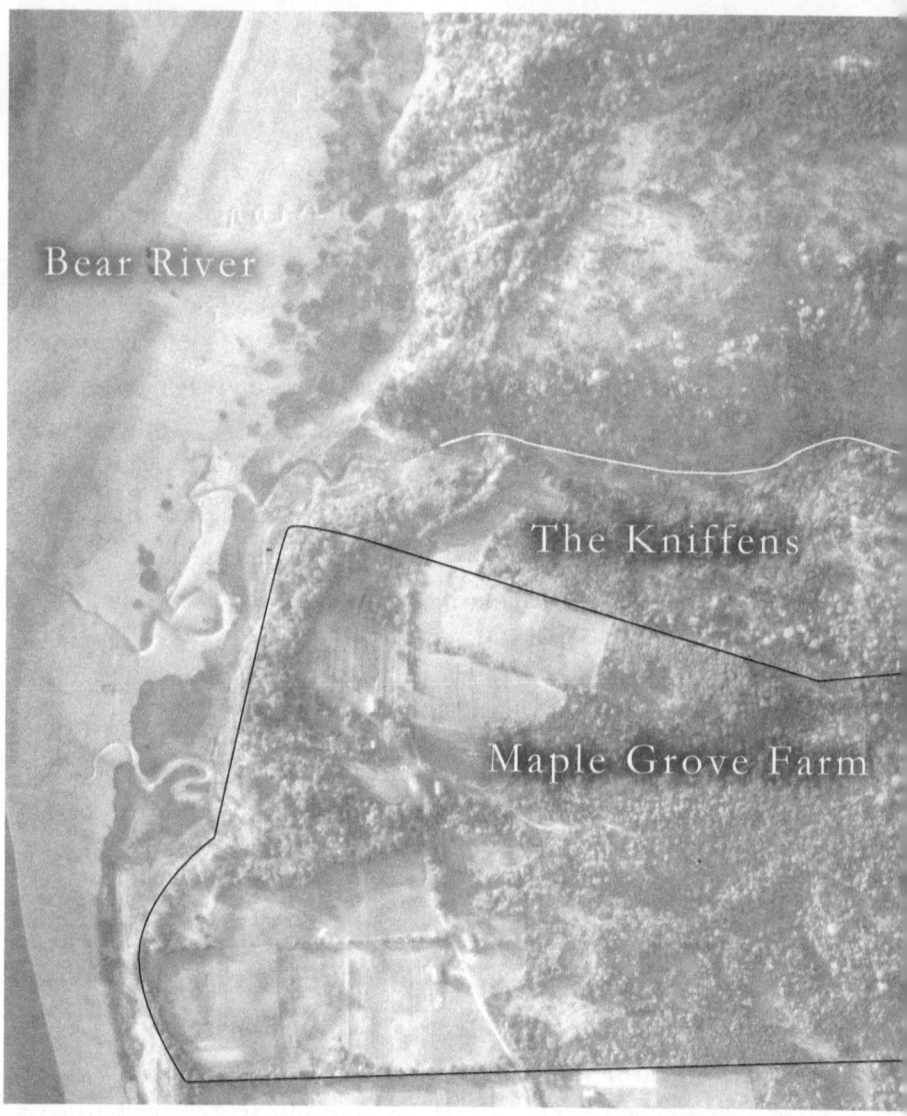

I obediently blew through cupped hands to encourage a flame while Douglas fed it twigs and small branches until the fire took hold, warming our tiny enclave. Douglas then gutted a trout, skewered it with a slim twig, and handed it to me to hold over the fire. The trout, served on twigs, was delicious. We had several, and as we ate, Douglas briefed me on all the foxes and deer and rabbits that would stop by the pool, how they came in turn and were likely waiting for us to leave. When the weather cleared up, he stuffed his schoolbag with trout, and we trekked back in the late-afternoon sunshine, the forest sparkling as if it were under a spell.

Kniffen's Brook

Douglas pointed out tracks, and bird and animal nests hidden to the untrained eye, part of that secret animal kingdom. Like sentries, birds called out our position as we paused to examine a curiosity or to pick flowers for Mother. When we emerged from the woods, we saw her sitting at the porch bunching vegetables, and that day we surprised her with two handfuls of flowers. What is it about memory that retains raindrops dripping through trees and dropping on my slicker? For most of that afternoon I sat in misery, listening to the steady thud, thud, plink, plink, but now it all returns with a wonderful softness.

Mary holding Joan, with Lorna

The span of many years has not dimmed the ghost-like memory of Mother, then so young, confronted by all the demands of babies, children and the farm. I can still faintly hear her firm warnings to watch the baby while she went to the barn for milk or to the gardens for vegetables. She was alone then and Uncle Peter had not yet arrived from Scotland. In those days, when two children became three, and the yearly propagation continued without letup, eldest girls cared for babies while boys helped out on the farm. Georgina Hill's mother had 16 children, the Woodworths had thirteen, and the Reades had the same, putting Evelyn in the same predicament as me. From the age of four, babies hung around my neck like albatrosses, drooling and burping between endless bouts of snivelling. I wiped faces and hands. I made spit curls all over their heads, hoping to make their hair curly, which I thought would be just the thing for a Marvin to have. I waved rattles at them and lugged them around like sugar bags. I wheeled them up and down the Chute Road, from the barn to the Red Astrakhan tree, over and over again, back and forth until I felt like a wind-up toy. For all my attentions, Mother called me her little mother, 'would my little mother like to hold the baby, feed him, wipe his face, you're such a good little mother.' I loved Mother's praise and needed it, so in spite all the misery they caused, I resigned myself to one baby after another, year after year, without letup.

Joan

When Joan and Lorna were two and three, they became fixated on cats, and I suspect the reason stemmed from Mother's telling them repeatedly to leave the cats alone. Mother worried about disease from scratches and bites and warned us when we went to the barn to, "stay away from those tigers." Lorna and Joan paid no attention and trundled about with kittens and cats dangling from their arms and shoulders. Mother put a stop to it, but the minute her back was turned, they would scurry about the pantry for brown paper bags to keep the kittens under wraps. Off they would run to the barn as fast as their little legs would carry them, and then they would toddle about, stopping every so often to look in the bag. One day Dad asked Joan, "What have you got in the bag, Little Jo Otter?" The two of them scurried off, but Mother caught up and said, "You just let me have a look in there," and "what's this?" She marched them back to the barn to empty the bag in front of snarling mothers. I was eight at the time and had Donald to take care of, but Mother made it my job to see that they stayed away from the barn and didn't snaffle any more kittens. I really think that this was the point when our sibling relationship deteriorated for good. We were never friends. I disliked being their proxy mother, they resented being ordered about by their sister, and this uneven arrangement established long-lasting friction points. Dad said that talking to Joan was like water off a duck's back, which was why he called her Little Jo Otter, a slippery character

Lorna

from Thornton Burgess bedtime stories. Mother would say, "She's as Irish as Patsy's pig." Lorna, one year older, was a very clever, determined child, and I often heard Dad deplore, "Dearie, that chald has to be either maimed or tamed." Mother would sigh, "She's just like my mother." It's strange how soon the die is cast, and how the passage of time can change so little.

Ordinary routine sloughs away minutes and hours as if they never happened, discarded and forgotten like flotsam and jetsam. My very early years were placid with no ripples except for the excitement of Dad's homecomings, always heightened by Mother's expectancy. Even those events happened enough times a year to become routine, but memory sharpened with Uncle Peter's arrival from Scotland when I was 3 or 4. What made his first day memorable was that usually Mrs. McCormick looked after us when Mother went to the village, but on this particular afternoon we were left alone with our brand-new uncle. Snow was falling heavily and it was getting dark, so Daniel and I kept running to the dining room window to look up McCormick's hill, anxious for Mother's return. When Uncle Peter went from room to room checking the stoves or lighting the lamps, he would come in one door and we would run out the other, but we regularly returned to the couch at the dining room window to urge Mother's return. At one point, Uncle Peter lifted the trap door in the hallway and went down to the root cellar, which caused us to worry. Then he puttered about the kitchen before returning to his cozy spot, reading in front of the fireplace. Finally, we spotted the lantern on the dray as it came down the hill, flickering through the heavy snow. We ran to the door as Mother stepped in, while Uncle Peter went out to unload the sleigh and take Harry to the barn. She had left a stew on the stove, and when she lifted the lid she screamed, "Oh my goodness." It was a stew the likes of which she had never seen, and it was not the one she had left on the stove. I looked in the pot as it bubbled away, blood red: red potatoes, red onions, red meat, and sticking up through the gory sight were beet roots. Uncle Peter had decided he would like to have beets, so he threw them in the stew. I didn't want to eat it but I did, and we ate it until it was finished. Uncle Peter declared, "It's no so bad at all!" I've never seen cookbooks mention it, but yes, there is such a thing as beet stew and it is red and rosy like Santa Claus, thoroughly ancestrally Scotch, only heard of in the MacGregor household.

From the minute Uncle Peter arrived, calm was unhinged and never restored. Although he was her brother, younger by a year, I don't think Mother liked Uncle Peter, and her irritation surfaced in stilted arguments. Dad was never impressed by his less-than-star-quality, and I'd often hear him mutter, "Caramba! That blasted numbskull!" My early impressions of Uncle Peter have faded except for one indelible memory when I stood watching him cut off a chicken's head for Sunday dinner. The deed done, the headless chicken fluttered at his feet splattering blood as Uncle Peter stood holding the axe. Seeing me watching, he called out in his burly, dogmatic Scotch voice, "Come wee Mary and I'll chop off your head."

I avoided Uncle Peter and was always running in the opposite direction. He would poke and tickle us until we screamed in pain and frustration and lack of control. Mother argued with him, telling him to leave us alone, so he called us cry-babies. Dad taught us never to utter personal comments, yet Uncle Peter constantly teased me about my stuttering, my freckles, my green eyes. If I cried, he laughed and said I couldn't take a joke. Well, perhaps I couldn't, but then neither could he when the joke was on him. Still, I do remember many times when he could be pleasant and even quite funny. He assumed a friendly veneer in the village and made the effort to fit in, attending committee meetings and lingering for the late-night revelry. And he did enjoy having babies around, though he never had children of his own. He would play keek (peek-a-boo) and dandle them on his foot, bouncing them up and down singing *A Wee Deoch an Doris* and *Come Peter Pan With Your Pipes and Play*. It wasn't that Uncle Peter was entirely unpleasant, but he was an interloper, and as long as he was there I wished he would just go away. I was too young to understand the reason for his being there, that Dad's health made it necessary.

Dad was very generous with Uncle Peter, paying him well and giving him all the benefits of being a family member. With no expenses to speak of, he invested in fashion. Large boxes of clothes would arrive from Barrie's of London: linen suits, camel-hair jackets, flannel pants (white ducks for summer), fedoras, and shoes with spats. Dressed like a Savile Row swank, he went prospecting at barn dances. I couldn't wait for him to get married and move along, but the whole miserable process took years.

The identity of the family was clearly divided as if destined by the stars. The eldest and dominant males, Daniel, Jim and Douglas dismissed me to an indeterminate entity of one. Lorna and Joan, always close, similar but dissimilar, lived in a world of their own with closed borders. Donald, David and Robert, the three youngest members later formed another male enclave. I stood between my brothers and sisters, a buffer zone, not inclusive in any group, there only when needed or noticed. I wonder what star hovered over my cradle. Was it the cold, lonely unwavering North Star, electing me to eventually become the anchor, necessary but rejected?

Lorna, Uncle Peter holding Robert, Donald to his left, Mary in back, Joan in front of her, and Scotty looking off-camera.

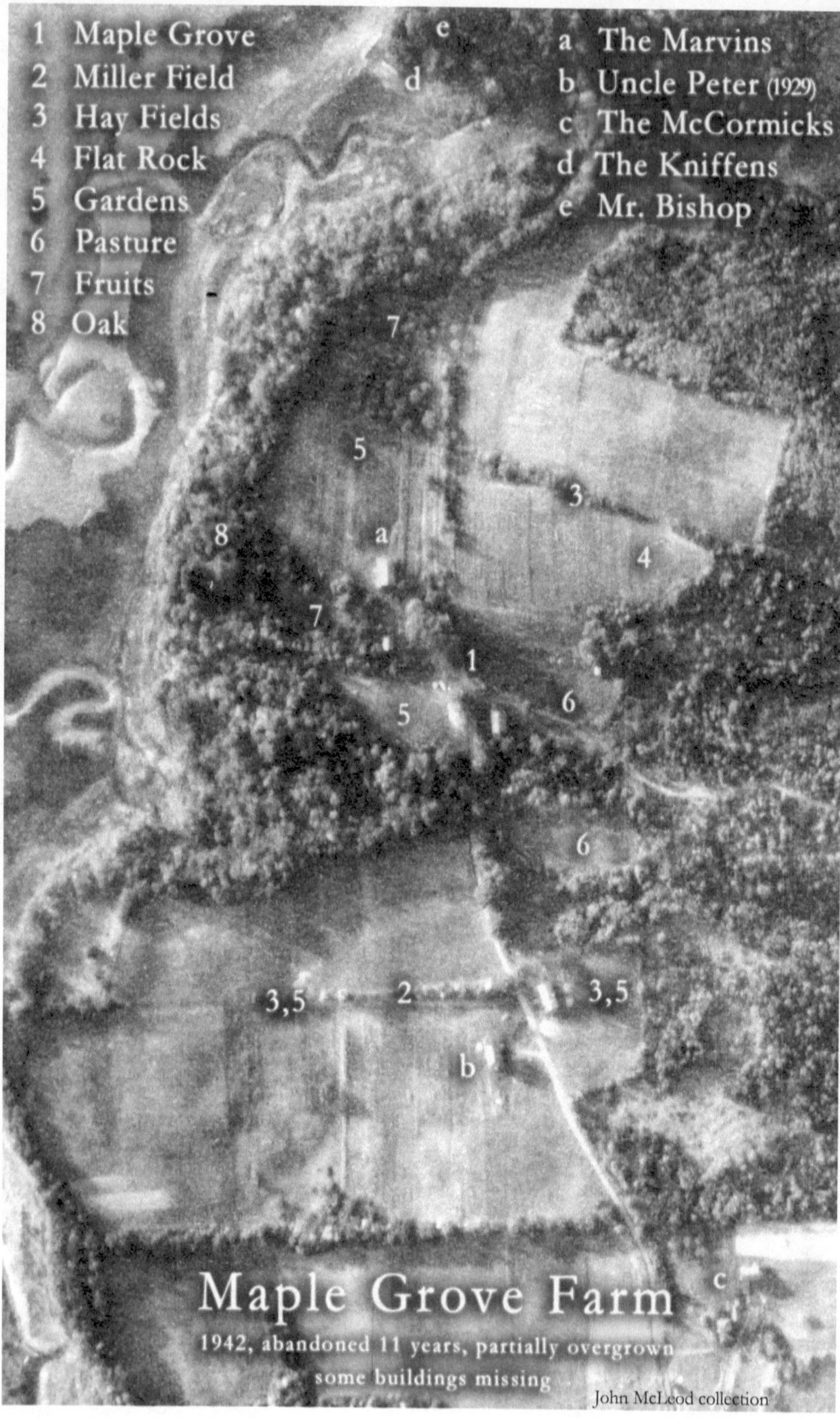

1 Maple Grove
2 Miller Field
3 Hay Fields
4 Flat Rock
5 Gardens
6 Pasture
7 Fruits
8 Oak
a The Marvins
b Uncle Peter (1929)
c The McCormicks
d The Kniffens
e Mr. Bishop
e
d
7
5
3
8
a
4
7
1
6
5
6
3,5
2
3,5
b
c
Maple Grove Farm
1942, abandoned 11 years, partially overgrown
some buildings missing
John McLeod collection

*A*FTER CROSSING THE VILLAGE bridge and passing the half-dozen stores on Main Street, you would mount Oakdene Hill, where a left turn at the top would put you on the Chute Road, two miles from Maple Grove farm. As you walked along, you could look steeply down to the river, while across on the Digby side, the River Road followed a similar route. A mile and a half down the road, after passing farm houses, fields and orchards, you would reach the Crossroads, where you could veer off towards Deep Brook, or angle down through a long laneway of maples and continue on to the top of McCormick's hill. From there, the Chute Road dropped down to evenly divide our farm. On one side, you looked up our pasture to the tree line of our woods, tipped by spruce trees. Up ahead you would see the steep hay fields curving down to meet the road. Looking towards the river was the Miller field gracefully sweeping down to the water's edge. Continuing on, you would pass a vegetable garden enclosed by trees, the apple packing house, the barn, and finally, the maple grove, canopied like a majestic green cathedral and leading to our modest, white-shingled house. Dad loved those huge trees and would often stand at the back door admiring them. There was something about walking through the maple grove, about coming and going through that lovely colonnade, sentinelled and domed by two dozen magnificent sugar maples.

The hills came to a hesitation at the house and spread out in an enclosed plain that held the long expanse of our vegetable gardens, the corduroy rows leading to a scaled-down apple orchard at the end of our property. The farm was cupped and held captive by the hills and a thick stand of oak that edged the river, thereby protecting us from the wintery blasts that blew in from the Bay of Fundy. When spring came and the gardens were planted, it was as if the soil had been warmed with mittens, because the seeds germinated so eagerly and bore so quickly that our vegetables always arrived first to market.

Dad was proud of his farm and would stand with his hands on his hips waxing rhapsodic about the maple grove, the gardens, the hay fields. As we walked through the stand of oaks along the river, he would effuse about their beauty and strength. Oak beams in castles stood for hundreds of years while brick and stone crumbled. Oak from our woods masted

Joe Warren picking strawberries in the gardens of Maple Grove farm, circa 1912. The orchards behind him were later much reduced.

English ships-of-the-line. Like the maples, the oak were hundreds of years old, and as children we would clasp hands to reach around their girth.

The scope of my early years reached from the top of Billy McCormick's hill, where only his chimney could be seen pushing up through the spruce trees, and down the Chute Road to the Red Astrakhan tree, which marked the beginning of the Kniffen's property. Nothing could be seen beyond the dense swath of trees and foliage. The road itself was like a magic ribbon tying the hill to the Astrakhan tree, disappearing mysteriously at both ends. Occasionally, a horse and buggy would trot by, kicking up poufs of dust before vanishing one way or the other. When the dust had flounced off to the side of the road and settled, the excitement of this unusual event remained like an echo.

Dad bought the farm from Joe Warren, and it was Joe who told my parents that our house was one of the oldest in Annapolis County—a squat, spacious, two-storey, uninspired structure of early immediacy architecture. Flowers crowded and abounded around it, the front and back doors embraced by June roses, ramblers creeping up the trellised corners, and blossoms blooming in between. Fronting the house and sprawling under two quince trees was Mother's rock garden, her pride and joy. Every year after whitewashing the house, Dad would paint the perimeter rocks that enclosed Mother's brazen bouquet of peonies, zinnia, heliotrope, nasturtium, lilies, daisies, baby's breath, forget-me-nots, sweet alyssum, hens-and-chicks, and many others. On hot summer days, a heavenly ambrosia wafted in through the windows to perfume our dining room and parlor.

Mother's garden was the best in Bear River, and in the summer when energetic tourists hiked from the River View Lodge in the village down to Kniffen's Hollow to laze on the beach, they often stopped to admire it. One of those charming tourists was Miss Clara Louise Crowley, a teacher from Brooklyn, New York. I was wheeling the baby in the pram when she stopped to chat and then asked if she could look at the flowers. Mother came in from weeding the gardens and insisted that she stay for tea. Beside Mother's rock garden was a tall Bartlett pear tree, underneath which sat our large, double-seated glide swing. In the summer, it served as our outdoor parlor, where visitors could relax in the shade for tea and conversation.

Robert finding his sea legs in front of the grapery.

Miss Crowley came back often that summer, and when she returned to New York, she sent me my first grown-up book, *Hans Brinker or The Silver Skates*. I loved that sad, wonderful story, and Miss Crowley became my first pen pal. I wrote my belaboured replies twice over for perfection before placing the two-cent stamp with exactitude.

Stationed around and about the house were the fruit trees: Bartlett pear, crab-apple, the cherry trees: Bing, Whiteheart and Dad's two prized Oxhearts, and the plum trees, Damson, Damask and the delicious Greengage, sweetest of them all. Behind the glide swing, the grapery fronted berry bushes that extended all the way down to the oak: blackberry, raspberry, blueberry, red and black currant, gooseberry. On summer days, we would fill half-bushel baskets and lug them back to Mother in the kitchen. The house would be drenched with the sticky-sweet aroma of boiling jams and jellies; the kitchen sweltering with the constantly burning wood stove. Dad used to say it was 'as hot as the hammered hinges of Hades.' Mother would be standing at the stove, stirring pots through clouds of steam, ladling oxheart cherries into heavy syrup, whole crab-apples into jars with cinnamon sticks. In the heat of summer, she would make our favourite red and black currant jams, quince and grape jellies, and a delicious crab-apple jelly for pork, slowly dripped through cheese cloth. I would hold out a thick slice of freshly baked, buttered bread for Mother to ladle out whole strawberries, so hot I had to blow on them.

In the house, couches sat stationed like lookouts at all the large windows, and my favourite couch was in the kitchen, positioned at the large, many-paned window. Looking out to the left were all the berry bushes, while stretching to the right were the rows of the vegetable gardens. The window took up most of the wall, reaching from the couch to the ceiling and showing in comfort all that was to be seen outside. It was like a picture in an art gallery, ushering into our kitchen every nuance of season and weather. Daniel and I watched rivulets of rain trailing down like quick-silver as downpours snapped at the many panes. Frequent fogs settled outside, breathing and pulsing like land-locked clouds. Snow piled up so high we couldn't see out, even by standing on the couch. At times, the window would frost over, and in our efforts to lick as many peep holes as we could, our tongues would stick to the panes.

We would pull them off and say 'ahhh' to examine each other's tongues and see if they were bleeding. When the snow on the roof melted, huge icicles hung down in shards, and Uncle Peter would answer the call to arms with a broom handle to shatter them before they fell and stabbed us to death.

When I was very young, this couch by the window was my entire world, so warm and comforting. I would play with my doll and listen to Mother sing as she prepared dinner or rolled dough on the table. I was loathe to leave it, and when Mother tore me away and pushed me out the door to play in the snow for the good of my health, I would sit in the snow and cry and cry until my bottom froze. Mother would come to the window and wave me inside, and I would crawl back on the couch, traumatized by the outside world.

Only during thunderstorms did the kitchen become menacing. Lightning would lace across the window and flash on all the copper pots and pans. It terrified Mother, and no matter how hungry we were, meals went uncooked while she cowered in fear and trembling under the hall stairs. She never got over that fear. Houses and barns burned to the ground during lightning storms because they lacked proper conductors or lightning rods. Children would talk in the schoolyard about so-and-so being burned out of house and home, lucky to be alive. One house burned down in the middle of a bridge game. The chimney flared, sparks lit the roof, and the ladies had to drop their cards and flee for their lives.

Daniel was once the hero of the day when, as we came through the maple grove after school, he spotted the chimney flaming like a Roman candle. Daniel rushed inside to alert Mother, who immediately began crying hysterically, so he ran out to the gardens for Dad. They raced to the barn for the ladder, and Dad put out the flame by pouring salt and baking soda down the chimney. I stood at the well cranking up endless buckets of water that the boys sloshed over to Uncle Peter, who lugged them up the ladder to douse the roof. For the rest of the day, we checked and rechecked the other buildings to make sure they were safe. We had heard how sparks could drift on the wind and land on a roof like deadly insects. The next day, Dad and Uncle Peter stood over the chimneys with long brushes, and soot came splattering down the fireplaces in billowing clouds, making a horrid mess. Then they noisily dismantled the stovepipes in all the rooms and took them outside for cleaning, adding to a mess that took days to clean up. In a house with two fireplaces, stoves in every room and kerosene lamps at night, we lived with a constant fear of fire. From the time we could walk, we were taught the terrible consequences of carelessness. And we always had an alerted watchfulness in case a toddler wandered too close to a fireplace or somehow reached up to a kerosene lamp, which could explode into flames on falling. Every evening, Mother would prepare the lamps for the night, washing and polishing the globes until they shone, carefully filling the base with kerosene, wiping them clean of dripping in case of a flare-up when she struck the match, trimming the wicks evenly so the flame would not fork and smoke up the globe, thereby dimming the light. When I was nine, Mother decided I was responsible enough to take over. I took inordinate pride in doing this chore perfectly, and I loved being praised for it. I was always very careful, until the time I almost burned the house down.

One evening I was alone in the kitchen preparing the lamps, and for the last one I had put in a new wick and was waiting for the kerosene to soak to the top so I could light it. In my impatience, I leaned the lamp over, unaware that in doing so, kerosene leaked onto the base. I placed the lamp among the others and struck the match just as Dad came in to see the lamp flare wildly. In a split-second he pushed me away so roughly that I fell onto the couch. He grabbed a rag, clasped it to the base of the flaming lamp, tore out the door and plunged it deep into the rain barrel beside the porch. Mother was bringing in clothes and the others were playing on the glide swing, so they saw the whole drama. I had almost done the unthinkable. Dad came into the kitchen without his shirt and sternly forbad me from ever touching the lamps again. That was the only time I remember his being really angry with me. My only defence for my stupidity was my tears, I had no other. My guilt turned into a nightmare, and the thought of the crime became as bad as the crime itself. Little sibling voices lulled me to sleep, 'You almost burned the house down, you almost killed us, you're stupid, etc.' Finally Mother warned everyone, as she usually did when there was an in-depth crime review by the holier-than-thou's, that if she heard one more word they would not live to tell the tale, 'mark my words.'

If the kitchen window was living art, then the huge stove against the opposite wall was nothing less than Cellini: rooted like a statue, rococo for the kitchen. It stood ponderous and plump, cluttered with nickel, enamel and friezed iron down to its Queen Anne knees. The stove burned day and night like an engine on a ship, resting only on summer evenings after the last cup of tea. Many times, company would arrive unexpectedly, and Mother would bank the fire, put the kettle on and quickly mix a batch of scones. After rubbing the top clean of stove black, she would dollop the scones out to be baked and turned, and by the time the kettle was boiling and the tea cups arranged on the tray, the scones would be done. Scones on the stove top was my first cooking lesson. We mixed the batter, and Mother handed me the spatula to turn those closest to the edge. This I learned long before I went to school.

In the style of the day, the stove stood on a tin platform, was backed by a tin-covered wall, and was topped by a ceiling of patterned tin, so the whole kitchen was more or less a warming oven. This made for a few scorching summer days, but in the fall when we came home from school soaked to the skin, or in the winter when we froze to the bone, the warmth of the kitchen was as welcoming as a fireplace. We would slip behind the stove with our hot cocoa, sitting with our backs against the tin wall and our legs under the stove. After the agony of the two-mile trek and the throbbing misery of the thaw, the penetrating heat cooked us until we glowed.

The kitchen was a large room made smaller by a multitude of cupboards and counters. Hanging on hooks and stacked on shelves was Dad's brass work gleaming gold in overstatement: copper pots and saucepans, large frying pans and stockpots, kettles, tea caddies and utensils. Our home was filled with brass work, but not for children to touch. The only brass we were given was our milk mugs, and that was to reduce the breakage of glasses. Babies showed early contempt for Dad's handiwork, banging them on high chairs and throwing them to the floor. Daniel, in a snit, once threw his against the wall and loosened the copper handle. Uncle Peter clumsily soldered it, and this offended Daniel's eye every time he opened his mouth to sip his milk. Although he tried, he couldn't switch because each mug hung on a hook under the counter, graded from youngest to oldest, and ownership could not be questioned.

Our breakfast table stood in the middle of the room, long enough to accommodate the family and doubling as a baking table with its enamelled top. Mother baked every day: cakes, biscuits, pies, scones, and numerous loaves of bread; every housewife did. With the house enclosed by flowers and fruit trees, the flavours of the season scented our rooms: apple blossoms and lilacs in the spring, roses in June, the bouquet of Mother's rock garden in the summer, the russet simmering of fallen leaves, all of them a taste of the outdoors coming in. But as lovely as the natural scents were, the aroma of baking had a human element that spoke to the soul like a mother tongue. It suited the indoors and somehow contained all the comforts of home. After school, when we stepped in the door defeated by the two-mile trek, the scent of Mother's baking touched our empty stomachs and turned a key. We would crowd around as she pulled her afternoon bread out of the oven and cut thick, hot slices that we slathered with butter and jam, food for the spirit.

Sitting beneath the side window that looked out through the maple grove was our sink, complete with the convenience of a squeaky water pump. That was as indoor as our plumbing got. Water for baths and wash basins had to be carried the rest of the way. Despite these meagre comforts, we were better off than others, whose pump stood outside and had to be thawed out with boiling water on freezing winter mornings. I shuddered to think of the effort in washing a dish. As it was, Mother ladled water for dishes out of the warm-water tank at the side of the stove, just as she did for our baths. She would line us up and plunk us in and out of Dad's copper wash tub, one after the other, just like the dishes. No lounging in foamy luxury for me. Other than a bath every few days, we cleaned up at the kitchen pump, or splashed our faces in the morning using the water jugs and basins by our beds.

I used to love watching Dad shave at the sink, swirling the lather in a wooden bowl of Yardley's lavender soap, dabbing his face and sometimes dabbing mine, thwacking the straight razor on a strap and deftly scraping away. I thought it quite the performance, and when he picked me up after clapping his face with Florida Water, he smelled wonderful. I wanted to smell as good, but on the farm with dirt and dust everywhere, cleanliness was a constant battle, next to impossible, much like Godliness.

Mother was not overly emotional about many things other than thunderstorms, children's cuts and Dad's comings and goings, but there was something else—Dad's eclectic choice of certain foods. When he came home from the village and announced that he had bought tripe, lambs' fronts, brains or sweetbreads, Mother would pale and leave the kitchen, closing the door to the hallway and the dining room. Every time he got them, Mother would say, "I wish you wouldn't bring those things home,"

and he'd say, "I like them Dearie, I like them,"

and she'd say, "You call that a delicacy eating things like that. It's barbarous,"

and Dad, "I'm not asking you to eat them."

One time she deplored, "Don't mention those disgusting entrails to me, Mr. Marvin," but usually all she ever said was, "Don't forget to wash the pot!" While Dad cooked his delicacies, she waited at the other end of the house, her nose twitching. Dad would putter about in happy anticipation. I can still feel the revulsion of looking into the pot of greyish, mouldy-looking brains, simmering to tenderness. And Dad, sitting at the kitchen table, his knife and fork poised, delicately portioning the shrivelled, wrinkled mass, then savouring it as if he had seen a vision. The sere, creamy-colored, rubbery-looking tripe was just as bad, as well as the cadaverous medallions of scallops. Mother classified scallops with the clams that bubbled away and pimpled our mud flats, nourished by the effluvia that flowed down river from the village. Though the Kniffens hosted clam bakes all summer and survived, not a single clam ever set foot at Mother's table. Once, Dad brought lobsters back from Digby, and Mother fled the kitchen in benumbed hysteria. We children watched with fascination as Dad plunged the lobsters into the pot of boiling water, pushing them down as they protested before giving in to their rosy fate. Dad cracked and probed the shells, and he and the boys demolished every buttery morsel. He begged me to try it, but I couldn't. The colour affected me, and in my mind I linked it with the vibrant blue of blue vitriol—both poisonous. After the meal, the finished shells lay piled on the platter like remnants of broken china. I didn't touch a lobster until I was 19 and was surprised to discover that lobster was my favourite food, but there was still no question about Dad's entrail cuisinery.

On entering our front door, you faced the stairs and a length of hallway that turned left to the kitchen. Fronting the house and on either side were two equally large rooms: the dining room to the left and the parlor to the right. In the dining room, the polished, dark oak table took up the middle of the room and was long enough to sit all 17 people when the unruly MacGregors arrived from Scotland. Until that time, the dining room was a place where good manners were observed in the stylized etiquette of the Old South. The boys may have been little barbarians outdoors, but they changed like chameleons at the dinner table, sitting in their bare feet and politely asking, 'May I please have this, would you please pass that, may I be excused from the table?' Dad insisted on nothing less, and any deviation earned his sharp rebuke.

At other times, the dining room table served as Mother's work desk, where she wrote letters, kept the accounts, ordered supplies, and completed all the paperwork necessary to keep a business running. Mother had a nose for numbers, and for that, Dad was grateful, because he did not. He admitted as much, and added that the farm turned a profit because of Mother's strict oversight. While Dad waited on payment for his brass work, Mother never tolerated accounts payable for our crops.

I often wondered just how divided our house was, because besides Dad's overly generous nature and his taste for certain foods, another point of contention was politics. In our house, religion was relegated to the status of myth, but you could say that politics was our religion, another conundrum. Dad loved to chat with anyone about politics and religion, but was noncommittal about both. Mother monitored British and Canadian politics closely via the Hansard and had named the boys after famous politicians, once family obligations were out of the way. Jim (James Rob) was named after Dad's father and the infamous Rob Roy MacGregor. Douglas and Donald's namesakes escape me, but they were also politically rooted. David (David Wallace) was named after David Lloyd George and the Scottish hero, William Wallace. Robert (Robert Ramsay) was named after Robert the Bruce and Ramsay Macdonald. The Helensburgh-born British Prime Minister Bonar Law was also greatly esteemed, but happily by-passed.

Mother and Dad were ineligible to vote in Canada until the 1930 election, when R. B. Bennett and Mackenzie King grovelled for the privilege of saving us from ourselves. Mother was in a quandary, saying, "I don't know which of these two sick-looking mushrooms to vote for." She finally made up her mind, and despite the sunny summer weather, clouds gathered that election day because the house was divided, with Dad saying, "Dearie, yew don't mean yew would skunk mah vote?!"

Mother laughed away and said, "I certainly would, and that's exactly what I'm going to do!"

Uncle Peter and Dad went into the village first. When they came back, Mother jumped in the buggy, tickled Harry's shank to turn him around and laughed at Dad's protest, "Dearie, maybe yew will change your mind?"

"Never, Mr. Marvin! Never!" She was wearing her new black, broad-brimmed summer hat with a huge red, overblown rose at the side. She had admired it in Mrs. Yorke's hat shop for a while before finally buying it. Dad never pondered a purchase; Mother always did. She trotted through the maple grove a happily franchised woman, still laughing when she returned. When I asked her what happened, Mother explained that she had put an X on a piece of paper. I still didn't understand. The whole exercise seemed like a joyous occasion with no more significance than a breeze from the Bay of Fundy, but I realized that my parents differed on something important.

Surrounding the dining room table were the same pressed-back chairs that sat in the kitchen, the parlor, the bedrooms, and wherever a chair was needed. If there was any pattern sense to our décor, it might have been traditional early 1920s Eaton's solid oak Canadiana, with a sturdiness that defied little boys. Chairs Mother ordered from the Eaton's catalogue for $2.00 now sell in antiques stores for $100 or more. Every home had them.

The dining room also served as Mother's sewing room, where she made quilts, rugs, curtains, slipcovers, linens, and anything else that could be cut from cloth, including most of the clothes on our backs. Knitting was nonstop, but took place in every room of the house. In those days, frugal homemakers needed these skills and would only pay for ready-made at a store as a last resort. In the pantry stood a flour barrel, refilled regularly, the bags always saved for quilts, rugs, even pillowcases.

Mrs. McCormick went one step further and spun her own yarn. One day she sat down at her spinning wheel and showed me how, adding that thrifty young women in her day all made homespun. A spinning wheel sat in our attic under years of dust, left by the previous owner. Mother's appliance of choice sat in the dining room corner beside the couch: her prized treadle sewing machine, flipping up from its own cabinet, black with elaborate gold stencilling to inspire the artist. Mother sewed like a wizard and could stitch up a dress or even a suit in minutes. Like the passing down of an heirloom, Mother taught me how to sew, how to knit, and when I was tall enough, she sat me down at the sewing machine. With one foot forward and one foot back, I slowly rocked the treadle as I mastered the art of sewing a straight line, allowing me to be frugal in my own home, which I most certainly was.

A couch stationed at the front dining room window looked out past Mother's rock garden to the Chute Road. Another couch at the side window looked through the maple grove to the barn. For as long as I can remember, I held babies up to these windows to drool and observe. While Mother sewed, I pointed out the landmarks of the farm as they gurgled and fingers left first impressions on windowpanes. Sitting in the corner between these two couches stood a bulging pot-bellied stove, the same as in the other rooms, made of solid, solid iron, built to last a lifetime, like the early Tin Lizzies that drove over ruts in farmer's fields and never lost a nut or bolt. In those days, there was a wonderful durability, even a morality to a product.

Beside every stove in the house was a woodbox, filled daily by the boys. With all the stoves and two fireplaces in the house, the background refrain on the farm was often a rhythmic chopping, sawing and splitting. Around Christmas time, Dad and Uncle Peter would take the old sleigh road into the woods for winter logging, after which, the timber had to be cut and cured, then split and stored in the shed to dry. It took muscle power to heat a house, which is why our second floor remained unused for years. But at the end of the day after all the hard work, the stoves kept the house cozy, and on quiet winter evenings when we lay on our stomachs reading, the soft hissing and snapping of the fire played an ode to contentment, like the purring of a cat.

Set against the dining room wall between the hall entrance and the kitchen door was a highboy filled with linens, while against the other wall was a long sideboard with a low mirror and shelves at each end. Cluttering the sideboard and sitting on every surface in the room was Dad's brass work, gleaming from the dark oak like a seam of ore: fruit bowls, jugs, cigar and cigarette boxes lined with sweet-smelling cedar wood, card trays with silver hearts, spades etc. in the corners, candlesticks, large oval trays with the etched crests of the Knights of Columbus, Oddfellows and other orders, desk sets of letter openers, pen and pencil trays, rocking blotters, letter racks and ink wells. Hanging on the wall were sconces for candles, holders for lamps and wall pockets for flowers. The list was endless, and the parlor held a similar display. Often when Dad was in Montreal, a crate would arrive from the railway station, and Mother would pull out the straw packing to reveal new kettles, pans, trays or bowls. At Christmas time, more brass would arrive, and on Mother's birthday, Dad always gave her something special, his best pieces.

When Dad was discharged from Netley Hospital in England, he gifted Mother with a vase of hammered brass that he had made from a shell casing. It was a lovely piece of work, often admired by visitors on the farm, though Dad claimed that since it was hammered, it hid a multitude of sins. I loved that vase for all of its hidden faults that no one could ever find. During the war, tinkering with brass was a common soldierly pastime, since empty shell casings littered the landscape. Soldiers would pick them up and fill empty hours by reshaping them into souvenirs, household goods, anything at all. Trench art, as it is now called, can sometimes be found in antiques shops, and bears witness to the ingenuity of bored soldiers, where shell casings sit transformed into items of everyday usefulness: jugs, ashtrays, candlesticks, oil lamps, or vases. Dad was expert at this hobby, not only because he was in the trade of fashioning metal parts, but also because he had trained as a coppersmith and was schooled in the arts. At Netley, the metal shops were made available to recovering soldiers who wished to continue this hobby, and St. Anne de Bellevue military hospital offered the same convenience. So when Dad went into St. Anne's to spend the winter, necessity became the mother of invention and destitution an inspiration. He began making brass work to finance the farm. Soon he was running a business, and for a number of years he worked out of a small shop on St. Catherine Street in downtown Montreal. His output was tremendous, and what Dad labelled brass work was diversified to include copper and German Silver. Henry Birks and Mappin & Webb on St. Catherine Street were the most prestigious jewellery stores in Canada, you might say the Tiffany and Cartier of Canada, and Dad made his market with their standing orders; they eagerly accepted all he had to offer. Every year they had a window display of his work, and when Dad came home for Christmas there would be a great discussion about it. Mother, full of pride, would say how she wished she could have seen it. Dad supplied other stores, The Handicraft Guild on Peel Street being one I recall, and he still had time for special orders and unusual requests. He made a baptismal font for a church in Montreal, and a swinging baby's cradle for a Captain in the Cunard Steamship Line. When he exhibited at the Canadian National Exhibition in Toronto, no one got a 'First' but him, and in the years he didn't exhibit, no 'First' was given because the pieces were not good enough. Dad's work was well known, but not in Bear River, where he was regarded as a farmer.

When the brass had to be cleaned, Dad would cover the dining room table with newspapers and gather the pieces together, making the room glow like a treasure trove. I always wanted a powder jar for my freckles, a frame etched with bluebirds for my portrait, and a cigar box for my jewels. Cleaning the brass was a tedious, messy chore that the boys avoided, but I enjoyed it because I rarely had Dad all to myself. As we buffed with Brasso and chamois, we would chat about all kinds of things, and Dad would often tell me about the piece he was cleaning.

Lady Byng was the wife of the then Governor General of Canada, she of the Lady Byng National Hockey League trophy for the most gentlemanly player, she of the foul mouth. Lady Byng wanted Dad's work and bypassed the stores to deal with him directly, striding into his shop armed with her own designs. Perhaps she had tired of silver and gold, but she liked brass and was the epitome of brass herself. Her conversation was splintered with swear words as she insisted that Dad make her designs to order. "No," Dad said, "absolutely not," he used only his own designs. I would have loved to have heard the exchange, so diametrically opposed: the hard-bitten, determined, upper-crust English woman of privilege, flailing against Dad's calm, lazy southern drawl, slightly puckish in pointless debate, knowing he would never give in. She promised she would never come back, and Dad promised he would make her something nice. Lady Byng stormed out of the shop and later sent her secretary with more designs to break down Dad's defences. Miss Eva Sandford was a lady, the perfect, cultivated foil to upper class crude. Dad told her, "Yew tell that old crock ah only use mah own designs."

Back came Lady Byng, storming in and swearing like a stevedore before getting to the point, "So, Marvin! I'm an old crock, am I?"

Dad said, "Your Ladyship, your secretary made a grave error."

Lady Byng laughed and said, "Blast your eyes. Let's see your designs that are so much better than mine."

Dad said she blasted his eyes every time he refused her designs, but he seemed thoroughly charmed by her visits, her God-damning and praising him as she smoked her cigars. It seemed like a strange way of doing business, but she scooped up everything he made and took it back to Government House in Ottawa. Dad was pleased when the notes she sent on Government House paper were so complimentary, and in such perfect English.

Another story Dad enjoyed concerned Lady Haig's portrait. One Christmas, Lady Dorothy Haig sent Dad her signed portrait in a gilded frame. She had been lady-in-waiting to Queen Alexandra, and her husband was the infamous Sir Douglas Haig, he who, in his spotless uniform, had once looked down at soldiers in the mud-filled trenches and called them dirty dogs. Dad was a friend of Camillien Houde, the mayor of Montreal, who according to Dad and all reports, was a very charming and witty man. Dad chuckled that Lady Haig had also given Mr. Houde her portrait that Christmas, but unlike Dad's, it was not framed, which Dad sometimes pointed out in friendly rivalry.

Giving one last buff of chamois, Dad would hold a piece of brass at arm's length in admiration. He loved his brass work and filled our home with it. He hardly needed the praise of others; he knew the value of his work, and that was his satisfaction. It seems strange that in view of his pride he never had a hallmark.

Opposite the dining room was the parlor, and like all the rooms of the house, it could never be considered elegant with its linoleum floor, papered walls, patterned tin ceiling, and heavy furniture. A long table filled the middle of the room, with couches at the windows, chairs all around, and books and brass everywhere. The windows were veiled with diaphanous white curtains, their pristine delicacy giving the room an elegance it didn't deserve. When Dad was home, he pushed all the curtains aside to usher in the raw uninhibited light, which to me only pointed out flaws and flecks of dust. But he wanted to observe the perimeters of his farm as if he were admiring paintings in a museum. The utility furnishings of the house hardly mattered when compared with the hills, gardens and trees. From one parlor window, he looked past three cherry trees and up the steep hay field to the sky. From the other parlor window, straddled by two prized, very old and very tall Oxheart cherry trees, he looked down the precision-rowed garden to the Red Astrakhan tree and the stand of woods edging Kniffen's Hollow. Even at Christmas when there was nothing but black scribblings above the snow and trees branches etching the sky, he could still see the baubled stalks of Brussels sprouts, ready for Christmas dinner. So Dad would wander through his home like an observer in a gallery with all the curtains drawn open to give full credit to the artist. Through the dining room windows were the quince trees and the maple grove. The children's bedroom looked out to the stand of oaks, their branches clutching each other like protective arms to hold off the cold winds that swept in from the Bay. The large kitchen window held the same view. When he lounged on the parlor couch, he only had to lift his head.

During the gardening season, Dad would come in from the fields, wash up at the kitchen pump and then relax or read on the couch while waiting for dinner. He would elect one of the 'little barbarians' to wind up the gramophone and then cuddle whoever wanted to be cuddled. The couch had big fluffy cushions and was large enough to accommodate an additional two or three toddlers. Behind it, the window sill was long and wide, so we often climbed over Dad to sit and play. With Dad away for half the year and out in the fields for the other half, we claimed him when we could.

At both ends of the couch stood two oak tables and two bookcases, both overflowing with books piled high. In fact, the whole parlor resembled a lived-in library, which it basically was. With no radio on the farm and TV years away, reading material offered our only means of escape. Large bundles of newspapers and magazines arrived weekly from the post office, and Dad was always mailing home boxes of books from Montreal. The clutter grew. The bookcases held our multi-volumed sets: an *Everyman's* collection of classics, a gilt-edged set of Shakespeare, *Nations of the World*, which Dad loved to browse through now that his globe-trotting days were over. And like all students of Ancient Rome, he revelled in Gibbon's *Decline and Fall*. Before Dad bought us the wonderful *Book of Knowledge*, our favourite set was *Nelson's Loose Leaf Encyclopaedia*. Oversized envelopes would arrive in the mail with updated information, and Dad would unlock the spine of the large volumes with a funny little key, inserting the new pages and handing us the old ones. Somehow it seemed like an exciting operation, and toddlers would demand the discarded pages to chew on, giving them their first impressions of the printed word.

All the Marvin children were reading and writing before we started school, and for proof of this, one only had to open any of the books in the family library to witness our scribblings. Early on, we learned to defer and appreciate by scrawling on fly leafs. Mother's beautiful, gilt-edged and embossed *Vicar of Wakefield* and *Rasselas* were covetously identified with all our names and ages as we perfected our writing skills. Even our Bible gathered footnotes. We did things like that.

Mother and Dad shared the same taste in reading, except when it came to religion and politics. Dad would occasionally peruse the Bible, while Mother religiously read *The Hansard*, the reportage of the House of Commons proceedings in Ottawa. She read other books and periodicals at leisure, but I'll always connect *The Hansard* with nursing babies. Every once in a while, Mother would suck in her breath, not because the baby had bit her, but because some parliamentarian had exposed his intelligence. She would exclaim, "Well, I never! Dan, would you just listen to this!" Dad would listen and say, "Dearie, an election is coming." Mother often asked Dad to buy her certain books, and on one trip to Montreal, she asked for Aristotle's *Politics*. Dad bought it, a slim, grey *Everyman's* volume, and he included for himself a book by Prime Minister Mackenzie King called *Industry and Humanity*. It was a big, fat, ugly, pea-green tome with too many pull-out charts that became blousy with reading. When it arrived, I flipped through the book trying to expand my mind, but I couldn't fold the charts back in properly, so I pulled them all out and burned them in the Franklin fireplace. When Dad finally found the time to sit down with his new book, I watched as he searched in vain for the charts and then exclaimed, "What in blazes!?" Blazes indeed. He called a family conference and I eventually confessed. "You burned them!? Confound it all, Sweetlady, why?" That was the first time I remember Dad reprimanding me, leaving a pea-green stain on my childhood.

Under the parlor window that looked down the garden rows was a lonely, black lacquered love seat: hard, caned and uncomfortable. Since no one ever sat there, it served as a repository for stacks of newspapers and magazines. Between this love seat and the couch was the coziest corner of the parlor. Two rocking chairs with petit-point cushions faced out from either side of the Franklin fireplace, while in front lay Mother's large, red shaggy wool rug. I spent many happy hours lying there on my stomach reading my favourite stories. On any given evening, we would be gathered like bugs on the rug with our books open in front of us. The red rug provided a meeting place of sorts, or in testy times, a council of toddler wars, hissy arguments, and age of reason jousting, but most of all, it provided a foundation of comfort, perfect for reading and peaceful exhaustion at the end of the day.

In the middle of the room stood a rock-solid oak table piled with magazines and cluttered with brass work: trays, bowls, boxes, a cribbage board, a large cigar box holding the mah jong game. Sitting in the middle of the table was Dad's chess board, the men poised in a game being played out by post cards. The cards piled up on the mantelpiece, checked and rechecked by Dad for placement of the men. Considering his long absences, it is a wonder that the board stayed untouched, but one of our earliest, strictest rules was never to touch the chess board—that and never to leave fingerprints on the brass. The boys found loopholes to every rule, but they always observed these two. Brass work glittered in every room, the polish unmarred, and the chess game continued undisturbed.

Underneath the table and attached to the legs were two book racks, and it was here where my earliest days of playing house took place. Daniel and I would push the books to the floor and set up our toys on either side of the racks. While I played with my tea set and dolls, Daniel's lead soldiers battled to the death. Amid gunfire and explosions, he would realistically break off arms and legs and twist off heads, piling the pieces in a fruit bowl. Eventually, Mother threw the remains in the stove so that babies wouldn't eat them and become casualties themselves. The battles under the table resulted in such carnage that whole regiments of reinforcements arrived every Christmas to continue Daniel's devastating wars.

The parlor was a large room separated from the children's equally large bedroom by heavy drapes that hung across a wide, arching doorway. Parlor bedrooms were common in the colonial style. In front of the dark, heavy-curtained doorway, almost blocking the entrance to our bedroom was Dad's oak and leather easy chair. In the corner beside it was the pièce de résistance of the parlor, the gramophone, establishing along with the sewing machine and the milk separator that we were mechanically up to date. The cabinet below held several racks of records, while a table off to the side was piled high with many more. Dad was always bringing home armfuls of records, so over the years the collection grew by the hundreds. We covered the classics in every which way: nocturnes, gigues, symphonies, concertos, quartets. I learned my essential Italian from these pieces, always spoken *con brio*[1]: *adagio, andantino, scherzo, oratorio*, and the full-bodied *rondo capriccioso*, after a beautiful piece by Saint-Saens. Mother and Dad loved to discuss music and would often play the same piece done by different artists, different conductors, or under different arrangements, comparing the effect of subtle changes in orchestration. Dad could never decide which he liked best, the piano or the violin, Rachmaninoff or Kreisler. With Mother, there was no question; opera was her first and only love. I grew up on a glut of opera, learning at a young age all I needed to know about magic flutes, tin soldiers, field mice and fallen women. I loved those magical performances, the records twirling dizzily, mesmerizing me into the opulent opera houses of the world. My favorite record was Luisa Tetrazzini singing "Caro Nome," from Verdi's *Rigoletto*. If Mother was busy and said,

[1] With spirit

"Oh just play anything," that was the record I sought out of the pile. "Caro Nome" made Luisa seem a bird-like creature, a hummingbird of infinite delicacy, when in fact at that point in her career she was giving her last concerts, admitting to her enormous weight, but grateful to be in voice.

Whenever Mother was cooking, cleaning or doing anything at all, she would have us play records and then sing along, eventually taking over herself. Mother was happiest when she sang. She had the need and compulsion of an artist, so the house and hills echoed with her beautiful voice. I can still see her sweeping the floor as she breezily sang Bizet's Habanera. Mother's voice was ingrained in our systems, a soft breeze blowing around our ears, almost reduced to a natural function, like breathing, barely noticeable. She sang in the barn while milking the cows, on the back step while bunching vegetables, in the gardens while hoeing and weeding. Her repertoire was endless with instant recall, and if she wasn't in the mood for opera, she sang the Scottish ballads she grew up with, or American classics by Stephen Foster and Edward MacDowell, beautiful dreamers and wild roses. Even when Mother called Harry from the pasture, she would cup her hands and sing out high and low, "Harrr-eeee," then again low and high, "Harrr-eeee," the pounding of the hooves and the end of the short song. Mrs. Kniffen always mentioned how lovely it was to hear Mother's voice filtering down through the trees to the Hollow. Often, tourists on their way to Kniffen's beach would stop and listen, and Mother, coming out of the barn or in from the gardens, would invite them to tea on the glide swing. We had many summer visitors, and one of our favourites was Mr. Benjamin Bishop, who had a tiny cottage high above Kniffen's Hollow. He was an older gentleman, a school master from New York City who had spent his long life as a patron of the performing arts. Many times I heard him say that he had heard all the great singers of the day at the Metropolitan Opera and none had a voice that equalled Mother's.

Through the heavy parlor curtains was the children's bedroom, large enough for three double beds with chests of drawers in between and tables at the ends. The centrepiece of the room was a mantled fireplace fronted by a large brick apron. At Christmas, the boys would fuel up and light toy train engines and watch as they bumped back and forth over the bricks.

Strangely, they observed the rules of safety with this dangerous toy and caused much more damage with the hammers and saws from their tool sets. To one side of the fireplace sat Mother's rocking chair, where she would cradle babies and sing Brahms' "Wiegenlied," "Shlafe Mein Prinzchen," "Jocelyn," "The Missouri Waltz," and all of those lovely Negro lullabies: "Shortnin' Bread," "Stay In Your Own Backyard" and so many others. It was all such a long time ago, but those songs still echo–so soothing.

On cold winter nights, we would sit in front of the fire with our hot cocoa and buttered cinnamon toast while Mother read Thornton Burgess bedtime stories. The whole cast of woodland characters was as familiar as old friends: Sammy Jay, Paddy the Beaver, Jerry Muskrat. How we laughed when Peter Rabbit scared off Reddy Fox by hopping about from under a hat. And oh, the worry when Danny Meadow Mouse was scooped up by Hooty Owl, only to escape his clutches and land in the Old Briar-Patch. When we began to slump, Mother would warm the flannel sheets in front of the fire and put us to bed. Our eyes would flicker with the shadows on the ceiling, and often stories never had endings.

Until I was 8, I shared a bed with Daniel, while Jim shared with Douglas, and Lorna shared with Joan. As we got older, this arrangement varied, because we often played musical beds according to the news we had to share. Our nightly forum was an in-depth review of the day's events. Trips to the village called for a full report: Did you have ice cream? Did Dad give you a penny? What candy did you buy at Mrs. Schmidt's? Who did you see? We kept close track of vital statistics. The boys often had a full day's worth of mischief to report, and we would lie in the dark giggling as they freely discussed every detail of their deceit and trickery, always followed up with the warning not to tell, "Or Else!" I wouldn't dream of it.

I often wished for a bed of my own in a room of my own, but then I never would have had the luxury of lying in the dark discussing every childish thought that fell into our heads. Sometimes, Mother would hear us whispering and giggling and she would call in with that loaded question, "Is everyone asleep?" Of course we were. Our nightly forum was a child's preserve, separate and inviolate, where we could freely theorize and philosophize. The dark held no fear as we eagerly expanded our little minds.

Between Mother and Dad's room and the kitchen were two equally small rooms. The pantry stood beside the kitchen, cluttered with boxes, barrels, and cupboards up to the ceiling. Next to the pantry and at the ell in the hallway was Uncle Peter's bedroom. A glance into his room, even if he wasn't there, seemed to say he was there all right. The room was almost claustrophobic, not only because of its size, but also because of the green vines that crawled over the wallpaper. I have never had green vines on my walls lest the jungle motif start furtively moving. Uncle Peter burrowed in there like a beast of prey in his jungle, waiting to catch us with his hairy gorilla arm as we rushed by. He would lie on his bed, banked by pillows, reading pulp magazines and smoking 'like a smoke stack,' as Mother said, as if he were steaming in his jungle. As I passed by he would say, "Come here wee Mary and show me your fernitickles (freckles)." I hated my freckles. Even worse, he assured me that only snakes had green eyes. If he was in his room, I always ran through the hallway as fast as I could, but Daniel, an early pioneer and ready to suffer, would call out, "Uncle Peter, I'm coming down the hall." He would run like mad and more often than not be caught by a hairy arm as he slid on Mother's hooked rug. Uncle Peter would tickle and torture him as he screamed for help, the uproar continuing until Mother intervened. And Uncle Peter's last words, "That will teach you."

The room barely contained a single bed, a chair and a small table. The table always held a can of tobacco with a beautiful girl in highland dress on it, the only indication that Uncle Peter was a connoisseur of feminine beauty. A narrow window looked past the gardens to the oaks, though I doubt the view interested him any more than the larger, more profound views of life. The table held a lamp, a pile of Zane Grey novels and other magazines made of cheap grey paper, which I presume were not worth the paper they were printed on, but provided education for idiots. Of a higher order were the lowbrow *Police Gazette*, *News of the World* and the *New York Daily News*. Uncle Peter probably nosed through the quantities of papers, periodicals and magazines that Mother and Dad subscribed to, but the above were exclusively his. Mother forbad us from sinking so low, but I am sure everyone in the house looked at them. I know I did when they were recycled to the outhouse. That's when my reading suddenly improved, when I started reading about Al Capone, my favourite gangster.

The *New York Daily News* vividly and pruriently detailed all of his exploits. Daniel was a voracious reader, and it was only natural for a young boy to be enticed by the gaudy cover of the *Police Gazette*. He quickly substituted it for Mother Goose, who flew out the window once for all. When he started school, he climbed out of the gutter and graduated to Zane Grey.

There were no pictures on Uncle Peter's walls, but a peg held his bagpipes, tartaned and tasselled among the vines. We were taught they were an object of respect, though when Uncle Peter was out, Daniel loved to take a sock at the bladder to hear a last rude belch. One of Uncle Peter's more obvious enjoyments was playing his bagpipes, and when the urge overcame him we were sent to close his door while all hell broke loose. The boys racketed up and down the stairs and babies cried. Sane children went mad. Mother shuddered. The noise was enough to raise the dead as he wailed those same ambidextrous tunes that droned at the battle of Flodden Field and at peaceful marches around town squares. When Uncle Peter's blood subsided, he would play his chanter or mouth organ, and Mother would join in, singing "The Road to the Isles," "Loch Lomond," and "Flow Gently Sweet Afton." I suppose Uncle Peter wasn't entirely sub-culture.

In front of Uncle Peter's bedroom and underneath Mother's hooked rug lay a trap door leading down to our root cellar. In the fall, Dad and Uncle Peter would wrestle large, burlap bags of vegetables down the narrow stairs: potatoes, turnips, parsnips, carrots, onions, and anything else that could last the winter. Without an icebox on the farm, I suppose you could say the root cellar was our fridge. It stayed cool throughout the year and breathed a crisp harvest aroma from all the vegetables and especially the apples. Dad had levelled most of the orchards, but every year we ended up with more apples than we needed: Bishop Pippin, Golden Russett, Gravenstein, Spy, Rome, Macintosh and several others. The only apple we didn't harvest was the Red Astrakhan because they were too delicate. Instead, we purloined them on the branch at the moment of maturity, every single one. We couldn't resist their melting deliciousness and would climb the tree to sit and munch away. Our only regret was that we had just the one tree. This delicate, rosy Russian apple with the snowy, melting flesh seems to have fallen out of favour and is now very difficult to find.

Stacked above the apple barrels and bags of root vegetables were shelves filled with Mother's preserves, hundreds of jars lined up and labelled in a delicatessen display: sauces, chutneys, pickles, chows, peppers, relishes, my favourite cauliflower and mustard pickles. In the summer when Mother was preserving, the stringent, cleansing odour of vinegar and spices for pickles wafted through the house, penetrating the walls and floorboards and tingling in our noses. Preserving was hot, hot work, spaced throughout the summer like heat waves. Every farm wife had to do it if the menu was to survive the winter. As each crop came in, Mother would skim off the cream and start chopping for chutneys and relishes. Ingredients had to be carefully cooked to the proper temperature, the jars and lids sterilized and then boiled again after being filled. I don't think Mother ever had a jar spoil on her, but she was always cautious when opening preserves, listening for the pop of the lid, taking a sniff and a tentative taste. If we bought canned food, she was doubly cautious, also checking for dents or bloating. Dad sometimes went moose hunting with Mr. Boyd and Ned McCormick, and on one trip, Mr. Boyd ate from a spoiled can of corned beef and died of botulism. It was a village tragedy. Dad was in St. Anne's at the time, so it was freely discussed with relieved emotions that he had not been with them.

Although we were surrounded by food, with no refrigeration, many fruits and vegetables had to be eaten fresh or preserved right away. When Dad butchered a hog, he took it to Mr. Oikle in the village for curing. Mr. Dukeshire handled beef. With no ice on hand, dairy products barely lasted the day, and strangely, milk would curdle into a lump during a thunderstorm. A cold drink involved a trip to the top of the pasture, where a spring bubbled up with ice-cold water. Like Jack and Jill, Daniel and I would go up for a pail of water when Mother made lemonade. With time and temperature leaving no other option on the table, farm wives busily dabbled in all the preservational arts. They pickled, salted, smoked and dried to save their summer labours and keep the winter blahs from creeping onto dinner plates. The off-season lack of fresh fruits and vegetables left a gap, barely noticed because Mother was a superb cook, despite her fixation on porridge every morning. The root cellar offered endless possibilities for soups and stews, bread was baked daily, fresh eggs and dairy were steps away, chickens awaited the chopping block, and preserves sat in reserve.

Our house had obviously been built for an expanding family, because all of the rooms were spacious except for the pantry and Uncle Peter's room. Until the MacGregors arrived, we rarely used the upstairs. Each of the five rooms was big enough for two double beds, and the largest room held three. The rooms sat like ghostly cubicles with their skeletal iron bedsteads and empty bureaus left by the former owners. Our voices were like echoes of a presence, and we closed doors quickly. Playing hide-and-seek and entering those empty, dusty rooms was boldly brave. When we were older and more courageous, Daniel and I would put a chair on the steamer trunk at the end of the hall, climb on top and lift a trap door to peer about the attic. It was empty except for a few dust-covered relics from years ago: chairs stacked on a table, a spinning wheel sitting in the corner, and boxes tied with string. Once on a dare, I climbed up to look in the boxes. Old pictures and keepsakes held lost memories, the leftovers of a life. Through a shaft of sunlight, dust drifted like stars in the heavens before passing into shadow.

Only two of the upstairs bedrooms were used now and then. Above the kitchen was Mrs. McCormick's room, made cozy by the rising heat from the stove. She would arrive with her suitcase and stay for several weeks, her yearly visit coinciding with the mysterious arrival of another baby. We were never allowed in the room, so it stayed neat and tidy, our one example of disciplined decor other than the attic. When Mother finished a quilt, a rug or a set of curtains, she would put it on display in Mrs. McCormick's room for a brief respite before sending it downstairs to be destroyed. For most of the year, the room sat like a page out of farm-house beautiful, warmed and waiting for the next baby.

One summer day while Mother was making jam, Douglas, still a toddler, was roaming about in his usual way and wandered into Mrs. McCormick's room. On the floor lay a small grate that you could open to access the stove pipe. Douglas lifted the grate and fell through. Mother heard a scream and looked up in horror to see Douglas' legs dangling over the stove pipe. She jumped on a chair and pushed his feet up, burning her arms on the stove pipe as she screamed at me to run up and pull Douglas free. I raced upstairs and lifted Douglas by his outstretched arms.

Such agony that little boy suffered. His whole bottom was burned, and he endured excruciating pain. Douglas slept with me while he healed, and his arms would crush my neck as he cried in my ears. Since it was summer, Mother and Dad decided it was best to cover his burns with Vaseline and let him run around with a long shirt and no pants. For some reason, Uncle Peter teased Douglas and me more than the other children. He shamed Douglas, and nothing Mother or Dad said could make a dent on 'that blasted numbskull,' as Dad called him. His teasing became worse when the burn healed, leaving Douglas' bottom wrinkled and shrivelled for quite a while. Uncle Peter would pull down his pants and laugh as Douglas cried. Once, when Douglas started school and we were walking home, Uncle Peter did this in front of our friends. I clearly remember hating Uncle Peter as I had never hated before. I screamed out, "Leave him alone!" as poor Douglas stood there with his pants at his knees, not even bothering to pull them up, crying his little heart out. I ran over and pulled up his pants, while Alice Copeland whispered to me in amazement, "Is that what boys look like?"

The bedroom opposite Mrs. McComick's served as Dad's workroom, holding an iron bed, his drafting board, and a table full of radio parts. Dad's early days of desperation on the farm were also the early days of radio, so he took the opportunity to make crystal sets and sell them. In those days, electric radios cost an arm and a leg, and the purchase of one prompted gossip and uninvited guests. For a fraction of the price, a crystal radio pulled a modest signal out of thin air using little more than a crystal, coiled brass and a wire strung to a tree. Ours sat on a table in the parlor, offering nothing more sensational than static. Not even the radio waves could find us. Still, the ultimate thrill on Christmas Eve was to tune in to the North Pole and hear Santa Claus ho-ho-hoing through a snowstorm.

I don't know how many sets Dad sold, but every once in a while, he would go upstairs, saying he was off to do 'a bit of tinkering.' The boys would follow along to watch and help, sitting around the table cluttered with boxes of cylinders, coils of brass wire, earphones, dials, and a key element called a cat's whisker. Dad would piece together a radio, explaining every step and letting the boys lend a hand. In a few short years, radios became affordable and electricity came creeping along the Chute Road, though it never quite reached the farm. Dad's final pronouncement on crystal sets was, "Ah am wasting mah tahm." Out went the equipment to the apple packing house for the boys to play with. They fiddled with dials and conductors and ran about with earphones clamped to their heads, pretending not to hear Mother when she called. Their hearing suddenly improved when she ordered them to the lilac bush for a tingler. On summer days, they would disappear into the woods wearing earphones, and I wouldn't be surprised if someone today discovered a set beside a brook. Dad needn't have worried about wasted time, because soon the boys were dabbling in elementary science and engrossed in the radio equipment. Building crystal sets was a popular hobby back then, so Dad ordered all the radio magazines. He showed the boys how to make speakers using various materials and how to amplify the sound using buckets. They made antennas out of saws, bedsprings, ploughs, anything at all. Experiments abounded, and that summer Daniel drifted down from the ozone long enough to find his vocation in the airwaves. Years later when he took to the skies, this one-time hobby allowed him to fulfil many times over his boastful claim that he would see the world.

From as far back as I can remember, Dad's drafting table sat in front of the upstairs bedroom window, comfortably positioned where he could look out past two very tall Bing cherry trees and down to the gardens. Tacked to the drawing board were large sheets of creamy drafting paper filled with Dad's intricate drawings. A table to the side held his rulers, callipers, compasses and delicate instruments set in velvet-lined boxes like expensive cutlery. We didn't understand the meaning of the word 'turbine' other than it was a type of engine Dad was trying to invent, but we knew its importance and that it took up a great deal of Dad's time. It seemed as regular and as necessary as milking the cows. On his return in the spring, he would pull one of the heavy rolls of drafting paper off the shelf, tack a sheaf to the board and place the others within easy reach. I loved looking at those drawings with their complex tubing and circular blades like a weather vane–Dad's dream so efficiently drawn out. Despite his intense concentration, it almost seemed like a leisurely pursuit. While we hovered and asked questions, he would lean over the drawings trying to bring this figment of his imagination to life. One day as I stood twiddling the callipers, I asked

Dad where he was going to put the turbine, in the kitchen or the barn. He chuckled and explained how the turning blades would power his invention. Daniel was leafing through a pile of old naval exams and showed him a drawing that looked much like the one he was working on. Dad said, "Sweetheart, it seems to me ah wrote those exams." On days when the weather turned, we would crowd around Mother on the old iron bed as she read from the *Boys Own* books or the *Book of Knowledge*. One rainy day while Dad sat bent over his plans, Mother read us *Tom Sawyer*, which had just arrived in a shipment of books. We laughed and laughed when Tom offered to show his toe in return for letting his friend whitewash a fence. I sat at the bottom of the bed leaning on a pillow, listening to Mother and staring up at the only picture on the wall, a framed portrait of Rachmaninoff cut out of the *Illustrated London News*. Rachmaninoff was Dad's favourite pianist, but, I am sorry to say, a very ugly man. I stared into his face all afternoon, being reminded by his presence that he was a great artist, and loving *Tom Sawyer* to this day.

I could never understand Dad's turbine, but another set of drawings read like the happiest of fairy tales. Page after page of blueprints held the house Dad was going to build for Mother, a stately Marvin manor with a double-doored entrance topped by a fanlight window; a wide, columned verandah layered with a sweeping balcony up above; tall windows bracketed by shutters. Daniel wanted a Captain's Walk, so Dad re-worked the roof. I spent hours poring over those drawings, following water pipes to the bathroom and spacious kitchen. I wandered from room to room, sitting at fireplaces and cushioned bay windows, watching the traffic on the river from the site at the top of the Miller field. Those simple lines sketched out my future, and I couldn't wait for the work to begin. I don't think I ever liked the farmhouse with its plain layout, rough edges and linoleum floors, so I latched onto Dad's dream house and my heart wandered off the way hearts often do, led astray by a mirage. Later in life when I was bouncing from one dismal dump to another, my mind would drift back to the old farmhouse and wonder what I wouldn't do for that full-sized kitchen, or all those bedrooms, or that huge parlor and dining room in a house all my own.

Looking down the Miller field from the Chute Road

As well as being divided horizontally by the Chute Road, the farm was also split vertically by a small brook. This brook originated high above our pasture at a spring that bubbled up with ice-cold water. It tumbled down through the pasture and took a sharp turn at the barn before arriving at the Chute Road, where it pooled under a bridge in a frame of rocks. From there, it flowed down through a colonnade of oak, paused at the trout pool, and continued on between the trees edging the Miller Field. At the bottom of the field, it drifted lazily past a stand of weeping willows before seeping onto the depressing spectre of our beach: rocky and pebbled on dark brown sand, still holding remnants of the ship building days—spiritless struts leaning into each other.

Milestones are not only made of cement blocks placed along highways; they can also be pools under bridges where children once played. I remember one particular sub-zero wintry day when I cried all the way home from school, unable to feel my feet and barely able to walk, unable to blow my drippy nose with my frozen fingers. When we got to the bridge, Daniel looked over the edge and told me that if he threw me into the brook I would be dead by the time he counted to three. I was a child riddled with fears, so I never forgot how quickly I could die. The painful misery of the two-mile walk from school in sub-zero weather was nothing as I glanced over the railing and saw those black bubbles peeping out of the blanket of snow like eyes. I never learned to swim, though I tried, and I have never set foot in water without remembering the count of three.

Things cheered up in the spring, and on the first hot days we would walk barefoot on the dusty road with our shoes in our book bags. At the bridge we would stop to wade knee-deep in the brook, or if we wanted to sit, the bank held a sward of soft grass and a stone seating arrangement where we could dangle our feet until they shrivelled like prunes. We called it the Bridge Brook, and it formed an idyllic pool edged with grass, wispy bushes, fern, and spear-like shoots tipped by tiny lilies. In season, we picked daisies, buttercup, myrtle, blue flag and the treasured mayflower in the damp, cool shade. Lily pads waited for frogs that sat perched on the island tips of rocks, all freshly green. Skippers danced on the water as dragonflies flitted dangerously. Elegantly-winged barn swallows swooped down for mud to build their nests under the eaves of the barn. Red-winged blackbirds rocked on slender reeds with mystifying buoyancy. Robins, finches, chickadees, wrens, cardinals, blue jays, red-capped woodpeckers, orange tanagers, orioles, and nut-hatches nested in the spruce, ash, birch, maple, elm and oak that enclosed the brook. To one side, genuflecting wild cherry bushes overflowed in the dappled sunlight. A steep embankment swept up to the barn, luxuriating in a careless array of wildflowers: chicory, aster, thistle, wild rose, primrose, Queen Anne's pungent lace, butter and eggs, goldenrod, wild carrot, lady slippers, blue vetch, sticky milkweed, weeds with prickles and burrs. Mother named every one of them for us. All of this flora and fauna at our feet and over our heads concerned us deeply then. Nature surrounded us and was busy throughout the day. I could never have had these memories of the loveliness of nature had I not lived on the farm I hated.

Jim, Lorna and Mary near the lilac bush

When we were young, we spent much of our summer at this pool. We were within calling distance, and Mother would occasionally ask, "Is everyone behaving?" I can't recall that we were ever bored or even quarrelled at the Bridge Brook. I must have made hundreds of paper boats for my little brothers to float. They would toss balls across the pool and be fascinated by the frogs and the sudden iridescent flash of a dragonfly. Lorna, Joan and I would gather dandelions and daisies, split the stems and deck ourselves with chains. We scrounged for every last wild strawberry, ripened to rubies with a delicious, pervasive perfume. If we were hot, we would refresh ourselves by drinking from the brook or jumping in the water to splash about. Our clothes would dry on our backs and we'd jump in again or sit under the bridge in the cool shade and dangle our feet. Sometimes I would just lie on the grass in a patch of sun listening to all the birds chattering away. The mood livened when Daniel, Jim and Douglas showed up. After having successfully destroyed every last Christmas toy, nothing remained but the glory of nature. They would splash each other, climb trees, gouge out spruce gum to chew, or swing on the bridge railing. If a horse and buggy came along, they would dash under the bridge to experience the momentary thrill of hearing the horse's hoofs on the planks above resounding and echoing. Farther up towards the pasture was a smaller pool where they collected skippers in jars and brought them down to the bridge pool. The boys thought that skippers were the one thing the pool needed more of, but they couldn't keep the frogs from eating them.

One of the mysteries of the Bridge Brook was the enormous supply of frogs' eggs every spring, suspended in the water like transparent clouds of tapioca. We would scoop them up in jam jars to sit on the kitchen window sill, or take them to school to observe their marvellous evolution, watching as the seemingly dormant, milky mass twitched to life. When the tadpoles emerged, we took them back to the brook, the hope being that we would soon have thousands of frogs. Year after year we were disappointed when it didn't happen. Dad finally explained that their mothers and fathers ate them. Parents eating their children didn't go over well with the younger ones, so he added that some escaped down to the river and turned into turtles. Oh yes, he said, he had seen many frogs-turned-turtles in Norfolk, Virginia, off the side of his ship when he was in training.

We loved our frogs. They were so adaptable to our small hands and felt like the softest silk. They sat on rocks, watching with knowing eyes and springing with childish playfulness.

After hesitating at the bridge, the brook bubbled down through a colonnade of oak to the trout pool, ringed by tall trees and a thick enclosure of ferns. The pool was much deeper than the Bridge Brook and had soft, cushioned banks of bright green moss and dried pine needles. The base of an old oak tree formed a comfortable nook where I liked to sit in the quiet shade on hot summer days. I would escape the family and take refuge at the trout pool, where I could be alone with my doll, sitting in privacy on the cool moss, the air delicately perfumed by last year's fallen pine needles.

The novelty of this pool was that it was home to a very foxy trout who had evaded years of my brothers' frustrated attempts to catch him. In the process of trying and vying to see who would catch him, they systematically fished the pool out except for the fat old trout. He weathered the mindless whim of heartless little boys and profited from their pointless carnage of earthworms. Like a mastermind, he cleverly nibbled worms right off the hook, and the boys wondered how a fish could do such an educated thing. They would pull their lines out and stare in amazement at the empty hook.

One day as we crossed through the woods with Dad, we stopped at the pool. There was the old trout, knifing across the sunbeams that latticed through the trees. Dad heard all about this wily nemesis and was so impressed by his cleverness that he forbad the boys from fishing there again. As long as we remained on the farm, so did the old trout. During one bedtime discussion, the boys struck upon a solution and called out, "Dad, can fish smell?" Dad's answer was, "Wha of course son. That's wha they have noses!" It seemed sensible to me then and it still does, though I don't know for sure.

There came a time when life was almost snuffed out of the Bridge Brook. Dad never left questions unanswered, so when the boys quizzed him about the Mediterranean and thereabouts, he told them all he knew. Their appetite for information was voracious; they absorbed nuggets and didn't let them go to waste. This time, they hatched a scheme and named it the Suez Canal. With shovels, pickaxes and crowbars in hand, they laboured in the pasture for days, digging and moving rocks to divert the flow of the brook where it turned at a right angle behind the barn. Only later did they realize that the cows might stumble and break their legs. No one thought to ask them what they were doing, though all the while Mother had a clear view from the kitchen door and through the maple grove. She was satisfied that they answered when called and were busy with manual labour. When it finally dawned on Dad to leave his work in the gardens and have a look-see, he was amazed and dismayed to discover that they were building their canal straight to the barn, which would flood out the cows and pigs. Dad pushed his hat back on his head and exclaimed, "Sweetheart (Daniel), do yew realize what yew have almost done?" They didn't care until he told them to fill it all in. Then the work was twice as hard and not half the fun. In no time, life along the brook returned to normal. Frogs gargled their night song, and the old trout bobbed and snapped at flies. Whenever we trekked up to the spring for a bucket of ice-cold water for lemonade, one of the boys would deplore, "there's our old Suez Canal."

Mounting the steep incline from the Bridge Brook, one couldn't help but notice an earthy pungency emanating from the barn, a conspicuous odour in evidence all along the middle of the Chute Road and down to the hitching posts on Main Street. To me, the barn loomed like an emporium of disgusting filth. It was never clean no matter how often the stalls were shovelled out and spread with fresh straw. Manure was heaved through the trap door to the side of the barn where it gathered in that monstrosity known as the manure pile, steaming and oozing like an ugly brown volcano, glistening white with crawling maggots. I loathed it and hated having to pass through the horde of flies that made it their home. Every spring the manure pile would be levelled and combined with whatever was dug up from the outhouse to be spread over the gardens. The stench was atrocious. Although we spent the summer running ragged and barefoot, I never, ever went into the gardens without my shoes. One day Dr. Campbell visited, and as he chatted with Mother in the gardens, he pulled a carrot out of the ground, wiped the dirt off with his hand and proceeded to enjoy it. I gaped in horror and offered to wash it for him, but he laughed at my fussiness and explained, "You have to eat a peck of dirt before you die." A doctor's homily.

Like every barn along the Chute Road, ours opened to an entrance hall wide enough for wagons and buggies to drive right in. Above and on both sides were the haylofts, full to overflowing, the delicate perfume of sun-dried hay wafting down to mask the earthy chemical odour of the cow stalls. The boys spent years of rainy days playing there, climbing the ladders and swinging from one loft to the other on the pulley rope, swinging and jumping like monkeys, burrowing underneath and tunnelling away to emerge elsewhere grinning and covered with straw and hay seeds. On the main floor opposite the stalls, a separate section in the back held old buggies and sleighs resting on rusty springs with no wheels or runners, their shafts and trappings hanging on the wall. My favourite was a very old, black buggy with a black oil-cloth top and windows, much like a Berlin or the village hearse, only smaller and neater. It was one of the few places I could go to be alone with my doll and drift away on my dreams. As I sat in that carriage, I was a princess times over, a queen with a king and princes by the dozen. I was Snow White kissed to life a thousand times and married just as often. I would seat myself in luxury and privacy, conjuring up all the lives I would lead, unaware that we can only live one. One day, I escaped to the barn, and when I opened the buggy door, a big black-and-white tom, one of the gang leaders, frizzed up, hissed menacingly and clawed his way past me. He scratched me badly, and I never dared go in that buggy again.

The cats were like gypsies, lurking on wagon seats and slinking in and out of secret places. Fluctuating batches of kittens and cats dragooned the mice and rats out of existence, though I never saw a single rat as long as I was on the farm. The cats were not allowed in the house and went wild in their own way, scratching and hissing. Mother always warned us, "Watch out for those tigers!" At times, a whole battalion would pop up like mushrooms and march around, then their numbers would mysteriously dwindle. They just came and went and we never knew where. Once, a sack of dead kittens was found on our beach, and being the event of the season, we thoroughly discussed it in our beds. There were certain things children instinctively didn't discuss with parents; we couldn't and didn't ask pointed questions. We finally assumed it was the sort of thing Uncle Peter would do. One day I innocently asked Uncle Peter if he liked cats, trying to get to the bottom of the sack of kittens theory.

He lowered his newspaper and said very definitely, "I love cats!" So I asked him if he liked kittens. He said, "I love kittens! And I like chickens too! I like to chop off their heads and eat them!" All said in a brusque, dogmatic Scotch voice.

An exclusive corner of the barn had several horse stalls, two of them reserved for Harry: one being his living quarters and the other one being his dressing room, gentleman that he was. Spikes held all his trappings: bridles, reins, blinkers, feed bags, curry combs, brushes, blankets and Dad's saddle. Old horse shoes nailed to his stall by previous frugal owners provided all the luck he would ever need. Often while we waited for Mother to finish the milking, we would wander over and feed him, meticulously measuring his oats, not too much or he would get frisky and kick his stall. Harry would hang his head over the door and observe us with his huge eyes while we petted him. He was as freshly scented as the hay he munched. We would talk to him about all kinds of things, and it was part of the conversation to hear him snort, to see his shoulders twitch and his tail swish back and forth in reply. Harry responded to all our praise and petting. The boys groomed him to pass the time, brushing and polishing his creamy coat. Daniel took pride in combing Harry's mane, done more carefully than his own. Harry would stand contentedly, never moving an inch. Mother assured us that Harry had his vanity. No matter how small we were, we had no fear of him. He understood us perfectly. When the boys were young and mounted him from the pasture fence, he never carried them at more than a slow, steady walk. Later, Daniel learned that piercing whistle by curling his tongue, and Harry would gallop to the pasture fence and nuzzle each of us in turn before giving one of the boys a ride.

Of all his belongings, Harry favoured his light, one-seater buggy the best. When he was harnessed and waiting for Mother at the back door, he would neigh and snort impatiently, wanting to make tracks. Mother would call to him as if he were a person, "I'm coming Harry." If she collected us after school, we would squeeze onto the single seat, and after mounting Oakdene Hill, Mother would give him rein to fly over the Chute Road, leaving ribbons of dust streaming behind. In those young years, our ultimate thrill was to race along the Chute Road at such speed. Mother only pulled in the reins going down McCormick's hill, letting him go again as he galloped over the Bridge Brook and tore up to the barn like a young colt. We would excitedly climb down and crowd around that magnificent animal, thrilled with our adventure, offering him water or oats, combing and petting him. Harry was pet heaven. To us, he was more of a person than a horse: loyal, gentle, as constant as a star. We often argued about whether Harry preferred carrots or hard bread, whether he liked Jim better because he gave him sugar cubes, or whether he liked boys better than girls, but the thing was, we all loved him dearly, and after Mother and Dad, Harry was the next best person.

Uncle Peter pulling Harry's one-seater. L to R: Daniel, Mary, Jim, Douglas.

The barn housed numberless pigs and nameless cows, all of them nourished as carefully as children. When Daniel and I were very young, we often accompanied Mother to watch as she milked the cows. We would sit in the hay at a safe distance in case a reflex action might cause a kick. Most of the cows were skittish and unpredictable except for Daisy, a creamy-colored patrician who accepted our lavish attention. Sometimes we sat on a huge squared oak timber that stretched the length of the barn and perhaps had missed its original purpose. Noisy sparrows crowded the entrance way, growing fat on hay seeds, while cats lurked nearby in the shadows. Barn swallows swooped protectively as their nestlings flitted about. Several times, we thought a barn owl had taken up residence, but Douglas said it was a horned owl just dropping in for a visit. All of nature made use of the barn at some point, finding comfort on cold winter nights or looking in to see what was on the menu.

As Mother sat milking, Scotty, our Scottish sheep dog, would poke his head in to see if the cows were ready for pasture. We would sit listening to the steady force of milk against the tin pail and the munching and mumblings of the cows as they waited patiently to get one of life's onerous exercises over and done with. Beside the grain cubicles were tin bowls, and when Mother was finished, she would fill them for the cats to encourage them to eat the rats, so that the rats, if there ever were any, would not eat the grain. Excess milk then went into the pig troughs. In the kitchen, Mother would strain the milk through cheesecloth and serve it over our porridge, then pour the rest into large pans, leaving it until the cream rose to the top. Later, a separator simplified the process down to a matter of seconds, just as long as it took to pour the milk into a bowl-like receptor. As the milk swirled, cream went in one direction and skim milk in the other. I had to stand on a chair to satisfy my curiosity. If we needed butter, Mother would then put the cream in the churn, a barrel-like contraption that hung from folding legs. It had handles like a baby buggy, and you pushed it up and down to shake the butter out of the milk. After removing the butter, we'd be left with tangy buttermilk, part of the pig's diet as well as ours. Milking was a relentless chore, done every day before sunrise: sitting and shivering by the lantern light on cold winter mornings, lugging the heavy pails back to the house through drenching rain and drifting snow, then doing it all over again in the evening, twice a day without letup.

With the morning milking out of the way, the cows were free to wander the pasture under the watchful eye of Scotty. He had replaced Ruff, our black and tan Airedale, whom Dad said had run off. We discussed this at our nightly forum and decided that Ruff would never do such a thing and had probably run off to the happy hunting ground. Uncle Peter proudly boasted that Scotty was a direct descendant of Old Hemp, the original Border Collie, a borderline genius and Scottish national hero. Uncle Peter insisted that Border Collies were the smartest dogs of all and could even understand what you were saying. It certainly seemed that way. When Mother told Scotty to bring in the cows, she only had to say it once.

Scotty

If she told him to go find one of the boys, he would do it, tearing off at full gallop. One day as we were playing, Scotty trotted up and singled out Daniel with unmistakable meaning. Daniel resisted, but Scotty stood implacable and marched him off like an officer of the law. Scotty was a busy dog with a full schedule, and I often wondered if he thought the farm was his. He was happiest patrolling the fields on his endless rounds, barking out orders like a captain on a ship. Cats slunk into corners, turning with a venomous hiss as Scotty trotted by. Wanderlust chickens scurried back to their quarters, Scotty's warning nipping at their heels. Even the pigs perked up, grunting in protest but taking direction. Sometimes at night, we'd wake to a barnyard brawl; a predator looking for a late-night snack. Dad would get the shotgun to investigate, only to find Scotty holding the field. Without question, he ruled over the animal kingdom. I marvelled when he rounded up the cows for milking, scurrying back and forth across the pasture, chasing down strays, nipping at laggards and staring down rebels. Back they would come, marching on the double-quick with Scotty barking time. A farm couldn't operate without a dog, so we crossed paths with many on our travels. The Rices, whom we rarely talked to, had an overly-friendly hound of questionable intelligence. At the Crossroads, stern Mr. Harris's miserable cur was always surly, often rude. On the Reade's dairy farm, their German shepherd suffered from the Prussian syndrome, efficient but belligerent. Only Scotty combined business and pleasure in perfect harmony. Border Collies are bred for farm work, so Scotty enjoyed the good fortune of doing exactly what he was suited for, a blessing upon man or beast.

One day when Mother was making lemonade, she asked me to go up the pasture for a bucket of ice-cold spring water. Douglas heard and offered to come along, promising to show me something wonderful on the way. Naturally I expected something wonderful; I could hardly wait. I asked for details, but Douglas wouldn't tell, he wanted to surprise me. Off we went through the pasture gate, and half way up the hill beside the brook we came to some boulders that we often climbed on. Douglas led me over to some flat rocks and handed me the bucket. The moment had come, that special moment. Using all of his strength, he flipped a large rock and said to come quickly for my surprise. I ran over and looked down at the dank earth as it seized up in a writhing, crawling mass of brown snakes, tangled together but quickly slithering in all directions, straight towards me. It was the most hideous sight I had ever seen. I screamed my head off, dropped the bucket and ran home paralyzed with fear. I never, ever went into that pasture again. As often as I had calmly walked past those rocks on the way to the spring, I never once suspected the hidden terror lurking below. Snakes were my worst horror story. When we were very young, Mother, Daniel and I were walking through the maple grove when a small green grass snake wiggled across the driveway in front of us, headed for the hot house. Mother let out a piercing scream at the pitch of her lungs and yelled at us to run for the house, properly instilling my life-long fear.

Whenever the boys had reached the limits of boredom elsewhere, they would escape to the apple packing house to hammer and saw and otherwise develop their talent for destruction. The apple packing house sat across the Chute Road from the barn, a two-story structure as large as our house, weathered and unpainted except for a red door between two large, multi-paned windows. By the time I was two or three, it had lost its original purpose and now served as a general storehouse for every implement a farm could ever need, and consequently, a stockpile of every tool a boy could ever want to play with. The farm was well-equipped when Dad bought it, a testament to generations of successful farming.

Stepping through the red door, to the left you saw a long workbench facing a multi-paned window. To the right stood a rickety, sluice-like apple grader, no longer used but misused in every which way by the boys. The second floor was only a half-floor, stuffed with tools and equipment like a hardware store. The boys liked to hang off the edge of the floor until their fingers gave out, one of them standing below to break the fall. Strangely, they never suffered any broken bones or injuries more serious than slivers and hammered fingers. When I climbed the plank stairs, I always stepped carefully, afraid of falling through or falling over. Since the half-floor also lacked a railing, I watched my step, even at a safe distance. Upstairs and leaning against the walls were rolls of chicken wire, barbed wire, screening, shiny black tar-paper that smelled of liquorice, rolls of soft, pliable haywire, the repair-all of the day. Nearby sat bundles of shingles, panes of glass, and rope coiled snake-like. Barrels held odds and ends of lost usefulness that we would pull out and puzzle over. Barrel staves lay stacked like kindling, handy for sword fights and impromptu batting practice. Barrel hoops would be given a push and bounce down the stairs before rolling out the door. One corner held the packing crates we used to ship vegetables, with extra slats and tin stencils to mark our name. The boys used those stencils to ink their stomachs in bold, black letters: D. Marvin, Bear River.

Downstairs, unused equipment hung on spikes like portraits of the former owners: old horse collars with the horse-hair stuffing coming out of cracked leather, the traces and reins all brittle. The walls were covered, nothing was thrown away, but hung on spikes displayed as frugal memory: saddlebags, whips, funny little goad sticks for oxen. I was fascinated by the heavy, silver-studded trappings for oxen, which we never had. It seemed strange that such lumbering, clumsy, even stupid animals should be so wonderfully bedizened with ornate collars, fancy yokes, and silvered tips for their horns.

Stacked against the walls and stored on shelves were all the tools needed to run the farm: hand saws, buck saws, picks, crowbars, scythes, rakes, hoes, shovels, post-hole diggers, the incubator, a seeder on two little wheels (my favourite tool), spiles and buckets for tapping the maples, a large round whetstone with foot pedal for sharpening axes and such.

Flush against the multi-paned window was the long work bench where many chores and much mischief was done. Standing upright at one end were several metal lasts where Dad repaired shoes. At arm's reach, boxes held shoemaker's tools, tacks, needles, and string that Dad waxed to sew leather. Attached to the opposite end was the bench vise, a favourite of the boys, its deadly brackets providing hours of enjoyment as they crushed all things breakable, particularly my dolls' heads. Their monstrous glee provided my first insight into man's callous disregard for women and children. I spent months of every year grieving the loss of my dolls while the boys would happily pull the glass eyes out of their pockets, or jiggle the voice box to hear the mournful cry. Before the year was out, every Eaton's Beauty doll I ever got for Christmas met the same fate in the apple packing house—her skull crushed in the vise.

Below the window and running the length of the bench was an array of built-in wooden boxes holding nails, screws, nuts, bolts, tacks, studs and every necessary hand tool: hammers, pliers, screw drivers, spanners, clippers, snippers, hatchets, drills, files, chisels, punches, wrenches, levels, planes, rulers, balls of twine and carborundums. There wasn't one item my brothers didn't make good and bad use of. From the time they dropped their rattles, they found more suitable toys in the apple packing house. I can still see Dad removing nails from the work bench with a claw hammer, telling the boys, "If you littah bounders are going to hammer nails, ah wish yew would hammer them straight."

For some reason, when Douglas was very young he liked a smooth steel punch that Dad used to sole shoes. Douglas kept it in his pocket and put it under his pillow like a treasure. One has to wonder why a young boy would cling to a piece of metal unencumbered by colour or design, of the plainest cylindrical form, merely tapered to a point of utility. Dad would be sitting at the bench searching through boxes and then straighten up and say, "Duggie Don, yew littah bounder, where's mah punch?"

If anything went missing, there was always a great scampering and wails of, "I didn't touch it," or "I put it back." I don't know what mischief Dad may have been part of when he was young, but he always seemed mystified by his children. Many times, he would shake his head and say, "Dearie, these children are destructive geniuses," followed by the dire warning that seemed to be directed more at Mother than the culprits, "Dearie, this rampant destruction has got to stop." And "Whea do theah get theah ideahs?" to which Mother always replied, "Not from my side of the family." A great deal of their apprenticeship was served in the apple packing house, and if they ever practiced anything but destruction, I'm not aware of it. It didn't occur to anyone to keep them out of there. On rainy days, the boys were sent to play there with the warning, "And don't destroy anything!" They sawed and hammered and made strange things to their heart's content, some of them blatantly nailed to the wall. They would spend hours planing a piece of wood for no practical purpose other than to produce a pile of shavings that they left on the floor. Dad's attitude was that the boys really were geniuses, though slightly destructive, and if he gave them enough time and opportunity, they would eventually prove it.

Beside the apple packing house, another brooklet bubbled up enthusiastically from a pile of stones at the side of the Chute Road. Downstream, it provided refreshment for the chickens as it pushed sluggishly past their quarters. The banks of this soggy little waterway grew lush in season with watercress, parsley and mint. On hot summer days, we would straddle it all the way down to our beach, parting the tall grass aside to feel the cool sponginess of the thick grasses beneath our bare feet. Eventually, a deluxe pig pen was built at the bottom of this brook. We never hazarded social calls on the pigs the way we did with Harry or Daisy, though we watched through the fence as they rudely edged each other, grunting and squealing over slops in the trough. Every spring we would excitedly watch from a distance as the sow lounged in the weeds, sunning herself with that certain insouciance inherent in pigs, while a line-up of brand-new piglets, refreshingly pink, nuzzled and suckled to their heart's content. On one of these visits, the boar broke loose from his pen and ran snorting up the river road. We fled screaming in terror as Scotty raced to the scene and quickly cornered him. Dad and Uncle Peter led him by the snout back to hearth and home.

Beyond the pigpen, the brook trickled through a stand of willow trees, the wispy branches hanging lazily like vines, useful for swinging from one bank to the other. The brook then dribbled on to the dismal spectre of our beach: a dank, narrow strip of pebbly sand edged with limp grasses browned by salt. The rotting remains of a wharf slumped to the shore, while the struts of once-sturdy trees stood like tired totems, leaning into each other at cross angles and ready to topple. Because of a slight bend in the river, our beach served as a catchall for everything the tides had to offer. Rocks snagged seaweed that snagged driftwood. Boulders trapped logs, wedging them in place, and they in turn trapped everything from lumber to old liquor bottles. The structure ended up looking like the work of a distracted beaver. We encouraged the clutter, because it meant bigger bonfires, especially in the fall after the clearing of the gardens. Dad and Uncle Peter would gather the beach debris, while in the gardens, we would fill the wagon with weedings, stumps, corn stalks, vines and any other combustibles we could find. The boys would climb on top for the ride down to the beach, where we heaped everything into a towering mass.

Our corn boils never made the social column like the Kniffen's clam bakes, but our bonfires had substance, people stepped back. Cool, crisp evenings meant nothing around a Marvin fire. Ours would be the last beach party of the season, so it was usually well-attended. We children would sit on logs, dipping our corn into lard pails of butter and observing all the adult activity. Mother would sing, Uncle Peter would unleash the bagpipes, while high above all the talk and laughter, flames would spike wildly as sparks drifted up to the stars.

Here, I must dwell on our outhouse, the farthest one could imagine from a fount of learning, yet I unashamedly admit that it was in the outhouse where I went on to advanced education. The outhouse was not as insignificant a building as it looked. In Bear River, public utilities inched slowly along the Chute Road. The telephone came to our farm a year or two before we left, electricity only extended to Truman Hamilton's, and the sewer line stopped just outside of town at Fowler and Loo Robinson's, so from there to our farm and beyond, every home had an outhouse positioned conveniently at the back door next to the wood shed. At the time it didn't seem unusual to have this sort of accommodation as well as chamber pots under beds for night-time and severe weather. I had no idea there was anything better because the same accommodation obtained at Oakdene School and the Trading Company, where one was doubly cautious looking down to the full tide gurgling below.

To get to our outhouse required a hurried run past Mother's rock garden, the well, the wood pile, the chopping block and the apple-packing house. There it stood beside our one and only MacIntosh apple tree, the branches hanging over the roof and tapping at the small window. When the apples were ripe, the boys would climb up and sit on the roof munching away, throwing the cores at anyone coming out from below. A bout of yelling would alert Mother and off they would run. Once, we came upon a gang of reprobate robins greedily pecking away at a few choice apples lying on the ground and fermented to perfection. They stumbled and bumped into each other, swooped recklessly and missed their perches, living for the moment without a care in the world or a serious thought in their heads.

The outhouse was white-washed every year, the floor covered with linoleum, the walls covered with left-over wallpaper, some years roses, and one year cheerful yellow daffodils, the same as in our bedroom. The two seats were regularly scrubbed with creosote, and lime was sprinkled beneath to give the structure a tart, antiseptic odor. In the corner of the outhouse, piled up in one last homage to print, was every bit of adult reading material man or child could wish for. I will try to remember some of the titles Mother and Dad subscribed to. The local papers were *The Halifax Chronicle*, *The Halifax Herald* and *The Digby Courier*, which also contained the one-page *Bear River Courier*. There was the *Montreal Gazette*, the *Hansard*, *Queen's Quarterly*, *Dalhousie Review*, *Family Herald*, the *Weekly Star*, *Canadian Home Journal* and the *Farmer's Almanac*. The American papers and periodicals were the *Chicago Tribune*, the *New York Times*, the *Herald Tribune* (crosswords done diligently), *Good Housekeeping*, *Ladies Home Journal*, *McCall's*, *Atlantic Monthly*, *Harper's*, the *Philadelphia Inquirer* (not the one today), *Literary Digest*, *Country Gentleman*, *Cosmopolitan* (much different from today—then it had class), *National Geographic*, the *Saturday Evening Post*, *Colliers* and *Liberty*. There were Mother's home papers from Helensburgh and Edinburgh, the *London Times*, the *Illustrated London News*, the *Manchester Guardian*, *Tattler*, *Punch*, *Woman's Weekly* and *The Universe*, an Irish Catholic paper that Mother and Dad loved because of contributors Hillare Belloc, William Butler Yeats and G.K. Chesterton, whose *Father Brown* detective stories the magazine serialized. Dad or Uncle Peter would bring a bundle of magazines and newspapers home from the post office, and Mother would snip the string and pluck out *The Universe* first. When we were tucked in bed and the drapes pulled between our bedroom and the parlour, Mother and Dad's voices would rise and fall as they read to each other the latest instalment. They discussed the clues in the *Father Brown* mysteries far more than doxology. Finally and to round out our learning was Uncle Peter's contribution: the *Police Gazette*, *News of the World* and the *New York Daily News*, not quite higher learning, but then it was the outhouse.

At first, children were only interested in the comics, and we often fought over them when the papers arrived from the post office. Everyone wanted the *Katzenjammer Kids* first, but there were many others we all liked: *Tillie the Toiler*, *Ella Cinders*, *Krazy Kat*, *Bringing Up Father*, and *Toonerville Trolley*.

Soon, we were sifting through the rest of the pile, and it was in the outhouse where we all went on to higher learning. I often had to stand and wait while Lorna and Joan, three and two, browsed through *Woman's Weekly* with their bloomers around their ankles. When Mother called to ask what was taking so long, they would protest that they weren't done yet. The pretty rooms and intriguing recipes took up a good deal of concentration and argument, "I like this one." "No, I don't like it. Mine is nicer." "I'm going to eat all these cookies." "I like cake better." When they began to read in earnest, they followed every single serialized romance that ran. I wasn't interested in serials that took months to end, but I did clip out enough short, saccharine poems to fill a poetry scrap book.

I think my serious reading began when Lindbergh flew the Atlantic. It was too exciting an event to forget because everyone talked about it, and the papers gave it front-to-back page coverage. On the day of the momentous flight, Uncle Peter was delivering vegetables in Digby and said he saw Lindbergh's plane passing only a few hundred feet overhead. When we realized the full importance of the event a few days later, we didn't know whether to believe him or to wonder if he was trying to grab at the coat tails of fame.[1] In any case, it was time I had a hero, so at seven years of age I found one and started snipping my way through all the papers and magazines to fill my scrap books. In the outhouse, I discovered a *National Geographic* devoted to Lindbergh, so I rescued it and treasured it for years. I especially liked a picture of my hero sitting on the nose of the *Spirit of St. Louis* with a monkey wrench. Underneath was the sensible quote that if you want something done properly, do it yourself.

The boys also got carried away by Lindbergh's flight, and for a while we all set our sights on the sky. Men and women were racing around the world setting records never thought possible. The sky was spawning strange new breeds: Zeppelins, Tin Geese and Seahawks. The boys' imaginations rose to flights of fancy, and at Christmas time, they meticulously glued their balsa-wood planes and buzzed about the house, swooping and circling like the Red Baron. Their dreams fell by the wayside when Dad said there was never going to be another war. Dad was wrong, and it was during another war that Daniel and Jim realized their ambitions. I later flew as a stewardess,

---

1 Lindbergh did fly over Digby, May 20, 1927.

eventually coming down to earth and sloughing away childish euphoria and heavenly misconceptions about the sky and the people in it.

Once the flurry of flying was over, there were so many other novelties for children to marvel at: cars, telephones, electricity, radios, movies, and the totally unbelievable rumour of television—it simply couldn't happen. Our pillows at night heard everything we said. They were a repository of every original thought we had: our dreams, our aches and pains, our vicious humour, all endlessly discussed before we took flight in sleep.

After thrilling to the miracles of the age and our Buck Rogers future, my outlook turned grim when I became involved in organized crime. The exploits of Al Capone and his gang of pug-uglies became an all-consuming interest and my reading skills improved dramatically. It all started with Uncle Peter's *New York Daily News*. Other papers like the *Chicago Tribune* were large and unwieldy, and the *London Times* was like tissue paper, but the *New York Daily News* was just the right size for a child, with short text and plenty of pictures. I was fascinated by Al Capone's ugly picture and all the ugly things he did. I read every word and simply couldn't believe that these hoodlums were roaming the streets of Chicago shooting people through restaurant windows, all because of booze, a new word in my vocabulary. At the Trading Company, Daniel and Jim heard rumours of rum-running in Bear River; boats slinking through the fog and barrels washing ashore. Names were mentioned with suspicion: the Rice boys and a few notables on Indian Hill. Daniel said it wouldn't be long before the shooting started. At our nightly forum, we agreed that Mr. Darres' ice cream shop was the likeliest hotspot, since Bear River didn't have a restaurant. Mother never let us read the *New York Daily News*, so I could only read about Al Capone in the outhouse. After frightening myself out of my wits, I would stuff it under the pile of magazines for my next visit. I might have been better off with serialized romances.

About this time when I was au courant with Al Capone's peccadilloes, a new girl came to my class and she had the flowing name of Dorothea di Geronimo. I was so enamoured by her name that when I got my annual Eaton's Beauty doll at Christmas, I named her Dorothea. But Dorothea herself fascinated me even more, because she was different and she came from Chicago.

She wouldn't talk to anyone and stood all by herself at recess, holding her skipping rope and ignoring all overtures to join in schoolyard games. She just stood there, sad, thin, dark-skinned with long black hair like a proud Indian who wouldn't deign to open her mouth to anyone. She lived above the offices of Clarke Brothers, across from the Trading Company, and when I picked up the mail after school, I would see her and wave, but she would turn away and listlessly skip. One day after school, Mother collected me to go to Barr's barber shop, and just before we crossed the bridge, a lady stopped Mother to introduce herself as the owner of the farm high on the hill across the river from us. I remember Mother laughing when the lady said that whenever she heard Mother singing, she would sit on her verandah and listen. As it turned out, this lady was Dorothea's grandmother. During the conversation, tears fell and Mother sympathized, while I opened my ears to hear all I could. I was stunned to learn that Dorothea's father was a gangster in Chicago and had been jailed for murder. I gaped in shock. It might just as well have happened in Bear River. Somehow I could never approach Dorothea again; she looked so frail and so sad and I knew her secret.

Out of fear I simply had to stop reading the *Daily News* and get on with my life. I concentrated on my reader, learning by rote *The Wreck of the Hesperus*, *Inchcape Rock*, *Tubal Cain*, *The Song of Hiawatha*, and *The Village Blacksmith* under his spreading chestnut tree. But before I washed my hands of the *Daily News* and gave myself over to poetry, I couldn't resist one last gruesome murder. One day while I was sitting in the outhouse, I opened the *Daily News* to page 3, and taking up the top quarter of the page was the picture of a happy, beautiful girl with light wavy, bobbed hair, sitting sideways with her knees up so she could fit in the page. She wore pretty shoes and a dress with a pleated skirt and a sailor collar. I thought she was lovely and was going to tear her out for my movie star scrap book. But the beautiful girl on page 3 was Helen Gordon, and for all her loveliness, she had been murdered, either strangled or bludgeoned to death. I forget the horrid details, but they traumatized me and I couldn't stop reading about her. It was one of the worst murders I had ever read about, as bad as Bluebeard, worse than Al Capone shooting people through restaurant windows. I couldn't get her out of my mind, and a terrible fear took hold of me.

I ended up having nightmares, which worried Mother, but I couldn't tell her they were triggered by my studies in sin.

Shortly after this terrible event, Mother asked me to take a pail of milk up to Mrs. McCormick after the evening milking because their cow had dried up and couldn't give milk. It was a warm September evening with the shadows falling and the sun dipping into the Bay. I didn't want to go, because I was seized with wild imaginings about Helen Gordon and murder in general. I took the pail and ran up McCormick's hill as fast as I could, and instead of taking the longer route up to their driveway, I climbed the steep embankment, digging my toes into the grass. I couldn't wait a second to get home, so I called through the screen door, left the milk on the porch and bounded down the embankment. At the top of the hill, the Bay looked like a pool of blood. To the left of the road, the Miller field was manicured clean, but to the right, the spruce woods were more forbidding than ever, full of squeaks and chirps from crickets and birds. I was so terrified I could hardly breathe, and I struggled running down the hill as much as I did going up. I ran so fast I didn't care about the pebbles hurting my bare feet, and I didn't stop until I raced through the maple grove and collapsed on the kitchen couch. I was a mess.

When the leisure of summer was gone and the dalliance over pictures displaced by school books, the stack of newsprint in the corner took on the clamminess and cold of the weather. We didn't linger. I admit that I learned much more in the outhouse than I should have during those tender years. Still, other than Uncle Peter's *New York Daily News* and his pulp magazines, the reading material was acceptably high-grade, except that the glossy pages were perhaps too high-grade for general use.

On the embankment under the lilac bush. Left to right: Joan, Uncle Peter, Mary (holding the bowl), Lorna, Daniel (in the shadows), and Jim.

The lilac bush grew in a blousy fashion on the embankment that lined the Chute Road in front of the house. Every spring, yellow finches returned to nest in its branches, and we observed their comings and goings as we played in the soft grasses that grew around it. When the lilacs achieved full magnificent bloom, their heady lavender fragrance would seep in through the windows like a sweet mist, perfuming the house with spring's arrival. Every year I took lilacs to my teacher, and on the way to school I would suck the sweet pollen from the tiny flower.

At the start of the 1924 school year, Daniel got his first spanking, a memorable event because until then we hadn't the slightest inkling of such a thing as discipline. Daniel's refusal to go to school developed into an epic battle of willpower, and Mother grew desperate. In her frustration, her eyes lit upon the lilac seedlings that generously sprung up around the parent tree. They were slim, lithe, supple reeds with the indication of a bud at the very tip. The older seedlings were sturdy and hard to break off. The younger ones were too small. The middle group was just right, not too hard, not too soft, slimmer than a pencil, and when rapped on the back of legs they tingled. Daniel deserved that spanking, and he got it with what Mother ever after referred to as a tingler. As corporal punishment evolved into a common occurrence, I would hear Mother's frustrated voice, "I'm not wasting my time with you, you little villain! Go to the lilac bush," and cries of, "I'll never do it again." Daniel always put on a great show of outrage, hopping and twitching like a Hottentot, crying as loudly as he could, refusing to say he was sorry and being sent to his room to meditate. When I would snipe, "You got a spanking," he would sneer, "It didn't hurt."

We were always sent to choose our own tinglers—a point of privilege and an added torment neatly rolled into one. Many times, the boys chose the smallest tingler they dared, handing Mother an insignificant twig. Mother would say, "You march yourself right back there and this time I want a tingler that will tingle." Back they would come, whimpering and pleading that they were sorry and would never do it again. The pantomime would continue, and onlookers with smirks of superiority would be warned, "And that goes for you too!" After one of Daniel's flamboyant exhibitions, they all fled to the swing and were laughing their heads off when Mother caught the drift on the summer air.

Do you mean to tell me you are laughing??" We were obligated to appear soberly chastened for a period of time after punishment. Jim called out, no they weren't laughing, Daniel was still crying. Daniel wasn't one to waste tears after the fact and Mother knew it.

The use of tinglers was reserved for blatant destruction or repeated disobedience. Otherwise, Dad had the bad, boring habit of sitting us down, not just the culprit, but everyone, and exploring every circuitous by-way of our evil little minds. In a crisis of dishonesty or skulduggery, arriving at the truth concerned the whole family. He would gather us at his knee, and half a dozen righteous little voices would iterate, "I didn't do it," "No, you're wrong, you did it, not me," "No, I didn't, Jim did," "Douglas did," "I'm telling the truth, Daniel is telling a lie, he always lies." Dad would gently say, "Ah know yew didn't do it, but as sure as God made little green apples we ah going to find out who did." He spent a lot of time searching for the elusive truth. I think the only reason I didn't indulge in lies the way my brothers did was because I didn't have the imagination.

It must have amused Mother to see Dad sitting like a philosopher expounding under a banyan tree, always about the same topic, the truth. And all his talking and gentleness, "Wha oh wha did yew do it? Confound it all, son, use your reason! It did no good!" In the end, it all seemed like a license to go ahead and do it again, whatever it was, and the boys usually did. If it hadn't been for the bugaboo of the tingler, they would have been animals. After these cozy episodes, of which there were so many, Dad would ask, "Now do yew have any ideah what a lie is? Bettah still, do yew understand the truth?" Daniel once answered, "The truth is a great big lie!"

I have no idea why we were so deceitful. Perhaps because Dad's exasperating polemics made it more fun to lie. Who gave Harry all those oats? Who took apart my last cigar? Who broke the windows in the hot house? Who took apart Uncles Peter's alarm clock and left it in the chamber pot? Who ate Mother's chocolates? Echoes of unsolved mysteries. No one ever did it. Wags might sagely define the truth, but for us it sprouted variations on a dozen different themes from as many keys as on a piano. Daniel's idea of the truth was to not admit it. When he was questioned, 'did you eat your mother's chocolates,' he relayed the guilt to the chocolates,

"They were there, Dad." Dad bought Mother a box of chocolates every Saturday night, which was shopping night for the entire village. She kept them by her bed, and the temptation was as strong as the pull of fate. It went on without letup for years, an established ritual. Dad would say, "Ah don't suppose any of yew littah barbarians ate your Mother's chocolates." All agreed and would say no to that positive statement. We were taught seeming equivocation. Dad would solve the problem, "The mice, Dearie, the mice." So the search for the truth went on and often resulted in the direct opposite. Many times after our fervent denials and distortions, the end result almost looked like the truth. The truth, carefully taught, got twisted out of proportion into an admirable vice. 'You told a lie' was like a badge of honour.

We used to love a simple dessert that Mother made with bananas, crushed pineapple and thick whipped cream. One day when it came time to make the dessert, Mother discovered that the bananas were gone. Dad opened an inquiry, and it was only natural that no one knew how the bananas disappeared. Dad persisted until Jim suggested that Joan might have been seen outside eating bananas, perhaps with the peels lying on the grass all around her. Joan denied everything. Early on, she was a loose prevaricator. Dad was determined, "For once in mah lafh, ah'll get that chald to tell the truth." His favorite name for Joan was 'Little Jo Otter,' and he often said she was as slippery as an eel. We all stood waiting and fidgeting, and after we had been asked one by one about the bananas and consistently voiced our denial, Dad sat Joan on his knee and said softly and kindly while she fussed with her doll, "Now Little Jo Ottah, yew can tell your old Dad the truth. Did yew eat those bananas?" Joan, her big blue Irish eyes as blank as could be, stubbornly said, "No!" Dad patiently explained right and wrong for the benefit of all, which he had parsed so many times before. Again Joan said no. Then he promised, "Littah Jo Ottah, ah will give yew another banana if yew will only tell the truth." He promised two bananas, three, four, and then it got ridiculous. We were all giggling while Dad said, "Little Jo Ottah, ah am going to get the truth out of yew if ah half to saw my leg off." Mother called from another room, "Mr Marvin!" Finally, he promised that if she would only tell the truth he would go down to the Trading Company and buy her a whole bunch of bananas.

"Don't yew want to tell your old dad the truth?" Of course not. It was more fun to lie. And by that time she was full of bananas, hardly interested in more. Dad resolved it with a laugh and a shake of his head. He often said of Joan after a losing battle for the truth, "Ah give up, she's as Irish as patsy's pig." Later that day, as Joan scrambled through the house clutching her doll by the head the way she always did, Dad stopped her and asked, "Wheah ah yew going Littah Jo Ottah?"

Joan answered without hesitation, "I'm going to tell a great big lie."

Mother and Dad laughed. After all, it was an admission of truth. Encouraged, Dad asked her, "Littah Jo Ottah, tell your old dad all about this great big lie."

Joan stood defiantly, looked Dad in the eyes and said, "I don't like bananas."

Douglas was different, but with the same directness, sometimes for the truth, sometimes against it. He could give a sensible excuse for wrongdoing, but like everyone else, there were times when he avoided the truth with a steady bulwark of lies. Dad would stand there at his patient best listening to repeated denials and snarly no's, and in the end he would throw up his hands, shake his head and say, "Ah wish yew would say yes once in a while. What in blazes Duggy Don! Do yew mean to stand there and tell me yew didn't do it when I saw yew? Why, ah'll saw mah leg off!" One day he called to Mother, "Dearie, these children are not only destructive geniuses, they are congenital lyahs." Faced with so many similar situations, Mother's reply was always, "They didn't get it from my side of the family." I think she was right. I couldn't imagine Grandmother saying 'I'll saw my leg off' to get a truthful answer.

I'm afraid that Dad was not a religious person. He was respectful, but his ancestry had given him a cant angle, hardly religious. He had converted to Catholicism to marry Mother, but religion hadn't taken root in either of them, so on the farm we lived like virtual heathens. Bear River had the full complement of churches, all of them packed on Sundays, but the little Catholic church was miles away on Indian Hill, too far to do us any good. To keep us au courant, Dad would gather us in the parlor on Sunday afternoons and read us our favourite Bible stories.

"Dad, read about the king who was going to cut the baby in half," or "Read about the queen who was thrown over the castle keep and eaten by dogs," or "What about the family that was cooked to death." We liked to be frightened, and the Bible was jam-packed with tales and myths so much scarier than the other storybooks he read to us. We'd sit and listen in wonder at the ghoulishness, "Why did they do it, Dad? Why?" One can be the most violent anti-Christ possible, but not even that can dull the bizarre dimensions of biblical tales: King Nebuchadnezzar eating grass like a cow for seven years, mad as could be; the parting of the Red Sea and the terrible imminence of drowning; Jonah being tossed overboard by his shipmates, and as if things couldn't get any worse, being swallowed by a whale; a man slaughtering a pack of children for making fun of his baldness; Salome dancing with nothing less than a severed head; horrid King Herod slowly being eaten alive by worms, the Hashemites, the Ammonites and all the other mites that left us baffled. Dad would read, stop and ask if we understood. What was there to understand? We all answered yes. We learned to lie. One Sunday while the rest of us yawned, Douglas kept repeating every paragraph or so, "Yes Dad, yes Dad, yes Dad," indicating he mindlessly understood. Occasionally Dad would ask for an explanation, and the boys would try to make sense of it all, 'how could a hand just appear and write on a wall?' 'How did it learn to write?' 'Did it go to school?' Thoughts skittered off in all directions as the hand made friends and played in the schoolyard. Mother, resting in the bedroom with the baby, would chuckle and go back to her newspaper and box of chocolates.

All my life I have been a doubting Thomas—if I couldn't see it, I couldn't believe it. I often said during some outrageous tale, "It's not true!" The boys would derisively counter that I was only a girl, no more, no less. Dad would humour them and say, "Give Sweetlady a chance. Now Sweetlady, what do you think?" My answer was always, "I don't know." That was the truth. I really didn't know. I didn't believe the unnatural, but I didn't know how to express an opinion during these extended discussions. And why did I think that way so young? I don't know. So I sat in the rocking chair holding my doll, my mind a blank, occasionally promoting debate by disbelief. The boys would clamber around Dad on the couch or sit on the window sill and speculate, "Maybe the Red Sea was like the Bear River, and they walked across the mud flats at low tide" or "maybe donkeys can talk; we talk to Harry all the time." And Douglas' concern over locusts, "They didn't do that did they Dad? You didn't eat locusts did you?" "Yayess, ah did son, ah did." One Sunday I was shaken out of my ennui by a frenzied debate about the end of the world. According to Kings, earth was scheduled to burn to a crisp in the year 2000. Daniel was visibly worried, saying the world would never end, and why would it just burn up for no good reason, and who would light the match, God wouldn't let that happen, would he Dad? "Well, son." And Douglas, "He let everything else happen." Dad was in over his head. Daniel went on and on until it got tiresome and I asked if I could go. Mother would call out, "Dan, they've had enough, let them go out and play." Another Sunday, Daniel decided it was possible to count the hairs on Jim's head, which he proceeded to do, but was forced to debunk the Bible out of boredom. We doubted Noah's ark. After Daniel the genius had toted up all the animals in the barn, plus hippos, crocodiles and elephants, he took out *Nelson's Loose Leaf Encyclopaedia* and filled pages in his scribbler. In the end, the ark was a big fat lie. The whys and wherefores of the Bible were just too much to swallow. We became early skeptics.

At that time of childish fantasy and fairy tales, Dad enjoyed telling other unusual tidbits similar to the family practice of turning frogs into turtles. Did we know that the best way to deal with an alligator was to put a handy piece of wood in its mouth, perpendicular, so it couldn't close its mouth and would mercifully drown. Whales were another problem, one whale in particular, a story Dad repeated on long walks home when my questions about his family became too pointed. He would suddenly cut off the subject and say, "Did ah evah tell yew the story of the whale that almost ate your old Dad." Yes he had, tell another one, but Dad would go on with the same old story. The hungry whale had followed their ship across the seven seas, with the cook throwing it all the food, then the cabin boy, then the furniture, and one by one all the sailors, who walked the plank straight into the whale's mouth. Only the Captain and Dad remained to navigate the ship up a Venetian canal where the whale got stuck. The starving Venetians ate the whale and boiled its oil. Dad and the Captain were hailed as heroes. Then he pulled another one out of the bag, one with terrible intonations, much like the Sunday afternoon Bible stories. He recounted a trip to China, where mothers were throwing baby girls into the Yang-tse-Kiang river. Oh, yes, he said, it was true. And it was. The boys thought it justifiable: girls are no good. Dad's stories were as ridiculous as those in the Bible and made skeptics of us all. As we walked home from school and listened to his tales of exaggeration, we weren't stunned by the moral laxity of natives in the South Seas, who ate each other and didn't bat an eye at having an uncle for lunch, "Why, Dad, why??" "Ah don't know son, but they did it religiously."

In the prime days of summer with the sun at its zenith and the wheat fields ripe, hired men would come down McCormick's hill for the haying, scythes in hand, red and blue kerchiefs around their necks. The scythe looked medieval with its long, curved staff and scimitar-like blade. For as long as I could remember, Bud McCormick, Aynsley Peck, Lou Albert, and Gus Copeland were our hired hands, doing the heavier chores when Dad was away. They were part of our family, eating at our table and telling us silly stories. After Uncle Peter arrived, we mainly saw them at haying time, when many hands were needed. We would run through the maple grove to renew our acquaintance. The big question for the boys was whether they would help this year, since they looked tall enough to swing a scythe. Haying was an exciting time with all the hired men on the farm and the urgency to get the crop in. The men would start at the top of the steep hay field in front of the house and sweep down like gladiators, rhythmically swinging, cutting in wide swaths. After a pause to wipe their brows in the sweltering sun, they would pull a whetstone from a back pocket, the steel ringing clearly as they sharpened the blade. Back and forth like pendulums they swung, sweeping down in waves, leaving rows of hay lying in their wake. At the bottom, with the field lined like corduroy by windrows of cut hay, they would stop at the keg for a drink of Mother's special summer beer, a haying-time ritual made exclusively for the hired men. When I helped Mother with the preparations, I liked to finger the crackling, tissue-paper hops, like leafy silver dollars. Mother would mix a pungent mash of hops, barley, malt, and molasses, and then strain it with boiling water.

Dad at the threshing machine. Harry is the taller horse on the right.

A delicious, mealy aroma would steam up, and we all took turns putting our noses over the pot for a deep, full-bodied breath. When the beer was ready, Bud McCormick would shoulder the keg and place it in a shady spot at the bottom of the field. We spent a lot of time running from one field to another with buckets of spring water and lemonade for the hired men.

I suspect that our farm was settled so early because of the hay fields, which were natural clearings. Beside the steep field in front of our house was an even larger field of rye and oats. Near the barn was a buckwheat field, and beyond the pasture and the cranberry bog, we planted timothy and alfalfa, also planted on the Miller field. Bear River wasn't good hay country, which kept farming small-scale. Many farms struggled to harvest every square inch of hay, and a poor crop left them in trouble. To keep the village going, as well as the lumbering operations in the backwoods, the Packet often docked at the wharf with a full load of hay. Bear River still ran on animal power, so hay was more important than gasoline.

With the scything done, the hired men would leave the mown hay to cure in the hot sun. We spent days tossing it with pitchforks until the sun had baked it crisp and sweet-smelling. There was always an urgency to fill the lofts before it rained. A sudden downpour would soak the fields, and the turning and pitching would have to begin all over again. Every farmer's nightmare was to have a harvest rot in the fields if the rains were prolonged. A farm couldn't survive without hay. I can still see Mother running up the field to help load the wagon before the onset of a storm. We nervously watched the heavy clouds rolling in from the Bay as we filled the wagon, later escaping with one load in the barn.

At that point of relief when the weather held, Harry would pull the spindly hay wagon to the top of the field, where Dad and Uncle Peter would scoop the hay with their forks and fill it to overflowing. The wagon seemed top heavy, making for hazardous trips down the steep field. Mother would urge Dad to be careful as he pulled on the reins and Harry inched the wagon down. When the wagon rolled safely on to the road, the boys would scramble up top for the ride to the barn. They assured me it was nothing but fun, so one day, I got swept up in the excitement and they pulled me aboard. It was much higher up than I expected, and when the wagon started moving, the hay shifted dangerously. The boys whooped and yelled, brushing against low branches and happily slipping and sliding with every bump in the road. I was terrified as I slid closer to the edge with nothing to hang on to but a handful of straw. People had been hurt falling off hay wagons. As we angled up the incline to the barn, I knew I was done for. I scratched and clawed as I felt myself slipping over the edge, but Daniel, my hero, reached down and pulled me to safety. My hayriding days were over.

At the barn, Dad would hitch Harry to the pulley, and the jaws of the forklift would bite into the hay, swinging back and forth until the wagon was empty and the lofts were full. Dad made us watch from a safe distance, but one time Lorna dashed out and ran directly under a full load, causing panic and screaming. Haying was a frantic time and there was always a great relief when it was over. The barn would be filled to overflowing and the fields left empty with stubble, prickling our bare feet.

The next chore was the threshing of the oats, barley and rye at Mr. Harris' farm. The boys raved about his threshing machine, insisting that I come along to watch, "You'll love it!" I did go once, my real reason being to visit Alice Copeland next door and play dolls with her. I cleaned myself up, polished my shoes and washed my one good dress, all set for a pleasant afternoon, perhaps even tea with Alice's Great Great Aunt Mary.

Mr Harris' farm stood at the Crossroads, fifteen minutes away, and when we got there, he sternly ordered children off his property; we could watch from the fence. Sensing opportunity, I asked Dad if I could visit Alice. He saw through my sly trick and said no, I had waited to ask and I hadn't been invited. What a disappointment! I was furious that he would deny me those few steps to see Alice when the boys could roam the woods all day long. I stomped off to sit in the shade, but the boys called me over, saying I had to watch from the fence, where Dad could see us, and besides, it was the best spot to watch the threshing. So what did I do? I kicked the fence and hung onto a rail, glowering in the blackest of MacGregor moods.

The threshing machine sat in the middle of the field chugging like a train engine. When Mr. Harris put it into gear, it rumbled to life, putt-putting loudly as a long leather belt whirred round and round. The ground rocked. Dad and Uncle Peter stood on the hay wagon with pitch forks and fed oats into a wide-mouthed funnel. The machine gobbled everything, moments later slewing kernels down a chute and spouting them into burlap bags.

The Pines Hotel, Digby

Straw and chaff whiffed into the air and gathered in a storm cloud that drifted downwind, straight towards us. The boys prepared in high glee. Straws in the wind stuck in my hair, and the chaff hit like a dust storm, coating me in the sticky heat. The boys joyfully rolled around until they were breaded like chicken, squawking and innocently explaining, "We thought you might like it." The little devils. I stood there disgusted with another facet of farm life. The things I wished for were antiseptically nice, not my dress full of chaff and my hair matted with dust. I longed for cleanliness, but on the farm, nature was always too close for comfort. I used to think the boys were so privileged, but whenever I joined them, the results were miserable. For years I wanted to go to the Pines Hotel in Digby to deliver a load of vegetables. On a day when the boys had disappeared into the woods, Dad finally gave in. My boredom began at the village bridge, already a long trip. I sat on the painfully hard seat listening to Harry's unhurried clop. Up the River Road on the Digby side, we heard the boys shouting from the top of the hay field, waving us on our way. Slowly, ever so slowly, we came to the outskirts of Digby and drove past miles of racks of drying cod that filled the air with the salty smell of the sea. It seemed like forever before Harry finally pulled up to the back door of the Pines Hotel, not even the front door. No-nonsense men emptied the wagon, Dad settled his business inside and handed me an ice cream cone. The boredom of the long trip home on that rock-hard seat was almost unbearable.

Hay fields

Looking across from the Upper River Road on the Digby side, 1972

Going to the threshing taught me, as I had been taught so often before, not to be jealous of the boys' privileges. When the threshing was over, Dad and Uncle Peter whacked their hats to dust off, sending clouds of chaff billowing around them. It was a hot, dirty chore that they were glad to be done with. They sewed the burlap bags shut and heaved them onto the wagon with a definitive thud. I could have walked the fifteen minutes home, but I sat on a bag of oats like a miserable lump, the wagon jiggling over the bumpy road. I was not happy at all. At home, Dad attended to his chores and then lectured me on basic honesty. It didn't change my attitude; the truth wasn't worth a fig. I was supposed to be satisfied with going to a threshing, but I didn't want the boys' freedoms, I wanted my own. The more I pasted snippets of elegance in my scrap books, the more I longed for the merest glimpse of modest luxury. We were taught that we got what we needed, that we mustn't ask for things, and if memory serves me, I don't think I asked for equal rights.

For children growing up on a farm, all aspects of farming become as familiar as nursery rhymes. By the time I started school at 5, I knew all about the ritual of the seasons: priming, planting, endless weeding, the urgency of haying and harvest time. I knew every farm and garden implement. I knew that cows had to be carefully milked on a regular schedule or they would go dry, and that singing to them always helped.

I candled eggs, looking for quitters or marvelling at the network of blood vessels twitching to life. I knew how to pick and bunch every kind of vegetable. I learned to snap corn off the stalk, not to tug or pull it. I looked under leaves for beetles and worms and those beautiful tiger-striped potato bugs, which I thought were as pretty as lady bugs. I knew which fields should be planted with oats, barley, rye, timothy (I liked that name) and alfalfa (I liked that name too). We planted Kentucky Wonder wax beans and Peter Pan peas. I learned about crop rotation: oats to wheat to corn, and then alfalfa to replenish the nitrogen. I knew more about the varieties of potatoes than my times tables. As a preschooler, I could have authored a primer, but I couldn't add one and one.

The vegetable crops were a constant preoccupation from the moment the gardens were plowed. Like earthy brides, they lay primed, ready to accept their seed and germinate in meticulous order. We watched for the miracle of the first delicately tinted pinpoints of new life pushing up through the dark earth, followed by the sturdy sprouts boldly asserting themselves, then the lush maturity. We would snip the perfumed pea pods and eat them then and there, or greedily pluck the first strawberries. It was disturbing when we moved the strawberry patch from behind the house to way down at the bottom of the Miller Field, past a field of Luther Burbank and Irish Cobbler potatoes. It was a very long walk for a strawberry. That was when I learned how to transplant the runners of the strawberry plant.

The days on the farm were filled with a rigid intensity, the alarm clock sounding out the first order of the day, followed by the rush to the barn to milk the cows. In a little while, Mother would be straining warm milk for our porridge. Throughout the day, chores piled one on top of another in unvarying orchestration: weeding, hoeing, spraying, picking—endless rounds from one urgent task to another. I recall seeing Mother seated by the hour, year after year, cutting potatoes into the wash tub for planting, each piece with the necessary eye. When she was rushed, instead of eating a meal she would grab a handful of oatmeal and put it in her hoover pocket to nibble as she hoed or bunched vegetables. One day I ran over to the chicken house and found her crying. She was sitting on the bench in front of the nests and the chickens were milling about, clucking at her as if she had done something wrong. I asked her why she was crying, and she said she didn't know what to do with all the eggs. Eggs could be gotten rid of in any number of ways, but I suggested that we eat them. Mother laughed through her tears. She would need an army to eat all those eggs. But our Sunday dinners required a full-blown chicken community. They had their brief experience and then had their heads chopped off.

As wild as my brothers were on their own time, when Dad needed them on the farm, they buckled down like hired hands, spending whole days among the row crops, thinning and scuffling with their hoes or choring around with Dad. I would look out and see them bent over their bushel baskets, slowly moving down the rows as they picked spinach, beans, peas, chard, eggplant, musk melon, chili peppers. When the summer rains came, vegetables still had to be picked and delivered. They'd be off in their slickers, the wagon covered with a tarpaulin and Mother calling out to Dad, "Don't forget Harry's raincoat!" He was pampered like a child. The boys spent days preparing carrots, beets, onions, lettuce, cabbage, anything Mother needed for delivery. She would be sitting at the back porch bunching vegetables and noting them in her account book. Dad would be loading the long wagon while everyone rushed here and there to help. At the height of the season, the farm ramped up to a full-scale family operation. We couldn't help but learn.

As the heat of the day settled into the soothing hush of evening, the animals would be brought in and put to bed, their feed measured out and hay forked into their stalls. After the last milking, Mother and Dad liked to take leisurely walks around the farm in a comfortable family ritual. Mother would sling the baby in a shawl and walk with Dad while we trailed behind, the evening dew cleaning our feet. Dad liked to admire the expanse of his farm, discussing the gardens as they matured into lush, ordered rows; perhaps he would plant this or that crop in this or that field next year; the hay crop was good, but maybe no Irish Cobbler potatoes next year. From the top of the Miller field, we would stop to watch the sun dripping into the Bay. At the Brook Bridge, we would lean over and drop pebbles, looking for activity. Sometimes a nighthawk would spring with startling suddenness from the damp evening grasses, whirring like a phoenix mounting to the moon, shrieking the last bird song of the day, its shrill cry followed by an orchestration of frogs and crickets. As the stars appeared, Douglas would urge Mother that she could see them better from the top of the hay field—they were bigger there. Well, the sky was bigger, and we could see lights across the river, almost down to the village. We would sit on the flat rock and everyone's fingers would jump across the heavens at a great rate, searching the sky for our favourites. Mother often made fudge before our walk and let it cool while we strolled. Uncle Peter, who had a terrible sweet tooth would call up, "Poll-eee, Poll-eee, there's no fudge left. I'm eating the last piece." We would tear down the hill, never sure if he was joking. Our last stop before bed would be the double-seated glide swing. With all energy and mischief expended, we slumped in useless heaps around Mother and Dad as they explained the constellations: mighty Hercules, Daniel's favorite; vain Queen Cassiopeia and her husband Cepheus; their daughter Andromeda chained to a rock and waiting for Perseus; Cygnus the swan stretched in flight across the heavens. The stars were so vivid and exciting then, our fingers tracing across the night sky in a pedestrian way, each constellation as familiar as the landmarks of our farm. We sat bunched together in the comfortable dark, swinging back and forth, and as the frogs chorused their sustained melodies, Mother would say, "Just listen to them! They love the night." In the summer they sang high and light, but as the air turned cool in August, their songs deepened into a muted profundo, melding with the snapping crickets and wonderfully defined by a delicate breeze through the trees and the soft obligato of the lapping river. All summer, this song was the last thing we heard before falling asleep. In later years, I lost track of the stars and their place in the heavens, only on occasion taking the trouble to lift my eyes and discover with renewed recognition the diamond brilliance of the North Star, still dangling in amazing symmetry at the end of the Little Dipper.

The summer constellations in their place over a photo of the Maple Grove gardens (2003). Bootes is pointing to the Big Dipper, then Corona, Hercules and Cygnus.

Daniel and Jim spent a good part of their lives flying, so they never lost their familiarity with the stars—sparkling mileposts as they buzzed around the world. They remembered, as I carelessly forgot, all they so eagerly learned on the glide swing. Douglas died at nineteen, and I often like to think that he just might be drifting among the stars that excited him so much, drifting and searching with his big brown doe-like eyes, still seeing the world with wonder, as he did when he was a little boy.

Above the Little Dipper is Cepheus on his throne, Andromeda chained to a rock, and her mother, Queen Cassiopeia.

Courtesy of John Marvin

Mother with Harry

A CLAXON SOUNDED FROM THE top of McCormick's hill, a clarion call announcing that the expected guests had arrived. Down they swept in a magnificent Ford Tin Lizzie, open to the elements and as brightly yellow as the daffodils that bloomed in April. In through the maple grove the lively machine purred before choking to a standstill amid an enthusiastic welcome. That was the first time I ever saw a car. Professor Smith of the Truro Agricultural College, corpulent and jovial with a snow-white beard, eased himself from his erstwhile saddle and offered a heartfelt handshake to Mother and Dad. With him was Dr. R. I. Donaldson, lithe and darkly handsome, immaculate in his blue suit with spats over polished shoes. After an equally warm welcome, he plucked up Daniel and plunked him behind the steering wheel, showing him how to honk the horn like a rubber duck, Daniel's first driving lesson.

I got the idea from Mother's sometime reminiscences that their time in Truro provided a slide rule for their future happiness. Mother and Dad were young and on their own for the first time, and college life bubbles with ideals. That was the period of la vie en rose, and their warm friendship with Prof. Smith and Dr. Donaldson was part of it. Our guests were passing through to Yarmouth for the ferry to Boston, where they would spend the Easter holiday with Dr. Donaldson's family.

Mother had set a light meal on the dining room table, after which everyone repaired to the parlor. That is when I saw Prof. Smith lean over the chess board and do what Daniel and I had been forbidden to do—he moved a man. Then Dad did the same. Prof. Smith chuckled and stroked his snowy-white beard as they both stood leaning over the board. Daniel and I watched, absorbed. The game suffered another hesitation when everyone went outside to walk through the gardens. I sat perched on Dad's shoulders as he proudly displayed the fields, primed and seeded. We toured the barn, where Daniel introduced Harry, and then went back to the parlor for tea. I was very young at the time, but even then the house was filled with Dad's brass work, which Prof. Smith examined and admired piece by piece. He was taken aback when Dad offered him any item he wanted, in the end choosing a cigar box as his parting gift.

When the time came to leave, we gathered around the car to look over its artefacts with enormous interest. Daniel couldn't resist honking the horn he had mastered. Dr. Donaldson's magnificent Model T was a perfect wonder: a double seater open to the elements, running boards with a tool box, and a mischievous crank that teased the car into a spate of hacking coughs, followed by relieved, purring chugs. The two guests mounted their horseless saddles amid great admiration for such a machine. I stood in awe and fear, holding Mother's hand as Dad cranked the engine briskly. His vigorous cranking to get a reaction seemed as uncertain as the future. After a few explosive coughs, the engine gasped and growled, signalling that send-off was certain indeed. Off it put-putted through the maple grove and up McCormick's hill, honking a last goodbye. It was an absolute miracle; an excitement that stuck like the tale of the flying carpet.

At the time, I can't recall having been in the village, so while I'm sure cars were on the roads, I hadn't seen them yet. Murray Harris (the taxi driver), the Trading Company delivery man, and even Dr. Campbell all still travelled via horse and buggy, though it wasn't long before they upgraded their mode of transportation. By the time I saw my first circus in Digby, we rode grandly in Murray Harris' taxi, a memorable event for many reasons: my first car ride; my first sight of Digby, that odiferous cod-filled metropolis; the fright of being in the same tent as lions and tigers; and the embarrassment of stopping by the side of the road to be car sick, my anaemic system having discovered an unhealthy side effect of progress.

Prof. Smith visited just the once, but thereafter, Dr. Donaldson, or RI, as Dad called him, would stop by on his holiday forays. We listened in high expectation for that brazen horn honking raucously over the countryside like a loose goose. Daniel and I would race through the maple grove to meet him as he swooped down the hill like a corsair. On he came, over the Bridge Brook, slowing down to pull Daniel onto the running board while I ran behind in the dust. Later, when he got a newer model with windows, a rumble seat and no crank, he would stop the car as we met him at the barn, and for less than a minute we cruised in style through the maple grove. It was heaven.

Murray Harris before the horse and buggy era. He's in front of Mr. Marshall's store, and the ox is trained to work on his own instead of the usual pairing.

I'm afraid our enthusiasm for Dr. Donaldson's visits was animated mainly by the lollipops he brought us. We never had treats when Dad was away, and only on Sunday mornings when he was home, so there were periods when we were starved for candy. RI never failed us. He would pretend he had forgotten them, knowing how greedy we were, but we knew that ploy and expected it. We knew they were in his pocket. The ploy and the lollipops were the thing. It's funny how good those lollipops tasted. I loved maple and spearmint; I could have licked them till I died they were so good. Without fail, RI also brought Mother a huge box of Whitman's Sampler chocolates, and to the discriminating palate of a three or four-year-old, they were the world's best. I always chose the Jordan almonds, two in a paper cup, so I would have a chocolate for later. Whitman's packaging remained traditional in appearance: a ribbonned hinge and a cross-stitched design, like an embroidered box. On the cover, a messenger boy in a skipped cap carried a cross-stitched box of, presumably, chocolates. No other company elevated the cross-stitch like Whitman's, a reminder of women's artistry. I loved those boxes and coveted them for my dolls' clothes. Even now I can close my eyes and dip my finger into a Whitman's Sampler, excitedly choosing the Jordan almonds, two in a paper cup. This revived memory is like a slim, flat stone skimming lightly over the water before sinking below the surface.

RI's visits were always short: a brief spate of excitement, the rush of pleasant, urgent conversation and laughter, perhaps a walk to look at the gardens, and then off to catch the ferry. There is no question that our emotions are born with us fully blown, and I realize that as young as I was, I gave my love extravagantly to a number of older men: Dad, our white-haired neighbor Mr. Kniffen, and without question, Dr. Donaldson. On one visit when Jim was two, an insignificant gnome who could barely walk, talk or think, I was extremely jealous of Dr. Donaldson's attentions to him. It really wasn't my fault that my love and adoration went overboard; he was so loving with us all.

One spring day before Dad arrived for planting and before Uncle Peter had arrived from Scotland, Mother arranged to have a hired man come and plow the fields, and on this particular day Gus Copeland showed up. Gus was very tall and thin with thyroid eyes, always with an old fedora pushed back on his head and always chewing a sprig of hay. When he spoke, he stuck his thumbs in his overalls and had the habit of nervously shifting from one foot to another. At breakfast, he came to the back door and told Mother that he couldn't plow because Harry was sick with the heaves, an ailment she had never heard of. Gus spoke hesitantly as he tried to explain the complications to Mother, who had no idea what he was talking about. Daniel and I were sitting at the table eating our porridge and listening to Gus' staccato delivery, which he finally cut short by saying, "Your horse is a dead horse Mrs. Marvin."

After her initial shock and confusion, Mother's natural calm vanished when Gus affirmed that the heaves were incurable. He said he had heard of a cure: take the bark of a hackmatack tree and boil it, but how to administer it, he didn't know, he had only heard. Mother asked how she could possibly go into the woods when she barely knew one tree from another. And how could she do without Harry, what if he should die. After a heightened discussion about hackmatack trees, Gus suggested a poultice of mashed turnips and went back to the barn to comfort Harry. With that, Mother just about flew off into hysteria, nervously deploring over and over,

"Dear, dear, dear. What am I going to do?" Daniel quizzed and harangued her, "What are the heaves? Horses don't die." All Mother could say was, "I don't know, I don't know." Then she simplified things by saying that Harry had a bad cold. She sent Daniel and I down to the root cellar, and we lugged a bag of turnips up the stairs, after which Mother put us in the dining room, warned us not to move, and closed the door. All we could hear was the loud, ominous thwacking of turnips being chopped and Mother crying as she talked to herself in sheer desperation. There were tears and recriminations that Dad wasn't there when needed and what would she do. When Daniel opened the kitchen door and asked if Harry was going to die, he took one look at Mother's reaction and quickly closed the door. Gus came in for the poultice and returned to the barn with a large pot of mashed turnips. Mother followed in tears, carrying a sheet and towels with safety pins pinned to her house dress. We watched them step into the barn and then stood on the couch glued to the window, waiting for the slightest movement.

By this time, Mother had transferred all of her fears over to us, and we were both in tears, with Daniel crying wildly in his overly dramatic way. The thought of losing Harry carried a terrible enormity. We loved Harry and took obvious pride in him, treating him with sugar cubes and carrots and endless care. He was gentle, even kind, not temperamental or unpredictable like other horses, his loyalty unwavering and unlimited. In our very young eyes, that beautiful animal was a living breathing human being in all but form, as permanent as a tree.

And on the farm, Harry was central to every chore, giving his energy fully to anything expected of him: plowing, haying, logging, hauling wagons full of vegetables for miles in every kind of weather. Horseflesh was more vital to a farm than a racetrack. In fact, the speed of the racehorse was a whim of the fast crowd, soon wearing him out with excess and putting him out to pasture, as indolent as the owners. Unlike the racehorse of burnt-out youth, the hard work of the farm horse kept him limber till he dropped of old age. A farm simply couldn't operate without a horse. Mother would be stranded like a rudderless ship. So we stood at the window nervously crying and trying to understand the terrible emphasis of the heaves and wondering what life would be like without Harry.

In the middle of this looming tragedy, a claxon sounded from the top of McCormick's hill, and down flew Dr. Donaldson. We were ecstatic. No visitor could have been more welcome. He stopped at the barn and immediately turned back to the village. Mother raced to the house in a frenzy. She was like another person, whipping the grey hooked rug out from under us, grabbing the red throw from the parlor couch, gathering up the kitchen rug and several towels before running back to the barn with all she could carry. Shortly, Dr. Donaldson returned from the village and rushed into the barn with an armful of blue and brown bottles. We waited and waited until finally Mother and RI emerged from the barn and came into the kitchen for tea. They sat in relieved exhaustion, Mother still worried and RI reassuring her. I had never seen another man's arms around Mother, but I did that day when RI hugged her as he got up to leave, telling her Harry would be fine. That was also the only time we didn't think to pester him for our lollipops. As he was walking out the door, he remembered and reached into his pocket—maple and spearmint. We took them greedily, and no lollipop ever tasted better. RI was the hero of the day and I was over the moon in love.

In a few days, Harry was back on his feet and receiving visitors. Daniel never forgot how close we came to losing him, and the incident carried over to his detailed concern about Harry's care. After a day of plowing, logging or haying, Daniel would carefully dry his coat and comb him, then make sure he had all that he needed and everything was placed just so. Harry was his one great love.

Had I been an only child, there are many incidents I would have forgotten, but we discussed the heaves endlessly at night. Daniel's overly dramatic flair emphasized events and gave them staying power. His obsessive sing-songing of words like hackmatack and his theatrical recounting on Dad's return marked the episode in time. I still don't know what the heaves are, I could look it up, but I'll go along with Mother's explanation given to curious little children: Harry had a bad cold.

RI's visits were snatched so quickly; he was always rushing to catch the ferry to Boston. That urgency capsuled our affections into a short time and space. His visits were like a light being turned on to high intensity, then off, then on again, and finally off. One day Mother opened a letter with the news that RI had gone home and was dying of pneumonia. Mother cried and cried; she was inconsolable. No one ever filled RI's empty space again. Mother was still in her 20s, but all her friends on the farm were greying or elderly. Never again did she have anyone her own age to share interests and ideas with.

In unearthing long forgotten memories of people and incidents, time emerges with a youthful verve. Those were very young years, not only for me, but also for my parents and the well-loved RI. His presence would flash back at odd moments, 'RI said this' or 'RI said that.' Dad moved the strawberry patch down to the Miller field as he had suggested. If Dad was considering a new crop, RI's opinions resurfaced—he helped regulate our fields.

After a time, the chess board with its deep ebony frame and gold inlay was packed up and hung diamond-like in the hall between two brass sconces. I suspect it was a wedding present, and I don't recall it ever being used again.

I have plumbed deeply to unearth grain by grain in their few words the faded miracle of people, emotions and a time, all hailed back into frail existence by a claxon sounding over a hill like Gabriel's horn, way up there. And Gabriel himself: young, tall, slim, dark and handsome, all Panama on bright summer days, white Panama suit, smiling in his Panama hat, and the shoes I wanted my father to wear, tan and white they were. That was all such a long time ago, but one never forgets first loves, flashes of smiles, lollipops, laughter and car horns over the hill.

Courtesy of Myrtle Selig

Mrs. McCormick

I don't know if 'McCormick's hill' was a proper designation, but that's what we called it, and that's where Billy McCormick lived with his wife. To the other side of us were the Kniffens, comfortably ensconced in Kniffen's Hollow. The Marvins had yet to acquire such status and lived on 'the old Warren farm.' In the winter when Dad was away and before Uncle Peter arrived, big, lumbering Bud McCormick was often our hired hand. He was Billy's cousin and sometimes lived up on the hill. After heavy snowfalls, Daniel and I would watch from the windows as Bud cleared the snow. First, he would drive Harry through the maple grove pulling a wide contraption used to haul logs from the woods. He would tamp down a path from the barn to the house, over to the outhouse, up and around the apple packing house, down to the river road and up to the chicken house. Then he would shovel for hours. We would watch Bud's beefy presence as he carved out our limited byways, and every so often he would toss snow at us as we stood at the window. We saw enough of Bud in the winter to make him seem like one of the family. He ate at our table and made us laugh with his silly stories, "The cows were talking about you two today." We never knew when to believe him. After lunch, he would go in to the village for the mail or groceries, then come back to saw and split wood or tend to the animals until the evening milking. During one fierce storm, Daniel and I watched from the dining room window as Bud struggled up the hill, snow drifting all around him like curtains closing. We were concerned, because drifts would tumble down the hill and gather at the bottom in deep pools, deep enough to swallow us whole.

In Bear River, winters were never as bad as they used to be, because at the drop of a snowflake, old-timers around the pot-bellied stove at the Trading Company would revive 'The Great Blockade,' a benchmark on the misery index, always recalled like a happy memory. It sounded like one of Dad's exaggerated tales, but no, it was all true: snow every day for a solid month, passenger trains stranded and then buried under drifts, the Bear River frozen solid, trapping the little Packet mid-stream; the whole Annapolis Valley, people and animals, a few snowy inches from starvation. Everyone shovelled for their lives, digging their way out of the house and over to the barn, then along the road to the rail lines to get the trains moving again.

Snow clearing still relied on muscle power, and after storms, Uncle Peter and the other men would gather with their shovels and teams of oxen to break out the road. At Hamilton's Corner, they often had to dig a trench that towered over our heads, just wide enough for sleighs to squeak through. Cars and trucks didn't travel the roads in the winter, and even sleighs had trouble with all the steep hills, especially in the village. At times, a brief thaw or freezing rain would ice the hills, making for a difficult climb and a treacherous descent. Once, a team of oxen slipped on Oakdene Hill, dragging their load downhill as the teamster jumped for his life.

Kniffen's Hollow filled in with snow every winter, closing the Chute Road and making us the end of the line. No one passed by, so those months were as empty and frozen as our fields, the only sound being the brittle bending and snapping of trees in the wind. Daniel and I observed the winter through windows, occasionally being pushed out the door to play in the snow for the good of our health. Mother would call out from the kitchen door, urging us to run about to keep warm, which we could have done just as easily inside. Winter days in those early years passed like blank pages, but the nights return in rich tones: sitting on the apron of the fireplace with our cocoa, the kinetic flames animating the scene as Mother sat in her rocking chair reading our Thornton Burgess bedtime story.

Every year before the daffodils bloomed, when cold nights turned into mild days, the sap in the sugar maples would run clear, announcing the last of winter and the first of spring. Bud would go into the apple packing house for buckets, wooden spiles and a drill to tap the maples. He started with the tallest maple in the grove, choosing a spot on the sunny side, not too close to last year's hole and above a big root. As he drilled, he would feel the turnings for the proper dampness before inserting a spile. All two dozen maples were hung with buckets to collect the slowly dripping nectar, another gift of the Gods from our beautiful maples. We would stand and listen as the maple grove echoed with a musical plinking like a dance from the *Nutcracker*. Maple syrup was a delicious expectancy, and we often put our mouths under the spout to let the delicately clear, faintly sweet liquid drip onto our tongues. On sunny days, the buckets brimmed, and we would carry them over to Bud, who stood at the fire stirring the sap as it slowly boiled down to a golden syrup. Mother always saved several jars for further refinement into maple sugar candy, poured at the delicate perfumed moment to harden in patterned madeleine tins. Every year, she sent maple sugar candy to Grandmother in Scotland. In return, we got Scottish rock candy sticks, and they too were a sign of spring.

Bud also attended another springtime ritual: the yearly incubation of the chicks, which required some expertise. The incubator stood in the apple packing house like a piece of misplaced furniture: a tall, polished wood cabinet with pull-out trays that held hundreds of eggs. After candling them to determine which eggs were fertilized, Bud would place them on the slide-out trays and light the attached kerosene heater. Then began the tedious chore of rotating the eggs so the chicks would not become misshapen and die. In a few weeks, a chorus of chicks would announce themselves from inside the shell, singing their one-note song. Like true pioneers, they would poke a small hole for a peek and then circumnavigate their tiny world by pecking around the shell to form an escape hatch. I found few pleasures in living on the farm, but one of them was the frequent opportunity to witness the miracle of new life. We watched in amazement as dozens of chicks emerged from the shell to begin their brief visit. They would quickly fluff up into cottony yellow balls, excitedly chirping about the thrill of it all. Bud warned us not to put them near water, because at the outset they had an irresistible urge to dive in and would drown. He placed a chick near a bowl of water, and sure enough, it went for a swim and had to be rescued. Bud's final chore was to separate male from female by examining their feathers, the only available clue. The chicks quickly evolved into fussy matrons, at which point I was done with them. Bud insisted they made good pets, that they each had distinct personalities, but I found them pushy, and I had to wonder where I fit in on the pecking order when they pecked at me. At the top of the heap stood the squawking, crowing roosters, nasty pieces of work with their razor-sharp talons, parading around like God's gift to women. Several times, we went to the chicken house in the morning and found a hen pecked to death, almost flattened–just another one of those nights. Was it rough justice or mob rule? The chickens ignored their erstwhile companion as they clucked and carried on, betraying nothing of their secret world.

Courtesy of Myrtle Selig

Billy McCormick

Billy McCormick and Mrs. McCormick were both white-haired and retired from whatever it was they had done. Both kept busy doing odd jobs and tending to their small farm. They had a number of children whom I never met, but sadly, their youngest, Ruth, was in her thirties and still had the mind of a child. Sometimes she would be home and sometimes not. On our walks home after school, we often met her coming home with the mail or groceries. I liked her and she fit right in with the rest of our friends. We were all children together and talked the same language. She was always smiling and laughing mindlessly, like a real hedonist.

Billy was chubby and cheerful, red-faced with a white moustache. As often as I saw him, I don't recall ever talking to him, but whenever he passed our house, we waved. If he was on his way to milk the Kniffen's cow, the boys would tag along, grabbing hold of the back of his wagon, digging their heels in and kicking up dust. Billy taught them how to milk, and whenever he dropped them off, they would be splattered with dried milk they had squirted all over each other. No matter what ordinary task the boys took on, they always embellished it with a mischievous flourish.

As often as she was able, Mrs. McCormick earned extra money by doing laundry in the village. She would hurry past us on our way home from school after finishing her day's work, so eager to get home that her little black boots would pump up and down. One day, I ran ahead of everyone to catch up with her and chat, and she told me the most unusual tale. At noontime her feet were sore, so she took off her boots, feeling that there was something in one of them. When she shook her boot, a small snake fell out, thankfully dead. Goodness gracious me! I never dreamed that a snake would stoop so low. Surely, the night was coming when one would slither across the bedroom floor and slip into my shoe. For a while, I shook out my shoes in the morning before sliding them on and wiggling my toes. And every time I looked at Mrs. McCormick's boots, I looked for snakes.

While our summer friends came and went with the season, Mrs. McCormick was a well-loved and integral part of our family throughout the year. Aside from frequent social calls and baby-sitting when Mother went to the village, she helped with the laundry, a demanding chore that often required two pairs of hands. Blue Monday began on Sunday evening, when Mother filled the copper wash tub with clothes to soak overnight.

In the morning after boiling enough pots of water to steam up the windows, she would shave a huge bar of P & G soap to melt in a pot on the stove. What followed next resembled a wrestling match: pounding and pummelling the clothes against the washboard, rinsing and wringing dear life right out of them. On a farm, dirt came and went through hard labour. A final rinse of blueing cancelled out the yellows for whiter whites. Winter and summer, our clothesline billowed like a ship at sea, except during downpours and blizzards, when the laundry hung inside to transform our kitchen into a clammy maze.

Despite the hard work involved, Mrs. McCormick's visits almost seemed like a social call, since they chatted all the while. I loved it when they stopped for tea, because Mrs. McCormick would hold me on her lap and let me use the sugar tongs to put the sugar cubes in her cup. She was wonderfully loving with little children. When it was time to go and if the weather was nice, Mother would sling the baby in a shawl and walk Mrs. McCormick home. I would carry the basket Mother always made up for her: freshly baked scones or bread, jam, a pat of butter and some vegetables picked that day. At the top of the hill, we would stop for last words and a look down the river. Mother liked to stand there and gaze out at what she said was, "a glorious sight!"

The top of McCormick's hill was a significant landmark on our two-mile trek to school. In the morning as we crested the hill, we would turn for a last look over our shoulders, down towards home and out to the Bay. After school, when we reached the top of the hill, we knew we were

Near the top of McCormick's hill. Photo by Mary Marvin, 1944

safely home and could stop to watch the Princess Helene sailing out of Digby, or the Flying Bluenose rattling across Victoria Bridge, or Captain Woodworth's Packet steaming out on the full tide, looking as if it were headed straight for Bear Island. We would wait for it to dip around a hill and reappear, bravely headed for the Digby Gut and across the Bay to St. John. Then the boys would curl their tongues and send shrill whistles down the hill. From down among the trees, Scotty would bark in reply and tear up to meet us, so fast he looked like a ball of dust.

One day when I walked home from school with Mrs. McCormick, she invited me over to tea, since Billy was moose hunting and she was alone. I was seven then, the right age for my first formal tea. It was also the first and only time I was in Mrs. McCormick's house. When Mother sent me up with a basket of food, I always stood at the door. Their house was lemon yellow with white trim and sat high above the Chute Road. A front verandah offered a marvellous view clear across the river. The kitchen was one very large room that seemed to be kitchen, dining room and parlor all in one. It was wonderfully light with windows all around to enjoy the view, but their kitchen stove was much smaller than ours and seemed unlikely to heat the large room when winter blew in. Perhaps that was why every fall we would see Billy banking the house with earth and snuggling it down with spruce boughs. Covering the kitchen floor and at every doorway lay all kinds of colourful braided rugs, and I suspect that Mother learned this craft from Mrs. McCormick. In every room of our house and beneath our feet we could pick out last year's ripped pants, old shirts, and stockings.

John McLeod collection

As we sat sipping our tea and nibbling buttered bread, Mrs. McCormick said she had something I might be interested in. She then opened a large, rough-hewn chest and proceeded to display her years of collected linens, laces and embroidery, all carefully saved and rarely used. One by one she took them out to show me. I had never seen such beautiful things; it was a dazzling treasure chest full of delicate antimacassars by the dozen, pillow cases bedizened by cross-stitch, tablecloths beautifully embroidered with flowers; quilts quixotically patterned with all the left-over materials of her life. Mother never had lovely things stored away; she used everything she had every day. Our best dishes sat on the breakfast table. Mrs. McCormick then informed me that every young girl should begin her hope chest so that it would be full on the day she married. This seemed like the right thing to do, so I dutifully prepared for my nuptials by going through an intense period of embroidery. For some reason, I felt a need to hurry, even though my prospects at the time were slim to none. Mother bleached all the flour and sugar bags I needed and kept me supplied with embroidery thread. I wanted to make tablecloths, but I couldn't do the hem, so my hope chest would be full of pillowcases. This proved to be a blessing when I learned that sugar bag tablecloths bordered on déclassé. But unlike Mrs. McCormick, I would never be able to save my pillowcases for my great-granddaughter's wedding. The minute I finished a piece, Mother sent it off to the front lines. Every single pillowcase made a beeline to our beds. My hope chest, which began life as a cardboard box, sat empty and alone before a brief stint as a dustbin, eventually ending up on a bonfire at a corn boil. Still, I had a vanity about lying on my pillow and letting my eye rest on my handiwork that I thought so perfect, especially my French knots, which had been such a problem. The boys objected to flowered pillows and picked at every single French knot until they all hung limply over my daisy stitch. As they lay in bed picking and pulling, I complained to Mother in my nasally lament. I did a lot of whining and carping, as Mother called it. We all did. Bone-tired and ready to strangle us, Mother called in, "I'll French knot every last one of you if I hear another word." Like an artist before his time, my work was never fully appreciated, but I found pleasure in sewing and was happy to learn an adult skill, one that children can easily enjoy. Because of Mrs. McCormick's rough-hewn, treasure-filled hope chest, I had a new impetus to life. Although mine went up in flames, I realized there was hope in a hope chest.

As well as helping with the laundry, Mrs. McCormick also ushered babies into the world. As wonderful as she was, I held her responsible for this unnecessary state of affairs and once asked her not to bring any more. Many times in my old age I have complained that I've always got what I didn't want in batches, and it all started then. Babies came every year without let-up or warning. We would be delegated to the upstairs bedroom to play, be quiet, and not to come down until we were told. The house would be hushed and then Mrs. McCormick would call us down to see the wonderful surprise: another bundle, all wrapped up in a fluffy angora shawl newly knitted in the fanciest of pale colours. Every time Mrs. McCormick brought a baby into the house, I felt a deep sense of abandonment. When Donald was born, another boy, of all things, it was just too much for me. Billy drove down to collect Mrs. McCormick after she had been with us for a few weeks, and as she was leaving I reminded her, "Mrs. McCormick, you forgot the baby." I was selfish and jealous. Since Dr. Campbell always appeared on the scene, I wanted to make sure of him when things began to look slightly familiar, so I asked if he would let me look into his little black bag. Nothing. He was only the doctor. Mrs. McCormick was to blame.

Courtesy of Myrtle Selig

Mrs. McCormick, with Ruth in the doorway

The path to Kniffen's Hollow, 2011

KNIFFEN'S HOLLOW WAS THE place I loved the best. It was like a secret that one discovers quite by chance, down a steep colonnade of trees, across a small bridge, along a narrow, oak-lined path, and out into a sunny clearing facing the river. Everything about the Hollow was magical: the brook bubbling through the pasture and out to the finely sifted beach, the sward of soft lawn in front of their house, the tall oaks strung with hammocks and swings, and most of all the Kniffen's themselves. The best part of it ended when I was five and Mr. Kniffen, over ninety, died. He was my first true love. He called me his little girl, and I had no idea of the hopelessness of my devotion or that he would ever leave me. He was always there, sitting in his rocking chair by the pot-bellied stove, his open arms warm and welcoming. He would pull me up to his cushioned lap, and I would settle into his arms, cozy and content. His long beard fell to his waistcoat pocket, as comforting as a down pillow. Across his portly chest lay a gold chain, one end latched on to a button hole and the other end slipping into a pocket holding his wonderful gold watch. He would gently remove his watch and hold it to my ear to hear the measured tick, then open it to patiently show me the second hand marking time. Sometimes, he would place it in my hand to feel its weight. Over his waistcoat he wore a cardigan, and in the pocket he always carried a small, brown paper bag of large peppermints. He would pop one in my mouth and I would hardly be able manipulate it around my tongue. I couldn't even describe his face, haloed by white hair, eyes behind glasses, a wonderful wheat-tinged beard, but he was rock-solid.

We had little or nothing to talk about, he had seen everything, I had seen nothing, but I wish I could tell you about the magic. Mother would walk us down, and as we crossed the bridge at the bottom of the Hollow, I would let go of her hand and run along the path to his front door, fleeing into his arms. No love is so well-remembered as first love, no matter how disparate.

My first memory of going down to Kniffen's Hollow seems to be substantiated by fear. It was an Easter Sunday and I couldn't have been more than 3 because Jim wasn't walking yet. Mother was sending Daniel and me down with a box of chocolates and a card. She wrapped the chocolates and tied them with a big bow in the middle so Daniel could carry them and take my hand. She tied the card in the same way so I could reach through the bow and take Daniel's hand. Off we went, hand in hand, dangling our gifts for the five-minute journey down the Chute Road. It must have been the first time I had gone anywhere without Mother or Dad. When we got to the Red Astrakhan tree, I looked down into the Hollow and then back to Mother standing in the doorway. Naturally, I panicked and cried that I wanted to go home, but Daniel held firm. My courage returned only when Mother came and persuaded me that Mr. Kniffen would give me a peppermint. Later in life, money became my moon, but in those early days it looked very much like a peppermint. Once we got to their door, empty arms enfolded us. Daniel would sit on Mrs. Kniffen's lap while I sat on Mr. Kniffen's. We were dearly loved by our parents, but I certainly had a fixation about Mr. Kniffen. I would crawl up on his knee, nestle in his long beard, and sometimes I would just fall asleep. At that young age, my favourite thing in the world was to sit on Mr. Kniffen's lap, hold his heavy gold watch, and suck on a peppermint that was too big for my mouth. We didn't have much to say to each other at our ages, precariously placed at both ends of the spectrum, but there was no greater excitement in life than visiting that loving old man.

Kniffen's brook tumbled steeply down from the woods on its stony bed before levelling out at their bridge and following the footpath to the house. The opposite bank had a small pasture and barn that housed their horse and cow. At the end of the path, the brook turned to avoid a wide swath of lawn that fronted the house. Edging this lawn stood several tall oak trees with hammocks slung between them and swings hanging from the branches.

We didn't have a hammock, so I loved to relax in comfort, looking up at the trees and listening to the brook. On the opposite side of the lawn in a sunny, secluded corner stood a eucalyptus tree,[1] its blooms as intoxicating as the heady mist from Mr. Clarke's apple orchards. The shade from this tree held tables and chairs where adults could sit and observe babies crawling about the lawn. Out on the far edge of the grass, the brook met up with the creek, an inlet from the river that formed a deep pool at high tide, almost like a swimming pool. Beyond the creek and spreading out along the river lay the Kniffen's magnificent beach of fine, creamy, sifted sand, where we played for hours on sunny summer afternoons. Kniffen's beach had class, like dining at the Ritz, while our beach was more or less the local stone quarry.

The Hollow was defined by two sheer, wooded slopes, one of which divided our property from theirs. Flush against the opposite slope was the Kniffen's home, large enough to have accommodated the family of four daughters and one son. Behind the house lay a bed of Lily of the Valley, almost obscuring the tiny white gravestones of three babies. The house was unadorned and Spartan except for an abundance of sunlight streaming in through the windows, making it light and bright and full of warmth and affection. Lamps on the walls had reflectors behind the globes, which ours did not. Pictures on the walls were delicate and small and not too many. In the front parlor and on either side of the pot-bellied stove were Mr. and Mrs. Kniffen's rocking chairs. Above, stove pipes angled across the room, in the summer dangling sticky traps for unfortunate flies. A seating arrangement of a couch, easy chairs and a coffee table completed the decor. A window above the couch framed the steep hill behind the house, showing the roots of tall trees, wildflowers and curious squirrels. The kitchen sparkled white, with everything in perfect, sparse order, while above the sink, a window offered a lovely view past their brook to the broad expanse of the river. Whenever we visited, Mrs. Kniffen made sugar cookies, a sprinkling of sugar and a single raisin in the middle. She would pick me up and sit me at the end of the long baking counter beside the sink, and I would watch as she mixed the ingredients and rolled the dough. Mrs. Kniffen always saved the final step for me, handing me the raisins that I carefully placed

---

[1] Eucalyptus would be unusual in this climate, but Mary insisted it was indeed the genuine article.

in the middle of each cookie. Daniel and I would hover in greedy anticipation as she pulled the tray out of the oven, and I don't recall any cookie ever tasting as good. After all these years, sugar cookies are still part of my Christmas baking, a sprinkling of sugar and a single raisin in the middle.

Mr. and Mrs. Kniffen wintered in Annapolis Royal with their daughter, Kate Woodbury, and during that time, Billy McCormick would house their horse and cow in his barn. I have one very early memory of a time when the whole picture of the Hollow was transformed into a surreal still-life after a heavy snowfall. The trees hung frosted and a heavy fog had rolled in from the Bay, muting our world in a dream-like silence. Dad had to clear off the Kniffen's roof, so he took Daniel and me along. He harnessed Ruff, our black and tan Airedale, to the box sled and lifted me in, placing me between Daniel's knees and tucking us in with a blanket. Ruff was excited and frisky, and Mother cautioned Dad not to let go of his rein or he might run off. I was alarmed because with all the snow and fog, we could be carried off to nowhere. Dad tramped ahead holding Ruff, the snow up to his knees. When we reached the corridor of trees leading down to the Hollow, we paused in front of snow-laden branches dipping low over the path and forming a tunnel, like an entrance to an underworld. The muffled quiet frightened me and I wanted to go home, but Dad calmed me and led Ruff down the steep path, brushing against snowy branches and filling the air with sparkling whiteness. At the bridge, the brook lay silent under the heavy snow, and along the pathway, oak stood like ghostly columns. The Kniffen's home was buried by a thick blanket of snow draping down from the cliff, and even the air seemed frozen under the icy shroud. As we peered through the fog, we noticed a large, unfamiliar shape looming at the river's edge. Dad wanted to investigate. He led us over to the river, where, in a scene from a fairy tale, huge shards of ice had pushed up into a jagged, crystalline castle. It looked haunted in the thick fog, filled with icy corridors and frosted rooms. The unease of that frozen structure reminded me of Hans Christian Anderson's *The Snow Queen*, a frightening story of cold suffocation that Mother had read to us one winter night. Daniel and I got the idea of licking peep holes in our frosted windows from the desperately unhappy Kai and Gerda. I loved that story and read it many times so I could be frightened all over again.

After the harsh winter, the first sign that spring had finally arrived was when Billy McCormick would pass by with the Kniffen's horse and cow, returning them to their barn. Then as the Woodburys drove by, Mother would scurry about the kitchen putting together a basket of vegetables, butter, eggs, bread, something she had baked, and a jar of preserves. We would run down with the basket, and it would be the most exciting thing in the world to race up the path and knock at their door. Mrs. Kniffen would call out, "Who is it?" but she knew who it was. The door would open, and we would rush into open arms.

Our excitement rose to a fever pitch when their other daughters, Mabel and Mary, arrived, signalling that summer had finally begun. Mabel and Mary were teachers out in the country, and every year they summered with their parents. We adored them. Daniel may have been drawing battle lines at home, but he did an abrupt about-face at the Kniffen's. The women doted on him, and Daniel was always on his best behaviour. Mabel, who was Daniel's favourite, would say, "Danny is such a gentleman."

Mother, knowing better would say, "I certainly hope so."

When Mabel had a clam bake, he would give up trips to Digby to gather driftwood and seaweed for the fire pit. He spent whole afternoons digging up clams on the mud flats. It was nothing for him to carry the heavy buckets and wash off the clams in the creek. He would do anything for Mabel, but if Mother asked him to feed the chickens or collect eggs, he slouched off as if suddenly drained of muscle tone.

In time, each child who came into the family loved the Kniffens. Lorna and Joan crawled up on their laps to show them their dolls. As soon as Douglas could catch a fish, he kept them supplied with trout, knocking at their door with the catch of the day. We vied for the privilege of running down with baskets of fruit, vegetables or a treat Mother had baked. Whenever the Kniffen women passed by on their way to the village, the boys would run out and escort them up the hill. I recall Jim, before he went to school, using his wiles on Mabel, rushing up to her and telling her she looked like a yellow bird in her new dress. Mabel hugged and kissed him and told Mother he was precious. I knew better. Like sap running in the spring, charms that had lain dormant all winter oozed from the boys when the Kniffen women arrived.

Since we only went down to Kniffen's beach on sunny afternoons, those days flow back full of brightness and warmth. Mother would take us down in the early afternoon when the tide was out and we could safely play on the mud flats or in the creek. We would race down the path and out into the sunshine for a glorious afternoon of fun. Mother liked to relax with the baby under the eucalyptus tree, sewing or knitting while chatting with the Kniffens. Our first stop would be the huge millstone that sat in the middle of the beach. In its energetic youth, the brook once powered a grist mill. The millstone was our hub, a gathering place throughout the day where we could sit in the sun and rest between adventures. On the hottest days, the millstone was searing hot, and we would take turns sitting on it for as long as our bottoms could stand the heat, then quickly jump off. The boys would sit squirming and twitching before hopping about to cool down. Then we would run off to splash and scream in the creek, or wade knee-high up the stony bed of the brook. We spent hours walking along the watery edge of the tide, searching like mudlarks for shells, sand dollars, or anything else that caught our eye, then gathering it together like treasure from the sea. I loved to dry off on the millstone, lying there soaking up the sun's warmth. On Kniffen's beach, I didn't feel a need to reach up to the ozone or escape across the Bay. I breathed perfect contentment. Sometimes I would doze off and then awake to the far-off sound of the boys yelling and screaming out on the mud flats. They would be running back and forth, slipping and sliding as they lashed at each other with ribbons of seaweed, their shouts rippling like waves of pure joy. The boys loved to roll around in the mud until they were completely covered, even their hair and faces. They called themselves chocolate babies, after the candies we got at Mrs. Schmidt's store. Often, they played in the sun so long that the mud baked and cracked all over their bodies like a reptilian shell. When Mother called them in for something to drink or a snack Mrs. Kniffen had made, they would come running over, grinning like gollywogs with only their eyes and teeth showing. Once, as we ate our sandwiches with cookies and lemonade, Mother shook her head and deplored that they were covered with germs from the entire village, and how would she ever get them clean. Mabel laughed and offered to clean them up in the creek when the tide came in, later sending them home with their clothes pressed and their hair neatly parted.

We would quickly finish our snack and run off to new adventures, but soon, the rising tide would signal an end to the fun. Mother's high, sweet voice would ring across the beach as she called us in. After a rinse in the creek and thank you's to the Kniffens, we would trudge up the hill, drained by the sun, as if its rays had scrubbed us deep-down clean.

I used to long for luxury and filled my scrapbooks with pictures of elegance, but not one beachfront house or seaside property sat among them, not with the glories of Kniffen's beach five minutes from home and a world away from the farm. Over the years, many events have faded or clouded over, but nothing has dimmed the brilliant sunshine of those days on Kniffen's beach. Such are the childhood memories that echo like screams of pure joy.

Strangely, the place I loved the best also traumatized me for life, but water has always bedevilled me, and these narrow escapes should be read as warnings from the gods to stay away, with Jim as the willing catalyst. In the late afternoon after a day of work, Dad would go down with a towel and a cake of soap for a swim in the creek, often taking the boys along to scrub them clean of the day's dirt. Twice I went with them, both times to my life-long regret. When the tide came in, it filled the creek to a deep pool that reached over Dad's head. The boys would dive in and roughhouse, and it all seemed like such harmless fun until one day as I stood on the grass watching, Jim snuck up behind me and pushed me in. He thought I should join the fun, but instead, I sank to the bottom. Dad pulled me out, sputtering and hysterical. Jim had been swimming since his crawling days, so he didn't understand my inability and resented Dad's stern lecture. I avoided the creek, but another day, I waded in to the river, first up to my knees, then up to my waist, and then feeling quite brave, up to my neck. When I called for everyone to look, Jim dashed in and pushed me backwards. In trying to gain my balance, I dug my heels into the sand and fell back into deeper water. A second time Dad fished me out, coughing and crying in absolute hysteria. My fear of water was complete, and I never learned to swim because I never forgot that strange, helpless feeling of drifting downstream with the gentle swaying of the tide. For a while after that, Jim and I moved in different circles. He was disgusted with my performance, and I was convinced he wanted me out of my life and his.

Shortly after Douglas was born and towards the end of summer, a large family gathering took place in the Hollow to celebrate Mr. Kniffen's birthday. All of his children came for the event; the only time I saw them together. Kate (Kniffen) Woodbury drove down from Annapolis with her husband and two children, Elizabeth and John. Ruth (Kniffen) Pratt and her husband arrived from the States, as did the Kniffen's only son, Venn. He was strapping and sandy haired, very different from the petite Kniffen girls. Mother bundled up Douglas in the pram and took Daniel, Jim and me down, each of us carrying a treat she had baked for Mr. Kniffen: currant squares, fruitcake, vinegar tarts, and his favourite scotch shortbread. Chairs and tables had been brought outside to the lawn, including Mr. and Mrs. Kniffen's rocking chairs. Guests swung on the hammocks and sat in chairs by the brook, everyone talking and laughing in the late afternoon sun. I sat at the fire pit with Mr. Kniffen, who was tending to the driftwood, burning it down to coals, then layering it with seaweed and amber ribbons of kelp. Little round baubles on the smouldering kelp hissed and cracked like pistol shots, providing entertainment for the boys. Mr. Kniffen sat at the centre of attention, not only because of his birthday, but also because he was preparing the clams. Everyone anxiously wanted to eat and good-naturedly joked with him, but he reminded them that you can't rush a clam.

Of the four sisters, I thought Ruth Pratt the most beautiful. Mabel, Mary, and Kate all had reddish-brown hair, but Ruth's was coal black and pulled sleekly back in a bun at the nape of her neck. She was fussily dressed, right down to a pair of black-and-white summer shoes that I decided I would wear when I grew up. Ruth was childless, and when Douglas woke up, she insisted on holding him. I watched her kiss him from one end to the other, and when she got to his feet, she put one tiny foot completely in her mouth before exclaiming to Mother, "Oh Mary, I could just eat him! I wish he were mine. Why don't you give him to me?" She was quite overcome in a slightly cannibalistic way, and she and her husband Vernon sat on the grass looking him over as if they had just opened a surprise package. I clearly remember Ruth's strange performance, not realizing that her excitement emphasized her tragedy. Ruth and Vernon were a handsome, slick couple who stand out in my memory: deftly line-drawn, cleanly and precisely, like the John Held sketches of the beautiful young of the flapper era.

The evening was filled with laughter and music and all kinds of food, but I was not happy at all because Elizabeth Woodbury, a year or two older than me, had claimed Mr. Kniffen for herself and was sitting on his lap. I was insanely jealous. I went over to Mother and said to just look at Elizabeth. Mother told me to stop my nonsense and sit on the hammock, whereupon Elizabeth dashed over and dumped me out, telling me I had to sit on the swing made of wooden slats, which was hard and uncomfortable. Instead, I ran to Mr. Kniffen, and he ended up with both of us on his knees leaning against his beard and glowering at each other. Mother wasn't impressed with my behaviour, but I didn't care. On later visits, I would see Elizabeth when Kate Woodbury stopped the car to chat with Mother, and we glowered still. I can't remember that I ever said a word to her again. We could never be friends.

The last time I saw Mr. Kniffen was when he walked up from the Hollow to visit Dad, who was hoeing the gardens row by row. It was a warm, sunny day, and as Dad worked each row, Daniel and I followed along, sitting in the grass and wildflowers of the embankment along the Chute Road. Mr. Kniffen came up the Road, looking old and tired. We ran to him, and Dad stopped hoeing as they talked, resting his chin on his hands at the top of the hoe, a familiar stance. They talked for a while, discussing the gardens, and then Mr. Kniffen jokingly said, "You immigrants don't know how to farm." Perhaps it was because Dad carefully prepared the seedbed and put bags of potash and other nutrients in the soil to doctor it up, or perhaps it was because Mr. Kniffen only had a hayfield and a small garden. In any case, Dad laughed uproariously, but the joke didn't register with me. Later, Dad laughed again as he told the story to Mother, who enjoyed it just as much. Daniel kept the incident alive by asking Dad what an 'iggerant' was, thereafter periodically bursting into sing-song, "Dad is an iggerant." Mother and Dad always seemed amused by the memory.

Mr. Kniffen's long life came to a close a few months later, and quite dramatically. Mother had told us that Mr. Kniffen was very sick and very old and we wouldn't be seeing him anymore. Reality doesn't come to little children just because they are told, especially when it concerns something as complex as life and death.

Mother could smell out a thunderstorm the way a cat smells out mice. She would say, "I smell it in the air." Immediately, she would see that the chickens were safely housed and that Scotty brought in the cows. She would call out, "Here, bossy, bossy, bossy. Harrr-eeee, Harrr-eeee." By the time the barn door closed, you would hear a distant thump over the Bay, rolling closer and closer. Lightning would pencil and flash across the sky, and the first rain drop would fall. Mother never allowed us into the kitchen, where the large window offered an open invitation for lightning to strike the stove, copper pots, pans, kettles, and our milk mugs, graded youngest to oldest. The parlor and dining room were off-limits as well because of Dad's brass. We were not allowed near windows or into bedrooms near iron beds. We couldn't even hold a spoon. Mother firmly shut windows and doors against the slightest breeze that might usher in the lightning, and, as she said, burn us to a crisp. We had heard of farmers finding cattle struck dead by lightning, lying beneath the tree where they had sought shelter. Silos would ignite; barns full of hay would erupt. When we started school and were caught in a storm, Mother warned us stay away from tall trees and to never, ever walk through the maple grove. Instead, we had to run up the Chute Road to the lilac bush, down the embankment and straight to the front door, which she quickly closed behind us as we stood dripping like drowned rats. We were then stripped, because our wet clothes were also a conductor. We couldn't even drink a drop of water. It's no wonder I was a child bedevilled by fear. Mother would corral us under the stairs and sit shivering, waiting for the house to be struck. Dad would humour her by saying he had seen storms far worse at sea and, "Dearie, ah survived! Here ah am!" Mother would tearfully grumble out of her dark haven under the stairs, "I'm not going to be struck by lightning if I can help it." When the storm had passed and the thunder could be heard faintly rolling off, Dad would say, "Come now Dearie, it's ovah," but she would sit waiting for that hush from a clear sky, "Dan, go away! I'm not moving an inch until the sun comes out." Finally, she would let Dad open the doors and windows, and the fresh breath of coolness would diffuse the clamminess. The boys would tear about with renewed energy after their captivity under the stairs. I can still see that wonderful, washed clarity as the sun came out brighter than ever and the grass, gardens, and maples sparkled with a glorious sheen—an overall beauty not seen in the city. Mother had grown up in a town, where the weather was merely an annoyance. In the country, there was a harshness to storms and a constant fear of nature. Mother never got over that fear. One distant rumble and she was alerted.

Dad was in Montreal the day Mr. Kniffen died. It happened in the early spring during a violent storm, with thunder and lightning crashing and the wind raging through the maples. It was one of the worst storms I remember, and later we heard talk of barns, silos and homes being burned or damaged. Mother shivered in hysteria the way she usually did during a thunderstorm. She had closed all the doors off the hallway: the parlor door, the dining room door, Uncle Peter's door and the kitchen door. Only a dim light filtered down from upstairs. We cowered under the stairs, Mother holding the baby, while Daniel, Jim and I sat on the floor, awaiting that flash of eternity. The storm seemed to stubbornly swing back and forth like a great pendulum. Lightning shattered all around us followed by pounding thunder as Mother exclaimed through her tears, "Oh! Oh my!! Oh my Goodness!! Oh dear, oh dear!! It's overhead! It's going away! It's coming back! Will it never stop! I've never heard anything like it! We never had storms like this at home!" Then a tremendous, splintering crash shook the house and nearly sent Mother into shell-shock. We thought it had hit the barn. When the storm rolled off, we looked out the window to see that the barn and the maples still stood. All the buildings and trees were the same as ever, but we knew that something nearby had been struck. The next morning, Billy McCormick stopped by after milking the Kniffen's cow and told Mother that Mr. Kniffen had died during the storm, and by strange coincidence, the oak tree he had planted as a boy was struck by lightning and rent from top to bottom, split like kindling.

Mr. Kniffen's oak was special because he had told us, as he had told his children, that he had planted it from an acorn before he went to school. Every time we went down to Kniffen's Hollow, I don't know why we did it, but we touched Mr. Kniffen's oak, often racing to see who could get to it first. It was a magnificent tree, as old oaks are, straight up to the sky, all those long years of growing and reaching. In the summer, as you lay on the hammock swinging, you looked up at this prized tree by the side of the brook. On the day of Mr. Kniffen's death, this lovely tree that stood by the pathway like his escutcheon, his coat of arms, was split down to the ground as if by a giant axe. It was stripped of its branches, and the ones that remained barely clung to the bole by strips of bark, bowing down to its roots in a strange contortion of grief. It seemed odd that Mr. Kniffen's oak should die with him, and Daniel with his wild imagination said it was haunted. Afterwards, whenever we went down to the Hollow, we still ran to touch some part of it, in a cautious way, as if it had a soul.

I had to believe that Mr. Kniffen was going away when a long, horse-drawn hearse, polished in ebony black with purple curtained windows, slowly came down McCormick's hill and passed by our house. Sitting on the high front seat were two men dressed in black topcoats and high hats. We watched from the front doorstep as it passed again, trailed by a retinue of mourners. We went around to the back door to watch the procession slip out of sight over McCormick's hill. That was the first time I was aware, in a vague way, of death. It was also the first time I saw a hearse, followed by all the people in black, everyone in tears. For some reason, the purple curtains gave me a sense of sickness and foreboding, and I have avoided that lenten, funereal colour ever since.

It happens in life that we must settle for much less than we had hoped for, but whenever I pass a candy counter and my happy eye sees those great big peppermints, I'll buy a few, and no amount of money could offer what I get from them.

Looking down to Kniffen's Hollow from the Marvin farm, 2011

With the return of all the Kniffens, the next member of our extended family whom we anxiously awaited was Mr. Benjamin Bishop, a courtly, aging gentleman, headmaster of a boys school in New York City. For the two months of summer, he returned to his tiny, dollhouse-like cottage high on the cliff above the Kniffens to rest his wings like a wise old bird.

As I look back, Mr. Bishop's facial features have faded, but his tall, slim frame still passes through my memory with dignity. I see a man striding past our house, nearing retirement, immaculately dressed in a pale blue seersucker suit, crisp shirt with silver arm bands, Panama hat on a bald head with grey fringe, cane over his arm, spats over tan and white shoes, the measured gait of age. On his return from the village, he liked to sit on the glide swing with Mother for tea. He was a mild, deferring, good-natured man, amused by little children. He was our true uncle.

Every year before Mr. Bishop's arrival, Billy McCormick would go up to his cottage to scythe the grass and straighten the trellised rose arbor that enclosed the tiny front lawn. Mrs. McCormick would clean up inside and hang the lace curtains on the two front windows. Lou Albert, one of our hired hands and Mr. Bishop's great and good friend, would hitch Harry to the wagon and collect him at the train station. At the first sound of the wagon rattling down McCormick's hill, we would excitedly rush out to meet them as they came through the maple grove, everyone in high summer spirits. Mother always had a light lunch prepared, and the adults would repair to the dining room for animated conversation. In the evening, she gave a welcoming dinner that included the Kniffens, the McCormicks, Stella and Jessie Harris, the Simons, and of course, Lou Albert. Children ate in the kitchen as the dining room rocked with conversation and laughter.

Mr. Bishop's dinner was often the first of the season and the most exciting, since it held the promise of many more to come. The Marvin parlor ran all summer long, inside and out, and everyone dropped by: old soldiers, friends from the village, guests from the River View Lodge, hired hands, passersby, and the dozen or so regulars of our summer family. Dad issued an open invitation, and his easygoing manner turned the farm into an outpost of southern hospitality, where guests received a warm welcome and could linger for as long as they wanted. When he attended to chores,

Mr. Bishop carried on like the well-seasoned host that he was, a veteran of New York salon society. His all-inclusive good manners and charm were as comforting as the shade under the Bartlett pear tree.

After Mr. Bishop's favourite dessert of lemon meringue pie, he would open a sack and distribute presents to everyone like a summer Santa Claus. Dad would get a book, Mother a box of chocolates, and for both of them a stack of records. He liked songs by the American composers: Vincent Youmans, Edward MacDowell, Stephen Foster, all those love songs, sweet and cloying, sung to enchanting ladies: Kathleen, Bonnie, Sylvia (who was she?), Jeanie with the light brown hair. We greedily awaited Mr. Bishop's arrival because we knew he wouldn't forget us. We watched for him to hand over to Mother a brown paper-wrapped package, knowing it contained a whole box of Beech-Nut gum, a full, glorious summer's worth of chewing. It was so much better than spruce gum gouged from trees, which you had to chew and chew to tone down the woodsy flavour. I can't remember many of the presents I received at Christmas, except for my dolls, but the wonder of Beech-Nut gum lingers still. Mother didn't approve of gum and strictly rationed when we chewed and for how long. But Mr. Bishop understood. How many times had he made reluctant school boys spit their gum into the waste basket? When Daniel and I started school, Mr. Bishop also started bringing us a full box of Farber's yellow pencils, not sold in Bear River. We were the only ones in school who had them. Pencils bought at the Trading Company could be slyly stolen from our desks with impunity, but Farber pencils were our unique status symbol and no one dared pilfer them. Merton Yorke and Roland Barrass could no longer boldly plead innocence. Those gifts were so special. When I see Beech-Nut gum or a golden yellow Farber's pencil, Mr. Bishop is there in the mists.

I first saw Mr. Bishop's cottage when Mabel Kniffen let me come along as she took up a plate of freshly baked cookies. A path from the Kniffen's back door led up the hill, but you had to grab small trees and bushes hand over hand to make the steep climb. We crested the hill and there it stood, straight out of a fairy tale: a white dollhouse with lace curtains, dwarfed by oak hundreds of years old. The huge trees formed a protective semi-circle, barely clinging to the cliff. Through an opening, you looked steeply down to the progress of the river. Mabel called out, and Mr. Bishop replied from inside, stooping as he came out the doorway. I was fascinated by the cottage and wanted to see inside, but instead he invited us to sit in his trellised rose arbor, which covered the front lawn in a rickety fashion. The arbor was like a small room, high enough to accommodate Mr. Bishop and wide enough for several chairs, a footstool and orange crates that held magazines. Outside the arbor, red ramblers strayed like outstretched arms, but inside they neatly climbed and twined through the trellis like Mother Nature's wallpaper. As Mr. Bishop sat down, he redirected several wayward vines reaching out for freedom, poking and reprimanding them like naughty pupils. Mabel offered Mr. Bishop a cookie, and they fell to chatting in the comfortable shade as the sun streamed through, leeching the roses of their very essence and filling the air with an intoxicating perfume. The meticulous gentleman seemed perfectly posed in his rose arbor, dappled by the sun, the operas and plays of New York replaced by the sleepy cadence of the lapping river and the breezy rustle of oak leaves.

Every fine sunny day of all those years of summers, Mr. Bishop would pass by on his way to the village for mail or groceries. We would gather around, trailing like appendages, escorting him from the Red Astrakhan tree to the Bridge Brook. When he returned from the village, we would invite him in like a playmate and an equal. Although I was shy, I never felt awkward around all the elderly people of my young years; we all seemed young together. As he sat down on the glide swing, we would crowd around, the boys anxious to show him their new sling shots, willow whistles or collections of rocks and bugs. He would help identify butterflies. Were they nice? Did Mr. Bishop like them? Would he like to see their tree house in the woods? Not today. He watched as Douglas shinnied up the swing rope to return a fallen baby robin to its nest, held carefully in his pants pocket. He listened to Douglas' excited recounting of how he had stalked a mother partridge and her brood. It was another day when he was late coming home and Mother sent us to find him. He had been following a mother partridge and her chicks when all of a sudden they vanished. He knew they hadn't gone far, so he lay down and waited for movement, staying still for a very long time. Finally, the mother partridge emerged from under his nose, crawling out from last year's leaves and passing right in front of him with her brood in tow. Douglas was amazed that the mother and her well-behaved chicks had been inches away and he hadn't seen them.

Another day, Douglas claimed in passing that of course squirrels ate from his hand, all kinds of animals did. Mr. Bishop was doubtful and challenged him. After fetching a handful of oatmeal, Douglas positioned himself near the first maple in the grove, cautioned everyone to be still, and gave a few creditable squeaks. We sat on the glide swing watching as a squirrel appeared and frenetically twitched up and down the tree as Douglas, who spoke squirrel fluently, mimicked its chatter. Daniel and Jim mimicked as well, mumbling in squirrel-ish tones, "Yes, I am hungry," "No, I'm full," "I love oatmeal," "No, I hate it.' After much debate, the squirrel jumped down from the tree and tentatively approached Douglas for his afternoons snack, but then Daniel and Jim yelled and hooted, frightening it away. Mr. Bishop was as determined as an old school master and dismissed them from the swing. All the while, Douglas never budged, poised with his hand extended. He resumed his chatter and we followed the squirrel's Shakespearean indecision, back and forth until it finally realized the act had worn thin. He stood up to Douglas' hand and nervously nibbled every bit of oatmeal. Mr. Bishop chuckled and shook his head. Later, Douglas demonstrated his slow, careful motions, adding that with squirrels, you had to talk in gentle tones, whatever that meant. We tried without success to lure squirrels in the same way until Mother forbad it when a squirrel nipped Daniel's finger. She warned us that an animal bite could cause lockjaw, so Daniel launched into a creditable demonstration, rolling around on the grass and clenching his teeth while Jim tried to pry his mouth open so he wouldn't starve to death.

I suspect that Mr. Bishop learned a great deal from the boys. I'm sure he observed more curiosities from them than he did as headmaster of his exclusive boys school in arty New York. Little boys there didn't hunt with slingshots or snare rabbits or wander through the woods for whole days. My brothers kept him amused as they rattled on about all their adventures in misbehaviour, things Mother wouldn't get out of them with a tingler. Mr. Bishop listened intently, hearing them out and chuckling at the little boys he so well understood. He must have been a very good headmaster.

Mother and Dad enjoyed Mr. Bishop's company, as did all our summer friends, and when they gathered under the maples for leisurely afternoon chats, the conversation drifted to the performing arts, everyone's favourite subject and Mr. Bishop's forte. At the time, rural life had yet to enjoy the spoon-fed sophistication of the live arts, outside of once-a-year Chautauqua and plays put on by talented locals, so listening to Mr. Bishop talk of New York nights was like taking a trip to another world. He had attended every opera, musical, play and ballet on Broadway from the Gay Nineties to the Roaring Twenties. It was the golden age, never since equalled, and he had seen every single star. He heard Caruso hit high C during his long reign at the Met. He saw Tetrazzini, Schumann-Heink, Nellie Melba, Maria Jeritza, every voice I had grown up hearing on the gramophone. As Mr. Bishop regaled us with tales from the Met, the printer's ink in my scrap books came to life. I sat enthralled. He spoke of revues at the Winter Garden, vaudeville at the Palace, the Zeigfeld Follies at the New Amsterdam. He attended every show by Gershwin, Hammerstein, Kern, Rodgers, and Youmans. He saw Marilyn Miller in *Sally*, the musical that began her long run as the queen of Broadway. If nothing new was playing, he would see the incomparable Al Jolson, who sometimes stopped a thinly plotted play to sing requests for hours. We were dazzled by Mr. Bishop's recounting of the fantastical *Wizard of Oz* and *Babes in Toyland*, but what stuck in my mind was Maude Adams as the infectious Peter Pan actually flying about the stage. It couldn't possibly be true. I asked him how she flew and he said it was a secret, even in New York. Only when pressed by Daniel did Mr. Bishop confess that it was an illusion achieved by wires and pulleys. He then said he had seen the great Sarah Bernhardt on stage with only one leg–another intrigue, compounded when we learned that she had been offered an enormous sum of money for the amputated leg.

Our summers were filled with visitors, and when the conversation and laughter ended, everyone seemed sated as if they had indulged in a good meal. Discussions over Sunday picnics extended past the milking of the cows and into the night, and if there were no lights, there were the stars. It seemed so comfortably exciting listening from our beds as voices filtered in through our bedroom window, lulling us to sleep. Long before I ever saw a movie, I saw the bright lights of Broadway.

One hazy afternoon towards the end of summer, Mr. Bishop stopped by for tea after his walk into the village, and as he was leaving he made an unusual request. He said to Mother that if she were in the mood to sing after supper, he would love to listen from his rose arbor. So many times he said he had heard all the best voices of the day and none compared to Mother's. He was always asking her to sing. She sang so much that it passed through us like a soft breeze. We children never realized how beautiful her voice was, but Mr. Bishop did.

After putting the babies to bed, Mother made fudge and left it to cool while we trekked to the top of the hay field, where a warm sunset glow spread across the hills like a luminescent haze. In the settling hush of the day, a dog barked in the distance, while far below, seagulls skimmed the river. The boys sat in an old gnarled apple tree that bore stunted fruit, relaxing on the branches as if they were comfortable chairs. I sat beside Mother, who stood on her stage, the flat rock. Without preamble, she opened her mouth and sang out as if her voice belonged to the hills. It trilled like a flute over to Mr. Bishop in his rose arbor and across the river to Dorothea di Geronimo's grandmother on her verandah. When Mother finished one song, she sang another, covering all of Mr. Bishop's favorites: "To a Wild Rose," "The Missouri Waltz," "I Dreamt I Dwelt in Marble Halls," "Beautiful Dreamer" and the lovely "Last Rose of Summer." I asked for "O Mio Babbino Caro," and then she sang "From the Land of the Sky Blue Water," a song so eerily beautiful that it sounded as if it belonged to the ancestors of the Micmac Indians. I only ever heard Mother sing that haunting song, but I can't help remembering it. I didn't quite understand the lyrics, so Mother explained that the young Indian Brave was courting his beloved by offering her a bowl of wheat. It seemed like an odd love token, but Mother's explanation made the wheat shimmer like gold. I suppose I thought it should have been roses or chocolates, but the tenderness was real, and no other lyrics gifted one's love in the same way. I asked her to sing it again. I can still see Mother standing on the flat rock singing her heart out that idyllic summer evening, her beautiful voice wafting over the hills like bells pealing. It may seem strange that Mother, so genteel, would just sing out with sheer joy to the hills and sky, but she was happiest when she sang, and music makes real artists compulsive.

THE MINUTE THE SUN and the warm breezes from the Bay had dried the mud on the Chute Road, Mrs. Croscup, who lived near the Waldec Line, would begin her summer forays, hiking at her great age to visit her friends. We would see her coming up from Kniffen's Hollow, a full-blown, energetic figure in heavy black mourning from her wide-brimmed summer hat to her black boots. A large black umbrella shielded her from the hot sun as she stalked along with her cane looking like a plump black mushroom. Daniel and I would run to meet her as she passed by to visit Mamie Walsh at the Crossroads, and Mother would call out, "Hello Buddy, drop by on your way home."

Mrs. Croscup would wave her cane and answer, "Yes, Mary dear, of course," and on she would flounce in full sail like the prow of a ship.

Mrs. Croscup had a happy, expansive nature that extended to every child in the family. She wasn't too old to hold babies, and as wrinkled as her face was and as gnarled as her fingers were, she seemed young to me then. Her enveloping arms would hold me on her cushiony lap, and her long black dress, pinned at the neck with a brooch, layered with lace, serge and summer bombazine over undergarments that rustled like taffeta, provided a cozy, tufted warmth. I would feel the rumble of her subdued chuckle as she chatted with Mother over tea. She was always happy, an age-old hedonist without a care in the world. Mother in her twenties and Mrs. Croscup in her late seventies seemed like sisters. They quilted and hooked rugs. She bathed and rocked babies. She sewed doll's clothes for Lorna and Joan. She loved us and we loved her.

Since many of our summer visitors were teachers: Mrs. Croscup, Mabel and Mary Kniffen, Mr. Bishop and Stella Harris, they nurtured the boys' insatiable, compulsive curiosity, never leaving questions unanswered. I can still see Mrs. Croscup relaxing on the glide swing under the Bartlett pear tree reading from one of Uncle Peter's penny dreadfuls while Daniel and Jim listened spellbound. Mrs. Croscup assured Mother they were good stories, and she usually got some before they were siphoned off to the outhouse.

Mother and Dad loved having long, involved conversations with Mrs. Croscup that delved into the early years of Bear River. Her German name indicated an ancestry dating back to the first inhabitants of the village, and many in her family had captained local ships. Her recounting of memories and stories went back to the mid-1800s. She had seen the youthful vibrancy of the village, when Bear River was renowned for its wooden sailing ships, their sleekness and speed taking them around the world. The few miles of the Bear River, the Rhine of Nova Scotia, bounced with activity, lasting until the era of iron and steel. Dad and Mother loved hearing about those early days when the little village grew wealthy and built large homes, now lonely reminders.

When Daniel and I were very young, one of Mrs. Croscup's stories fascinated us so much that it seemed to evolve into a tale straight out of Scheherazade. For many years, Captain Woodworth's Packet, the *Bear River*, plied up and down the river bringing weekly supplies to the villagers, unloading its wares on the wharf by Mrs. Schmidt's store to fill the half-dozen shops. The Packet looked like a saucy washtub with its one smoke stack, and when we heard its shallow toot approaching from Bear Island, we would race to the top of the hay field and sit huffing and puffing on the flat rock, waiting to see its progress from behind the maze of trees. We would watch until it disappeared beneath the hill near the exhibition building. What happened after that was an open-ended story until Mrs. Croscup told us her tale. She had embarked on the Packet and sailed down the Bear River and out to the patch of blue water between the hills, then across the Bay of Fundy to finally disembark under the rocky promontory of the port of St John, New Brunswick. Along the way, she had savoured Capt. Woodworth's fish chowder, as famous as the Packet itself. It was the best fish chowder she had ever tasted, the fish caught right out of the Bay as they sailed along. And not only that, she had also taken the ferry from Yarmouth to Boston. She had travelled the world. It hadn't occurred to our little minds that Dad had sailed the seven seas and Mother had crossed an ocean. With Dad, there seemed to be nothing we could pinpoint as solid adventure outside of exaggerated tales meant to amuse and confuse us. And as for Mother's adventure, it never occurred to us that she had any, being rooted in her kitchen.

Daniel seized upon Mrs. Croscup's roaring adventure and would beg retelling time after time. How the Packet had rocked on the rough Bay and survived was an absolute miracle, and how Mrs. Croscup had lived to tell the tale seemed utterly fantastic for this old lady. One day Daniel was going to sail the Packet, the ultimate journey for a 4-year-old. At the time, the village still had several beautiful schooners skimming down the river, but as sleek as they were, they hadn't the exotic charm of that squat little indestructible tub.

Daniel's amazement simmered down on his first trip to Digby when he saw "the largest ship in the world," the Princess Helene, which displaced the Packet considerably. But he never forgot Mrs. Croscup's amazing journey and relived part of the excitement several years later. One day Dad, Captain Morgan and Captain Woodworth were chatting on the wharf while I waited with Dottie Morgan, sitting on the step of Mrs. Schmidt's store and eating her candy. After the chat, Dad and I walked up to Dr. Campbell's with Dottie and Captain Morgan, while Daniel was invited by Captain Woodworth to come aboard the Packet for a bowl of fish chowder. Later, Daniel had good reason to rave about the steering wheel, the stove, the ship's complement, and the chowder. He couldn't wait to equalize his experience with Mrs. Croscup.

The Packet caught in the ice not far from Maple Grove farm.

For all of our years on the farm, Mrs. Croscup's son Eugene supplied us with a wide variety of fresh meat for our table. Daniel called Eugene's horse-drawn wagon 'the meat house' because of its shed-like structure on the back with tiny louvred windows for ventilation. I thought it looked like the village hearse. Eugene would open the back door, and inside would be a cupboard full of gore: long rods with hooks holding a bloody mess of fresh meat: sides of beef, red and raw; whole lambs hanging in effigy; those terrible blobs of liver and kidney; Dad's favourite, brains and tripe; plucked chickens with their heads and feet still on. Eugene would slice off a steak, or cut a roast or a chunk of meat to chop up for stew or grind into hamburger. My favourites were all the fish served fresh from the Bay: cod, haddock, herring, tuna, halibut.

Often, Eugene would drop his mother off at our house, promising to collect her at the end of the day. His business took him far afield, and if he couldn't pick her up, Dad would hitch up Harry and take Mrs. Croscup home. It was a long trek at the end of the day for an elderly lady, but only fifteen minutes by horse trot. Eugene was very considerate of his mother, and in return for small favours, he would give Mother the extras of the day that he knew she liked: baby beef, halibut, or Gaspereaux salmon. Once, he brought her a large mackerel, insisting that she would like it, but Mother insisted that she wouldn't because it was a scavenger. Mother took it and stuffed it and everyone loved it. Sensing Mother's wariness, I didn't try mackerel, not until years later when I found out that Eugene was right. Another time, Dad came home from a hunting trip with a rump of moose meat. Mother with her delicate tastes said no, never would she eat it. She offered it to Eugene. Mrs. Croscup eagerly tried to convince her to keep it, but Mother was adamant. She packed Mrs. Croscup off with her usual assortment: treacle scones, vegetables, a freshly baked loaf of bread, jam, and a great rump of moose. Mrs. Croscup happily accepted Dad's bounty and said she had a number of colonial recipes in mind, one being moose meat mince meat pie. Mother reeled at such savagery. Moose meat in a dessert would never happen in her house. But it did. On Mrs. Croscup's next visit, Mother humbly ate moose meat mince meat pie, and she agreed with Dad that it tasted quite as wonderful as the ones she made with suet.

In a few years, Eugene appeared with a truck and the same meat house sitting on the back, somewhat elevated and accommodated by steps, all of which appeared very elevated in our eyes. Until then, only Mr. MacIntyre's car motored along the Chute Road, so Eugene's jerry-built meat house suddenly had prestige, ranking him among the village elite. The meat man and the village tycoon travelled the same road in the same way. Years later, we had a milk man, an ice man, a bread man, but Eugene was the last of the meat men, offering any cut of meat delivered fresh to your door, a convenience unheard of today.

Ned McCormick (son of Billy) and Dad moose hunting.

I always thought of Mrs. Croscup as the grandest of ladies living in a big, beautiful home with surroundings to suit her dignity. She just seemed grand. It so happened that when I went to Alice Copeland's birthday party, her best friend Louise Harris and I became best friends. At the party, Louise and I joined forces to find all the jelly beans wrapped flamboyantly in cellophane and hidden in the nooks of trees and other obvious spots, the winner receiving the prize of a lollypop. We played tag, hide and seek, may I, and the paper chase before settling down to a birthday feast of sandwiches, cake and jell-o, all laid out by Alice's sister Eileen and Ethel Reade, both in high school. I had a wonderful time at my first ever birthday party, and best of all, Louise promised to have her mother invite me over to play. I eagerly waited for Louise's mother to call, which she soon did, giving instructions for me to meet Col. Harris at the end of a certain hay field, where he would collect me in his car. Louise was an only child, and Alice briefed me about her lovely home, all her clothes, and her huge collection of dolls. I suppose I became overly excited about the visit because I turned it into the most exciting day of my life. Like a dog-tired housewife, I thrilled at the chance to escape the house and babies to see how I should really be living.

It was hot and sunny the day I walked down Kniffen's Hollow clutching my doll. I crested the hill in front of Mr. Bishop's cottage, and from there, the Chute Road ran straight out to the Waldec line. Cicadas pierced the air as I walked along in the dry heat, the pulverized dust in the ruts of the road puffing and powdering my polished shoes. One always avoided the grassy area between the ruts, liberally sprinkled with horse manure. The dusty road seemed endless, and in a while I became confused because all the fields looked alike. After passing a clump of trees, I came to a weary old farm house, weathered and grey. Leaning fence posts held up loose strands of barbed wire. Slipped boards left gaping holes in the barn. On the listing verandah, an old lady sat in a rocking chair fanning away the heat. I kept walking, but then I heard that wonderfully familiar voice calling my name. It was Mrs. Croscup, no longer in her crinkly taffeta, no longer in her imposing black to emphasize her magnitude, but sitting in a house dress, rocking and fanning, looking very tired. On one of the happiest day of my life, I was suddenly sobered. How could it be that Mrs. Croscup was so poor, living in the shabbiest house on the Chute Road, all alone and so far from company? The walkway to the house was a loose arrangement of wooden slats that sagged into wrinkles in the ground. Tall grass and nodding flowers crowded the path. As I stepped onto the verandah it creaked, crying out for repairs. From the kitchen, the aroma of raspberry jam wafted through the screen door as Mrs. Croscup rested her ample weight in her rocking chair, cooling herself with a black fan showing faded flowers and dangling what might have been a gold tassel, now a shaggy brown. I explained my purpose, and she checked the kitchen clock, telling me I had time to sit and chat. We talked about birthday parties and raspberry jam, and then she gave me my bearings—straight ahead to a crossroads at the end of her field. I picked up my doll and walked off, lost in a jumble of emotions.

Shortly, a car approached from the Waldec Line. It was Col. Harris with Louise. The door opened and I climbed in to the world of a favoured only child. Her bedroom sprawled over the plastic wonder of polished hardwood floors. A windowed nook held a writing desk and painter's easel, both awaiting inspiration. A cushioned window seat crowded with dolls looked out to a golden, waving wheat field. Her pillow-covered bed stood like the lap of luxury, banked by night tables with electric lamps. Louise opened a door and showed me her cupboard full of stylish clothes. She had toys, clothes, shoes, and all pampered elegance a child could wish for. We burrowed into the window seat and pulled out movie star dolls to dress. Then we lunched at Louise's small table and chairs under a tremendous oak tree that cast a cool shade over the manicured lawn. In comparing our lives, the only similarity I found was that Louise had a list of complaints as long as mine. Whatever else we dined on, all I remember was something we never had at home: creamed peas. Later, I raved about creamed peas, but Mother reminded me I was doing well enough with plain old buttered peas. I never had creamed peas again. My peas have always been buttered.

That was one of my charmed days, impossible to forget: a taste of the life I wished for, a silly dream, meshed with Mrs. Croscup, not in her indelible black, but even more indelibly defined in her house dress, rocking on a sadly weathered verandah, looking out at the overburdened grey weariness of her farm. Surely the farm had prospered once, but all those years of endless chores amounted to little more than tired resignation.

Not far from the Croscups lived Mrs. Abner Chute and her twin sons Abner and Miney (Minard), all of them aging and poor. They were silent, lonely figures. Occasionally they would drive by in the summer, Mrs. Chute sitting in the buggy between her two sons. She was a tired, wispy, birdlike woman wearing rimless spectacles, dressed in widow's weeds with a pancake hat tied under her chin. Her two sons seemed just as old, both of them shy and remote, both of them with no upper teeth. Other than a hello in passing, only once did Mrs. Chute accept Mother's hospitality. It was a very hot day and Mother saw her coming up from the Hollow holding a large matchbox in front of her. Mother said, "Poor soul, she must be going to the village." By the time Mrs. Chute had reached our farm, she had already covered a good distance. Mother invited her in to the kitchen for tea while Uncle Peter hitched up Harry to take her to the bank, where she was going to deposit the pennies in her matchbox. The infrequency of passersby left images more defined than if there had been a great flow of traffic. Mrs. Chute is still pigeon-holed in my memory, so tiny and fragile with her matchbox of pennies and Mother's epitaph, "Poor soul."

Several years later, on a day when the boys had fled to the woods, they ranged so far that they emerged at the dilapidated premises of Abner and Miney Chute. Elderly Mrs. Chute had passed away, leaving her shy, middle-aged twins lonely orphans. When they occasionally drove by, they looked thin and shabby, and even their horse seemed neglected. The Chute brothers weren't home that day, so Daniel, Jim and Douglas boldly went into the house, snooped around and then went out to the barn, where the chickens were scratching about, looking busy. Douglas, in one of those moods, decided to catch a chicken and kill it with his bare hands, which he then did by wringing its neck. To see that it was doubly dead, he drowned the unlucky bird in a nearby brook before tossing it to the bank, thereby masking the deed as a swimming accident. They moved on, ranging across the countryside like an invading army until they ran straight into Mrs. Croscup on her farm. She called out to them and asked Daniel to take a bunch of rhubarb home to Mother. We grew everything on the farm but rhubarb, which Mother loved. For some reason, Mother had warned the boys within an inch of their lives not to go beyond Kniffen's Hollow, so Daniel, wary of punishment, gave Mrs. Croscup the surprising news that Mother didn't like rhubarb anymore, she had stopped liking it. With that, he cancelled out rhubarb tarts, rhubarb custard meringue pies, rhubarb jam, rhubarb preserved with ginger root, all our favourites. At night in bed, they whispered the details of their busy day, ending with a warning not to tell, or else. They showed neither sympathy nor concern for the Chute brothers or their hapless chicken, lying brookside in all the indignity of death. They went to sleep happy and slept like lambs until one fine morning when Mrs. Croscup alighted from Eugene's meat truck, her arms filled with her precious peonies and a generous bunch of rhubarb. Daniel twitched. The spectre of the Chute chicken hovered nearby. Immediately, Mrs. Croscup called for Daniel to take the rhubarb to Mother. He was trembling like an aspen leaf and whispered to me that she was going to tell. This happened during Grandmother's epic visit, and she was furious that Daniel stuck to Mrs. Croscup's side like a burr all afternoon. Grandmother could not abide little children listening in on adult conversation, so she sharply dismissed him, several times. Daniel wouldn't budge. She didn't understand that we had never been dismissed from Mrs. Croscup's company. Besides, we loved Mrs. Croscup far more than our newly-minted grandmother. All that afternoon, Grandmother angrily eyed Daniel as he sat by Mrs. Croscup's side waiting for the axe to fall. I waited too, but Mrs. Croscup was as loving as ever without the slightest hint of a shadow. She proved her loyalty to naughty boys that day. Daniel shuddered for a while, but after she left, he stated confidently, "I knew she wouldn't tell."

Douglas was almost six when he strangled Abner and Miney Chute's chicken, but truth to tell, every Sunday we witnessed the slaughter of chickens on the chopping block and then savaged them down to the carcass at the table, everyone licking their chops. It was a religious Sunday ritual, the demise of another chicken, accompanied by French fried potatoes.

From as far back as I can reach, there were certain patterns and people who were born into my family from June to September. You could say that my father established this pattern with his constant comings and goings. The Kniffen's, Mr. Bishop and Mrs. Croscup were more or less relatives, and we were more possessive of them than the relatives we were soon dealt. Even the hired men seemed to belong to us: Lou Albert, Gus Copeland, Archie and Aynsley Peck, Bud McCormick, arriving in the spring to prepare the gardens and returning for haying and the harvest. Eleven summers it was. Eleven summers of a child's eye view of a closely knit family that came and went like my father. They were long waits: fall, winter, spring, and then with the finches that returned to nest in the lilac bush, our family would gather again and life could settle into that comfortable pattern. When we tripped out of school singing no more pencils, no more books, no more teacher's nasty looks (there were many versions) summer could finally begin. Those two months were all the excitement we needed. No toy, nothing else was as exciting.

Many years later in Ottawa, I had my first dinner in the main dining room of the Chateau Laurier with everything so perfect: soft music, a red rose in a silver vase, my first love sitting opposite me. He plucked the rose out of its silver vase and handed it to me, my first red rose. I thought that dinner would supersede the luxury of any meal I could ever imagine. Now I only remember that I sat there, and, well, the red rose. It is the summer picnics under the maples that burst forth in the sun. I hear a distant echo, tapping like a knock on a door—it's Dad, hammering in the apple packing house, making a crate for a shipment of cabbage. We rush in and drag him away, all of us excited and barefoot. Then we would race down to invite the Kniffens and breathlessly run up to Mr. Bishop's, drawing everyone in like puppets on a string. It was a frantic anticipation fraught with complete abandon, all of us so young and excited. We would rake the grass and set the large table cloth—four stones at four corners, the cushions and little tables placed just so. And the rivalry to carry things out: dishes, cutlery, pepper and salt, all of us swirling like paper boats in a whirlpool. Dad let the younger ones sit with him while the rest of us played musical chairs, sitting with our favourite people. Daniel claimed Mabel. It was an accepted fact that he would marry her when he grew up. I would sit with Mrs. Croscup or Mrs. McCormick, but if Douglas or Jim deserted Mr. Bishop I might fill in. Mother and the Kniffen women would bring out the food as everyone approved excitedly: whole Gaspereaux salmon à la hollandaise, roast chicken with Mother's wonderful bread sauce, freshly shelled new green peas in thick cream and butter, huge pans of cauliflower au gratin baked in buttermilk, new potato salad with fresh shallots and homemade mayonnaise, mounds of salads, Mother's pickles and preserves, freshly baked bread, scones and buttermilk biscuits, strawberries and blueberries thick with cream, ox-heart cherries in syrup with whipped cream, Mr. Bishop and Dad's favourite lemon meringue pie, cakes and cookies to enjoy with the last cup of tea. The day would spin itself out as the flow of conversation and laughter paused only for Mother to sing. Those picnics weren't over in an afternoon; I am still nibbling at crumbs.

A MERE MONTH BEFORE **DANIEL'S** fifth birthday, he was well prepared for his first day of school, which he was led to believe would be the experience of his life. Mother and Dad were convinced he was a genius. He was reading Mother Goose to me, and that was proof enough, but Dad also had him reciting Mark Antony's speech to the Romans, Horace at the bridge, Napoleon at Radisson and The Raven above the door. He proudly performed for Mr. Bishop and the Kniffens, and his genius was smiled upon, particularly by Daniel himself. The prospects were enough to inflate the pride of any parent before the fall. The fall came early that year. No one had the slightest inkling that Daniel was a monster. It just suddenly evolved, and the only conclusive symptom was school. Dad had walked him the two miles to the village to initiate him into the daily ritual, and Daniel had given the odd hint that he might not like school and that his legs would hurt, but no one paid any attention. On the morning of the first day, the backlash hit like a slap in the face. Dad couldn't find Daniel, he had to drag him out from under the bed and struggled to get him dressed in his new suit and shoes. He then pulled the little savage between his knees and said in his creamy 'listen to me son' voice, "Now Sweetheart." Daniel exploded and stamped his feet, "Don't call me Sweetheart. That's not my name." He had suddenly become twice the boy he was. Dad held him firmly by the shoulders and repeated in his low but firm voice, "Now Sweetheart, one thing is as sure as God made little green apples, today is the day yew ah going to school." Dad, until the day he died, never called Daniel anything but Sweetheart. He left Daniel on the bedroom chair wailing away, while Mother exclaimed in the kitchen, "That little villain." Dad said to let the little barbarian blow off some steam, but Mother knew how long that could take. She picked Daniel up, plunked him at the table and read him the riot act. He stared at his porridge, refusing to eat because school made him sick. Uncle Peter, a noted scholar in his day, actively encouraged academia. I wished I could go too, but Daniel had already officially told me: girls can't go. This, at such a young age, an extension of his male dominance and the need to keep women ignorant. I had acceded because like Mother, I thought he was brilliant. Daniel then started crying that he wasn't going unless Wethat (that was me) went too. Wethat, a contortion of Sweetheart, is what he called me for years.

Mollifying stopped, replaced by threats. Daniel screamed back, and then a startling thing happened, something that had never happened before: Mother lifted Daniel off his chair, turned him over and spanked his bottom soundly. He was outraged and fought back like a tiger. Dad spoke severely, saying that no matter what, he would be going to school. Daniel pleaded that his legs would hurt. He cried without let up, bawling his eyes out that I had to go with him. The household suffered a change that morning. Perhaps that was the time and place I was won over to parental guidance–something to be feared and respected. Mother ended Daniel's breakfast by his pulling chair out and propelling him to the door. As a last defence against academia, he latched on to the door handle and screamed for dear life while Mother pried his fingers loose one by one. She then mercilessly gave her fledgling the heave-ho, and Daniel stood at the doorstep wailing to the heavens. Dad dropped his school bag over his shoulders, took his hand and proudly walked through the maple grove, his son and heir crying and screaming, "I want Wethat to come with me!" Although I dearly wanted to go with him, my interest in school was quickly waning.

Dad came home happy, assuring Mother, "Dearie, the little bounder is in school," No sooner was this said than Daniel appeared at the door with grimy rivulets of tears running down his face. He had fled the scene at recess and was boiling over in a murderous rage. He didn't like his teacher, Miss Withrow, because she had red hair, and he would not go back unless I went with him. Daniel had given school and Mamie Withrow the once over, and on the first day he decided once was enough. Didn't he like his new little friends? No, he hated them! Mother despaired. It hadn't occurred to her that after all the concentrated preparation, her little prodigy would give up on learning so soon. I have a hunch that at this point, Mother wanted him out of her life during the daylight hours. He was experimenting with loose ends by pinching and punching me and stabbing my arms with pick-up sticks. There was no doubt he was becoming obstreperous.

The next morning, Daniel staged a repeat performance, and the next day, and every day after that. Dad drove him in, walked him in, talked and reasoned with him, but Daniel dismissed higher learning. An hour or two of schooling was all his genius could endure. If Miss Withrow confined him at recess, he fled the classroom the second she turned her back.

Shortly, Dad had to leave for Montreal, and the minute he was out the door, Daniel launched into open rebellion. From the break of dawn as the cock crowed, the pantomime began. Mother had to drag him out of bed as he clung to the frame. He refused to get dressed, his clothes had disappeared, he didn't know where. He hid in cupboards, cowering like a house cat, evicted with a broom. Every step required a mounting threat. At the table, Mother pointed the wooden spoon, "Finish your porridge or you'll get what's good for you." Daniel lowered his eyebrows and locked his jaw. He would stall by meticulously dividing his porridge into quarters and then eighths until his bowl was a web of milk channels, then he'd spoon it section by section. I discovered that this was the best way to get through porridge. After time enough to eat, Mother would lift him from the table, drop his school bag over his shoulder and oust him with a shove, slamming the door without so much as a fare-thee-well. Then one day while Uncle Peter was harnessing Harry, he found Daniel lounging in the hay. He promptly drove him in to school for his afternoon ABCs. After picking up groceries, Uncle Peter returned, thinking the problem solved. Not so. At a bend in the road, he came upon Daniel, a lonely figure trudging the road of life, his face mapped by a muddy stream of tears. Another day, Mother glanced out from the kitchen and was startled to see Daniel glowering back at her from a window in the apple packing house. She went to collect eggs and found him roosting among the chickens, eating his lunch. She found him hiding behind a maple tree, eating his lunch. On her way to the barn, for some reason she looked way up and spotted Daniel in the branches of a maple tree, eating his lunch. He ignored Mother, so she left him there, knowing the coming rain would force him down.

At our nightly forum, I learned the horrible truth about school. He poisoned my mind so that a year later I was prepared for Miss Withrow's pointer, which she had been regularly applying to Daniel's fingers. When Uncle Peter found Daniel in the barn one morning, he drove him in and deposited him at Miss Withrow's door. She told him that Daniel was incapable of learning, no school could teach him, and he was unfit for society. It turned out he was a little barbarian after all. Mother exploded. Why didn't he answer Miss Withrow? He didn't have to; she already knew the answer. Why did he run away? Because no one else liked school.

Then one day in the middle of our morning dustup, as if heaven smiled, Mother's eye lit upon the lovely lilac bush. She broke off a branch the thickness of a pencil and applied it to the back of Daniel's legs. Tinglers did no good at all; they only heightened Daniel's adrenalin. Mother would hold him with one hand and wield the tingler with the other as they swirled about like an eddy. After a few lucky hits and umpteen misses, she would slump into a chair, battle-weary. Once, when I dashed over to rescue Daniel, Mother turned on me and whacked the back of my leg. Having sampled the tingler, I retreated to a corner and cried my eyes out. The house was unravelling. Everyone had tried everything. Even I pleaded with him, "Sweetheart, please go to school." He warned me with a pointed finger that if I ever called him Sweetheart again he would kill me. I gathered up enough courage to tell him he couldn't kill me; I was impossible to kill. Finally one day after another breakfast-table scuffle, Daniel returned in the middle of a venting downpour, banged on the kitchen door, and stood there with his school bag, looking like a drowned rat. Uncle Peter was the first to crack, "For goodness sake, Polly, he isn't even five yet! A year won't make a difference, let him stay home." Mother gave in and life assumed a sudden calm. I was overjoyed. By Daniel's fifth birthday on September 24th, school was a thing of the past. After three good weeks, he had absorbed little, if any schooling and lots of discipline, which hardly left an imprint. He sloughed off punishment as a parental aberration. Mother still wanted him out of her hair, so she continued his education in the dining room. His first day of school was history, the next one was approaching fast. She sat him at the table with pencil and paper, closed both doors to the public, and had him do times tables and ABCs morning and afternoon. For edification, she plunked a big, fat *Bulfinch's Mythology* on the table to copy out cautionary tales. During his confinement, every time Uncle Peter looked in to smile, Mother would sharply order him out. One day on closer inspection of Daniel's work, Mother discovered that Zane Grey had replaced Bulfinch. Uncle Peter had slipped him one of his pulp magazines on life in the Wild West. The sturdy moralizing of *The Fox and the Grapes* and *The Crow and the Cheese* didn't register with Daniel, but once he settled into Uncle Peter's shoot-em-up penny dreadfuls, his mind expanded. From there he graduated to the *Police Gazette*.

Memory received a severe jolt on Daniel's first day of school. What a nasty little boy he was. The incident was emphasized by Mother's reasoning, frustration, tears, threats and finally the last resort, clearly recommended in the Good Book, with her ever-distracted reminder, "This is going to hurt me more than it will hurt you." And there standing in the background, blooming so gracefully by the Chute Road, housing little yellow finches in the summer—the lilac bush—the renewable dispenser of the rods that would not spoil the child and instilled fear of oneself. Howls and yowls and refusals to be sorry, cries of, "I don't like you anymore Mother," then honest appraisal bred of mischief and tears. Although he claimed the tinglers never hurt, Daniel cried louder than anyone else. It put him in full drama. The boys were a devious lot, and after warnings of 'don't do this' or 'don't do that', they would go ahead and do it, only to beg Dad, "Don't tell Mother." Dad would intone stoically, "No son, yew must learn your lesson." It was almost biblical. When Dad said, "Go to your mother and tell her the truth," it meant punishment to the fullest extent of the law—the tingler. Discipline often got complicated. Many times Mother would call back, "I've more to do with my time, Mr. Marvin. I'm sending him right back to you!" Naughty children were often shuffled back and forth. Mother was patient and fair-minded about the use of tinglers, and when she was too busy she'd say, "Go upstairs and I'll attend to you later." She would forget that Daniel was waiting with his tingler, and after little or no soul-searching, he would call down, "I'm still here Mother, when am I going to get my spanking?" Remembering her lapse of memory she would say, "Just this once I'll let you come down, but remember…" A hollow threat. Out he would come triumphant.

Dad never lifted a finger to us, claiming his hand was too heavy. Mother often wailed that her children would hate her forever and it was all Dad's fault, but I recall Daniel's possessiveness as we fought to sit on Mother's lap when she read our bedtime stories. Losing out, I would slump on the fireplace apron, consumed by the bitterness of complete and utter neglect. The little demon would not give up what he never could. Mother needn't have worried about any lingering resentment, because by the time Daniel was in his teens, he and all the boys were unfailingly kind to her, polite and deferential, always the perfect gentlemen.

Several months later came that crucial time of year when Santa Claus was used as a bogeyman to browbeat us day in and day out that we had better be good. If we didn't stop the nonsense he would fly right over our house with all those toys; no down the chimney for us. We learned that he could be good and he could be awfully mean. Santa's reputation was made in this way weeks before Christmas when Daniel went into Mother's top drawer and carefully examined every tiny detail of the lovely gold watch Dad had given her as a wedding present. There it lay in pieces on the bedroom floor, irreparable, and I had followed along as Daniel surgically dismantled it. Mother was devastated, inconsolable. She had so few pieces of jewellery, and so little about the farm was delicate. The gold watch was a special treasure and could never be replaced. The empty gold casing sat in her bureau tray for years. Uncle Peter sympathized, lifting his feet off the rung of the Franklin fireplace and taking his nose out of his Zane Grey to say, "Polly, why go on? Dan will get you another one." Mother iterated, "That little villain," her favourite remark about the apple of her eye. Daniel protested that he only wanted to see how it worked. Nevertheless, he spent time upstairs in solitary and was told by people in the know that Santa Claus would leave something for everyone but him. This came as a shock to all of us, that Santa would do such a thing. Daniel screamed down the stairs, "I hate Santa Claus."

The one thing that really upset Daniel was not Mother's ignoring him, which she did all the time, but Uncle Peter's doing the same thing, starting at the breakfast table, which was a different bowl of porridge altogether. Daniel didn't examine his conscience long enough to shed tears over a mistake, but when Uncle Peter snubbed him for days, the pre-Christmas season of good will around the house as he sat snivelling in corners became a limited version of the Bridge of Sighs. He was unrepentant, he was miserable, and when I reminded him that he only had to say he was sorry, that did it. Sorrow for something he had done brought out the worst in Daniel. He exploded and said, "Alright, I'm not going to speak to you either, and you can't sleep with me." He then got busy beating up me and my doll. Uncle Peter reached into the tangle of arms and legs, grabbed Daniel by the scruff of his neck and the seat of his pants, and transported him in that ungainly position back up to solitary, where Uncle Peter's voice rose and fell.

He came down and calmly took up his position with his feet at the fire and Zane Grey in his hand, back to his winter mood of grey indifference. Soon, all was quiet again except for my sniffling and mumbling. Daniel had never hit me before and I was upset, he had hurt me. Shortly, he came downstairs and apologized, even to me–a revelation. Daniel kept his promise and never again laid a finger on me. With that, calm returned to the house, and it had the wonderful aroma of Mother's cakes and shortbread baking in the oven. Christmas was on its way.

As much as we esteemed Santa Claus, Christmas meant one thing above all else: Dad's return. Homecomings no matter what the time of year stirred up a wonderful anticipation, but Dad's return at Christmas filled the house with excitement beyond endurance. Early on, the whole business of coming and going became a permanence, a resignation to a way of life. Even in the summer, it seemed like fall or winter or the end of a season when Dad left, with no assurance that the season would ever return. The brightest summer days washed into pastels and grey, fixed by Mother's tears. She was alone with the burdens of the farm and not sure if her husband's health would persist beyond the next visit. The lonely whistle of the train rattling over Victoria Bridge was always there to remind us, a dual signal of hail and farewell, never completely one or the other. Those haunting notes accentuated the loneliness we suffered. I always ended up crying, so did Mother. Tears, tears, always tears of love. The loneliness and longing underlined those happy returns. Dad's returns were renewals.

The Flying Bluenose crossing Victoria bridge from Digby.

That year was special because Mother let me go along with Daniel to meet Dad on the Digby train. It was a grey, bitterly cold, blustery day as Uncle Peter bundled us into the sleigh, sitting us on one buffalo rug and covering us up to our noses with another. Uncle Peter slapped the reigns and we climbed McCormick's hill, but instead of going through the village to Bear River station, we turned at the Crossroads for the mouth of the river. In those days, the D.A.R. (Dominion Atlantic Railway) made stops all along the line, so Dad often got off at the bridge and walked home. At the bridge, Harry pulled the sleigh up to a high point where the Basin lay spread out before us like a map, Digby to the left, Annapolis Royal to the right, and the steep slopes of the Digby Gut in between. A cold, biting wind swept in from the Bay driving sheets of snow up the river. Uncle Peter said I should stay covered in the sleigh, but I jumped down to be with Daniel. We stood at the tracks with our noses tucked in our scarves, stomping our feet and trying to stay warm as the cold crept down our backs like frost spreading on a window pane. Finally, we heard the train chugging in the distance, wisps of smoke rising above the tree line to mark its progress. A shrill whistle gave a warning as the train emerged from the trees and rumbled across the trestled bridge, pushing a frightening momentum that blew through me like a shock wave as it passed. I had never been so close to a train before, and by the time it squealed to a stop, the cold had been shaken out of me. Several people stepped down, and then Dad appeared in the doorway, his wide smile with that slight space in the middle. He jumped down and wrapped his arms around us, kissing me on the forehead and wiping my tears as those long months of pain melted away. After a quick hello to Harry, Dad tucked in beside us, and Uncle Peter gave a 'git-up.' Off Harry flew, frisky and snorting, haunches rippling, hooves crunching the snow, the Swiss bells on his harness tinkling like Prokofiev's "Troika" as we raced across the frozen countryside. Down McCormick's hill we swooshed and in through the maple grove, where everyone stood waiting at the front door. Mother rushed into Dad's arms with a kiss and more tears and we excitedly crowded around. Then, straight into the dining room where Mother had laid out the homecoming meal. After months of quiet dinners and Dad's empty chair, he took his place at the head of the table. Though we never said grace, every one of us counted our blessings.

After the euphoria of Dad's return had settled into a contented calm, Daniel came to me with a serious concern. Dad never returned for Christmas without an armful of parcels: boxes of candy, chocolates and all our other Christmas treats. When we met him, he only had his club bag. With no Christmas candy, what about our presents? Had Mother and Dad talked to Santa? Daniel was a worried boy. Later that day, Uncle Peter came back from the train station with two steamer trunks on the sleigh, one of which he and Dad placed in the dining room to sit idling in a corner—an odd situation for investigation. Daniel and I poked and probed but were stymied by the padlock. The next day and without explanation, Mother shunted us up to Mrs. McCormick's room and closed the door, telling us not to come out until called. Why all the secrecy? Curiosity was painfully strained. Daniel and I snuck downstairs. The dining room door to the hall was closed, so Daniel stationed himself at the keyhole. I tiptoed around to the kitchen, but that door was closed as well. Daniel scurried in with the breathless news that he could see Mother and Dad taking things out of the big trunk. What kind of things? He didn't know, he would go back and see. Through the door, I heard Mother and Dad whispering and laughing and then what sounded like the whistles of a rubber duck. Well this was just too much to endure. I wasn't conniving enough to peer through keyholes, so I opened the door and caught Mother and Dad with their noses in the trunk. They furtively scrambled, dropping things into the trunk and quickly closing the lid, but at a glance I had seen everything. Dad sent me upstairs, and I reported back to Daniel. The table was filled with a cornucopia of candy: boxes of chocolates, ½ lb boxes of Eaton's Christmas candies, chicken bones, crunchy glazed nuts, barley sugars that took days to suck away, and best of all, those tiny amber fish that nipped the tongue and seemed like epicurean bravery to suffer and enjoy. I loved them. There were wooden boxes of blood oranges, figs, and another favourite of mine, dried raisins packed on their vines. Straw packing littered the floor and the table overflowed with more brass work, a new set of dishes, Christmas decorations, books, records, and boxes of cigars. Understandably, there were no toys; Santa Claus would attend to that. Daniel exclaimed in relief, and we returned to our games, happy in the knowledge that we would celebrate Christmas in the traditional way, with oodles of candy.

From the time Daniel and I were walking, we loved to play hide and seek. The house had many good hiding places, especially upstairs with all the unused bedrooms. As simple as it can be, hide and seek is a highly excitable game, and with the heightened emotions of Christmas time and Dad's being home, we were thoroughly wound up. As Daniel counted time, I tipped about for the perfect hiding spot and decided to slip behind the dining room door to the kitchen, which for some recent reason was being held open by the highboy pushed in front. I crawled under the highboy and then, through a sliver of an opening, I peeked behind the door and discovered a cache of Christmas presents, obviously not put there by Santa. Boxes of toys sat piled high, with skis and snowshoes leaning against them. All the candy that had previously vanished magically reappeared. My Eaton's Beauty doll sat among a group of lesser toys, not alone atop the Christmas tree where Santa Claus always placed her. And I really had heard a rubber duck after all! I scrambled out in shock and nimbly rolled under the couch, waiting to be found. I was stunned. Immediately, I realized the worst. Santa Claus disappeared in a flash, done in by a rubber duck. I sucked my thumb and thought about it. Santa Claus was deviously my own father perpetrating a lie. My world subsisted on that lie and now nothing remained but the naked truth. I abhorred the truth as if it were a dastardly lie. I had to deal with this bombshell, but I couldn't tell Daniel. He would blab to everyone and the shock waves would lay waste to our parlor on Christmas morning. I would have to conceal my trauma and live with the guilt of knowing something I shouldn't. So parents told lies just like we did, and not only that, they told the biggest, most shocking lie of all. My spirit was crushed. I couldn't believe anything anymore. If a child couldn't have faith in Santa Claus, out the window goes Mother Goose.

The next day was Christmas Eve, and as usual we were awakened at midnight to honour that fraudulent porcine myth, Santa Claus. Dad would turn on the crystal radio, and through a maze of static that sounded much like mouse scratchings, we'd hear the world-wide message from Santa Claus at the North Pole urging all little boys and girls to be good and that he was on his way. No sooner was this said than we heard Harry's Swiss bells ringing vigorously at our front door. Mother and Dad urged us to excitement by saying that Santa Claus had decided not to come down our chimney this year, but was knocking at the front door. What an act! Daniel argued logically that he couldn't possibly be on the radio at the North Pole while banging at our front door. Mother and Dad pretended outrage that he would malign Santa Claus. We were formally lined up for the welcome, and in the door came none other than Uncle Peter properly ho-ho-hoing about the big joke, stuffed with pillows and wearing a Santa Claus suit that was much too big for him. Sure enough, he had a bag filled with toys I had already seen. Meanwhile, Mother and Dad were actively promoting this not entirely likeable uncle as the provider of Christmas wishes. When he stopped being gruffly jovial, he asked if I had been a good girl, as if he didn't know. I said, "Yes, Uncle Peter." I was quickly hushed like the all time party-pooper and told to offer Santa Claus a plate of shortbread and Christmas cake, which I did. Santa Claus asked me if I had helped my Mother bake them and I replied, "Yes, Uncle Peter." Mother and Dad feigned shock and said I mustn't say such a thing, but I persisted, saying that I could tell by his tie, MacGregor tartan, a present he had opened that very afternoon. Uncle Peter quickly adjusted his loose-fitting beard, but chaos ensued because Daniel and Jim started screaming, "It's Uncle Peter," as they tried to have a good look at Santa Claus' tie. Uncle Peter distracted the boys by showering them with gifts, and in a flurry of fraud, Mother and Dad said that Santa had to visit children all over the world. Quick as a wink, the last Santa Claus slipped out the door, rattling Harry's sleigh bells and banging on the side of the house like prancing reindeer. Shortly, Uncle Peter returned, shaking snow off his hat and overcoat, deceitfully asking if Santa had shown up, still trying to baffle us. That insight gave me my first glimpse of how grown-ups got caught up in fantasy as well.

My Eaton's Beauty doll topped the tree as it did every year, but the surprise was gone, the glamour had faded. Still, I was devoted to my dolls like any little girl, though I suppose I could have been labelled somewhat obsessive and possessive. I adored those mute, inanimate soul mates, so beautiful and serene. When I held something so lovely in my arms, I could whisper and talk to them as I could to no one else. They held my secrets and my tears. It was so easy being with them, and inexplicably, like a mad person, I was happiest more or less talking to myself. They represented all that was beautiful and genteel. As more and more babies came,

I struggled to keep my dolls perfect, but what was the use when Lorna and Joan cried and Mother would say, "Let them play with it for a while," just to keep them quiet. I'd watch them carelessly fling it on the grass or play with it in the sand and my heart would sink, knowing I couldn't rescue it without a fuss. Dad would tell me that I was older and had to give in to the younger ones, that I mustn't be selfish, I must share. I admit I had a fixation about my dolls. They were mine, the only possession I cared about, and I didn't want anyone else touching them. All to no avail. My release of their shabbiness to careless, insensitive hands was a yearly heartbreak. And then the final ruination in the apple packing house and the sad, tearful parting. Once my dolls were gone, little joy was left. Dad would say never mind, I would get a new one at Christmas. It went on from one year to the next. Only when I hugged my new doll did the ache go away, and on Christmas day I felt that renewed protective jealousy.

Despite Daniel's poor performance that fall, he got everything he wanted. That Christmas set a benchmark as Dad outdid himself, supplying Daniel with snowshoes, skis, a toboggan, everything needed to get him out of the house and out of Mother's sight. The boys also got the (yearly) Meccano set, a (yearly) tool set, a (yearly) train engine that was lit with fuel (a dangerous toy), more soldiers, pick-up sticks and steel puzzles. What intrigued me most was his oil painting kit, a large wooden box replete with everything the advanced artist would need: numerous brushes, shiny palette knives, metallic tubes of paint, several canvases. If a child showed the slightest sign of latent talent, Dad would nurture it. I suppose he saw Daniel's doodles and scrawls in books and on walls and detected real art. He often said to Mother, "Theah must be more than mischief in that littah barbarian." When Mother looked over the paint set, she decided it suited an older child and would be saved for later. Such a blow-up! Daniel, then into the fourth year of his terrible twos, screamed and stamped his feet—it was his and he wanted it. Daniel had a point. The rules were you couldn't just snatch away Christmas presents on the day of and hide them again. Mother relented. Daniel picked it up and ran around the house holding it importantly like a briefcase in one hand with his tool set in the other. Mother warned him that under no circumstances was he to open the tubes of paint. A warning was all he needed.

After stuffing ourselves at Christmas dinner, we had a period of recuperation, and as was usual for privacy, Mother sent us upstairs to play while the grown-ups relaxed. The boys carted their toys up to Mrs. McCormick's room, which had been spruced up with Mother's new patchwork quilt and hooked rug. I went into the connecting bedroom with my new doll and dishes and the other usual things I got: books, art supplies, sketch pads and clothes. One by one, the boys played their toys out. The Meccano set was tried with the result that it would never be complete again. Tinker toys were tolerated for just so long. Steel puzzles were spread out on the floor, some pieces lost forever. Rubber ducks and bunnies squeaked, horns and whistles and mouth organs blew. All the while Douglas, at 2 rowdily cried, "Me, me, me." I recall a lot of cheap Chinese toys that were finished and done with on Christmas day. Tiring of pick-up sticks, they poked each other until Mother heard the ruckus and came up to take them away. Daniel then opened his tool set, only to be stopped in his efforts by solid oak. The hammer echoed as he pounded a nail, and the saw rhythmically tried to make headway on the leg of a chair. I asked him what he was doing and he screamed, "This wood is no good!" He preferred the soft wood of barrel staves in the apple-packing house. When Mother asked, "What's going on up there," the answer was, "Nothing," and Mother's reply, "I hope so." How much mischief could three little boys of 5, 3, and 2 make? They culled through their toys one by one until all of them were played out and put aside except for one: the paint set. Suddenly, children became dutifully subdued. Once in a while Mother would call up, "Is everyone behaving?" She should have known that an orderly quiet was the basis for mischief, especially when they replied with too many ready assurances of goodness. My only interest was my new doll. She meant everything to me to the exclusion of brash little brothers who were barely tolerated, so I was happy to have the quiet and ignored their hushed whispering.

Relaxed and rested, Mother and Dad came upstairs and into my room, smiling and happy. Then Mother stepped through the connecting doorway and fell back with a scream that echoed through the house. Uncle Peter ran up the stairs while Mother and Dad froze in their tracks. Dad gave his usual expletives, "Caramba, what in blazes have we heah?" Uncle Peter added a disciplinary tone, "Och, yoo weeee blackguards!"

Mother burst into tears and ran downstairs helplessly crying as if Christmas had suddenly died. Every wall had been vividly splotched as high as fingers and brushes could reach, and Daniel, Jim and Douglas blended in perfectly. They had emptied every tube of paint and coated the bed, chairs, rug, commode, walls, the inside of the cupboard and themselves. Douglas sat on the bed with a tube he had just emptied on himself. Clothes, bedding and Mother's hooked rug were blighted. Mother bewailed her months of hard work. She cried and cried and called upstairs, "It's your fault Mr. Marvin. I told you, but oh no, you wouldn't listen. Now you see how clever your son is." Daniel stood there covered in paint like a blot on society.

Dad and Uncle Peter scooped up all the toys and threw them out after their one good day. That was the Christmas the boys wound up with no toys except for the broken remnants from other years. Mother's rug and patchwork quilt were thrown into the porch and somehow later emerged in not bad condition. Uncle Peter tried to restore Mrs. McCormick's bedroom, but it remained splotchy for years until it was painted and prepared for Grandmother's arrival. Dad plunked the three little barbarians in the copper bath tub and scrubbed them youngest to oldest. All the while, Mother cried her eyes out and mumbled, "Oh Dear, dear, dear, this is dreadful, oh my goodness, I should have known this would happen." Between gasps, she called from the bedroom that if Dad left a drop of paint outside the bedroom she would leave the house and never come back, and she hoped she never heard Merry Christmas again. That was the only time I ever heard Mother criticize Dad. She went to bed and stayed there, only getting up for company until Mrs. McCormick arrived for one of her extended stays.

That night Daniel came to bed and put his arms around my neck, practically strangling me, whimpering in my ear, "It wasn't my fault." Mother's punishment, which afforded her the least effort, was prison-like solitary confinement behind a closed door with absolute quiet for reflection. It didn't work for Daniel, but he got it anyway. Being a menace in the house, he was then thrown out the door to tackle the elements. He plowed about the yard in his snowshoes, tapping on the window and performing minor feats to show how clever he was. He went hunting in the woods through the deep snow with Dad and Uncle Peter. He hauled his toboggan to the top of the hay field and swooshed down with Dad, bumping over the Chute

Road and swishing across the gardens to the oaks. He spent hours climbing to the top of the hay field with his skis and tearing down madly. Mother nervously observed his recklessness from the window, saying, "Dear, dear, dear, I hope he doesn't break his neck." Soon he was flying down expertly, whooping and laughing like a hyena. When it looked easy enough, I thought I might try so that Mother and Dad could marvel at me. Daniel strapped the skis on, gave me a push, and off I flew, terrorized. I couldn't stop, I couldn't steer, and I was afraid to fall, so I veered off, pulled like a magnet to the only tree at the bottom of the hill, which I crashed into, knocking myself out. Dad carried me into the house and the whole trauma about my head started all over again. He forbad me from skiing, and I waited twenty years to try again.

Uncle Peter on the hay field with Ruff.

During the holiday season, a number of friends would come by to visit Mother and Dad: Major and Amanda Simon, Jessie and Stella Harris, Joe Warren, and Dr. Campbell, who asked if Santa Claus had brought me my pretty new doll.

"No," I informed them, "there isn't any Santa Claus."

I was corrected, "Oh, that simply isn't so. Of course there is a Santa."

"No," I persisted, "there isn't."

Guests looked dismayed as they championed Santa Claus. Amanda Simon, expertly prying and slightly domineering in her strident way, wondered where my doll came from if not from Santa. I told her what she wanted to know,

"From behind the dining room door." Mother broke down and laughed her tinkly laugh. Dad had not been brought up with little children, so he wore a look of bewilderment at my deviousness. He then explained that when every little girl grows up, she finds out there is no Santa Claus, but I mustn't spoil it for the younger ones. The younger ones crawling about were in no mental shape to be concerned with anything other than what they could find on the floor and put in their mouths. Goodness knows we were lectured on the truth, but having admitted the fraud, Mother and Dad were actively contriving to promote dishonesty for the sake of the world view. The awful truth was a bold-faced lie dribbling down generationally. The Bible, mythology, fantasies and children's stories are filled with the most outrageous tales, settling in little minds and warning them to tell the truth, but truth, if it can be told, is a many splendoured thing, like love and spider webs.

When I told Daniel, he was disbelieving. Then after considering his seniority, he was outraged that I should know before him. Later, he fell in with some discerning 5-year-olds in the schoolyard who saw everything they needed to know in cupboards and under parents' beds. Gossip at recess put Santa in full perspective, creating cynics so early in life.

Daniel and I lied to the younger ones, and the golden aura of Christmas carried on. Santa Claus existed for years. Dad collected Christmas lists, put them in an envelope with a stamp and was off to the post office, so he said. Daniel would say, "He'll never get that letter!" The innuendo flew over the younger one's heads, while Mother turned to snicker. They found out later on, having turned into proficient prowlers at Christmas time. Perhaps Santa Claus unmasked makes philosophers out of little children, and perhaps it made me the heretic I am today.

No Christmas was more disastrous than that one. And because it was so traumatizing, it's one of the few Christmases I remember. Two weeks later, Mrs. McCormick arrived for a protracted stay, and on January 18, Lorna was born. Dad stayed for Lorna's birth and then returned to Montreal, while Mrs. McCormick remained with us until Mother was back in the harness. Shortly afterwards, Uncle Peter found his alarm clock in pieces in a chamber pot.

John McLeod collection

I MUST TAKE YOU INTO the village along the Chute Road, passing each home briefly on my way to school. I can't remember ever going into the village until Mother and Dad took me in to prepare me for the two-mile walk to school. It was a sunny day, and since I was alone with Mother and Dad, the long walk almost seemed like a privilege. I wore my new dress and shoes, and at the outset I learned something significant from Uncle Peter. After he handed me a nickel, a magnificent sum, which I tied in my handkerchief and stuffed in my bloomer leg, he then added, "Every wee lassie should have mad money in her knickers." I couldn't agree more. Then, as if the gift of a nickel wasn't enough, Dad also promised me my first ice-cream cone at Mr. Darres' ice-cream parlor. Along the way, I stopped frequently to wipe off my new shoes with my handkerchief, but by the time we got to the village my heels were blistered and I was crying, not only in pain, but also in shame of having to go barefoot. Dad hoisted me onto his shoulders as we passed Mrs. Zinck's big oak tree at the top of Oakdene Hill. We walked down past Will Brinton's and the Anglican Church, pausing in front of the schoolyard for a good look at Oakdene. Then and there I said I didn't want to go to school, and then and there Mother said, "I'll have no more of that nonsense. You're going to school whether you like it or not." Dad promised me I would like it. We continued down the hill, past the Trading Company and across the bridge, where I could see the river between the planks. Up Chapel Hill was Mr. Darres', where Dad plopped me on a white iron chair at a white iron table. I ate my ice-cream out of an elegant silver dish, lined, curiously, with paper cones. By the time I was finished, I had developed a life-long passion for ice-cream and begged for more. The thrill of ice-cream far surpassed the walk to school. Dad let me share his cone, and in my frenzy of greed, I ate the end of that wonderful cookie cone and ice-cream dribbled all over my dress. Dad wiped me off and called me a silly goose.

After our treat, we crossed Main Street and went into Dr. Campbell's to have him patch up my heels. Whatever it is that keys into our psyche and souls and nascent desires, by the time Dr. Campbell had washed and bandaged my feet, I knew what I wanted to be. Goodbye to being a lady who baked pies—I was going to be a doctor. That was the first time I had ever seen a doctor's office, and I was transfixed the minute I entered. The room was full of sunlight, and the atmosphere breathed of pure, distilled antiseptic. Glassed-in cabinets held shelves lined with white linen towels, on top of which lay hundreds of polished silver instruments, shining like curious cutlery. Several of them looked similar to tools in our apple-packing house, so I asked Dr. Campbell why he had saws and hammers. He explained that the saws were to saw off legs. I looked over at Dad, stunned. So it was true, legs really were sawed off.

In 1925 when I started school, the vibrant youth that had once flowed from the village and crested down the river had ebbed into genteel old age. The Chute Road registered house by house the rise and fall of the wooden ship building era. Some of the more stately homes were peopled by lonely, white-haired widows who rattled about all by themselves like one pea in a pod. Other homes showed the stamp of long neglect, grey and devoid of paint. Of the twenty-five homes from our farm to the village, only three had school-age children. Three houses were occupied for short periods of time and thereafter, blank windows revealed hollow shells, our running feet echoing on deserted verandahs. It was a street of old people where it seemed that children strayed almost by happenstance. I knew the homes well, walking back and forth to school twice a day in every kind of weather, watching as age laid its unmistakable finger here and there.

Our two-mile trek began as we scurried through the maple grove with our book bags and lunches and Mother calling out not to be late. Scrambling up McCormick's hill, we'd pass Billy's house high above the road, and then we'd turn for a quick glance back from the top of the hill, down the river and out to the Bay.

Two minutes on was the Rice home. Their barn sat level with the road, and behind it lay a spread of pasture sweeping up to the woods. On the river side, the edge of the road sheared down into a sand pit and seemed dangerous for traffic, but the road held, and I never heard of anyone plunging over the side. The Rice home rested sharply down on the only accommodating level, halfway to the river and surrounded by gardens and hay fields. One saw their roof and a rough path leading up to the road.

Mr. Rice was a widower with four sons. There was never any neighborliness, except for the time Uncle Peter fired shots in the air when the sons snuck down the Miller field and raided our strawberry patch in the dead of night. Scotty was the night watchman barking his alarm. At other times their impossible dog would stray over to our barn and start barking. One dark night it howled at our back door, so Mother, not knowing how to shoot a gun, took one of Dad's tobacco cans and pitched it out the bedroom window. Miraculously, without seeing where she aimed, she hit the dog and it went off whimpering. She laughed that it was the only time she had ever aimed straight.

One day on our way home from school, a lady walked along with Alice Copeland and me wanting to know all about us. I was taught not to talk to strangers, so Alice was the spokesman, telling all she knew. The lady said she was Mrs. Rice, but she was much younger than Mr. Rice, who had an aging, grizzled appearance. She gave out the information that she was a maid at the Pines Hotel in Digby, and from her description it seemed like a lovely place to work; I suddenly wanted to go. She was very friendly and invited us both to her house where she would give us something nice. We followed along like overly-willing lambs and waited by the front door. Mrs. Rice handed Alice a compact, a real powder compact, and she powdered her nose immediately. Mrs. Rice then gave me what looked like a smaller compact, but it was empty with no mirror, no powder and no puff. I refused it, but she insisted I take it. I asked what it was for, and Mrs. Rice said it was for pills. I was disappointed, because a pill box didn't have the cachet of a powder compact, and at 6 years of age I needed cachet. I went home thwarted, while Alice went home powdering her nose, which she continued to do at recess, lunch, and once during class. When I got home and showed Mother my very own pill box, she was livid. She sent me right back with Daniel, the pill box, and a message to Mrs. Rice that I could not accept gifts from strangers. Sometimes I'd see Mrs. Rice sitting in the window just looking, but shortly she disappeared from the history books, leaving the Rice home a male preserve.

I don't know if the rumours were true, but they certainly did persist that the older and more adventuresome Rice boys supplemented their income by dabbling in the rum-running trade, a proud Nova Scotia tradition by the time I learned about it. Ships that once sailed the Grand Banks for cod now dropped anchor off of Boston and New York along Rum Row, where an impromptu fleet gathered at the legal limit to wait for nightfall like blockade runners. Talk at the Trading Company made rum-runners seem quite swashbuckling, but the Rice boys looked like your garden variety farmers. Still the rumours persisted.

One summer, the youngest son, Clive, was swimming in a lake a few feet from shore when he playfully rocked a canoe filled with friends, causing it to tip. The boys in the canoe couldn't swim and had to be rescued, but one boy drowned and his body couldn't be found. All the neighbours responded to the tragedy and rode out to the lake to help recover the body. Dad rustled through the apple packing house for some sort of equipment that he piled on the wagon along with the shotgun. He harnessed Harry and left with Uncle Peter and Daniel, returning very late. As Daniel explained in bed that night, the boy's body should have floated to the surface as it filled with gasses, but that didn't happen. Men fired shotguns over the lake hoping the concussion would dislodge him. Then they rowed back and forth across the lake with grappling irons in an effort to snare the body. It was some time before they found the boy only a few feet from where he had drowned. Daniel was a good swimmer and didn't understand how someone could drown in such shallow water. I knew. A black wreath hung on the Rice's front door, and Clive was quickly put on trial and sent off to jail. He was just a teenager, and we often saw him putting the cattle out to pasture as we went to school. It seemed sad passing by after that.

A few paces along, the road dipped down to a plank bridge high above Rice's brook, and then it angled straight up to the Crossroads through a lovely avenue of maples, forty on either side. Years later and for the usual reasons, the avenue was renamed Lover's Lane.

The avenue of maples (2011)

We emerged from the maples having completed our climb, already a lengthy hike, and from that point on, the Chute Road ran level, etched into the side of gently sloping hills high above the river. The Crossroads was really a fork in the road: one road veering off to Deep Brook, and the Chute Road heading into the village. Alice Copeland lived on the road to Deep Brook, two houses up from the Crossroads. Her father, Gus, often worked as our hired hand, and I always knew he had a daughter my age, but until I started school, I had no idea she lived only fifteen minutes away. We had a lot of catching up to do. My only real happiness that first year of school was in meeting Alice at the Crossroads so we could walk together. Without delay, we jointly declared ourselves each other's best friend.

Alice's family was long resident, and I learned much of the history of the village from her, that is, the salient points sifted down from adult conversation. Alice made sense. At five, she was wiser than I—she had travelled the Chute Road and could knock on the doors of relatives and family friends. She knew everyone and liked to stop off on the way home from school to say a friendly hello and be rewarded for her sweetness and charm with a treat, as she expected. And who could not treat a pretty little girl?

It was Alice who briefed me on the who's who of the Chute Road: Mrs. Brinton had the best chocolate cake, Truman Hamilton had the best apples (Kings), and old Mrs. Chute had the most wonderful molasses taffy. We bypassed the affluent Clarke homes; one didn't beg from the rich. I eagerly accompanied Alice on her social calls, but eventually Mother discovered our devious practice and lectured me on beggary. Alice continued her old habit, while I followed the letter of the law by standing off to the side and waiting to share a bite.

Alice had other local information I couldn't possibly be privy to: the woman who went into conniptions bearing a dead baby; the orphan girl who was held hostage in a dungeon for years; the Annie Kempton murder and subsequent hanging; the mulatto whose head was cut off by the wood-sawing machine, the same man who came to saw our wood after winter logging. We were kept in the house and watched from the dining room window as two horses hauled the long machine up to the log pile. It chugged and puffed as belts whirred and the sizzling saw sliced logs to fit into stoves and fireplaces, all thrown higgledy-piggledy into a pyramid pile.

The arrangement of the Copeland household appeared to be the most unique and pacific theory of relativity. Great Great Aunt Mary was very old and more infirm than her friends, Mrs. Crosscup, in her late 70s and hiking everywhere, and Mamie Walsh next door, who travelled the Chute Road in her horse and buggy and worked at the telephone office with Miss Liske. Aunt Mary had her own self-contained and cozily appointed apartment just off the parlor, and it seemed the most unusual thing when Alice told me she had to knock for admission.

Some homes, no matter how ordinary, have an air of tranquillity stamped on them from the foundation to the chimney, and the Copeland house was one of them. It was a white, salt-box style house with dark green trim, comfortably settled beneath tall trees. Flowering shrubs lined the perimeter of a generous swath of lawn, making it all seem very neat and orderly. Inside, tasteful furniture complemented the polished elegance of honey-coloured hardwood floors, floors that ran up the stairs and straight into Alice's bedroom. There is no doubt that when I was young I had a fixation about hardwood floors, the foundation of luxurious living. Without them, none of my dreams were possible.

One Saturday, Alice invited me over to play, and we went up to her room and dressed her dolls, particularly the ones I liked, the rosy-cheeked Campbell's Soup dolls that came monthly in *Good Housekeeping*, a magazine Mother didn't subscribe to. At 6, I realized that Alice's household had certain items ours lacked, like Minards's Liniment (The King of Pain), Scott's Emulsion (For Sound Bones, we used it later), Palmolive soap (we were devotees of Lifebuoy), peanut butter, and *Good Housekeeping* magazine. After playing, we went downstairs and I waited in excitement and anticipation of meeting Great Great Aunt Mary, whom everyone adored. Alice knocked, and a clear voice said, "Come in, dear." The apartment was large and inviting, filled with warmth from the pot-bellied stove. Beside the stove, Aunt Mary's rocking chair faced a large window that looked out past the lawn to the road. Aunt Mary was fine-boned and frail, crowned by a halo of white hair. She sat knitting in her rocking chair while a cat purred on her lap. She put her knitting aside as Alice crawled on her lap, and the three of them rocked entwined, Aunt Mary, Alice and the cat, all rocking and stroking in perfect contentment. I sat on the couch enveloped by cushions while Alice detailed me for Aunt Mary. She sent Mother warm regards and then offered us tea, reaching for a kettle on a trivet that swung over the stove. In one corner, a pantry with glassed-in cupboards held kitchenware, while the counter below held bowls of fruit, jars of tea, and tins of biscuits. The entire arrangement seemed ideal; everything one needed for snug seclusion. We sipped our tea and chatted like old friends about school and teachers until Alice's mother called us in for dinner. That evening, I had my first taste of baked beans with Boston brown bread served fresh from the oven, hot enough to melt butter—so exquisitely sweet.

At the Crossroads lived Mr. Arthur Harris, notable because he threshed the local wheat. He was a widower who lived in a nice house, white with green shutters. A high hedge lining the road obscured the house and continued across the bottom of a large hay field. Mr. Harris was a remote, surly man whose wife had died long ago at the birth of their only child, Arthur, who was so retarded that he could never go to school. He was a grinning, bearded child who craved company and would stand at the front hedge when we came home from school, waving happily and trying desperately to communicate. He would be ecstatic when we stopped to say hello or gave him our school drawings. Daniel and Jim sometimes teased him, he unaware, happily slavering. Daniel wheedled out of him the information that they only washed dishes in his house on Fridays, fish days. Daniel repeated with great hilarity what he thought was a witty sally and learned in the usual fashion (lilac bush) that infirmities were tragic and not funny. He perfected his humour in solitary confinement. When Mr. Harris remarried, Arthur was sent off to the insane asylum. In passing homes like the Rice's, Mr. Harris's, and others where tragedies had occurred, an emptiness pervaded like an aura of life suspended, yet with a strange continuation. It hardly helped when Daniel, always in step with the spirit world, insisted these houses were haunted. We would say, "Poor Clive," or "Poor Arthur in the insane asylum." We never thought to say, "Poor Mr. Harris," though I'm sure his life had been a strange continuation.

Stella and Jessie Harris also lived at the nexus of the two roads, both of them retired teachers. A tall hedge fronted their property, giving it an air of privacy and hiding a large salt-box style house with arched driveway. In behind was the usual garden, hay field, barn, horse, cow and chickens. Alice told me that Mrs. Harris was an heiress, and whatever that was, I believed her. Stella and Jessie were good friends with Mr. Bishop, so in the summer when he was resident they often attended our dinners and picnics. Mother and Dad enjoyed their company, but to children they seemed distant and strait-laced.

In the spring when our windows were open and the curtains drawn out with the breeze, we often heard Stella playing the piano. It sounded wonderful, and whenever the music drifted down we would stand and listen like spies. Daniel was transfixed. We were both taking violin lessons at the time, but now he wanted to play the piano. One day after school, we walked along with Stella, and Daniel really lathered it on about how beautifully she played. He waxed enthusiastic, oozing charm like a gigolo the way he did with older women. Stella was tall, thin, grey and always seemed remote, but she fell for Daniel's charm and told him that if he took piano lessons, he could stop by after school to practice. Mother assumed the gesture was payment for the cigarette case Dad had given Jesse, so Daniel won the day. He got his weekly piano lessons with Inez Baird and practiced on Stella's piano after school, with time out for a chat over cookies and milk. Then began the never-ending arguments about a piano–he wanted one of his own and he wanted it badly. The great piano debate went on every morning at breakfast. Mother, who was not much of a conversationalist at times like this would say, "Just eat your porridge or I'll piano you!" He was reminded he was doing well enough with the bicycle Dad had just bought him. Daniel was a lucky boy, because not only were cars a rarity along the Chute road, but so were bicycles. I wondered about charm and persistence and squeaky wheels that only got squeakier.

Though she never allowed him to ride his bike off the farm, Mother made a concession for his Saturday afternoon piano lesson in the village. The bike was full-sized, and even with the seat lowered all the way, Daniel still had to stand to pedal. He'd make desperate headway climbing up McCormick's hill, then labour along through dirt and gravel until finally reaching the macadamized section of the Chute Road from the Clarke homes into the village. Coming home, he would fly down McCormick's hill and through the Maple Grove, stopping with a dramatic sideways flare to announce his arrival. Naturally I wanted to experience the thrill, but Dad told me bicycle riding was unladylike. I had to agree when in an unguarded moment, I took the bike and sped off in a flight to freedom, minutes later almost skidding into Mr. Larimore's team of oxen. I couldn't hide the disaster because I came home scraped, scratched and bleeding from head to toe. After my experiments with biking, skiing and swimming, Dad suggested a pattern might be forming.

Next door to Stella and Jessie Harris' and almost hidden behind an overgrowth of bushes stood elderly Mr. and Mrs. Chute's home: grey and weathered, propped up by the name of the road and not much more. Alice's mother was friends with them because Great Great Aunt Mary and Mrs. Chute had known each other since grade school. Alice liked to drop in to say hello, and Mrs. Chute would hug and kiss her and give her a treat.

One day after school, Alice induced me to walk up the rutted path, our last call of the day, the purpose of our visit a piece of molasses taffy. The front lawn overflowed with weeds and bushes growing so high and so dense that they obscured the front verandah. We went around to the back verandah, which was piled with implements and items of lost usefulness. Alice climbed the stairs and knocked on the door, calling out, "It's me, Alice." From inside, the old Chute dog barely woofed a welcome. The door opened and Alice stepped inside while I waited until a very old lady covered with a shawl called me in to be recognized. The kitchen held an unbelievable clutter of objects, two very old people, and one very old and somewhat smelly shaggy dog, all in the latter stages of mobility. Mr. Chute lay ill on a couch beside the warmth of the stove, while Mrs. Chute sat with her cane hooked in her rocking chair. I was gently quizzed, "Oh yes," she said, I was of the new family in the Warren farm. They were a lovely, gentle couple pleased to have our company. I looked around the kitchen, fascinated by the clutter and disorder, but most of all by the heavenly, perfumed scent of dried fruit. It was the sweetest smelling kitchen, because hanging from the ceiling from wall to wall were strings of sliced apples, pears and plums, all drying out like the Monday wash. The aroma was as intoxicating as apple blossoms in spring. I had never seen anything like it and couldn't imagine all that shrivelled fruit being good to eat, but it was. Alice and I made a habit of visiting that year, mainly because Mrs. Chute had two items on the menu that no one else did: molasses taffy, and chocolate fudge with nuts. On that first visit, Mrs. Chute let us take a piece of taffy, neatly wrapped in wax paper and sitting in a bowl on the overcrowded table. It all seemed so special. As I closed the door with my taffy in hand, Mrs. Chute called out, "Goodbye dear. Be sure to visit again."

The next winter, their farm stood deserted, leaving a sad vacancy, another empty house along the road. There were no tracks through the deep snow, no smoke curling up from the chimney. Later, I visited Alice one Saturday when the whole family was involved in pulling taffy. We buttered our hands and pulled and folded over and over until the precise moment of snipping. It was tiring work, and I realized what a chore this delicacy must have been for those two lovely old people. Molasses taffy was wonderful.

Directly opposite Jessie Harris' and dipping down from the road was an empty W.G. Clarke house at the end of his last apple orchard, a home for a hired hand, beige with brown trim and a wide verandah, a nicer home than ours. In all my years of walking back and forth to school, it was only occupied for a few short months when Jimmy and Tooney Trimper parked their dented, rusted, faded red truck out front and moved in with their six children. Having that nice house and a truck, despite its appearance, gave the two older children, Florence and Jimmy, both in my grade, the impression that they were high class. We were still in the horse age and so was everyone else on the Chute Road except for Mr. MacIntyre. Despite owning a truck, the Trimpers were, in fact, terribly poor. Their clothes were faded, wrinkled and threadbare, either too big or too small. Half of them had no shoes, and even their hair seemed tattered. We tried to ingratiate ourselves to the newcomers as we walked home, but the children were both suspect and circumspect. Jimmy was difficult to draw into conversation and Florence chose her words carefully. Their poverty made them defensive.

When Tooney took work in the village, Florence had to leave school to look after the four youngest. Walking home from school, we would see all the grimy, raggedy, shoeless little Trimpers playing at the side of the road and peering like meerkats, waiting for their parents. Alice and I wanted to be friendly with Florence, we felt sympathetic and would ask when she was coming back to school. We tried to involve her in school trivia, encouraging her that on Arbor Day we were going down to the hollow opposite Oakdene to plant trees and picnic. She rarely responded. Then one day while all the little Trimpers were stationed at the side of the road, as usual eating Mr. Clarke's apples from his orchard, Alice and I and the boys stopped for a few words. I felt sorry for Florence, always holding the baby with her thin arms, and if there was anything I understood it was holding a baby, which I would be doing as soon as I got home. With nothing else to say and wanting to be nice, I said that her dress was pretty, which it wasn't. Having a native intelligence, she immediately saw through my blatant deceit of flattery and hoidy-toitedly told me, "Us folks has a better sugar bowl than youse folks has," whereupon the boys burst into derisive laughter at the revelation of such an unusual status symbol. The war began immediately.

The little Trimpers, all dominantly, wildly male, and despite their tender years and thumb sucking, sprang into action by hurling stones with deadly accuracy. Alice and I fled in terror to the Crossroads amid screams of, "Youse folks is poop," and "Youse folks is snots." The boys took up the gauntlet and shouted, "So are you." Out of range, the boys screamed the golden rule taught at home and school that one shouldn't throw stones. It only encouraged them. We vowed we would have nothing more to do with them, but they hadn't finished with us. The next day, every last Trimper stood waiting for us armed to the finger tips, screaming the same old invective and showering us with stones. The littlest warrior would try to throw, but his stones fell behind his back and the boys would laugh. This state of emergency continued for a few days, so we stayed on the other side of the road and ran for our lives. According to the winds of war, they'd scream 'youse folks is snots' or 'youse folks is poop' or 'youse folks is no better'n us folks'. We neither confirmed nor denied it, we ran. Coming home from school, Jimmy Trimper would run past us to forewarn and forearm. It was frightening approaching the Trimper stronghold, and Alice and I would huddle together for the daily race to safety. Our boys couldn't respond in deed, so the little dominant male Trimpers, already infused with the smell of victory in a one-sided donnybrook, became quite bold. They were feisty and fierce and the wicked little toddlers tried to follow suit. We would scramble off to echoes of the defining four-letter words while the boys taunted, "Sticks and stones may break my bones, but names will never hurt me," and "I'm going to tell my father." At this point, Dad was at Camp Hill hospital and Mother refused to listen to tattle-tales because too often it emerged that Daniel was the culprit. She often said, 'just stay out of trouble, it takes two to quarrel etc.' and more significantly 'don't come home complaining about your teacher or you know what I'll do!' In fact it only takes one to quarrel, so the Trimpers held the field, reviling and stoning us as well as scabrously labelling us.

Then one afternoon Tooney stood waiting for us with a warning to stop throwing stones at her kids. Tooney was a fierce but sad lady. Where and why she acquired such a name is lost. She was a tiny emaciated woman with hollow eyes and no upper teeth, which made her lisped orders almost unintelligible, "Youth kidth thtay on tuther thide of the road."

At other times, the meaning of what she lisped at us was lost and we'd stand in puzzled suspension. Sometimes we'd see their old red truck rattling into view and we would stand in the grass and weeds of the ditch, getting the benefit of their billowing dust. As the truck passed, we'd see Tooney packed in the front seat with the little ones, her thin arm hanging out the door, at the end of which her fingers held a cigarette. She not only smoked, she hung her arm out the door to announce the fact! Alice and I whispered about the sinful cigarette. It was shocking in an era when such a thing was unheard of, especially on the Chute Road, where if elderly widows didn't look like Queen Victoria, they at least acted out the tail end of her era. Only one other jezebel smoked: Tilly Comeau, who lived above Mr. Chute's jewellery shop and had three children but wasn't married. They said she smoked cigars. But that was on the Digby side. I sometimes saw her leaning on the doorway when I went to the post office. Another day the Trimper truck came rattling down the road with the whole family piled in. Tooney shouted down as best she could, "Youth kidth get off the road or we'll run you down," to which all the little Trimpers who had learned plain English shouted in passing 'youse folks are poop, snots and poop-poopy doop up the road and out of sight.

When Dad returned from the hospital, as always he lent a listening ear. We recounted our misadventure and how the Trimpers were very poor, faces grimy, raggedy hair and clothes, no shoes and winter approaching. It was also at this point that Daniel began his several weeks long campaign for a truck. If the Trimpers were poor and had one, why not us? Dad reasoned patiently, "Sweetheart, a truck can't plow mah gardens." Dear Harry, I learned a lesson about the farm and horses: one couldn't exist without the other. Daniel persisted. He'd start at the breakfast table, seriously badgering Dad, "It would be great for going to the Pines hotel and hauling vegetables," not to mention hauling us to school. Daniel's morning harangue lasted long enough to make it indelible. Mother's nerves were the first to go. She didn't often shout, so we sat up, "Now you listen to me you little villain, I'll tell you what you'll get, you'll get a tingler instead of a truck. And that goes for a piano too. Eat your porridge!" So he ate his porridge, dividing it into milky canals to eat in geometric order.

Dad always agreed with Mother and assured him, "Son, we ah not keeping up with the Trimpers." After Dad had heard all about the sugar bowl war, he decided a social call was in order. Until then, he had seen neither hide nor hair of Tooney nor had the pleasure of her repartee. He loaded bags of potatoes and root vegetables in the wagon and went off to visit the lady of the house. No one was home, so he left everything on their verandah. Tooney's pride was dented.

The whole crisis came to a rough climax when Daniel biked into town for his Saturday piano lesson with Inez Baird. His return was not unexpected. The whole Trimper family had been properly alerted and lined the road in a gauntlet, led by Tooney wielding her broom. Daniel's bike was almost too big for him, his feet barely touched the pedals, so he had to stand like a jockey, swaying from side to side, urging the bike on unsteadily over the gravelly road. At the precise moment of ambush, Tooney pounced like the wicked witch, flailing away with her broom while Daniel cycled for his life. He saved himself by hightailing it through Jessie Harris' driveway and sped off shaken by the thrashing. Triumphant, Tooney waved her broom and called after him, "You little thnot. You tell your old man not to leave hith old potatoes on my verandah," amid a chorus of, "Your father is a snot," and "Your father is a big poop."

This latest skirmish prompted Dad to engage the mercurial Tooney in a tête a tête. Again he took along a few bags of potatoes, knocked on their door and launched into the purpose of his visit, whereupon Tooney ordered him off her property, "You old thnot, youse folks think you'r better'n us folks and on top of that, get those old potatoes off my verandah." Dad persisted. When Florence came to the door, my age, thin and holding the grimy baby, Dad's heart melted. He lectured the children on throwing stones, which they miraculously heeded. Dad laughed that the tattered little urchins brazenly eyed him, and he was worried they were going to bite him. The next day he went down to Mr. Marshall's store, where he always outfitted the boys, and bought shoes and clothing for the Trimpers. Mother made up a parcel of old clothes and Daniel dropped everything at their door and ran like mad. The next day all the children were wearing their new shoes and clothes, clad for the fall chill.

Thereafter they stood by the side of the road watching us traffic by, not throwing stones but still with a residual reminder, "You're snots." Then one day on our way home from school, their truck passed by with all their belongings piled high. Florence and Jimmy stood in the back and Tooney sat in front with the younger ones, her thin arm dangling out the window, a cigarette between her fingers. We silently and solemnly watched their departure; no stones, not a single swear word. Stella Harris later told Mother that Tooney had contracted tuberculosis and went into the Kentville Sanatorium.

Tooney was the first liberated lady along the Chute Road, and Alice and I discussed her endlessly. Tooney had spark. We were sad to see her go. The house was not occupied again, and Mr. Clarke's last apple orchard behind it was left untended, the apples unpicked.

I used to long to have as much as Alice, she was so favoured, so indulged by her parents and Great Great Aunt Mary and relatives in the village. I wanted the same, but the Trimpers haunted me because I saw first-hand the poisonous contagion of envy. Dad once said to a neighbour, "Mah children won't get what they want but what they need." I suppose I didn't mind Dad's policy, because for some deep-down reason it made sense. After the Trimpers moved away, the fierce defensiveness of their poverty left an imprint, and I could never forget how Dad's kindness carried with it the sting and humiliation of charity. I wondered about the dangerous game of giving and getting.

The Clarke orchards, looking towards the Bay.

Passing the Trimper's, we walked along looking down to Mr. Clarke's extensive apple orchards. All the orchards behind all the homes from the Crossroads to the village belonged to Mr. W.G. Clarke. We had been taught that we mustn't touch the apples, and we never did. But many times after school we hiked through those orchards, especially in springtime when the delicate perfume of apple blossoms filled the air like a heady mist. Alice and I leisurely searched for the first crocuses, hyacinths, daffodils, myrtle and the heavenly narcissus. But most of all, I eagerly scouted through the woods for the elusive, delicately scented Mayflower. I waited every spring for the fleeting wonder of this lovely flower. The sweetly haunting scent could never be replaced, not by lilacs, violets, apple blossoms, the June roses flanking our front door, the pungency of all the flowers in Mother's rock garden, or the perfumes in her top drawer.

The next stop on our route was Truman Hamilton's for the coveted King apples. Mr. and Mrs. Hamilton were a lovely older couple, both white-haired, so much like Mr. and Mrs. Kniffen. Their home sat perched on a small hill, the front door level with the road but the sides of the house sheering down. We'd climb the high plank stairs to their windowed back porch where barrels of various apples blended to a delicious perfume. Mrs. Hamilton would welcome us in and get polite information about our families while we waited to be asked if we would like an apple.

If she suggested a yellow pippin or a russet, we would hesitate and she would give in, saying she knew, we wanted the Kings. We always did. They were a huge apple with a wonderful, orangey taste.

Down their driveway was a large barn where the hundreds of barrels of apples from Mr. Clarke's orchards were readied for export. During the harvest, we'd see Mr. Larimore's team of oxen or the wonderful Dan Hamilton hauling wagons full of apple barrels in to the barn. Of all the horses in Bear River, and there were many because everyone had a horse, only two had personality and intelligence: one was Harry and the other was Dan Hamilton, getting on in years and very much an elder statesman. We were always on the lookout for Dan, and any time we saw him on the road, Truman Hamilton would stop so we could pet him. Mr. Hamilton had no need to rush at his age. He would climb down from the wagon and hold the bridle while we clamoured around Dan, our small hands patting and petting him. Dan had a recognizable personality and enjoyed our conversation as we stroked his mane and let him nuzzle us. We adored him; he was the nearest thing to Harry. Sometimes on our way home from school, if Mr. Hamilton was working around the barn, we would dash down and ask to see Dan to fuss over him and put our hands through his stall to pet him. After our visit, Mr. Hamilton would send us up for a cookie or an apple. We would race up the hill, where Mrs. Hamilton would be waiting for us as we clomped up the back stairs huffing and puffing.

Sadly, Mr. Hamilton had to endure the tragedy of putting his wife in a home because, as he explained to us why we wouldn't be seeing her anymore, when she got up one night and turned on the light, she went blind. Then one terrible day, we got to school and the Reade girls told us that Dan was dead. Mr. Hamilton, in his distraction, forgot to close the trap door on the barn floor and when he drove in, Dan plunged down, breaking his legs. Mr. Hamilton had to shoot him then and there on the barn floor. Another dreadful blow. We were almost afraid to say hello to poor Mr. Hamilton. He looked so sad and much, much older. Alice Copeland and I became overly dramatic and cried over Dan until Mother said to stop the nonsense. One of our concerns was where and how a horse was buried. I cried even more when Uncle Peter assured me that Dan had been carted off to the glue factory. Shortly, Mr. Hamilton left and the house remained empty.

All of a sudden, there was an unwelcome emptiness as we rounded Hamilton's corner. Part of our young lives had been snatched away and the corner stood still. The Hamiltons were so much like loving grandparents. We talked about Dan for a long time after that, and it was always 'poor Dan.' We liked to look for him on the road, and meeting him was one of the nice things about our walk to school. Nowadays children look for other treats but that was one of ours. It was an age of innocence for little children and we chose our horses like we chose our friends.

Opposite Truman Hamilton's was another of Mr. W.G. Clarke's empty homes, a nice house up a steep hill and hidden by rocks and bushes. It was only ever occupied for a few months by a teacher, a friend of Alice's family. We stopped by once or twice for peppermints. She could no longer teach, because one day she pulled a boy up from his seat by his ear and ripped it. It seemed that in those days, the worst of crimes were committed by teachers wielding pointers and settling scores with little ruffians. The home took on her aura and was held in contempt by passing children long after she was gone. Her legacy remained: a little boy's torn ear.

Five minutes past Truman Hamilton's were two homes directly opposite each other, both of them neat, lemon coloured houses with white trim. Major Simon's modest property dipped down from the Chute Road, while on the other side, Fred Reade's expansive dairy farm swept up to the skyline. Mr. Reade was the local milkman, and before he modernized I'd often see him delivering milk from the back of his jitney, the milk cans in full sight and quarts dipped out with a huge dipper.

The large Reade home sat a short walk up from the road and was fronted by apple and cherry trees. Vegetable gardens followed the road down to the end of their property where they had a huge barn, a chicken house and an ice house. In the winter, we would see Mr. Reade in his wagon hauling large blocks of ice to be lowered into sawdust, eventually to be delivered to the village ice boxes. Behind the house, hay fields and pasture for the dairy herd crept up over the hill. At the back door of their house, a vicious, barking German Shepherd ranged back and forth on a chain nailed to a tree. Dad advised Fred Reade in a neighbourly way that if it ever escaped he would shoot it.

The busy dairy farm was neat and efficient, the pasture full of cows, the house full of children. The lively, loud-mouthed Reade brood ranged through every grade from kindergarten to high school, all ten of them. Back then, babies often came by the bushel, and at school, families loomed large, forming clumps at recess. Walter, the oldest and still in high school, helped in the creamery, delivered milk and put the cattle out to pasture. Ethel, the eldest daughter, was her mother's helper until she left to live with relatives in the States. Evelyn, my age and one of my best friends, became the resident little mother and had to rush home after school to look after all the babies. Since we suffered the same affliction, we spoke the same language, noted for its whining and carping.

Mrs. Reade had the tuneful name of Zella Maude and weighed in at close to 300 pounds. Occasionally when Mother walked home from the village, Zella Maude would call out, and Mother would stop to pass the time of day. Mrs. Reade was always eager to chat, and I suspect she led a lonely life opposite the fussy, fenced-in Simons. Mother felt sorry for her physical imbalance, explaining that she was so cumbersome because of a thyroid condition. She added cryptically that having ten children didn't help, and though the gist of the remark flew over my head, I agreed on principle.

Mother sometimes hesitated over our association with the Reades, but they were all pleasant and sociable except for the tempestuous Lois, undisciplined and noted for her sauciness. After visits from their American cousins, Lois would do her best to establish the latest vogue in colloquialisms. She'd spice her conversation with: shut your trap, you're nuts, so's you're old man, oh yeah, you're a liar, you're a horse's a—, you're full of s—, and others with the word darn, which was considered as crude as the word damn by every church-goer. Lois was difficult, like the last angry man. She'd see me in school and for no immediate reason say, "I hate you Mary Marvin." I'd rebut with, "I hate you, Lois Reade." Her jealousy was spiked because Alice, Evelyn and I were all in the same grade and walked home together. Three was company. Edged out, she didn't dare get mad at Alice or Evelyn. One morning as we were all walking to school, the Marvins, the Reades, Alice and her sister, we passed the Potter's, high above the road, and Dorothy called for us to wait up as she came down the hill with her sister Connie. We all stopped and waited in front of Loo (Lucy) Robinson's, who was on her verandah shaking out a rug. Lois Reade tolerated no hesitation from anyone and shouted up to Dorothy, "We can't stand here today, tomorrow and the next day waiting for you, you horse's a—!!" Loo Robinson straightened up and invited Lois to come over so she could give her a good shaking too. Ethel assured Loo, "You'll have to catch her first." All the Reade children were noted as free thinkers who eschewed their mother's discipline by running away. I passed one day as Zella Maude stood in her doorway yelling at little Fred, a year younger than Lois, "When I catch you, I'll whip you."

Mother and I were walking home from the village one sunny day when Zella Maude, standing at her kitchen door with the latest baby, called out and insisted that we come in for tea. As often as I had passed by their house, I had never been inside, and the one thing I enjoyed was seeing other people's homes. The kitchen was cavernous and bright with a breeze blowing in one door and out another. White towels hung on a clothesline strung the length of the room. A huge stove sat in front of a long table covered with towelling and countless upturned milk bottles glaring like crystal. On the floor, a stack of shiny, sterilized milk pails stood beside equipment cleaned and ready for the next milking. Mother took the baby from Zella Maude's arms and sat down, putting it over her knee and rubbing its little back until the baby brought forth a healthy burp. They both chuckled. I had never seen Mother holding any baby but her own. Zella Maude pulled the largest cake pan I had ever seen out of the oven, and she then cut me a square of delicious, buttery cake. When she sat down to talk with Mother, Evelyn came in and invited me to sit in the living room. The house was as neat as a pin with no evidence of toddlers or babies anywhere, not a rattle or a toy or even a book out of place. I didn't think such a thing possible. As a rule, toddlers trailed a path of destruction. Suddenly, Evelyn was twice the little mother I was. She played a tune on their piano and showed me her favourite books, but what really impressed me was a huge stack of movie magazines sent by American cousins, sitting on the table like a pot of gold. Years before I saw my first movie, I was thoroughly versed in the who's who of Hollywood. Living on a farm with pigs and cows and outhouses created a real need for glamour. We sat down and studied the photos, every page filled with stunning beauties and handsome heroes. Were there ever such beautiful young people so artfully photographed?

One year, Mrs. Reade returned from the States amid great excitement because she brought back their little cousin Paula, who had made the rotogravure section of the newspapers as one of America's most beautiful babies. On our way home from school, we all tried to observe this four-year-old phenomenon, seated on the culvert by the sidewalk dressed in old style clothes with a hat, purse and ladies' shoes, posing like a petulant pro. She was beautiful in her amber ringlets, and wishing to ingratiate myself I said, "Hello, Paula." The tiny termagant snapped, "Shut up!" I quickly learned my place on the totem pole in the presence of fame.

After our visit, Mother marvelled at Zella Maude's efficiency. How did she cope with the business and all the washing up of equipment and milk bottles and how did she keep such an immaculate house with such neatly pressed children. It must have been a tremendous job with all the children and toddlers, beleaguered by the yearly appearance of yet another offspring. Passing by, I would see her large frame laboriously tending the gardens, a full clothesline fluttering in the wind, a baby screaming from the buggy, the German police dog barking, and children yelling all around.

Across from the Reades was Major and Amanda Simon's pretty, lemon coloured, white-trimmed house and neat lawn, all enclosed by a pure white picket fence, saving them from the onslaught of the energetic Reade children. Amanda would have none of them, although she did buy the Reade's dairy products. She was a lean church woman, gruffly proper, continually complaining about all those children, all that barn, all that smell. Sometimes when Mother and I walked home from Barr's barber shop, Amanda would come to the gate for a word, and as the joie de vivre of the Reade children pierced the conversation, her face would pucker up like a squeezed lemon. At other times, her nose would twitch and she would sniff down the road at the Reade's huge barn as if it had committed an affront to all common decency. Amanda yearned for the pristine white of the pearly gates.

I liked the neatness of the Simon's home, cocooned by a picket fence with no barn or out-buildings to mar the prettiness. Still, the home seemed forbidding, and Alice and I never, ever hazarded knocking on their door to say hello. I'm sure Amanda would have quite rightly reprimanded us for begging food.

We saw a lot of the Simons because of Amanda's love of music and the Major's recounting of the Great War. They'd pop down on a Sunday and Dad would welcome them into the parlor for tea and conversation and much too much singing. Amanda was a serious member of her church choir, an ever-deluded aging songstress with a floundering tremolo. She would pass us on the Chute Road singing to the high heavens, oblivious of even the birds. Her musical delusions burned with a youthful zeal that no one could tame. I can still see her sitting in our parlor, the object of her visit to hear our latest batch of records. Unabashed, she sang with the best. I can't get the "Barcarolle" from the *Tales of Hoffman* out of my mind, sung by Madame Schumann-Heink and Louise Homer, whose contralto voices Amanda thought best matched hers. It's a dreamy, mesmerizing song that Mother sang as a lullaby, played on our gramophone far too often because of Amanda's fixation. Dad could barely sit still. At beach parties or clam bakes when Amanda sang, he would grit his teeth and hiss under his breath, "Wha oh wha doesn't some kind person choke that canary?"

Major Simon was chunky and red-faced and stated his facts like an army man. Many times, Dad would stop for a chat on the way to the village, and the Major, a furious man in the ordinary run, would grow redder in the face whether you agreed with him or not. Dad loved discourse and would talk to him about anything, eventually egging him on to a state of explosion. They looked like they enjoyed themselves, but it all went over my head. I would sit in the wagon while Harry snorted and swished away flies with his tail. The conversation simmered down when the talk turned to farming. The Major was a keen gardener and considered himself something of an expert. Perhaps he was, and Dad was happy to listen, but the Clarke orchards ran behind their house, so the gardens were quite modest. But every fall, the Major would polish and primp the cream of his crop and march them across the river to do battle at the Digby County Exhibition.

He took special pride in his prize-winning yellow tomatoes, and his vegetable rows were trim and precisely regimented, the army way.

Major Simon never relinquished his military rank or stance with his jodhpurs and leather puttees, underarming the least of weaponry, the swagger stick. When he strolled down for a chat, we'd hear him coming, thwacking his ever-present swagger stick on his leather puttees. Mother thought him pompous and full of himself and wondered exactly what war he fought in. But he did fight because when General Bremner visited in the summer, Daniel would listen outside the parlor window. He told us in bed at night that the Major had said there were no rats in the Russian trenches because the Russians ate them all. Clean as a whistle the Russian trenches were. When the Russians begged for used tea bags, they got them when the British troops were finished with them, and when the grateful Russians were finished with them they ate them. Tea and rats! No wonder I had nightmares.

Daniel was so intrigued by the Major's stick that he whittled an appropriate branch and strode about with it under his arm, whacking his leg authoritatively and occasionally whacking mine. That was its purpose, he explained to me, so I told Mother about his army training. Mother said to him very calmly, "Let me have a look at that stick." Daniel proudly handed it over, and as quick as a wink Mother whacked him, "There. Now you've had a taste of your own medicine." She snapped the stick in two and threw it in the stove. The army flew right out of his mind. The training was too rigorous.

Of all our visitors, the Major and Amanda were the least approachable to children. We were circumspect and studiously polite and I most certainly never sat on the Major's knee, nor did I dream that I would. I couldn't adore him the way I did Mr. Kniffen, Mr. Bishop or even Dr. Campbell. Nor could I stop and answer friendly questions and chat as I did with Mr. W.G. Clarke, who owned the Trading Company, or Mr. Burns Clark who owned the River View Lodge. They were all the first of my elderly loves. I hope this is not shocking, but the moment we gasp our first breath we are a miniature entity complete with that most dominant of emotions outside of murder.

The Potter's brook today, still with the flowers and bulrushes.

Passing the Reade farm, we came to a brook lined with flowers that trickled down between two hills. It paused at the bottom in a soggy stand of bulrushes before seeping over to the side of the road to fill a watering trough, the only one along the Chute Road. Whether Harry needed it or not, he always stopped for a quick drink, and neither Mother nor Dad had any say in the matter. On his own time, Harry would veer over to the trough and noisily slurp away. Dad never interfered, saying that Harry enjoyed the comfort of habit just like we did. When Harry was done, he would give a shake of his head and a snort to announce his satisfaction. Sometimes when Harry stopped for refreshment, we would look up to see Dorothy Potter and call out a hello. The Potters lived high on the hill in a yellow and white house fronted by bay windows and a broad verandah. Dorothy's father worked for Mr. Clarke, who also owned their home, and I used to think she was so lucky living there, even though the path leading up to the

house was steep and gravelly. You struggled climbing up, but once there, you had a beautiful, breezy view clear across the river. In the spring, Alice and I would stop at Potter's brook and follow it up the hill, picking the flowers that grew in abundance on both banks. One sunny afternoon, we crested the hill and were surprised to find ourselves facing a large apple orchard in full, fragrant bloom. It was like a secret garden, cupped by hills with long blossomed laneways. Falling petals drifted like butterflies, flitting in the afternoon sunlight. The orchard was older, filled with taller, sturdier trees covered with ancient bark, so behind the blossoms it seemed forbidding. We skirted the orchard, afraid to enter, as if we were on the edge of a fairy tale, and when we turned to leave, we rushed down the hill, unsure of what we were running from. The Potters were surrounded by orchards, and Dorothy said that in the springtime, they opened their windows to let the fragrance fill their home, and at night it settled like dew while she slept.

The largest of Mr. W.G. Clarke's continuing apple orchards stretched from Major Simon's all the way to Mr. Clarke's house, the orderly rows sweeping down to the river, one after another for almost a mile. In the spring, the light in the orchards softened into an impressionist painting, with faintly pink blossoms accenting the misty green of the leaves. Halfway along, two maples framed a break in the orchards where a laneway led down to a house on a sunny hillside plateau, another Clarke home for hired hands. For a time, Mr. Larimore lived there, and when he left, Ernie Baker took his place, and then the house stood empty and alone among the orchards.

Farther along, we came to three houses in a row, the first being another Clarke house, white with green trim and a large verandah, occupied by Fowler and Loo (Lucy) Robinson. Fowler tended Mr. Clarke's orchards, and when we walked past them after school, we would call out to him and listen for his reply returning like an echo. The Robinsons were middle-aged and childless, but for a year or two they cared for Billy Brown, who might have been a relation. We first met Billy when Loo ushered him out the door to join us on our way to school. Billy was Jim's age and very shy. We made our introductions and quickly got acquainted, learning that for

The two maples still look down to the Larimore/Baker home, but the orchards are gone, replaced in part by vineyards.

some reason Billy's parents were unable to care for him and he would be staying in Bear River for a while. Thereafter, Billy would stand waiting for us in the mornings, and he quickly adjusted to his new life the way children always do. If anything, Billy thrived in Bear River, making friends and always scoring at the top of his class. Fowler and Loo beamed with pride at school plays and concerts. The Robinson house took on new significance and we were always on the lookout for Billy. If we called out at the orchards, he and Fowler would hallo from down among the trees where they were working. When the time came for him to return to his parents, everyone was saddened and Billy seemed reluctant. Then, shortly after he left, Billy had an attack of appendicitis and was rushed to Digby hospital, where he died on the operating table. We couldn't believe it. With so many elderly people in the village, death occurred at an alarming rate, and thoughts of the departed soon faded, but when someone our own age died, their memory stuck, as if it wasn't ready to leave. In passing the Robinson house, a snapshot would flash of Billy waiting out front. At the orchards, we still called out once in a while, and Fowler's reply would echo back through the trees, full of overtones.

Fowler Robinson spraying Mr. Clarke's orchards.

Nova Scotia Archives and Record Management

Next door to the Robinson's was Mamie Marshall's home, grey and stripped of paint, having suffered the ravages of age and weather and economics. Her family had seen the best of times. An affluent relative lived in a large home in the village, and Mr. Marshall's general store was a smaller rival to the Clarke Brothers' Trading Company. Mamie Marshall sat lonely and old at her window, daintily dressed in ruched collars and brooches and long skirts brushing her boots.

Beside Mamie Marshall's stood a white clapboard house with green trim, occupied by the Reades, an elderly, genteel couple, parents of Fred Reade the milkman. Although it was ordinary by any standards, I felt drawn to this house almost from the moment I saw it. I liked the macadamized path leading past the neat lawn to a front porch enclosed by lilacs, a windowed alcove up above. I liked the den and parlor windows framed by clematis and orange blossom. And I liked the glassed-in back porch that looked across to the lovely Clarke home next door. The house had a coziness in its compactness that beckoned from every window.

Mr. Reade had been principal of Oakdene School. He was a handsome, erudite, distinguished gentleman, always suavely dressed from his grey fedora down to his grey spats. Mrs. Reade was a delicate, white haired, once-beautiful patrician lady. She would inquire about Mother and send her regards, reminding us to ask her to drop in for tea. Many times on our way back from the village, Mr. and Mrs. Reade would stop Mother and chat while I sat waiting on the culvert out of hearing range. At other times, they would insist that Mother come in for tea, and I would be sent home. Later, Dad would hitch up Harry to the jitney and collect her. Eventually, lively conversations with Mr. Reade extended over long walks down to the farm. I thought it nice that this distinguished gentleman would visit, something he never did before. Then Mr. Reade's afternoon walks brought him down to the farm, and his visits became ritual. There is no doubt that Mother welcomed company and discussion as much as Dad, except whenever Mr. Reade arrived, Dad was never home. Mother chatted with him over tea and would invite him back by saying, "You must come when Dan is here." Finally after one visit, Mother's irritation surfaced. She wondered aloud why he always appeared when she was alone. Her dilemma could have easily been solved had she known that Mr. Reade was stopping me on the way home and asking the common question, "How are your parents?"

"Fine, thank you."

"And how is your Mother?" telling me she was a very beautiful woman.

"And your Father?"

"Oh, he was in Montreal or Halifax."

Then one day while Mother and I were hoeing and weeding a row of carrots, we looked up and there he was again. Mother was livid, "Well, I never! Here comes that old palaverer again." She fumed about him walking all the way down to the farm and weren't there other places he could walk. But you can't stop a man from walking. On he came between the garden rows in all his formality: grey fedora, cane over his arm, hat doffed, arm extended for a handshake and a courtly kiss. Mother was in no mood for a tête a tête over the carrots and ignored his handshake, staring at him stonily and curtly dismissing me to the house. When I looked back, Mr. Reade had turned towards home, never to return. Mother swept into the dining room and sat down to scratch off a letter, dipping her pen in acid and mumbling to herself with undeniable determination. She wanted the letter mailed immediately, but Daniel protested the long walk to the village; couldn't he just hand the letter to Mr. Reade at his home? Mother exploded and said that if he didn't post the letter, he would experience the thrashing of a lifetime. Since she couldn't trust a child like Daniel, I had to go along to see that the post office got the letter. It was a long trek on a hot summer day, and Daniel complained bitterly about this latest injustice, compounded by all the others he listed off. In fact, Mother, Daniel and I were a microcosm of righteous indignation. The situation confused me, especially Mother's rudeness to such a nice man, but now in my old age and after having ironed out the wrinkles of human nature, I can see that for all his charm, Mr. Reade was a snake in the grass slithering down that row of carrots. And Mother—the prey of this devious charmer. Still, when he wasn't exhibiting the best of man's failings, he was a very nice man with his courtly, old-world manners. Shortly afterwards, Mr. Reade died of a heart attack, and as we passed his house a large funeral wreath hung on the front door.

Mother's warm friendship with Mrs. Reade continued, though she spent her winters with a daughter in the States. The house would sit empty until her return in the spring, when the Reade children would be turned out in new clothes and have American scribblers and other school supplies to establish their superiority. After school, Mrs. Reade would be watching for the gaggle of children to appear on the road, and she would come out to meet us with a plate of fudge or ginger snaps. A lucky grandchild would be favoured to stay, and she might ask another to run home and get her eggs or butter, and everything would seem like a privilege for those concerned. Then one year, she left in the fall to remain in the States. After a brief occupancy by an elderly couple, another black wreath hung on the front door and the home remained vacant.

Despite death and abandonment, the house retained the palpable warmth of its past owners, an emanation of kindness and happiness, tea and ginger cookies and the aura of bygone elegance and refinement. Fred Reade kept his parents' home well-tended: flowers in spring, the lawn neat and tidy, and the windows polished like mirrors so I could look through and imagine my life behind those lace curtains.

Mr. W.G. Clarke was the richest man in town and lived in a white, verandahed mansion next door to the Reade house. The Clarke family ranked as one of the wealthiest in the province, so I was told, and the three brothers, Willard (W.G.), Wallace (W.W.) and Bernard (Burns) were the town tycoons. Their family origins dated back to the founding of the village, but it was the business acumen of the Clarke brothers that breathed life into Bear River, forging the character of the small village and ushering in decades of good old days. They started out with a logging operation making squared timber, that original Canadian export, backbone of the building trades. As they expanded their land holdings, they built a mill at Lake Jolly that quickly grew into an entire lumbering community, shipping everything from plank and lath down to clothespins and dowels. In the village, they bought a loading wharf, warehouses, and offices until that side of the river was known as Clarke's Corner.

W.W. Clarke

W.G. Clarke

Shipping turned into shipbuilding, which turned into overseas trade that came back to fill the shelves of the Trading Company. They built the Packet to run local errands and keep the village well-supplied. Their reservoir kept the water running and their hydro plant kept the lights on. The Clarke businesses employed hundreds, which bolstered every other line of trade. But by the time I started school, the firm had dwindled, the brothers were elderly, and the bulk of their carefully amassed wealth had vanished, lost in a few short years on an all-or-nothing pulp mill.

The homes of the three Clarke brothers were the largest and most elegant in the village, their architecture an attractive, subdued antebellum. At that young age and never having travelled farther afield than Digby, I thought them grandiose in the same way I thought the centre of the village was as big as things got. Later, I found out that as mansions go, they were quite ordinary by city standards. Still, they comfortably housed the large families of the day with plenty of room for hired help. As my mind expanded, I also realized that for a rich man, Mr. W. G. Clarke's home retained a certain modesty. Originally a practical, unimposing structure, subsequent additions and embellishments raised it in rank. The attraction of the house lay not in the building itself but in the sweeping, two story verandah embellished with columns, railings and rounded stairways. My mind could never resist wide verandahs, glassed-in porches, and bay windows fronting book-lined dens. I dreamed of escaping the farm, and it is in the nature of dreams to swirl about in the best luxury we know.

Although their grounds were unimpressive, meagrely flowered and mostly bushed, the Clarke's did have a tennis court, and this was enough to signify status. In the spring I'd see workmen dragging a roller to level the court, then kneeling on the grass to manicure every square inch. When the net went up, the stage was set for the summer performance of the village elite. Women graced the court in immaculate whites with caps and pleated skirts, while the men dashed about in white pants and V-neck sweaters. They thwacked the ball back and forth, and endless games of tennis were followed by tea and sandwiches on the verandah served by maids wearing black and white in the spring, pale blue and white in the summer. I was thrilled and aspired to sandwiches served by maids on my verandah.

Courtesy of The Bear River Historical Society

Behind the house, the grounds sloped down to a large barn where apples were stored for shipment to the West Indies. Below, the woods fell steeply down to a wharf where their schooner anchored. We often saw the white sails slipping down the river, the last of the Clarke sailing ships. By all accounts, Bear River's finest ship was the *Ethel Clarke*, lost some years ago but still praised as 'The White Swan.' Ethel was the second of Mr. Clarke's four daughters and had drowned when she was twelve. She was swimming behind the school with friends when her foot caught in the underpinnings of a boat slip. A distraught Mr. Clarke came running from the Trading Company and in his grief, carried her up Oakdene Hill and home.

Clockwise from top left: Ethel, Edith, Josephine and Annie, the youngest.

The other three daughters were all married and all approaching middle age: Mrs. (Josephine) MacIntyre, Mrs. (Edith) Cunningham and Mrs. (Annie) Fraser. The MacIntyres lived across the road with their two children, Nancy and Billy, both in high school. The Cunninghams were childless and lived with W.G. Clarke. I would see Mr. Cunningham working away at the Clarke Brothers office on Main Street, his head bobbing above the half-frosted window. He also owned a lumber mill at the Head of the Tide that he somehow retained after the pulp mill debacle, bankruptcy being an art among the elite. Years later, he was still perfecting his art, scrambling in the dead of night to remove equipment before the bank foreclosed. Otherwise, Mr. Cunningham was notable for having introduced the Boy Scouts to Bear River, causing a sensation among the village tenderfeet. The local troop seemed to be his main interest in life, and for years I would see him marching packs of uniformed half-pints out to the backwoods to enjoy the black flies and mosquitoes.

For a time, the Frasers also lived at the Clarke home with their two children: Mary-Ellen, a year or two older, and the impossibly handsome Clarke, who was in my class. My teacher once scolded me for staring. Sadly, I would remain thwarted, because Mr. Fraser had recently returned from a government posting in Ireland and was packing up the family for Jamaica, where he would be the Canadian Trade Commissioner. He had worked for Clarke Brothers until the collapse and then landed on his feet in the Foreign Service. Mother recalled a time when he clerked at the Trading Company, but with Dr. Lovett a Member of Parliament for Digby-Annapolis, people joked that a jump to the diplomatic was top-notch grocery trading.

I remember the first time I met Mr. W. G. Clarke–I remember it very well. I had just started school and Dad collected Daniel and me to go down to the Trading Company. We went into Mr. Clarke's office at the back of the store, beyond the dry goods departments, the part of the building that was anchored directly in the river. Seeing us, Mr. Clarke slipped down from his stool and came to the wicket. Dad introduced me, and Mr. Clarke asked to shake my hand. He removed his pince-nez and reached through the wicket as I stood on my tiptoes. In my awkwardness I gave him my left hand, and Mr. Clarke corrected me, "Not a Scout's handshake," he would like my other hand, the right one. I was embarrassed because in those days, you didn't forget the formality of good manners. I had shaken many hands in my five years and knew the proper hand. He escorted me to Ralph Purdy in the grocery section to choose a lollypop, a ritual he performed for me many times. Elderly gentlemen knew how to charm little girls, and in those days, nothing charmed like a lollipop. I liked Mr. Clarke and I liked meeting him with his old-world courtesy of the handshake. As I look back at that period, it seems that young and old were never very far apart with the established courtesies. Whenever I met Mr. Clarke with his pince-nez and his crispness, I always felt very important shaking his hand. He was a well-respected man throughout the province. Mother or Dad would meet him on the road and launch into friendly discussion, walking along slowly. Several times, Mother and Mr. Clarke finished their discussion on the sidewalk in front of his home while his two daughters, Mrs. Cunningham and Mrs. MacIntyre, sat on the verandah. I thought it strange that they never came down the few steps to say hello. For as many years as we passed the Clarke home, I don't recall Mother ever speaking to them. They had met when Mother joined the doyennes of society on her one and only foray to the Ladies Aid sewing circle. She sang for them, but had to decline in ignorance when they requested cowboy songs. Dad would stop and chat with them in passing, but Dad spoke to everyone. I would say a polite how-do-you-do or good afternoon as I met them on the road, two plump, middle-aged figures who always asked how was my father, never my mother. They would walk on, affecting the current fetish of the walking cane among the women of the Bear River rich. The showy flourishing of the cane died out for lack of favour among the farmers wives.

At the River View Lodge, where 'Grandma' Clarke lived. (Clockwise) Mr. W.G. Clarke holds his grandson, Billy MacIntyre. Mrs. W.G. Clarke. Mrs. Clarke (W.G.'s mother 1824-1924). Mr. MacIntyre. Mrs. MacIntyre.

High on a hill opposite the Clarke home was the MacIntyre's bungalow with its lavish, well tended grounds, the nicest along the road. A meticulously manicured lawn arched up the hill, divided by a zigzag flagstone path lined with blazing red rhododendrons. To the right, a driveway swept up a curved path flanked by tall poplars. To the left, a large duck pond cupped in stone sat enclosed by flowered bushes. Parked in front of the house was a yellow roadster, the only car on the Chute Road. I suppose the nucleus of the village began at this part of the Chute Road. With other homes, grounds were devoted to vegetable gardens and hay fields. Barns housed the necessary horse, cow, perhaps a pig, always chickens, and nearby sat the woodshed and outhouse. Fields were for stock, not flowers and lawns.

Mr. MacIntyre, a son-in-law of Mr. W.G. Clarke, was the dreamer and schemer behind the pulp mill, built at the mouth of the Bear River. The mill's chief failing was an inadequate supply of fresh water to clean the pulp, so the village council rubber-stamped a pipeline to run water from the Head of the Tide, through the village and up the river to the moribund mill. Dad was outraged, because without his approval or even notice, the Clarke consortium of sons-in-law proposed to high-handedly cut a swath through our oaks. Strange men came to survey and argue. Immediately, Dad saddled Harry and galloped into the village, but if he made a point at all, it was ignored. Early the next morning the sawing and chopping began at the far end of the Miller field. It was as if a war had broken out. Uncle Peter, who could always be depended upon to work up a temper, grabbed the shotgun and fired shots in the air. The men stopped cutting and sawing and Dad galloped back to the village. The alarm and confusion went on for days. Nothing but talk, talk, talk about the pipeline. In the end, construction went ahead, leaving an ugly, fat-bellied insinuation snaking across our beach.

Besides saving the pulp mill and the town, the pipeline was just wide enough to walk on, making it a useful shortcut home. We had been warned to come right home after school, but when baseball came to town we had to witness the spectacle. We had also been warned not to dare walk on the pipeline the way the workmen did, but that's what we did. We'd watch part of a baseball game, then take off our shoes, put them in our book bags,

Pipe line from East Branch to Bear River Pulp Co's mill at mouth of Bear River, Nova Scotia made of Douglas Fir 2 ft. in Diameter, 5½ miles long.

and race along the pipeline in our bare feet to catch up with the others. It made for a hazardous shortcut, and I often got slivers because the pipeline was wooden. If we had fallen off the high trestles bridging valleys, we could have killed ourselves. I couldn't bear to look down from heights, so I would slip down and walk along the logs atop the trestles, grabbing the clamps on the steel ribs hand over hand. When the pipe line touched down on solid ground, I'd crawl up on top and run along to catch up with Daniel, nervously doing my balancing act.

The pipe-line operated for only six months, but was talked about for much longer. Edging through town, the cross-patch trestling held up the snake-like pipeline to the sky like a creosoted burnt offering from the people of Bear River, a more or less tarred memorial to their lost savings, bankrupt village coffers and the absentee Mr. MacIntyre. He ran off below the border. His name was mud. Of course it spilled over to the schoolyard. Billy and Nancy MacIntyre were both in high school at the time. One day Billy was dressed to kill, so John Harris, son of the taxi driver, yelled out, "Hey Billy, where did your father steal your white duck pants?" The family soon followed south, and the lovely, rusty red and yellow trim bungalow high on the hill sat empty for most of the year. After all this time, parts of the pipeline still exist for children to crawl through, and no one would suspect that those remains represent Bear River's biggest scandal.[1]

[1] Perhaps there were still sections at the time of writing, but now you will only find the occasional iron hoop.

Beyond Mr. Clarke's was a hayfield that sloped down to offer a lovely view of the village. We often stopped to watch ships coming in on the flood tide. Every ship that docked was a village curiosity: her name, her cargo, her home port. If we lingered too long, we could run down the hill to a narrow path that cut through the woods and came up behind the school. The path still clings to the hill, a useful shortcut for late schoolchildren. Beside this hay field stood Wal (W.W.) Clarke's beautiful home, with a Captain's Walk and columns everywhere. W.W. had four sons, one of whom died young. After his death, the family moved to the wife's home in the village and did not return. W.W. stayed in the background of the Clarke businesses and was said to be more involved with the church and charitable works. He was a larger, more imposing man than W.G., though just as pleasant. One son taught out west, while the other two sons had worked at the pulp mill before leaving for Montreal. W.W.'s. house sat empty for long stretches, and we would detour onto the semi-circle driveway to run across the wide wraparound verandah, peering through windows into elegant sitting rooms, the furniture draped in white sheets and frozen in time.

Next door lived the elderly Mrs. Troop, her large house stripped of paint by years of weather, looking as if it were ready to topple down a risky hill. Mrs. Troop was very frail and would sit at her window with its raggedy curtains stroking a very large grey cat, much larger than any in our barn, so it seemed much more dangerous. Yet there it sat, calmly accepting her petting and never once turning to hiss and scratch. I marvelled. Mrs. Troop lived alone and liked to see little children going home after school. I often saw her smiling and waving. One day she stood at her gate and asked if I would run down to the post office and mail a letter. For the favour, she gave me five cents, a fortune. I can only recall several times in those young years when I had money in my hand and that was one of them. It didn't matter that I had to walk home alone, because I went in to Mrs. Schmidt's store and bought a bag of dulse[2], blackballs and my favourite honeymoons, pocketing the change for more candy later. When I got home Dad was furious, and the next morning I had to knock on Mrs. Troop's door and return the nickel.

2 Mary raved about dulse, how all the children loved it and she did too. On a family trip to Nova Scotia, she bought some for us, and we were less than impressed. It's basically dried seaweed, an acquired taste, eaten like potato chips but very nutritious.

I didn't mind, because I understood the explanation of not expecting rewards for small favours, especially from elderly ladies like Mrs. Troop. It was her cat. I had a terrible fear that the minute Mrs. Troop opened her door I would last no longer than a mouse. Whenever Daniel saw a cat slinking along the road he would stamp his feet and tear after it, saying, "I saved you!" I returned Mrs. Troop's nickel and survived only because her cat was between meals and sleeping. After that close call, whenever I saw a cat's pink tongue daintily licking flexed claws, I assumed it was about to eat and the menu was me. I ran.

Opposite Mrs. Troop's and high above the road lived Mrs. Hennigar, whom we never knew. A few paces on was the River View Lodge, with the Annex across the road. Mr. and Mrs. Burns Clarke ran the Lodge, the building not as ornate as the other Clarke homes, but the grounds rather elegant, treed with cherry and apple orchards in back. It still stands as it was, still accommodating tourists, and still with the magnificent horse chestnut tree on the front lawn, every spring festooned with its templed bloom, then shrugging off the faintly pungent flowers to cover the ground like late snow. It was the only chestnut tree on the road, and the boys waited for the ripened, prickly-covered mahogany nuts to make their annual yo-yos. When that interest waned they stuffed their book bags and used the chestnuts to score direct hits at recess and scatter screaming children.

After school, elderly Mr. and Mrs. Clarke often waited in front of the Lodge to smile and talk to us. Mrs. Clarke would have a plate of cookies, fresh from the oven and still warm. I don't think Mr. Burns Clarke had an equal share in the Clarke Brothers business. He seemed to amble about at his own pace, never as involved as W.W. or W.G.. I often saw him helping out at the Trading Company, but for the most part he seemed content to busy himself at the Lodge, taking in tourists in the summer and lodgers in the winter. I don't recall anyone else ever inviting Mother to a formal tea, but Mrs. Burns Clarke did several times, sending us home with invitation cards. I once went with Mother to their annual Strawberry Social. It was a bright summer day with the grounds decorated in an elegant al fresco arrangement: linen-covered tables sparkling in the sun with crystal and silverware, flags and banners fluttering in the breeze. Polite music accompanied the chit-chat of fashionable guests from other towns, the ladies holding fine china with gloved hands, young ladies doing the same. I mingled in my good dress and polished shoes, always boys' shoes, on Dad's insistence. One table offered delicate sandwiches with tea and lemonade. Another table held strawberries with whipped cream, whole strawberries on custard tarts, double-decker strawberry shortcakes oozing crushed strawberries between the layers and topped with whipped cream. The centrepiece featured a huge crystal bowl of strawberry punch with whole berries and their little green leaves floating on top. We supplied the Lodge with fruit and vegetables all summer long, and the strawberries had come from our fields, and I had helped pick them in those very same shoes.

Oakdene teaching staff, 1930, left to right: June Schmidt, Grace Hubley, Flossie Dunn, Vera Heisler, Margeurite Baird, Clyde Brown (Principal).

Next door to the Lodge lived Mrs. Schmidt in her gingerbread house with twin gables and all the trimmings. Every child in the village knew Mrs. Schmidt because her variety store near the bridge had all the candy you could ever wish for. Mr. Schmidt had died years ago, leaving his wife to run the store. Their daughter, June, worked as a governess in Boston, and when she was home, she would help out behind the counter. I always strung along with Alice when she went to Schmidt's, and since June was a relative, she would stuff the bag for Alice and include a blackball or a honeymoon for me. June was tall, not petite, her bobbed black hair framing a ready smile.

Eventually, she joined the staff at Oakdene and taught the younger Marvins. At recess, I would see her playing tag in the schoolyard with an excitable group of grade ones. At school concerts, I would see her gathering children like a mother hen. Younger siblings raved about Miss Schmidt, how she made them laugh, the fun projects they were doing. On hearing this, I felt cheated out of my youth. In my day, grade 1 involved trial by fire with Miss Withrow wielding her pointer as a handy aide-mémoire.

At Oakdene, the patriarchy was in final fling, so Principals were men and the teachers were single women. Most of our teachers were quickly swept off their feet and out the door, but June never married, not even after the rules relaxed. Her career at Oakdene spanned forty years and generations of Bear River children, all of whom reserved for her that special affection one can give only to a favourite teacher.

The old Methodist church, and the Annex behind it. (2011)

A very old building stood opposite the Schmidt house, looking like a large shed, weathered and stripped of paint, but with tasteful trim around the small windows. Alice said it was the original Methodist Church and had been moved up the hill a long time ago to make room for a larger structure. It seemed too small to serve as a church, but I suppose in those early days when the faithful gathered in parlors and barns, it was one step closer to heaven. The tiny church was still in the business of sending souls on their way, playing its small part as a storehouse for coffins.

The last house on the road stood a few paces on, the old Chute house, likely the reason for the moniker 'Chute's Corner' and perhaps the reason for the 'Chute Road' as well. The house bulged with bay windows that looked down to the village from the top of Oakdene Hill. It was built by a Captain Chute, who had the seaworthy name of Horatio Nelson but went down with his ship many years ago. The current owner was the elderly Commodore Chute–another nautical name I loved. His rank implied service on the high seas, now nothing but happy memories if one keeps in mind that the Chutes had the bad habit of sinking with their ships. Trade at sea became trade on dry land when he opened a general store at the wharf, his schooner docked nearby to stock his shelves. The Commodore was something of a patron saint at Oakdene school for having saved five youngsters from drowning on five separate occasions, right outside his store. At the first cry of alarm he would dash out the door and dive into the river to pull out another sputtering child. Now in his golden years, the Commodore earned his keep as a building mover, which didn't seem like steady work. Buildings in Bear River generally stayed put, except for the old and decrepit little Methodist church. Imagine our surprise when we learned that Mr. Harris' drugstore, now resting comfortably on stilts, had once sat on solid ground across the street. Dad then informed us that buildings were on the move all across the province and the Commodore was one of the few who knew the trade. Yes, the Commodore said, people and their houses could barely sit still, and why shouldn't they move on to greener pastures? I didn't see why not, but moving buildings hardly seemed like a job for the elderly. The Commodore assured us that after teaming up a train of oxen, all he had to do was tickle them with a goad stick. Why, even children could move buildings. He liked to tease us. I would see him yukking it up with the hotel crowd outside the Grand Central, his brother and aged mother among them. The family owned the hotel, and sometimes when we went in to the village, I would check to see if it was still there. It's gone now, likely inching its way down a country road.

I don't know if Mrs. Zinck was related to the Commodore, but it was she who lived in his house. Oakdene Hill was a steep climb for an elderly lady, so Mrs. Zinck often asked Alice and me to mail letters. After Dad's rebuke I had to refuse her reward, but all was not lost, because

Alice and I made a pact that she would collect the money. We would run down the hill to the post office and then rattle back across the bridge, straight into Mrs. Schmidt's. Mrs. Zinck was one of many elderly widows in the village who lived all alone in big houses. She was dignified and stately, very much like Mrs. Burns Clarke, Mrs. Schmidt, Mrs. Romans, the widow of the Royal Bank manager, and Miss Van Buskirk of the Trading Company—like many of the grey-haired, well-dressed matrons of the day wearing brooches and pearls and black ribbons around their necks holding watches or gold fountain pens. They maintained tradition with calling cards and regular 'at home' sessions, the tea poured from silver into fine china. Their style, early 1900s, skipped the flapper era of the 1920s and survived with sophisticated reserve into the 1930s.

At the corner of Oakdene Hill stood a very tall oak hundreds of years old, arching across the road like the village gateway. In the winter, teenagers would drag their sleds to the top of Oakdene Hill and start their downward plunge at Mrs. Zinck's tree. The more reckless would mount even higher, up to the Oickle's. They would careen down, turn at Mrs. Zinck's oak and then swoosh down to the village, past the Trading Company and along Main Street. Then they would reverse their route from the Digby side, down Chapel Hill and across the bridge. Luckily, no one skipped over the wharf and into the river, but we heard reports of loaded sleds spilling out at Mrs. Zinck's tree or plunging into the gulley behind Mr. Yorke's smithy.

Below Mrs. Zinck's was Will Brinton's house, a white cottage with green trim. He clerked in the grocery section of the Trading Company, just down the hill. The Brinton's lawn spilled down an embankment and was bolstered at the road by a long stone wall that wedged down the hill, ending at the entrance to the Anglican Church. The stone wall was wide enough to walk on, and every single child happily marched along it and jumped down at the church. It was one of our simple pleasures. Oakdene stood next door to the church, so after school, our first stop would be to see Mrs. Brinton, Alice's Aunt Fanny. Alice would engagingly say hello and be rewarded with a piece of chocolate cake or a soft molasses cookie. As we climbed the hill, we would alternate bites and discuss cake versus cookies, molasses taffy versus chocolate fudge with nuts, and king apples versus all the rest.

John McLeod collection

Looking down Oakdene Hill from Mrs. Zinck's tree

Looking up Oakdene Hill from in front of the school, 1944

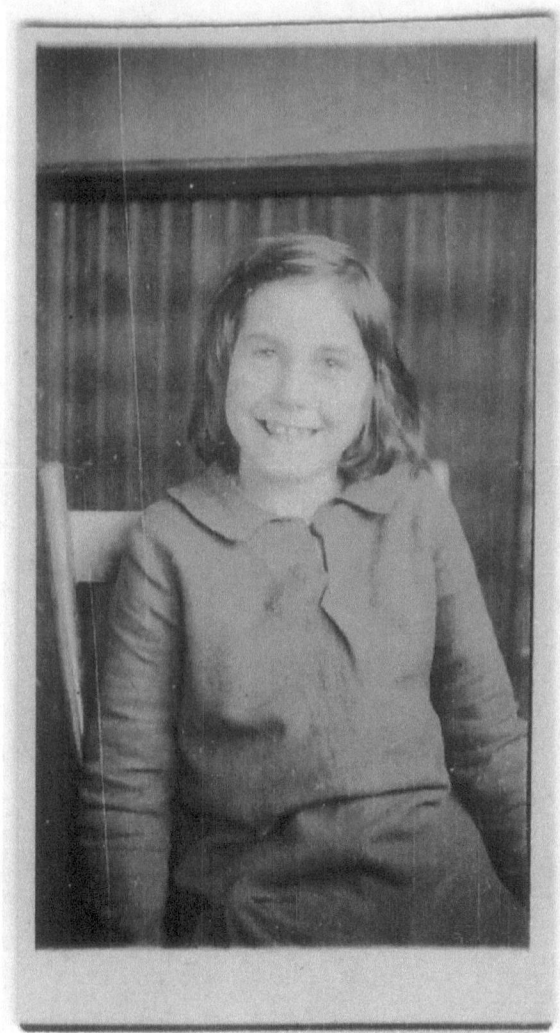

Mary at Oakdene.

*O*AKDENE SCHOOL WAS NAMED for a very fat, motherly oak hundreds of years old and standing in the corner of the school yard. The tree still stands as I knew it in 1925 on my first day of school, and I suppose children still play underneath it, enjoying all the same games children love: in and out the window, London bridge, may I, hopscotch and tag. We spent many happy hours racing around the schoolyard yelling and screaming, little girls taunting little boys, little boys terrorizing little girls. These things will never change.

Bear River had several landmark trees, and children in the schoolyard knew all about them. In front of Oakdene, a gully sheared down to the Tupper brook, which gathered in a pool in front of Bear River's oldest sawmill. Beside it stood a tall poplar, one of several in the village, and local myth held that this tree had grown from a walking stick. A traveller, having walked all the way from Halifax, paused beside the brook to refresh himself and was so taken by the beauty of his surroundings that he decided to put down roots, planting his walking stick in exclamation.[1] Daniel and I tested the theory by planting several likely looking sticks, but nothing took root. Daniel then suggested that we try Dad's walking stick, since it had sufficient mileage. Dad happened upon it poking above a row of cabbage and brought it into the house, baffled. Oh yes, he said, the stick had taken root, but only after many years. Dad's exaggerated tales had polished our scepticism, so I opted for the more likely explanation: that homesick Hessian soldiers had the poplars shipped over from Germany.[2]

Behind Oakdene and across the river was Clarke's Flats, where Bear River's first cherry tree was planted, brought over by an Englishman many years ago. By some accident of climate, the tree and its descendants thrived to the point that Bear River was crowned the 'Cherry Orchard of Nova Scotia.' But attached to the original tree was a curse that if it was ever chopped down, blight would descend. The tree was chopped down and blight ensued, putting a crimp in the Cherry Carnival.[3]

1 Mr. George Harris. When he sold the land, the deed said that the tree should not be cut down, but it eventually was.
2 People still insist it grew from a walking stick.
3 The tree, which apparently grew to an immense size, was planted by William Sutherland in the 1700s, and the curse also involved the lack of recognition for he who brought it over. I thought I should mention him. Happily, for the first time in memory, a number of trees have recently sprouted up from the original roots.

I didn't care for curses or myth and preferred the unquestioned status of Oakdene's oak, the largest in the province (largest girth). That wonderful tree was as much a part of the village as the river. Longfellow's Evangeline oak had nothing on ours. Its roots spread under the school and bolstered the foundation, bracing the pillars and beams. At recess it served as home base for tag, while up above, boys swung from the branches. At lunchtime, we sat on its knuckled roots eating our sandwiches. We loved that tree, and so has every Bear River child for the last 100 years.

The Mill Pond and Bear River's first sawmill. Behind it is the famous poplar. To the right is the Oakdene oak.

Oakdene school was a composite of all the one-room school houses that peppered the valley—one teacher in one room, all grades. Oakdene was much more commodious: a three-story building with eight classrooms, each room with two or three grades taught by one teacher, each grade having an allotted time slot, the time slots sliding back and forth all day long. Clever children could finish their work, listen to the next lesson and eventually earn a promotion in the half-year, thereby avoiding the prosaic norm. It must be remembered that at the time the coffers were empty, but the school provided all that was necessary: a warm furnace tended by Daddy Chalmers; a lunch room where the Ladies Auxiliary served hot cocoa; a new library with Encyclopaedia Britannica, courtesy of Mr. W.G. Clarke; and clean washrooms with sinks, though the indoor-outhouse regimen still obtained: toilets were frightening holes that fell away down the back of the building. All in all, we had everything we needed.

As young as the teachers were, and some were teenagers just out of Truro Normal School, they were all very good. If a boy left school after grade seven to work on his father's farm, he would have been thoroughly grounded in the three R's and well-groomed in proper decorum. Teachers inspected behind ears and under fingernails after the Lord's Prayer and the national anthem. Pointers wiggled over sloppy ABCs in our penmanship books and tapped at runaway notes in our music books. Memories were honed daily by spelling bees and lengthy poems. Sentences were parsed to express precise thoughts, and above all, language was polite and proper. Letters from a hundred years ago show how exacting the schooling was.

After the chaos of the previous September, Dad was primed for more trouble, but when the time came, Daniel and I marched off to school without a fuss. I remember that first day very well. Just as we got to the top of Oakdene Hill, a sudden blowing of horns and whistles and shouting rose up from the village. I naturally thought it had to do with my going to school, but Dad explained that the last wooden ship built in Bear River was being launched.[4]

Oakdene School stood between the Anglican Church and Mrs. Yorke's hat shop, which stood beside the Presbyterian Church. The back windows of the school looked out to the Anglican graveyard on one side and the extended Presbyterian graveyard on the other side. When I started school, my seat was by a window where I could observe funeral processions and burials. At times I completely forgot my work and watched the priest motioning at the grave as the mourners lowered the casket. Miss Withrow would startle me out of my reverie by slamming the pointer across my desk or rapping my knuckles. I was a child consumed by the puzzle and eventuality of death, and Oakdene was surrounded by cemeteries. Across the road and beyond Mr. Yorke's smithy, Mount Hope sat high on a promontory, the largest of Bear River's cemeteries. From our desks, we could watch as the horse-drawn hearse slowly mounted the hill trailed by black-clad mourners, who looked like passing shadows themselves. When Gerry Rice died, his classmates marched in the cortege, too young to understand.

[4] Mary was very clear about this, but all launchings made the local paper and this one did not. It might have been a smaller boat, or a repair.

One day we were in the auditorium practicing hymns around the piano for school closing when someone whispered that Janie McCormick was being buried. She had died of scarlet fever. It was a cold, rainy day, and I looked across to Mount Hope and saw a group of dark figures standing by an open grave. Dad often went moose hunting with Ned McCormick, and Janie was his granddaughter. I had only seen her once, when Dad stopped at the Trading Company for a chat. Mr. McCormick was holding Janie, who couldn't have been more than three. She was the most beautiful little girl with blond curls and blue eyes. As she hung her head over her grandfather's shoulder, we smiled at each other. I reached up to touch her hand and she playfully pulled it away, laughing. It seemed so strange that such a beautiful little girl should die and be buried, someone I knew. For some reason, we were singing a Christmas carol for school closing, 'Love and joy come to you, and to you your wassail too, and God bless you and send you a Happy New Year.' I cried as I watched Janie's burial, and Miss Withrow snapped that I would have to get over my crying because it was a very bad habit. To this day, that carol reminds me of grey skies, cold rain and a family standing motionless at a small grave.

Courtesy of Bob Benson

Looking to the back of Oakdene, with the two churches on either side. In the foreground is the Clarke wharf will a full load of lumber waiting for shipment.

My opinion of Mamie Withrow had been formed by Daniel, and I had a whole year to think about her. Mamie Withrow's opinion of me had probably been formed in part by Daniel's unorthodox performance, still a lively memory. Any teacher would be twice shy before welcoming such a challenge again. She sat Daniel in the back with Merton Yorke. I was put in the front seat, so I kept looking back to Daniel for reassurance. I had no idea there were so many children in Bear River, none of whom I had ever seen before. Miss Withrow warned me to look straight ahead and to pay attention, but I looked back again, and she rapped the pointer over my knuckles. I was terrified. She seemed overpowering, and I can only remember being afraid to look up to her stern, unyielding form: tall, red haired, pasty faced. I needed to see Daniel, so I kept looking back until Miss Withrow rapped my knuckles again. Then Roland Barrass, a sly opportunist seated behind me, stuck a pin in my bottom and I screamed at the pitch of my lungs. Mamie Withrow had had quite enough of me and told me to lay my hands on the desk. She then whacked them soundly with the pointer and told me to put my head down on my arms, not to look up, and to stay that way until called. I don't know how I did it, but I fell asleep, perhaps to get away from myself and the terrible mess I was in. I awakened to the pointer rapping on my desk and Miss Withrow telling me to stand in the corner. She ignored me for the rest of the morning despite me having my hand up to go to the washroom. In time I disgraced myself and stood in a puddle of tears. After school, Dad sat in the buggy waiting by the oak tree. He didn't need to ask if I liked school; my condition said it all. He'd gone through this once before. Dad said, "Poor Sweetlady," and opened up a bag of lollipops. My troubles vanished. Daniel and I immediately began arguing over spearmint and butterscotch until Dad said, "Why yew littah bounders, yew have one second to make up your minds." To this day, spearmint lollipops take me back over that dusty, crunchy road, coming home from my first real slice of life. When I got in the door Dad called out, "Dearie, ah've brought yew a real lave skunk," the final humiliation of that memorable day. Dad always called me the sweetest things he could think of, but that day he called me a skunk. I cried all over again. I was too young to express my terror and humiliation, but it was there all right. I just stored it and never talked about it.

As Mother bathed me, she asked if I liked school and I said yes. Did I make friends? No. What did I learn? I didn't know. Did I have a nice teacher? Yes. At the dinner table, Dad thought maybe I should stay home for a year, but I begged and begged. No matter what, I wanted to be with Daniel and to get away from babies. Daniel said he hated Miss Withrow, which was more or less what Mother expected from him after last year's performance. She said firmly that if she ever heard one complaint about the teacher she would know who to blame, and it wouldn't be the teacher, "So don't come home telling tales!" I wanted to sleep with Mother and Dad that night, but the answer was no. I asked to sleep with Daniel, but Jim said no. In the end Daniel came to sleep with me and we talked about Mamie Withrow and Roland Barrass. I told him why I screamed, and Daniel promised to stick a pin in Roland Barrass as soon as possible. That proved to be more difficult than one would think. Roland was frenetic and wily, as oily as a fox. Only the high school boys could handle him, playfully holding him at arm's length and watching him squirm like a worm. He knew what Daniel's sidling up to him meant, so months passed before Daniel finally cornered him and paid him back with interest. Before that happy day, Roland Barrass, the only son of the Baptist priest in a Baptist town, evolved into a holy terror. One day he snuck up behind us, threw our hats in the oak tree and pointed at us, screaming for all to hear, "Pope lovers!!" Daniel and I looked at each other, puzzled. We had no idea what a Pope Lover was. If we had known what a Pope was, a Pope lover might have thought it very nice. Roland's slander made no sense, even after he took the time to explain that we were Catholics. We had never been to church and had no idea what a Catholic was, so we still didn't understand. Roland ran off as confused as we were. As it turned out, we were the only Catholic children in school, information that likely passed from the school registration and filtered through the Baptist parsonage into refined name-calling.

In class, I worked hard to have everything perfect in my scribbler, but my hesitancy and stuttering annoyed Miss Withrow to the point that she took an active dislike, a novelty that left me a little rattled. While she gently corrected other students, if I made the slightest mistake she kept me in at recess to write lines or to fill the blackboard with acres of ABCs. Day after day while the screaming horde played outside, I was deep into penmanship.

Oakdene school

Miss Withrow would carefully scan my work line by line for mistakes, so out of simple survival and a desperate need to get out and play, I approached perfection. Mine was a scribbler for the ages. Miss Withrow would hand it back to me with a grudging nod, but then when Roland pinched or stuck me and I screamed out, she would pounce like a spider and whack my hands with the pointer, her ever-present appendage. I hung my head in despair, the class pariah. I was afraid to speak, nothing came out, only tears. It was only when Mother was bathing me and noticed my scratched bottom that I had the gumption to tell on Roland. I showed her my bruised fingers, and she was horrified that Miss Withrow had punished me as well. Mother mobilized. The next day, she marched in after school and had me brief Miss Withrow on the pox that was Roland Barrass. Daniel concurred. Miss Withrow, with her fiery, uncontrollable red hair and pudgy nose, eyed Mother stonily. I'm sure she didn't know what to make of Mother, a new breed of farmer's wife. Mother was beautiful, petite and feminine, sure of herself, she never raised her voice, but was as incisive as a surgeon's scalpel in her choice of words. It wasn't difficult for Mother to pinpoint the Irish-Orange antipathy that seethed in Miss Withrow, and Mr. Gilliatt, the principal.

She had seen these simmerings before, and it was all understandable in the Irish-English-Scottish parameter, where history often got a little silly. Miss Withrow was sobered by Mother's visit, and whatever Mother said to her while Daniel and I waited outside, I could see she was not pleased. She kept her pointer off my fingers and moved me away from Roland, but not before one last incident. Throughout the day, Miss Withrow would call students up to her desk to inspect their scribblers, and as we stood waiting, our eyes could take in every item on her desk, including a little dish that held clips, pins and a big brown George V penny that sat there invitingly. It disappeared, Miss Withrow questioned the class, and as you would expect, no one had taken it. Of course Roland had it, but his nerves gave out, so he slipped the penny under my seat with his foot and screamed, "There it is!" This was a big surprise to me. As he pointed it out, I couldn't deny a thing because I had started my crying all over again. Miss Withrow had to change her tactics, so she exhibited me in front of the class as nothing less than a hardened criminal, the village desperado. All I could do was snivel and shake my head no, but Miss Withrow said yes, I was a Judas Iscariot who denied the plain truth. I lacked insight into the decline and fall of Mr. Iscariot, but on principle, I snivelled some more. But before Miss Withrow could convince me of anything, a girl stood up and told on Roland. One George V penny was trading at 30 pieces of silver,[5] so the mantle of Judas fell upon the young scion of the Baptist parsonage. Miss Withrow left Roland to suffer the ravages of his guilt while she turned to me with a stern lecture on the truth. I went back to my desk more confused than ever, proof positive that I must have been learning something.

With all my screaming out and being whacked by the pointer, my stuttering and incessant blubbering, it was only natural that I be shunned from schoolyard society. Children whispered and pointed fingers at the local pariah, and it was quite a while before I made a friend or even wanted one. Without Daniel to put my arms around and cling to, I probably would have become a mental case before my fifth birthday. Through a telescoped look back into the world of 5 and 6-year-olds, I can only wonder about the wholesomeness of mother's milk and the cradle. The schoolyard provided a training ground for Grade 2 skirmishes and subsequent wars.

5 A quick reminder: Judas betrayed Jesus for 30 pieces of silver.

School that fall provided us with a number of shocks, not the least of which was the two-mile trek to get there. Before Dad left for Montreal, it was sheer luxury when he hitched up Harry to the buggy and drove us comfortably to school. Billy McCormick or Truman Hamilton might drive by and thoughtfully give us a lift, but those occasions were rare. Once, Mr. Cunningham picked us up at the top of Oakdene Hill and drove us in his Ford car all the way down to the Crossroads. This happened only once, spawning hopes it might happen again.

After Dad was gone, we reluctantly trudged through the maple grove, fortified by porridge and muffled against the wind that made itself felt full force the moment we mounted McCormick's hill. When the fall rains came, we walked the two miles through heavy downpours, soaked to the skin, our boots wet and heavy with caked mud. The agonies of winter were on their way. Occasionally, Uncle Peter would wrest himself from the bear-like slumbers of the basically lazy man that he was and drive us in, but we knew we couldn't depend on his favours. Best of all was when Mrs. McCormick came to help with the washing. She would watch the babies so that Mother could hitch up the sleigh and drive us in. Those are the winter days I remember so well, the buffalo rugs covering us up to our frozen noses, Harry dancing along to his Swiss bells, hooves rhythmically crunching the snow. The winter storms were severe, at times clogging the roads so much that Harry had to jump the drifts, making the sleigh heave and zigzag dizzily. If the drifts at Hamilton's corner reached Harry's belly, Mother would decide not to press him, and Daniel and I would grin from beneath the buffalo rug as we turned for home. When the sleet blew in, it covered everything with a cold, crystalline delicacy, and every movement of every tree would pop and snap as if whole branches were about to come crashing down. Harry would leave his splintered hoof-prints, and the sleigh would slip and slide along the road, slithering down Oakdene Hill with Mother pulling hard on the reins. When we stopped, I would throw off the buffalo rug and jump down from the sleigh, running as fast as I could to the school door, as if I were eager to embrace academia.

For most of the winter months, we got ourselves to school as fast as our legs would carry us. McCormick's hill was often coated with a sheet of ice, and we would slip and tumble down, making little headway.

Mother, watching our progress, would call from the back door to hurry or we would be late, which we often were, or to hurry or we would get cold, which we already were. After cresting the hill, we scurried along the open road high above the river, the winds pushing and needling us. Drifts piled up at Hamilton's corner, and often we could barely struggle through, the snow up to our shoulders. Daniel would skirt the drifts looking for a breach and then bravely plow through, cutting a narrow trench. I would follow his footprints, and once through, we would race along where the wind had blown the road clear. Our only hope was that as much as we hated school, it was there, and we gratefully rushed down the hill the moment we passed Mrs. Zinck's, climbing the staircase exhausted, having overcome one ordeal to face another. At times, we got to Hamilton's corner and couldn't get through, not even by detouring through the fields, so we would turn back, hoping Mother would understand. At home, falling snow would pile up to the eaves, imprisoning us for days. Uncle Peter would dig himself out the door and shovel his way over to the barn to tend the animals. An open door would usher in a gust, flickering the lamps like a warning to stay inside.

Sometimes at school, the Ladies Auxiliary would rush into the classroom to bundle us up and whisk us out the door before a sudden, blinding storm blew in. Men would have teams of oxen hitched up to break out the roads, but beyond the village, snow buried the road for days. I spent the winter months crying with the cold, stamping my feet and clapping my hands to convince myself I still lived and breathed in this miserable world. Daniel would assure me that if I didn't hurry I would freeze to death. "Yes," he would say, "that's what's going to happen to you. You are going to freeze to death." If Uncle Peter was really convinced that a storm was blowing, he would don his snowshoes, carry Daniel's snowshoes and meet us on the road. He would hoist me on to his shoulders and I would no longer have to worry about whether my lifeless feet would carry me another step. They dangled in limbo until the merciless thaw. In those days, little girls wore woollen leggings and overstockings that covered our shoes before we put on our boots, but I can't remember them ever keeping me warm. Often, fierce storms would burst in before we got out of school, and the drifts at Hamilton's corner would tower over our heads. Then we had to take the longer route home, freezing more than ever. We would detour down the tree line that divided Mr. Hamilton's from the Simons and then follow the lesser drifts along the woods that protectively edged the river. We plowed ahead, now and then plunging down to our armpits, the snow going up my bloomer legs and down my stockings, caking in my boots. I wonder how I survived my fifth year, and probably did only because Daniel valiantly pulled me out of drifts and sinkholes and constantly reminded me I was about to freeze to death. I can't imagine what Mother went through waiting for her children to come home, looking out the window at the heavy snowfall, drifts tumbling down McCormick's hill and darkness closing in. As we struggled up the river road, sinking hip-deep every step of the way, we'd look up to see Mother poised at the window. She would haul us in the door and pull us apart, wrapping us in heavy blankets and sniffling in sympathy as she rubbed our hands. With our cup of hot cocoa, we'd slip behind the stove to defrost inside and out. Dinner followed quickly, and then she would tuck us into bed by six o'clock for stories and lullabies. Life was nothing less than Spartan. Mamie Withrow once asked each child what time he went to bed at and called me into question when I answered 6 p.m. Mother promptly informed her of our schedule in a note. I could only expect humiliation in her class, and there was no question the pressure was exhausting me. My only respite was crawling into oblivion at 6 p.m.

That first winter I was late for school often. I couldn't run as fast as Daniel and he couldn't wait for me, so I would straggle in and have to stand in the corner until recess. Alice Copeland was the teacher's pet, she went to the right church and had a brother and sister in high school to protect her, so when she arrived late, Miss Withrow let her stand over the hot air register. I never could, so I would shiver in the corner away from the heat with my fingers and feet tingling in pain. Miss Withrow ignored me, and I would stand there so long and be so tired and I would have my hand up so long to go to the washroom that it would ache. In time I disgraced myself and I would stand in a puddle and cry silently. I was either in a puddle of tears or a puddle of something else. I was definitely the soggiest child in the class. This happened two or three times, and I had to wait in agony and embarrassment for lunchtime to stand over the register and dry out. I hated myself. Mother was disgusted as she stripped me, and I tried to explain that

I had to stand in the corner all morning and I did have my hand up. Mother donned her armour and confronted Miss Withrow once again. Years later when I was grown and discussing Miss Withrow, Mother said she finally told her that if she did one more cruel thing, she would see that she lost her job. Instead of standing in the corner, I stood at the blackboard printing out those wretched ABCs. Finally, Miss Withrow resolved my lateness by sending me up to Mr. Gilliatt. I had no idea of his punishment, but I was petrified as I looked up past his fat stomach to his glasses. He told me to hold out my hand, and the black strap came down so heavily that it pushed me to the floor. The pain ran up my arm like a shock and my hand hung limp. Then he sternly told me to hold out my other hand, and again the heavy strap nearly pushed me to the floor. Mr. Gilliatt dismissed me with a warning to be on time, and I went downstairs to sit in the cloak room until I stopped crying. The sting of the strap on frozen fingers was something to remember all my life. I slunk into my seat at the front of the class, holding my hands and withered by the humiliation. Several times that fall I visited Mr. Gilliat. When he strapped my hand so hard that it bled, Mother saw the marks and again confronted Miss Withrow and Mr. Gilliatt. She wrote the Department of Education, and when Dad returned at Christmas, there was a lot of running into the village and Dad hugging me and kissing my hands. At least I was his pet. Shortly, Mr. Gilliatt left the school and Mr. Steadman took his place.

My only real joy that first winter was in being sick. In those days before penicillin, parents carefully watched every cold, but we honestly hoped for them. We welcomed chicken pox, measles, mumps, pink eye and even

Courtesy of The Bear River Historical Society

whooping cough, though the coughing made us helplessly gasp for breath. I enjoyed being cozily stuffed into bed with toddies, Scott's Emulsion and even Sloan's Liniment, which scalded inside and out but made you smell properly disinfected. Mustard plasters were molded to my chest, warmed camphor oil poured in my ears, Friar's Balsam steamed through my nostrils and poured down my throat with a teaspoon of sugar, all followed by a healthy dose of Casagara to purge my system. To be happier while sick, I weakly asked Mother for Minard's Liniment (The King of Pain), because that's what Alice's mother used. Alice was right; it was good. I enjoyed that creamy white emulsion as if it were ambrosia. Free of school, home in bed, suffering, itching and coughing my last agonizing breath, I was a happy child to be avoiding the miseries of Miss Withrow. Then Dr. Campbell would come by to look me over, hand me my tongue depressor, and pronounce me cured. Back to school I would go, trudging the long road of life and learning. No sooner were we dosed up and cured than it was time for the springtime ritual of sulphur and molasses, an ugly blob sticking to the roof of your mouth, more or less anchoring the cure for summer.

Eventually, I mastered the art of arriving on time, and as I climbed the stairs I could look up to the large clock on the wall and smile. By the time one of the high school boys had finished pulling on the bell rope, I would be at my desk, anxious for the learning to begin, but not before the all-important salute to the flag, the pledge to country and empire, "God Save the King," "O Canada," a few choice hymns, bible readings and the Lord's Prayer, at which point some straggler might wander in and take my spot in the corner of shame. How far I had come.

Oakdene high school class, 1926.

Once I cleaned up my act, I eventually made friends with Alice Copeland. At first when I went to the lunch room, I sat by myself in a corner. I suppose I was so used to corners that I thought I belonged there. I would eat my lunch and observe the stuffed birds and snarling animals in glass cases. For fun, there were posts where I could swing around and around until I was dizzy and falling down. Then Alice would leave her sister's stylish high-school friends and sit with me. I loved her for it. Everyone wanted to be with the high school crowd, all so pretty and perfectly turned out in the latest fashions and hairstyles: the Woodworth girls, the Dunn and Morine sisters, beautiful Eileen Baxter, and Nancy MacIntyre, younger, but already a favourite. Instead of holding back after school to walk with Daniel, I would hurry to catch up with Alice and the other girls: Dorothy Potter, Nancy MacIntyre and the Reade girls.

Courtesy of Bob Benson

I loved it, because the walk home was my first chance to listen to girls' talk, which was essentially boy talk. After the Reade girls turned up their driveway, Alice, her sister Eileen, and I could chat until we parted at the Crossroads. Alice was very sweet, my first real friend, and we talked about everything. On hot spring days, we would take our lunch and walk down the Yorke's driveway, squeeze between a high wooden fence and sneak into the Presbyterian graveyard. There we would sit comfortably on one of the low crypts and eat our lunch, adding and subtracting dates on tombstones. We had a certain simpatico for the babies who had died much too young. The steeple on the church was topped by a hand pointing to heaven, where little lost souls surely found their way. On those hot sunny days it seemed so peaceful and pleasant, the air scented by the lily-of-the-valley that grew so abundantly between the graves. From our seats in the graveyard, we could look up to see Merton Yorke and his red-headed brother, Denzel, eating lunch by their kitchen window. They lived with their grandmother during the school year because their home was quite far away on the other side of the river. Merton was older, bolder and somewhat wiser since he had missed a year of school because of childhood illness. He was a blond, handsome boy who thought he was smarter than everyone else. Well, he certainly did know a lot more, despite wallowing at the bottom of the class every year. Across from the school, Merton's father had a blacksmith shop where he shod the village horses and the men stood and chatted. And Merton listened. Behind the Yorke house, his grandfather had a wagon shop where men stood and chatted. And Merton listened. His grandmother had a hat shop in the front of the house, where ladies primped with indecision and chatted while making up their minds. The vicissitudes of village life spilled out and Merton heard everything. Mother loved hats and could never pass by without going in, "for a quick look." Mrs. Yorke would bring out a hat that was, "just for you Mrs. Marvin," and Mother would have to try it on—another summer confection full of tulle and berries, flowers and birds.

I liked watching Mother dress for the village, dabbing her ears from a vial of perfume and reaching to the end of her bureau for one of her hats, stacked on a stand that looked like a tall layered cake. Mrs. Yorke's hats were filled with all the goodies that a hat was not a hat without: tulle veils (veils were in then); cherries, red and ripe; birds, if not the whole bird, then their tails or wings; assorted flowers, and often, dominant roses. Crowns and brims were filled to overflowing, waiting to be plunked on a ladies crowning glory.

While Mother primped and posed in front of the mirror, she enjoyed lengthy conversations with Mrs. Yorke, and on one visit, Merton boldly stood in the doorway watching and listening to everything. I was furious that he wouldn't stop staring at Mother and concentrating on what she said. Mrs. Yorke pulled Merton to her side, proud of her little grandson, and asked if I knew him. Didn't I just! I uttered a grim, "Hello, Merton." He once told Alice that he knew what girls looked like. How he came by this information he didn't say, but Alice screamed at him to go away and that her mother said he was a bad boy. I don't know what happened to

Merton when he grew up, but he certainly had a nose for news, and he was well positioned right in the middle of it all. He had a habit of hissing in little girls' ears and saying nothing, then telling other little girls he had told a secret, which naturally peaked their interest.

When Mr. Robinson died, Merton heard every single detail and then he certainly had something to whisper about. At the top of Oakdene Hill was a dark green, white trim house that clung to the elbow of the road. The back of the house was bolstered by timbers that kept it from tumbling into the gully that extended down Oakdene Hill and past Mr. Yorke's smithy. Dad's friend, Colonel Jefferson had lived there, and when they moved out, their cousins the Robinsons moved in. Mr. Robinson became very ill and when he died, Merton said his body exploded all over the room. Merton thrived on such frightening news, and every little girl in the schoolyard was sticking her fingers in her ears and running away from him. At seven years of age, Merton had the mind of a savage.

And then there was Mr. McNaught, the one-time manager of the pulp mill. What a terrible shock when he committed suicide by hanging himself in his garage. Just to be sure of things, he left the car running. No one had ever heard of such a thing, and we discussed it in hushed tones in the schoolyard.

Merton and Denzel's grandparents, Mr. and Mrs. Yorke, in front of their home. Along the road are 'six of the best cherry trees in Bear River', so they said.

The village suffered many tragedies brought on by accident or misadventure, but the taking of one's own life was seen in a more serious light. People said he was distraught over the loss of his wife. Others blamed the demise of the pulp mill. He had recently become our insurance agent. The spectre of Mr. McNaught hanging in his garage was never allowed to fade thanks to Merton, who would illustrate the scene by lolling his head over and hanging his tongue out. One day, Alice and I were eating our lunch at the school entrance when Merton joined us and demonstrated by slapping his hands on the steps exactly how Mr. Robinson's feet sounded when his ghost paced their verandah every night. Merton's mind flew off into fantasy when he talked about all the village ghosts that popped up at night. He would awake to whispering, sobbing, and faint cries for help, reason enough to go to the window for a look-see. Down below would be the who's who of the graveyard milling about like death warmed over, passing through tombstones and trees, aimlessly wandering as if they had nothing but time. We told him they were harmless, but Merton countered, "What about Mr. Alcorn?" Merton's grandfather had worked on his carriage, the same carriage that Mr. Alcorn was seen to fall dead from as he drove down the road. Merton insisted a ghost had snuck onto the carriage while it was in the shop and later strangled Mr. Alcorn as they drove along. We were always fleeing Merton. We still ate our lunches in the graveyard because it never seemed like anything more than a quiet, peaceful place, despite Merton's wild imaginings. We had no fear of the dead resting in their graves; people were the real problem.

Another day, Merton and Denzel joined us in the graveyard, and Merton wanted to tell us a joke about a bitter end, which we didn't want to hear, not after Mr. Robinson. We stuck our fingers in our ears, and what followed was a bout of pulling and pushing and tearing about the tombstones to escape. The roistering subsided long enough for Merton to tell the joke, which he promised would be funny. I have never been able to tell a joke that didn't end up as simple-minded mumbo-jumbo, and even now I don't think I can get it right, though a number of times in my young life when I slyly repeated it, I could hardly finish it before doubling over in laughter. As I recall, it concerned a fat lady walking through a field when a vicious dog spied her and gave chase. Just as she mounted the fence, the dog jumped up and bit her end, so she died a bitter end. I don't know if it was the play on words or the ridiculous picture that was so funny, but Alice and I screamed with laughter. Our lunches in the cemetery ended when Mrs. Yorke heard us squealing and giggling. She called out for us to leave immediately and weren't we ashamed of being so disrespectful and what would our parents think. Merton and Denzel ran off while Mrs. Yorke berated Alice and me. Even worse, she reported us to our teacher, who asked for the guilty to raise their hands. Merton and Denzel sat smugly, almost assured of their innocence. Alice had backbone and was not about to see those two little devils hide behind faux wings, so she admitted our crime and told on them as well, which probably saved us from the pointer, since Alice was the teacher's pet. Alice was a confident child made of sterner stuff than I. A reprimand brought me to tears and I suffered for my guilt. It gnawed away at my imperfect soul.

There was also a question of respect for the dead on the school premises, down in the basement, in particular, where a skeleton hung from the furnace pipes right beside Daddy Chalmer's chair. Years ago when the town doctor died, his daughter could find no good use for the skeleton that hung in his office, so she gave it to the school. Mr. Chalmers was the janitor, tall, thin, elderly, very calm and very nice. He would slowly patrol the halls with his hands in his pockets, always chewing, ever watchful for messy children. Everyone liked and respected him, referring to him as Daddy Chalmers. One day Daniel induced me to sneak down to the basement to see the skeleton. Daddy Chalmers was having his usual after-lunch snooze, so we stealthily tip-toed down the plank stairs, Daniel first. The furnace radiated a stifling warmth in the musty, shady basement. Daddy Chalmers was sleeping in his chair, melding in with the shadows and dust, while the startling milk-white bones of the skeleton looked more alive than he was. I shuddered at the sight of him comfortably snoozing in his tipped-back chair, shadowed in the protective company of some forgotten and misbegotten soul. The thought seized me with terror and I ran up the stairs as fast as I could. Daniel followed, but when he got to the top of the stairs he shouted, "Boo!!" as loud as he could and slammed the door. Daddy Chalmers was used to children's curiosity. He came upstairs and ambled down the hallway, hands in his pockets, calmly going about his rounds.

I knew Mamie Withrow didn't like me, and she probably hated Mother, but somehow Daniel always avoided her discipline, and at times it seemed as though she even liked him. I should have expected it. Daniel had charms like a box of chocolates, and no woman could resist. Mamie forgave and forgot most of his mischief, but not the time he displayed his very precise art work. Daniel liked to play with Dad's compasses and perfect his talent for drawing intersecting circles, which he would then vividly colour. In time he became bored and enlarged upon the perfection of circles by dealing with the human body. Daily, he drew dozens of little men in his own likeness to varying degrees, and what parts of their bodies were not circular he streamlined with semi-circles, or less. Every exterior part of the human body was, if not accurate, at least as meticulous as he could make it, à la Da Vinci or Adam in the Sistine Chapel: ears, eyes, fingers, toes, perfect circular nipples and belly buttons, et cetera. Needing to keep Daniel constantly preoccupied, Mother would hardly glance at the many little boys in the altogether and say, "That's nice, do some more." At times she would urge him to save them for your father. Dad, in an off-hand way would say, "Wonderful," as if familiarity with Daniel's genius generated indifference. At that young age, Daniel understood the real value of art—to be shared. He'd say to me, "This is my best one. I'll give it to you." Great artists must exhibit, so when Daniel went to school, he willingly shared his efforts with Merton Yorke. Merton saw real potential, and though he didn't have a compass, he did well enough free-hand on the back page of his scribbler. The two of them held their work up to share with the back-seaters amid sniggers of appreciation—the reward of lesser art. It was no revelation to the boys, but a real eye-opener to horrified little vestal virgins. Miss Withrow intervened and was aghast, promptly sending them to Mr. Steadman with the evidence, whereupon Mother got a note with Daniel's art work enclosed. At first I thought she was crying in despair, but instead she had collapsed in a chair and was laughing hysterically. Until then, Mother had never discouraged Daniel's brilliance, but all she said was to leave Dad's compasses alone. At school, little girls called Daniel and Merton dirty boys and ganged up at recess to discuss the salient points of Grade 1 erotica. I don't recall that Daniel ever drew again. He gave up art and concentrated on Merton Yorke's low-class humour.

Over the next few years, nothing much happened, and I learned my lessons out of fear, waiting for the day when I would get out of Miss Withrow's class. Although I never liked her, she was a very good teacher, and I do remember how much I enjoyed the books she read to us after lunch, which likely fostered my love of reading, stories like *Mrs. Wiggs of the Cabbage Patch*, *Rebecca of Sunnybrook Farm*, *Little Black Sambo*, the Elsie Dinsmore books and many others. I suffered Miss Withrow for two long years until that blessed day when I took my seat in Lexie Hatfield's class. She was pretty, tall and slim, and wore her jet-black hair in a Dutch boy bob, flapper style. Lexie (Alexandra) had no favourites and everyone loved her.

That year, I sat by a window that looked across the street to Mr. Yorke's smithy, and when my mind wandered, it would drift down to the shooting flames and the musical ringing at the anvil. Several times I looked down and saw Dad chatting by the fire. He alternated between Mr. Yorke and Ben Hill for Harry's shoeing. Flossie Dunn was a teacher whose father ran a smithy on the Digby side. He once refused to shoe Harry because Dad had kept his business on the Annapolis side. Dad had not been accommodating, so now it was his turn. When we went to have Harry shod, I rather liked sitting in the buggy and peering in to the shady interior. Mr. Yorke would pump the bellows to heighten the flames, stirring up a nest of sparks as he pulled the red-hot iron out of the coals. The anvil would ring like Handel's "Harmonious Blacksmith" as he hammered and shaped the shoe for a custom fit. Then he would bend down and hold Harry's hoof in his black leather apron for a quick manicure, filing briskly before securing the shoe with long, square-headed nails. It seemed miraculous that Harry didn't feel a thing. Out he would clomp with his shaggy fetlocks, ready for the dusty road.

From the same window, I could look down the gully to the Tupper brook, which divided Oakdene Hill from Mount Hope. The brook paused at the old sawmill behind Mr. Yorke's, where a dam formed the Mill Pond. There, boys could swim, or fish for trout, or catch frogs to spring on little girls. The whole school went down on Arbor Day to plant trees and picnic by the pond. Alice and I often went down at lunchtime to sit in the sun or pick flowers for the teachers. In the winter, the pond froze thick enough for the lucky few who had skates. Otherwise, boys would clear the snow for hockey games,

The Yorke house beside the Methodist church. In 1925, the Methodist, Presbyterian and Congregational churches became the United Church, which explains its several names in this book.

played with improvised sticks and pucks. At my desk, I sometimes heard the hollow clanking of ox bells as teams hauled timber up to the sawmill, and that would be the signal for boys to wander over for offcuts to make sticks or bats. Cardboard boxes from the stores were handy for sliding down the hills that surrounded Oakdene. At lunchtime, the winter scene resounded with an invading army of screaming children overrunning the hills, sledding, throwing snowballs and swinging hockey sticks. After snowstorms, I would look down from my window to see oxen dragging logs chained together in a v-shape to break out the road. Our lessons were accompanied by the jangle of sleigh bells flitting up and down the hill, and when I recognized the heavier chorus of Harry's Swiss bells, I would look down to see Mother or Uncle Peter swooshing by.

In grade 6, I was in Flossie (Florence) Dunn's class, and that year I sat by a window that looked out the back of the school and up the river. Throughout the seasons and in every kind of weather, I watched the rise and fall of the tides, in and out, as if the ocean were taking long, deep breaths. At high tide, the river broadened into a boulevard for all the traffic that coursed up and down: powerboats, steamers and the lovely schooners, the tips of their yardarms reaching to the hills. Sometimes, the Packet

The Packet towing a barquentine, photo taken at Oakdene.

would chug by like a locomotive, towing a loaded schooner out to the Bay and trailing a heavy black streamer. One spring at log-driving time, men assembled a huge timber raft and floated it down river like a desert island. After concentrating on my studies for a while, I would look up to see that low tide had exposed the river to be little more than a trout stream. Large schooners would sit high and dry, clinging to the wharf. They reminded me of swans, graceful in the water but ungainly on land. Meanwhile on the mud flats, patches of sea grass lay like tousled hair, the seagulls pecked for leftovers, and the clams got on with their day.

Below my window stood a small patch of playground where girls skipped and played hopscotch. Brazen boys would jump through on their way down to the playing field, one of the few pieces of level ground in the village. Bear River sat in the saddle of steeply rising hills, so you were either going up or down. The front and backs of houses stood at odds. Dr. Lovett's front door sat level with the street, but a step out the back door would be a 40-foot fall into his tennis court. Across the street at Dr. Campbell's, one had to climb steep stairs to enter his office. The villagers built their homes wherever they could put a notch in the side of a hill, and everyone was more or less a cliff dweller.

Nova Scotia Archives and Record Management

Low tide at the Clarke wharf.

The playing field was fronted by the river, so every year it flooded during the spring run-off, forcing children to higher ground. Otherwise, the field remained the exclusive preserve of the baseball players. For that glorious hour and a half at lunchtime, the hills rang out with the excited shouts of children as the crack of the bat put the ball in play. The boys would call out warnings as home runs scattered our hopscotch games. Prodigious hits to the opposite field crashed through a row of oak and into the Presbyterian graveyard. At low tide, foul balls plopped into the mud flats, but at high tide they splashed into deep water and set sail for the Bay. Players would race to the shoreline and unleash a torrent of stones to coax the ball back to shore. Pant legs would be rolled up for the advance into knee-deep water, while other boys would bring up long branches held in reserve for this eventuality. They snared most balls, but not before some brave soul had taken a soaking. Occasionally, a ball would evade their efforts and sail off to adventure. I suspect that a cache of old baseballs sits at the bottom of the Bay of Fundy.

After school, the young men of the village baseball team practiced and played while onlookers lined the embankment of the steep hill, shouting their excitement. After watching our first baseball game, Daniel and I anxiously wanted to play. We loitered after school and learned the rules, but Dad thwarted me with that common refrain: baseball was unladylike. I didn't mind, because I had no intention of setting foot on that damp soil, not only because of the overflow from the river, but also because of the ominous seepage that occasionally oozed down the hill from the school outhouse. When the Cherry Carnival brought the merry-go-round to that damp sports field, I stood well off, listening to the haunting calliope music as the horses galloped up and down.

The Carnival evolved from the midsummer harvest of that fruit, when families would pour into town, rent a tree and pick it clean. Picnics in the orchards soon included games, music, and before long, a parade to make everything official. Cherry Sunday became a full day of fun, once church was out of the way. The Carnival suffered a hesitation when blight cut into the orchards, but Bear River was nothing if not the Cherry Orchard of Nova Scotia, and enough trees survived in gardens and back yards to keep up appearances. The Reades had a number of cherry trees, so did the River View Lodge. Merton Yorke bragged about his grandfather's cherry trees, saying they were the best in Bear River. They were nice enough, six of them lined up in front of the house, but not nearly as nice as Dad's ox-hearts. Merton was always so eager to one-up, and he did succeed on occasion. One Sunday morning, he and his brother were sitting in their brand new car waiting for their father. Merton, never one to sit still, got out to stretch his legs just as another car came hurtling down Oakdene Hill, its brakes gone. Merton scrambled for cover as it smashed into the Yorke car and somersaulted, launching its two occupants out the opened roof. The Anglican and Presbyterian churches both emptied, and when it was discovered that no one was hurt, both claimed credit for the miracle, since prayers were being offered at the time. The Baptists across the river scoffed. Mr. Yorke was then modernizing his smithy into a car repair, so it was a simple matter of pushing the cars down the driveway, the joke being that it was no way to get customers. This happened just before school started, so Merton won kudos for the best summer story, though his brother, who suffered the impact, had little to say.

The Yorke cherry trees survived the crash after a fluttering of leaves, and during the cherry season, we would see Merton and Denzel crawling among the branches and filling baskets. No one dared climb their trees, though all boys were expert in the art of pilfering fruit: a quick shinny up the trunk, the toss of a few pears down to waiting friends, a shout from the

Swimming races at the Cherry Carnival, 1920s, looking to Chapel Hill.

owner waving a shotgun, and a mad dash across a field and over a fence. Legend had it that years ago one farmer did fire his shotgun, and Dr. Lovett had to pick birdshot out of a backside. The village boys made good use of their fruit-gathering skills at Carnival time by hiring themselves out to pick cherries and then running in the obstacle races.

On calendars hanging on walls across both counties and around the Bay, Cherry Sunday stood out as a red-letter day, not to be missed. Tourists, friends and relatives timed their visits for Carnival day and stuffed the little village full. Boatloads of revellers would wave to us as they passed the farm and sped towards the village. Along Main Street, storefronts stood patriotically draped in red, white and blue, the banners, flags and bunting waving in the breeze to greet the throng. The day began with a Calithumpian parade, meaning that people could show off their silly side. Amid horns and whistles from onlookers, the brass band opened with a raucous din as it marched down Main Street like precision traffic. Horses festooned in tribute to the cherry blossom pulled wagons ridiculously disguised as trains, buildings or storefronts. More wagons had people in costume acting their part, while clowns hovered nearby, acting up. They struck randomly, offering balloons or squirts of water to inquisitive children, their natural prey. Trucks and wagons became floats and passed by en tableau, illustrating scenes like a window display: Indians poised with tomahawks, oblivious of a sea of palefaces; farmers hoeing the same old patch of ground;

Cherry Carnival, 1925. The black horse is Bob and the grey horse is Rocky.

woodsmen mechanically chopping. Another float featured the local barbershop quartet, their delicate harmonies lost in the commotion. The crowd would give a visiting band from Annapolis or Digby a polite interlude, likewise for the Masons, always dignified in their top hats and aprons, like Cordon Bleu chefs out for a stroll. The Boy Scouts marched meaningfully, and after the baseball team had tipped their caps and all parade possibilities were exhausted, it was time for the games to begin. The clean-up crew would remove every horsey remnant from Main Street, a helpful prelude to the foot races: 50-yard dashes, obstacle courses, sack races, three-legged races. The popular horse races took place in a field on the edge of town, where husbands with money to squander had better odds of avoiding their wives. When the high water came in, onlookers lined the wharves for canoe races, canoe tipping, swimming races, the greased pole, and one year a novelty called 'landing the human fish', which described it perfectly. Bands played from the bandstand and excitement percolated all day long. At one point, the woodsmen took over with logrolling and a manly display of wood chopping. I loved it. Throughout the day and at various points in town, the ladies fed the hungry mob with meals, snacks and treats. Every year, one group or another staged the Carnival and collected the proceeds. One year, it was the baseball team, which had just formed and was representing the village in motley make-do's. Another year, the village needed fire-fighting equipment; it had been a number of years since the last inferno and people were getting nervous. The highlight of the afternoon was a life-or-death baseball game against Digby, Weymouth or Windsor, our one-time shipbuilding rivals. The highlight of the evening was a play put on by locals in Oakdene Hall, followed by a dance for the adults, thus bringing the Cherry Carnival to a close, a year's worth of fun packed into one day. Then Main Street would slip back into its comfortable routine, accompanied by the buzz of flies and horses quietly clopping along.

The top floor of Oakdene held the large assembly hall where we staged pageants for Halloween, Christmas, Easter and Empire Day (celebrating Canada in poem, play, skit and song). School choirs, quartets and orchestras performed for the village, and since every child in town took music lessons, recitals occurred with numbing frequency. At other times, locals gathered for plays during Chautauqua and the Cherry Carnival. Chautauqua travelled from town to town like a circus, once a year bringing entertainment and edifying speeches to the hinterland. Otherwise, the village entertained itself. Alice's sister Eileen was an active thespian, so on our walks to school she told us all about the busy Bear River theatre scene. Amanda Simon sang in a minstrel show, playing Madame Queen and singing a song called, "Spress Yo'seff." The Major acted with a group called The Pastime Players in *So This Is London*. June Schmidt starred in *Patty Makes Things Hum*, and they toured the valley to rave reviews. Staid Jesse Harris played in *Yimmie Yonson's Yob* about a suspect Swede. Mr. Dukeshire, the basso profundo village butcher, did a song and dance act in blackface that left the crowd in stitches. The whole village was in on the act. No committee or church meeting ended without a performance. Every week, some group staged a spectacle. And on the night of a big play, the entire village stuffed into Oakdene Hall. Most sat in the audience, some had to stand, and the rest trod the floorboards of Oakdene.

Not only did Oakdene Hall serve as a hub on par with the Trading Company, but the entire school occupied the village as a pastime of sorts. Trustees made sure the money was well spent, the School Board made sure the teachers were teaching, and the Women's Institute made sure of everyone. The Ladies Auxiliary served hot cocoa at lunch, interloped among the classrooms, and looked for dust in corners. Churches made sure we were en route to heaven, and nurses and doctors made sure it would not be too soon. The Home and School Board accommodated pushy parents, and since everyone paid their school tax, everyone put in their two cents' worth. Oakdene lay like an open book, with the *Bear River Courier* printing everything, even students' marks, making one's intelligence a matter of public record. Luckily, Merton Yorke set the bar low.

The same oversight obtained for the village as a whole. Since it straddled two counties, Bear River never had a proper town council. Instead, the many volunteer groups kept things ticking with frugal efficiency: the Board of Trade, the Masons, the Oddfellows and Rebekah Lodge (the women's branch), a multitude of church groups, the Agricultural Society, the Great War Veterans Alliance, and the all-powerful Women's Institute, simply known as The Institute, or, as some men slyly put it, The Institution.

Mr. Yorke was a constable, our only visible sign of the law. Ralph Purdy, who clerked at the Trading Company, was a health warden when he wasn't on stage. We had fire inspectors and livestock inspectors and custom collectors—a place for everyone and everyone in their place. Special committees sprang up like mushrooms in response to problems or projects: street lighting, sidewalks, the war memorial. Like the trestling under Main Street, committees and sub-committees bolstered the little village: the Roads Committee, the Cleanup Committee, something called the Publicity Committee, the Health Committee, which met for the benefit of young ladies.

Governance called for a continual involvement, not just the ticking of a box on election day. Evenings were busy, and everyone got roped in, everyone but Mother and Dad. Dad was away too often and Mother was too frazzled at the end of the day to run the village. But Uncle Peter became a director of the Red Cross, which got him out of the house. At school and according to grade, the Red Cross Club had the 'Happy Hearts', the 'Busy Bees', and the 'Live Wires.' Uncle Peter used his pull, and then he used his push to make a Live Wire out of me. I was on my way to solid citizenry.

Nova Scotia Records and Archive Management

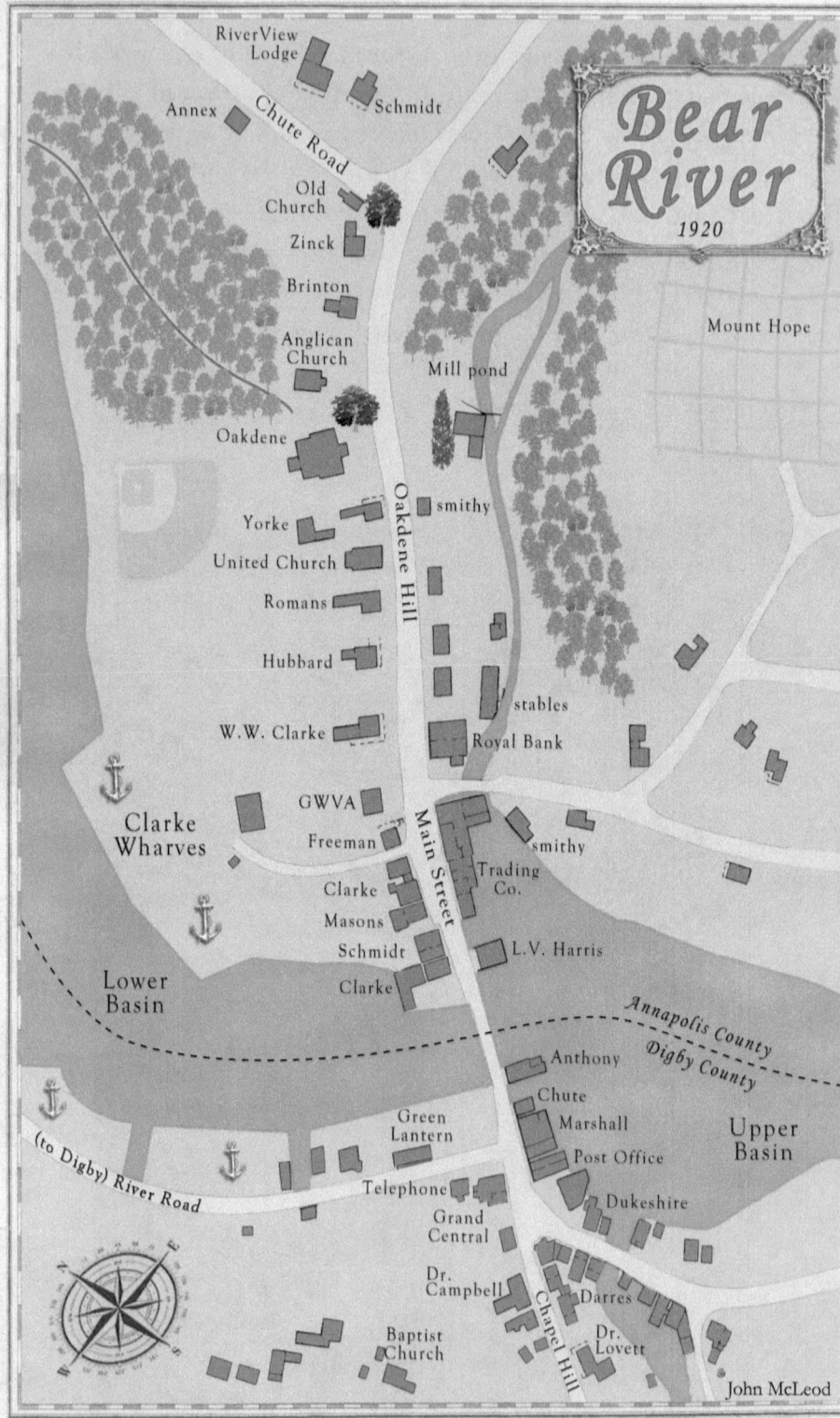

BEAR RIVER WAS A dockside frontier town of indefinite architecture, if it could be called architecture at all—not a scroll or a column or a curlicue in sight. A door was simply a vehicle to be opened, a window to be looked in or out of. Perhaps the lack of embellishment indicated the practicality of the builders that has kept the buildings standing on their pinions for over a century. One may question their wobbly strength, yet the slippery fringes of the twice-daily tides swirl away as always and nothing has collapsed into the poisonous mud flats.

Initially there was a concentration on the immediate needs of the citizens: the spires of the several churches upheld the faith of the few hundred worshippers; the half-dozen stores kept them well supplied; Dr. Lovett and Dr. Campbell preserved their health; visitors stayed at the Grand Central or the River View Lodge—all very compact, just what a small town needed. Those who craved the hedonism of the jazz age made their way to Digby for movies, dance halls and fine dining. There was none of this excitement in Bear River, except for Cherry Sunday in July and the fall exhibition of local crafts and cattle judging. Otherwise, gatherings were in church halls or the school auditorium. There was a dearth of thirst quenchers, and the only watering hole other than Mr. Darres' ice cream parlor was Mrs. Copeland's temporary tea shop. One day after a trip to Barr's barbershop, Mother and I made a day of it by paying a visit. We climbed stairs at the side of the Trading Company and entered a long, narrow, almost cavernous room, the bare floorboards echoing our footsteps. Mother allowed me anything I wanted, and I made my selection from a small counter holding cakes, cookies and sandwiches wrapped in white napkins. We settled in to a small table by a window, and Mother nodded polite hellos while I discovered the infinite utility of the pleasant interlude.

The W.W. Clarke house, with a moose head on the verandah

Outside, the view looked up Oakdene Hill to the jewel-like home of W.W. Clarke, lemon yellow with white trim and a wide, embracing verandah scooping around the house. I could never decide which of the lovely Clarke homes I wanted to live in. Next door, perched on an embankment and accommodated by high stairways were the large homes of the widowed Mrs. Hubbard and Mrs. Romans. Since these homes were so high up, one could only see the windows and porches that preserved their details and privacy. Across the street in the Oddfellows building, the Royal Bank managed the village finances, while through a side door, Dr. Roop maintained the village teeth. Behind the bank, a long livery stable held dozens of stalls, where horses could be parked in inclement weather, protected from rain and snow while their owners conducted business in the commercial hub. In temperate weather, Mother would leave Harry at the hitching post in front of the Trading Company. There he could gaze at the old cannon barrel that stood quixotic at the corner, sentinelling the store—was it a memorial or an artifact?[1]

---

1 An artifact. The cannon barrel is said to be a relic of the Fenian raids (1866-1871). The Fenians were a rogue element of American society, Irishmen who hated all things British, and to prove it they wanted to invade Canada, and they did. Nova Scotians armed themselves, but never had to fire a shot. The cannon barrel sits there still.

Courtesy of The Admiral Digby Museum

Up Oakdene Hill. Left is the GWVA, right is the Oddfellows building with the Royal Bank on the main floor, front right is the cannon barrel.

Mr. W. G. Clarke's Bear River Trading Company was a sprawling emporium full of everything needed to make life perfect: lollipops, dolls, toys, scribblers, dresses, shoes, anything and everything for the needs of people and animals, all served with that old-world courtesy, free with every purchase. The Clarke schooners sailed the world, returning with fashions from New York and London, pongee silk and kimonos from Japan, tea from China and India, candied ginger from Jamaica. My little girl wonder whirled dizzily round and round.

Entering via the door at the cannon barrel, we stepped into the dry goods department, which looked like a panelled library with its dark oak display cases, drawers, cubicles and a long polished counter fronted by twirling stools. I will always retain the excitement of walking in and breathing that perfumed luxury of newness: new clothes, new shoes, everything fresh and new. Overtones of perfume wafted through the air: roses, violets and lemon verbena in ornate decanters, waiting to be carefully dripped into vials. Behind the counter were floor-to-ceiling shelves stacked with bolts of every kind of material: serges, satins, ginghams, cashmeres, homespun, broadcloth. Presiding over this treasure trove was the genteel Miss Van Buskirk: tall, grey-haired, slim and spectacled.

She would efficiently heft bolts of material onto the counter, flip-flopping them out and deftly scissoring. Mother often chatted with her at length, so I would slip off my stool and browse, looking at ribbons for my hair, gloves, shoes, or purses to hold all the clutter of necessity.

Through an archway at the side was the grocery department, where the air livened with the penetrating scent of the river. Huge barrels lined the wall, fat and tubby, filled with silvery herring packed glassy-eyed. Other barrels held dried cod smoked to a pungent amber, cod flattened into salty cardboard remnants, pickled salt pork and other briny substances. Behind the long, L-shaped counter, Ralph Purdy and Will Brinton stood at your service, green visors shading their eyes, pencils permanently latched behind ears. I loved it when Ralph Purdy hung his bushy moustache over the counter and handed me a hard candy, a piece of heaven for a small child. Sometimes he would give me a lollypop, and I would be in rapture. As clerks filled orders, we stared in fascination at the large brass weight scale, the springs and levers aligning to take the measure of all things. The cash register was just as intriguing with its pop-up numbers, slide-out drawer, and a tune that rang like cold hard cash. Bolted to the counter was a sturdy iron frame holding a double roll of brown wrapping paper.

The Trading Company in the 1920s, "the best general store in western Nova Scotia." The dry goods entrance is near the cannon barrel.

From a spool near the ceiling, a piece of twine dangled down like a stray thought, occasionally tapping at Will Brinton's head. Wheels of cheese lay stacked under glass at the ell of the counter, while overhead hung sides of bacon on large hooks. Ralph Purdy would lower a slab and slice it, always with the rind left on. After a glance at the scale, he would swipe a piece of paper, reach up for the twine and spin a neatly tied bundle. Then a quick scribble on the package, and back behind his ear the pencil would snap. In those days, brown paper covered most purchases, so a trip to the village ended with a stack of parcels wrapped like presents from a sensible Santa: cold cuts and soup bones, socks and school supplies.

In front of the counter and in the middle of the room stood the pot-bellied stove, the conversational hub of the village, its radiating warmth exerting a magnetic pull on the men of Bear River. In the winter, a seating arrangement of apple barrels and packing crates made it the coziest spot in town. Men would come and go as they went about their day, but the conversation carried on with a life of its own. The door would swing open with a wintery blast as one man left and another man entered, shivering and clapping his hands as he approached the stove. The brief draft would prompt concern about the cold, and all would agree

To the left is the Trading Company. To the far right is Mr. Freeman's leather store, Clarke Brothers is the next two buildings, then the Masons.

to another log on the fire before another word could be spoken. One of the men would delicately open the iron door, fearful of singeing his fingers, then toss in a log and rustle the coals with a poker. Their comfort thus assured, the men would carry on discussing all their favourite topics: the latest cars; steamships; the stock market; Jack Dempsey's fights; the gangsters of Chicago; Mackenzie King and the looming election. I remember thinking how everyone seemed so brilliant in debate. Despite the heightened discussion about headlines, the only real interest came down to the operation of the farm: the revolving seasons, too much rain or not enough, feed prices rising and crop prices falling. During spring plowing, the farmers always complained about their crop of stones. Over the course of the winter and in defiance of gravity, buoyant fieldstones would mysteriously surface from some rocky reservoir, lurking like leftover turnips to crack plowpoints. Long before the green-up, rocks were the first crop of the year, as welcome as weeds. Farmers would load them onto a low sled called a stoneboat and heave them onto a rock pile, Sisyphus-like.

With all the hills and rocks, Bear River was not good crop country, so farms remained family-sized, growing the basics and not much more: potatoes, corn, turnips and such. When Dad broke ranks to sell chili peppers and purple eggplant, he shocked the pot-bellied crowd. People bought them, but not in Bear River. The Trading Company, true to its name, gave credit for crops and shipped them off to market in St. John or Boston. In those days, general stores were clearing houses for anything a farmer had to sell. Sometimes I would see our produce for sale in the Trading Company, and other times I would see our crates being loaded on the Packet for parts unknown. During the hunting season, the Trading Company took in venison and moose meat; during the butchering season, they took in hogs. Butter and eggs were currency like dimes and quarters. One popular story told of a difficult customer, a farmer down on his luck. He brought in a few pounds of butter and the clerk credited his account. Later, the clerk opened up the butter to find a rock inside, which he returned in a later purchase.

Once when I went with Dad on a delivery, he explained that ever since the war, the cost of everything had been rising, while the prices farmers got for their produce had been dropping. The larger farms in the province compensated for lower prices by delivering more crops using McCormack harvesters and other machinery. This was why Dad decided to specialize in early market gardening. Others like the rock-butter farmer had not adapted and found themselves selling their produce at ever-lower prices. They thought the Trading Company was cheating them, but Dad said Clarke Brothers gave top dollar. And Mother always mentioned how generous they had been during Dad's early days of destitution. The Trading Company knew everybody's struggle and strife, but it was also common knowledge that they carried the debts of many farmers. Back then, customers put most purchases on account, and everyone ran a balance, Dad included. I don't ever recall him paying in cash, though I often went along when he paid down his balance. At the back of the store and behind a wicket, Mr. W. G. Clarke's high desk sat beside a wall safe large enough to walk into. I always wondered about the detail on the door of that safe, and one day Mr. Clarke took the time to explain it: the tasteful gold lettering and elegant geometrics surrounding a pastoral scene of two boys going fishing, every element bearing some significance to the firm. That door carried an obvious pride, a reminder that every dollar behind it stayed true to those two boys.[2] Mr. Clarke, who seemed much older then, was in a reminiscent mood that day as he discussed the changing business climate and the inevitability of the catalogue companies. In villages across Canada, Eaton's and Simpson's catalogues were making inroads with lower prices and a larger selection. Meanwhile, the general stores had to carry on like the local bank, giving customers long lines of credit, not charging interest, and absorbing frequent write-offs. I once heard an exasperated clerk say yes, he would match the Eaton's price, "and I'll give it to you in four days," the time it took a mail order to arrive.

Other than offering unlimited credit, the Trading Company stayed competitive by bringing in goods from overseas. Shelves lining the walls of the grocery department were filled with exotic tins and jars: English jams, huge boxes of German biscuits, the 10 lb boxes of imported chocolates that Dad bought for Mother. Against the back wall, burlap bags of coffee beans from South America lay stacked beside 50 lb bags of flour, sugar and cornmeal. Nearby stood a bulwark of barrels: molasses from Puerto Rico, pickles, hearty pilot biscuits and crackers. One tale told of a clerk who

2 There's a picture on page 594.

closed up shop but didn't notice an open spigot on a barrel of molasses. He returned in the morning to find the floor coated an inch thick. Another story involved Mother's brother John, who had died of his war wounds. Years ago, he visited Bear River and was chatting in the Trading Company when an Englishman piped up that the Scots couldn't fight. Uncle John disagreed by picking him up and dumping him in the pickle barrel. Uncle John offered to pay for the pickles, but the clerk laughed it off, saying his pickles were tougher than that.

Beyond the grocery department was a section with kitchenware, household items, and the beautifully-crafted Micmac supplies: buttery-smooth leather goods, soft and beaded; fragrant sweetgrass baskets, a scent of summer fields; expertly-carved woodworking, from knick-knacks to axe handles. For the sportsmen, they made fishing baskets, trumpet-like moose calls, even birch-bark canoes. Guides were essential to hunting parties and could be hired at the Trading Company. The Micmac were renowned for their tracking skills, so it was a decided advantage in the tourist trade to have them right there. With the pulp mill gone, logging camps disappearing, and farming a death wish, tourism was our last gasp. We had the Micmacs, we had the moose, and we had the backwoods creeping into our backyards. From his moose-hunting trips, Dad knew several guides, and he said that as well as being expert woodsmen, they were also marvellous storytellers, entertaining everyone at night with tales from the beginning of time. There were also the usual ghost stories about long-lost hunters and dead bears holding a grudge, but I do recall one story about a logjam. The Micmac were unusually sure-footed and excelled at log driving, often working the large drives in Maine or New Brunswick. Log driving was wet, dangerous work, done during the spring melt to get the timber down river to the mill. With long pikes in hand, they would poke and prod the logs downstream, scampering among them like water spiders. At the pot-bellied stove, I heard about a huge logjam in New Brunswick. Thousands of logs filled the river, backed up for a mile by a pick-up stick arrangement lodged in a waterfall. Jams were often caused by one obstinate log called a 'jam dog', and this time it came down to one young driver of unusual courage volunteering to chop it free. After shaking hands and saying goodbye to his friends, he tiptoed onto the jam, swung his axe at the log and ran for dear life as the creaking mass burst like a broken dam. He survived, but once or twice we heard of a driver perishing, swallowed up by the logs and never found.

Hardware and farm implements filled the far end of the store, while spilling outside was a feed section for animals and nutrients for the gardens. Nearby stood Bear River's only gasoline pump, the gas shipped in smelly barrels and unloaded incident-free at the Packet wharf. Customers needing kerosene brought their own jugs and filled them by turning a hand-cranked pump on a barrel. Everyone had kerosene lamps then, even those with electricity, because the power shut off at midnight. Electricity was priced by the light bulb, water was priced by the tap, and the pipes didn't extend to the stores above the river. Once, when Mother took too long with Miss Van Buskirk, I had to use the washroom and looked down in horror at the river swirling below. I grimly held on to the seat so I wouldn't drop through. For the benefit of all, the Bear River's twice-daily tides came in and scrubbed the mud flats spotless, much like the mythical river Alpheus, diverted by Hercules to effect a quick clean-up.[3]

When Mother finished her shopping, men would heave 100 lb bags of feed on to our wagon, and we would continue along Main Street. In the front of the Trading Company was the luxury of a concrete sidewalk. Other stores still had wooden planks that became slippery with mud. Main Street was unpaved, blowing dust in the summer, bogged with mud in the spring and fall, and the ruts freezing solid in the winter.

Beside the Trading Company and standing all alone above the water was Mr. Harris' Drug Store. There were many Harrises and Chutes in the village, perhaps related, but seemingly unrelated. We were always running in the drugstore to have film developed or to fill Dad's prescriptions for aspirin. Mrs. Harris seemed the prickly type, posed behind the heavy oak counter with her red hair and stringent smile. At her back were shelves filled with powders and potions in large glass jars, labelled in Latin to compound the mystery. I recognized some names from the chemistry lab at school, where boys were always trying to blow something up. Other jars held strange herbs and extracts, like the elements of some ancient art. And some jars didn't seem to belong at all: licorice, cinnamon, chrysanthemum (an essential ingredient of spelling bees).

3   The fifth labour of Hercules was the cleaning of the Augean stables.

Glass showcases held neatly stacked displays of emulsions, pastilles and patent medicines. Minards's Liniment cured man or beast of life's ills. Lydia Pinkham's compound (18% alcohol) promised to lift women out of various crises. Beecham's pills modestly claimed to clean out your liver once and for all. Dr. Chase's Nerve Food could either calm them down or fire them up. Pharmacy bordered on alchemy, seeking to turn the elements into that elusive elixir, not of youth, but of simple good health.

The Harrises had two red-haired, somewhat noxious boys, Walter and Lenfest. Several times they pilfered from the store and distributed the goods in the schoolyard: cough drops, pastilles and other poor substitutes for candy. Each time, they earned themselves a thrashing from their father, who had to measure his reputation as carefully as he filled a prescription. Mr. Harris was a slight, serious man who didn't make a point of chatting with children. I would see him in his back room filling prescriptions, poking his head out once in a while to quietly ask for an ingredient. He looked like a chemist in his white coat, surrounded by jars and vials, carefully grinding with a mortar and pestle. On a wall at the front of the store hung a 'show globe', a glass jar filled with coloured water, displayed to instil confidence that the pharmacist was indeed an expert.[4] Dr. Lovett confirmed as much one day as he wrote a prescription for Dad. We were sitting in his office and he mentioned how glad he was to have Mr. Harris; that a good pharmacist was a life and death necessity. Bear River had always done without until one day Dr. Lovett tired of making his own prescriptions. He lacked expertise and worried about killing his patients off so soon after curing them. He canvassed about for a pharmacist and found Mr. Harris, convincing him to quit the city for our rural charms by offering to set him up in a store of his own in a town full of customers. He fit in perfectly, and several years ago while making inquiries, I was happy to hear that Mr. Harris, into his eighties, was still busy in his back room, quietly measuring and mixing.

Across from the Trading Company was the Great War Veteran's Association. Dad would go in every once in a while with a letter in hand to see Captain Morgan, head of the local branch. Bear River was filled with returned men, many who came back wounded and now had to battle bureaucracy.

---

[4] Before the mortar and pestle symbol, show globes designated a pharmacist.

In my class, it seemed as though everyone's father had fought. Clarke Fraser's father had been seriously wounded; so had Lawrence Henshaw's. Merton Yorke's father came back, but not the brother. Mrs. McCormick had a son buried in France and wanted to visit his grave but knew she never would. To bring the men home, if only in name, the Women's Institute campaigned for years for a war memorial that they were funding with bake sales and quilting bees. One year, they hung a series of celebrated war paintings in Oakdene and charged admission. Every fall, they ran the poppy campaign, the poppies made by the men of Camp Hill. I often wondered if Dad had a hand in any of them. I never asked. Year after year, as time pulled one veil after another over the war, the old soldiers fell. Uniformed men would march the casket up Mount Hope and form up at the grave. Then a lonely last post would sound across the hill to Oakdene. We heard every note.

Among their other duties, the Ladies Auxiliary of the GWVA also ran a tearoom for the shoppers who swarmed into town on Saturday nights, when the stores stayed open until midnight. In those days when most Canadians lived on a farm, the Saturday night shopping spree was a small-town tradition, the highlight of the week and not to be missed. As small as Bear River was, it served as the commercial centre for many outlying communities: the lumber camps, the Micmac reservation, Victory, Morganville, Clementsvale, Lansdowne and all the farms in between. For farmers, a week full of long days in the fields offered no more society than the mumblings of cows and other animal chatter. Farming was lonely work, and one tired of nature and her many moods. Sanity required humanity and the structure of civilization. So every Saturday night, the country came to the village to sell, stock up and socialize. One summer night Dad took us in, and I was amazed at the transformation on Main Street. It was like the Cherry Carnival, with buggies and wagons crowding the street, the brass band playing from the bandstand, and people everywhere. Busy wives scurried from store to store, a list in hand and a husband in tow. A group of men stood at the wagons, their banter rising gleefully when a wife summoned one of the gang from a storefront down the street. In the Trading Company, men stood around the stove, while a counter full of clerks briskly filled orders. Outside, farmers unloaded produce: vegetables, butter, eggs, and poultry as Ralph Purdy, pencil in hand, quickly inspected the goods and agreed on a price. After Dad had the boys carry our groceries out to the wagon, he let us wander Main Street while he chatted with friends. At Mr. Darres', a group had gathered around the radio. The Green Lantern was showing a movie. People stood talking and laughing in front of Mr. Marshall's store. Nearby, horses stood patiently at their wagons, munching on feedbags and eyeing all the activity. Occasionally, a whinny from the stables would prompt a reply at the wagons; everyone was catching up. In looking back, Saturday night shopping resembled a church bazaar–a pleasant exchange of money and conversation with everyone far removed from the cares of the week.

At nightfall, Dad pulled up the wagon and we climbed aboard. Harry lugged us up Oakdene Hill, past the school until we were high above the lights of the village. By the time we turned on to the Chute Road, the bustle of Main Street had been replaced by night noise and a thick, heavy curtain of darkness. I had travelled the Chute Road at night once before, when a full moon and fresh snow lit the way, but this night offered no such vista. It was very dark. Harry clopped along through a shadowy canyon of trees, while overhead, a reclining crescent moon hung like an ornament. We sat in the creaking wagon, peering into the darkness and looking for landmarks. Houses passed by in swatches of black, the road ahead a faint ribbon of grey. At the orchards, the road opened up under a dome of stars–ancient heroes fixed in their place like a moral compass, a vast menagerie ruled by noble Pegasus, the winged horse, Harry's only rival. Ursa Major[5] led to talk about bears and all our other late-night predators: foxes, coyotes, bobcats, lynx. Once, we heard of a bear taking a Sunday stroll through town, thinking he fit right in. Several times, a moose wandered through someone's gardens, looking for a change in diet. There he was, the monarch of the glen, posed on stilts high above the carrots. But you could never trust a moose because they liked to come charging out of the bush for no good reason. The boys loved to frighten me, and that night Daniel swore he saw antlers. Then he heard a grunt, yes, a bear, a hungry one, he could tell, why did we have to be carrying groceries? And who knew what the Micmac were up to. Nighttime was busy, with one half of nature out to eat the other half.

5 The Great Bear, home of the Big Dipper

Daniel and Jim then reminded me of all the rumours that filtered in from the backwoods about cougars and timber wolves; people had seen tracks. Dad said no, not in Nova Scotia, they were probably large bobcats or coyotes, which seemed just as bad. Dad then asked, "Did ah evah tell yew about the dancing rabbits?" Yes he had, and it was the strangest thing. One night, he came to a clearing and saw dozens of rabbits running in a circle under a full moon, jumping and circling in a scene from a square dance. Dad's story seemed almost supernatural, but I believed it because Douglas had seen tracks when he went fishing in the mornings. Why did they do it? Dad couldn't say; they might be mating, or playing, or maybe the moon had cast a spell–it could do that. As we rattled past the clearing in question, we looked for movement, but a mist had settled in like a night mirage. The clearing, so familiar in the daytime, seemed haunted with its shadowed walls and ghostly floor. At the Crossroads, we angled down into the pitch-black cavern of the avenue of maples, where I couldn't see my hand in front of my face. Dad lit the lantern for Harry to cross Rice's bridge, and our shadows stretched and jumped between the trees like puppetry, animating the scene so that the darkness itself moved. Even at the farm, the landscape had shifted, and we raced inside for the comfort of our pillows. Night changed everything, draining all colour and leaving a shaded underworld, ruled by a restless, meddlesome moon.

Sunday mornings when Dad was home meant one thing above all else–lollipops–bought Saturday night and distributed Sunday mornings if we had been good, which we always were, even if we hadn't been. For the rest of the village, Sunday mornings meant church, and everyone attended. Perhaps there were other Catholics in the village, but I didn't know of them. If there were, they would have had to wait for the one Sunday a month when Father Mackay motored in from Annapolis Royal to conduct service at St. Anne's on Indian Hill. To get there, one had to go beyond the village to the Head of the Tide and up a steep hill on the Micmac reservation. I suppose we could have made the effort at some point in our dozen or so years in Bear River, but we never got around to it. Besides, we already had a Sunday ritual. Mother rested in bed with her cafe au lait and a book, while Dad stood at the stove making our favourite breakfasts. After breakfast he gave us our lollipops, and if we didn't eat them right away, we could save them to get us through the Bible reading. Still, when the Sunday bells rang across the hills in their jangled chorus, it sounded as if God Himself was swooping down for a visit and perhaps we should be there. And the churches looked so pretty with their crisp white clapboard, lined like the pages of an untold story, topped by a steeple pointing to heaven in exclamation. I preferred the columned elegance of the Baptist steeple, windowed like a Captain's walk and topped by a gold dome. It promised a heaven done in seaside colonial, the rooms tastefully filled with Chippendale, Queen Anne, and Dad's brass. The Presbyterian and Anglican churches opted for the modesty of a simple spire, which only incurred God's wrath via repeated lightning strikes. When we quizzed our friends about church, their answers made it seem like just another chore. Alice attended the Presbyterian Church and could only recall sitting, kneeling and singing. Evelyn Reade attended the Baptist Church and could only vouch for the snacks after service. I didn't bother asking the children of the clergy, who strode the school hallways by divine right. But I did like the Reverends with their pleasant hellos as they went about their daily rounds. I was taken aback when they acknowledged me by name in spite of my heathen status. They seemed like everyone's favourite uncle rather than an emissary of the Almighty. They cheered on the baseball team and handed out prizes at the Cherry Carnival. At the Trading Company, they shopped for their wives and chatted at the pot-bellied stove. At school, they strolled through classrooms with the Inspection Committee and offered kind encouragement at concerts, plays and graduation. We saw a lot of the clergy, but this only added to the mystery, because they seemed to occupy another dimension, like artists taken by the muse. They attended every village function, but always as observers. They were neutral but not, quoting cryptic passages to offer moral fibre. Like God in the universe, they were everywhere but elusive. And that collar around their neck–like a blank space where something should be. Dad said yes, they had one foot in another world, but then he explained that the Reverends were doctors of the soul, and their work could be just as important as Dr. Lovett's. This made sense, because we often saw a Reverend and a doctor riding out on a call, sometimes racing by like an ambulance, off to a lumber camp or a lonely farm. On the Chute Road, we would see

Rev. Barrass or Rev. Mack visiting shut-ins or entering a sick house. They would mobilize the ladies of the Visiting Committee, who would march up the steps with baskets of food. Upon review, they might activate the ladies of the Charity Committee, who would smartly knock on the door and step inside. In Bear River, you couldn't be sick in peace, not until you took those first fragile steps and the Women's Institute could announce in the social column that you were back on your feet. Through quiet council, the church attended to the village, body and soul, this world and that. To finance these efforts, the parishioners held dinners, teas, garden parties, plays, and concerts—enough to exhaust anyone's charitable urge. Then on the seventh day amid bells and choirs and Ralph Purdy at the organ, God would drop in for a look-see and smile. The clergy and congregation could take stock of their efforts and be pleased. After the service, children played games or attended Sunday school, giving the parents time to chat over tea and snacks—a sociability as enjoyable as Saturday night shopping. Later in the day when the Kniffen's horse trotted by, Mother would call out for them to join us for dinner after the Sunday afternoon lull. Despite our laggard status, church infused Sundays with a soft, reflective calm. Even the air seemed quiet. I still had no desire to attend, but I thought it nice that others made the effort. Years later when we returned to the fold, I asked Dad why, and he said, "Sweetlady, it's good for the soul."

The Baptist church today, from Mount Hope

At the corner of the GWVA property stood Mr. Freeman's leather shop, where he sold harnesses and collars and all the trappings for horses and oxen. We didn't have oxen, but many farmers did. Much of the local economy was still ox-driven. We often saw teams lumbering down the road, twinned by a heavy wooden yoke. Mr. Larimore once explained that teams were paired for life from a young age and took years of training. He then demonstrated the use of the thin goad stick and called out the strange 'gee' and 'haw' that all teamsters used. The oxen responded, left and right, and then stopped after a common 'whoa.' Many farmers preferred oxen, and I often heard horses-versus-oxen debates in the Trading Company: horses were smarter and more adaptable—with the advent of cars, oxen had difficulty breaking their training to keep to the right. Yes, but oxen didn't mind the chemical spray in the orchards. But horses could take the heat at haying time. Oxen were cheaper to care for. Horses were faster. Oxen were less excitable. That was true; horses could bolt on a whim, overturning carriages and launching their equally surprised occupants into the ditch. People got hurt. Harry would never dream of doing such a thing, but on the road, Dad sat ready with the reins, alert to every twitch of Harry's ears. One had to read a horse's moods and know what kind of a day he was having. Dad knew. He grew up in the saddle in Virginia horse country. Oxen were out of the question. I once watched an ox being shod at the smithy behind the Trading Company. Ben Hill led the ox into a stall and looped slings under its belly to hoist him up with a pulley. The building creaked and I stood back, not because of the ox, but because the building clung to the riverbank in a rickety fashion and didn't seem likely to bear the weight. As Ben Hill hammered the curious, half-moon shaped shoes, he made small talk with the ox. One didn't work with an animal and not chat with him; that would be rude. Besides, animal talk was everyone's second language. On our travels, we spoke to many horses, dogs and pigs, or at least said hello in passing. I had never paid oxen much attention; they just didn't seem the conversational type, but there the ox stood, holding its own with Ben Hill. After the shoeing, the owner took possession, and the huge ox seemed almost child-like, only better behaved. I never questioned Harry's superiority, but I decided that ox and horse both had their place, and the advantages of either stemmed from a good owner.

Oxen pulling the pipeline float at the 1924 Cherry Carnival. It won first prize. To the left is Mr. Yorke, Merton and Denzel's father. To the right is Mr. Harold Davis, Isabel and Bobby's father.

Between the smithy and the Trading Company, a stone bridge arched across the Tupper Brook, which ran into the river after tumbling noisily down Oakdene Hill. Directly opposite on the Digby side, the Wade Brook followed a similar course. These two brooks defined the initial placement of the village by providing water power for grist mills and saw mills. Water power thrived at the Head of the Tide, where the power plant and several mills operated, but the village grew up around these two brooks for reasons that likely made perfect sense in those days of urgent practicality.

Opposite Mr. Freeman's and across the road that led to the Clarke wharves were two buildings housing the offices of Clarke Brothers. In passing, I would see men coming and going and heads bobbing above half-frosted windows. Next door was the Masonic Hall, also called the Keith Lodge, after Alexander Keith, a prominent Nova Scotia beer baron. His brewing skills made no inroads in Bear River. The Masons were an all-male bastion, holding their meetings on the second floor, seemingly secretive, but out on parade in their top hats and aprons whenever civic pride was called for. Their cohorts, the Oddfellows, were housed above the Royal Bank and opted for a flamboyant, military look, complete with spiked helmets. I once asked Dad about these groups, and he explained that aside from charitable works, they acted as a mutual support society. In those days before welfare, people insured themselves. As a veteran with a pension, Dad didn't feel the need to join, but anybody could, and membership offered security against calamity.

For most of our time in Bear River, the main floor of the Mason's building served a variety of part-time purposes but could never find its niche. The vacancy marred the small-town perfection of Main Street; the two plate-glass windows stared wide-eyed in hope. Then no-nonsense Mrs. Hubley blew in from the prairies like a change in the weather. She put her hands on her hips, looked around and decided that what Bear River needed most of all was fine dining. And she was right. She swept out the store, put curtains and fresh flowers in the windows, set the tables, and as quick as boiled asparagus[6], 'Ye Friendly Tea Shoppe' was catering to the dining public, a swank step up from the boarding house fare at the Grand Central, where the special of the day usually boiled down to grub. I didn't know that a woman could open a business just like that. Middle-aged Mrs. Hubley suddenly seemed daring and modern. I suspect there was no Mr. Hubley on the scene and that the vicissitudes of marriage had released her to the restaurant trade. With few options open to women back then, the one thing they all knew how to do was cook. So courtesy of Mrs. Hubley, progress swept through the village, west to east. Bear River had its first real restaurant and the change in menu caused a sensation. Our Main Street frontage beckoned unblemished, the Masons now sported a feminine touch, and women were inching their way into the business world, even if they weren't quite out of the kitchen.

Courtesy of Bob Benson

Ye Friendly Tea Shoppe

6 Emperor Augustus' favourite saying. Mary loved *I Claudius*.

Next door to the Masons, elderly Mrs. Schmidt's variety store presented a similar facade, gable end out, Greek temple style, with two large plate glass windows framing a doorway–19th century storefront vernacular. Inside, left and right, long glass counters stood in front of shelved walls. In those days, all the stores had similar cabinetry, giving them a polished, oaken elegance. On one side, curved glass showcases highlighted a selection of unnecessary necessities: games, puzzles, decks of cards, colouring books. In the back, a fragrant corner of tobacco supplies tempted the men. Women didn't dare. Along the opposite wall, large, pattern-stamped linens for embroidery hung like unfinished paintings. Cubicles held needles, thimbles, scissors and other tools of the trade. Beneath the glass counter lay a rainbow display of thread, bouquets of ribbons, pristine lace and other fripperies for the dedicated seamstress. Bulging packets of wool awaited busy fingers. If a housewife had time to sit down, she picked up her knitting. Mother knitted all of our sweaters, leggings, mittens, caps, and scarves. We spent the winter wrapped in wool. She often dropped in for supplies, and while she chatted with Mrs. Schmidt, I would wander over to the long table that ran down the centre of the store and held every child's heart's desire, a cornucopia of candy: slabs of golden taffy, mounds of dulse, large squares of sponge toffee, barley sugars, chicken bones, every flavour of lollipop, and a dazzling array of glass jars holding penny candies and other jumbled jewels.

The bell above the door would ring to announce a customer, a youngster clutching a coveted nickel, about to make one of life's most important decisions. At the table, his knitted brow betrayed a sudden interest in fractions and long division. Fingers counted out times tables. Mrs. Schmidt knew all about little children and their calculating ways. She would offer hints that less of this would buy more of that. I suspect that Mrs. Schmidt taught more math than Miss Withrow. And children listened, no fidgeting, no yawning, math suddenly mattered. With each selection, she would reach into jars to fill one of those wonderful little paper bags that fit so perfectly in a child's hand. If he was someone you knew, he would offer a honeymoon or a blackball. Friends always shared candy–the cornerstone of companionship. Every child remembers those early trips to the candy store, a first lesson in the value of money.

From promotional material for the pulp mill, showing a busy wharf and the 'Clarke's Corners' section of Main Street. Beside the packet is the bandstand,

Courtesy of The Bear River Historical Society

then a Clarke warehouse, Mrs. Schmidt's, the Masons, Clarke Brothers offices, another Clarke office and Mr. Freeman. LV Harris' drugstore is bottom right

Beside Mrs. Schmidt's, a Clarke warehouse faced the wharf where Capt. Woodworth's Packet moored. The Packet kept a busy schedule, sailing back and forth across the Bay to St. John, delivering lumber or apples or whatnot and returning with the weekly needs of the village. Bear River had many ships to call its own, beautiful schooners and barques named after locals, some living, some dearly departed. Everyone followed the progress of these ships like proud parents, but as lovely as they were, none captured the heart of the village like the Packet. It wasn't sleek or graceful, it looked like a tugboat, but its proper name was the *S.S. Bear River* and it had personality. The Packet was irrepressible, scooting about the basin like Scotty in our pasture. When it returned from St. John and rounded the last bend before the village, its cheerful whistle echoed between the hills, and everyone took note, even children in classrooms. The curious would wander down to the wharf to see who had come in, what the men were unloading, and perhaps to hear the news from across the Bay–these things were important. At his perch on the bridge stood Capt. Woodworth, quietly overseeing everything and looking the part in his blue blazer, peaked cap and bushy white beard. I suppose the Packet took its personality from Capt. Woodworth, because the two were inseparable; you could not imagine one without the other. His brother had captained the original *Bear River*, a schooner that plied the eastern seaboard, but it sank with all hands. When Clarke Brothers built the

Captain and Mrs. Woodworth, parents of thirteen.

Packet and revived the *Bear River* name, all they needed was a Woodworth at the helm. The Captain readily signed on and piloted the ship to the end of his working days. Although the village didn't have a mayor, you could say that Captain Woodworth was our fitting ambassador, respected and admired at every port around the Bay. When the Packet was moored, Dad loved to pass the time of day with Capt. Woodworth and all the sailors who gathered at the wharf to yarn. The old sea dogs were like houses on the Chute road, weathered and stripped of paint, firmly rooted and filled with memories. After school, Dad would collect us, while Capt. Morgan of the GWVA would be waiting for his granddaughter Dottie, who was in my grade. Both of her parents were dead, so it fell to Capt. Morgan, an elderly widower, to look after her. We would trail behind as Capt. Morgan and Dad chatted on their way down to the wharf. They had shared the same hospital ward at Camp Hill. The Captain always handed Dottie a penny for candy, so she and I would run into Mrs. Schmidt's and then sit on the front step that ran the length the store, eating candy and watching the Main Street bustle. After a while we would join the men. Daniel was going to sail the world, so he sat listening for every bit of information he could latch on to, to be digested and reproduced later. Bear River lore was repeated often, everyone knew the stories: the terrible storms rounding Cape Horn, dead calm in the horse latitudes, transatlantic races, the rivalries going on for years.

The Packet towing a schooner with a full deck load, 1931.

Capt. Rawding was over ninety and talked of having to crew ships in far-off ports with the shadiest characters on the waterfront, renegades from every country in the world. He took on the whole mutinous lot and then fought them for control of his ship. Local dealers would supply a crew, sometimes depositing unconscious, unsuspecting drunks on board. Captain Rawding took them all, and as was the custom, turned them into sailors, but not without a struggle. Captains often had to rule with a clenched fist. Once, the *Ethel Clarke* lost its entire crew in Buenos Aires. Another captain was stuck in New York with a loaded ship and a mutinous crew locked below deck. He had the ship towed out to sea and sailed for the Far East, taming the men along the way. One old sailor had worked on a slaver before the American Civil War and spoke of the terrible treatment meted out to the captives, usually ending in a watery grave. Daniel's favourite story was the world-famous mystery of the ghost ship *Mary Celeste*, built in a village on the Bay and found drifting in mid-ocean by a Bear River ship. The Captain stepped aboard to find an empty ship, meals half-eaten and nothing disturbed. Speculation was endless; it goes on still.

Another popular story told of a Captain who travelled with his wife and her cat. They left Bear River with a load of Clarke lumber and sailed for South America, straight into a mid-Atlantic hurricane. One by one, the masts cracked and crashed to the deck in thundering heaps. Waves washed overhead, tangling the fallen sails and rigging, but the Captain stuck to the wheel and the ship rode out the storm like a piece of cork. The next day and for a month afterwards, the crew sloshed about the deck of their slowly sinking ship, piecing together a lifeboat and diving for supplies from the sunken hold. Then on a day when the waves passed unbroken over the deck, they stepped into their makeshift lifeboat, rigged with sails and a small cabin for the Captain's wife. According to later reports, it turned out that their ship stayed afloat for some time, falling in with a flotilla of weeds and drifting about the shipping lanes making a nuisance of itself. Meanwhile, with a compass and the stars to guide him, the Captain sailed the lifeboat across open ocean and straight into a lively Caribbean port. Locals gathered to greet the unusual vessel, and after hearing the tale, carried everyone off in triumph: the Captain, his wife, the crew and the cat.[7]

---

[7] *Florence B. Edgett*, 510 tons, built in Bear River, 1890, sunk in 1902. Capt. Kay took his wife, a crew of nine and Whiskers the cat 1450 miles by lifeboat to St. George, Grenada.

One of the village's best-known sailors was Captain Parker, buried at sea years ago in the Far East. He captained the *Tamar Marshall*, Bear River's largest ship, and on one trip across the Pacific, he took credit for a dramatic rescue. A ship had foundered in mid-ocean after a storm, barely kept afloat by its cargo of lumber. For a week, through gales and rough December weather, the crew clung to the rigging without food or water, their exhaustion complete. At one point, a wave washed a sailor into the sea, but the Captain jumped in and saved him. Then on a stormy day that surely would have been their last, Captain Parker spotted the stricken ship on the horizon. Through rough seas, he pulled alongside and plucked the full complement of frozen sailors from the rigging, thawing them out in time for their Christmas dinner.

The *Alpheus Marshall* **(1096 tons)**

The last of Bear River's great captains was the town dentist's father, the aged Captain Roop. He had shipped out in his early teens and quickly rose in rank, eventually sailing the clipper ships. At the first opportunity, he switched over to steamers, but had the bad luck to be docked in a German port at the outbreak of war. They seized his ship and tossed him in a prison camp for the duration. On his release, he then had even worse luck and contracted 'sleepy sickness' (not sleeping sickness from the tse-tse fly), which broke out after the war and left victims in a terrifying, trance-like state. He recovered after a year and fled to the high seas, his whereabouts a village curiosity as he sailed from port to port looking for lost time.

Harry Morine was several grades ahead of me, barely a teenager, but he wanted to see the world and shipped out with his father. It was around Christmas time and the ship ran into a storm one night. Harry was crawling along a spar when a wave swept him into the icy blackness. They never found his body, and Harry's father returned at New Year's with the terrible news. His sisters were devastated—their only adored brother. No one blamed Mr. Morine for taking Harry along, because everyone agreed that the son was just like the father, who, as a teenager had disappeared one night, shipping out and not returning for years. In those days, ships sailed for every port, so restless boys could jump aboard and see the world by the time they were twenty. That's what Dad did. Many boys had gone to sea in their early teens and in a few short years were piloting a ship, like Captain Roop. For those with seawater in their veins, the comings and goings of the ships exerted a pull as strong as the tides. But not on me. I was a sailor's daughter born with a fear of the water, and a few near-drownings made that fear permanent. I knew I would never sail. I couldn't even step down to the wharf with the river gurgling below and the Packet heaving with the pulse of the river. Nor could I cross the bridge without fear. I ran across as fast as I could, the planks rattling loudly and the river all too evident between them.

Towing the Ethel Clarke, above and right.

The bridge was built to swing open so ships could navigate between the upper and lower basins. Then we would see large schooners being helplessly towed through by a tiny powerboat, the sturdy bulwarks inching by close enough to touch, the wide spars passing overhead cradling their neatly bundled sails. The *Tamar Marshall* was almost wrecked minutes after launch when a trick of the tides got it stuck in the bridge. As the quickly receding tide lowered the bulwarks towards the pilings, a cracked hull seemed certain. Only a frantic chopping of the bridge timbers saved the village from a terrible loss and a withering humiliation. Another ship grounded herself seconds after launch, slipping off the blocks and across the basin to the opposite shore, earning the captain dubious recognition.

Throughout the shipbuilding era, the Marshall name predominated. Alpheus Marshall built many ships, among the largest of the day. The best of them he named after his wife, his daughters, and himself, all with a likeness of the namesake carved as the masthead. They sailed the world, returning from exotic ports to fill his store with exotic merchandise. The Marshall schooners made early history, still talked about in the 1920s, world famous with enviable records. Memories flashed over the short-lived wonder of the finest Marshall schooner, praised for its speed and craftsmanship but wrecked on a reef before proving itself to the world. What was left of the illustrious history of the sailing ships? The days of glory stood sadly recalled, all dressed in grey.

The *Ethel Clarke* (433 tons) on the blocks at the Benson yard. Bear River's largest ship was the *Tamar Marshall* at 1270 tons.

Courtesy of Bob Benson

From the bridge, you looked across the upper basin to the remnants of the Marshall shipyard, once the busiest of the half-dozen yards. Little remained of it other than a muddy clearing at the water's edge, but apparently that is all the yards ever were. For a hundred years, logs floated down river to be plunked on the beach, where men would pick up their axes and start squaring timber. In the spring, the riverbanks looked like an assembly line with a dozen ships on the blocks, the skeletal frames rising to form primal hulks, dwarfing the nearby houses. The village bustled to one great purpose as blacksmiths hammered, sailmakers stitched, and carpenters rhythmically sawed. Mr. Kniffen, a Master Builder, told Dad how the tangy scent of sawdust filled the air, as welcome as the apple blossoms. The best of the Master Builders was Captain Benson, known for his skill throughout the province and beyond. Generations of Bensons oversaw the largest Bear River ships, taking their lines off of small wooden models that a child might play with, seeing in those simple curves a complete set of blueprints. Many Bear River ships were built for interests in St. John and elsewhere, so they sailed down river and never returned. The local fleet was begun by the merchants, their schooners trading up and down the eastern seaboard before returning to fill the shelves of their stores. Soon, the larger merchants, the Chutes, Harrisses, Marshalls, and Clarkes were building ships that sailed the world. In those days, Canadian-built traders covered the oceans, and chief among them was the great Bluenoser fleet. Nova Scotiamen were world-renowned for their speed and craftsmanship, racing and often beating the American clipper ships, the best of which were built by transplanted Nova Scotians. With their smaller crews and larger cargo, Bluenosers turned a tidy profit, causing a mad rush to the mud flats as towns and villages across the province jumped into the shipbuilding gold rush. The great Maritime advantage lay in the bounty of virgin timber standing mere miles inland. With a ready supply of craftsmen skilled at dinghies and dories, towns were soon launching three-masted schooners, brigs, and barquentines. As each ship sailed, shareholders followed them as closely as the stock market, and the payoff could be just as lucrative. After several voyages, the initial investment turned a profit, and ships often sailed for a decade or more. On the other hand, few ships carried insurance, and they sank with depressing regularity.

Shareholders often included the tradesmen who built the ship, so a loss might cripple a community. Bear River's first ship was said to be the *Temperance*, sunk without a trace on her maiden voyage. But the glory days were very good to Bear River and they went on for many decades. As steel hulls and steam engines ended the age of sail, the village could sit back and reflect with satisfaction on a productive youth—well over a hundred ships to its name. Then, just as nature was reclaiming the yards and new memories were crowding out old ones, Clarke Brothers announced the building of a three-masted schooner, the *Castano*. Like the arrival of a late-in-life child, everyone greeted the news with delight. After years of doing repairs and refits, Bear River craftsmen, once the best in the province, would reclaim their crown. Men trekked deep into the woods for the perfect trees to lay the perfect keel, and as the ship rose from the stocks, it sparked hopes and long-lost dreams, like a second chance at love. At the launching, everyone proudly declared it the finest Bear River ship ever, though the next one would be even better. The village waved the *Castano* down river for its maiden voyage to Cuba, and that was the last they saw of it. Reports came in of a terrible storm, and then word that a steamer in the Gulf of Mexico had passed a ship floating keel up. Was it the *Castano*? Possibly, they weren't sure. For a while, rumours surfaced about this or that ship in some far-off port looking very much like the *Castano*, but such reports were common. Many ships had sunk without a trace, some going down with hundreds aboard, only to resurface through inspired storytelling. So the *Castano* joined the *Temperance* in the great fleet of mystery ships that sailed among the shadows, the last of the Bear River schooners.

Across from the school on the Digby side was Clarke's Flats, home of our first cherry tree, another one-time shipyard, now the site of a Benson sawmill. Rumour had it that Captain Kidd, the pirate who was hanged in London and then left hanging in a dockside cage for years, had once sought refuge in Bear River before the village was settled. Locals long suspected buried treasure and zeroed in on Clarke's Flats, but their nocturnal diggings yielded only sore backs and lost sleep. Dad said the treasure had come and gone, that it wasn't to be found in buried chests, but above-ground, in the magnificent ships that traded around the world, bringing work and wealth to the entire village.

Courtesy of The Bear River Historical Society

Lake Jolly

As the shipbuilding era ended, Clarke Brothers put their extensive timber holdings to good use by building a lumber community at Lake Jolly. In the fall after the crops were in and the fields prepared for the winter, farmers would leave the comforts of home to spend winter in the rough confines of a logging cabin. The backwoods of Nova Scotia were dotted with lumber camps cut out of the wilderness to serve the sawmills. The men would shoulder their axes and trek out to the deep snow where they would chop and saw. Horses and oxen would sleigh the timber to the riverbanks, and come the thaw, log drivers would ride the spring freshet as the meltwater carried the logs to the mill. Such was the rhythm of rural Canada.

At Lake Jolly, the timber was finished into any number of items, and caravans of oxen would haul it to the village and down to the loading wharves. We often saw men stacking planks one by one into giant sheaves. Old-timers recalled a time when the wharves overflowed with lumber and the excess had to be stacked along the roads, making the village look like a lumber yard. Ships lined the wharves, their rigging threading the sky, ready to set sail for Boston, New York, Havana and Buenos Aires. But after 30 years, the forest had thinned out, leaving pulpwood as the primary resource. The Clarke sons-in-law built the pulp mill with an eye to launching Bear River into the industrial age, but the mill relied upon a new salt-water

Courtesy of Bob Benson

The pulp mill, also showing proposed shipbuilding. The Packet is at the wharf and the 'Flying Bluenose' is in the background.

cleaning process that hadn't been tested properly. It failed miserably. The infamous pipeline was then built to bring fresh water in from the Head of the Tide, but it froze in the winter and didn't supply enough water. The whole fiasco failed in a year after barely producing enough paper to file for bankruptcy. What looked like incompetence to some was seen as a swindle by others, especially the villagers who had trusted the Clarke name with their life savings. If it was a swindle, then Clarke Brothers was the primary victim, because they had mortgaged every single asset for the mill. After 50 years of carefully manicured growth, all was lost and the great firm of Clarke Brothers collapsed in a heap. While creditors sifted through the wreckage, the Trading Company carried on with W.G. in his office. W.W. kept busy with his good works. Mr. Cunningham retained his mill by the skin of his teeth, and Mr. MacIntyre fled to the U.S. bearing most of the blame. Then a suspicious fire destroyed the mill at Lake Jolly, dooming the settlement. Soon, it stood like a ghost town, waiting for Boy Scout excursions and hunting parties to stroll through empty streets past empty buildings. Backwoods lumber villages like Victory, Franklin Lake, and Morganville saw the writing on the wall and put their affairs in order. Occasionally, we would see oxen hauling lumber down from Cunningham's mill, but most of the time the wharves sat like vacant lots.

Villagers stood on the timbers to fish, poised like sentries. Boys jumped in the water, screaming and splashing the way they've always expended their restless energy. With the village reverting back to the farming community it had been at the outset, the only industry that showed any vital signs was Mr. Rice's tombstone works at the Head of the Tide. The 1920s, which began with the pulp mill and renewed hope after years of war, devolved into a nightmare of bankruptcy, lost savings, and discarded dreams, tossed aside like a losing hand.

Logging near Lake Jolly

Across the bridge on the Digby side, timber cribworks shored up the government wharf, with wide-open spaces extending along the waterfront to Main Street. Apparently, this had been the site of Bear River's most recent fire some years ago. Four or five stores had collapsed in flames, scarring Main Street, but considering that Digby, Weymouth, Windsor and others had all in turn been burnt to a crisp, fortune had indeed smiled. It was a freezing cold night, which is when this sort of thing usually happened, and the river was frozen over, but a vigorous performance by the bucket brigade saved the village. On a smaller fire years later, they further limited the damage with the judicious use of dynamite, blowing the top off a building but otherwise saving it. Mr. Rice of the tombstone works took the credit, dynamite being his tool of choice.

Sitting beside the bridge and braced by stilts stood a large building housing young Mr. Anthony's general store. Bear River once boasted five general stores, in the good old days before the great dwindling. The Anthonys were charter members of the village elite, quitting their circle only to visit relations in Boston, Montreal and Ottawa. They often took along their precious Billy, who bragged in school about the rarefied air on Beacon Hill, Westmount and Parliament Hill. Mrs. Anthony was a pleasant, precise lady with a flair for music. She sang, she played and she taught. Her church choir was the best, her classes were the best, and she taught the best pupils. As per the custom, she involved herself in village affairs, and though other ladies had more status and substance, Mrs. Anthony carried on like the queen bee. I suspect that Mother's differences with the doyennes of society extended to Mrs. Anthony and her store. I recall a hushed conversation with Dad implying that Mother had stepped in on one of the village ladies engaged in a little extra-curricular activity. Who it was, I don't know. The lady slandered Mother the way guilty parties often do, and the frost settled in. I suppose the truth eventually filtered out, because the word 'secret' has no meaning in a small town. People and their patterns become as familiar as your own, and the slightest change, real or imagined, is a gateway to gossip. So for whatever reason, the Anthony's store existed on the fringes of our society, and then it didn't exist at all. The humiliation of bankruptcy played out in public, with announcements and auctions and squabbles over scraps. The school orchestra lost its conductor when the family decamped across the Bay to St. John, leaving old Captain Anthony to gaze upon an empty store when he sat at the Packet wharf.

The Anthony family tree was cluttered with captains, and he had opened the store years ago after retiring from the sea. Like other merchants, old Captain Anthony owned a schooner to stock his shelves, the *Valdare*, which traded up and down the east coast. For thirty years the *Valdare* plied this route, first for the Anthonys and then for the Clarkes, until shortly before the bankruptcy, the *Valdare* sank on its way to Boston. In the brief time it took to cross the Gulf of Maine, it got trapped in a terrible nor'easter, the first of the season and a little bit early. Everyone heard the story of how the crew battled the storm from afternoon into night, struggling through torrents of rain, the waves cresting above the sails before swooping down to lift the ship high. The schooner pitched and rolled until the masts bent back in the wind and snapped like twigs, sending timber, sails and rope crashing to the deck. Draped in a tangle of sails and rigging, the ship was blown like wreckage hard onto a reef far offshore, where the waves pounded it into the rocks until the hull splintered. The men struggled with axes and bare hands to untangle the lifeboat, prying it loose and heaving it overboard, only to have it swamped by a wave. Without another thought, they jumped in and bailed for their lives. They sat in water up to their knees and rowed beyond the reef before settling in to the steady up and down of huge waves. All night long they rowed, swamped as they crested a wave, bailing desperately as they slid down into the trough. At dawn, the storm ebbed, and they spotted a lighthouse on a small island several miles offshore. With the last of their strength, they rowed through terrible coastal currents before finally landing and collapsing on the rocky shore. All eight crew members survived. The lighthouse keeper took them in and nursed them back to health. After a week, the men set out in their boat for the journey back to Nova Scotia, singing as they rowed.

At times I would see Captain Anthony sitting at the Packet wharf chatting with the other old sailors, all of them tough as leather. When Dad was a boy, he often saw Civil War veterans sitting in the town square. He said they were like another breed of men, and to me, those old sailors were of that breed.

Next door to Anthony's was Mr. Chute's watch repair, while a few paces along was Mr. Marshall's general store, the Trading Company's competitor. Alpheus Marshall was named after his father, the shipbuilder. He built two *Alpheus Marshalls*, both of them wrecked, their first namesake being dashed to pieces in a storm off of England near the Isle of Wight. As it so often does, luck came bundled that day, the good with the bad. In the nearby village, Sunday Mass was in session when the parishioners got news of the wreck. They had no difficulty interpreting this heaven-sent hint and bravely rowed out through high seas to save the entire crew, all two dozen of them clinging to the wreckage in a terrible state, injured and barely alive. God was pleased and the ship's cargo of foodstuffs subsequently washed ashore, keeping the village well-fed for months. I don't think Alpheus Marshall *fils* ever sailed, and perhaps it was just as well that he didn't.

Mother and Dad dealt equally with the stores for certain items: Mr. Marshall's for boys' clothes, boots and rubbers; Mrs. Schmidt's for sewing supplies; the Trading Company for everything else. With all the polished counters and general neatness of the Trading Company, it was obviously more prestigious than Mr. Marshall's, a cluttered emporium with narrow aisles and casually piled merchandise. Still, general stores in those days usually had the look of an overstuffed warehouse, and if you wanted something, they had it buried somewhere: corsets, snuff boxes, spinning wheels, you only had to ask. Because of the clutter, men didn't loiter at Marshall's the way they did at the Trading Company, where parliament was always in session, but it was a general store, a talk shop.

Next door was the Post Office, with two wickets and Queen Victoria staring down from the wall. Impatient customers joked that even Edward VII and George V waited in line. The Post Office was a busy place because at the time, the great Maritimes diaspora was just gearing up, and relations were spreading out across Canada and down to the 'Boston states.' Family and friends were almost dearly departed but for their letters that faintly recalled fading voices. Our Postmaster was Mr. Harris, a patient man often quizzed by the anxious and the elderly, "They said they would write. Are you sure it isn't there?" "Can you check again?" "Maybe it's in that pile over there." Daniel and I were just as bad. When we started school, we were always running in to see if Dad had sent a letter.

Courtesy of Bob Benson

Mr. Harris would shake his head and say, "Nothing today, son," but sometimes he would furrow his brow and feign surprise at an envelope sitting off to the side. We would greedily grab it to study Dad's sharp, angular script cutting across the envelope as if it couldn't wait: 'To Mary Marvin, Bear River, Nova Scotia.' When we got home with our precious cargo, Mother would drop what she was doing to read aloud. Dad usually wrote about the brass he had made in his shop on St. Catherine Street, who his customers were and what was happening in busy Montreal. Best of all was when he mentioned each of us by name, giving us simple instructions and reminding us to be good. After Mother had read the letter, we would examine it as if it held more than words on a page, as if pen strokes and smudges could give us a glimpse of Dad. Mother would place it with the others in the brass tray on the dining room table, and while we ate, we would read out passages and try to fill in the blanks. There were always blanks. Dad's letters sustained us during those long winter months of waiting. Letters were lifelines.

Opposite the post office was the Grand Central Hotel, not to be confused with Grand Centrals in New York, Paris, and London. Still, in its day it did cater to the globe-trotting crowd, often hosting a full house of sailors fresh from New York, Havana, Rio, and Buenos Aires. Surely they found the village a little low-key, but I never heard of a single instance of rowdiness or misbehaviour on their part. I have no idea how the sailors entertained themselves other than by visiting Mr. Darres' ice-cream parlor. One has to assume that like everyone else, they enjoyed a little peace and quiet now and again.

Behind the Grand Central on the River Road stood the Western Union telegraph building, where sentences were parsed to the bone, nouns and verbs and not much more. Dad often preceded his comings and goings with a terse message, 'arriving Montreal tomorrow stop meet at station' always with the word 'stop' butting its way in among the bad grammar. After a quick word count to set the price, Miss Landers would calmly tap out the message like a nervous tic. Shortly, the sounder would give its staccato reply. The exchange seemed unreal, like a séance with a talkative ghost.

On the second floor was the telephone exchange, operated by Miss Liske, a fixture in the building since the days of the telegraph. She lived alone on the Digby side in a house overlooking the village, not far from the Baptist church, where she had been a fixture in the choir since the days of the telegraph. Daily, Miss Liske walked down Chapel Hill, down, down, straight into temptation. The telephone lines buzzed with all the news that was fit to whisper, and wags had pinned her as the town gossip. But if she was, then she was first among equals, because it was common knowledge that everyone listened to everyone else. As lines were installed up Chapel Hill and along the Sissiboo Road, up Oakdene Hill and along the Chute Road, the quietly curious picked up their telephones and joined the fun. We finally got a phone a few years before we left the farm. What a fantasy object that was! Mother would lift the earpiece and turn the little handle at the side to ring Miss Liske, then ask for the Trading Company and place an order just like that. When the phone rang, we counted the rings to know who it was for. I once caught Daniel and Jim listening to Mrs. Walsh and whistling into the phone. Mrs. Walsh asked Daniel, "What's your name, little bird?" He hung up laughing, thinking that because Mrs. Walsh was so old she would never find out. She called right back and the boys scrambled to answer, "No, Mother is not here. No, Dad is not here. Oh no, we wouldn't do a thing like that." I was threatened not to tell, or else. Mrs. Walsh was a wonderful lady who lived next door to Alice Copeland.

Miss Liske at the switchboard and Millie Parker at the telegraph. c 1910

In a little while she called back and I answered, "Yes, Mother and Dad are both here, but in the gardens." Down I went to give Mother the good news, and as expected, the boys got their marching orders, "You get yourselves down to the lilac bush, you little villains, and I want tinglers that will tingle!" Mother didn't tolerate busy-bodies or tattle-tales, which made her a minority of one when Dad was away. I would see Miss Liske primly walking down Main Street, stopping here and there to chat. Mother said she was like a loose cannon. But people have to talk about something. I was never privy to any of the details, but the worst of it was likely the same old hanky-panky that has kept the world spinning for so long.

Local news fit to print was put out by the Women's Institute, who published the Bear River Courier, a one-page supplement in the Digby Weekly Courier. It provided the usual fluff: who went away and who came back (supplied by the tell-all taxi drivers), who won at bridge and who won at tennis (supplied by the winners), who was ill and who was well again (supplied by concerned doctors). Miss Liske and the listening public supplied the asterisks.

Across from the telephone exchange was the Green Lantern hall, a barn-like building used for meetings, and more importantly, movies on Saturday night with Gertie Barr at the piano. The movies were oldies, even for back then. Those who wanted to swoon over Rudolph Valentino and Ramon Navarro had to visit the Bijou Dream in Digby. The Green Lantern was so named because it originally showed lantern slide shows, which it still did on occasion. Before documentaries, there were talking tours with slide shows to educate and entertain: an explorer back from Africa to discuss his adventures; a soldier recounting the war, things like that. The Green Lantern was where I saw my first moving picture. It was a hot day towards the end of the school year, that special time when leniency was granted for field days and other treats. We paraded down Oakdene Hill and across the village, raising dust like an army on the move. Teachers herded us into a darkened room and we settled down to witness the wonder. Immediately, I was frightened out of my wits because it was a film of a raccoon and an unusually large snake, which I naturally thought was in the room. The mood lightened when Charlie Chaplin appeared, whom I also thought was in the room.

Later, I attended a short matinee and bravely sat in the front row. Gertie Barr, who clipped hair at her father's barbershop, fluttered by in pale chiffon and scarlet lipstick, straight out of a movie magazine. She sat down at the piano, and as the screen flickered to life, she embellished freely, trilling to Mary Pickford's butterfly lashes, rumbling a baseline to the villain's footsteps, striking a chord as Mary quailed, pounding out a crescendo as the hero rode to the rescue. Such excitement! Her performance amounted to a medley of the classics, but Gertie played with gusto and likely stirred and spurred the emotions of her audience more than any recital by Rachmaninoff or Rubinstein.

Up Chapel Hill was Mr. Darres' ice cream parlor, always a big hit, then a small hotel run by Aileen Seamone's parents, and then Murray Harris, the deliveryman and taxi driver. Poor Murray Harris. His truck missed a corner one night with his unsuspected ladylove on board and sadly, he was killed, leaving a wife and three children. His girlfriend was a young teacher, and while she was in the Digby Hospital recovering from her injuries, she sent a poem to the Digby Courier, which Mother read. I was absolutely captivated by the sad, whispered romance, which I thought was quite all right. The deathless lines still stick, 'As I lie on the flat of my back, what gems memory holds.' I was so young then it seemed worthy of Mother Goose.

Looking up Chapel Hill, Mr. Marshall's store is to the left, Dr. Campbell's is the white house in the middle, the Grand Central is to the right.

Murray Harris had energized the taxi trade when he upgraded from the horse and buggy and began motoring customers out to Digby, Clementsport, even Weymouth, later picking them up if need be. People were thrilled because everyone had family scattered across both counties, but buggy trips took too long, a whole day or more. Now in under an hour, Miss VanBuskirk could visit her elderly father out in the country, Dad could take us to the circus, and the Digby hospital was a short drive away. None of this applied in the winter, when snow clogged the roads. Like the finches returning to the lilac bush, a sure sign of spring was a car skidding down a muddy road. The state of the roads was a subject of conversation as worrisome as the weather—fair or foul. From the sounds of it, the village had only recently smoothed out the wrinkles, sparing tourists a bone-jarring buggy ride from the train station. But with the river lined by steep hills and cut by intersecting brooks, our roads had to dip and turn sharply to make a grade. Eight roads gathered like a spider's web at the village, one lane, dirt and gravel, no lights or guardrails. Sections edging the river were notched from crumbly slate, and some steep downward curves looked like one of life's turning points. When cars and trucks came roaring down the roads, they had no difficulty pinpointing the trouble spots. After terrorizing the horses and oxen, they skidded and tumbled down gullies. People got hurt, some died, like Murray Harris. Deep Brook, Moose River and Joggin Bridge all had the same problem. Roads that were good enough for the horse and buggy became hazardous at higher speed. The committees met, raised the money, and work crews widened the path for progress to come lurching down the road, two steps forward, one step back.

Steeply up Chapel Hill and on opposite sides of the road were the offices of Bear River's two doctors: Dr. Lovett and Dr. Campbell. Dr. Lovett was the senior of the two, well-respected and well-loved. Besides having organized the Board of Trade and served on every committee in town, Dr. Lovett was notable for his term in Ottawa as Member of Parliament for Digby-Annapolis. People still laughed about the election night revelry when they hoisted him above the crowd and the bonfire threatened to incinerate Main Street. For those few years, Bear River shared the national stage, not that anyone else noticed. I thought it something special when I shook the hand that shook the hand of Prime Minister Mackenzie King, Mother's 'sick mushroom' and Canada's pre-eminent mother's boy. Dr. Lovett lost the 1925 election, though Mackenzie King and a desperate gang of Liberals clung to power by hook and by crook. He never ran again, but both Dr. Lovett and his wife remained active within the Liberal party. Senators and MPs would drive in for a visit, sending a ripple of the old excitement up and down Main Street. I gathered from his chats with Dad that Ottawa had disappointed Dr. Lovett and he welcomed the return to medicine. In that, the village was lucky, because no doctor showed more devotion, and his tenure lasted the rest of his life. For over fifty years, he cared for the village and all the outlying communities, attending births and deaths, sickness and injury. From my seat at school, I would see him leading burial processions or standing by an open grave. On his rounds, he would stop for a chat, but when he clipped by in his carriage, we knew he couldn't be delayed. He owned several serious-minded horses and often worked them like race horses, tearing out to lumber camps to treat accidents, up Indian Hill to deliver a baby, out to a lonely farm to give final comfort. Day and night through driving rain and howling snowstorms, he answered the urgent call. In the winter, he would swoosh by in his sleigh, and if the drifts on the back roads became too high, he would put on his snowshoes and tramp for miles through the woods. Lakes, frozen and half-frozen offered short-cuts,

Dr. Lovett

while neighbours hung lanterns to mark the route, or offered a change of horse to speed him along. Operations were impromptu, done on kitchen tables and barn floors, on people and animals. His first patient was a dog, and he once told Dad that animals made better patients than some villagers. If time allowed, he would take a patient to the Digby hospital, which occupied the floor of a hotel. Or he might accompany them to Victoria General in Halifax for more serious care.

When Dad first came to Bear River, Dr. Lovett attended the family until his stint in Ottawa. Dad still liked to drop in for a chat, and I sometimes went along. We entered off the front veranda into an oak-y office lined with cabinetry, the shelves busy with books and jars of powders and potions. A leafy window looked down a ravine where a brook could be heard bubbling away beneath the greenery. Dr. Lovett once said that every amputated limb, even fingers and toes, received a proper burial behind his house, an old superstition to speed healing. Dad and Dr. Lovett

Mrs. Lovett with the catch of the day.

would set to talking about the village, medicine, anything at all. He was quick with a joke and a wry chuckle; he had seen the human comedy. When the talk shifted to politics, I would sit in the chair swinging my legs, understanding nothing. Mrs. Lovett often popped in to say hello and to give Dad something for Mother, a box of chocolates and a card. Mother would return the favour with jars of preserves. Once, Mrs. Lovett introduced her grandson, Lewis Sutherland, polite and handsome but no Clarke Fraser. The Lovetts had two daughters, both grown up and moved away. Mrs. Lovett was a daughter of Alpheus Marshall, the shipbuilder. She had a schooner named after her, the *Josephine*, as did her sister Annie, wife of W.G. Clarke. Their mother's namesake was the *Tamar Marshall*, Bear River's largest ship, modelled after a Man o' War, people quipped. Despite a prodigious amount of shipbuilding, it seems the Marshalls sailed in name only, and were happy to stay put in Bear River. Mrs. Lovett preferred the backwoods, and her celebrity lay in her hunting prowess.

Dr. Lovett with two unidentified Micmac guides, unfortunately cropped.

She was an outdoorswoman extraordinaire with the trophies on the wall to prove it: caribou, bear, moose. The men of the village deferred; she was a crack shot and that meant something. We would see her on her horse, trotting down Main Street like the town sheriff, quick with a nod and a pleasant hello. Mrs. Lovett was a busy woman, the founding president of the Women's Institute, active in every club and committee. With the added prestige of having entertained the Ottawa elite, you might say she was Bear River's first lady. It could not have been easy being a country doctor's wife, because marrying one meant becoming his secretary, nurse, pharmacist and fill-in when he was out on call. Young brides apprenticed on the fly, attending every type of illness and operation. Mrs. Lovett's voice had a deep-down kindness after witnessing the full panorama of life. She often accompanied her husband to visit sick children, always bringing toys or a treat. She also handled his accounts, and it was common knowledge that they had more IOUs and write-offs than a general store. In those days when people paid for their medical care, payment happened when it could and sometimes not at all. The Lovetts often had to accept chickens, vegetables and small favours. The remainder was credited to a growing reserve of goodwill that bears interest like an annuity to this day.

Veterans Affairs covered most of Dad's medical expenses, and because of Dr. Campbell's ties to the department, it was he who attended to the family. So many times, Dad and I would climb the steep side-stairs to Dr. Campbell's office. I looked forward to those visits when he would sit me on his knee, probe the dent in my forehead, look down my throat, and present me with the coveted tongue depressor.

As I look back on that first visit to Dr. Campbell's and my intense emotions before I was five, I really was a smitten toddler. As Dad and Dr. Campbell chatted, I wandered over to the glass cabinets and examined with studied fascination the shiny implements, laid out on white towels and looking as if they held a wizard's magic. It was wonderfully mysterious. I felt that Dr. Campbell had hidden powers like no one else in Bear River and I decided I wanted to be like him. I wanted to be a doctor and have an office just like his with all those instruments. I would bind and cure everyone, look in ears and up noses, and present tongue depressors so that everyone would love me as much as they loved Dr. Campbell. While Dr. Campbell bandaged my blistered heel, his son Jimmy, a year younger than me, watched and sucked his thumb. He was a shy, pale, sickly mother's boy whose overpowering love was tucking him back into the cradle. Later I heard Mother and Dad ruefully discussing this lonely, only, overly-loved child. To me, Jimmy's situation seemed ideal. What was wrong with being an only child in the village in a big home with no cows or pigs or chickens in the back yard and a father like Dr. Campbell who could make the whole village better? Dr. Campbell often drove down to the farm to chat with Mother and Dad on the glide swing while Jimmy clung to his father's side as if we were savages to avoid. We made no inroads on his shyness. Eventually, Jimmy sucked his thumb so hard and for so long that he had the worst case of buck teeth in town. Mother wondered why the only son of a doctor would be in such a condition. After Dr. Roop left town and Bear River was without a dentist, Dr. Campbell did what he could for the village, but Mother said she would rather pull her own teeth than trust Dr. Campbell. She was not above trashing social icons, so Dr. Campbell foundered at the bottom of his pedestal. For a time, Dad pulled the boys' loose teeth with a string and the door handle, slamming the door to the cheers of little barbarians.

Dr Campbell was there for all our physical problems, and even more so in the summer when our gardens were flush. He could drive down anytime for anything he wanted, so he never lacked for eggs, fruit or vegetables. Dad would kill a chicken for him or let him dig his own potatoes. When Mrs. Campbell sent word she wanted fruit for preserving, the boys scrambled through trees and bushes to pick them. Mrs. Campbell never came to the farm, and Mother rarely saw her, she being of the elite. She was a strange woman, a compulsive talker but dogmatic, of the no-nonsense mold. I thought her silly when she asked Dad to come into her kitchen to marvel at the jars of gooseberries she had preserved. There they were, all lined up on the counter like trophies, the contents straight from our farm. Mother's preserves were second to none, but they went down to our root cellar without comment, ignored until we ate them. Dr. Campbell didn't suffer as Dad's friend. He got brass work when he asked for it, and in those strapped times, we were likely one of his few paying customers. I remember handing him the envelopes myself. This became an issue a number of years later when he relocated to Halifax.

When I left Dr. Campbell's after that first visit, my future seemed assured. Instead of becoming a brat like Daniel, I got involved in all the medical aspects of my siblings' recklessness. I pulled out slivers and saturated fingers with iodine to prevent lockjaw. At the first sign of blood, I rushed to bandage cuts, iterating, "I'm going to be a doctor." Mother and Dad said I would have to make another choice because ladies did not become doctors. It was all I could think of so I persisted. When Dr. Campbell joked with Dad about a two-hour moonlit trek through the woods to deliver a baby, I had second thoughts. Then on my first trip to Halifax, I saw a woman not only driving a car, but a car with doctor's plates. Dad said yes, she was one of the few, and my dream was reinforced.

When Donald found his sea legs and was searching for life beyond the cradle, he wandered down to our dump, where bottles and trash were thrown down a steep embankment. The grapery fenced it off, but Donald wiggled through and fell down. He limped home screaming and dripping blood from a wide open gash across his instep. Mother was hysterical, not knowing what to do, so she sat down holding Donald and helplessly cried. It was the biggest medical moment of my life. I filled a basin with warm water, and while Mother held him, I washed his little foot thoroughly with soap to clean off the grime. I filled the basin again and poured in brown creosote, which turned milky, and I washed the foot again. Ignoring Donald's screams, I poured iodine over the large wound, the flesh looking curiously larded. Then I tore cheesecloth into strips, wrapped the bandage and pulled it tight, drawing both ends of the wound together. More bandages, more iodine and more screaming concluded my first major operation. Mother waited for lockjaw, while I tended to my patient daily. When Dr. Campbell came down for vegetables after a holiday, he examined Donald's foot and said he couldn't have done better himself. I indulged in such pride. Years later, Donald was studying in Quebec City to become a lawyer, and to pay for his education he joined the Army to fight in Korea. On his application, the neat scar along his foot was his only identification mark. He had no idea how he got such a large scar, so I told him of my medical prowess at nine and my wistfully lost dream. Wandering off to Korea earned Donald three more scars.

I rather like to remember my first trip to Barr's barbershop. Dad often trimmed my hair when he did the boys, but on this Saturday, Mother insisted that I go with her to Barr's. Off we went to be shorn in the style of the day, and when we returned, Dad gaped in shock, "What in blue blazes has happened?" Mother and I were quite happy with the new arrangement. For me, it meant no more braids, no more hair being pulled in the schoolyard or sticking in the heat. It was cut exactly like Alice Copeland's, up to my ears and across my forehead. Later I would add spit curls across my cheeks, vamp-like. Mother had no further need of her tortoise shell pins and pretty amber combs that sat in a tray on her bureau. How often had Dad brushed my hair. How often had he brushed Mother's, so soft and luxuriant, Dad always telling her how lovely it was. He got used to things.

Going to Barr's wasn't quite like having afternoon tea, but it always made for such a nice, pleasant interlude in our humdrum lives. Barr's looked like any other barber shop, beckoning with its candy cane pole, but inside it catered to the basic beautification of the entire village, combining a beauty shop and barber shop all in one. Mrs. Barr and her daughters, Olive and Gertie, ran the shop when Mr. Barr was indisposed. Gossips recounted Tine's (Valentine) legendary bouts with John Barleycorn and his ensuing recoveries. I don't recall anyone calling him a drunk–it was always referred to as 'Mr. Barr's problem'. Others had the problem as well. The Anglican minister Rev. McLeod had his problem. His son Hinson, in high school, whom everyone said was a chip off the old block, had a problem at barn dances, specifically when he lay splayed in the hay. At recess on Monday mornings, he bounded in the front door, his recovery better late than never. Alice said he was handsome, so I took a good look, and yes, he was darkly handsome, but handsome is as handsome does. McLeod & Son were on the road to blue ruin.

Barr's occupied the upper floor of the building next to Dr. Campbell's. We climbed steep steps up to a long verandah that fronted the shop and offered a wonderful view of the village. The same view obtained inside the shop, because the front wall was entirely windowed. So inside or out, you could look up Chapel Hill, across to Dr. Lovett's, down to the post office, across the bridge and along the street to the Trading Company. One could survey the entire commercial hub of the village from Mr. Barr's elevated verandah.

Inside and opposite the length of window, six sturdy swivelling barber chairs faced six white enamel sinks. Wide black straps hung on hooks, ready to sharpen razors folded in safety. A mirrored wall ran the length of the room, lined with bottles and jars in antiseptic blues and greens. A select row of shelves held personal mugs with stubby shaving brushes lounging inside. While men reclined beneath a sheet, Mr. Barr would deftly whip foam out of mugs and lather faces into biblical relics. There they lay, peacefully attended, soothed by the flip-flop of the razor on the strap, honed to the point of ministration on the village necks. For toddlers, Mr. Barr placed a board across the arms of the chair and hoisted the screaming subject into position. Tears of, "No, No," as the little terror became embroiled in a show of howls and fisticuffs. With every break in the action, Mr. Barr would quickly snip. Then in a flurry of white sheet, the little tyro would run out the door and down the steps clutching the coveted lollipop, a screaming disaster. Trailing behind, his doting mother would hold close a few precious locks to be preserved in lockets and keepsakes.

The ladies section occupied the far end of the room, where hair was marcelled with deep waves and kiss curls like Clara Bow, or bobbed like Louise Brooks, the idol of a certain style. A display by a window held everything necessary to practice the refined alchemy of beauty: jars of emollient, creams, tins of salve, emery boards, clippers, manicure kits, men's astringents to be clapped on faces, brilliantine to be clapped on hair. Wafting over the shop was the refreshing perfume of soaps and talcum powder. How delicious it all smelled! Barr's was a place of elegance, a place where beauty touched me. Except for the spittoon.

I had always noticed the wide-rimmed brass bowl sitting just inside the door, splotched and filled with a dark, tar-like liquid. I wondered what it was and why it was there. Nearby stood two chairs and a low table stacked with an exciting collection of movie magazines—lexicons of beauty and style filled with stunning women and handsome men. I preferred to wait my turn so I could have more time to leaf through the magazines. One day while I was flipping pages, lost among the stars, a man came in and with unusual accuracy, spat tobacco right into the brass bowl at my feet, which I then learned was a spittoon. I gulped to stabilize my system and was revolted for all time. I never sat by the door again.

In the village, I would see men opening their penknives, cutting a chunk from a dark square slab and popping it in their mouths. They'd stand tall and spit and spurt to punctuate sentences, staining moustaches and beards. Splotches on the ground embellished the ambience left by horses and oxen. Every once in a while, a young man whose name I forget would stroll by with his wheeled dustbin and handy shovel, removing any imperfections and restoring Main Street's dignity.

When my turn came, Olive or Gertie would cheerfully call me over to join the ladies. I would climb up onto the board to be covered in a crisp white sheet and cranked up to blissful elevation where I could look in the mirror and admire my transformation. Then a clip clip, snip snip to the polite conversation of the ladies. The Barr women were fitting advertisements for the shop, as beautifully dressed and coiffed as the stars in the magazines, though their scarlet lipstick caused comment by the old guard. In those days, it spelled a certain careless insinuation. The roaring 20s readjusted perspective and scooped up the younger generation–another vigorous culture war that sizzled emotions. Despite their outré lipstick, the Barr ladies were very genteel, and if you listened to them with eyes closed, they could have been presiding over afternoon tea. They chatted politely about the issues of the day: Rudolph Valentino, such a tragedy; Charlie Chaplin, wasn't it shocking; Fatty Arbuckle, guilty or innocent? Then a few snips for perfection, a whisk or two of the brush, and a dusting of scented powder. I would turn to observe myself in the mirror, a lesser version of Louise Brooks. I loved the feeling of being momentarily bathed in the aura of beauty. I would jump down from the chair, perfumed and pampered, all set to go back to my earthy surroundings of barns and outhouses.

At times when the shop wasn't busy, Mother would linger for tea with Mrs. Barr while I caught up on my reading. She was a gentle lady who whispered Mr. Barr's indiscretions in Mother's ears, which were whispered throughout the village. Mrs. Barr told Mother of her ongoing struggle to keep her husband on the straight and narrow, but when she went to bake a cake, she opened the cupboard to find that he had finished off her vanilla extract. He even misapplied his Bay Rum aftershave. Mother whispered back, "...not for children's ears," and tea was gulped. "..now that was strange," I thought, "why would Mr. Barr drink vanilla extract??"

John McLeod collection

Despite a degree of risk, the boys preferred to be clipped by Mr. Barr. He would flip the white sheet and ask, "Well young man, what'll it be today, a shave or a haircut?" They would squirm and squeeze their eyes tight as Mr. Barr took a bearing before pausing to chat with the waiting men. He was a thin man with glasses and dark hair, and his fidgeting made Mother wonder if she was putting the boy's lives in danger. Even when he had undergone a periodical drying out, his recovery played havoc with his nerves. He would anxiously reach for a cigarette or cigar and puff prodigiously as he snipped, pausing for occasional sips from a cup of what surely was tea, motioning in broad circles with the scissors as he chatted. If Daniel gave an unrepressed ouch, Mr. Barr would caution him not to move and then daub the wound with a styptic pencil. The waiting men would snicker knowingly and offer Daniel encouragement, "Steady, son." One day Mother tsk-tsked at what she said was a patchwork quilt made with the clippers, telling Daniel, "It doesn't matter, you can't see it." Another day when Daniel came home with an unevenly designed trim, Dad had to get out his clippers. Daniel decided he would like paths clipped across the side of his head like a Mohawk Indian. Jim wanted a swath cut from ear to ear, and Douglas wanted a big bald spot. Mother took a picture, one of the few I still have: Daniel with his usual smirk, ready to burst out laughing, Douglas in the pyjamas he liked so much he wore them all day, Jim holding Scotty to a pose, and Uncle Peter with Verna, his newly intended. Immediately after the picture, Dad shaved their heads clean. Daniel then remembered a nugget of information from the Bible and decided it was an ideal time to count the hairs on Jim's head. They rolled around on the grass while Grandmother observed from the background, "They're not all there, those two." Later in the afternoon, everyone trooped down to Kniffen's beach, and Mother took more pictures of the family group, all the Aunts and Uncles with Daniel, Jim and Douglas standing proudly in front without a stitch on. When Aunt Elsie went to the drugstore to collect the pictures, Mrs. Harris handed them over with a broad smirk. She was usually rather acidic to match her brittle red hair. Afterwards, when she realized why, Aunt Elsie laughed her head off, but Mother wasn't amused at the invasion of privacy and fired a broadside, "And what was the point of her smirk? She is married and has two boys, both of them with vicious red hair just like hers."

The Board of Trade once asked Dad to build a plaster model of Bear River because they were considering bringing in the railroad on a spur line down the river. After the pipeline fiasco, Dad feared for his oaks, but the Board was considering the River Road on the Digby side. But the iron horse would have trammelled the horse and buggy right into the river, and in the end they let the railway bypass the village. Bear River remained recognizable en route by a modest, dull-red siding at the mouth of the river. From the village you could hear the trains whistling across Victoria Bridge, and that was as close as progress got. Even cars seemed out of place.

Cherry Carnival. circa 1910, in front of the Grand Central.

As I look back, from the vantage point of a child there was an inherent lethargy to the village: large and lonely houses with widows rocking at their windows; homes suddenly becoming empty shells; horses and buggies slowly trotting by, the hollow echoes like memories of time gone by. The humble hamlet still maintains its inflated and elevated footnote: The Switzerland of Nova Scotia, almost like the claim of deposed royalty, proud but bankrupt. Today the debt of old memories is paid by the original charms of the lovely river, the rising hills and the verdant forests. That remains. Castles do crumble.

Courtesy of The Bear River Historical Society

Grandmother

I **WAS IN MY SIXTH** year, or to be exact, my sixth year and seventh month when I was made aware that I had a grandmother. Events and information never filtered down to little children in our busy household. What we knew outside of fairy tales was absorbed in the schoolyard or on the way to school. Upon reflection, Mother was tending her sixth baby, my sister Joan, and she had enough to do starting the day and getting us off to school without keeping us abreast of the family tree. Grandmother's picture never graced our walls to establish her identity as our worthy progenitor. She was so remote she was nameless, and so were my aunts and uncles. We learned their names on arrival, but where they emanated from other than a taxi was not known until I learned there was another country besides Bear River. Scotland was somewhere down the road beyond Digby.

One night when I was very young, long before I went to school, Mother was reading her home papers by the fireplace after our bedtime story. She suddenly screamed out for Dad and began crying inconsolably, saying over and over, "My poor father." She had read of his death in the paper before Grandmother or any of her family could sit down and write her. I was too young to ask questions, but she was sad for a long time. So I knew Mother had a father whose death caused many tears. And I knew Mother sent parcels and received them from 'My Mother.' For years I watched Mother knitting, pulling threads on linen table clothes she embroidered, stitching the edges of fine linen handkerchiefs and packaging them with yearly quantities of maple sugar candy that she had taken days to make. I only knew they were going 'home.' If mail came, a parcel of rock candy, scarves and tams, it was from home. No one was identified, and if they had been, they might as well have resided at the post office and had no more substance than a postage stamp. Only recently having learned to write our names, we were hardly able to cross-examine.

Although Uncle Peter lived with us, to me he seemed more of a hired hand and never consciously registered as a relative until later. I pinned my devotion and the possessiveness of relatives on the Kniffens, Mrs. Crosscup, Mr. Bishop and Mrs. McCormack. Alice Copeland had never mentioned grandmothers either. It was Great Great Aunt Mary who provided the pennies for her candy, held in the thumb of her mitten or tied in a handkerchief and stuffed in her bloomer leg. Along the Chute Road, the only obvious sentiment about grandmothers was displayed by the Reade children when their grandmother returned from the States bringing gifts and summer clothes they proudly displayed. When I later found out that Major and Amanda Simon were grandparents I couldn't believe it–it seemed highly unlikely and a gross distortion of the truth.

Then all of a sudden, such activity! Mother and Mrs. McCormick papered, painted, scrubbed and refurbished. Every empty room upstairs was transformed into the modest elegance of Eaton's catalogue, not Victorian, not Edwardian, but Eaton's Catalogue, that enduring oaken era. Coming home from school, I stepped into a house that smelled pungently new. No explanation was given or asked for; house beautiful was its own reward and that was all I needed to know. Truth would come in its own good time. Beds were covered with new mattresses and linens, windows were covered with filmy curtains. New washbasins, jugs and chamber pots sat atop new commodes. Painted floorboards were covered with sheets of linoleum, and beside each bed lay one of Mother's hooked rugs, formerly placed higgledy-piggledy downstairs.

Mrs. McCormick's room was held in reserve, but Dad's room, used for making radios and working on the turbine, was redone and feminized. Out went the drafting table and radio parts. All that remained was the passepartout picture of stony-faced Rachmaninoff. He was re-hung, but his unwavering Siberian stare was definitely out of place among the tiny roses now embowering him. By the bed, Mother placed the large hooked rug with wild red roses, previously in the downstairs hall, the one we slid on running away from Uncle Peter's clutches. With all the refurbishing and beautification, Daniel decided a move was in order. He chose his new lodging only to be told no, our grandmother was on her way.

Who this grand person was remained to be seen. We were badly informed. In fact, we weren't informed at all. Soon, appearances made up for lack of detail and she needed no further definition.

How often we remember notable firsts. They flood the mind in a jumble: first best friend, first kiss, first love, and first relatives. For the big day, Mrs. McCormick came to help, and I stayed home from school to watch the baby. The dining room table was laden with food, but at one point Mother wondered if she had enough desserts, so she quickly stirred up a bowl of jell-o. At that point of my life when passions were few or undeveloped, I did have a passion for jell-o, and I greedily licked the waxed paper packaging clean of crystals. Mother had me take the bowl up to the spring where it would cool quickly, and before I placed it in the brook, I enjoyed the enormous satisfaction of drinking a few good gulps of warm jell-o. I haven't had jell-o in a long time. I must see if my passions have cooled.

Since Dad was in Montreal at the time, he met the MacGregor clan as they docked: Grandmother, the four aunts: Elsie, Nan, Cathy and Ellen (Ellie), and the three uncles: Douglas, Jim and Alec. From Montreal they entrained overnight through the forests of New Brunswick to the lesser metropolis of Saint John, there to embark on the Princess Helene and sail across the Bay of Fundy to the negligible metropolis of Digby, there to entrain on the Dominion Atlantic Railway and alight with their baggage at Bear River station, a siding backed by forest. They piled into Murray Harris' taxi, and once the MacGregors had travelled from the station to the village centre with its half-dozen stores, the hind quarters on stilts in the river, their vision of Canadian cities and towns had tunnelled. Almost immediately the teen-aged uncles, Jim and Alec, who had noticeably loud mouths, were saying, "Give it back to the Indians."

In through the maple grove they came that jolly day in May—callooh, callay! Uncle Douglas dismounted and led the procession with bagpipes blazing. Uncle Peter and Harry followed, hauling the wagon with all the trunks, one of which surely belonged to Pandora. After alighting from Murray Harris' taxi amid hugs and hellos and a confusion of Gaelic, Grandmother asked where the loo was, a word I had never heard. Mother said in English, "We have no loo, Mother." Grandmother was nonplussed,

"You have no loo!?" Mother repeated, "No, Mother we have no loo." Grandmother snapped, "For goodness sake, what on earth do you have?" It didn't sound friendly. Mother said, "We have an outhouse, down there by the MacIntosh tree." Grandmother couldn't believe it, sputtering 'you don't mean to tell me you live like this' and on and on, well into her first misconception of life in the colonies. Mother informed her that as well as the outhouse, we had chamber pots on top of the commodes in every bedroom. The MacGregors gasped. I thought all those brand-new, top-of-the-line chamber pots would be greeted with delight. So we watched Grandmother, in a very chastened mood, trip down the long path to discover her objective, which Mother had papered with bright yellow daffodils.

With 17 people in the house, it was a well-trodden path, and I don't know why I found it so funny when I watched Grandmother or the aunts on rainy days tearing down to the outhouse like mad with slickers over their heads. Every foray to the outhouse several times a day was a very public private exposure. Over and over they walked down the path, past Mother's rock garden, down the small embankment, past the well, the wood pile, the chopping block, the apple packing house, and there it stood, where Grandmother could hear the geese and ducks honking and quacking in their smelly quarters, and the hundreds of chickens and roosters clucking and crowing in theirs. It wasn't exactly a sonorous destination. Grandmother would shudder and look miserable, "This is not even civilized, Polly." However, as much as Grandmother complained, she was lucky she only endured the summer months. Had she stayed for the winter, she would have had memories frozen in her mind for the rest of her life.

When the MacGregors first sat around the dinner table, we hovered in high excitement, staring at them and listening to their strange accent. Mother's accent was very light, almost musical, and at that point we didn't know Dad was a failed American, so his accent was colloquially Canadian. Initially, the conversation covered topics of a general interest: Helensburgh, friends, and relatives whose names I promptly forgot, except for Aunt Kate, Aunt Ruby, and then Aunt Maggie, at whose mention the teen-age uncles gleefully sputtered that she now had a moustache. Daniel thrived on unusual information and let out an uncontrolled guffaw. Grandmother dropped her cutlery, but before she could open her mouth Dad said one word, "Sweetheart," a stinging rebuke, since Daniel's worst humiliation as long as Dad lived was to be called Sweetheart. Friends jeered and he socked them. Daniel never realized how loved he was. Grandmother looked him over and said, "Come here, laddie! Hold out those filthy hands!" She looked in his ears, "I see potato sprouts! You've got fly spots and cherry juice all over your face! Don't stand there and tell me you washed up. Off to the kitchen sink!" Daniel discovered he had gained more than a Grandmother and resisted this new authority by protesting, "But Grandmother, this is clean dirt!" That was the last time Grandmother tolerated back-talk. She checked and criticized us equally, but somehow Daniel always managed to prey on her surviving emotions.

From the moment the noisy MacGregors set foot on the farm, children lost their identity and were relegated to the sidelines in a congealed mass of inquisitiveness. The mores of the day were now strictly applied: children should be seen and not heard; children should speak only when spoken to. Every room in the house was overrun by these strange people. We had lost our territory. If I went into the parlor to see and hear all I could, I was told to go out and play or to watch the baby. If I sat on the couch in the dining room after I had been excused from the table, Grandmother would dismiss me from the adult preserve of the after-dinner chat. Strident MacGregor voices and opinions filled every room with debate and controversy on every subject headlined in the home papers. They thrived on arguments nasty or nice. The machinations of the British government gave them fuel and fired them up so much that they blazed over the dinner table while masticating their meals like savages eating hot coals. It seemed impossible that Mother belonged to this clan. One highly combustible subject was The Vote. Men in the British Parliament, their chests plastered with medals earned by shooting each other up all over Europe, felt that bestowing the vote on women was even more dangerous than what they had suffered. Termagants and hoydens were marching up and down the streets of Helensburgh and all over the Isles demanding The Vote. They shouted and screamed, tore off their clothes, chained themselves to gates and fences and stoned policemen, who carted them off to jail to show exactly what the world was coming to.

That's where the old battle-axes belonged, said the infallible MacGregor men, who were basically ignoramuses except for Uncle Douglas. They aligned themselves against Grandmother and the aunts and stood their ground waving knives and forks across the table. Neither the MacGregor men nor women gave an inch. Good manners and southern decorum were thrown out the window to the heliotrope and nasturtium. Mealtime conversation graduated by degrees from family and home turf to the beauty of Loch Lomond, the Gare Loch, the Trossachs, and then on to trouncing politicians, back to the Scottish wars, forward to the miseries of the farm and Canada before ending on a high note of religion, which put an end to anyone's idea of heaven. Mother always ignored heightened emotions, but Dad had the unfortunate habit of waiting for an issue to settle before relighting the fuse. A string of remarks would sizzle around the table before coming to a halt with one of Dad's defining comments, then a brief vacuum before the explosion. Chairs would scrape back, brass work would be heaved against the walls, all followed by the acrid aftermath. Dad expected nothing less. I never understood. It was just another mealtime.

When Grandmother took possession of her bedroom, she was met by Rachmaninoff's stony stare and Tartar eyes. Being a woman of quick observation and decision she demanded, "Who's that?" Wanting to make myself seen and heard by my brand-new grandmother, I ingratiatingly said, "That's Mr. Rachmaninoff, Dad likes him." Grandmother hissed, "Well, I don't! I'll not have that ugly man in my room." As quick as a wink she plucked the picture off the wall and threw him out the open window. Grandmother threw a lot of things out the windows that summer. As she unpacked her large, wicker hamper, her first concern was the placement of the family portraits. At the time, we had only five pictures hanging on our walls, all in the parlor: Mother and Dad's wedding picture in a dark oak frame; Ardencaple Castle in a smaller, less imposing frame; a large signed portrait of Dorothy Haig in a lovely gold frame; Daniel in his bare feet squinting in the sun; and Maria Jeritza, Mother's favorite opera singer, her beautiful face framed by her lovely hair stuck with a large red rose, dressed for the part of the Marschallin in *Der Rosenkavalier*.

We had plenty of space for more pictures, so Grandmother chose a spot next to Ardencaple Castle for Great-grandmother McCullagh's heavy, oak-framed scowling portrait. Luckily, this was beside the parlor door, which always stayed open with an easy chair pushed against it, so Great-grandmother remained a mystery. She looked sullen and Moorish, even suspicious, a braid around her head and a shawl around her shoulders. No one ever praised or blamed her so I have no way of knowing how she was regarded or loved. I only know that in our family she remained hidden behind the parlor door as if she had fallen right off the family tree.

The same heavy oak frames held pictures of Grandfather, with his sensitive, poetic face and Uncle John in his highland regalia. These she lovingly placed on the opposite wall on either side of the Franklin fireplace. After all the hammering and hanging, Grandmother took a good look across the room at the sweet, patrician face of Dorothy Haig with her meticulously coiffed white curls and asked, "Who's she?" Mother explained that Lady Haig had given Dad her portrait as a Christmas present when she was living in Montreal. She had been a lady-in-waiting to the Queen and was the wife of Sir Douglas Haig, Commander-in-Chief of the British Forces in World War I. This brought on the first of Grandmother's momentous explosions. She loudly demanded that Lady Haig's picture be taken off the wall immediately, right now! She would not have that woman facing her husband and most of all her dear John, God bless his soul, may he rest in peace. He had died of his wounds and even though dead, he didn't spend all those years in a prisoner of-war camp and fight with the bravest of the brave to have to face the wife of Sir Douglas Haig, he who had heartlessly looked down into the muddy trenches and called boys like her John dirty dogs. That picture would come off the wall! Our peaceful parlor had only ever heard lullabies, Thornton Burgess' bedtime stories and Mother and Dad reading to each other. Now, the walls began to seethe as our newly hung relatives in their over-sized dark frames took up the fight from across the room, with Great-grandmother McCullagh waiting in reserve. For some reason, Dad refused to give in and insisted the picture remain in its place. Like Mother, Dad easily gave in to inconsequential things, so it was surprising that Lady Haig stayed in our parlor and was not moved to the bedroom, as Grandmother suggested.

The dining room table became a battleground where Grandmother exposed Sir Douglas Haig for all he was worth. Things simmered along in this fashion until Maria Jeritza acted up in Vienna and did a perfectly unladylike thing: she spat in a rival's face at the opera. I was sad to see Jeritza go, she was so beautiful, the only beauty on our walls, but Mother simply would not tolerate someone spitting on her walls. Out she went. The artists were gone. Then Mother had an idea and moved Lady Haig to Maria Jeritza's blank space. Hers was the first face you saw as you entered the parlor, but Uncle John was spared the sight of her. Grandmother never gave up, it wasn't in her nature, and she would hiss, "I can't stomach that woman's face."

Grandmother's appearance was her one great deception. She was petite and pretty and as meticulous as a bandbox. No one would have suspected that she was the mother of ten. She even looked helpless. I don't recall her ever lifting a finger on the farm. Grandmother's energies had their natural exploitation in the rearing of her ten children, and with that phase of her life over, she seemed to slough off every last fledgling from the nest. In fact, she didn't have a nest any more. There is no doubt Grandmother was unhappy, and with this unhappiness, her mind became deftly incisive to a cutting edge, especially concerning Dad and the farm. Her tongue cut like a pair of scissors, snipping away until she had shredded a subject. But as much of a crab as she had become, I don't recall her ever raising her voice. To compensate for her Irish heritage, she had become an inveterate student of Scottish history, subsequently boring little children at dinner tables and sometimes spoiling their meals. I could have learned a lot of Scottish history from her, but I came to hate it as much as she hated the Irish. Marrying Peter MacGregor was not the only reason Grandmother loved Scottish history. Simply put, she discovered that an antecedent was the famous, infamous Rob Roy MacGregor. It didn't matter that he was a light-fingered bounder with cows and sundry as well as peoples' lives. He was in the history books and she liked that. Although he was long dead, she sympathized with him in the present tense, excusing his dastardly deeds brought on by the foul MacFarlanes, and she could spit in the face of King James. "Aye," she would say, "he's one of the really great MacGriggers."

And then, when she cleared away the scrub and branches of the family tree and climbed to the very top, there she discovered to her great delight, recorded in the mists of time, King Alpine. What more could one ask of heritage? This took up a great many meals worth of discussion, supercharged by Dad's southern drawl and sly humour as he pulled out her chair, "Yewr majesty," followed by a bow. Staking one's claim to royalty in the backwoods of Nova Scotia seemed a little uppity, especially with the line diluted by the centuries down to the merest soupçon. The information rubbed off on Daniel, who staked a claim of his own. He would hang from the branches of maple trees while grown-ups idled over tea, pompously yelling at the top of his lungs, "I'm the king of the castle and you're the dirty rascal." One day Grandmother, sick and tired of that rendition, popped her head out the window looking like a ferocious owl and said, "You cheeky wee beggar, I don't want to hear any more of that nonsense."

Although I paused over Grandmother's pride in her adopted ancestry, there was no question about her pride in Grandfather. She freely stated that she had married far better than any of her sisters. Grandfather owned a landscaping business and was chief gardener at Ardencaple Castle with a dozen men under him. He was also piper for the laird and played at all the great occasions at the castle. She praised him often with tears in her eyes, and it seemed to me he was a far greater man than Rob Roy McGrigger. In fairness, Grandmother was in deep mourning for Grandfather, as she was for the rest of her life. She breathed her grieving every minute of every day, and in discussing Grandfather, it was the only time she was ever tender. She'd dry her eyes and wonder why only the good die young. Why? Why? Life never answered her question. Every time she mentioned 'my dear Peter', she crossed herself saying, 'may he rest in peace, he was such a good man, a wonderful man, a kindly man, a gentle man', he hadn't a single fault– he was a saint. The minute she arrived on the farm, his large framed picture was hung in the parlor where she would sit and gaze up at it as if it were an icon, fingering her rosary beads. His picture stood on her night table, always turned towards her for a last look in the evening and a first look in the morning. I'm sure she dreamed of nothing but him. With his death nothing and no one else mattered. Later on, she followed the stock market as seriously as she studied the Scottish wars, but that came some time later. She blamed Dad for bringing her to this God-forsaken country, though she knew full well it was Grandfather's wish. She said a thousand times that summer that she never should have left home, she never should have left her dear Peter, may his soul rest in peace, all alone and forgotten in his grave. She couldn't even go to church to pray for him. The little church of St. Anne's on Indian Hill was miles and miles away on the reservation. After a Sunday trek back and forth, her first visit was her last.

And then there was Uncle John, her eldest son who had died in Vancouver from his war wounds. The sun shone as brightly on him as it did on Grandfather, and she grieved for him with as deep a sorrow. She never expected death or accepted it, she wasn't prepared for it, but it became her whole life.

Uncle John's picture hung in the parlor, a teen-age boy standing proud in full highland regalia, a gun at his side, ready for war, already serving. "My poor John, may he rest in peace," and Grandmother would tamp her eyes. "I never should have let him join up. What was it all worth?" It was repetitive. All she had left was a picture and a letter from the nurse who had tended him as he died, which she read over and over, as painful as it was. For many years, she sent the nurse money to put flowers on his grave. But it was a lonely grave and he was part of the Pacific coast, an alien shore. It was easy enough for the government to cross him off their roster once he was dead. The government had no heart, but she had hers and it was breaking. She decided she would make the government pay for her dead son until the day she died. He wouldn't be written off with that last pension cheque. It was on the farm in the summer of '27 that she began her crusade of many years, petitioning the government for Uncle John's pension. I suppose the reason I remember it was because of her tears of outrage with every reply repeating their denial. She discussed it over and over. How dare they think a young boy's life was only worth being killed? Dad would say in his gentle fashion, "Motha, it does no good to brood," but she would lash out at him. She had made up her mind.

As I looked at Uncle John's picture, with all the talk about him, I pulled back the faintest memory of someone with a strange limp giving me a piggyback, and then he was gone. I couldn't have been more than three. The years went by and Grandmother hounded and haunted Pensions—tenacious, argumentative and sad. The government may have felt they had a tigress by the tail and that the war they were waging with her had lasted far longer than World War I, but she had given her son and they had reneged on payment. The years would go by and she would make them remember John MacGregor. Finally admitting her claim after fifteen years, they gave her a token pension of a few dollars. It didn't ease her pain. All she could say was, "My poor John." When I was grown up and visited her in Montreal and she told me that Pensions had conceded, I wondered why she had let Uncle John's pension take over her life like an open wound, and for a pittance. But I was young then.

Grandmother, Aunt Cathy and Grandfather

Grandmother

From the day of Grandmother's arrival, I had been nervously curious about her large wicker hamper, because when she first opened it, she noted meaningfully that something special waited inside for Daniel and me. Although Grandmother seemed formidable from the moment she set foot on the farm, for that promise of something special I was prepared to love her. But first, the family portraits had to be hung, and that took some time. While the hamper rested in the upstairs hall, we endured the daily expectation of the wonderful surprise awaiting us. Only at Christmas time did I experience such delicious panic. Finally after all the fuss about the family portraits, the great day arrived and we crowded around in eager anticipation. For Daniel, Grandmother reached into the hamper and unearthed a heavy wooden case, opening it proudly to reveal a violin made by the best violin maker in Helensburgh, so she said. It was a large, heavy instrument with aging information glued inside the F-hole. Daniel was ecstatic. He scraped away on the flatulent strings and begged for lessons immediately.

For me, Grandmother pulled back the lower strata covered by a woollen blanket and revealed my wonderful treasure: a MacGregor tartan kilt handed down through her children to the very last one, Uncle Alec, and now she was handing it to me. A skirt worn by a boy, five boys, Uncle Peter included. I hated it. I didn't even want to touch it. So that my feet would grow properly, Dad insisted I wear boys' shoes, and now I had a matching skirt. I sullenly accepted my heirloom accoutrement as Mother nudged me and then nudged me again to say thank you. I had been looking to expand my wardrobe beyond my one good dress, but again the gods reminded me: be careful what you wish for. I clomped through the schoolyard in my boys' shoes and my uncles' hand-me-down skirt wrapped around my waist like a towel and held together with a silly blanket pin. It was the only kilt at Oakdene and an instant curiosity: 'why does it need the pin,' 'can't your mother sew it up?' 'I've never seen anything like it!' It was too soon for me to be trendsetting; I hadn't the poise or the panache, so I shrivelled in humiliation. Daniel thought the pedigree of my skirt hilarious and laughed that I was wearing not just second-hand, but sixth-hand, worn by all the uncles and maybe Grandfather too. His urge to blab was bubbling over, so I suggested that since my skirt had been worn by five boys at least, perhaps he should be wearing it as well. The thought of Daniel marching through the schoolyard in kilted splendour made my predicament seem not so bad after all. Besides, it did seem strange that all the uncles should have a kilt, I should have a kilt, and yet Daniel did not. I offered to ask Grandmother, why the oversight? Was Daniel a MacGregor or not? Perhaps she could fit him with a matching tam at Mrs. Yorke's hat shop. Daniel visibly wilted and pleaded that we close the subject. The secret of my ancestral skirt was safe.

As I stood at the wicker hamper holding my vintage kilt, Grandmother then announced with a smile that she had a very special gift for me that I must take very good care of. She then held up a large pillowcase and, as if she were pulling a rabbit out of a hat, produced a giant antique doll. My heart fell. It was as big as my sister Joan, who had appendages like an octopus, and it was just as dirty looking, affirming that it was indeed old and antique. The yellowed, lacy dress had obviously been part of some baby's wardrobe, burped on and washed times over. The plaster head had scrolled hair, painted eyes, and nicks on the nose and ears. Its spongy, sawdust body was stuffed into a greyish covering sprouting plaster arms and legs missing fingertips and toes. Grandmother pushed the grubby monstrosity into my arms and said that since it was antique I couldn't play with it. She needn't have warned me. It seemed to be my lot in life that I could never keep my dolls pristine for the world they inhabited. I was bitterly hoodwinked.

The doll was so big that it fascinated Lorna, and she immediately laid claim to the behemoth. I was made to share my dolls, and for once I had no objection; I was glad to do it. Then Grandmother spotted Lorna through the kitchen window playing with it in the sand, feeding it mud pies and making it more antique by the mouthful. She rushed out to rescue it and placed it in the parlor on the tapestried love seat we never used, issuing a warning that it was to stay put. The boys pounced quickly, devilishly disembowelling it on the spot and laughing at the dangling arms and legs. When Grandmother stepped into the parlor for a few quiet moments with her dear Peter (may he rest in peace), she found the doll splayed and spilling sawdust, somewhat demobilized. I was on the kitchen couch holding the baby when she stormed in, outraged and emphasizing with a pointed finger that she was thoroughly disgusted with me for not keeping an eye on it.

I couldn't stand the doll, so I put it on one of the chairs in the bedroom to sit and wait on death row. Naturally, it disappeared, and when Grandmother asked me where it was, I was sure I had no idea. Then on a trip to the outhouse, she spotted some familiar tidbits lying on the ground. Sleuth-like, she picked up the trail and followed it into the apple packing house. There, dangling lifelessly from the vise was her beloved doll, its head crushed. Grandmother came in to the kitchen carrying the remains, basically drawn and quartered. She was livid and demanded answers. There was no doubt her doll had a rough go of it, but I tried to explain that it was just the way things worked around here. Her lecture gave me pause to appreciate what people gave me out of the goodness of their hearts and to cherish possessions on that premise. I suppose I more than anyone should have understood the doll's significance.

I don't recall Mother's defence of me to Grandmother; no one ever crossed her, but after one of Grandmother's harangues that I was an ungrateful wee lassie, Mother said collusively behind her back, "Never mind wasting tears over the dirty old thing. I'm glad it's gone, it was probably full of germs." I think it was then that Grandmother's reserve of generosity froze, because after that desecration she promised she would never give me another thing. She didn't, and I hardly got a pleasant word. Out of guilt, I avoided crossing her path except to say good morning or good night, as was required. Grandmother kept her promise until she was ninety-six, when she gave me the powder jar Dad had made for Aunt Elsie. She kept her promises well. Of course, promises are made to keep.

In spite of his handiwork with the vise, Daniel proved to be the fair-haired boy, and Grandmother's peak was somewhat mollified when she saw how eagerly he wanted to play the violin. One antique was saved and that is a wonder. It would be impossible to tally the number of toy pianos, xylophones, horns, Jew's harps, ocarinas, mouth organs, whistles, and flutes that the boys demolished from one Christmas to the next with no obvious sign of skill beyond destruction. If they felt an urge to produce their own music, they whittled a willow twig and worked on it until it could produce one note, which showed nothing more than a lack of talent. Mother and Dad were convinced that Daniel had a hidden cache of musical potential, so he began lessons right away, before school closed.

His interest quickened when he developed a passion not only for the violin, but also for Inez Baird, a teacher who charmed the citizens of Bear River by organizing a rhythm band. Daniel was smitten, but the love affair ended when Miss Baird left to marry a minister.

At first, Grandmother was edified on hearing Daniel's daily devotion to his scales, and in no time he was playing "Mary Had a Little Lamb" with conviction. I watched as she patiently listened to his efforts and heaped him with praise, so I asked for lessons as well. But it was a foregone conclusion that music was not my forte. I couldn't sing high, I couldn't sing low, leaving me with one wobbly octave. When Dad asked us to sing "La Marqueta" for a nickel, I desperately strained for the high notes that Daniel sang so sweetly. At the dinner table, the MacGregors freely discussed my lack of a musical gene, and Grandmother said under her eyebrows, "If I were you young lady, I'd leave that violin alone." The more I was discouraged, the more I was determined to prove everyone wrong. Dad, always quick to encourage an interest, finally said I could, if that was what I wanted. Soon, the general consensus was confirmed and all agreed that I would never make the concert stage, "You're no Yehudi." Grandmother encouraged me not to practice one hour a day. When I insisted that Miss Baird told me to, Grandmother said outright, "You don't need to, you're not musical." I knew I had no talent, but I refused to give up. Daniel helped me as we fiddled around that summer. It was all a matter of jealous competition.

With all the daily irritants in a house of 17 people, Grandmother soon tired of Daniel's repetitive "Mary Had a Little Lamb." The accolades petered out, replaced by an edgy, "Daniel! That will do! Och! I've never heard such a noise." Then I would tune up and work my scales, up and down, searching for those elusive notes until every draw of the bow scraped at Grandmother's exposed nerves. Such was the state of the art. She ordered me in no uncertain terms to put the violin down, and I'm sure she would have gladly taken it out to the apple packing house. In the beginning, Grandmother thought she had done a good thing, but no good deed goes unpunished. She finally conceded, Och, it was chronic and she was sorry she gave it to him.

When school started in the fall, Daniel couldn't wait to resume his lessons. I wanted them as well and begged so much that in spite of money being recklessly squandered, Dad gave in. Miss Baird offered encouragement, saying she saw signs of potential. But it all became a curse when Daniel made me carry the violin and its heavy wooden case in return for his sharing. I stumbled along with it slung around my neck like the proverbial albatross. When my strength failed me, I dragged it along the road or plunked it down and ran, leaving it for the horses to trample. Daniel would chase me down me and pinch me in punishment, accompanied by his disciplined warning to pick it up, Or Else! 'Or else' being a cornucopia of unpleasant alternatives. Through thunderstorms and blizzards, I dragged myself home with that leaden burden like *The Man With The Hoe*, 'bowed by the weight of centuries,' longing for a Bridge Of Sighs, not to throw myself over, but to get rid of another of Grandmother's valued antiques.

I stuck with the violin in spite of it all, so I do have Grandmother to thank for my musical education, which continued uninterrupted until I left home at nineteen. Mother would be singing, records would be playing and underneath the classicism would be my twangy dissonance. I knew I was no Menuhin, as Grandmother so often reminded me, but at least I appreciated one of her antique gifts.

I never knew the meaning of the word antique until I was older and saw the word on a store window. I looked in with distaste at the display of dirty, grimy old things. At the time, my scrap book bulged with clippings from the *London Illustrated News* and *Women's Weekly* showing my favourite rooms of my future dream home, taken from the stately homes of England, basically antique. Our own complement of household belongings came brand-new and direct from the Eaton's catalogue, $1.00 each for kitchen chairs, I saw the price in the catalogue when Mother ordered them. They were new, but it wasn't long before I viewed their ordinariness as if they were antiques. A voice far in the back of my head said, 'no, no, I'll never have them.' And what did I do when in dire straits later in life? I went down to an antiques shop and got those very same chairs for the elevated price of $4.00, very antique and very much in need of repair. I sat in praise and comfort of the mighty oak, and I sat on them until a few years ago. As far as antiques are concerned, it was long ago established in my mind that someone else's trash is not my treasure. I've always liked the new and unused, even though my home is full of trash.

MOTHER AND DAD WERE very good to Grandmother. They deferred to her as the matriarch, and except for Dad's sly humour, they overlooked her arguments, tirades and bad manners. Dad took Grandmother and the aunts on trips and let them charge whatever they wanted at the Trading Company. When Aunt Nan saw a hat she wanted at Mrs. Yorke's, Mother said of course she could buy it and even tried it on herself. Every sunny Saturday they strolled down to Barr's for bobs and marcelles and to have their nails manicured. Grandmother said you could always tell a lady by her hands. I suspected there was more to it than that. When Dad went to Montreal, he brought back several pieces of brass work for Grandmother, which she accepted in rare good grace. He gave the aunts white gold watches with tiny diamonds and black straps, and made a brass powder jar for Aunt Elsie. He stopped at St. John for bolts of material, including a homespun in beautiful robin's egg blue, and Mother spent hours at the sewing machine and hours more on the glide swing putting finishing touches on dresses and skirts, but she never wore any of them. That summer must have cost Dad a fortune, but I never heard a word of complaint.

Dad made a powder jar for Aunt Elsie because she took a relentless ribbing from the uncles as the only left-handed member of the family and the only one with freckles. Uncle Peter would say to her, "Is that you Elsie? I can't see you for your fernitickles." Aunt Elsie would toss her head in the grand manner and say that freckles were a sign of beauty, "And I am a very beautiful woman!" Now that was the sort of enlightenment a 7-year-old freckled girl like myself needed. When she dressed to go to the village, she powdered her face so heavily that the teen-age uncles teased her that the powder could be scraped off with a trowel. Uncle Peter would say, "Och! Surely this is Elsie's ghost before me." She didn't care. She was tiny, dainty and fastidious, and I, for one, thought the powder made her glamorous. I loved watching as she dabbed her face. She would ask if any freckles showed, and if I pointed one out she would say, "Oh, dear!" and take the puff and dab my nose. She promised that when she was finished with the box of Coty powder, with its pretty powder puffs all over it, she would give it to me. She kept her promise, and that was one of the wonderful things that happened that summer. There was something so out of the ordinary about opening that empty box and inhaling its faint perfume, a definition of the undefined. It transported me beyond the farm and my bare feet and grimy dress stained with baby's burps. I loved that box and for years I kept it up on a shelf holding my embroidery needles, beyond the reach of children. My lovely dolls barely lasted a summer, mishandled and mutilated, but for years I treasured that silly little cardboard powder box with its soft bouquet.

Aunt Elsie and Uncle Peter

Aunt Nan came to Bear River in the throes of love, never for a moment dreaming that it could be as doomed as death. She placed Evelyn Thompson's picture on her bureau and adored it like an icon, her adulation steeped in exquisite sighs as her face lit up like a moonstone. Aunt Nan's rapture rubbed off on me and I adored him as well. There wasn't much love around the house at that time so I latched on to Evelyn Thompson in my dream world. Not only do I still remember his name, but I can still see his dark handsomeness: that slick, brilliantined hair, the three-quarter profile, perched on the corner of a table with one leg casually swinging. All too soon the old maxim about absence making the heart grow fonder proved to be an outright lie. Out of sight was out of mind, and Evelyn Thompson, that perfectly handsome louse, found a likely substitute and was going to marry her. And he did. Aunt Nan wilted visibly day by day, and when I, unsuspecting since no one had informed me, picked up the picture to admire him, Aunt Nan screamed in hysteria, "Put that picture down and never dare touch it again!" I ran out of the room.

A few days later, after refusing to eat or associate with the rest of the family, she took the picture and smashed it to the floor. Then, seeing that Evelyn Thompson was now staring at her with the sidelong glance of a gigolo, she hysterically tore him to bits, shaking and trembling all the while. She took to her bed and refused to move, clutching her soggy handkerchief and sobbing to the ceiling, "Why did we ever leave home?" If anyone went near her or talked to her, she moaned in sepulchral tones, "Leave me alone." Her only actively conscious effort was to go to the outhouse, which caused children to flutter with excitement. We silently stared at her progress back and forth, not daring to say 'Hello, Aunt Nan'. It occurred to me that Aunt Nan was doing a lot of things that I would be reprimanded for, but curiously, even Grandmother was noticeably restrained. Mother and Dad sympathized; let her cry all day and starve herself and stare at the ceiling. Then one afternoon while everyone was sitting at the kitchen table having tea, Aunt Nan suddenly rose from her bed screaming, raced down the stairs, tore through the kitchen and out the screen door, running as fast as she could past the grapery, the strawberry patch, the raspberry and blackberry bushes, headed straight for the river, which at that point in the day was safely at low tide.

Such an alarming turn of events! We all ran after her only to find that she had stopped short of the mud flats and was sitting on her haunches, hugging an oak tree and crying into its trunk with her broken heart, as if that hefty oak could afford her the only solace to be found in Canada. Dad tried to pry her loose, but she held fast. My brothers giggled, so Mother sent them up to the house with a warning. Everyone was sent away, even Grandmother, leaving Dad to reason with her. In a little while they returned, Aunt Nan still sobbing, Dad's arms holding her gently. I still remember Dad sitting beside her on the kitchen couch, stroking her hair the way he did his children's and telling her it was going to be all right, insisting that she eat and have tea. I'm sure the only thing that would have given her any hope was to get away from Bear River, and perhaps he promised her that. Grandmother's inscrutable wisdom was, "There are as many fish in the sea as ever came out." Fish? At a time like this? Under normal circumstances I liked Aunt Nan, she was so pretty and sweet, but there was no question her natural gaiety was gone. In off-moments, her big brown eyes gazed past everyone and bored holes through walls. There was no longer any excitement about going to the post office, walking all those miles to the village and back. She didn't bother. I learned early on that love is uncertain with certain people and could make a young girl lose her mind, as Aunt Nan most certainly did. It was her first love, as desperately tragic and sad as a flamenco love song, and they are the world's saddest.

Aunt Nan, Uncle Peter and Mary

Aunt Ellie (Helen) was Uncle Douglas' twin and seemed quiet and vacuous, like me. Looking back, I can see that she was timid and shy and daunted by the whole clan of MacGregors, who were so sure of themselves and didn't mind saying so. She pouted and Grandmother would say, "If you don't mind opening your mouth, would you mind telling me what's wrong with you." She would give the proper answer, "Nothing." As often as not, Grandmother would say, "Then don't go around with that look on your face." The few times I remember her asserting herself, they backfired.

One day everyone was preparing to go to a barn dance, an event for the young and vibrant. In the midst of all Mother had to do, Aunt Ellie asked Mother to make her a dress for the occasion. Mother went down to the Trading Company and came home with a bluish-teal crepe and a pattern in the recognizable style of the twenties: scoop neck, no sleeves, no waist, up to the knees and a frill hanging down vertically instead of the traditional horizontal. Mother was a wizard with the sewing machine, and she sat down and zipped it up in no time. It was a beautiful dress and Aunt Ellie was thrilled. She couldn't wait to wear it to the dance, so she wore it to the dinner table. Then, in the middle of a typical mealtime fracas, she dropped her bread and butter on her lap, leaving a large grease stain. The Scottish wars suffered a hesitation as Aunt Ellie became hysterical and burst into tears. Off came the dress for Mother to fix. She put the flat irons on the stove and scurried about for brown paper to blot the stain, but nothing worked. At the end of a long day, Mother was sick and tired of everything, her household was out of control, so she told Aunt Ellie that she should have been more careful and to wear something else to the dance. Aunt Ellie was inconsolable. The grease stain took on new dimensions, and she began to suffer seriously. Grandmother was commanding, "Will you stop that! I said stop it! Stop it and I mean it! Off with you! Off to your room and shut the door! If you hadn't been so clumsy! It's your own fault!" Later, while Mother was nursing the baby, she asked me to put the flat irons back on the stove and to bring her the large Indian basket that held snatches of material. She got busy manufacturing more frills that effectively hid the grease spot. Aunt Ellie pieced herself together in time for Murray Harris' taxi to bundle them off to some barn. The dance didn't cheer her up and she pouted at the table for days.

Then one dinnertime after all the rattling discussions and amid compliments directed at the other aunts for their delicious meal, Aunt Ellie announced that she would make a chicken stew. She'd never made one before, but she knew how. Jim and Alec, the teenaged uncles, weren't very nice, they never were, "There'll be a blue moon in the sky before I eat your chicken stew; it would kill me stone dead," or "You'll have to eat it yourself, I value my life!" Grandmother's only discipline for those two was, "Hold your tongue!" It did no good. Even I could see that Dad was out of his element preaching peace to this bunch. When Aunt Ellie started to cry, Dad begged her not to, and she miraculously cheered up when he promised her two dollars to make the stew, "Theah is nothing I like better than a good chicken stee-yoo." This was news to me, because we never had chicken stew. We had Irish stew and had it often, we had roast chicken almost every Sunday, we had chicken croquettes with parsley sauce, chicken soup and chicken this and that, so I suppose Mother thought enough was enough.

Early next morning the stew swung into high gear when several Wyandot and Plymouth Rock hens lost their heads on the chopping block. We all sat at the kitchen table plucking and singeing pinfeathers. I eagerly listened as the aunts' conversation bounced around the table. Dad cleaned the chickens, removing those horrid giblets and the pearl-like string of unhatched eggs. Then we were shooed out of the kitchen, leaving Aunt Ellie alone with a huge pot and no one to interfere.

Come mealtime, everyone gathered for the pièce de résistance, which turned into a piece of outright resistance. The chicken was tough, the vegetables half cooked, the dumplings heavy and soggy, all of it held together by a glutinous, lumpy gravy. The uncles had been out in the gardens and were hungry, so it was no joke and they were rude. Grandmother was not one to give credit where it was not due, so she made her point. Mother never commented on hopeless situations and she surely had a thousand things on her mind—the next meal for seventeen people was coming up. Dad was the only one in a good mood and said it was the best chicken stee-yoo he had evah tasted. As he said this, the whole onion he was tackling bounced off his plate and rolled across the table in front of Daniel, who picked it up and returned it to Dad's plate. Then it bounced off a second time and Dad said, "Mah, oh mah, that is one lively onion." Everyone started to laugh, and Aunt Ellie crumbled, leaving the table in utter despair. Uncle Jim reminded her over his shoulder, "And you got two dollars for this insult." We were forbidden to leave the table until we had finished everything on our plates, and then we had to tell Aunt Ellie how much we had liked it. I didn't dare have another chicken stew for years, so I assumed that Aunt Ellie's was the definitive effort and a good reason to steer clear.

Later, Aunt Ellie was hauled out of the bedroom cupboard where she had sulked for days. She was told to get that look off her face. No one ever knew what was wrong. Grandmother would say, "I'd like to ask what's the matter with you now?" The correct answer would be, "Nothing," and Grandmother would say, "It's just as well. Then just get a pleasant look on your face for a change." I was too young to be sympathetic and could only see that she was hurt and remote. Lorna loved her, and she was always so gentle with little children, playing games and keeping them entertained for hours. Aunt Ellie never married and lived with Grandmother until her death. In those later years and in a mollified mood, Grandmother would say, "Ellie is so good to me." The praise came much too late to give a young woman's character a boost.

There was a tremendous amount of cooking that summer, much of it done by the aunts, who found they had nothing better to do on the farm. While Mother had the usual preoccupations of nursing the baby, bunching vegetables for market and managing the accounts, the aunts kept busy by vying with each other in the kitchen. They were all marvellous cooks, even Aunt Ellie had her moments, but pretty Aunt Cathy excelled, and this preoccupation eventually became her profession. Aunt Cathy was a careless optimist who seemed to take everything in stride, calmly doing her needlework or sewing pretty voile dresses. In the kitchen, she often took over from Mother, and then our menu assumed a distinctly Scottish flavour: Dundee cakes, potato pancakes, roly-poly, soda bread, jam cakes, short cakes, fruitcakes, suet pudding, Spotted Dick, treacle tarts, vinegar tarts, Scotch pancakes for tea, pies and fools for dessert. Since we had more eggs than we ever needed, there was a plenitude of custards, heavenly meringues and puddings, the Queen of Puddings—my new favourite. There were Scottish recipes perhaps untranslatable into plain English: cock-a-leekie, stovies, toad-in-the-hole, mince, barley soup, Scotch eggs (a new mystery), and wonderful puff pastry for beefsteak and kidney pies. Oatmeal was a rampant cultural artifact, as solid as Scottish history. Though far removed from their home turf, the MacGregors remained staunchly patriotic in their cooking.

For me that epic summer, the kitchen became a hub of excitement and confusion, a dizzying combination. When I sat on the couch by the large window holding the baby, it was the first time I could listen to women's conversation without being banished. I finally felt as though I had equal privilege with the boys. It wasn't just the event of the summer, it was the event of my life. The aunts were well-educated and included me in the conversation whenever they could. As they chatted, their busy fingers sewed or knitted, and since I had just taken up the craft, they would pause to show me stitches or little tricks. They were always cooking, and since I knew where everything was, I felt important as they listed off ingredients for me to gather. Sometimes, as Aunt Cathy rubbed the stove top with paper to remove the stove black, she would have me get started with the mixing, and soon I was making my first Lardy Johns. Those were my first real cooking lessons, and I felt so proud when I put them in the oven and closed the door, the aunts looking on in approval.

Perhaps because the aunts had no social life on the farm and no hope of one unless they buggied out to some barn miles away for dances with the local yokels they ridiculed, they enjoyed rumbling about the kitchen, perhaps trying to satisfy a primordial yearning that they decided wasn't about to happen just yet. As I look back, cooking certain foods were about the only thing that made them happy, and haggis made them happiest of all. In a moment of unbridled enthusiasm, they decided it was high time for haggis, the very name striking an unfriendly, sibilant note in my recollection. When confronted by certain foods, Mother's natural calm vanished, and she was adamant that there were two things she simply would not abide: blood sausage and haggis. Grandmother was appalled at this heresy, and concluded a stirring patriotic discourse with, "Many's a time you ate haggis and liked it," while Mother replied, "Only because I had to."

Aunt Nan satisfied my curiosity about blood sausage, saying it was fresh blood cooked in sheep intestines and it was delicious. I thought I would die. Even today I turn my head at cold meat counters. Aunt Nan then revealed the mystery of haggis: ground mutton, oatmeal and onions, all neatly bundled in a sheep's stomach, and it too was delicious. I immediately added haggis to a list that included blood sausage, jellied tongue, headcheese, and all of Dad's grisly delicacies.

At the dinner table, the prospect of haggis highlighted the binge of Scottish history and politics that we digested with every meal, stirring the MacGregors to a nationalistic frenzy. To avoid a Scottish civil war, Mother conceded the kitchen with her usual caution, "And don't forget to wash the pot." The next day, Eugene Crosscup drove in through the maple grove with his meat truck. Basins in hand, the aunts skipped out the kitchen door to examine the delicacies hanging on Eugene's meat hooks. They selected a variety of cuts and topped it off with a huge slab of liver. Liver–my nemesis; I should have known. I was an anaemic child with a weak stomach and had been force-fed liver for years, which only added to my run-down condition. When I was sufficiently sly, I would slip the leathery liver under the table to be disposed of later. I can still see myself scraping the fried onions carefully off the liver, and then in the middle of a Scottish eruption, slipping it off my plate and into my bloomer leg. I didn't care about the mess it made, as long as my plate was clean. And oh! the triumph as I fed it to Scotty. No one was any the wiser that the dog's health was improving. There would be no way to escape liver in haggis.

In a celebratory mood, the aunts began grinding the meat as blood spurted fitfully over the table. Tears and sniffles followed as they chopped onions, clenching phosphorous matches in their teeth to combat the scent. They floured a cotton cloth and fingers tenderly spread the pastry on top. Then they seasoned the meat mixture with this and that, blessing it with quantities of oatmeal before lovingly dumping it on the pastry. I couldn't watch as they encased it all in a sheep's stomach, but as the whole great, humongous mass took shape, I knew I could never eat haggis, and if forced, I would die a uniquely Scottish death. "It'll be a great haggis," the aunts agreed in a wave of patriotic over-euphoria. Of course it would! All haggises are. They securely tied it with string and deposited their objet d'art in the large preserving pot to bubble on top of the stove. It was a big one. But the more I thought about haggis as it bubbled away, the sicker I got, and I finally stumbled into bed with violent pains. Mother was sure I had eaten green apples, the usual reason for summer pains. Knowing I was safe in bed, I suddenly felt better, and what's more, as a sick child I got my favourite food, pap. I then realized I possessed a wonderful defence mechanism to protect me from any number of foods; such a timely blessing.

When I think of pap, I always think of the warm comfort of the sick bed, the attendant loving concern, the undivided attention to the exclusion of other children. Only then did I become the only child I always wanted to be. Pap was a dish of exquisite simplicity: a slice of freshly baked bread (and bread was baked daily) lightly toasted over the open lid of the stove, buttered, placed in a bowl with boiled, creamy milk, and sprinkled with amber crystals of Demerara sugar. Unfortunately, when I think of pap I also think of haggis, that one-time event linking the two foods in extremis.

Luckily, the gluttonous MacGregors savaged the whole bulbous mass, so there was no danger of leftovers. Even so, in my mind, I really did eat that haggis. Thereafter, I suspected everything the aunts concocted with ground meat. Nothing was safe anymore, not mince, not shepherd's pie, not Scotch eggs, nothing. I approached the table with unease.

I used to wonder why the Scots wore kilts. Why they ate blood pudding. Why ever did they eat haggis? Why did they put oatmeal in everything? Why did they eat skink? One day as Daniel was being chased out of the kitchen, he asked the aunts what was for dinner. Grandmother dismissed him, "Off with you laddie, you'll find out when you get to the table." Aunt Elsie happily added, "We're having skink." Sitting on the sidelines with the baby, I shrivelled. Daniel's curiosity ignited because it could only mean one thing–skunk. "I don't want any," he snarled. Daniel asked Mother if we were really going to have skunk for dinner and Mother snapped, "Just stop being silly." So he asked Dad, who shook his head and said, "Son, wheah do yew get your ideahs?" Mother had to drag him to the table. No, he'd never eat skunk. "Sit there if you know what's good for you, you little villain, I've had enough." Aunt Elsie brought a large platter of creamy haddock to the table and served each plate with a small volcano of mashed potatoes, the crater filled with buttery haddock in sauce,

Uncle Douglas

much like what we always had and no surprise. Skink was definitely not skunk. Years later, Grandmother reminisced in her old age, 'Och, do you mind the time this or that? And the time you thought you were eating skunk.' She enjoyed Daniel's mischief. It made memories.

In the process of getting over the trauma of Aunt Nan's ill-fated love, we suffered more midsummer madness when Uncle Peter fell in love. And even worse, he fell in love with Uncle Douglas' brand new girlfriend, Verna Parker, a teacher from Shubenacadie whom they met and sparred for at a barn dance. In these volatile circumstances, there was nothing to do but get on with the business of pummelling each other out on the dance floor. They battled for the redoubtable Venus, thereby shocking civilized barn dancers, causing a local disgrace and raising questions about recent immigrants. Love among the MacGregors was a serious business. They came to the Sunday breakfast table badly bruised, as surly as bears and looking like two raccoons. They ate in silence, looking neither left nor right and being especially intolerant of little children, who were told to go away and stop staring. Not knowing the details and only seeing the results, every child in the house asked, 'Uncle Peter or Uncle Douglas, what happened to your eyes or your nose or your cheek?' The answer was, 'You just never mind what happened to my eyes or my nose or my cheek.' Grandmother was the only one not at a loss for words. She was at her outraged best, claiming that your poor, dear father, God rest his soul, would be turning over in his grave, which gave me pause to uncomfortably wonder. Uncle Douglas conceded surprisingly quickly and could have saved himself some bruises and black eyes, because it wasn't long before he was sitting on Mr. W. W. Clarke's verandah swinging with the maid, whom I thought had the exotic name of Loretta. She was dark, pretty and very shy, and when I passed Mr. Clarke's jewel-like home, I'd look way up and see her in her maid's uniform shaking out a mop or polishing windows.

Uncle Douglas was my favourite uncle, the handsomest and the gentlest. By any standards he hardly fit the MacGregor mold, fraught with stinging fragments of Black Irish. He was soft spoken with a quiet sense of humour that he never tested on Grandmother the way Dad did. Upon arrival, he worked the gardens with Dad from morning till night with a diligence that Uncle Peter lacked. Uncle Douglas and Dad got on well. He seemed to enjoy the work, vastly different from the decorator (plasterer) he was in Scotland. Since the arrival of the MacGregor clan, love and marriage became a significant issue, so I asked Uncle Douglas at the dinner table if he were going to marry Loretta. His jaw locked and he said he would never marry. Not him! Never! He did. Later, when Uncle Douglas returned to Scotland and married Teresa, he was the only family member Mother wrote to, and the only one I wrote to as well. I suspect he was very much like Grandfather, a gentle soul.

Naturally, Mother was curious about the enticing Venus who had won Uncle Peter's heart, and we all laughed when Uncle Douglas said she was tall with big feet, a crooked nose and a dimple in her chin. He was right. Verna towered over Uncle Peter, and I definitely did not approve of this unromantic coupling. In short order and while he still bore the wounds of having fallen in love, Uncle Peter created a minor sensation by announcing that he would be marrying this beguiling siren whom he had discovered in a country barn. This was a bit of a shock, even suspect. Still, having battled to the near-death, the prize could be nothing less. Uncle Douglas speculated on who the best man would be, but seemed more concerned about whether his nose was broken. We children bubbled as if it was the most exciting thing since Eve ran away with the apple. Marriage was not an ordinary occurrence along the Chute Road; it had gone out of style years ago. Abandoned farms stood beside the homes of elderly couples and lonely widows; there was no choice, no one was young any more.

They planned the wedding for next summer, but after all the discussion about receptions and honeymoons, one problem remained: exactly where would we put Verna? I asked Mother if Uncle Peter was going to move out; I needed to know. Grandmother heard my question and sniffed, "Why should he move when this is his farm." When Mother didn't hazard a correction, I was left wondering.

There was another troubling occasion when Mr. Harrow, recently of Scotland, visited the farm uninvited, perhaps having heard we were harbouring a Scottish enclave. People often just showed up and Mother and Dad were always glad to have them. I thought Grandmother would be delighted to see a countryman in full regalia, but his dark green tartan was not MacGregor.

He was very tall and burly, very dark with black eyes and a black beard that covered his features and made him look ferocious. As Grandmother described him, "What a sight!" Moreover, his booming voice exaggerated every Scottish burr, irritating Grandmother's precise diction to the extent that she said, "You can't be Scotch Mr. Harrow, I don't understand a word you say." He tried to explain that he came from the Highlands somewhere, but recovered the conversation by taking it to a more satisfactory level. He told Grandmother that Uncle Peter had a lovely farm and knew how to farm successfully. "Oh yes," Grandmother went on, raving proudly, "there was nothing in the beginning but Peter made it what it is, and now it's the best farm in Bear River." Mother and Dad never said a word. My mind swirled in an undercurrent. Was the farm Dad's or Uncle Peter's?

I also remembered that day because Mr. Harrow brought along his daughter Hannah, and trying to do my share of the polite thing to do, I could think of nothing else but to demonstrate my attempts at cartwheels. Daniel had been coaching me; he wheeled about the grass like a dervish, but I could never get my feet over my head. I flailed around and around in full view of everyone seated under the Bartlett pear tree, my legs frantically striving for balance, my dress over my head and showing my bloomers. I heard my name in a southern drawl and went to my room in meditation of what young ladies never did. Days later, Mother and I were on our way to Barr's barber shop when Mr. Harrow hove into sight: kilt flipping, too tall, too dark and somewhat fearsome. Mother sucked in her breath and said the definitive Scottish expletive, "Och!" There were how-do-you-do's while Mr. Harrow offered his hand and simpered his delight at seeing such a lovely lady. During the conversation he said to Mother, burring away, "Och, I canny believe yoorrr Scot Mrs. Marvin!"

"Oh really," said Mother, "how so?"

Mr. Harrow went on, "Nae, I canny believe it, why ye hae nae accent."

Mother cut him short, "I'm just as Scotch as you are, only where I come from we talk properly. Good day Mr. Harrow." Mother walked me off quickly, schooling me in the art of the not-so-subtle snub. Crossing the bridge Mother hissed, "I have no time for fools." Mother was unforgiving; he had visited twice and should have known. That evening at the dinner table, Mother said she didn't want to see Mr. Harrow on her farm again.

Dad solved the problem of Uncle Peter and Verna by deciding to build the uneven love birds a home of their own. He immediately bought the strip of land above the Miller field between our farm and McCormick's. It was a gorgeous piece of land, cleared and ready for planting, sweeping down from the Chute Road to a stand of trees along the river. The new house, the barn and the land would be Dad's wedding present. He then brought his drafting table out of the apple packing house to draw up the plans, placing it in the downstairs bedroom in front of the window looking down to the oaks. For weeks, he spent every spare minute poring over the creamy drafting paper, the precise many-angled drawings evolving into a new house. After a day of haying, weeding, picking vegetables and shipping them to the Pines Hotel, sawing wood and milking cows, Dad would sit down at his drafting board with his children clambering all about him, everyone anxious to see what Uncle Peter's house would look like. I was fascinated and enjoyed watching him. The house would sentinel the whole of Uncle Peter's property at the top of his hill, edging the Chute Road with a beautiful, broad view clear down to the river. Every joist, timber, two by four and slat was measured to the inch, meticulously drawn and then added to a tally in a notebook like the ones that held his engineering exams. When Dad finished the house inside and out, replete with every shingle and every bush, he decided to paint it with my watercolours. I saw what he was doing, but I didn't question him. When he was happy with the result, he called Mother, "Dearie, ah have finished, come and have a look-see." Mother gave a look and screamed with laughter, saying the house looked wonderful but the colours were not Verna's style. The roof was purple, the house was pink and the whole landscape was shot through with a rainbow of contradictory colours. He insisted that the roof was brown. It was then that I discovered Dad was colour-blind.

The digging of the cellar began immediately. A house had once stood on the site and burned down, leaving an indent that simplified the task. The first problem was getting the teenaged uncles, Alec and Jim, to lift a finger. Dad had no use for them because they rarely helped with the chores, and when they did, they were surly and uncooperative. They pouted when he refused to take them in to the village, and then they thoroughly soured, mumbling regularly about giving the country back to the Indians. I didn't like the teenaged uncles and I knew I never would. They had inherited the superiority complex of the motherland and looked upon us as colonial bad genes. Back home, they never had to do anything more strenuous than blacken their boots, which suited Grandmother just fine. I was amazed that she had encouraged their laziness to the point that it took root. She saw everyone else's faults so clearly, but her all-seeing eye had a blind spot and passed over those two louts. Uncle Peter had been similarly coddled, but now he had a fiancé waiting on a house and the prospect of a 'wee bairn' or two. The pressure was on after years of idling by the Franklin fireplace, and I suspect he was experiencing sticker shock at the price of love. He and Grandmother sparred in acidic debate about the teenaged uncles, and this eliminated all their good mornings and good nights for a while. But Uncle Peter prevailed, and after evening chores, everyone dug until last light. The teen-aged uncles moaned that their backs were broken, but no sympathy issued forth. Instead, a new and improved Uncle Peter stunned the dinner table crowd by advising them that there was nobility in work. I hesitated over a mouthful of mashed potatoes and decided that the nobility in question stemmed from helping Uncle Peter rather than the work itself. His life's journey was shipping him off to the land of responsibility and he balked at the solo passage.

When the foundation and cellar of Uncle Peter's house were finished, Dad hitched up Harry and took him to the lumber mill at the Head of the Tide, where the wagon was piled high with wood, barrels of nails, bundles of shingles, windows and doors. Pinney Henshaw, who was married to Verna's sister Elsie, was hired to help build the house and managed to stay sober until it was finished, but no sooner was he on another job than he fell off a roof, quite inebriated, and was killed. It was a village tragedy. For years, I had been feuding at school with Lawrence Henshaw, a zealous Boy Scout afflicted with do-gooder syndrome. On the day of his father's funeral, Lawrence's desk sat empty. Every child looked over to Mount Hope and watched as the soldiers carried the casket up to the grave with Lawrence following behind. 'Last Post' sounded, and the notes filled the

Clarence 'Pinney' Henshaw

classroom as we leaned over our books. Bear River had many veterans, and some carried their burden of memory with a limp. The long reach of the war eventually claimed them.

With weddings come the inevitable in-laws, and several weeks after Uncle Peter's announcement, Mother was surprised by a visit from a coterie of Parkers. In tow with Verna was her mother, her two sisters, Ruth Parker and Elsie Henshaw, and Aunt Loo Robinson, none of whom Mother had met. The swirl of activity cheered up the aunts and Grandmother took over. As usual, her preliminaries included ushering me out the door with instructions to walk the baby until further notice. I trudged back and forth, pushing the carriage down to the Red Astrakhan tree, back past the house, up to the barn and down to the Bridge Brook, again and again over the same terrain, watching with the eyes of a hawk for some development. Finally, Mother called me in so the ladies could inspect the baby. I listened like a spy at the dining room window as they marvelled at Joan's accomplishments, namely sucking on her toes and uttering inarticulate sounds. Then as everyone was leaving, I heard Mother say she was awfully sorry about the tea—a strange thing to say. Mother was fussy about her tea, it had to be scalding hot and if it wasn't scalding hot it wasn't tea, it was dishwater. Verna's mother had gulped her tea and promptly burned her mouth, sputtering and coughing and raising a kerfuffle. She burned her mouth so badly that she could neither eat nor drink and went home to Aunt Loo's a virtual cripple. Mother was sympathetic, but, I noticed, amused. That Saturday night, Mrs. Parker could not indulge in Aunt Loo's baked beans and Boston brown bread. On subsequent visits, Verna was not loathe to mention her mother's suffering and how long she took to heal. All Mother could do with passing reminders was to laugh, laugh right out loud. Mother was up against an impossible situation on the farm, and the introduction of the Parkers was another compound fracture. On sizing up Verna, Grandmother laid the groundwork for dislike, "She's an arrogant one, that one." She was.

DESPITE THE CONTINUAL WORK of the farm from early morning until our evening walk through the gardens, we enjoyed many welcome respites beneath the Bartlett pear tree when summer visitors arrived. Even though children were often relegated to the sidelines, these visits brought sporadic waves of excitement, washing over our summer months and painting them in brightly-coloured hues. When the Kniffens finally arrived to fill the Hollow with their warmth, and Mr. Bishop had settled into his aerie high above, only then was our eager anticipation of summer rewarded with a full complement of family.

That year, the MacGregors began the summer the same way we always had, with Mr. Bishop's Beech-Nut gum. He strode through the maple grove with those wonderful brown paper packages tucked under his arm: records for Mother, a book for Dad, Beech-nut gum and Farber pencils for us. When the gum was opened, the aunts and uncles dove in and then sat about the parlor chewing like contented cows. We children kept saying, "It's good, isn't it?" while Grandmother looked on in disgust, "If only you could see yourselves, you should take a good look and see yourselves as others see you." She thought it the height of vulgarity and didn't mind saying so in front of Mr. Bishop. Nevertheless, Mr. Bishop and the Kniffens saved the summer for Grandmother and the aunts. Visits gravitated up and down the Hollow throughout the season. They liked to sit in the dappled shade of Mr. Bishop's rose arbor where they could discuss the arty side of New York. Then they would troop down to see the Kniffens and swing on the hammocks or sit on the soft lawn in front of the beach. If they saw Mr. Bishop or the Kniffens coming up from the Hollow, they would all amble off to the village, returning later for tea under the Bartlett pear tree. Grandmother was at her social best with visitors, and I must admit that she exhibited a somewhat sudden joie de vivre, her high, light voice sweeping up in laughter. The aunts were no slouches either; they were convivial, made friends easily and loved to laugh. The aunts lionized Mr. Bishop, and Grandmother declared him the wittiest man she had ever met. It seemed his worst fault was that he was old and unsaleable on the MacGregor marriage market. He enthralled them with tales of the Met, the bright lights of Broadway and the sheer wonder of New York, warning them of premeditated New York nights full of plays and operas, his squiring them like the suave, well-seasoned boulevardier that he was. The Aunts loved it, they were practically gone. I went too, a waif in my bare feet holding a drooling baby.

I don't recall that Dad ever said a word about the States during those conversations. He never revised Mr. Bishop's information and never joined in. Surely he must have seen New York on his travels, but it was as if he had divested the stars and stripes from his soul and had never been anything but Canadian.

The MacGregors more than made up for Dad's silence, recounting trips to Edinburgh and London to see D'Oyle Carte productions of Gilbert and Sullivan, plays by Sir James Barrie–Peter Pan rising above the floorboards, and another play they raved about titled *Mr. Pim Passes By*, which in later years I tried to find but never could. They talked of plays and operas in Glasgow and Helensburgh, pantomimes at Christmas, and even Mother's concerts were recounted enthusiastically. It seemed their world was nothing but music and theatre. Now, they were doomed to trot off to Digby for Saturday movies, though they still managed to swoon over Valentino and Raymond Navarro. Summer afternoons would drift pleasantly along as everyone chatted over tea while the aunts vied with each other in the kitchen, returning in minutes with trays of tarts or biscuits.

When the Kniffens, Mrs. Croscup or Mrs. McCormick stopped by, tea under the Bartlett pear tree would turn into a picnic under the maples. We would run to the gardens to give Dad and the uncles the urgent news. I can still see everyone quickly washing up at the sink, the kitchen pump squeaking noisily. We would rush out the screen door to take our place. It was so much better than sitting at the dining room table. For all the right reasons, the green shade and fresh air lightened mealtime conversation, and even Grandmother simmered down. Still, as gracious as she was with visitors, beneath her gaiety lay undertones, like sitting near a tack. One Sunday as everyone sat outside listening to Mother sing, Mr. Bishop said to Grandmother at the end of a song that he had heard all the great voices of the day and none compared to Mother's. By this time, Mother and Dad were to blame for Grandmother's miseries in Canada, so she had to administer pinpricks. In that airy voice of hers she said, "Oh, I don't know, I always thought Nan had the better voice." Whenever Grandmother was abrupt or sharp, Mother would whisper, "Don't pay any attention." Ordinarily I didn't, but this remark rang like a fire bell. Aunt Nan's voice was good, but it didn't compare. Grandmother's venom stung. That was the only criticism of Mother's voice I ever heard. Mother sat as if she didn't hear a thing, and a silence briefly settled until Dad said, "Dearie, Wha don't yew sing The Wearing of the Green." Even I knew what it meant. The aunts smirked, waiting for the explosion, but in the middle of Sunday afternoon company, Grandmother showed rare restraint and deftly turned the conversation.

Joe Warren was an older man whose family had once owned our farm. Mother and Dad always warmly welcomed his visits, and we would hear easy discourse and laughter filtering out the parlor window. Grandmother liked him too, but called him an old palaverer because of his courtliness. Actually, she was so tiny and Joe was over six feet, so he had to bend to her like a courtier. I liked it when he stopped me on the street and shook my hand, a grown-up gesture and a levelling courtesy. It may seem silly today, but I was taught to greet grown-ups with good morning, good afternoon and how-do-you-do, but never hello and hi like the Reade children, who learned all their colloquialisms from their American cousins. I was always very comfortable with this formality, which reached back beyond Edwardianism to Victorianism and hung on in the refined atmosphere of the village elite.

Joe lived on the Digby side, so by the time he arrived at our farm, it had already been a creditable hike. Sometimes he would bring along his two adult children, Rosalind and Wyman, and then the parlor would buzz. They were very witty and entertaining. I loved it when Rosalind came, because she always claimed the baby for the duration of the visit. For those few hours I had my freedom, but with so little practice, I had no idea what to do with it. Since having company was excitement in itself, I took my usual spot in the kitchen and helped out. Joe loved Mother's Scotch pancakes, made in a minute, the size of a dollar, served with jams and whipped cream. Mother always sent him home with a generous supply of his favourites. Guests never left empty handed.

One day Joe visited when the June roses were in full fragrance at the front door, and as he was leaving he asked Mother if she had ever seen his Aunt Charlotte standing by the roses, which she had planted. Aunt Charlotte, we then learned, had died of tuberculosis many years ago. The spinning wheel in the attic belonged to her. Mother and Grandmother were amused despite Joe's assurances that succeeding generations of Warrens had been visited by her–yes, right where they were standing. Daniel's curiosity was piqued. Had Joe seen her? No, but he wouldn't have minded meeting her. We were used to Biblical emanations, burning bushes, etc., so it hardly disturbed me and I put it out of my mind. Not Daniel. In bed at night, we discussed Aunt Charlotte and he was right, it did seem odd–were ghosts real or weren't they? He asked Grandmother what she thought, and she said bluntly, "I think you're a wee bit off," while everyone else at the table laughed. And then it happened. While everyone was sleeping soundly, Daniel went in to the kitchen for a snack, and there she was at the door barring his way, none other than Aunt Charlotte, a very old lady in old-fashioned clothes who stood determined. Daniel said he felt a cold breeze and ran back into the room screaming. He jumped into bed and grabbed my neck in a stranglehold, at which point I woke up screaming. I had been having a few nightmares about snakes and bugs, so screaming in the middle of the night was the norm. On principle, the other children joined in. Dad and Mother and all the MacGregors gathered around and listened to Daniel's gibberish. They wrote it off as a nightmare, treated with that time-honoured solution: a dose of Casagara. Then it happened again. Aunt Charlotte appeared in our bedroom. Feeling a cold breeze, Daniel awoke to see her busily flapping the sheets up and down, and when he tried to grab them she snatched them away. He screamed and yelled and called for help, strangling me all over again. What a night! Daniel babbled, wide-eyed with terror, and the MacGregors thought it a great show. The next morning, Grandmother said with disgust, "Och! you're not all there. It's just your imagination." One would have thought that Grandmother, being Irish, might have fallen in with Daniel and Aunt Charlotte, there being pixies and little men in her ancestry. How they all teased Daniel. He was furious at being the butt of so many jokes and said, "There are too many people in this house," as he ran outside to cool his nerves on the swing.

It didn't take long for Daniel to get back into high gear. When Dad's friends visited, they talked war, and that's what he liked—no cows or crop rotation for him. Old soldiers remembered every step they slogged, and it is to be wondered how they could ever forget. They sang their marching songs and talked about the war as if it were to be the last war. Grandmother cheered up on these visits and dove right in without a qualm. She was intelligent and enjoyed an audience, and not only an audience, an argument. Her high, light voice could be heard happily discussing every campaign and battle of the war. The aunts, making tea in the kitchen, would smirk that she was in her element. Grandmother knew as much about Dad's naval operations as he did. She told him all about the Dardanelles and Gallipoli and that bounder, Churchill. She knew the whole Mediterranean theatre. She was conversant with the progress of the army from start to finish as if she had been in the thick of it: Paschendale, The Somme, Vimy, and don't talk to her about Wipers (Ypres) or the left bank of the Marne. She was in the trenches with her son John (God rest his soul). She had been in the PBI (Poor Bloody Infantry).

One occasional guest was General Bremner, a tall, tweedy Englishman,[1] rather restrained and severe looking. He had served many years in India, and his stiff English stance and upper crust mumbling under his clipped moustache, his strutting about as if he were inspecting great armies prompted Mother to call him a silly ass. The General had several claims to fame: he had introduced pheasants (or maybe grouse) into that part of the province; he had, in his youth, helped introduce ice hockey from Nova Scotia to the rest of Canada; and what was much more fascinating to us, he had survived the war with a hole in his head. It was over his temple, about ¼" deep and was impossible to ignore. For Daniel, the hole in General Bremner's head was something of a mental preoccupation. Whenever the General visited, we discussed in our beds the miracle of being shot in the head and surviving, never once thinking of Dad's wounds.

The one joy of Daniel's life was adult conversation, so one afternoon when the General visited, he asked Dad if he could sit in the parlor. Normally, children never entered the adult purlieu, and we had to collect details by stealth, which only encouraged us to be deceitful.

---

1 Actually, he was Canadian.

Daniel would plant himself outside the parlor window where General Bremner's booming, drill sergeant voice spilled out loud and clear as he expounded on the opulence of the Raj, the contemptible Hun, and the craftsmanship of Micmac hockey sticks. That day, Daniel was allowed in the parlor on the condition that he sit quietly and not open his mouth. But that's what he did. He sat in open-mouthed wonder, staring at the hole in General Bremner's head. Dad noticed and curtly dismissed him. When the General left, Dad took him aside, but Daniel deflected, "I couldn't help it Dad, I was mesmerized." Mother was always quick with connecting paragraphs, "I'll mesmerize you if you ever stare like that again. I'll mesmerize you with a tingler." We had gone through periods of trying to mesmerize each other the way we had seen at the Chautauqua plays at school. We tied objects to a string and swung them back and forth, waiting for oblivion and wondering what would happen if we couldn't wake up. Uncle Peter said it could be done, but no one ever swooned. Daniel decided it didn't work on children.

Shortly after the General's visit, Col. Hamilton from Middleton was expected to stop by and pick up a copper tea kettle Dad had promised him. This news had Daniel hopping about with excitement and sheer delight, because Dad had warned him, hoping he wouldn't revert to type and stare, that Col. Hamilton not only had one arm, but better still, a glass eye. This was something we had never heard of. Once, a man came to the farm with a patch over his eye, so the empty space was hidden. The black patch looked like a mourning symbol. Daniel's information spread like a news flash, and we thrilled at the prospect of seeing such a thing. Dad, sensing trouble, decided to brief us before Col. Hamilton's arrival, hoping to avoid the humiliation of General Bremner's visit. Unfortunately, he briefed us so well that the glass eye became even more fascinating. As Dad explained, Col. Hamilton popped the eye in and out, and for the most part it looked normal except that his eyes crossed at times. We were amazed. Did it roll around? Did it fall out? He couldn't see out of it, could he? The pain of wounds was not even considered. I was awestruck that the glass eye could be just put in and taken out at will. Would wonders never cease! Dad got the drift from Daniel's in-depth questioning and threw up his hands,

"Sweetheart, ah am warning yew within an inch of your life and that goes for all you littah barbarians." An empty threat. As usual, Dad's warnings were permissive. When he urged us to tell the truth or he would eat his shirt or saw his leg off, what happened? Everyone chose the better alternative. Mother settled the situation by warning us to be on our best behaviour, to play nicely with the two Hamilton children and show them the chickens and cows. Despite Dad's ground work, Daniel was primed for Col. Hamilton's visit in the usual way. Under ordinary circumstances, the arrival of company stirred up excitement, but this visit caused an absolute sensation. I desperately wanted to see that glass eye. But it was all too bad for us, because when Col. Hamilton arrived with his family, Dad quickly ushered them into the parlor while Mother shuffled us off to the sidelines, telling us to be neither seen nor heard. Luckily, the children didn't want to play with us and stuck to their parent's side. Being a boy of quick decision, Daniel jumped at this opportunity. On the pretext of getting the children to come out and play, he snuck into the parlor while we hovered outside waiting for his report. The adults were so engrossed in conversation that Daniel remained undetected until Dad glanced over and saw him staring open-mouthed and studying every movement of that mesmerizing glass eye. Again he was abruptly dismissed, and out he gleefully ran. We crowded around for first-hand information. Yes, it was amazingly real, and yes, the Colonel had no difficulty at all in crossing his eyes. Well this we simply had to see. Poor Dad. All of his warnings were useless, because when it came time for Col. Hamilton to leave, there we were, half a dozen children poised strategically at the door with a clearly delimited curiosity. Dad tried to scatter us but we couldn't move, we were mesmerized. Daniel later got the benefit of Dad's disgust, but for once he defended himself with the truth, "Dad, I just couldn't help it." In bed at night, we thoroughly discussed the ins and outs of glass eyes. The way we laughed as the stars came out made it seem as if the ravages of war were funny. What couldn't you do with a glass eye, just think of the places you could put it, the fun you could have with it. We discussed it endlessly. We were such little devils.

In payment for the copper tea kettle, Col. Hamilton gave Dad a bottle of Haig & Haig Scotch whiskey in an elegant three-cornered bottle. We never had liquor in the house except at Christmas time when Dad bought Harvey's Bristol Cream for Mother to soak her cakes and flame her plum pudding. I suspect that Dad's health kept him abstemious, so Col. Hamilton's pretty bottle sat unopened on the parlor shelf, almost forgotten until one Sunday afternoon when Major and Amanda Simon paid us a visit. In through the maple grove they came, the Major with his prized yellow tomatoes and Amanda energized by her church choir. They settled in to the parlor and sipped their tea, but when the Major caught sight of the bottle, all thoughts of tea flew out the window. After a polite interval, the Major exclaimed in mock surprise, "Why Dan, you son of a gun, you have a bottle of whiskey and you haven't offered me a drop," which Dad promptly did. He sent Daniel up to the spring for ice-cold water and told the Major he was welcome to help himself, which he promptly did. Since an offer wasn't forthcoming, Amanda decided to be ignored no longer and said, "Well I just might like some as well." Grandmother straightened up. Mother shifted in her chair. Neither of them touched a drop, and they assumed that no lady ever would, and certainly not whiskey. That particular day I was given a chocolate to wind up the gramophone and watch the baby in the connecting bedroom, so I was privileged to witness the performance through the parlor curtains. Amanda, who was a mezzo (or a basso profundo, really), loved listening to our records and loved singing along to them even more, so she promptly tuned up and let loose. There really was no stopping her, though I could see that Dad would have enjoyed putting his hands around her neck. Grandmother, who sang beautifully, had not yet had the pleasure of Amanda's voice, so the impromptu recital came as a rude shock. Mother assumed that the Major was tone deaf since he never stopped her nonsense. Eventually and inevitably, Amanda asked for Offenbach's "Barcarolle," her favourite aria. I put it on and we all listened as she crooned along with Madame Schumann-Heink's undulating, faraway voice. It's funny how music is such a palpable connective in recall: Amanda singing, a baby mewling, a rocking chair squeaking, and Dad singing along, da-de-da,da-da-da,de-da. I remember Mother recounting that Madame Schumann-Heink had seven children and nursed her babies backstage of the world's opera houses. I had seen enough of that. It seemed so backstage. What fingerprinted the "Barcarolle" firmly in my mind was that the disenchanted of Middle Europe who had seen enough of this world were playing it on their gramophones as a sort of last rite before flinging their bodies into the Danube, the Dnieper or the Rhine and floating away from their miserable existence. It became a European cathartic, and I would hear remarks like, 'another victim of the Barcarolle.' For years, I had a childish fear that Offenbach would compel me to throw myself into the Rhine of Nova Scotia. It all came back to me a few years ago listening to a Met performance of the *Tales of Hoffman* with Tatiana Troyanos, her deep and lonely voice reaching up from the depths of a hypnotic river, waves seductively lapping over my memory.

As the "Barcarolle" drifted off, Amanda sat rocking in its wake before gulping her drink and calling for an encore. I cued the record and played it again, and again, and again. Amanda's voice became louder and her tremolo more uncontrolled as she growled out one "Barcarolle" after another. I was fascinated by the transformation and wondered if she would soon be rushing headlong towards the river. Between bouts, the Major was back in the trenches: a thousand-yard stare, sentences suddenly dropping off. The MacGregor women sat open-mouthed and speechless; the Poor Clare hadn't prepared them for this. When Mother got up to leave, she passed through the parlor curtains and told me, "Don't play that record again." Then she called me away from the gramophone to help in the kitchen. With suppertime nearing, Mother bristled, "I'll not be serving dinner to those two. They're getting tea and they're getting out." Amanda carried on though; she had the soul of an artist and just couldn't help herself. When Dad came in to the kitchen, he whispered, "She murdered the Barcarolle again." Later, he revised his opinion, "Dearie, that wasn't murder, it was wholesale slaughter." Dad was enjoying the visit, but it couldn't go on, not with Mother clicking her tongue in disgust, a menacing prelude. He went back to the parlor, but before he could give the Simons their marching orders, Uncle Peter returned from the village after his Sunday ritual of a trip to the drug store for the newspapers. He would deposit the hefty bundle in the parlor, and adults would leisurely sift through the stack while children waited on the sidelines for the comics.

On this day, Uncle Peter went into the parlor and took a look at the Simons, sinking into their chairs like ships going down. He picked up the remnants of the bottle and retreated to his bedroom for a Scottish siesta, taking the life of the party with him. On cue, Dad suggested a tour of the gardens and ushered the Major out for a promenade among the cabbage. The aunts poured some tea into Amanda, stood her on her feet and escorted out the door, where the fresh air prove a little too rich for her blood. She bobbed and weaved until the Major rescued her for an unsteady stroll through the maple grove. Arm in arm they walked like two grey-haired lovers, holding each other up more lovingly than I had ever seen. We watched them hobble up McCormick's hill while Grandmother tsk-tsked, "They're a right royal pair, all right. And on a Sunday, no less. Polly I hope I never see the likes of them in this house again."

Mother said, "I hope they make it over the hill."

The aunts were giggling and performing unsteadily, "More tea? I think I will, thank you."

As the Simons crested the hill for the long walk home, Mother turned to Dad, "Well, Mr. Marvin, there goes your brass tea kettle."

Oh, the table-talk at supper that night! If Dad thought ill of someone, he rarely showed it, but Grandmother said she did not like the Simons, in so many words. We all laughed at her comments, and for that brief spell everyone forgot their differences. "With a voice like that she sings in a church choir? Is it not chronic? They'd never darken my door. Polly, why bother with them? Why not have friends your own age?"

Mother said they just appeared one day, "What can you do?"

Despite all the talk and shock, I couldn't grasp the effect from the contents of such a small bottle, and such a pretty bottle at that. I knew all was not well with the Simons, but I wasn't sure why. I could only equate their condition to the dizziness I felt after eating green apples. I still thought the bottle quite elegant with its tricorn shape, so I asked Mother if I could keep it; I would put flowers in it. Mother snapped, "Certainly not. No daughter of mine is going to collect whiskey bottles." Dad closed the subject by saying he had enjoyed himself, the Simons had enjoyed themselves, so the bottle had gone to good use, "Another victim of the Barcarolle."

O N ONE OF **MOTHER'S** forays in to the village, she met a very nice lady whose name I forget, so I'll call her Mrs. Smith. Of all the people Mother knew, Mrs. Smith seemed to be the only one close to Mother's age. She was early widowed and quite well-off, having moved into a brand-new home built just for her on the Digby side. Mrs. Smith wanted Mother to visit and promised to call for her on a certain afternoon. Mother was eager to see the new home with its hardwood floors, frosted French doors, chandeliers, and best of all, a kitchen with an electric stove. I had never heard of such a thing—an electric stove that didn't burn wood. I anxiously wanted to see Mrs. Smith living antiseptically alone in her grandeur, so far removed from the conditions I was doomed to exist in. On the day of the visit, I washed my annual yellow summer dress (as opposed to my annual red winter dress) and hung it out to dry with my socks. Grandmother was going as well, so after all the ironing and pressing, I ironed my dress, still damp, polished my shoes, scrubbed myself clean, combed my hair and pinned it with a barrette. I always liked to present myself to Dad because he would call me the sweetest things he could think of. On this day I was his magnolia—a happy transformation from the 'smelly wee lassie' that Grandmother called me when the baby burped on me. When Mother saw me standing by watching her preparations, dabbing her neck with lemon verbena from a vial, patting her hair and putting on her watch and ring, she gave me instructions to watch the baby and be the best little mother I could be. My heart fell. At the time, my fixation with hardwood floors was in full swing, and I simply had to see that stove. Mrs. Smith arrived in her Model A Ford, and after pleasantries, Mother and Grandmother stepped into the car. I broke down and begged Mother to go, pleading that I wanted to see the electric stove, but her answer was no.

If I was despondent as they drove off through the maple grove, I was even more so when they returned. Grandmother sat at the kitchen table recounting detail after detail to the aunts, and I listened with as much curiosity as they did. Grandmother was impressed, and when she was impressed, that was as good as royal assent. On and on she raved about the silver, china, furniture and floors; 'the most elegant tea she had in Bear River.' I was a disappointed opportunist whose opportunities flitted away. And it showed. When Grandmother finished, she turned to me with a sharp reminder to get that black look off my face. On closer inspection, she called me a dirty wee lassie because the baby had burped on me, pulled at my hair and drooled all over me. I was a wreck. And another humiliation, "Don't be a nosy parker. Run off and watch the baby."

I'm not sure exactly when Grandmother became disenchanted with me and I with her, but I think it happened on the first day, almost at the first moment. I wanted her to like me, or at least to talk to me the way she did with the boys, but there seemed to be no way to impress her. I had nothing to say. I only opened my mouth, played with my brace on my two front teeth and stared warily. I would say a hesitatingly polite 'good morning' and 'good night' as we had to, but I cringed before her authority: 'Close your mouth, leave your teeth alone, stop your staring, sit up straight.' One day, I was sitting on a blanket under the Bartlett pear tree trying to pacify Joan, who was crying because of teething. It irritated Grandmother so much that she called through the dining room window, "Polly, if that were my child she'd soon stop that baby from crying." Mother's reminder that the baby was teething only brought the usual reply that she should have more control over her children.

Many times that summer, I would pretend to go to the outhouse and then sneak behind the apple packing house, jump the brook by the river road, climb past the chicken house, race across the cabbage field and run in to the stand of oaks where I would collapse by the trout pool. Alone and unseen in the cool shade, I could sit with my doll on the soft moss by the oak tree and cry and say out loud, "I don't like you Grandmother, you're not nice." There wasn't a corner of the house where I could go to hide. There were too many MacGregors who were too brusque. I hated their Gaelic secrecy so I wouldn't understand. There were too many boys who went everywhere, saw everything and got all the treats. There were too many babies and I didn't like them either. "Would my little mother like to help me feed the baby, wash his hands, wash his feet? Would my little mother like to hold the baby? I don't know what I'd do without you." If there was one thing I learned that summer, it was to hate. It took hold and interfered with the way I really felt. Basically I was a romantic who dreamed of everything and everybody being as pretty as pictures, but there were too many people around to dislike, and they deserved it. I was in the wrong house, with the wrong family, and I definitely had the wrong relatives. The woman I wanted to be was pasted in my scrap book, and I thought she looked like Mother. She lazed luxuriously on a chaise, dressed in a filmy white gown down to her slippered toes, hands indolently drooped and a satisfied look on her lovely face. That picture was me in a dream. When I was grown and studying art, the dream sputtered to life when I discovered that the lovely lady I admired had the languid name of Madame Recamier. Because of my meticulous clipping, she had remained nameless all those years. Well, we simply don't get to be other people, but I always wished I could have a Recamier couch in my boudoir.

From a young age, I had a clear idea of the home I would live in and the rooms I would walk through: spacious, honey-coloured floors with slim-lined Pembroke tables beside embracing wing chairs, nothing bulky, all of it far removed from the Eaton's catalogue. In a corner of my mind was a piano where I would sit and play. I dreamed that dream a lot. I fantasized about living in any one of the large, tall-windowed homes in the village. I pictured the comfort and elegance I would indulge in behind those lace curtains, the rooms as inviting as the ones I clipped out of magazines. But my dreams were paper dreams pasted in my scrap books with inferior flour paste glue. As I turned the crinkly pages, they crackled, and my beautiful rooms became ugly and worn. Handsome heroes turned old and jaded with hideous wrinkles. Madame Recamier looked tired and bitter. Even Yehudi Menuhin and Ruggerio Ricci, both my age, became old men, posed in sailor suits with their little hands clutching violins. I was a drowning child grasping at straws, and I learned the true meaning of dreams, not the dreams of snakes and spiders in my nightmares, but the ones floating up to the ozone after a thunderstorm, where the air was light and sweet.

At the trout pool, the cool air held the delicate scent of pine needles, and I would breathe deeply as I lounged in comfort and solitude at the base of the oak, alternating between dreams and despair, talking to my doll, wishing I were an only child living in a big house in the village, far removed from nasty MacGregors. After a while, I would hear Mother calling for me from the back step, and I would scurry back into the bosom of my over-extended family in our over-crowded home. Like a needle lost in a haystack, I was there. And I knew I was loved.

From *Phil May's Gutter-snipes*, 1896

Another sunny day, Mrs. Smith arrived to take Mother to her cottage in Deep Brook for the afternoon, and this time Mother let me come along. I sat in the back seat of the car in feverish anticipation of observing the life I would live one day. Instead, the cottage held the same disappointing mish-mash I was used to: linoleum floors, faded chairs covered with antimacassar that only added wrinkles to their age, walls heavy with the family tree. My deep-rooted reaction was that my walls would never have oval portraits with convex glass hanging like thyroid eyes—no men with beards or moustaches, and certainly no portraits of stern matrons, firebrands of the home. I would have only beautiful people on my walls, or animals.

A number of ladies sat at the lunch table, and after the meal, Mother excused me with the suggestion that I play with the children next door. They were all teenagers busily involved in a game of croquet. I couldn't intrude myself, so I sat on a step and watched. After a while, I wandered off to the outhouse, down a slope and hidden behind some bushes. Like the cottage, it was scruffy and slipshod: a single unit, unpainted and stung by years of salt from the Bay. I scuttled any thoughts of a seaside cottage; indoor plumbing underlined all my dreams. But then when I opened the door, I gasped with delight as I feasted my eyes on a huge pile of all the glossy English society magazines of the day, magazines we didn't subscribe to. Every page featured all the beautiful homes of all the beautiful people. The crowned heads of Europe stood posed in their jewels, perfect portraits à la Cecil Beaton. Ladies and children were delicate, doing interesting things; the men as dashing and as handsome as princes should be. That was the day and the moment, as I sat in Mrs. Smith's outhouse, that I became a closet royalist. I lugged an armful of magazines to a sunny spot out of the breeze and began flicking through the pages, wishing I could tear out my favourites but knowing I couldn't ask. In the background, the piano accompanied Mother as she sang. I loved those Scottish songs and hummed along as I flipped through page after page of upper crust strutting and swaggering.

In a while, the teenagers came looking for me. They had decided to go sailing and were asked to take me along. It was still too soon after my near-drownings on Kniffen's beach, but I went with them, afraid to show fear. Besides, I had a passion for yachting. During the 20s, there was keen competition for the America's Cup, and Sir Thomas Lipton's races caused a ripple of excitement in our home. He was the originator of Lipton teas, a self-made millionaire and a Helensburgh native, so the MacGregors praised him like one of the clan. Though old, he cut an imposing figure with his snow-white hair and moustache, clad in pure white racing togs, standing on the deck of his yacht against towering, billowing sails. I thought Sir Thomas and his yacht and the whole business of sailing was too, too glamorous, and yes, I pasted that old man in my scrap book.

I approached the wharf with renewed determination to conquer my fear of the water, but I faltered at the outset. One look down at the heaving, lurching boat and I seized up with terror. Thereafter, I took notice when terror struck, but on this day I let a teenager convince me to take his hand and step aboard. I couldn't find a good place to sit, so I grabbed hold of a rope railing that encircled the boat and watched as the teenagers scampered about like seasoned pros, unfurling sails and handling tackle, calling back and forth as happy as clams. They neatly manoeuvred the boat as it dipped and raced out to the Bay on a stiff breeze, the waves frothing by like passing clouds. Farther out, the water became much rougher, spanking the boat up and down and splashing all over me. I wanted to find a drier spot, so I let go of the rope and promptly slid on my leather-soled shoes to the middle of the boat, where I couldn't find a thing to hang onto. Above, a sail swung unsteadily on a boom, and when someone shouted to duck,

I slipped and fell. With nothing else to hold on to, I scrambled over and clutched the corner of a box-like structure in the middle of the boat, holding on as I have never held onto anything in my life. I didn't move from that position for the rest of the trip except to pull my knees up to my chin. It seemed like hours that I clung to that box, afraid to loosen my grip or shift my position. All the while, the teenagers dashed past me in their squeaking sneakers with the sea legs of old salts, and the faster the boat clipped along the happier they were. After an eternity, we finally made the turn for home, which caused the boat to list treacherously, angling higher and higher. Everyone scrambled into position and hung off the edge of the boat to keep us from keeling over, while I clung to my box in grim terror of sliding into the Bay. As I stared into the black water rushing below me, I cried my last tears. The boat then stabilized and plunged back down, smacking the water as a wave washed overhead, thoroughly drenching me. I knew I would never sail again. Sunny days with idling yachts are scenes of deep deception. Dad said that the Bay of Fundy had some of the roughest waters he had ever sailed on, and it was the only place he had ever been seasick.

At the dock everyone scurried about their chores, while I sat glued to my favourite spot, my numb fingers frozen in position around the corner of the box. A thoughtful young man helped me to my feet, but at the gangplank I seized up once again. I was terrorized and traumatized, convinced I would drown at the water's edge. What a spectacle! He finally carried me piggy-back and safely deposited me on dry land just in time for me to retch and get the whole trip out of my system. Mother had enjoyed her afternoon and looked happy as she met me stumbling up the incline to the cottage, urging me to hurry because we were ready to leave. She looked at me, soaked and snivelling, and said, "Goodness gracious me! You look like a drowned cat. Did you have a nice time?" I could only mumble a monosyllabic, dejected yes. Mrs. Smith laid out a towel on the back seat and I collapsed in a soggy heap. At home, I trudged in the door and crawled into bed, sinking into oblivion with my last nervous twitch. Mother assumed I was bilious as well as anaemic, so liver was back on the menu. Strangely, not even Dad suspected that I might have been sea-sick. It took me a long time to recover from that afternoon, if ever.

After my experience at Deep Brook, I preferred to forget about Sir Thomas Lipton in a very fickle way. I'd look at his yacht and get sick all over again. The only happy note from that afternoon was in discovering the crowned heads of Europe in that lonely, ramshackle outhouse. And I still remember humming along as Mother's voice drifted out on the breeze like a song to the sea. Afterwards, Mrs. Smith came by once or twice more, but Mother never returned the visits, being too busy for a social life that wasn't rooted in her kitchen.

Another day, Mother and Grandmother went off to visit Mr. Bishop, and I was allowed to go along. I had never been inside Mr. Bishop's sparkling white doll's cottage with its frilly white curtains, but as I crossed the threshold I expected perfection. Instead, I stepped into a shady interior of bare necessities. To the right, a long, rough-cut counter led to the sink and pump. Along the opposite wall, a shelving arrangement of stacked orange crates held dishes, cutlery and Mother's jams. Wall sconces held kerosene lamps, and at the far end, a door led to the outhouse. The middle of the room had a pot-bellied stove with a Spartan arrangement of spindly chairs and more house-beautiful orange crates filled with books and magazines collected over the years. To complete the dismal décor, the bedroom at the far end of the room was hidden by a grey blanket strung across on a rope. Mother and Grandmother sat on the chairs and I sat on an orange crate as the adults fell to talking. At one point in the conversation, a surprising sneeze came from behind the blanket, indicating Lou Albert, Mr. Bishop's close companion and our hired hand, safely excluded from the conversation but curiously included. I decided I didn't like Mr. Bishop's cottage and asked Mother if I could go home. I was disappointed that this erudite gentleman from the great city of New York who spoke of plays and operas should live in such stinted dimensions. The dream-like cottage was deceitfully two-faced, as deceitful as a dream. I went out and sat in the rose arbor and then went home to my child's world.

*P*ICTURE IF YOU WILL a beautiful sunny day, full to overflowing with summer, the sky high, pale and shimmering, finches chattering in the lilacs, robins perched in the maples, swallows darting to the barn with their beaks full of mud, roosters making their presence known in their strident way, almost daring us to kill another chicken. Opera drifts out the open windows, mingling with the clinking of dishes as the aunts clean up after lunch and chat in Gaelic. A baby in a carriage mumbles and gurgles. Every flower in the rock garden and around the house is blooming and oozing its essence. The vegetable gardens can't wait another minute to be picked, and that's what Dad and the uncles are doing, filling bushel baskets that the two teenagers are bringing to the back of the house for me to wash. Mother is sitting on the step bunching carrots and beets. Daniel, Jim and Douglas are loading the long wagon with baskets of new peas, spinach, lettuce, onions, peppers, green and yellow beans. When the wagon is full, Mother tallies every quart in her account book and hands the bill to Uncle Peter, who whistles for Harry from the pasture. Pounding hooves race down the hill and pause at the brook, where Harry refreshes himself before trotting through the maple grove and taking up position in front of the wagon. The boys climb aboard with Uncle Peter, grinning as they rattle down to the Miller field for a load of new potatoes from Dad. From there, they'll head off to Digby on their almost daily travels around the world. On a day like this, one would say all's right with the world, but farmers know it is always brightest before the storm.

For some reason, after they loaded the potatoes, Dad didn't let Douglas go to Digby, so he stalked off with all the fury of a four-year-old and barricaded himself inside the outhouse. It wasn't long before everyone was banging on the door. The aunts were agitated. Grandmother was furious, "That wee blackguard, I know what I'd do with him!" Mother pleaded, not too pleasantly, "Are you coming out or will I have to give you a good sound thrashing? Answer me! Are you coming out?" The answer was, "NO!" Mother sent me off to the Miller field for Dad, saying as she so often said, "I've more to do with my time. I'll deal with that little villain later." I told Dad that Douglas was holed up in the outhouse and wouldn't come out and everyone wanted to get in. Dad stuck his fork in the dirt, pushed his hat back and laughed. When we got to the outhouse, Grandmother and the aunts were on edge and pleading, but the answer was still a surly, "NO!" Dad rapped on the door, which he could easily have pushed in, "Duggy Don, yew littah boundah, come out!" The answer was still, "NO!" Dad said, as he always said when Douglas was in his 'no' mood, "Ah wish yew would say yes once in a while." Then a strange grinding sound came from behind the door. Dad asked, "What in blazes ah yew doing in theah, son?" Douglas said, "Nothing." He was doing nothing of the sort. We shifted our gaze down as the tip of a drill poked through the door and kept turning, kicking out shavings until it bored a hole right through. I never saw Dad laugh so hard; he doubled over and almost collapsed. Grandmother and the aunts were furious. Douglas opened the door, dangling a large drill, his hand barely covering the round handle. It must have taken quite a determined effort to stand there and keep drilling with all the threats coming from outside. The aunts dashed in and stuffed the hole, while Grandmother misconstrued Douglas' intentions, calling him a right royal wee blackguard for wanting to spy on people in the outhouse. Dad asked, "Duggy Don, wha in blazes did yew do it, son?" Douglas' sensible answer was, "I wanted to see if someone was coming." The outhouse was a busy place, so he put the hole at eye level from where he sat. There, he could see clear up to the back door as he rustled through the pages of *National Geographic*. Dad shook his head and chuckled, ending the episode by hoisting Douglas on his shoulders and taking him down to the Miller field. Later, Dad came in for some aspirin, saying he had laughed so hard he got a headache. When I told Mother what Douglas had done, she giggled helplessly into the bread dough she was kneading. Grandmother and the aunts weren't impressed. They didn't think it funny and nodded in agreement that Mother should have more control over her children. Grandmother's children never experimented with her rigidity, so they couldn't have understood.

With 17 people in residence and guests almost every day, we were busier than the River View Lodge. Maple Grove farm was booked solid. The kitchen ran all day long from one meal to the next, with barely a pause for clean-ups. Mother and the aunts worked in shifts, heaping great quantities of food onto platters and lugging it in to the dining room to be devoured in minutes by the starving horde. The logistics of feeding 17 people three times a day must have been daunting, and I'm sure our bill at the Trading Company soared. Delivery men would arrive with large orders, including all of Grandmother's favourite foods, kept in supply to keep her happy. Although she complained about everything else, Grandmother had nothing but high praise for Mother and the aunts' cooking, and deservedly so. The food at our table was gourmet, and Aunt Cathy truly was a wizard in the kitchen. I suppose it was at Maple Grove farm where she completed her apprenticeship, because shortly, she became the personal chef to the wealthy Stewart family in Montreal, owners of Macdonald's tobacco.

The MacGregors weren't used to rural isolation and were always encouraging guests to stop by or to stay for dinner. They eagerly accepted, and Mother and Dad didn't mind because company stabilized mealtime conversations. After dinner, everyone would gather under the Bartlett pear tree for tea, which included coffee, lemonade, cakes, cookies, etc. Guests could linger as long as they wanted, and I often woke up late at night to the sound of laughter at the glide swing. From the early morning milking until late in the evening, the farm percolated like a rustic retreat. All day long, the water pump squeaked, dishes clinked, the screen door slammed, and the chatter of activity echoed throughout. The house didn't have a quiet corner for a moment's reflection, except for perhaps the attic, though Aunt Charlotte was in no mood to socialize. Despite the heavy traffic, the house ran smoothly, other than frequent bottlenecks at the outhouse, the kitchen pump, and the outside pump. Our whole bathroom system was out of kilter, and lineups often required the use of wash basins and the dreaded chamber pots, which marked a return to the stone age for the MacGregors. Grandmother's baths took on the performance of a farce, bringing the entire kitchen area to a standstill. Uncle Peter would drag the large copper tub into the pantry and fill it with every drop of water from the hot water tank on the stove. Grandmother would arrange her towels, soaps, perfumes and powders on the counter and close the door with a smart bang. Inevitably, Uncle Peter would rap on the door, "Are you still in there Ma?"

Grandmother would snarl, "Get away with you, Peter!"

And Uncle Peter, "How long will you be Ma? I've got indigestion and I need some soda and cream of tartar." He did it every time. They were so much alike.

At other times after coming home from the village on a steaming hot day, Grandmother would bathe in her room, and when she was finished she would save her steps by heaving the water out the window. Her room was above the side parlor window, so when we heard a sudden downpour, we knew that Grandmother was finished. When Dad had company in the summer, Daniel loved to sit by the open window and listen to whatever adult conversation drifted out, to be repeated when we went to bed. All along the side of the house was a soft, grassy embankment where we liked to play and roll down. One day while Daniel, Jim and Douglas were eavesdropping outside the parlor, Grandmother heaved her dirty water out the window and soaked them, just like they used to do in olde London. It didn't dampen their spirits and they ran off singing, "It's raining, it's pouring, the old man is snoring." Grandmother enjoyed their performance so much that she doused them several times that summer and would lean out the window saying, "It serves you right you nosey wee parkers!"

Douglas caused a lot of confusion that summer with his extended explorations. Mother would call and call and send Daniel and Jim trudging back into the woods to find him. One day, he went missing from before dawn until after the evening milking of the cows. The whole house was in disarray with Mother crying in near hysteria and Grandmother reminding her for the umpteenth time that she should have better control of her children, "That one's a right royal wee blackguard if ever there was one," and she knew what she would do with him. Dad saddled Harry and galloped down to the Waldec Line and then into the village. Daniel, Jim, the aunts and uncles hallooed across the fields, up Kniffen's Brook and into the woods. Then with night closing in and all hope almost lost, Douglas came lumbering up from Kniffen's Hollow, dead tired after a long day of adventure, carrying his usual bunch of wilted wildflowers and dragging a long, slim branch that he had whittled smooth. A crowd gathered, but Douglas ignored everyone's nervous concern and presented Mother with her flowers. He then handed her the tree branch, saying he had made her a nice, long tingler that she could use while sitting down. After the frenzy of fear, there was a frenzy of laughter. Dad picked Douglas up and said, "Duggy Don, yew fraghtened ten year's growth out of your old Dad." Douglas always brought flowers, and Mother didn't mind that they were past their prime. She would put them in a tea cup above the sink, and sometimes in the busy kitchen she would look at them and recall his thoughtfulness.

At almost 5, Douglas was coming into his own and didn't deviate on his quest for learning. He was so intense. One day while Mr. Bishop and Grandmother chatted on the swing under the Bartlett pear tree, Douglas crawled by on all fours with his nose in the grass, refusing to satisfy anyone's curiosity. Grandmother watched Mr. Bishop, who was looking on in amusement, and she said, as she so often said about questionables, "I don't know what to make of that one. I don't think he's all there." Mr. Bishop assured Grandmother that she had exceptional grandchildren and that Douglas was a budding naturalist. Douglas stopped to announce, "It knows where it's going!" about a wandering, pioneering bug. Grandmother kept her nose above nature, and when Douglas would ask, "Guess what I have in my hand Grandmother?" she would lean sideways over her chair and hiss, "Away with you, you wee beggar." He would open his hand to show her Japanese beetles, or June bugs, and once when he surprised her with a praying mantis she almost lost her false teeth.

One day we came home from school, and there behind the apple packing house were Uncle Peter's new pets: a dozen or so ducks and two hefty geese, all quacking and squawking, making a lively racket along with the roosters and chickens cackling and crowing and the seagulls screaming up and down the river. Uncle Peter had corralled them in their brand-new rickety chicken-wire quarters complete with apple barrels lined up and filled with straw for comfort. The ducks and geese caused a lot of trouble that summer, and in short order they were liked no better than the chickens. When grain was thrown in, the geese took it as an insult and literally bit the hand that fed them. Their quarters became as noxious as the pig sty, and Mother wondered why chickens weren't enough. Uncle Peter proved he was no carpenter, because it wasn't long before the chickens, ducks and geese were all flying their coops. The obstreperous gander was unruly, chasing and bullying children smaller than himself, while all the other loose and lively birds took to running about and poaching, even up to the kitchen door. Since visits had to be made to the outhouse first thing in the morning, there was no escaping that first fine, careless rapture of the roosters, geese, ducks and chickens welcoming rosy-fingered dawn. When Grandmother discovered that she had to watch her step as well as hold her nose when she ventured thereabouts, she just about had a conniption, "Is this no dreadful! Is this no rank! Is this no chronic!" Uncle Peter promised, "Ma, one of these fine days you're going to have a grand and glorious goose dinner."

Dad soon decided it was high time that our fractious flock had their wings clipped. With Dad and four uncles to do battle, it was a foregone conclusion that Homo Sapien would triumph over Gallus Gallus. Amid squawking and flying feathers, the teenaged uncles were the first chicken-livered defectors, pecked and clawed and showing drawn blood. Grandmother feared that her two youngest were on the verge of lockjaw, so she dabbed their wounds with iodine until they looked diseased. Dad, Uncle Douglas and Uncle Peter soldiered on despite their wounds, while we children sat at a distance enjoying our afternoon amusement. The real wrestling began with the geese. The ducks were submissive, but the geese showed muscle. It finally took three grown men to bring the gander under control: Uncle Peter grabbing the neck, Uncle Douglas holding the feet, and Dad doing the clipping. As the sun set, all of nature gently acquiesced and any fears were banished that Dad would have to reseed the gardens.

With a few hundred chickens, plus the ducks and geese, we had no shortage of eggs, so Dad got busy frying duck and goose eggs for our breakfasts. He countered our objections by saying he had eaten eggs as small as robins' eggs, sucked all kinds of other eggs, and even ate seagull eggs, which tasted fishy. A tentative taste of a duck egg, much richer than chicken eggs, convinced me that there was no need to reinvent the egg. Next came the larger goose eggs. Dad's oversized copper frying pan easily held a dozen goose eggs, and whatever it was lined with, it cooked food beautifully, particularly bacon and eggs. As I passed through the kitchen for breakfast, I stopped by the stove and was revolted to look into a pan full of palpitating, sputtering goose eggs. I scratched geese and their eggs off my list, much like the Vatican's proscribed list of books—too nasty for consumption. Porridge didn't seem so bad after all, despite Dr. Johnson's definition of oats: fed to horses in England and people in Scotland. Uncle Peter said the horses showed good taste. When Mother objected to goose eggs, Dad gave in and decided to let the goose do whatever she wanted with her eggs. Naturally she sat on them, but there was no anticipation of goslings because the incubation period had long since passed. The goose sat and sat, patiently waiting for tomorrow, which never comes.

When Daniel asked what would happen to the eggs, Dad gave the surprising reply that eventually they would explode from internal combustion. This was the sort of high drama Daniel thrived on. He saw circumstances far beyond what they were, enlarged, out-sized, somewhat volatile. In bed at night, he thrilled to the idea of the goose being blown out of her apple barrel. He spent his last thoughts of the day lying on his pillow tilting at goose eggs. He conjured up a conflagration, revelling in the heady excitement of the goose being blown to smithereens, leaving nothing but feathers and a gizzard. Our beds shook with devious delight.

Daniel revealed vast stores of patience during his vigil at the goose coop, urging the process along with his incessant sing-song incantation of 'internal combustion.' Finally, he decided that things had gone on long enough, he couldn't wait any longer and would do something about it the very next day, a Saturday. I wanted nothing to do with it. Saturday night was shopping night in the village, and if we were good we got lollipops after breakfast on Sunday. The boys didn't care because they always filched Mother's chocolates, but I wanted my lollipop.

The big event happened that afternoon while Grandmother was in the outhouse. As she walked the well-trodden path, she heard the geese honking and the boys laughing, so she shooed away the lot of them. The minute she stepped into the outhouse, the boys took their sticks and did some vigorous poking until every egg did a pouf, filling the air with a thick layer of rotten-egg gas. Grandmother staggered out of the outhouse and up the path, leaving the boys in stitches. I was in the kitchen watching the baby when Grandmother stumbled in hacking and coughing. She leaned on the table and rasped, "Those vile weeee blackguards." The smell had nearly knocked her stone dead, and she launched into a tirade at Mother about her out-of-control children. Mother thought it was funny, and when Dad rounded up the culprits, he put his hands on his hips, shook his head and asked the silly question, "Did yew littah barbarians do that?" to which he expected a truthful answer. The boys stonewalled,

"It wasn't me, it was Daniel." "It was not, Jim poked first." "No, Douglas did." "I didn't do anything, it was them." "No, I watched." Their idea of the truth was as elusive as quicksilver. It fuelled Grandmother's conversation, and she knitted her eyebrows every time she observed her grandchildren. I was never casually comfortable in her presence, not even when I was grown, when I still tended to be studiously polite, but early on, the boys wormed their way in to a casual rapport with her. The cockles of Grandmother's heart felt a mid-winter thaw as they tried to please her like a favoured guest, bringing her things and chatting about their tree houses, trout fishing, and adventures in the woods, and to my amazement, she listened. She even listened to their goose story. She had never smelled rotten egg gas, and although forgettable, she told them she would never forget it. Even though the eggs didn't blow up, for the boys the event was like an ode to joy before sleep overcame them. And then, from pillows, "Dad, why didn't the goose blow up?"

"I'm not sure, son, but it's mighty disappointing."

They turned it over in their sleep until their wicked little minds hit upon a solution, and then they concocted a slew of recipes using a few rotten goose eggs, any old chicken and a handy firecracker.

It was around this time that the hens suddenly stopped laying as they should and seemed to be taking a summer vacation. Daniel reported the news to Mother, but she never believed a thing he said and went to see for herself. As she mounted the embankment from the river road to the chicken house, she could see that the hens were sitting underneath their quarters cooling off in the shade, their eggs lying all around them like mushrooms. The boys crawled under and collected the eggs, but there were far too many to use. Before Mother could decide what to do with them, the boys had pasted the barn door. Dozens of smashed eggs dripped down in the hot sun as hordes of flies from the manure pile buzzed around the corner to partake of the feast. Dad's worst punishment was to stand with his hands on his hips, shake his head, threaten to 'saw his leg off' or 'eat his shirt' and ask in amazement, as if it couldn't really happen, "Did yew littah bounders do that?" As usual, they gained traction with half-truths, "It was Daniel who said let's do it" "Jim thought of it first" "No, Douglas, you threw them." A straight answer was out of the question.

'Who left the pasture fence open so the cows had to be corralled halfway to the village?' 'Who fed them green apples so they stumbled around like drunks?' 'Who left all that fertilizer mixed with bran and blue vitriol down by the brook?' No one ever did it. 'Who sawed the branches off the ox-heart cherry tree?' Well there, the truth came out. The branches lay on the ground with Daniel seated among them, eating the cherries at the end of the branches he couldn't reach. There was no denying it. "Mah cherry tree!! Do yew realize what yew have done, yew littah boundah? Yew have ruined mah tree!!" Daniel didn't realize and didn't care, he was full of ox-heart cherries. Grandmother was in a state of utter disbelief, "Och, I've never heard of such a thing. That greedy wee blackguard. I've never seen the likes" Dad's punishment was duly delivered by proxy. Mother was unwillingly assigned the case and simply said, "Go to the lilac bush." The punishment of a few whacks of a tingler hardly fit the crime, but Daniel learned his lesson, only to learn it again another day.

At the top of the Miller field on Uncle Peter's new property stood a rickety structure surrounding a well, and Dad's warning that if it collapsed we could fall in and drown kept us away. This had happened years ago to a boy on a nearby farm. Beside it stood a building, empty and ignored for years, and Dad's warning that it was nearing collapse also kept us away. The building was a half-sized version of our apple-packing house with one large, many-paned window. For some unknown reason, Dad had temporarily cut off diplomatic relations with Daniel, so he, in a snit, sat down with a pile of stones and methodically picked off all but two of the small windows. There was no need to investigate because Dad caught him red-handed, "Caramba! Do yew mean to tell me that yew deliberately broke twenty nahn windows?" For once, Daniel defended himself with the truth, "No Dad, I broke 28." Dad pushed his old fedora to the back of his head and stood in the heat wiping his brow, incredulous and hardly able to grasp such wicked dedication. He recovered and called for Mother, "Dearie, this rampant destruction has got to stop! That littah barbarian goes to his room. Ah don't give a hang for how long, just don't let him loose for a while." Shortly, the building was razed to make way for Uncle Peter's house, and Daniel deplored that he had to sit in his room for breaking windows and now the whole building was being pulled down.

Another day, Daniel came home dog-tired after digging clams on the mud flats for Mabel. He enthusiastically recounted his day, so Mother capitalized on his good mood by sending him out the door with Jim to pick a half-bushel of black currants. The weather was blistering hot as the sun beat down, and in a little while, they returned lugging the basket between them. I was on the kitchen couch holding the baby, while Mother and Grandmother were sitting at the table preparing dinner. The screen door opened and Daniel, in a foul mood, dumped the whole basket of black currants across the kitchen floor and said, "There are your old black currants!" Without a word, Mother flew out of the kitchen like an ill wind. She chose a better tingler than usual and the bedroom above the kitchen echoed with all the familiar sounds and phrases of upheaval. Grandmother had never, ever suffered a moment's disobedience from her ten children and claimed there wasn't a child she couldn't manage, "but Och! This one staggers the imagination." She tiptoed around the black currants and swept them up with leaves and broken twigs. Daniel was confined to Mrs. McCormick's room for days, and since Mother was busy making jam, it was as hot as sin with the stove pipe next to the floor and the sun at its sizzling best. Mother would send me up with his three meals a day, and he was only allowed out to the outhouse. His meals were served cold: cold porridge, cold pancakes, cold stew. One day he told me, "Tell Mother my dinner's cold!" He still wouldn't apologize, and when I pleaded with him, "Why don't you just say you're sorry." he said, "I'm not." He leaned on the window sill all day. Dad would open the bedroom door to say, "Good morning, son, ah yew going to say yew ah sorry today?" No response. Dad would say, "Yoar Mother is right," and close the door. One day Dad said, "Sweethaht, ah want an apology today." Daniel snarled, "Don't call me Sweetheart." Then Mother cut into her busy schedule and appeared at the doorway in a measuring mood. Daniel took the hint and quickly apologized.

Bad behaviour abounded that summer, and even I got into the act. Lorna, and later Joan, were always snaffling cats from the barn and hiding them in paper bags, so one dull day the boys decided it would be just the thing to sit in a circle while everyone took a turn slinging the bagged kitten over our heads. I wasn't having any fun in life, so I joined the family circle.

By the time the bag got to me, claws were hanging out and the bottom was soaked. When I slung the bag, the kitten flew out, landed on a rock in Mother's garden and lay inert. Lorna screamed at the pitch of her lungs that I had killed her kitten. In moments of horror I freeze, and I froze then. Mother and all the MacGregors rushed to the scene and crowded around as the kitten gradually revived. I slumped into the background, paralyzed by what I had done. Mother eyed everyone and angrily demanded an explanation, prompting my backstabbing siblings to expertly snitch. Pointing fingers singled me out as a coldhearted kitten-killer. The MacGregors gaped in shock, itching for rough justice. I could hardly get myself to the lilac bush for one of the few spankings I remember, and Mother kept asking me why I would do such a thing. I couldn't answer. She sent me to my room and I ate alone. Grandmother said she wouldn't have believed it, "You're a crrruel wee lassie." Every time Lorna got near me she reminded me in her baby voice, "You almost killed my kitten." Everyone got off Scot-free, and the boys played on my guilt by taunting me in sing-song, "Mary almost killed a kitten." Even Douglas chimed in, having just recently wrung the neck of the Chute chicken. I suffered for a long time. Worst of all was that Mother ignored me for days, even though I tried to make up by being more diligent with my chores. When Dad came home after a brief visit to Montreal, he heard the grim tale from all sources and could see I was the local pariah. When he said with displeasure, "What's this ah heah about yew, Sweetlady?" I ran into the bedroom and cried and cried. Dad was too gentle to let anyone suffer, and in his usual method of extracting the truth, detail by detail, it boiled down to another dimension. When he asked why I didn't speak up, I didn't know. His knowing the truth didn't make my guilt any better. For years after that, contented purring and plaintive meows made no inroads on my affections. Cats and the witches they consorted with were bad, bad luck.

Once all the exotic eggs were dispensed with, the time came for the ducks and geese to be eaten as Uncle Peter had intended. Besides, a gang of rowdies had taken to ambushing Grandmother and nipping at her heels as she scooted to the outhouse. I don't know why this rogue element singled her out, but she was infuriated that the miseries of the outhouse were now compounded by a gauntlet of ducks and geese armed to the teeth. Another day they formed up in a phalanx, barring her way. She demanded that they be put to the sword, right away. It was a massacre, but no different than what went on every Sunday. We had developed a certain insensitivity and occasionally attended the weekly sacrifice. Like spectators in the coliseum, we would sit on the embankment looking down to the chopping block, casually observing as Dad or Uncle Peter entered the arena dangling the unfortunate bird by its pedal extremities. The antagonists would briefly spar, one determined and efficient, the other flailing, then a brief pause before the thwack of the axe, etching the chopping block with crimson streaks and feathery fragments. The boys exhibited a ghoulish delight when a headless chicken managed to shrug off its affliction and recover to wander about. We discussed these events endlessly in bed at night. Oh yes, they would tell me, some chickens had run off to the woods and were still there, wandering around with an axe to grind, looking for a head, any head.

As I crawl back into that bed I shared so long ago, I can see how collusively male those three little boys were. They seemed so wicked. They had hundreds of acres to expand their mischief, and that summer with the house in turmoil, they were free to commit their own crimes. They'd be out from early morning, ranging over the countryside, resting at their tree houses and fishing holes, appearing at the edge of the woods at the end of the day. At our nightly forum, I'd hear all about their adventures as they recounted and plotted for the next day, 'we'll do this or we'll do that.' For a long time I wanted to see their tree house, but I was told, "No, you're only a girl." I never disagreed. I almost lost my listening privileges when I learned that they were making pipes out of acorns and straws and smoking crumbled leaves. I said I would tell and they offered to kill me. Then the teenaged uncles took to going along, helping with the tree houses and filching cigarettes from Dad's tobacco can. The boys said I would tell, so Uncle Jim reminded me that if I opened my mouth, he himself would kill me, stone dead. Discipline was maintained. Grandmother monitored the chores of the teenaged uncles to the point of laziness, but she wasn't aware that their idle hands were latching on to mischief and cultivating a bad and continuing habit.

After a week or two, the ducks were dismissed in orderly fashion, accompanied by strawberry shortcake. But the gander was a different matter altogether. When the day of dispatch arrived, everyone was busy, so the task fell to Uncle Peter. The boys gave up a trip to Digby with Dad to witness the spectacle. We stood on the woodpile as Uncle Peter manoeuvred the heavy bird onto the block and wielded the axe, but the gander quickly sized up the situation and dodged the blade, snake-like. As Uncle Peter pulled the axe out of the chopping block, the bird pecked its way free and turned to fight. The boys cheered as the combatants squared off, circling and hissing. The morning wasn't turning out as either of them had expected. Uncle Peter wrestled the bird to the ground, and in a swirl of dust, pinned him and tried to finish him off then and there, but the gander writhed free and attacked, scoring several clean hits. Uncle Peter regained his feet and rebounded with a wild swing and a kick. He feinted left and right before grabbing the bird like a set of bagpipes, and in a move cribbed from a Morris dance, twirled and stepped lightly to the chopping block before deftly placing the gander's neck for a mighty thwack. Callooh, callay! A battle worthy of a Scottish dance. We cheered as Uncle Peter wiped his brow and gave a definitive, "Aye!" Headless and spurting blood, the gander conceded, but he wasn't done yet.

Mother had a deep rapport with her kitchen, and when she saw the gander, she said in her prescient way that she would have nothing to do with him. She ceded the kitchen to the aunts, who needed another challenge. They had just finished the cherry season, during which time they did everything imaginable to that versatile fruit: pies, tarts, jams, trifles, all served to guests on the glide swing, which was becoming a haven for hungry passersby. The meal would be well-attended, so the aunts rustled about the kitchen in their usual excitement on gourmet occasions. After outlining a menu filled with biscuits, breads, salads, sauces, every possible vegetable and copious amounts of dessert, they focussed on the meat of the matter. They plucked and gutted the gander, but then discovered that there was still a lot of bird and no pan large enough to hold it. A rummaging through the cupboards yielded nothing, so they finally settled on a large, shallow pan used for baking rolls. After seasoning and stuffing the bird, they covered it with greased paper, only to find that it was too heavy to lift.

Dad and Uncle Douglas were called in to hoist the behemoth into the oven. It was a big one. But no sooner had the aunts started on the vegetables than ominous wisps of smoke began streaming up from the stove, and when Aunt Nan opened the oven door, smoke billowed out and filled the kitchen. The shallow pan was overflowing with fat, which threatened to prove that where there was smoke, there was fire. The aunts tried to pull the bird out, but discovered that it had expanded and wedged itself firmly in the oven. As I stared at the smoking, steaming bird, all I could think of was internal combustion. Daniel would get his wish and the gander would have his revenge. Aunt Cathy and Aunt Ellie nervously called out the door for Dad, while Aunt Nan, who had already suffered enough hysteria, just about flew off into madness once again. Aunt Elsie only ever got upset about stray freckles, and simply said, "Oh Dear." She took a carving fork and gave me my first roasting tip, "You pierce the goose to release the fat," information I have never needed to use, until now. She stabbed the bird with the fork, and grease spurted all over the oven, making even more smoke. Mother, who was sitting on the glide swing with Grandmother catching the summer breeze, saw her kitchen clouding over and called out, "Is everything alright in there?" The aunts called out, "Yes, Polly" as Dad and Uncle Douglas hustled in to pry the bird out of the oven. What a mess! The Aunts scrubbed the oven and collected jam jars full of grease, lining them up on the kitchen table like noxious glue. Aunt Cathy called out to Mother, asking her what to do with all the grease. Mother said to throw it out, but when pros and cons were up for consideration, it was normal for Grandmother to differ. She said certainly not; that wonderful goose grease could be saved to rub on our chests when we had colds. We had many unpleasant things rubbed on us when we were sick, but the thought of goose grease sinking deep into my chest horrified me. I added goose to my proscribed list, and by mealtime, my stomach unsteadily agreed.

The aunts rallied to save the dinner, which turned out to be grand and glorious after all. Mr. Bishop, the Kniffens, Mrs. Croscup, Jessie and Stella Harris, the Simons, Mrs. McCormick and Joe Warren all attended, and the sounds of revelry filled the dining room. Children ate in the kitchen, and if we didn't like the food on our plates, we could feed it to Scotty. He was a good dog who never liked the gander, but didn't seem to mind him in the end.

Later, the party moved outside, and as the stars came out, we listened from our beds as Uncle Peter, the aunts and even Grandmother regaled the guests with tales of the MacGregor ducks and geese: the squawking and skirmishing, making a thorough nuisance of themselves, not unlike the rest of the clan. Grandmother recounted her outhouse adventures, the aunts laughed at their kitchen catastrophe, and Uncle Peter replayed the battle of Chopping Block Greene. Even the gander turned out to be quite alright, and everyone agreed when Grandmother said, "Aye, he was one of the really great MacGregors."

Despite the demise of the ducks and geese, Grandmother's outlook continued to worsen. As the horseflies, mosquitoes, cows, pigs and chickens all merged with the summer heat to heighten the daily metamorphoses of the farm, there was nowhere she could go without a whiff urging her home to the Highlands. She'd say, "Och, I'll bless the day I leave this farm." Before that blessed day, Grandmother showed promise as a budding farmer by urging an immediate cleanup, starting with the mess left by the ducks and geese. She supervised as the teenagers removed all traces of Uncle Peter's erstwhile pets, after which, they rolled the apple barrels down to the beach to be burned. Then she ordered Uncle Peter to tidy up the wood pile after several logs had rolled down and chased her along the path to the outhouse. Next, she got busy on the pig sty beside the barn. It offended her every time she walked to the village. It would have to go, right away. The pigs were delegated to a new area under the grapery ridge edging the river road, in a small field full of weeds and thistles. She began cleaning up the marshes, so to speak. There were arguments, and she quarrelled with Dad as if she were in permanent residence, as if she were the owner. After one sizzling dinnertime conversation, she said to Dad, "It's plain to see you don't know how to run a farm." Dad said with his slow drawl, "Motha, mah own motha ran a tabaka fahm and ahm sure you could do just as well." Grandmother rattled her cutlery and made everyone sit up as if stuck with a pin, saying, "The day I leave this place can't come soon enough." That was good news to us and we asked, "When, Grandmother?" From then on, we constantly discussed Grandmother's leaving. The teenaged uncles gave us hope with reminders that they would be going to Montreal. We didn't care about the undertones, only the solution of going.

*T*HAT SUMMER WE HAD snipe pie, and though a child's memory can become opaque and distorted, the event of snipe pie is still as current as the fact that I was named after my grandmother.[1] How could I forget either? One day Dad went hunting with Douglas and shot a brace of partridge. He hung them on a nail in the back porch, and there was a great discussion at the table about how long they should cure. The smart-alecky teen-age uncles jumped in and said they should hang until they rotted and the maggots had their fill. If Grandmother told them 'will you hold your tongue' once a day, she told them a hundred times, but they always felt their cleverness was too good to be ignored. Lorna had cried at the table when they told her, oh yes, those were flies in the Spotted Dick she had just eaten, and flies tasted just like raisins. Spotted Dick vanished from our table. Mother covered the partridge with cheese cloth and said they would be eaten tomorrow. We discussed maggots when we went to bed, as we discussed everything our opinionated relatives had to say.

Two partridge were hardly enough for a table of 17, so Dad decided to shoot snipe on Kniffen's beach and make a pie of them, a novelty to us all. I jumped at the chance to get away from babies and asked Dad if I could come along. I should have known better. When the boys learned how to trap rabbits with a wire snare, they took me with them once, and only once. I watched in horror as the rabbit came out of its hole and helplessly strangled to death. Mother always sent rabbits up to Mrs. McCormick, but for Grandmother she cooked a rabbit stew, promising never to make it again. I was excused from eating it and still am.

On the day of the hunt, the sun shone so brightly on the beach that I could barely see the low flights of snipe skirting the edge of the incoming tide, flashing by in silvery, rippling streaks. Dad sat me on the millstone with the dire warning not to move one inch. With everyone safely in position, Dad and Uncle Peter's guns cracked and resounded along the river as the birdshot tore into the flights of snipe like a hard rain, dropping them to the sand with jarring finality. Dad never allowed my brothers to handle a gun, but they got caught up in the hunt, pulling slingshots out of their back pockets and aiming with deadly accuracy. When Dad and Uncle Peter called a pause, the boys scampered out to retrieve the fallen birds, hurrying back

---

[1] Her middle name, Elizabeth.

with the tiny claws clamped between their fingers. They wanted to put the dead birds on the millstone, but I wouldn't budge, so they lined the snipe up on the sand in front of me. Dad called out another warning and the air shattered with the sharp gunfire cracks. At one point when I was relaxed and not paying attention, Dad fired his gun near the millstone. The concussion stunned me, and as I screamed, my voice sounded terribly far away. For a while, my ears were filled with ringing and the sound of whispers. It wasn't hard for me to realize the danger of the hunt and the ferocity of a gunshot with its incense-like smell of cordite. Nor could I forget the delicately beautiful birds spread before the millstone as if sculpted in the sand, looking with their ebony eyes and tied with ribbons of blood. It was something I never wanted to see again.

When Dad prepared the snipe pie, I avoided the kitchen, but I did look in to see the small stripped bodies, no bigger than sparrows, packed like sardines in the large ceramic baking dish. As Aunt Nan rolled the pastry, Dad pared an apple and inserted a thin sliver into each tiny cavity. I couldn't eat the snipe pie, though I did eat the delicious, gamey partridge; its fate hadn't occurred to me.

We were no sooner done with snipe and partridge than Dad got a wild urge to make sauerkraut. "It's simple," he said. He brought home a barrel, which he scrubbed out and turned to the sun to dry, warning the boys not to dare crawl in. It wasn't a small barrel like the ones apples were shipped in. Oh no, it was a huge, heavy, seasoned barrel like the ones in the Trading Company that held salt cod, or like the malmsey casks seen in old movies of bygone times in which wicked people drowned other wicked people. There would be a lot of sauerkraut.

As we entered the dog days of summer, the aunts became as petulant as Grandmother. There were nasty little rows behind bedroom doors, and Grandmother issued regular reminders to 'get that black look off your face.' They needed a venue and the sauerkraut operation was just the thing. Aunt Ellie was hauled out of the bedroom cupboard where she had sulked for days, pouting like Aunt Charlotte's ghost. Aunt Nan had stopped crying over Evelyn Thompson, but still looked tragic in repose. She could only be content for a few short hours. Happiness was a rare thing in that part of Annapolis County.

Dad's enthusiasm swept them up, and everyone seemed to be in fine fettle as they joked and laughed while chopping cabbage and looking for worms. Grandmother, as expected, was not impressed. She had said many times that it was a peculiar thing to see a man in the kitchen, and she intimated very strongly that it was a character flaw. When Dad served one of his creations, Grandmother would acidly ask, as if referring to his brass work, "So you've been tinkering again," or "Is this your handiwork? I'm not sure I want it." Our dinner table had suffered a few food blowups over mashed potatoes. Dad loved to embellish them with Digby chicken (herring), herbs or chili peppers. Grandmother took mouthfuls and gasped. By this time, I had enjoyed years of hot peppers, so I thought them wonderful. Grandmother said she was sick and tired of Dad's nonsense. Nothing, but nothing, ever fazed Dad's love of cooking. He good-naturedly kept on cooking the way people keep on loving and hating.

After all the cabbage chopping, they shredded it and placed it in the barrel between layers of salt. Dad then rolled the barrel into the root cellar, where it was left to ripen like fruit on the vine, and unfortunately, long after. It quietly fermented into a pickle, like the whole family picture, and then developed a certain insidiousness, not unlike the MacGregors.

In the meantime and to cheer them up, Dad took them on trips to Halifax and the beautiful Annapolis Valley, waxing rhapsodic along the Evangeline Trail about Longfellow's famous poem[2] on the expulsion of the Acadians. "Good," said the MacGregors, "we're glad they're gone." They liked war, so he took them to Fort Anne in Annapolis Royal, where the French and English had slugged it out for a hundred and fifty years, with the Micmacs landing the occasional blow. It was the first Scottish settlement in North America, the whole province was named after them, Canada began there.[3] "Give it back to the Indians," the teenagers reiterated. He took them to Digby, but Grandmother warned Dad for his trouble, "Don't you ever take me there again! The smell is enough to knock you dead! It fairly reeks!" I was always fascinated by the racks and racks of cod drying in the sun, lining the road into town and smelling of the sea as I have never smelled it since.

2 *Evangeline, A Tale of Acadie*. Henry Wadsworth Longfellow, 1847.
3 Before Quebec, the French colonized Port Royal (later Annapolis Royal) in 1605, beating the Plymouth Rock Pilgrims and the Jamestown Virginians by years.

Drying cod in Digby

In time the house took on a disturbingly earthy odour, and day by day it became more pronounced. Mother was especially sensitive, more so when the lippy teenaged uncles suggested it could be boots, chamber pots, or a dead rat between the walls. It was decided it had to be a rat, but what could be done since the walls couldn't be torn out. The teenaged uncles said that the rat would mummify and then you wouldn't smell a thing, that's what would happen.

When the rains came to clamp us indoors, everyone would be lodged in corners and on couches reading, sewing, knitting, playing chess or cribbage. Inevitably, the MacGregors' ancestral urge would beckon like the call of the wild and they would dismiss children from the parlor, push the furniture aside, and skirl the bagpipes, launching into Scottish reels and sword dances with broom handles. As they swirled about the room in their wild pantomime, curious children would stare past the heavy drapes that danced and flipped at our feet. The house throbbed. I was amazed to see Grandmother tearing around our parlor hiccing and hooting. When she sang 'Scots, wha' hae wi' Wallace bled' with her arm up in the air, slashing as if she held a sword, you could swear there wasn't a trace of Irish in her. She was a MacGrigger, right enough–royal's my name, and don't you forget it. They were wild, those MacGregors. Exhausted, they would collapse on couches and wonder about the rain. Someone would start up the gramophone again, alternating Caruso, Tetrazzini and Jeritza with that detestable Scottish gnome Harry Lauder.

In the midst of all this song and dance, Dad decided the time was ripe to feast on his sauerkraut, so he put a pot on the stove to gently simmer. The minute the aroma of sauerkraut wafted through the house and announced itself, the truth was out. That was no dead rat, though no one could tell the difference. Imprisoned in the house and gasping for air, the MacGregors loosened their tongues and tossed nasty comments around like boomerangs. Everyone paled as Dad enjoyed his sauerkraut in happy but lonely isolation. He declared it a delicacy. Grandmother tore into Dad, telling him he should never be allowed in the kitchen, "You're daft, you should have your head examined, the smell is enough to kill–stone dead, etc. etc.," before ending on a current theme, "This God-forsaken country reeks." Dad tried to calm her by saying that sauerkraut was an acquired taste, much like haggis. Grandmother's head just about exploded. Haggis was central to Scottish ritual like a hallowed relic, its organ meats and other grisly delicacies served up as a blood bond, a sacrament. Grandmother was done with Dad. Mother ordered the sauerkraut out of the kitchen and out of the cellar, "Out! out! out! and wash the pot." It made her sick! sick! sick! and never again, not ever would she have that awful stuff in her house. She never did.

The next day, Dad and Uncle Peter rolled the barrel up a board and onto the wagon, securely tying it down for delivery to Mr. Dukeshire's meat market, where, as agreed upon, he would sell it to the unsuspecting citizens of Bear River. Dad said that since I had been good, I could come along. It would be just the two of us, and we would conclude our business with ice cream at Mr. Darres'. Occasions like this called for cleanliness, so I scrubbed up, put on my good dress and polished my shoes. Dad hoisted me onto the wagon seat like a lady, and off I went, bubbling with excitement. I knew what to expect, but the excitement was always new. Nothing unusual ever happened except I felt happy and free. After Harry hauled us over McCormick's hill, he would clop along in his leisurely, measured gait. The creaking wagon would bump along the washboard road until we got to the Crossroads, where the road smoothed out with gravel that snapped at the wheels. Unless Dad stopped to chat, Harry would amble along at his own pace, veering off to refresh himself at the watering trough near Potter's. Those trips had a sameness to them, all rolled into one, but not the trip with the barrel of rotting sauerkraut gurgling and fermenting behind me, much more lethal than the small potfull Dad had enjoyed the day before. On the way, Dad stopped for a few words with Major Simon's young cousin, Cyril Burns, who had recently arrived from Germany to live with them. He hallooed from below the Major's garden where he was tending his beehives. Cyril was a towering, magnificent, athletic blonde. He looked so fearlessly romantic, like the Norsemen of myths, all covered with bees. I adored him because he provided us with little wooden honey combs. I had a passion for eating the wax. Dad called for him to come up and give an opinion, and who better? After a whiff Cyril said, "Ist deef-runt, is nut like Cherman!" And Cyril would know.

As Harry clopped along, the sauerkraut plopped and gurgled, sending up escaping whiffs. I concentrated on Harry's haunches, hoping I wouldn't be sick to my delicate, unpredictable stomach. When we arrived at the meat market, Mr. Dukeshire bounded up on the wagon to inspect his consignment and immediately fell back holding his nose, saying, "Dan, this is best load of rotten sauerkraut I've ever seen!" Dad defended his sauerkraut by saying he had eaten it for dinner and believe you him, it was delicious. Mr. Dukeshire was a hearty man and laughed his head off, asking Dad to take his advice for the good of his health and don't eat any more. Rather than take it home and start a revolution, Dad suggested dumping the festering mess right there, underneath the meat market. The river made a short incursion under the planks, and the tide would soon get rid of it. Dad's suggestion horrified Mr. Dukeshire, "No, Good Lord! No!" He quickly suggest crossing the street and rolling the barrel down the embankment behind the post office. That's what Dad did. The barrel bounced and banged into the Bear River mud flats, spewing sauerkraut along the way, adding to the effluvia that Mother thought was so unhealthy for the clams. It was early afternoon, long before the tide came in, and there was only a trickle of a river, so the sauerkraut spread out on the banks of the river to rot even more in the hot sun. I was sick with embarrassment.

We left Mr. Dukeshire laughing away and wiping his eyes with his butcher's apron. Dad tied Harry to the hitching post at the post office and we walked up to Mr. Darres' ice cream parlor for our treat. Then we went across the street to Dr. Campbell's for Dad's prescription of aspirin.

Dad enjoyed a good joke, even on himself, so he told Dr. Campbell every offensive detail of his culinary fiasco, including the nasty remarks from his in-laws. They laughed and laughed. I don't know if Dr. Campbell was the local health officer, but then he said something like, "You mean to say you dumped it behind the post office, right in the middle of the river? I must have a look." Dr. Campbell asked me what I thought about Dad's sauerkraut, and I confirmed that Mr. Dukeshire said it was rotten. Another hoot. Dr. Campbell assured Dad that since he had survived his rotten sauerkraut he would live to be a hundred.

I begged Dad not to tell anyone about the sauerkraut, but when we got to Major Simon's, he and Cyril were gardening out front, so they immediately heard the whole unsavoury story and thought it a great joke. Cyril, with his heavy German accent and uncertain English, questioned Dad to make sure, "Ist nut goot? Nein? Nut Goot?" Though Dad brought it on himself, I hated everyone for laughing at him. As we left, the Major gave Dad some of his prized yellow tomatoes. The Major bragged without shame about his English broad beans and his yellow tomatoes, both prize winners at the fall fair. Mother said his vegetables were all he had to brag about. The Major might have been vying with Dad over his purple eggplant, which the village would have nothing to do with, and his chili peppers, which Amanda claimed almost ruined her voice. Whenever I handed the Major's tomatoes to Mother, she would say, "Oh, him and his yellow tomatoes!"

On the way home, Dad smirked to himself, musing what Mother would say. No sooner did he get in the door than Mother asked, "Well, Mr. Mar-vin, (she was always formal when she was either very happy or very mad) what did Mr. Dukeshire have to say about that mess you took him?" Dad started laughing and wheezing so hard he could barely tell the tale and promptly collapsed on a chair. I piped up that Mr. Dukeshire said it was rotten. When Mother got the whole story she shook her head in dismay. Amanda Simon would spread the word and the village wouldn't doubt her because the evidence would be festering behind the post office. Then Mother began to laugh and collapsed in the chair on Dad's lap. They were in hysterics, and finally Mother said, "Thank goodness there are tides twice a day."

As expected, Grandmother gathered momentum from the previous day, and even though the danger had passed, it seemed that it was just beginning. "Polly! I'll leave this house and go back to Scotland if I ever see that man in the kitchen again. He could have killed us as easy as not!" On and on she went. The teen-aged uncles were as rank with their jokes as the sauerkraut until Mother warned them she never wanted to hear that word again. Eventually the unsavoury facts filtered through to Merton Yorke's eager ears, and he yelled at recess, "Mary Marvin, your father makes rotten sauerkraut." Daniel socked him.

Dad couldn't have been aware that it was rotten because not only was he colour blind, but his sense of smell was also very poor. When I was older, he would have me smell meat as it came into the house. I used to wonder why he used Pinaud's Violette and Florida Water after-shave, but in time Mother and I both wore it as well, perhaps as a reminder of sartorial perfection. Years later when Mother was in a reminiscent mood, discussing sauerkraut and perhaps sadly recounting the high points of her marriage, she said she had never bothered to ask Dad where he had learned to cook, and for goodness sake why had he learned to eat brains and tripe, etc., all those terrible things. Probably, she said, with his Mexican girlfriend in Vera Cruz when he was stationed with the American Navy. "And there couldn't possibly be a recipe for snipe pie. It had to be something he dreamed up, thinking he was a great chef. You were too young to remember." Aunt Cathy, now an alert eighty-eight, still remembers that highlight. Such things memories are made of.

I don't know how old Cyril Burns was, but he was so blond, so blue-eyed, and so tall–the handsomest man in Bear River. He marched through the maple grove like a young god in all his virility. The nubile aunts admired him as much as I did, and for me he took over where Evelyn Thompson left off. Cyril towered over my father's 5'7" and dwarfed the MacGregor uncles to insignificant trolls. When he visited in the waning days of summer when Grandmother had given her last smile in Bear River, he was like a ray of sunshine, always bringing us lollipops and honey. His use of the English language in his hesitant German was even more endearing.

To our young ears, ya and nein were as sophisticated as when we teased Dad to say car, a word that seemed to improve as he obliged us by smiling and saying cah.

Cyril bought himself a motorcycle, the only one in Bear River, and we would hear him buzzing along the Chute Road or across the river on the road to Digby—buzzing like his bees. At the end of a visit when he was ready to go home, we watched with wonder as he mounted his noisy chariot and thundered up McCormick's hill as if he were headed for the clouds to join his real cousins, the Valkyries.

We loved Cyril's visits because he was the youngest of our guests, all the others being middle-aged or old-aged, which often necessitated our being neither seen nor heard. Cyril pushed our swing high enough to touch our toes to the branches of the maples; he carted children about on his shoulders and swung us around until we were dizzy; he made us guess which hand held the coveted penny, which he then gave to the winner. He enjoyed being with our large family, helping with any little thing, bringing an armful of wood or a bucket of water, digging potatoes or bunching vegetables. He helped the aunts wash the dishes, putting them in a good mood as they momentarily forgot the miseries of Canada. He always arrived on sunny summer days, and the aunts would spread a table cloth in the shade of the maples, sit him down and hover attentively as they eagerly stuffed him with treats. He would entertain them with stories that ended in bursts of laughter, and then, on provocation, playfully chase an excitable child until capture, or push us on the swing, urging us higher.

I only ever heard snatches of company conversation, but one day I hesitated when Amanda Simon's voice raised in righteous resentment as she told Mother of having to measure loaves of bread so that Cyril would not have an extra slice, and the Major had to preserve his whiskey by pencilling descending levels on the bottle. Turning on such a tenuous pivot, Amanda's charity turned cold and exhausted itself, grinding out to the last crunch as surely as the mills of the Gods. Cyril was thrown out of the house with his beehives, not for purloining candlesticks, but for a slice of bread, a stale and crumbly pivot. Though Amanda Simon had graduated from the same Victorian school of outrage as Grandmother, the level of the crime puzzled everyone. Over the dinner table, the MacGregors thoroughly discussed the strident Amanda, and as frugal as the Scots may be, they are not mean. Everyone found Amanda's attitude abhorrent. We discussed it at our nightly forum and it made no sense. We stuffed ourselves with bread, slathering it with butter, jam or molasses. The boys mangled loaves for sandwiches when they went fishing early in the morning. Mother pulled fresh bread out of the oven daily, and eating it held no fear. We were in complete sympathy with our hero.

Immediately, Cyril set up housekeeping in a tent beneath some willow trees between the river bank and the road to Digby, directly across from us. He took his beehives with him, and to complement his motorcycle, he bought a red rowboat. We discussed his choice of territory, because despite his being told that spring would bring floods and ice that could pile up and crush him, Cyril insisted that he liked having the river at his door, steps from his morning swim. At high tide he would row across to see us, at low tide he would tramp across the mud flats, and at other times he would swim across. One late afternoon when we were all down on Kniffen's beach cleaning off the day's dirt, Cyril saw us and swam across on the full tide. I stood on the millstone and never once took my eyes off him as his head bobbed up and down and his powerful arms pushed aside the water. I couldn't imagine anyone so strong. He stayed for supper and regaled the aunts with stories, but later, Grandmother spoke her mind and thought him vulgar for sitting at the table in his bathing suit. As the sun set, he plunged into the Rhine of Nova Scotia, and much like Leander braving the Hellespont, swam off to his Mount Olympus, his tent under the willows on the River Road to Digby. We watched him swim back and waited until he reached the shore. The boys thought it great to be able to scream goodnight to him at the pitch of their lungs. Atop the hay field they whistled and hallooed for the fun of it, "Cyr-illl, Cyr-illl, are you there Cyr-rilll?"

When winter closed in, Cyril relocated to a fishing cabin down the river, but come spring he was back in his tent tending his bees. The boys called across and we'd see him waving. But it wasn't long before the Bear River, the Rhine of Nova Scotia, claimed Cyril's life, ever after assuming the same deadly uncertainty as the mythical rivers Styx, Acheron, Rubicon, and the Rhine of the Lorelei, where Cyril swam as a boy. He joined his gods in Valhalla. His gods loved him and followed him. One early spring evening when the weather was rough and the water choppy, Cyril took his rowboat in to the village for supplies. On his return, the boat was swamped and he drowned beneath the waves. When he didn't show up for Saturday shopping, his friends began to worry. We couldn't believe he had drowned. Why didn't he swim to shore when he was such a strong swimmer. Dad said, "Poor devil, he should have known, especially when the water was rough." Mother said it would have taken less effort and been more sensible to walk to the village. Cyril's death was traumatic and we discussed it endlessly. In thinking back to the time I almost drowned on Kniffen's beach, I would seize up and hold my breath, feeling the stifling snuffing out of Cyril's life. At night we talked about Cyril, and Daniel's active mind explored more byways than a spiderweb. Ever since his nodding acquaintance with Aunt Charlotte's ghost, who was in quiescence until the June roses bloomed again, the supernatural had become entrenched in his mind. It was an uncomfortable preoccupation, and he constantly wondered about Cyril— would his ghost sit under the willow trees or would it swim up and down the river. Daniel didn't stop. I would lie in bed hiding under the sheets, my skin crawling with goose bumps. Daniel insisted that if God were everywhere and couldn't be seen, why not Cyril? So he asked Dad, who said, "Well son, that's a different matter." I didn't want to believe in ghosts, but I couldn't be sure, so to protect myself I traded beds with Jim. It was much easier listening to Douglas talk about what the animals in the forest were up to, more or less a continuation of Thornton Burgess bedtime stories.

After Cyril's death, we passed the Major and Amanda's neat, lemon-coloured home with deep feelings of approbation. We loved Cyril and felt a strange unease knowing we would never again see him thundering down the hill on his motorcycle like a ray of his pure blond sunshine. When we got to the top of McCormick's hill on our way to school, we would look across the river to Cyril's tent, collapsed like a fallen tomb stone.

If Cyril's ghost could have been anywhere, perhaps a spot more appropriate than the river or under the willow trees would have been at the bottom of the Major Simon's garden, dipping into the woods where he kept his beehives. That spring, his bees returned to exactly where they had been in the first place, and soon the Major was bringing us honey to spread on our toast. We still called it Cyril's honey.

John McLeod collection

*I*T'S HARD TO KNOW what possessed Grandmother to be such an inveterate student of Scottish history. Perhaps that's the way turncoats show their new-found loyalty, by being overly sincere. To her, Irish history was an unnecessary mess, but at the wheeze of the bagpipe's bladder, she would rise up and sing, "Scots, wha' hae wi' Wallace bled, welcome to your gory bed," waving her hand and slashing the air, on to bloody victory. At the dinner table, the Battle of the Boyne, Bonnie Prince Charlie, and Robert the Bruce's helpful spider got lumped in my stew like toxic tidbits. Much worse was the fate of Mary Queen of Scots. After arguments and rude interjections about her succession, flight, and imprisonment, there she knelt on our dining room table, being hacked at twice by the headsman's axe, her little Skye terrier cowering under her red petticoat, the axe severing the last sinewy bits and pieces before her head could roll into the basket, blood spurting and lips still quivering a prayer. It didn't help that Dad was carving roast beef at the time. These historical meals were endlessly upsetting for an anaemic child with a nervous stomach.

In the beginning, I wanted so much to sit at the table with grown-ups, but now I was sick of it. I didn't want to hear them anymore and I wished they would go away. Who cared about Loch Lomond, the Trossacks and Garelockhead? Bear River was nice enough for me, though I'd only really seen the Annapolis side. Edinburgh, Glasgow and London were dream cities compared with Digby, Annapolis and Halifax. And oh! the beauty of the Highlands, the Lowlands, the Clyde. Canada, Canada, Canada was slung across the table like leftovers for the pigs. Even the Indians received black umbrage, those same gentle souls who came to our back door selling baskets. I couldn't understand their fierce nationalism, which seemed overly sincere. And yet Canada was where they were, and here they chose to stay. It was the first time I felt the stamp of the Canadian flag on my psyche.

All of this unappetizing history at the dinner table couldn't go on, even though Dad said himself that he liked a good controversy. It had to end, and it did end quite suddenly when Dad added to the gore by saying that the Scotch originally wore bags instead of kilts and they ate their young. A scream of terror came from Mother's end of the table as Douglas grabbed her for protection and cried, "Is Grandmother going to eat me?" This was not humour, it was sacrilege. The shocked aunts held their breath as Grandmother rose from her seat like a storm swell and hissed acidly, "Mr. Marvin, why don't you go back to your slaves in Virginia!" As she barged out of the room, she grabbed a copper jug, and with a surprisingly good arm, wound up and pitched it at the wall, denting it badly. Dad called it his Arabian jug, and it was a lovely piece, copper with a brass handle. As long as I polished the brass work, that dent reminded me of Grandmother's history lessons, exactly what I wanted to forget.

As August ended, Grandmother was fed up and took no pains to hide her feelings. If Dad was in the room, she pointedly ignored him. I knew she didn't like him and it bothered me. There had been sporadic moments of civility, but now she seethed with outright hostility. At the table, when Grandmother snapped at children over minor points of order, Mother would get up and excuse herself. Dad would carry his cup of tea out to the glide swing. He seemed weary and sick. He would stretch out and lie on the swing while we crowded around. Shortly, he would rouse himself for chores, wandering off with the boys trailing behind. It was the busy time before he left, with as much work to do at the end of the season as at the beginning. Gardens had to be cleared; corn stalks raked to the end of their rows; bean vines pulled and piled so we could sit and empty the beans from the dried, papery pods. Turnips, cabbage, potatoes, carrots, beets and squash all had to be piled in heaps, then bagged for sale or storage in the root cellar. One afternoon, the cows deviously escaped from the pasture and snuck into the turnip patch, resulting in pale orange milk. This novelty delighted us as we stared into our brass mugs at the miracle of peachy turnip milk. Mother said it would make lovely butter.

With so much to do, Dad simplified things when he suddenly excused himself from finishing Uncle Peter's house. It was a nice, solid structure with three floors, a windowed side porch, and plenty of room for an expanding family. Mother would have loved a brand-new house, especially since ours was devolving into a fixer-upper. Uncle Douglas, good scout that he was, had agreed to do Uncle Peter's walls before he returned to Scotland, where he had been a plasterer, or, as they called it, a decorator. He had finished the downstairs, so one evening, Dad, Uncle Douglas, and I walked up to have a look. Dad and Uncle Douglas were poring over the plans, which were pinned to a large board on two wooden horses, when Uncle Peter and Verna came in, not suspecting that anyone was there. Uncle Peter asked Verna what she thought of her new home and she said, "I love it, but Marvin has too much to say about it." I was about to go and say hello, but I stopped and looked at Dad. He acted as if he hadn't heard a thing, but without a word, he casually took the thumb tacks out of his plans, rolled them up and walked out the front door. Uncle Douglas and I followed. Dad never set foot in the house again. Fifteen years later when I visited Uncle Peter, the upstairs was still unfinished.

Despite my qualms about the MacGregors, I was sad to learn that Uncle Douglas would be leaving. He was my favourite uncle, so considerate and gentle with Mother, always doing her small favours. Still, he was a MacGregor, and if justifiably aroused, his warring heritage would surface. But it was not to his discredit that he dealt with Uncle Peter for filching his girlfriend, or that he nearly throttled Mr. Chute out of existence for taking his watch chain, honour being a plaything among rogues and thieves.

With school looming, Mother remarked that I looked like a ragamuffin and needed a haircut, and since Uncle Douglas had errands in the village, she suggested that I go along. An outing with my favourite uncle seemed like just the thing, so I spruced up in anticipation of a pleasant afternoon. After delivering a load of vegetables to the Trading Company, our next stop was Mr. Chute's store to pick up Uncle Douglas' watch. For his birthday, Dad had given Uncle Douglas a green gold Waltham watch with a magnificent chain that lay across his waistcoat.

Uncle Peter's house almost finished

The crystal of the watch broke when he and Uncle Peter beat each other up over Verna's affections, so he took it to Mr. Chute for repair. On picking up his watch, Uncle Douglas asked where the chain was. Storm clouds gathered when Mr. Chute said there was no chain. Temperatures rose when Uncle Douglas insisted that there most certainly was. The pace quickened until their loud shouting tumbled out the door and rolled across Main Street. Mr. Chute was adamant and unyielding. Uncle Douglas refused to leave without his chain. A dangerous calm settled briefly when Mr. Chute stopped arguing, sat down at his repair table and ignored Uncle Douglas, whose face turned as red as the MacGregor tartan. Reason had run its course. Uncle Douglas jumped the counter, grabbed Mr. Chute by the necktie and proceeded to throttle him, calling him a lying...thieving...blackguard with every wrenching wring of the necktie. This being my first strangulation, I froze, paralyzed as I watched Mr. Chute flail bug-eyed. In the middle of this uniquely MacGregor moment, Uncle Douglas spotted a folding display board on a desk, and there on a hook hung the chain. He dropped Mr. Chute, who fluttered to his chair like a falling leaf, and grabbed his chain, holding it in front of me and asking me to confirm that it was indeed his. I was in no condition to know a chain from a cherry blossom, so I cried, "I don't know," and ran out the door. I leaned against the side of the building and did what I do best, I blubbered. The door opened and out stepped Uncle Douglas straightening his tie, all set to be spiffed up at Barr's for the Saturday night dance with Loretta. Olive, Gertie and everyone else in the barbershop heard the sordid tale. They hooted because Uncle Douglas told a lively story, taking centre stage to demonstrate with his tie how he wrung out Mr. Chute like the Monday wash. Going to Barr's was usually a highlight of my life, but not this day. As I stared in the mirror, the luxury of being perfectly coiffed and dabbed with perfumed powder merged with the image of Mr. Chute gasping and flailing puppet-like. After that debacle, I avoided looking in at Mr. Chute's jewellery display. He was always at the front window smoking away as he repaired watches, sitting behind a heavy green curtain halfway up the window so you could only see his head. He lived on the Digby side with his spinster sister and had taken over the shop years ago when his father died. I didn't see much of him after that and paused to wonder when he died of pneumonia the next winter.

One evening at the dinner table after all the significant subjects had been pushed aside like plates of old bones, Aunt Elsie wondered why handsome, elderly Fulton Parker had never married. A roar went up. Elsie was on the prowl. No, No, she was just wondering, after all, he must have money. Fulton Parker looked like the financier Otto Khan, very suave and handsome. He was always turned out like a band box, dressed in grey from his grey fedora down to his grey spats. He was very nice to us, and Dad often stopped to chat with him in the village. On occasion, I would see him escorting the elderly Miss Van Buskirk of the Trading Company, so surely he could make a maid happy, and why not? However, Grandmother emphasized that Fulton Parker was old enough to be Elsie's father, even her grandfather, and heaven help silly young girls who married silly old men. Aunt Elsie had left a boyfriend in Helensburgh, not sure whether she liked him or not, but since prospects in Canada were so poor, she wondered if an old boyfriend was better than none at all. Not a single prospect in Bear River could build a castle commensurate with her dreams. She said she did not want chickens in her back yard, yet every house along the Chute road and into town had chickens, a horse and buggy, and a cow. Where there were people, there were animals. She took in all the barn dances and had seen quite enough of farmers. She cancelled out the few young teachers simply because they didn't make enough money: John Henniger, young Mr. Wal Clarke, Truman Hamilton's son, and Henry Romans, who was spoken for. Alice Copeland told me that she would marry him one day, if he would have her. Doctors were out for the same reason. Dad regularly supplied Dr. Campbell with vegetables and chickens, but many of his patients were barely scraping by. Ministers were out too. For a Catholic girl, priests had nothing to offer but prayers. Aunt Elsie sighed and the conversation moved on. Then, as Grandmother was propounding about The Vote, she looked at me just as I plucked the loose brace from my two front teeth and put it beside my plate. It sickened her to see such a thing, and she ordered me to take it away, immediately, out of her sight, right now. She threatened to send me away from the table for good and rasped, "If you'd keep your tongue where it belonged, that nasty thing wouldn't be necessary." Aunt Elsie then dispensed with The Vote by saying she had heard that Dr. Roop, the new dentist, was terribly handsome.

A single, young, handsome man and not a farmer but a professional was unheard of in Bear River. This demanded further investigation. She dressed carefully, powdered every freckle out of existence, and determinedly accompanied me to Dr. Roop's to have my brace tightened. It was Aunt Elsie who hammered home to me that getting married was vital to the salvation of the single woman, as I then was. Dr. Roop fixed my brace and fixated Aunt Elsie. Whether Dr. Roop was better off than anyone else didn't matter; she was smitten. Since I hadn't noticed Dr. Roop's qualifications before, Aunt Elsie briefed me on the way home. He was, as she said, marvellously tall, his hair was marvellously wavy, he had marvellous blue eyes, he was marvellous—his dimples, his smile, his perfect teeth, and that voice, "Oh my!" He was Evelyn Thompson all over again. Because of Aunt Elsie's ravings about Dr. Roop's curly hair, his smile, his eyes, I took notice of handsome men as I never did before. I began to look at Dr. Roop as a paragon for a 7-year-old girl, and for a while he hung in my mind in a gold frame. Dear Dr. Roop who gave me lollipops. This went on until I lost my brace when Daniel banged my head on a massive snowball we had rolled. I couldn't find it, and Mother said, "Oh, well, it'll show up in the spring."

The MacGregors teased Aunt Elsie relentlessly about Dr. Roop, but she didn't care a fig. When Mabel Kniffen stopped by one day to announce their end-of-season clam bake, Elsie was ecstatic to hear that Dr. Roop would be attending. The clam bake was to be their biggest ever, but we were devastated to hear that it would also be their last. The Kniffens were leaving the Hollow and would not be returning.

On the day of the party, the boys spent all afternoon slipping and sliding across the mud flats looking for bubbles and digging up a multitude of clams. They gathered piles of seaweed and driftwood for the fires, and then cleaned the clams in the creek, throwing them in buckets of water with corn meal to purge the sand. For the bonfires, Uncle Peter cleared the gardens of corn stalks and took a wagon load down to the Hollow along with burlap bags of corn. It was the event of the summer, and excitement bubbled everywhere. The Aunts were busy in the kitchen baking a full menu of desserts. I was delegated to look after the baby, so I sat on the glide swing watching a steady procession of horses, buggies and cars pass by.

As the hollow filled up, they parked along the Chute Road, around our barn and up McCormick's hill. Stylish strangers poured out of vehicles and passed down to the Hollow, their talk and laughter following them. With so many people arriving, Mother put our kitchen at Mabel's convenience, and Aunt Elsie prepared a huge cauldron of coffee. It was Dr. Roop who arrived to take it down, and who should be at his side but a lovely blonde whom he introduced as his fiancée. His eye did stray, though, because as soon as he saw Lorna, dressed in her new green-and-white gingham rompers, he picked her up and didn't let her go. As long as he was there, he carried her around and sat her on his knee, examining her dirty doll as she docily observed him with her big green eyes. They were smitten with each other and Aunt Elsie was out of the picture. She sighed her last disappointed sigh, "Isn't he marvelous." The last good man in town.

At dusk, I went down with Mother and Dad, and as we approached the Hollow, the revelry filtered up through the trees like the ocean's roar. I had never seen so many people in my life. Every inch of lawn and beach was filled with people talking and laughing. Some were swimming or sitting by the bonfires or dancing to the gramophone. Others gathered around the fire pits that smouldered away, layered with a bed of seaweed for the clams, corn and lobsters. We spotted Daniel running about with driftwood for the fires, feeding them liberally and stirring the logs as they buzzed with sparks. Dad took my hand as we threaded through the crowd. It was my first big party and everyone was so happy and nice. Mother found the Kniffen women and fell to talking. I sat with Dad, wedged between his knees. Mr. Bishop, Major Simon and Fulton Parker were enjoying a lively conversation amid clouds of pungent cigar smoke. Lexie Hatfield, Flossie Dunn and June Schmidt rushed over like birds landing and sat with the men. They were courteous and accommodating to the young ladies, who enjoyed the chivalry and looked so elegant in the flapper styles of chiffons and beads and pretty shoes. Lexie Hatfield was starry-eyed about New York and quizzed Mr. Bishop, who responded in his native flamboyance about the most exciting city in the world. I was fascinated by a group of energetic young ladies who were taking turns dancing the Charleston on the millstone. The gramophone played "Red, Red Robin" and

"Has Anyone Seen My Girl" as they fluttered like moths in their filmy chiffons, dancing themselves to exhaustion as the gramophone wound down. They spun themselves out like the ballerina that twirled atop Aunt Nan's musical powder box. As the records changed, couples would jump up on impulse and dance in the sand. Amanda drowned out one song, and I giggled when Dad whispered in my ear the same old hope that someone might choke that canary. Uncle Douglas arrived in his usual high spirits, clutching Loretta's waist like a predator. Uncle Peter arrived with Verna, and the boys clamoured around her. She was robust and healthy, but had a delicate air about her, gently laughing as the boys softened her up with compliments. Nearby, the tiny Aunts bantered loudly with some men, their laughter roaring out of them. The large pile of records on the millstone was becoming disorganized, so Mabel asked me to look after the gramophone. I sifted through the records, playing the current favourites and taking requests from people, who rewarded me with fudge or chocolates. Olive Barr asked for "Ain't She Sweet," and Amanda's voice rose above the raucous din, wavering unsteadily, "Ain't she sweet, from her head down to her feet." Her freewheeling overtones suited the dance-hall disorder. Several talented locals offered a medley of songs from a performance at Oakdene hall, cleverly improvising with imaginary props. Cyril Burns did his bit too, which everyone loved, singing 'My Blue Heaven' in his deep guttural German accent and terribly off-key, "Yust Mollee und mine, und babe make tree, mine bloo hav-vun." Everyone asked for an encore and got it, but then they said no, no, no. Uncle Peter and Uncle Douglas pitched in with their bagpipes, which brought howls of despair when they wobbled off-key with Cyril. The MacGregors all had good voices, even the teen-aged uncles, so they gave a creditable performance of the tartan top ten. Daniel took over the gramophone when Mabel asked me to help refill the tables with food and do other small chores that let me comfortably wander. I took a pail of butter over to the fire pit where guests were nibbling corn and gulping clams. Others sat on logs chatting or staring into a large fire pit that glowed with embers and coals like a seething stained-glass window. I joined them and stared down, down, into a fiery underworld. Then I sat on the grass transfixed by the dancers on the beach, their kinetic shapes outlined by the bonfire, flaring and splintering against the flames in a tribal tableau.

When Mabel asked Mother to sing, I went over to listen as she sang ballads and Uncle Peter vamped on his mouth organ. Then during an aria for Mr. Bishop, Dvorak's "Song to the Moon," I suddenly realized there was complete silence, as if the party was over. All of those strangers who had been talking and laughing and shouting over each other had stopped and were training their eyes on Mother. For some reason I was uncomfortable with the silence, even embarrassed, yet there she stood singing her heart out so confidently, her lovely voice floating down the river on the night air. Then Uncle Peter and Uncle Douglas skirled their bagpipes for the high-stepping MacGregors. They hicced and hooted as others joined in and swung the aunts round and round. Uncle Peter obliged by shifting up-tempo into a ridiculous Scottish square dance with Uncle Douglas calling out the moves in a thick brogue. The aunts were hilariously hick. When the air turned cool, Dad gathered us up, and as we climbed the hill, Uncle Peter's bagpipes crashed through the trees. In bed, we lay in the dark listening to the music and laughter echoing up from the Hollow like a fading dream. It was a wonderful party; the biggest and the best in all my years.

Low tide at Kniffen's beach (2011) looking towards where the house was (right) and up the river towards the Bay.

The next morning a quiet cast hung over the Hollow, as if it were empty already. Daniel went down to help clean up the beach and burn the rubbish. Mother prepared a last Sunday dinner for departing friends, and that day the dining room was closed to children. Mr. Bishop got his favorite lemon pie and left with a supply of Mother's jams. Later, a truck passed by with the Kniffen's belongings, all those wonderful years hauled away in a truck. Kate Woodbury sounded the horn of her Model T Ford, and Mrs. Kniffen, Mabel, Mary and Kate bid a tearful farewell. Mabel was Daniel's first love and he kept insisting, "You've got to come back," but Mabel said she didn't think she would. The Kniffens were Mother's only real friends, and she was terribly sad at this final parting, crying as the car climbed McCormick's hill. Later, little things made Mother remember this or that, but there were always empty spaces. The flow of conversation and laughter left with the season and never came back. A cool emptiness crept up from the Hollow and whispered hauntingly in our ears.

John McLeod

*A*s soon as the Kniffens left, a noticeable pall fell over the house, and the MacGregors acted as if their lives were as empty as the Hollow. Grandmother lost her facility for wit and charm, and in dealing with her family, she assumed she was dealing with idiots, never more so than on the day religion reared its ugly head.

It all started when Merton Yorke told Daniel that Mr. Henderson, the pastor for the Jehovah's Witnesses, would be holding a baptism right in the Bear River. Merton explained that everyone would be wrapped in sheets, dunked in the river and then they would be ready for heaven. Merton wanted Daniel to accompany him, could he go? At the dinner table, Dad casually said he didn't see why not. Daniel was giggling in high glee–all those Bear River worthies wrapped in sheets, and he and Merton on the sidelines. Then Mother snapped, "Certainly not. Certainly not with Merton Yorke." Not one to sweep baptism under the rug, Daniel wanted to know exactly how one was baptized and for what purpose. Grandmother stepped in with the dire warning that unless one was baptized, one would never get to heaven, ever. And where would one go? Hell, of course, that awful place. This opened up a whole new set of circumstances for us. Apparently, there was a lot more than wind up above, and a whole lot more to be avoided down below. Worried, Daniel asked if he was baptized, and Mother said yes, and so was I. But then she announced, as heaven crashed down on our mashed potatoes, none of the other children had been baptized in the church. She had done it herself at birth, as was allowed by the Catholic Church in certain circumstances. That's when the eruption occurred. Grandmother spewed that her grandchildren would not be brought up as heathens and heathens they would be unless they were properly baptized by the church. "Your poor, dear father must be rolling in his grave," his usual reaction despite Grandmother's repetitive 'may he rest in peace.' All the aunts and uncles were shocked at the omission and nodded their heads gravely; it was a disgrace. Mother explained that she could hardly take babies in the wagon to St. Thomas' in Annapolis in the dead of winter; they were baptized well enough for the time being. Grandmother then soared off on another one of her religious rants, gaining altitude as she described in detail the frightening sermons preached by the Jesuits back home. She followed up with a recounting of all the other bombastic performances in the pulpit; the pounding and fulminating about death and destruction as the rewards of sin. Grandmother said she sat in her pew and shivered, while Grandfather, a true Scot, feared they would have to put more money in the collection plate to repair the pulpit. Oh, yes, said the aunts and uncles, they all remembered it like a fond memory. The thought of Grandmother shivering in her pew put church in an ominous light. Religion clearly had a few bones to pick.

Although we were familiar with the more lurid tales in the Bible, not to mention the Greek myths, Bluebeard, and the deadlier quirks of the human comedy, our religious training was essentially nil. There had been an earlier blow-up when I came to the breakfast table and Grandmother asked me if I had said my morning prayers. I answered truthfully that I only said my prayers in school and school was out. I didn't quite understand the Lord's Prayer and thought that trespassing meant not going into someone's woods. Grandmother had to correct me for saying harrowed, a farm word I understood, instead of hallowed. In those days, everyone went to church, and our exception was a relief, despite Grandmother's overtures to perdition. As the bells of all the churches rang across the hills like Bizet's "Carillon," we would race to the top of the hay field and watch the Kniffen's horse trot by with everyone properly posed in their carriage. Work still went on like any other day of the week, but Sundays meant freedom, especially sunny days with picnics, and the only taint of religion was the bloody sacrifice of another chicken on the chopping block.

Daniel and I were relieved to know we qualified for heaven, but Grandmother's dogmatic pronouncements made us fear for the younger ones, all to be severely dealt with by God Himself. It really disturbed us. We were called heathens so often and so pointedly that Dad said he would believe we were heathens when we started eating each other. Grandmother countered nastily, "I don't know what you should have to say about your children being baptized, you're nothing but a turncoat." Dad had become a Catholic to marry Mother. With that chilly remark, Mother and Dad gathered our plates and let us finish our meal in the kitchen, where we could think and talk like normal human beings. After that, children were weeded out from the MacGregors at mealtime and we enjoyed the equilibrium of regained territory, if only at the kitchen table. We did a lot of whispering.

Grandmother's baptismal tirades intensified during what became a month-long struggle over the fate of my siblings. She badgered Mother daily that she was leaving soon and wanted the matter settled. There was Mother nursing a baby, bunching vegetables, making jams and pickles, rushing her life away to find enough minutes in the day, and Grandmother was fired up over the state of our everlasting souls. Finally, Mother stated very plainly that she was too busy to bother and she simply didn't care; the children would have to make do with the baptism they had. Grandmother countered that the little wretches would not be carted off to perdition on her watch. She had been raised on Irish suffering and damnation, so the fires of Hell burned ever-bright. She and Uncle Peter trotted off to St. Thomas' in Annapolis Royal, where Grandmother harangued Father Mackay with tales of our heathen shame, easing up on the debauch only when he agreed to trek into darkest Bear River. She returned triumphant, announcing that Father Mackay would be visiting Maple Grove farm for the express purpose of giving every last little Marvin a ticket to heaven, though conditions still applied. In two shakes of a lamb's tail, Father MacKay rose in rank until he was in with the angels, floating high above any rumours involving the watering holes of Indian Hill. And if the celebrations on St. Anne's Day[1] got a little out of hand, well, it was all in good faith. Mother and Dad agreed to the baptism, but the younger ones were alarmed when Daniel asked if they would be wrapped in sheets and dunked in the river. The aunts reassured us that a baptism was a happy event, even festive, like Easter or Christmas. The prospect of candy calmed everyone down. At this point, the MacGregors took over, and if Mother existed at all at the time, I forget. She faded from the picture. In the kitchen, the aunts had a reason to cook again, while Grandmother launched another clean-up. The teenagers mowed the grass and tidied to pastoral perfection, though the manure pile still marred the main approach, seething like a hideous evil.

A day or two before the baptism, on a sunny September afternoon, Grandmother and the aunts decided on a trip to Barr's. They wanted their hair and nails done, they still had some shopping to do, Aunt Elsie had seen a hat at Mrs. Yorke's, and perhaps they would stop for tea at Mrs. Copeland's. Dad generously allowed them to charge whatever they wanted,

---

1 Patron saint of the Indians

and they had generously accepted. This was never questioned until years later when Mother sadly wondered. The mellow weather put everyone in a seasonable mood as they ambled off in the late-summer heat, chatting and laughing in expectation of a pleasant afternoon. Dad had taken the boys to Digby, and the uncles worked in the gardens, so Mother had a peaceful interlude with the kitchen all to herself to make her pickles. The house hadn't been this quiet for months. As I sat watching the baby and listening to Mother sing, I wished the MacGregors would just go away so the house could always be like this. In a little while, the Trading Company delivery man arrived with Grandmother's order: Scotch marmalade, English biscuits, her special brand of tea (not Lipton's), and among other things, a jar of pickles like the ones Mother had just made. In the root cellar, dozens of similar jars sat on a shelf, so Mother thought it was a mistake and sent the pickles back. Soon, everyone returned and sat around the kitchen table in a happy mood, recounting the afternoon while Mother prepared the evening meal. As usual, the aunts discussed everything: where they went, whom they saw and what was said. Parcels were opened and displayed, each with a story attached. Aunt Elsie got her hat, and Mother tried it on. At the Trading Company, they chatted at length with Miss Van Buskirk. At Barr's, Olive and Gertie gave them all the Hollywood gossip. At Mrs. Copeland's tea shop, they learned that she would soon be closing down. When the conversation waned, Grandmother got up to check her food order and quickly discovered that her pickles were missing. Mother said she was sorry, but she thought it was a mistake and sent them back. Grandmother hissed, "How dare you countermand my order!" Everyone froze. Mother looked tired and stood there wordlessly, not quite ready to care about a jar of pickles. Grandmother flared, "When I order pickles, I order pickles. How dare you! How Dare You!!" She then lifted her tiny, perfectly manicured hand and slapped Mother across the face as hard as she could. Mother withdrew in shock, and the room went silent as she stood for a moment, then turned without a word to the bedroom. I followed and watched as Mother wordlessly turned her cheek to the mirror and put her hand up to her face. She then calmly returned to the kitchen to get on with the meal. Aunt Cathy, always so sweet and helpful, urged Mother to sit down and she would fix the meal, but Mother stood silently at the stove, not moving.

The aunts rallied, saying, "Polly, I'll do this" or "Polly, you're tired, let someone else do that." They were so kind. Later, Mother sat in the bedroom nursing the baby, silently rocking. I sat with her until she told me to go in to dinner. At the table, I warily eyed Grandmother, waiting for an eruption and being told to stop staring. I suppose it was at that point that I stopped fearing Grandmother and started hating her. I couldn't believe that anyone would do such a shocking thing to my mother. As a child, I was unable to express my feelings and could only compare her to the porcupine in the maples that Dad had shot for our safety. Never again would I be comfortable in Grandmother's presence.

That night when Mother kissed us good night, I kissed her cheek and said, "I don't like Grandmother." Mother said never mind, but I felt I was given license to hate. In bed, I told the boys everything, and they agreed that we'd be better off if Grandmother would just go. Instead, early the next day Dad packed his club bag, and Mother walked him to the end of the maple grove where a taxi stood waiting. I ran after them because Dad had left without my kiss. He told Mother he had a lot of orders for brass work to fill and they would be his last. He also said emphatically that he would not be back until Grandmother was gone. She had been vocal about leaving, but still had her nose to the wind trying to find direction, either Halifax, Montreal or back home to Scotland. Dad said he would find her a place in Montreal, but one thing was certain, he would not be back until that woman was out of the house. He left Mother in tears, and as we walked back through the maple grove, I could feel her helplessness and inability to cope with the whole fractious lot of MacGregors. Afterwards, she became as silent as a shadow except where our behaviour was concerned.

On the day of the baptism, Mother sat in the background, almost like an intruder, calmly nursing Joan. Meanwhile, the MacGregors tore about in full fling, setting tables and chairs under the maples, placing dishes and cutlery just so. Every child was scrubbed clean, primped to perfection and lined up for inspection like sacrificial lambs. Amid all this activity, I was sitting at the top of the stairs, just sitting there like a turnip without a thought in my head, no incentive to move up or down. Grandmother was in her room talking to Aunt Nan, and when she opened the door, she brusquely snapped, "Off you go. You should be out playing instead of listening at doors, you nosey wee parker." I scurried off, hurt by the way she always talked to me. I ran out the front door, up to the lilac bush and along the Chute Road, running as fast as I could. At the Red Astrakhan tree, I turned to look back. No one had seen me, so I ran down the steep path until the stillness of the Hollow slowed my pace. The quiet seemed unnatural, and I felt a deep sense of desertion, as if I had stepped into a graveyard. Even the brook bubbled mutely. My shoes echoed across the bridge, and twigs snapped loudly as I walked along the path. After touching Mr. Kniffen's oak, I went over to the house. It seemed small; its blank, curtainless windows betraying a lifeless shell. On the verandah, I stood on tiptoes and peered into empty rooms stripped of linoleum and showing bare floorboards. At the base of the cliff, the tiny babies' graveyard with the one fallen tombstone seemed sad; it wasn't that way in the spring when the lily-of-the-valley bloomed. I wandered over to the beach and sat on the warm millstone, basking in the sun and watching the incoming tide. I was a happy child in minutes. Then I flopped on the soft grass under the eucalyptus tree and lay there listening to the birds chirping, the brook bubbling and the lapping of the river. It was so peaceful: no Gaelic, no chanters, no harsh tones, nothing but lying on the soft grass and listening to the world. After a while, I realized I had better get back. When the Kniffens left, we were forbidden to go into the Hollow alone because people had heard bootleggers off-loading one night. I stepped up to the front door for a last look through the window, but when I absently touched the handle, the door opened. Sunlight streamed into the parlor through the front windows, and as I stepped inside, I suddenly felt all the warmth and comfort of this once-loving home. All that remained was the pot-bellied stove, where Mr. Kniffen had rocked me against his straw beard. The floors echoed an eerie emptiness as I wandered from the parlor to the kitchen to Mr. Kniffen's room, a mere cubicle. I had never seen the second floor, so I tiptoed up the stairs and looked down a narrow hallway. The back of the house was dark, and all I could see through the windows were the roots of trees climbing the cliff, so I went into the front bedroom where the sun poured in. I stood at the window looking out to the river. Across the Hollow, the wooded slope edged our farm. I turned to go, but then my eye caught a flash of something in the closet.

The door was ajar, and when I opened it, there on the floor stood a huge stack of *Good Housekeeping* magazines. In a spasm of sheer joy, I opened one up, and yes, it still had the Campbell's Soup doll. Alice Copeland's mother subscribed to *Good Housekeeping*, so every month she got a new Campbell's Soup doll with a new wardrobe. I couldn't wait until she brought the latest one to school. There, in that closet was every paper doll I had ever longed for. I dragged the pile into the room, sat down in a sunbeam, and began tearing out each and every one. I loved that cuddly little doll with its beautiful cut-out clothes. I carefully tore out page after page until I must have had a hundred, and as I tore out the last one, it was as if the bell tolled midnight. I realized I had better get back. I pushed the stack of magazines into the cupboard, stuffed the dolls in my bloomer leg and ran back as fast as I could, wondering where to hide my illicit cargo.

After climbing up from the Hollow, I sneakily circled around to emerge at the maple grove, approaching the house cautiously and fully expecting a criminal investigation. Instead, I was stunned to learn that the baptism was over and done with and no one had missed me. The MacGregors were sitting around the table finishing off the last of the meal, pleased with themselves as the saviours of souls. Aunt Elsie pushed the baby into my arms, and I asked Daniel for a report. He said it was a dull performance with no candy, and certainly not on par with the spectacle the Jehovah's Witnesses had promised. For a few late afternoon moments, Father Mackay had splashed each child with water, gulped his tea, and lingered only as long as the MacGregors could detain him. He excused himself for other duties and bolted up McCormick's hill, probably headed to Indian Hill to lift a few spirits. The leftover table-talk was still in full swing because it so happened that Father Mackay had written a book called *The Rape and the Lock*. The MacGregors were thrilled at having met a real author, and a man of the cloth at that. The subject of rape had not yet been broached at our table, so I assumed it was a good thing, what with all the fawning and obvious admiration of our local spiritual guide. The title remained a mystery until years later when I was deep into poetry and wondered just how many of the early poets Father Mackay had overly-appreciated, Pope[2], Swinburne and the like. The line still sticks, 'from too much love of living.'

2 Alexander Pope. *The Rape of the Lock*, 1714.

To protect my dolls, I hid them in my book bag and spent many secret hours at home and school carefully clipping. I enjoyed giving life to my Campbell's Soup dolls with their scrubbed, apple-chubby cheeks, bright eyes and Dutch bob. Eventually, Lorna and Joan found them and left them in tatters, the torn tabs of their clothes turning them into raggedy waifs. When I complained, I was told that they were only scraps of paper.

The rectification of our heathen souls did not make Grandmother happy. She had mounted the cause like Don Juan of Austria conquering the infidel, but victory trailed its tatters. Her attitude was steadily downgrading, and at odd moments she would sit in the parlor staring at Grandfather's portrait and fingering her rosary beads. Thus ended the great baptismal war–over in an afternoon and forgotten for years. The significance of our souls waned and was not visited upon us again until my teens, when we joined the herd and I became a religious zealot.

A few years ago, I asked Aunt Cathy if she remembered that slap. She looked surprised and said, "You were so small, I wouldn't have thought you'd remember." There was a particular emphasis to that day. In our minds there is a registry, and no matter how distant, events can be retrieved from pigeon holes. We slough away the insignificant, but indelible incidents are stored as we saw and heard and smelled them. Even now, I can still recall Mother's shocked reaction, her breath being sucked in, and the astringent aroma of pickles.

The Trading Company delivery wagon. To the left is the cannon barrel.

*A*LTHOUGH THE BAPTISM WAS over and the little ones would not have to face the fiery gates of Hell, we still weren't out of the party season, because Uncle Peter had announced a corn boil in honour of his beloved Verna. On a crisp, early fall evening, Daniel and I went down to our beach to enjoy the festivities, the only family members to attend because all the MacGregors had taken to feuding. Tables full of food were positioned around the fire, where a large cauldron of corn bubbled away. The significant thing for me was that I was allowed to drink coffee to stay warm. Daniel and I sat perched on a log high above on a grassy embankment where we could listen like spies to the adult conversation. The first thing we noticed was that the men were passing around a bottle of something; a most unusual rite. The party quickly geared up to its jovial best, and Uncle Peter, not one to let heritage rot, got busy on the bagpipes. An explosion of sound wailed up and down the river, alerting the dogs. After the salute to Scotland, the guests enjoyed bouts of eating and drinking and outbursts of song. At intervals, the bottle circulated freely amid laughter over nothing. At one point, the crowd saluted the happy couple as Uncle Peter and Verna danced. The bagpipes skirled a sentimental dirge, and then a more cultivated musician brought out his harmonica. Everyone sang along to the favourites of the day: "Bye, Bye Blackbird," "Has Anybody Seen My Gal," "The Red River Valley," "Beautiful Ohio," and a song about some man finding the girl of his dreams in a five-and-dime store. Amanda Simon injected a serious note and piously launched into "The Old Rugged Cross" with her tremolo contralto as commanding as the bagpipes, all of which did nothing to control the level of hilarity. I hated it; who sings about death at a corn boil? Everyone politely let her finish her last wavering note, and a few jolly men said Amen. Uncle Peter added, "There's nothing like a good hymn in the middle of a wild party." After the nod to heaven, Amanda decided that since a chill was coming in from the Bay and the party was winding down, it was time for a nod to the King, so she ridiculously launched into "God Save the King." Major Simon joined in, and then everyone else tagged along except for a loud cockney Englishman named Ernie Baker, a hired hand of Mr. W.G. Clarke's, who sang an entirely different song at the pitch of his lungs, something about his Auntie Florence. Whatever his differences with the King of England, Daniel and I thought it hilarious. When the song ended, Ernie Baker shouted into the night, "God soive Earnie Biker, oi soiy!" He threw a lard pail into the air, and it fell on to the rocks, echoing several last, tinny notes.

There's a haunting sense about end-of-summer nights when the sky is black and the stars hang low. Sounds are softer: the crickets and frogs; the muted, muffled flight of night hawks; a voice carrying across the water. After the drenching heat of summer, there is a coziness about cool breezes from the river and the smell of burning drift wood, presaging the cruelties of Atlantic winters.

With Dad out of the picture and Mother on the sidelines, the house quickly slid into turmoil as the MacGregors sparred nonstop. Like love gone wrong, everything irked, and no one cared to hide the fact. Uncle Peter and Uncle Douglas seemed destined for a repeat performance of their barn dance skirmish. The bad blood returned when Dad and Uncle Douglas walked out of Uncle Peter's house after Verna's remark. Uncle Douglas considered the subject closed; he would not lift another finger, but Uncle Peter felt he was owed a fully plastered house and didn't mind saying so. Meanwhile, Uncle Peter and the teenaged uncles were edging towards war as they argued daily over chores. Breakfasts evolved into nasty affairs whenever Uncle Peter reminded them to saw wood or chop kindling or shovel out the cow's stalls or clean the chicken house. They weren't afraid of Uncle Peter and seemed to be threatening him when they shouted, 'I don't have to do as you tell me. If you think I'm shovelling manure, or doing this or that, you're daft. I'm telling Ma.' The teenagers had him over a barrel and they knew it. Uncle Peter needed their help with his house, and Grandmother refused to see her boys working Dad's farm. This ignited a fiery exchange between Uncle Peter and Grandmother, followed by a cool silence that lasted years.

Because of Grandmother's coddling, the teenager's work ethic never took root, and whenever they did do something, they affected an arrogant reluctance. While my brothers scooted about and quickly completed their chores, the teenagers stumbled over simpler tasks, finishing with injured expressions and developing a finely-tuned sense of injustice. Bringing in wood seemed to be all they were good for, but the finer points of stacking it beside the stoves escaped them. They refused to kill chickens, their ancestry hadn't caught up with them yet, but they didn't mind eating those chickens. One day, Uncle Jim, in a voracious mood, said to Mother over his chicken bones, "Polly, you should have another chicken for dinner. I could eat a whole one myself." Mother said she would cook it if he killed it.

As the family portrait splintered, the aunts lost their zest for life and took to sleeping in late, retiring early, and commenting on the cold wind and rain blowing in from the Bay. Aunt Nan had nothing better to do, so she started grieving for Evelyn Thompson all over again, while pouty Aunt Ellie vanished into closets. Grandmother's prickly attempts to revitalize them only led to nasty rows behind closed doors. Not even Thanksgiving dinner could budge them out of their ennui. One day Aunt Nan revived herself and appeared in the school lunchroom with a treat. I withered as she singled us out one by one for a bowl of stew, ladled from a lard pail just like the ones everyone filled with slops for the pigs. For the first time ever, Merton Yorke held his tongue. I would have stabbed him with my spoon if he had said a word.

Mealtimes were testy affairs, and our dining room was all set to host the next Scottish civil war. We listened from the kitchen table as sniping and skirmishing led to the occasional blow-up. Once, we looked in to see the uncles standing and shouting at each other, Grandmother and the aunts pitching in, and Mother staring at her plate. Then, just as the whole warring clan was about to devour itself, Uncle Douglas stepped in and took charge. Suddenly there was peace. I marvelled. Even Grandmother acquiesced. I don't know what he said or did; perhaps it was the same no-nonsense approach he used in Mr. Chute's watch repair, but the teenagers responded, getting buckets of water, collecting eggs, feeding the chickens. They never once questioned him. He gave orders and they ran. Uncle Douglas also took charge of Mother, who seemed rootless in her own home.

I liked the way he did favours for her and ordered about in his soft voice, not strident like the other uncles. He would take things out of her hands, vegetables, dishes or something, and say, "Polly, you are going to sit right down and take it easy and have a cup of tea with me. Wee Mary, you make us a cup of tea." Over and over again he would tell her, "Polly, this is no life for you. It's too hard. You've got to get away before it kills you." Leaving the farm was my dream, but I was disturbed to hear it put in those words. Mother just sat there listening, not saying a thing.

So calm returned to the breakfast table. It was a rushed but peaceful time of day with Grandmother and the aunts sleeping in. Uncle Douglas would come to the table, taking over from Dad's hymn to the morn by rubbing his hands and saying, "Och, it's a braw day, the lark's in the heavens and all's right with the world." Douglas, a budding ornithologist, would put a cloud in the sky, "There are no larks in Bear River."

"Well now," Uncle Douglas would list off a number of unlikely birds: penguins, parrots, cockatoos, ending with, "What about chickens?"

"Not in the sky." We loved him. He often hitched up Harry and drove us to school, sometimes collecting us afterwards on rainy days. But the days we had to walk to school were a different matter altogether. The minute we stepped over McCormick's hill and out of sight, the teenaged uncles would grab our book bags, or push and shove us. They didn't like school, they didn't like the long walk, and they didn't like us. If I told them to stop and that I was going to tell, they would remind me what would happen if I breathed a word: they would kill me–stone dead. To emphasize the point, they would throw stones at us as we ran to escape them. We'd be out of breath as we met Alice Copeland at the Crossroads, where the uncles behaved, since Alice would be sure to tell her older brother. Often we were too late to meet up, so we just kept running as the stones buzzed by. We didn't dare look back, we just ran. Eventually, we'd catch up to Alice or simply outrun the uncles, who didn't have the stamina for the long hike. After school, we'd walk home in the protection of the group: Nancy and Billy MacIntyre, all the Reades and the Copelands. The uncles would lurk behind, intruding like unwelcome guests, smirking menacingly. On reaching the Crossroads, we would scurry down the avenue in a mad dash to safety, the uncles hounding us all the way.

One day before the cold weather set in and their knees got frost-bitten, the teenaged uncles decided to show the natives a thing or two by going to school in their kilts. What a pratfall. I knew what would happen and I was glad. At recess, little rowdies laughed and jeered, and what they really wanted to know was whether the uncles had anything on underneath. Inquisitive little boys boldly ran up and lifted their kilts. The uncles had a hard time keeping their skirts down, hopping this way and that in a variation on a sword dance. They didn't dare turn their backs. It was a terrible recess with cracked knuckles and banged heads and little children retreating in tears. The yelling and screaming stopped only when the principal appeared at the door, looking down his fat stomach on a suddenly peaceful scene. Knowing what would happen the minute he left, he sent the uncles home to get properly dressed.

I never got over the embarrassment of being related to those two. I avoided them at school by turning corners and turning my back. After the schoolyard melee, I never wanted to wear my kilt again. To be seen wearing the same skirt as my uncles was a crippling humiliation. When I stomped into school wrapped in that old horse blanket, I felt all the cruelties of being a fashion faux pas. I wanted to tear it to rags. I wanted to be sent home to get properly dressed. Luckily, one day as I crawled along the pipeline it caught on one of the clamps and ripped, and that was the end of my antique MacGregor accoutrement.

One balmy Indian summer Sunday, the teen-age uncles announced at the breakfast table that they would be attending church, which was so out of character as to be a shock. Naturally, this change for the better required a change of clothes. I used to wonder why there was such vanity and pageantry when the uncles paraded in their kilts. They were like ladies dressing for a ball. I found it a ridiculous pantomime: the frilly shirt; the pleated skirt; the leather trappings to buckle up; the diamond socks with garters and a dirk; the shoes with buckles; the waistcoat, jacket, tam, and scarf; and especially that ridiculous sporran dangling in front of the whole masquerade—a well-skirted uncle. After much primping, they marched down the stairs smelling of Florida Water, their hair slicked down with brilliantine to a glossy roué-shine. Grandmother attentively brushed off their jackets and gave her final approval, "Aye, they're a bonny pair."

They strutted like peacocks in all their plumage, ready to show off their immigrant status. Off they went to great fanfare, since church-going in our house was a new and noteworthy event. Mother encouraged them, "Don't forget to say your prayers," while Uncle Peter called out in his witty way, "Keep your skirts down and your socks up." All good advice because earlier, Daniel, Jim and Douglas had shinnied up the maple trees and were roosting on the branches with their sling shots. I had been warned not to say a thing if Mother called for them. They were tired of how the uncles were treating us on the way to school, so they schemed and plotted like the cattle thieves of old for an opportunity to strike. They were fast developing the survival tactics of their ancestors. As soon as the uncles walked into the maple grove, the boys fired a deadly barrage. The uncles didn't know what hit them as they howled in pain, holding their necks and dancing jigs as they reached for their legs. They twirled about in their skirts, and, I might add, nothing is more fashionable for a Scotsman than the twirling of his kilt. The house emptied as everyone ran out to see what the commotion was all about. The uncles were in no mood to turn the other cheek, yelling at the boys that when they caught them, their lives wouldn't be worth two cents, they would be killing them stone dead. The boys laughed from high up in the branches and launched the odd volley to spur the uncles along. Grandmother was in great shape, demanding, "You come right down you wee blackguards and believe you me I'll thrash you myself." Mother reminded the uncles that they were only getting a taste of their own medicine. Off they went in foul moods, rubbing their necks and knees, dropping hints over their shoulders of imminent war, their bright red MacGregor tartans swishing back and forth like the tails of dangerous animals.

They returned in a better frame of mind, but Grandmother went into convulsions over her tea when they said they had gone to the Baptist church. This was one way for a Catholic to get to Hell. Indian Hill was the only place to find Him. "What would your poor, dear father say, God rest his soul." Of course he'd do another turn in his grave; he did a lot of that. Grandmother sputtered in horror when the uncles argued that the Baptist church was closer. In her stubborn Irish fury, she excoriated the Baptist church, even though most of Bear River was Baptist, the schoolyard was full of Baptists, the Kniffens and all her friends along the Chute Road were Baptists. She was bedevilled by Baptists, and we, the only Catholic family in the village, non-practicing at that, had nothing to offer but invective. It was the perfect microcosm of the bigger definition of religion. After Grandmother had finished casting stones, I wondered if there really was something wrong with Baptists. Of course, the uncle's motive was transparent. It was not religion they yearned for, but the beautiful Marian McLeod, daughter of Reverend McLeod, whom they fawned over at recess and talked about constantly. It was an arrogance that they openly showed their feelings when it was expected that Marian would marry a Toronto businessman on graduation. Nothing fazed those two.

The Baptist church just might have done the uncles some good, but Grandmother denied them their chance at redemption. The teenaged uncles were done for. Grandmother assured them they would never get to heaven. I knew it. The uncles didn't care about getting into heaven, but they did want out of Bear River, so when Grandmother hinted that Bear River just might be in their immediate future, they found their fear of God and pestered her, "You're not going to leave us, are you Ma? Please don't leave us here."

As Indian summer faded into All Saints Day, we wondered why Grandmother was taking so long to leave. In bed at night, Daniel and I speculated about every sign and portent, and we fell asleep sustained by that dreamy eventuality. Finally at the dinner table one evening, Grandmother announced that she would be leaving for Montreal with the aunts, but Uncle Jim and Uncle Alec would be staying to finish the school year. Mother then added, "Your father is coming home next week." A great cheer went up as we let loose with joy unconfined. Grandmother might have preferred a more subdued reaction, but we simply couldn't wait to wave goodbye. The only sour note was that we would be saddled with the teenaged uncles. They slumped in their chairs, devastated and near tears, whimpering, "We want to go with you, Ma."

Shortly, Grandfather and Uncle John's pictures were removed from the parlor wall and carefully packed in the wicker hamper. For some reason, Great-Grandmother McCullough's picture remained to lurk behind our parlor door. Uncle Peter took the trunks and wicker hamper to the train station.

Dad mailed tickets for the train to Digby, the Princess Helene across the Bay, and the overnight train from St. John to Montreal, where they would step into their home on Oldfield Avenue, which Dad had rented and furnished. He had kept his promise to Grandfather, but if Grandmother was grateful, she held her tongue, and her tongue was as mute as her pen for years.

It was a brisk November day with the trees stripped bare when Grandmother finally took her leave. Clutching her handbag, she grimly stepped into the taxi and stonily waited for an end to the sentimentality. The boys had raked a huge pile of leaves and were enthusiastically rolling around in them. They jumped on the swing, arcing higher and higher, putting on an athletic show in relieved excitement. They kept saying goodbye, trying to extract one from Grandmother until she got sick and tired of Daniel's repetitious "Goodbye Grandmother, Goodbye Grandmother, aren't you going to say goodbye to me?" She snapped, "That's enough out of you, you've said your goodbye!" The teenaged uncles hovered, hoping for a change of heart, wailing, "Ma, I want to come too. I don't want to stay here. I hate this place." She had said her piece to them earlier, so she ignored them too. They were being dropped off the family tree for the nonce. Uncle Douglas and the aunts showed genuine fondness and gratitude as they hugged Mother and said goodbye. They bundled into the taxi, the door slammed shut, and off they drove through the maple grove. No bagpipes, no waves, no tears, we just stared. When the taxi crested McCormick's hill, we gave a cheer and did a ring-around-the-rosie at the pile of leaves, singing, "She's gone! She's gone!" until the surly teenaged uncles pushed us down and we scattered.

As I look back, I realize that the placid flow of my early life left few traces, like the satisfied awakening from a refreshing sleep that holds no memory. It is the exclamation marks that cause the mind to stop and register, and the summer of Grandmother was full of them; exclamation marks that couldn't possibly qualify as nice commas notching off the humdrum. Every day was like the click, click, click of a cog in my mind. Memory was honed that summer. I can still hear the rattle of cutlery on plates as hands flew up in the air; a teaspoon agitating a cup–the vote, the vote, the vote;

a chair scraping back and brass work ringing against the wall; eruptions and disruptions, misunderstandings and catastrophes. What a summer! Much evolved out of Grandmother's six-month visit. She was a highlight and had staying power.

But I mustn't be too harsh. It would be arbitrary of me to label Grandmother as an unfeeling rabble-rouser; unfair because my memories are childish, and I must bear in mind that she was the conscientious mother of ten children. She had cared for them, and every one of them deferred with consideration and affection, as strange as it seemed to me. It must have been a difficult decision to leave her beloved Scotland with her whole family and cross an ocean to a strange country. She gave up her home, church, friends, and for what? It was made immediately clear. She would have a room in an old house with a few treasured belongings in a wicker hamper. No wonder she pitched Rachmaninoff out the window. Grandmother was so meticulous and exacting with her delicate sensibilities that she never could have adjusted to farm life: all those dirty chickens, dirty pigs, dirty cows, and we children weren't all that clean either. She couldn't stand messy little faces spread with jam or molasses or whatever else was on our bread. When Mother came in from the gardens, her hands and hoover brown with soil, Grandmother would lament, "I can't see you leading this kind of life, Polly." Above all, Grandmother desperately grieved for Grandfather, as she did every day for the rest of her life, succeeding him by 54 years. Never once did she mention his name without saying 'May he rest in peace' or 'God rest his soul'. Nothing and no one could ever replace him, not her children and certainly not their children. His sad-eyed roto faced her always and she breathed life into that image. She adored him and there was little love left over for anyone else. I suppose her children understood because they adored him too.

I actually heard Grandmother laugh once when the joke was on her. Mother was telling about a time back home when Grandmother got caught up in her orating, standing with her back to the open kitchen door, holding a bowl of soup and waving a wooden spoon. She lost her balance and tipped out the door and into the back yard, landing with soup all over her and both feet up in the air. When Mother saw Grandmother's feet in the air and the spoon still pointing, she couldn't stop laughing.

Even when she helped her inside and cleaned the soup off her clothes, Mother was still hysterical with laughter, so Grandmother hauled off and slapped her face. When her sisters saw Mother laughing harder than ever, they laughed too, and then Grandmother joined in. They laughed again as I listened, but Grandmother insisted, "It wasn't funny!"

Grandmother in Montreal

I can't say that life improved all that much with our reduced contingent of kinfolk. The depression that Grandmother created was still with us; she had left it behind. As soon as Uncle Douglas was out the door, Uncle Peter and the teenagers resumed their battle royale. With all hope gone, the teenagers came to the breakfast table in a Black Irish mood, surlier than ever: "you can't tell me what to do," "over my dead body," "not on your life." The picture changed when Dad returned from Montreal and sat in on a loud breakfast. Uncle Jim was sounding off to Uncle Peter, so Dad told him to get his school bag and get out. When Dad looked at Alec, he included him too. Alec said, "I didn't say a word," and they both protested that they hadn't finished breakfast. Dad assured them they were going to starve for a change, just get off to school, and by the way, forget about lunch. The natural thing happened; they took our lunches in exchange for the same old death threats.

When Dad returned, there were a number of chores that Uncle Peter had left untended, the most unpleasant ones being the levelling of the manure pile, the cleaning of the outhouse, and the spreading of the whole horrid mess over the gardens for fertilizer. The teenaged uncles had bitterly complained about their chores, but they soon realized how antiseptic chopping wood could be. They paled in disbelief as Dad led them off to the barn. From the kitchen window, I could see them wielding their pitch forks and filling the wagon, trudging over to the chicken house, to the outhouse, and then to the gardens. The stench was atrocious. Afterwards, they rinsed their rubber boots at the back door, threw their clothes in the wash pile, and came in to clean their formerly lily-white hands at the kitchen pump. Uncle Jim snarled under his breath, "I'm not about to forget this." Dad was at the stove attending to his favourite hobby, and I was on the couch with the baby when Uncle Jim hissed to Alec, "This whole place is a crock of manure." I couldn't believe it, our happy home a crock of manure. The remark fell upon Dad's ears, who casually walked over and laid his heavy hand on Jim's shoulder, buckling him to the floor. Dad said quietly, in his lazy, southern manner, "As yew were saying, son?" Uncle Jim replied post haste, "Nothing! Nothing!" Dad walked back to the stove, absolutely dangerously calm. With one powerful grasp of the shoulder, Dad established his authority. They never tested it again.

The uncles then began a healthy correspondence with Grandmother, sending regular reports to the enemy camp and receiving instructions that they furtively burned in the kitchen stove. Grandmother wrote to Mother that farm chores were too difficult for the latent spies. The poor things hardly had the stamina to face tomorrow and the long trudge to the halls of learning. She said Dad could do his own dirty work if he would only get out of the hospital long enough. Grandmother never believed in Dad's war wounds since he was alive and her son was dead. Mother was visibly hurt by that letter as she read it to Dad. She urged him to send those two to Montreal, but for some reason, Dad stalled. Since Grandmother wouldn't have them, they got it in their heads that they would return to Scotland. Every time they were asked to chop a piece of wood or feed the chickens, they threatened to leave. Mother and Dad wished they would and said so. The price of a ticket was the problem, but Dad said he could get them work as stevedores on a cattle boat. At the dinner table, he would observe their black eyebrows lowered in a straight line and drawl, "Mah boys, ah really want yew to be happy. If yew like, tomorra ah'll take yew to Halifax harbour and put yew on a boat for home. It'll be rough on the North Atlantic this time of the year, but ah know yew'll be happy." Dad spelled it out for them as he reminisced about his Atlantic crossings: blinding snowstorms with 100 foot waves crashing over the deck, men washed overboard, battleships tossed about like toys for days on end while the men inside reeled, barely knowing up from down. Dad laughed to himself at the recollection. The teenagers sat silent; they only had to look out at the snow piling up to the windows. Canadian winters came as a shock to their systems, because in Helensburgh, snow only lasted long enough for a day of fun. On the Chute Road, we plowed ahead through blizzards, leaving the uncles behind as they struggled through snowdrifts. After school, they sat shivering at the dinner table, still in the process of thawing out, barely able to lift their forks. Uncle Peter would warn them about hungry timber wolves as they ran out the door to the outhouse. You battled through wind and snow just to get there and risked being blown past the river road and up to the chicken house, missing your objective. Once inside, you sat shivering in frigid isolation, your breath billowing in the dark, the stack of ice-cold newsprint there to remind you that life is often one misery after another.

Uncle Jim and Alec then decided that by some miracle they would be transported to Montreal for Christmas. Surely their own mother would want to see them at the table for Christmas dinner. Believing it would happen, my brothers and I were happy and said, "Good, I'm glad," and anything else that tumbled into our minds. We informed Mother who said, "Oh, is that so?" indicating it was highly unlikely. Dad's only reaction was to send them out to saw logs, chop wood or split kindling. Finally they asked outright, and Dad said certainly, if Grandmother would provide the tickets. A flurry of correspondence ensued, and they excitedly opened letters only to learn that Grandmother was in no mood for seasonal sentimentality. Their Christmas would be quiet, but white.

Seething under winter conditions and somewhat displaced by their own mother, our resident orphans retreated into a dark, moody choler, an inveterate MacGregor trait. At the dinner table, their demeanour became stylized: black, lowered eyebrows, burning eyes, speech that hissed from the side of their mouths. They were miserable, they pouted, they protested their bitter lot, their bread was always falling buttered side down. Dad only had to calmly say, as he did many times; "Son, if yew like, yew can pack your bags and ah'll take yew down to Halifax harbour tomorrow morning." We wished it would happen. They faithfully sent dispatches to Montreal, and judging by the look on Mother's face when she read a letter from Grandmother, Maple Grove farm was a penal colony. Mother would suck in her breath and read passages out to Dad. The wretches were deep into espionage. On our walks to school, the surly teenagers would push us into snow banks, rub our faces in the snow, and pitch snowballs as we outran them. When Dad drove us in, he would tell them they had to walk, reminding them that the exercise would be good for their brains, and who knows, "Yew might become geniuses." They would leave early and we would trot past them. I was glad. Anything that made the uncles miserable made me happy.

So with winter swirling all around, our household seethed like a hot spring, and the bubbling MacGregor-Marvin feud gathered steam, far from over.

The teenaged uncles caused a lot of trouble during their overly-long stay, but one skirmish was all my fault, I won't deny it, and the commotion I caused still stings.

With the farm ready for winter, Dad was off once again to Montreal, and since Christmas was mere weeks away, he pocketed numerous lists and told the younger, more gullible members of the family that yes, he would be speaking to Santa Claus himself. Excitement spurted from all directions, but the event of the season was Uncle Peter's decision to give Verna an engagement ring for Christmas. The choosing of the ring was a family involvement, and everyone pored over the Birk's and Mappin & Webb catalogues, turning pages and offering suggestions. Those luxury catalogues heightened my attitude on local love, and I was carried away with the idea of the happy surprise awaiting Verna on Christmas morning. Uncle Peter decided on a white gold filigreed mount with a single diamond, paired with a matching brooch. We were overly excited and re-examined the ring in the Birk's catalogue. I could hardly wait to see it on Verna's finger. When the package arrived, everyone crowded around Uncle Peter as if it were one of our own presents. The ring was utterly precious: a flashing diamond set in sparkling white gold, posed in the box on deep blue velvet. I bubbled with the excitement, and it was one of the few things that made me happy about Uncle Peter. Shortly after the ring arrived, my teacher, Lexie Hatfield, a friend of Verna's, asked me how the lovebirds were doing. So what did I do? I told her all about the ring. My information passed through the grapevine to Verna, and that Saturday night when Uncle Peter met her at Aunt Loo Robinson's for the ritual meal of baked beans and Boston brown bread, he got the surprise he least expected. On Sunday morning, the sky fell on my head. Uncle Peter exploded. He ranted and raved, and then Verna pointed her finger and sternly reprimanded me. I was a case for the justice department, and like a criminal with no recourse, I was ready for the guillotine. I was too shocked to even cry, and when they had finished, it was no comfort when Mother cautioned me about giving information to inquisitive grown-ups, who were twice as bad as little children, not only for asking, but for tattling. That was the first time I remember committing a grievous error, but I learned a valuable lesson about betraying trusts, good for a lifetime.

From that day on, every time Uncle Peter saw me he'd say, "Och now, here's the wee blatherskite!" I didn't understand the word, but I knew full well its meaning. The teenaged uncles picked up the word and took it to school. Mother asked Uncle Peter to stop, but it was no use. Finally, she angrily reminded him that Lexie Hatfield should have known better, and that he and Verna should know better than to bear a grudge against a child. She never wanted to hear me called a blatherskite again. So Uncle Peter and Verna became very, very frosty and ignored me entirely. The humiliation was withering and I cringed in their presence.

The business of tittle-tattle progressed, and more people heard all about my unsavoury character. I would be scorned till the day I died. I felt guilty when I saw Loo and Fowler Robinson on the way to school. I felt guilty when I stepped into Lexie Hatfield's class. I felt guilty when I saw Verna's sister, Elsie Henshaw. And I came close to murder when I looked across the classroom at that insufferable little smirk, Lawrence Henshaw. No doubt he had broadcast the details to the class and probably delivered the cautionary tale to his Boy Scout troop. Merton Yorke would blab mercilessly, so my name would be raked over the coals at the smithy and tossed down the hill to the Trading Company, where the men likely had a pickle barrel waiting for me. Roland Barrass would tell his father, who would sermonize on godless gossip-mongers, and the faithful would nod their heads knowingly, no names necessary. Best of all, Elsie Henshaw was good friends with Miss Liske, so really, the whole village was covered, likely out to the lumber camps. I expected the Women's Institute to be coming for me with a warrant. Even within the family, baby voices reiterated, 'you almost killed my kitten, you almost burned the house down, you ruined Verna's Christmas.' I didn't plan anything; things happened because of others, and because of others I decided I would have nothing more to do with them. I would tell my multiplying siblings to go away and leave me alone. Perhaps that guilt made me a confirmed loner so young, except for my confidences with Daniel. Because of being hit over the head with a crowbar and the fear that I was mentally retarded, I was encouraged to talk, but the fallout from the ring debacle made me feel that there was no need to open my mouth unnecessarily again. I would hold secrets like a sphinx and leave the talking to those who liked it.

Uncle Peter and Verna never forgot my childish error, nor did they ever forgive me. I had tarnished the glow of their love, intruding myself like a bad omen at the most sensitive time of their lives. The sparkling diamond on Verna's third finger, left hand, and the brooch over her heart were lifelong reminders. I was never comfortable in her presence again. Whenever my eye faltered on Verna's finger, she would twiddle her ring, and when I looked up, she would be watching to see me blush with guilt. I hated that twiddling finger. When Verna came for Sunday dinner and deliberately wiggled her ring, Mother pointedly sent me out of her presence. Verna had become a MacGregor.

When Dad returned for Christmas that year, Daniel spotted him coming down the hay field, his arms filled with Christmas packages. We lay in wait and mobbed him as he stepped in the front door. The train had let him off at the bridge and he was tired from the long walk, his brown wool suit nicked at the knee from barbed wire. The boxes promptly vanished, but the boys solved the mystery and came to bed with lumps in their cheeks. When the theft was discovered, Uncle Peter threatened to write a letter to Santa Claus. Then he took another stab at me by saying he knew someone whom Santa Claus wouldn't be bringing anything to. Around the table it was who, who? Well, Santa Claus knew. This brought a hoot from Daniel, "We know who Santa Claus is. It's you!" This prompted an outburst of tears from the younger ones. Uncle Peter never gave us anything, not even a lollipop from the village, so they knew what to expect. Mother settled the issue by truthfully saying that Uncle Peter lied, pay no attention. Our resident Santa Claus was a liar.

With Dad home, the house returned to normal. The MacGregors subsided into corners, and the euphoria of an approaching Christmas gave life that seasonal sparkle. Though many Christmases are lumped together in the usual exhaustive excitement of feasts with turkeys, trifles, cookies and candies until distended stomachs put half the little Marvins out of commission for days, that particular Christmas was clearly identified by Georgina Hill's shimmering, silken tie.

Every winter, Mother knitted me a red wool dress, and that year she did a beautiful job, giving it a full, flared skirt and caped collar. On a morning when I appeared at my yuletide best, Lexie Hatfield stopped me on my way to class and looked me up and down. Then and there she said she had to have me for the Christmas play and that was the dress I must wear. As easy as that, the part was mine. I was to be the ingénue thespian of the Grade 12 play. Immediately, my friendship with Alice Copeland suffered a fracture when she said, "I'm smarter than you. I should have gotten the part." She cold-shouldered me for days and I was hurt. On hearing the news, Mother and Dad were thrilled, even amazed, and they promoted it as the event of my life, which I suppose it was, other than being hit in the head with a crowbar. What I liked best was that I would be Marian McLeod's little sister—Marian, the most beautiful girl in school with her lovely, wavy red hair. The glow of her beauty would reflect on to me. I was convinced I would be the theatre's darling, awash in the footlights as I bowed to waves of applause. Surely, I would be ready for Chautauqua, perhaps even rivalling Mr. Goldsmith, the one-armed pianist. What a wild dream. My first order of business was to browse my scrapbooks and decide which of my beautiful actresses I would be. I'm not sure why, but I finally settled on Bebe Daniels. Next, I had to learn my one line, which I practiced in front of the mirror and repeated for days over my porridge. On the big day, the younger grades would have their party in the afternoon, but I, a star, would shine at night. After school, Mother put me to bed, later waking me up to be primped for the floorboards of Oakdene. She handed me a brand new pair of red stockings from the Trading Company, and then as a treat, she let me open one of my Christmas presents. Aunt Cathy had sent me a pair of crisp, white linen bloomers, elegantly edged with two inches of lace. They fit perfectly. No other girl in school had real lace on her bloomers, I was sure of it. After I put on my red dress, Dad brushed my hair and gift-wrapped me with a red velvet bow on top. With a twirl for approval, I was all set for my debut as a seasonal accessory.

That evening was also special because it was the first time I went into the village at night. I sat on the front seat of the sleigh under the buffalo rug between Mother and Dad, the preferred spot. Daniel wedged into the back seat between the teenaged uncles. It had snowed all day so the landscape was blanketed white and bright. I remember looking up to the sweep of black sky and the brilliance of the stars: Orion the Hunter, his sword held high; faithful Sirius, the dog-star, poised on the alert.

The runners of the sleigh squeaked through the fresh snow as Harry pulled us along, jangling a tune on a new set of Swiss bells, his Christmas present. There were high spirits all around: Dad chatted with Harry, Mother and Daniel pointed out their favourite stars, the teenaged uncles wondered who had picked their names for presents, and I rehearsed my one line. As we slid down Oakdene Hill, Dad pulled hard on the reins and stopped in front of the school, where all the sleighs were manoeuvring for the drop-off. Dad took Harry down to the stalls across from the Trading Company, while we made our way upstairs with the throng. Oakdene hall glowed with the golden hue of the season as parents mingled in clumps and students circled the tree, looking at presents to see who had drawn their name. Every year, the high-school boys would go up Tupper brook and chop down the tallest tree they could find, whooping in triumph as they carried it down Oakdene Hill like natives returning from the hunt. We would spend days decorating the tree with cranberry strings and crepe paper cut-outs. Branches, boughs and wreaths would be artfully arranged around doors and windows, adding to the forested feel and giving the room a woodsy aroma. As a final touch, the teachers would hang all the presents on the tree, so that when the students arrived, they could finally discover who had drawn their name. The tree stood floor-to-ceiling, filled with a dazzling array of presents and bearing oranges wrapped with candy in tissue paper. Nearby, the stage presented a wintery scene, minus the bitter cold. The evening began with patriotic formalities, a nod to heaven, and a wink to Santa. Then after sketches and songs by the other grades, the stage was set for the main event. The play's the thing to touch the conscience of Christmas. The scene was a living room, and Lawrence Henshaw and I were the two household children—Lawrence Henshaw, my nemesis. We were seated on a sofa with our props: a book and crackers, and while we waited for our cues, we sat with our heads together reading the book and eating the crackers. My joy of literature was so intense that I became engrossed in the story I was supposed to be reading and the crackers I was supposed to be eating, while ignoring the play I was supposed to be following. My cue only registered when Lawrence reached behind me, pinched my bottom and hissed, "Stupid." Marian casually repeated my cue and ad-libbed to the Christmas tree while I grabbed my book and dashed up to deliver my deathless line.

What I didn't know was that when I closed the book and brought it up to my chest, I had gathered up the front of my skirt. I walked up and bubbled to Marian about something I overheard, something wonderful about Christmas, so the whole village got to see the tittle-tattle of the month in action, and as an added bonus, they got the benefit of my new lace-trimmed bloomers. Marian calmly took the book to flip through the pages, and my dress dropped, restoring my dignity. Somehow, when she handed the book back to me, I knew my error. I returned to my seat amid controlled laughter. I was a hit. As I sat down, Lawrence hissed again, "Stupid." He strode up to say his line louder and clearer than I did—a true thespian. His mother sat in the audience along with Ruth Henshaw, Aunt Loo and Fowler Robinson, Verna and Uncle Peter; the whole gang of looming in-laws who knew of my noxious character. Everyone saw my latest faux-pas, but for some reason, I didn't care. I went back to reading my book to the exclusion of Lawrence Henshaw. There would be no need to ever talk to him again.

Lawrence Henshaw

Alice heard about the play and was curious about my bloomers, but our friendship never recovered after that. I couldn't ignore what she had said so clearly. I don't think I had a best friend after that. My best friends became my scrapbooks—mute soul mates, repositories of dreams with no harsh words, just like my dolls. And memory, where has it gone?

It's as if that line of prop dialogue, repeated so often and so perfectly, has been pinched right out of my mind. It's still there, elusive but not gone, adhering like an embarrassment. Never again did I aspire to acting or high drama. That phase of my life was over. Later, Uncle Peter and Verna dredged up the spectacle, but my lack of interest seemed to close the subject.

The long evening of entertainment ended with great excitement when Santa arrived amid sleigh bells and ho-ho-ho's as he handed out all the presents on the tree. That was the year Dad made a piece of brass work for every teacher in the school. It was a lovely gesture and he received a lot of attention because of it. For me, twice in one day I had an orange and candies wrapped in red tissue paper and tied with a ribbon. When it was time to go, Dad pulled Harry up to the entrance, and I climbed into the sleigh utterly exhausted. I was curious about my performance and asked Mother if she thought anyone noticed? Daniel guffawed, but Dad said I delivered my line perfectly, which was good enough for me. I crawled under the buffalo rug and sniffed my orange. We were all pleased with our gifts except for Uncle Jim. Georgina Hill had drawn his name and given him a beautiful tie of pale sunset colours: pale pink, pale blue and pale mauve flecked with gold thread, colours I had seen hanging over the limpid Bay on waning summer evenings. To Uncle Jim it was no tartan, and when he opened the box he hissed under his breath, "N-gger colours." As we started for home, Uncle Jim was still in a funk and exclaimed loudly, "I'll never wear that N-gger tie." Immediately, Dad stopped the sleigh, turned to Uncle Jim and said, "Son, Ah nevah want to hear yew talk like that again." Mother was livid and warned Jim that if he ever dared opened his mouth to hurt Georgina, she would see to it that he apologized and a whole lot more. The term was common back then, though Dad never used it; he would say Nigra. Even we used it when we chose sides for games in the school yard, singing, "eeney, meeney minie moe, catch a N-gger by the toe." But the way Uncle Jim used it was ignorant and vicious. The Hills were the only Negro family in the village, Loyalist settlers from all the way back. The Hill name was in the Book of Negroes, so they had fought in the Revolutionary War and won land, land paid for with blood. They helped build the country, and here was Uncle Jim, just off the boat with nothing to offer but his arrogance.

Georgina's father, Ben Hill, had a smithy behind the Trading Company where Dad often took Harry to be shod. Once, while I waited in the buggy, Georgina sat studying by the kitchen window, so we waved and smiled, though we had not yet spoken. The Hills were a family of 13, and I knew they were poor by the size and condition of their grey house, connected to the smithy and sitting on the banks of the brook that fed into the river.

In the sleigh, Mother reminded Uncle Jim that it was an added expense to buy that tie and Georgina had chosen it very carefully. Dad slapped the reins and the sleigh pitched forward. I can still conjure up the blackness of the sky, the stars so clear, the cold frost, the warmth of the buffalo rug up to my nose, wedged so comfortably between Mother and Dad. Everyone along the Chute Road had turned out their lamps and gone to bed, leaving a crisp, black and white stillness. The sleigh hissed through the snow as Harry rhythmically clomped and snorted, his Swiss bells ringing like Christmas as we flew along the road. I was terribly tired and yawned as the stars fell down, down, and I closed my eyes until Dad carried me into the house.

The next morning Dad was busy at the stove wielding his spatula and flipping buckwheat pancakes. Whenever Dad was home in the winter, Mother rested in bed while he made breakfast, and he always made something delicious, never porridge or cream of wheat. The custom with pancakes was that whoever ate the most won money, and this time it was 25 cents, a magnificent sum. While Dad cooked, I ran back and forth serving the struggling combatants. Daniel and Jim were sure they could win but collapsed in lumpy heaps, leaving Uncle Alec and Uncle Jim to soldier on. They were all discussing the Christmas party, and at one point Uncle Jim got up from the table to go to his room. He came into the kitchen, surly as usual, and pitched Georgina Hill's tie into the wood box by the stove, snarling "This is only fit to burn. I'm not wearing N-gger colors." I didn't know what I would do with a tie, but I immediately grabbed it and asked Dad if I could keep it. Dad ignored me and just stared at Uncle Jim, hands on his hips with that calculating look on his face. He was holding the spatula, and for a moment I thought he was going to use it on Jim. Instead, he handed it to me, grabbed Uncle Jim by the scruff of his neck and guided him across the kitchen, Jim's feet barely touching the floor.

Dad roughly shoved him into the pantry and stepped inside, closing the door behind them with a bang. There were whacks and thuds and yowls of "No, no, I never," while Dad spoke in controlled hisses. The boys rushed in to listen at the door, giggling in high glee and scattering when the door opened. Uncle Jim emerged looking dishevelled and turned to go upstairs, but Dad ordered him back to the table to finish his breakfast. Getting beat up must have been good for his appetite, because he wolfed down his pancakes in a fury, saying he needed the 25 cents to get out of Bear River. Uncle Jim won the contest, and Dad paid him, telling him he was glad the money was going to a good cause.

When I took Mother's café au lait in to her, she asked what on earth all the fuss was about. I told her that Dad had beaten up Uncle Jim, and she said, "Oh good," and went back to her reading. In the kitchen, I was admiring the tie with its diagonal wide stripes of wonderful colours and asked again, "Isn't it beautiful Dad, can I have it?" Dad said, "No, Sweetlady, ah think ah'll take it." He picked it up and put it on. When Mother rustled into the kitchen for another café au lait, Dad turned to her and she smiled, "Mr. Marvin! My, you look handsome in that tie. What lovely colors. I hope you'll wear it often." And he did, every day for Uncle Jim to grind his teeth. Dad always slicked up for the day, even when gardening, so it wasn't out of character to wear Georgina's tie on the farm.

That spring, when the warm weather came with the birds and the daffodils, Dad sometimes walked in to the village for the mail and would wait outside the school to walk us home. One day as we stood by the front steps of Oakdene waiting for the full complement of Marvins, Georgina Hill stepped out the door. I remember that moment so well. Dad had his walking cane in one hand and slipped his other hand up to his tie, then lifted his hat to Georgina. She smiled broadly, gave a slight curtsy and skipped off. I was so proud of my father and I loved him for wearing that beautiful tie. It hung by his bureau with all the others, accenting their provincial dullness. And then when it wasn't worn anymore, it hung on Mother's bureau for a long, long time. I like to think that Georgina's tie never wore out and was never thrown out, but wafted off brand-new in all its dazzling colours to some kind of memory heaven filled with Dad's gentle southern charm.

I CAN'T REMEMBER ANY OTHER details of that particular Christmas other than my acting debut, Georgina's tie, and Dad beating up a quasi-child. Dad went back to St. Anne's and we went back to school, suffering the wrath of the teenaged uncles along the way, rushing home to Mother and the warm kitchen, aching and complaining like bitter old men until we thawed out behind the stove. After the chores were done, the pigs fed and the cows milked, a stillness settled in on winter evenings that emphasized the loneliness of the farm, never noticed when Dad was home. We would read in the parlor while Mother filled out order forms at the dining room table and Uncle Peter burrowed into his cowboy stories at the Franklin fireplace. When he tired of Zane Grey and the old west, the only thing left to do was blast the house alive with the bagpipes and make the baby cry. The plaintiff wail pulsated through the walls while the uncles hicced and hooted and flailed about like maniacs. Then they would take out their chanters and sing about what was really on their minds, that noble cultural artefact: war, war, war. When the bagpipes gave their last gasp, it was back to Zane Grey in front of the fireplace, while Mother repaired the damage with Thornton Burgess bedtime stories.

One severe winter night when Dad was away, Mother said that since it was so cold, Daniel and I could sleep with her, a treat we always enjoyed. We loved the coziness of lying in the dark and talking to Mother about all kinds of things, much like we did at our nightly forum. With all the cares of the day put aside, Mother would relax and chat with us in a way she never could during the day. It seems that in those young years, we did most of our learning just before falling asleep.

We didn't have bed-warmers, so on the coldest nights, Mother always warmed the flannel sheets in front of the fire. After she warmed the bottom sheet, we would quickly jump on it to preserve the heat while she warmed the top sheet. That night as I lay watching Mother hold the top sheet up to the fire, I thought it odd how the flames reflected on the ceiling in such a strange way, hovering almost ghost-like. Daniel had to investigate, but as he got up, he looked out the window and gave a cry of alarm. We rushed to the window to see Mr. Bishop's cottage blazing away like a torch on its high perch. We stared in silence as the flames fanned and spiked wildly, silhouetting the trees and casting the sky with a broad orange glow. The scene played out in complete silence. Within minutes, the flames died down, and then nothing, no glowing embers, not even a wisp of smoke, just the darkness of the forest, which didn't seem to register the change. We had heard of barns and silos mysteriously burning in the night, but this happened so quickly and so quietly that we could hardly be sure we even saw it. We crawled into bed, but Daniel's emotions accelerated under stress, and he was in no condition for sleep. He wanted to know how the unoccupied cottage could burn, and on such a cold night. Mother's explanation that perhaps a mouse chewed some matches seemed unlikely. It was frightening to think that a building could burn so quickly. How would people ever escape in time? And there had been fires all around us: the flat rock at the top of the hay field was once a front step; the cellar indentation of Uncle Peter's house indicated a similar fate. As usual, Daniel's imagination carried over to the supernatural. Had people died in those fires? Would Uncle Peter's house be haunted like ours? Where would Aunt Charlotte go if our house burned? And what about all those silo and barn fires? What happened to the animals? What if Harry, his beloved alter ego, got trapped? Daniel would save him. Mother always agreed, "Well, of course you would, Harry's part of the family." She patiently answered one question after another as Daniel's mind was possessed to wonder about fire in all its forms. As I lay there listening, watching the shadows from the fireplace dance on the ceiling, I thought about the tiny, dollhouse cottage. We had always been so excited when Mrs. McCormick went up to prepare it for Mr. Bishop. It was as if he was bringing summer with him. I pictured the flames shrivelling those frilly lace curtains and creeping among the orange crates, lighting the dark interior brighter than it had ever been before. And I could never forget that strange spectral glow hovering on our ceiling, as if the ghosts in the cottage had fled to our house.

After the long winter months of being cooped up inside, cool mornings turned into afternoons of fresh blue skies, announcing that something wonderful was about to happen. At school, I'd sit at my desk looking out the window at icicles dripping in the sun, and I'd feel that urge to escape, that there was somewhere I had to be. On our way home, we would check the progress of buds on our favourite trees, or gather around crocuses bravely pushing up through the snow. Along the Chute Road, brooklets bubbled up, running clear over their stony bed. Sometimes we would spot tiny fish darting about, amazed that they had survived the winter freeze. In the trees, familiar birds would announce their arrival, calling to us through the crisp air: swallows, jays, chickadees, nuthatches, and my favourite, the Ruby Kinglet, a tiny, elusive bird that issued a torrent of song. Douglas cautioned us to be very quiet to hear all three parts. At the Bridge Brook, we would hang over the edge looking for the return of our frogs. One day we came home and there was Dad, home for good, Mother said. We crowded around excitedly, not sure what it meant, just happy he was home and life could begin again.

Throughout the 1920s, for seven months of every year and despite continuous headaches, Dad hammered his brass, silver and copper artefacts in his workshop on bustling St. Catherine Street. Finally, the years of constant hammering took their toll and he closed his shop. Two large wooden crates were shipped home to rest in a corner of the apple packing house. One crate was opened but never emptied, topped with sheets of brass, silver and copper. As I pulled back the metal sheets, I could see strange hammers and other unusual tools. The tiny ball peens seemed too delicate for the common nail. The other crate held shears, lasts, files, rasps and other tools that were removed and piled in a jumble on the work bench. Tossed aside and sitting amid the dust was a stack of over-sized design books filled with drawings and cut-outs, never to be used again. As I looked at the clutter of tools and the carelessly placed crates, I couldn't possibly understand what the end of that period of Dad's life meant. When I asked if he would make any more brass work, his reply was succinct, "Nevah."

The partly-sheared sheets of brass, copper and silver would lose their lustre, now without a purpose. What might they have become? Hanging on the wall above were the cracked leather trappings for oxen and horse collars with the stuffing coming out, all finished and done with. Dust would gather on the table as it had for years, settling on the jumble of tools embellished by wood chips and sawdust. On top, spiders would artfully spin their gossamer, silken threads with a view of the flies buzzing at the many-paned window.

Years later in Montreal, I was browsing at The Handicraft Guild, next to the Mount Royal Hotel, and I asked the elderly clerk if she ever had any brass work since there wasn't any on display. She said no, so I mentioned that they had once sold my father's work. Surprisingly, the lady remembered Dad and his work, even after all those years, and moreover, she offered to sell anything I had to part with. I was happy she remembered Dad so well.

There is no doubt that Dad had an overly-generous nature, and there also is no doubt that this was a friction point with Mother, especially concerning his brass work. Mother would stare in shock when visitors casually asked for some item they couldn't afford, expecting to get it for free. With Dad they succeeded. I remember once when Dad stood talking with Jessie Harris at the Crossroads and offered him a cigarette from the case he had made of German silver. Jessie admired the craftsmanship, so slim it slipped unnoticed into Dad's vest pocket. He asked if Dad could make one for him, so Dad simply gave it to him despite protestations of payment.

When Dad closed his shop, several pieces of finished brass work returned with the crates of tools. Mother bristled because the Simons had ordered another piece without having paid for the previous ones, always the largest and most expensive. I would hear her telling Dad that they simply had to pay, and I suspect this was one reason why the friendship waned. Mother's reminders trailed Dad out the door as he and Daniel went off to deliver the brass. Dad returned without payment. Instead, the Simons had invited him to dinner. Mother flew into a minor rage, "After all these years!" How much brass had they ordered and how many times had they dined uninvited, never once returning the favour. And to think that they had hosted all those bridge nights for the rest of the village, but oh no, nothing for the Marvins. Daniel piped up that Amanda had met them at the door, ordered them to take off their shoes, and they had advanced no further than the hallway. Mother's deadly silence stilled the room. She recovered in an ominous whisper, "Indeed! So you had to take off your shoes!" Dad pleaded with her to accept the invitation, but she told him no, never. She would not be sitting in her socks surrounded by unpaid brass, "And that dinner had better not be considered payment, believe you me!" Instead, Dad took Daniel and me. I was thrilled at the prospect of my first formal dinner. As per any soirée, I scrubbed up, washed my one good dress and polished my one pair of shoes.

Entering the Simon's house with its electric chandeliers shining over glazed hardwood floors was like stepping into a dazzling ballroom. It was the most elegant house I had ever been in. We dutifully removed our shoes as Major Simon invited us in to the parlor, whereupon I promptly slipped and fell on those polished hardwood floors of my dreams. Dad picked me up and deposited me in a large, wing-backed chair, while he and Daniel sat on the sofa. Daniel sat open-mouthed, ready to gulp in all the adult conversation. I sank into my chair and got busy redecorating my dream house. The parlor was large, airy, and elegant with frosted French doors, a piano in the corner, French provincial chairs embroidered with petit-point scenes, slim tables hovering nearby, and a cozy window seat looking past the woods to the river. Here and there, Dad's brass work shone like gold: on the tables, on the piano, piled on the dining room sideboard. The dinner table was fussily set with silver and china on virginal white linen, and in the middle of it all stood Dad's candlesticks. The collection surprised me; they had the biggest and the best cigar boxes, trays, bowls, and jugs. I could see Mother's concern. For dinner, Amanda served everything I liked: a succulent roast pork with roast potatoes and corn, the Major's yellow tomatoes, which I decided were not as tasty as our full-blooded red ones, and his prize-winning English broad beans, buttered and cooked to perfection. They were so good that, in my enjoyment, I licked my fingers, prompting Dad to flick his napkin, nipping my wrist. I bent over my plate in shame. Then I sinned again by asking for a second helping of broad beans.

We were taught never to ask for things, but I couldn't help myself and earned a second silent rebuke. Still, nothing could dim the elegance of the evening. Amanda's house sparkled with a crisp, uncluttered cleanliness, just like my dreams; no kerosene lamps or linoleum squares, no wet clothes drying out over the stove. In my excitement, I tried to tell Mother all about it, but she wouldn't listen. As she bent over to kiss me good night, she said, "You just forget about English broad beans." Later, I heard her say to Dad, "I hope you enjoyed yourself Mr. Marvin, you paid for it." Mother was right. In the end when the friendship was over and the brass still unpaid for, Dad said forget it.

On summer evenings after all the children had been put to bed, I often had to stay up and watch the baby while Mother and Dad weeded the gardens. One evening while I was tending Donald, who was several months old, a car pulled in to the maple grove and out stepped John Jefferson's parents. John Jefferson was an insufferable little brat with a finely-tuned sense of supremacy. Colonel Jefferson introduced himself and shook my hand before going down to see Dad in the gardens. I invited Mrs. Jefferson to wait in the parlor, but she looked our house up and down and refused, so I went inside to get the tea started and left her standing by the back door with the mosquitoes. I knew our house suffered from creeping decrepitude, but Mrs. Jefferson wasn't exactly living in a modern miracle either. The old house on their farm was so dilapidated that they had set up in an unused museum–a building too old to be a museum. She was a tiny woman and very well dressed, certainly a contrast to Mother, who arrived in her dirty hoover and muddy shoes, excusing herself that she couldn't shake hands because hers were so dirty. Mother invited her in to the house, but again Mrs. Jefferson made her reasons obvious and refused. Mother came inside saying, "Is that so," an expression she used when she was shocked by the world and planning her next move. I mixed the scones and arranged the teacups while Mother prepared for battle by washing up at the kitchen sink and putting on a clean hoover. When the men walked in from the gardens, they found Mrs. Jefferson alone at the back door swatting mosquitoes, so Dad came into the kitchen puzzled. I explained that I invited Mrs. Jefferson in, but she preferred to wait outside. Dad then asked about tea, and Mother flared like an extinct volcano, "Indeed! I'll not be serving tea in this house tonight!" But she did and I helped. Mrs. Jefferson came in with her husband, and when they sat down, the Colonel announced that he had brought his wife down to see Dad's brass work. Mrs. Jefferson was very effusive, saying she had seen Dad's work in friends' homes and simply had to have a piece. She was ignoring Mother and using her wiles on Dad, who had the bad habit of picking up small pieces and handing them over to admirers for the asking. Mother had seen enough of that nonsense and often testily reminded him, "You may be working for nothing, but I'm not!" So Mother jumped in like a black widow spider and announced to Mrs. Jefferson at the outset, "All the brass work you see here is mine and it's not for sale." With that, I was sent off to bed. By this time, Daniel and I were sharing Grandmother's old room; he had a bed in one corner and I had a bed all to myself in the other corner. We could whisper across the room until we exhausted our little minds, and I could look out the window to my favourite place, Kniffen's Hollow, where the sun left the last of the day's warmth. I was fascinated by Mrs. Jefferson, and being a victim nine times over of what killed the cat, I snuck downstairs into the large bedroom, which was separated from the parlor by heavy drapes and held three double beds, two of them with two children apiece. I slipped into the last bed with Lorna and Joan, beside Dad's drafting board, and I listened like the spy that I was. Dad led everyone into the kitchen with its display of brass and copper pots, pans, kettles, bowls, jugs, and all our cups hanging on hooks under the shelf. The procession then led to the dining room with all the fruit bowls, cigar and cigarette boxes, cribbage boards, ash trays, card trays, a large, round tray that held the mail, and the Arabian copper jug with brass handle that Grandmother had thrown and dented. When everyone marched from the parlor into the bedroom, I covered my head and held by breath, listening in amazement as Mrs. Jefferson whispered excitedly to her husband that she must have Mother's candle sticks and picture frame, which incidentally held Mother's picture. She begged Dad, "But you can make more anytime," despite Dad's having made it clear that he was finished making brass work. Dad had given the candle sticks and picture frame to Mother for her birthday, the last brass he made for her. The candle sticks were lovely: fluted with a square, lead-filled base and bevelling around the edge, each with her initials. The square picture frame had rounded corners etched with little birds, which Dad said were bluebirds. Mrs. Jefferson refused to give up and only turned to Mother when Dad emphasized that the brass belonged to her. Mother said flatly that she could never give her husband's presents away. Back they went to the parlor, only to return to the drafting table, where Dad removed the plans of the house he was going to build for Mother. Col. Jefferson was also planning to build and asked for a closer look at the plans. As Dad walked out of the room, he noticed a third lump in the bed and sharply sent me upstairs.

After that, the drafting table remained empty for some time. I liked looking at the columned verandahs and the long glassed-in side porch where everything could be seen in comfort through all kinds of weather, the sort of thing Mother liked. Dad studiously pored over the plans until everything was perfect, everything but the location. I pleaded with him not to build it on the farm. He hadn't decided. Although I knew the answer, one day I asked Mother if Col. Jefferson had the plans for our house. Mother was sweeping the kitchen floor and stopped in her tracks. She was furious and could just kill Dad, because as often as Col. Jefferson was asked, he would not return the plans, not even when Dad went to Annapolis Royal to get them. Then he gave the improbable story that they had been stolen.

A sort of desperation set in after that, as if I would be stuck on the farm for the rest of my life. I used to dream of going across the Bay on the Packet or of sailing off to somewhere on the Princess Helene, we all did, but those house drawings were a solid structure rooted in the ground. We excitedly watched Dad draw Uncle Peter's house, and now it would be our turn. I felt my prayers had been answered on that creamy drafting paper. At a glance, our life became genteel. There were pathways and bushes and not a cow in sight. Dad wearily said he would draw a new house, but instead, he unrolled the plans for his water turbine and tacked them onto the drafting board. I saw our future evaporate with those house plans, and I assumed that things would always be the same. At nine, I was too young to know that things never stay the same. Although Mrs. Jefferson didn't get any brass work that evening, she did find a Marvin home that she liked. I suppose our dream house is standing somewhere in Annapolis Royal.

I SUSPECT THAT THE PLAN with the teenaged uncles had been to move them onto Uncle Peter's farm after his wedding and somehow, in some way, turn them into farmers. But Uncle Peter's wedding kept getting delayed, and besides, he saw what they were good for and wanted nothing to do with them. Neither did Grandmother. She was adamant; distance had improved them to the point that she liked them just where they were. Dad's only hope was that they would resign themselves to their fate in Bear River and perhaps learn a thing or two so he could pawn them off on Uncle Peter. But after a full year in the fields, their defects had solidified into character flaws, especially with Uncle Jim.

The next spring after the last patch of snow had melted into the dank earth, the gardens sat ready to be primed and planted. With Harry harnessed to the long heavy wagon, Dad and the three uncles tramped down the river road in their rubber boots, shovels on their shoulders, down to the beach to pile the wagon full of the rich effluvia from the village. My brothers grinned like gremlins from the empty, creaking wagon, eager for the opportunity to get filthy. One might say the very soul of Bear River was thrown upon our gardens. At the end of the day after having plowed and disced the gardens, the teen-aged uncles were old men. Spring had brought on premature old age. But just when the vernal season was urging all of nature, human and inhuman, to do things they had no control over, the very next day, a sunny Sunday, the two teenagers felt an overpowering urge to go to church. We all thought the previous two-and-a-half mile walk had exhausted their search for God because they hadn't mentioned church since, not until this particular Sunday when they swept out of their room in full regalia, kilts swishing behind them. Were they turning over a new leaf? No, it was the same old leaf. If they got down on their knees and prayed, they wouldn't have to get down on their knees in the gardens. But who in good conscience could keep them from honouring God. Mother said it might do them some good. Dad didn't think so. He was out of patience with that useless pair and said as much. But then, just as the last little hope was fluttering away, Uncle Jim, by some miracle of persuasion, got himself elected president of the new calf-raising club at school. Dad was stunned; we all were. Dad never failed to kindle an interest, so Uncle Jim got Buttercup to look after, Daisy's new calf. Daniel dearly wanted

Buttercup because he belonged to the Garden Club and needed the extra points. His bitterness was brief. Uncle Jim mistakenly thought that a pet calf was much like a pet dog, so he tied a rope around its neck and took it with him everywhere, despite its reluctance to leave its mother. Off Uncle Jim went to the beach for some peace and quiet, but Buttercup put on such a disturbing performance, without letup, that he was forced to bring her home. As they were walking back, poor little Buttercup, in her hunger and distraction, stepped on Uncle Jim's foot. He went berserk. Ignoring high office, he let his heritage surface and hobbled to the apple packing house for a sledge hammer, swearing to kill Buttercup, stone dead. The boys screamed, calling for Mother and Dad, hugging and protecting creamy, honey-coloured Buttercup with her melting eyes and spindly legs, bleating and starving and minutes away from a ritual Scottish slaughter. Dad was beyond disbelief and simply shook his head. Daniel got Buttercup after all.

The calf-raising club needn't have feared their President's unorthodox methods, because his tenure was brief. One day after school, Uncle Jim told me that instead of walking home with everyone else, I was to go with him to the post office. I argued that he could get the mail himself, but he insisted, warning me to do as I was told. I walked along wondering why it was so important, and it seemed even less so when there was no mail and all he did was snarl at me for sulking. At Rice's bridge, he told me to go under the bridge because he wanted to show me something. I said no because there was nothing to see and I didn't want to get my shoes wet. He insisted and tried to pull me down, but I cried and made such a fuss that he let me go. He was furious and went down by himself, telling me to follow. I ran. At Rice's pasture, I climbed an embankment edged with bushes and hid, waiting until Uncle Jim ran past in a fury. I followed slowly, watching from a distance until I saw him enter our kitchen door. When I arrived, Mother was visibly upset and could see that I had been crying. I told her in front of Uncle Jim what had happened and he shouted that I was lying. An ominous quiet settled over the house. Dinner time was glum and we were sent to bed early. The next morning, Mother sent us off to school without the uncles. I was relieved because I had been dreading what might happen on the way. I was afraid to look over the breakfast table because I knew there were black looks over certain porridge bowls.

I had no idea why they were kept home and didn't connect it with the previous day. That afternoon when we came home from school, the teenaged uncles were gone, off to Montreal and auld lang syne. Daniel and Jim, the clever little gossip mongers of the family, wheedled the information out of Mother that Grandmother wanted them in Montreal right away. None of us, including me, was any the wiser. It was only when I was older and the media freely delved into every quirk known to man that I put two and two together. I was the unwitting catalyst.

The teenaged uncles had the idea that Montreal was utopia, but they soon discovered the sort of utopia Grandmother had planned for them. The minute their feet touched the ground at Windsor Station, they learned to their dismay that Grandmother had jobs for them, and not only would they be earning their own living, but they would also be paying their room and board, leaving them with the merest of pin money. Uncle Alec soon took up with Allyne Reid, a wealthy wild child from Upper Westmount. For the sake of modesty, Alec and the wild child soon married to propagate more wild MacGregors. Allyne was the first modern hoyden in the family, while Uncle Jim, whom I never saw again, became the first devoted drunk. To his credit, he became part of the backbone of the Canadian Army. Grandmother ignored his indiscretions, lost jobs, hapless marriage to the unfortunate Barbara, and after his death would look at his picture and say, "He looked lovely in his uniform." Then he was picture perfect.

Although we were thrilled to see the end of the teenaged uncles, things hardly returned to normal with Uncle Peter still there like a spread of cactus. I couldn't wait for him and Verna to take up residence in their half-finished home so they could exist like two love birds billing and cooing silly names. She would coyly say 'Petee', which I thought a kindergarten affectation, and he, thinking he was the supreme wit, would look up to her height with the eyes of a conqueror and call her 'Verniticle.' But the wedding kept being delayed, and it seemed like we would never be rid of the last lingering MacGregor. They certainly took their time moving on. Uncle Peter balked at setting up housekeeping until the danger of being saddled with the teenaged uncles had passed. Only then did he ever-so-slowly inch his way out the door: choosing furniture, moving his possessions, and finally that day of deliverance when he emptied his room. He still showed up for dinners, but the house was ours again. One thing I remember from that period, and it is a very vivid remembrance, is of being able to go into the house without hesitation or fear, of not having to rush upstairs when the air was blue, of coming home from school and hearing Mother singing, of knowing that life had slipped back into that comfortable old order. It was so much better without them. No more Scotch accents, no more bagpipes and tartans and schottisches and hooting and black looks and wretched history. No more Harry Lauder. No more of Uncle Peter's favourite song, "The Big Rock Candy Mountain," where they hung the jerk who invented work. Mother hated that record so much she broke it three times. Hearing Tetrazzini sing "Una Voce Poco Fa" was like the air being cleansed, pure and sweet, the harshness all gone. I no longer envied Alice her Great Great Aunt Mary or the Reade girls their grandmother, or anyone else their relatives. There was no more curiosity left, at least on Mother's side. I did wonder now and then about Dad's side, even though he was as willing to dismiss his family as Mother now dismissed hers.

With the home back to its natural state, our only regret was that our true family couldn't share in our blessing. The Kniffens were long gone, Mr. Bishop only stayed a week at Stella and Jesse Harris', and Mother said that Mrs. Croscup had gone away. Mrs. McCormick's last baby was David, born that spring, and I was very sad when she told me she wouldn't be coming around anymore. She wasn't feeling well, her working days were over. It seemed so strange not seeing her every week; she had been part of the family for as long as I could remember. She was such a gentle, loving person, the grandmother I always wanted. So Maple Grove farm, which had always existed on the outskirts of society, became a Marvin preserve, still referred to as 'the old Warren farm.' Visitors were few and I only recall several from that time.

Flossie Dunn, whose father had once high-handedly refused to shoe Harry, was Jim's teacher that year, and one day she flew down to our house in her father's Tin Lizzie, her beautiful red hair aflame with outrage. "Just look at this," she said as she handed Mother the smuttiest of smutty notes, packed with row after row of the four-letter word of the day, unmistakably signed, Jim Marvin. The kitchen was in disarray and Mother was wearing her usual hoover, mussed and crumpled at the end of the day. She moved a pile of clothes from the couch to make room for Flossie to sit down. Flossie was carefully coiffed, carefully dressed and carefully arrogant, implying that Jim's offense might be a family failing. She refused to sit down, saying that she had no time but wanted Mother to know just what kind of a child Jim was. Mother said, "Well perhaps you don't have time, but I do." She sent me off to find Jim, who came in protesting his innocence. Without preamble, Mother sat him at the table with pencil and paper and had him sign his name. Mother only had to look at the note to know that Jim hadn't done it, and Flossie should have done the same. She had the good grace to apologize, but flared at the thought of this foul-mouthed fugitive, vowing to collar him and correct his grammar. Mother credited her efforts but questioned her methods, returning the family favour by lumping the Dunns in a heap and promising never to trust Harry to the likes of Mr. Dunn. Jim was in good enough hands, though, and I spent a year in Flossie's class. She was tall and slim, an expert ear-puller and a stickler over syntax. I often saw her poised behind the wheel of her Tin Lizzie, her beautiful red hair falling behind her in waves as she went about her rounds, Bear River's keeper of the King's English.

Over the years, Zella Maude Reade had often seen Mother passing by on the Chute Road and called her in for tea. Mother always reciprocated with an invitation, but with the dairy business and ten children to care for, Mrs. Reade had little time to spare. Then one scorching summer day, she did return the visit, her only one. She arrived exhausted from the heat and the long walk, and in tow was the detestable Lois. We had long ago made it plain that we didn't like each other, and our friendly acknowledgement was always one of mutual hatred. Lois was a nasty child who liked to throw stones and remind everyone of their stupidity. She wasn't happy about being there and told me right away, "I don't like your house." I saw her point but wasn't about to agree with her. Mother suggested that we play outside, but Lois wouldn't budge from her mother's side. Then Mother asked if I would like to show Lois my doll, my lovely Dorothea. I wasn't keen on the idea because I kept Dorothea in her box and took her out only on special occasions. This was not one of them.

My innovative system originated the year before, when just before he left, Mr. Bishop stopped by and found me on the swing crying my eyes out because the boys had destroyed my beautiful Pauline. I tearfully mumbled how they had taken her to the apple packing house, cracked her head in the vise and tore out her voice box. Mr. Bishop had indulged children's woes for many years, so he patiently listened in sympathy and promised to talk to the boys. Then he suggested that when I get my next doll, I should ask Mother for a special place to keep her and take her out only on special occasions. That Christmas, all of my dreams came true when I got the most beautiful of all the Eaton's Beauty dolls: the bride, my beautiful Dorothea. I was delirious when I saw her atop the Christmas tree shimmering in her satin wedding dress. Dorothea restored my faith in humanity—so beautiful with her lovely porcelain face and lashed eyes. I couldn't believe my luck; she was Eaton's Beauty's best. I decided to follow Mr. Bishop's advice. Mother let me keep Dorothea in the bottom drawer of the dining room sideboard, and she issued a general warning that no one could touch her. Mr. Bishop gave such good advice. I had my heart's desire as I looked at her safe in her box and talked to myself.

I didn't want to show Lois my doll but was at a loss to entertain her. Mother wanted us out of her hair, so I agreed. I took Lois into the dining room, opened the bottom drawer and pointed out Dorothea, lying there among the tablecloths. Lois was impressed and asked if she could see her out of the box. I agreed, but added that only I could hold her. I opened the box and carefully untied the ribbons around her feet and waist. Then as I lifted her out, Lois grabbed Dorothea and in the flick of an eye, wrenched her head so violently that it lolled forward and fell to the floor. I shrieked as Lois threw Dorothea down and screamed at me, "I hate your doll." I ran upstairs in tears. Never had I cried so hard in all my life. The beatific Dorothea, never played with and rarely out of her box, suffered the same fate as all the others. After that, she lay beheaded in her box. Then her clothes were stripped for Lorna's doll before a final trip to the apple packing house. Mother was furious with Lois and sympathetic with my grief, but when Christmas rolled around that year, she told me I was too old for dolls. I suppose it was time I grew out of a phase that filled me with so much sorrow. How I suffered for my Eaton's Beauty dolls.

DAVID WAS MOTHER'S LARGEST baby and had been born with his feet severely turned inward, which Dr. Campbell labelled 'club feet.' Mother and Dad were devastated by this deformity and took Dr. Campbell's advice to consult a specialist about having his feet straightened. Dr. Acker of the Children's Hospital in Halifax recommended that David be admitted to the hospital and have his feet put in plaster casts, possibly for a year. He also mentioned the likelihood of an operation. Mother and Dad hesitated over Dr. Acker's advice, but finally agreed to have David admitted before he started walking.

I wouldn't have minded all the other babies being shipped out, but David was different, and I was heartbroken that he would have to go into the hospital. I loved this blonde, blue-eyed boy, and he loved me. As long as I held him or hovered nearby, he had the sunniest, most placid disposition of any baby I had ever seen, yet when Mother picked him up or when I was at school, he reverted to type. I suspect it was with some relief that Mother said he liked me better than her. She would say he waited for me to come home from school and was unhappy all day long. His clinging made me possessive, and I suppose I developed quite an emotional attachment to David. Day by day, as his crawling became more experimental, his condition became increasingly upsetting. When he finally pulled himself up at a chair and turned to me with a smile, proudly wobbling on his crooked little feet, I couldn't help but cry. On the day of departure, Mother insisted I come along because she couldn't take David without me. I remember looking out the dining room window and waiting for the taxi while Mother sat at the sewing machine putting the final touches on the pair of pale blue rompers that David would wear for the trip. After she had dressed him, he put his arms out to me and was mine for the whole trip except for nursing.

That day I took my first train ride, and the thrill of it still resonates: the large plush seats, little towns passing by minutes apart, tea and sandwiches in the elegant dining car. It must have been a late afternoon train, because we stopped overnight in Windsor and continued on to Halifax the next morning. I remember the crisp white sheets of the upper bunk, Mother in the lower bunk nursing David, sated and sleepy. Dad had been admitted to Camp Hill Hospital a week or two prior, so he met us at the station and took us directly to the hospital. Tears and more tears as the nurse took David, his arms reaching out to us. He cried his little heart out as I waved goodbye, the echoes following us down the hallway. I never saw Mother so overcome; her shoulders shaking as she sobbed.

That was a strange day of contrasts, because life for me was suddenly full of the most wonderful surprises. Halifax was huge, and I couldn't believe the number of cars and trams. The streets and sidewalks were packed, and stores went on for blocks on end. Dad held my hand and taught me how to cross at the streetlight, a leap of faith in front of all those idling cars. He guided us in to a drugstore, where we sat at a polished oak counter and had a sandwich for breakfast. This was my kind of drugstore, because one counter held tremendous glass jars of candy, while underneath was a sprawling display of chocolate—a candy for every ailment. For a more effective cure, one could cross the room to the ice-cream counter.

Dad had arranged for Mother and me to stay in a boarding house on Spring Garden Road, the home of a lovely older lady. She welcomed us in to her large home, plush with Victorian elegance: carpeted floors, velvety sofas, tasselled lamps, softness all around. Upstairs, I stared in awe at the bathroom with its porcelain tub and sink, both with hot and cold running water. And the toilet was an absolute marvel. Mother showed me how to pull the chain, my first lesson in flushing.

Shortly, Mother and Dad returned to the hospital, leaving me with some colouring books and in the company of two office girls who were home for lunch. They took me to their room and made scrambled eggs with onions on a small two-ring burner, served with bread and butter. The meal was delicious, and they treated me like an honoured guest. They were small-town girls, just like me, and they had no trouble convincing me that the life of a big-city career girl bubbled with excitement. They had good jobs, nice friends and several boyfriends. No, they could never go back. I agreed. Why ever would they want to?

Before Dad left, he had given me ten cents, a new record, so when I couldn't lie down and sleep, I decided to go back to the drugstore and buy some candy from those huge exciting jars. I snuck down the carpeted stairs and slipped out the front door. I knew I shouldn't, but the big city beckoned. Everything seemed straight out of a story book: the tall buildings leaning over the sidewalk, trams rattling down the middle of the road, store windows filled with intrigue. Halifax was a busy city of wonders. I strolled along Barrington Street, looking in windows and enjoying my freedom, when who should I bump into but Mother and Dad, as if it were a small world. Dad took my hand and disciplined me grimly but gently, giving me a frightening lesson about little lost souls. He then took me into the drugstore, lifted me onto a twirling stool, and the man behind the counter produced my first ice-cream sundae, a confection that defied reality. How could I ever go back to plain old ice-cream?

After our treat, Dad announced that it was time to show his two ladies the town. We walked through the commercial core, the streets lined with tall buildings set in brick and stone. Dad loved architecture and explained all the details he found interesting. Columns in front of the court house stood like a set of principles. Banks implied Greek temples, holding a sacred trust. The university referenced the classics, beauty from symmetry. A great stone cathedral rose like the rock of ages, built on unshakeable faith. When I spotted a woman driving a car with doctor's plates, I asked him, and he said yes, she was a doctor. I was astounded that a woman had trespassed on men's territory and reminded Dad that I was going to be a doctor. He said he didn't see why not, but Mother warned me that it would mean more babies. After a thrilling tram ride and a visit to a museum, we climbed Citadel Hill to look the town over. Dad pointed out ships in the harbour: huge ocean liners, battleships, and steamers bringing cargo from around the world. Mother said it reminded her of home. Then Dad pointed out Camp Hill Hospital, not far away. It seemed strange that Camp Hill actually existed. For so long, it had been just a name, nowhere in particular. I looked at the buildings, but couldn't picture my father living there. Off to the side was Camp Hill cemetery and I looked away.

Down Citadel Hill, we stepped through the tall, ornate gates of the Halifax Public Gardens. I had never been in a park before and hardly saw the point since nature was running rampant on the farm, but here, it was trimmed and tamed, neat as a pin. Even the ducks were well-behaved, quacking politely, not rude and demanding like the hicks on the farm. Huge beds of flowers lined the walkways like painter's palettes, and Mother kept exclaiming over and over, "It's glorious, it's glorious." Gardens made her happy and these were superb. High atop a large fountain stood a mythical woman draining a jug, whom Dad said had been turned into a fountain when her husband died. A soldier kept watch atop another fountain, his rifle now a useful perch for sparrows. Statues of goddesses were stationed here and there, gracefully overseeing their domain. We sat in a gingerbread style bandstand and then wandered over to a lake where a swan sailed about. Dad said the park was a formal Victorian Garden, and to qualify as such a thing required two swans and a bandstand, among other things. He added that the lake was named after a man who had been hanged for murder, right over there—not a requirement of a Victorian Garden. And in the early days, a gardener with a fine head of hair was captured by the Micmacs. They wanted his scalp, but on discovering that he was bald, they settled for his wig and let him go. Dad knew the park well, saying he visited often. Mother was in rapture. I had never seen her so relaxed and happy. For those wishing to escape their cares, the Halifax Public Gardens are still there as I knew them, a glorious example of Victorian Garden order and grace, one of two in Canada.[1]

Boer War Memorial, Halifax Public Gardens

1 The other one is in Victoria, British Columbia, naturally.

That evening, Dad took us to the Green Lantern, my first meal in a restaurant, and the luxury was exquisite: royal red plush, deep carpets, a uniformed waiter showing us to a candlelit table sparkling with silverware and crystal. I sat down and proceeded to gawk. Every table had elegant gentlemen sitting with jewelled ladies. It was like a scene from my scrapbooks. Especially intriguing was a stairway leading to another railinged level where diners up there could watch diners down below; a whole new level of sophistication. I simply had to see more, so without any immediate need, I excused myself to the ladies' room. It was like stepping into Madame Recamier's boudoir. A lighted dressing table held powders to smell nice with, tissues for one's nose, and lotions for delicate hands. Nearby stood a full-length, three-panelled mirror to see myself front and back. Marble sinks with hot and cold water faced a long mirror lit by frosted light bulbs. The counter held fragrant soaps and towels for the wash-up, while behind, private cubicles had toilet paper on rolls. Mother came in and dragged me out, but then and there I decided I was a city girl. Goodbye to shivering in drafty old outhouses and struggling over squeaky water pumps. I yearned for marble. After dessert when Dad asked how I enjoyed everything, I said I loved it and we should move to Halifax. Mother always corrected boldness, but that time she didn't say a thing. She suited that restaurant, she belonged there, we both did.

Barrington St. and the Green Lantern in the '40s, third awning from the left.

After dinner, Dad walked us back through streets bustling with early evening excitement: trams filled with passengers, shoppers hurrying home. A line of street lamps pointed the way to our boarding house. That was a marvellous day of firsts, and Halifax became my dream city. For years I would fall asleep thinking of the elegance of the Green Lantern, willing myself to dream of being surrounded by such luxury. Years later when I was 22, I revisited the Green Lantern, and my dream evaporated as I sat in a diner at a Formica table, no royal red, no white linen, no formally dressed waiters, all of it gone except for the plagiarized name of my dreams. But dreams can never keep their shape as they drift like clouds before passing over the horizon.

The next morning, we returned to the hospital. David lay anchored in his crib with both legs in plaster casts, holding his arms out to me and crying. Dad picked him up, the nurse put him back and ushered us out. At the train station, Dad seemed ill and quiet. He was going back to Camp Hill and reassured Mother that he would visit David every day. Mother was distraught, worried that David might never walk. While we stood on the platform waiting for the train, I spied a penny on the track and reached down for it. Dad whipped me back, and a second time I learned a serious lesson. He kissed my forehead and lifted me onto the train. The trip back was quiet; Mother looking out the window, troubled and sad. We didn't know how long David or Dad would be in the hospital and whether either of them would get better. Driving in through the maple grove was not like coming home at all. Later, I told Daniel about Halifax, but he didn't believe me, likely because I had overstepped his seniority by getting there first.

Three months later, just before school started, Mother and I made a quick return trip to see David. Dad was still in Camp Hill and met us at the station. If leaving David was sad, seeing him again was unbearable. He just stared at everyone, like a thin little orphan, lying in his crib with both legs pinned down in heavy casts, no longer a happy, sunny baby. He ignored Mother and Dad and lifted his arms to me as if I had betrayed him, his face pale and unsmiling. I burst into tears. He was so changed, so wan and pale that I asked Mother, "Is he dying?" Mother, never mean with her tears, let them burst forth. The nurse assured Mother that he was a perfectly healthy baby, and in time he would stand on his feet properly.

Seeing David in his crib in that room full of crying babies was my first real trauma. All those little cribs looked like cages. When we got back to the boarding house, Dad and Mother talked things over; they weren't happy. Dr. Acker recommended a protracted stay of a year or more followed by an operation. Dad didn't mind the expense, but he doubted Dr. Acker's methods. Mother was torn, but I begged Dad to bring him home. Finally Dad decided that he would treat David's feet himself, and if it didn't work, then he would bring him back to Dr. Acker. One thing he did not want was David's feet being operated on. Once Dad made his decision, I was happy, but Mother kept asking him if they were doing the right thing. Dad reassured her, "Dearie, let's just try it. I have a feeling it will work."

Shortly, Dad returned from Halifax with David, his little legs dangling in plaster of Paris casts. He had gone into the hospital a chubby, happy baby and returned a pale, thin little waif clinging to Dad. Immediately, Dad removed the foul and odorous casts and placed him in the oval copper wash tub for his first real bath in months. He sat with his legs straight out, unmoved, almost insentient. We crowded around the tub while Mother and Dad tried to encourage some emotion, but he sat there bewildered, hardly aware of us, without even a whimper. After the bath, Dad began his massage therapy, repeated two or three times a day for two years. Out would come the wash tub and basins of warm water to soak his twisted little feet, Dad's gentle fingers patiently probing and massaging and manipulating. He would push David's legs up and down and bend his knees the way babies discover and taste their toes. I asked Dad why David stood on his outer ankles, and he explained that the inner ligaments were shorter, and what he was doing would lengthen them. He was constantly standing David up and placing his feet and encouraging Mother, saying, "Look Dearie, he's standing on his feet."

In a year, David was wearing his first sturdy boots and trundling over the lawn as we took turns holding his hands. It was a miracle to us all. I wanted this pretty little boy to be perfect and eventually he was. He wore special boots while the rest of us roamed in bare feet all summer, but he never went back to the hospital, and later, no one would have guessed he had what Dr. Campbell termed club feet. Years later it was all forgotten and David, so young, never knew.

Donald, David and Robert

Although I had a vague awareness of Dad's injuries, I never thought of him as being anything but healthy. To me, he was indestructible. He worked from morning till night doing all the heavy chores of the farm, every bit of it sheer physical effort. As a child, I had no understanding of how fragile his health was except to get a cold compress for his head, a glass of water for his aspirin. Dad's health was never discussed. Besides, I had pains of my own: I was bilious, anaemic, I sometimes fainted, I had frequent cramps that were diagnosed as growing pains, I suffered the vagaries of the weather. I was a child, impervious to the real pain of others. Hospitals had no meaning other than absence. When Dad left St. Anne de Bellevue for good, I assumed he had been cured and that phase of his life was over. That first summer was like every other, and when Dad would come in holding his head, take some aspirin and lie down, we thought nothing of it because that was what he always did. Many times after a hard day, he would come in exhausted, take his aspirin, throw himself on the parlor couch and say, "Dearie, I haven't got the gumption I was born with."

When the fall came and the crops were in, we were all set for Dad to pack his club bag and leave, but it didn't happen, and our lives settled in to the most unusual calm. Instead of having to rush out to the gardens, Dad would let Mother sleep in and make our favourite breakfasts: Welsh rabbit, enormous omelettes, curry hash, buckwheat pancakes. Mother's unstinting reliance on porridge and cream of wheat made winter mornings one unpleasant task after another, but Dad's menu turned breakfast into a treat. When he wasn't in the kitchen, he would putter around the house taking care of chores in his orderly naval manner. In those days, men didn't cook, and they certainly didn't clean, but Dad liked to stay busy. It seemed right that Mother should rest in bed with the baby. She didn't have to milk another cow or shovel another stall. Dad would make her café au lait, and I would take it in to her, sipping along the way. At the time, there was a wonderful café au lait called Martha Washington's, made with condensed milk. A teaspoon or two in hot water was delicious, so delicious that I didn't bother with the hot water and would sneak into the pantry to scoop teaspoons right out of the can.

If Dad didn't have too many chores, he would hitch Harry up to the sleigh and drive us to school, picking up Alice and the other children along the way. Sometimes the sleigh would be packed to the runners with a mob of screaming children. On the coldest days or if it snowed, we could always count on Dad to be waiting for us after school. We would scamper across the schoolyard to the comfort of the buffalo rugs, and it seemed like only minutes before we were home. The ritual thaw behind the stove was replaced by games and reading before dinner. Having Dad home on those cold nights took away all the loneliness of living on the farm. That winter set a new benchmark of contentment.

The spring of 1930 began with the usual frenzy of plowing, discing and raking, but no sooner were the gardens seeded than Dad suffered a bout of headaches, and they became so bad that he took to his bed for days at a time. Dr. Campbell made house calls, stepping into Dad's darkened bedroom, while I wondered what on earth was going on. That was my first real awareness of Dad's poor health, and I realized how oblivious I had been. Thereafter, I made mental notes of all the times he reached for his aspirin or sat reading in his chair, his elbow resting on the arm as he constantly massaged his forehead. Again and again that summer, Dad was bedridden, and the house took on that strange suspension of sickness. As summer wore on and Dad's headaches continued, I honestly wished for the fall rains so the hard work would end and Dad could rest.

After Dad cleared the gardens that fall, I heard many discussions with Mother about the farm and whether the effort was worth it. When Dad left St. Anne de Bellevue, he came home with a pension, 100% disability, enough to live on comfortably. Along with the proceeds of the farm, we should have been doing well, but crop prices had crashed and the farm was turning a loss. On top of that, Dad was in debt, he always had been. His finances never recovered from those early years when his health had been so poor. Then as the family grew, money drifted out the door the way it always does: insurance and educational policies for each child, the expense of hired hands, farm equipment and Uncle Peter's generous stipend. And there was no doubt Dad was extravagant. The summer of the MacGregor clan must have cost him a fortune. He sponsored their immigration, paid for their crossing, was far too generous during their visit, and financed their move to Montreal. Then came the expense of Uncle Peter's house, land and equipment. So with the farm losing money and piling up even more debt, why carry on? The Soldiers Settlement Board had offered to buy the farm back and leave Dad free and clear. Many farmers were talking about selling out, and they didn't have a pension to fall back on.

When Mother and Dad voted for the first time that summer of 1930, the whole business of the election seemed as if it was over and done with in a day, but I realized I didn't understand its significance when angry farmers began slinging Mackenzie King and R.B. Bennett's names in the mud, coupling them with a word I had never heard before: Depression. They were reviled up and down the Chute Road as the authors of the calamity. In the Trading Company, men talked in hushed tones about what had happened to so-and-so. Cash money became scarce, and farmers were trading their produce for less than it cost to grow. Old-timers threw in that old canard, Confederation, saying it forced Maritimers to trade with Montreal and Toronto instead of Boston and New York. Yes, but things were no better down there. People were worried. Strangers started coming to our door begging for potatoes or a few ears of corn. Dr. Campbell asked for chickens because his patients couldn't pay. Everybody wondered, 'What is going on?' No one knew.

In discussing the farm with Mother that fall, Dad said he could not be idle and sit at home collecting a pension. He wanted Maple Grove to be the Marvin farm, built to last, like the settled estate of his youth. The family was born there, that was important to Dad, and the farm would be his legacy. Besides, Dad enjoyed farming. On our evening walks, he admired his fields in the same way he admired his brass work, paying them the same compliment, "Sweetlady, there's beauty in a straight line." He liked experimenting with crops, trying something unusual to bring in more money, always tinkering. He once said he had shown the farmers how to farm, implying that he made no friends along the way, also implying that he didn't care. Maple Grove was the best farm in Bear River, even Grandmother saw that. We were first to market, we sold everything we grew, and we had all the best clients. So in the end there really wasn't any question; Dad decided to work through difficult times as he had done before. The pension would back him up, and soon the farm would be turning a profit again.

I CAN'T EXPLAIN HOW WE children became aware of Uncle Peter's underlying bitterness, but one instinctively knew without ever hearing an argument or a discussion; it seeped into our bones. He seemed to have lost interest in us and no longer teased us. I knew that he expected Dad to finish his house, but there seemed to be a flaw in his thinking about the possession of the farm and equipment. He was nursing the mistaken idea that after years of doing the chores of a hired hand, our farm was his as much as Dad's. There was a lot of discussion about the animals he wanted in his barn. Nothing on our farm was his, yet he laid claim. Dad bought him a horse, a harrow, a plow, and he had free use of all the implements that Mother and Dad had worked so hard to buy. He had his house and property, but he worried about his finances. Still, he seemed insulted when Dad suggested that he buy a new overcoat at the Trading Company instead of ordering it from Davie's of London. Dad gave him the unused furniture in our upstairs bedrooms. He installed Uncle Peter's new kitchen stove and we all watched as he lit it, the draft drawing perfectly. Dad let him cut all the trees he needed from our woods, and the sawing machine buzzed away, cutting a supply of wood that we stacked in his cellar. A home had once stood on the property, so the well was already drilled, and Dad installed a large pump over the kitchen sink, a modern convenience. The new outhouse was close by, nestled beside his barn, which housed Jock, a selection of pigs, cows, and as many chickens as he needed. It was all very cozy. Although the house remained unfinished upstairs, the newness and airiness of the high view made it seem orderly in a way that ours wasn't. We were crammed in by hills, trees and buildings. Uncle Peter had little to complain about. He had a brand new house, land stretching down to the river, animals and tools; far more than Mother and Dad started out with, all without spending a penny, but he wasn't happy, it wasn't enough. When Uncle Peter and Verna appeared for Sunday dinners, they assumed a frosty familiarity, but they didn't mind eating the food Mother put on the table. How can I describe their guarded attitude? They were like children of wealth waiting for the will to be read, only to discover that they would be getting one miserable dollar. They were marching to their marriage bed stung by the burden of ungrateful relatives, unconscious of their worth.

1931 began with the news that Uncle Peter would definitely, absolutely be marrying Verna that summer. It seemed like he meant it this time. But Uncle Peter was in a bit of pickle because he was striking out on his own in the middle of a Depression. This must have come as a rude shock because he had not yet been tempered by harsh reality. From the comforts of home, where Grandmother had mollycoddled him, he fell straight into the bosom of Maple Grove farm, where for eight years he had a roof over his head, all he could eat, and responsibility for nothing but his chores. In the winter, he used those months of free time to study up on the old west. Self-improvement would come in its own good time. But nothing is forever, and love has a way of zeroing in on the pocketbook. His first bold move was to ask for a share of Dad's pension, harbouring delusions that he had earned the same rights as a war veteran. Dad was flabbergasted. But Uncle Peter wasn't finished; he was just beginning. Next, he claimed that part of our farm was his, which part he didn't say. Again, Dad said no, a word Uncle Peter wasn't used to hearing. He then suggested that the two farms be run as some sort of collective. Dad was adamant, sharing was out. He agreed to help with chores, as all farmers did, but that was it. Uncle Peter was dreading having to stand on his own, a novelty coming a little late in life. As winter wore on, the battle lines formed, and Uncle Peter seethed in his spacious quarters, thinking traditional MacGregor thoughts.

As soon as the snow melted, Dad began preparing the gardens, but the strain brought back the headaches, as bad as ever. Our worst fears were quickly realized. It seemed that every few days he was in bed, and Dr. Campbell made regular house calls. In between, Dad would rush out to the gardens, trying to make up for lost time or to get ahead of things before the next bout. I remember having the distinct feeling that things couldn't go on, that something had to happen. Something did happen, and in the midst of all the upheavals that spring, we got another shock when Mrs. Johnson, whom we had never met before, arrived to take up residence in Mrs. McCormick's room. Dear Mrs. Johnson with her silvery top notch, one upper tooth, and Scottish brogue. She would become such an important part of our lives. We instinctively knew to be better than usual, but the sad part for me was that her visit culminated in another baby. On April 27, 1931, Robert was born, another boy.

Shortly after Robert's birth, Daniel and Dad were cutting logs with the cross-cut saw while Uncle Peter was harrowing the gardens with Harry and Jock. For some reason, Uncle Peter started swearing at the horses and then began beating them with a stick. The frightened horses strained at their traces until Harry reared up on his hind legs and let out a piercing animal cry. He dragged the harrow with Jock, ready to stampede, but Uncle Peter held the reins. Dad was livid. He ran over to the gardens with the cross-cut saw and pitched it at Uncle Peter, cutting his arm badly. Uncle Peter cradled his ripped and bloody arm and furiously shouted at Dad that he would see him off the farm. I stood at the kitchen window, shocked. That was the only display of temper I ever saw from Dad. Daniel and I agreed that Uncle Peter deserved what he got because no one had ever laid a finger on Harry. Horses had to be treated like favoured children and to beat them was unthinkable, vicious. Dad came into the kitchen for his jar of aspirin and spent the evening reading and massaging his forehead. The next day his headache worsened, and when we came home from school, we were told to keep quiet because he was resting in the bed. The next day was the same, and after a week of Dr. Campbell's visits, Mother told us what we already knew: that Dad would be going back to the hospital. It seemed that Uncle Peter was keeping his word, and I wondered just what he said when Dr. Campbell dressed his arm. For Dad to be leaving in the spring and under such a cloud seemed ominous. There was an uncomfortable uncertainty, like the end of the world that had been predicted in the newspapers. Other partings seemed almost normal, Dad always came back, but in my child's mind that day, I thought he never would. I stood by the taxi waiting for my kiss as he walked through the maple grove with his club bag.

That spring with Dad and David in the hospital, my finer emotions got lost in a strange entanglement of negativity. I felt nothing but contempt for Uncle Peter, and that contempt sustained me. I developed an intense, oppressive, depressive outlook. I was a nihilist, an active negativist. Nothing was good anymore; I hated everyone and everything. Mother's constant chores distanced her from me. I was merely a little mother, exactly what I didn't want to be. I only existed in my scrapbooks filled with worthless paper cut-outs. With an attitude like that, it wasn't long before I got myself into enough trouble to call my character into question.

One day we came home from school while Mother was cleaning the kitchen, so she told everyone to stay outside and play until she was finished, everyone but me. I had to take the buggy and walk Robert. That was the last straw. I was always being singled out for chores while everyone else got to play. I wheeled the buggy up and down the Chute Road, hating babies, siblings and life in general. As I returned through the maple grove, I boiled over and gave the buggy a shove, sending it careening down the path. Realizing what I had done, I ran to catch up, but the buggy hit a rock in Mother's garden and flopped into the flowers with Robert screaming under his blankets. Everyone saw it. I marched myself to the lilac bush, and the back of my legs tingled for days. I kept my socks pulled up. I was a budding criminal, and Lorna reminded me, "You almost killed the baby the way you almost killed my kitten." At least Dad was beyond recall. My guilt stared me in the face and apologies did no good. Mother ignored me for weeks except for short, sharp orders. I tried to explain that I didn't mean to do it, but she reminded me for ever and all time that people mean exactly what they do, make no mistake. Perhaps the next time I was in a bad mood it would be just as well to think twice before, rather than after. So for a while I swallowed lumps in my throat and worked hard at my chores to regain Mother's approval, the one thing I couldn't live without.

That silent punishment gave me the best lesson I could have learned, because I had time to think things over, and I opened my eyes to Mother's endless burden. I would come home from school and the wash tub would be resting on two chairs, still filled with clothes. In the basin by the sink, diapers would be soaking, while baskets filled with damp clothes sat waiting to be ironed. One day on my way home from school, I saw Mrs. McCormick on her verandah, so I cut off from the others and told her that Mother needed help, could she please come over? She explained that she couldn't, she was getting too old and too tired, but she would visit. She did come, and she told Mother what I had said. I didn't mind, because Mother was not well that spring. I cannot imagine what it was like for her to be alone on the farm with eight small children, Robert a newborn, David in the hospital, and Dad sick. She was in and out of bed, and a lot of chores went undone. She had less and less time for us and bedtime lost its ceremony. Lullabies and stories were replaced by a quick lights out.

One day I was watching Robert at the end of a row of vegetables while Mother weeded the gardens. I looked away, and when I turned back, Mother was gone. It seemed so strange, and I became more alarmed as I called and called for her. When she lifted her arm and motioned above the rows, I ran over and sat her up as she asked for a glass of water with Urasal, that useless cure-all Dr. Campbell had been prescribing for years.

I don't know how we managed that spring, but the sense of crisis eased when Mrs. Johnson came to stay for a few weeks. That brief respite allowed us to settle in to the familiar pattern of life without Dad. When he left for Camp Hill, the gardens were seeded and ready for the boys and the hired men to take over. As bad as it was to have Dad away for a whole summer, it was a pleasant surprise that we coped and the farm survived. Dad made brief visits home for haying and to bring in the crops. Mother called in the hired men or traded favours with Uncle Peter, but for the most part, Daniel, Jim and Douglas took over. They cared for the animals morning and night, they weeded, cut hay, and one time they took it to be threshed, which startled Mr. Harris. At 11, 9 and 7, the boys became farmers that summer. Suddenly, Daniel was ordered and efficient, arranging the chores of the day, shuffling us from one field to another, bringing in the crops Mother needed to ship and then delivering them. I never expected as much, but Daniel magically transformed. Mischief and bad behaviour were gone and forgotten, and Daniel became as kind and considerate to Mother as Dad was. The house realigned and we all followed his lead, establishing a pattern that would last for years.

We didn't see much of Uncle Peter that summer, and for that I was grateful, because whenever he did show up, he was surly, even rude. It was obvious that he wanted the farm to fail, and it irked him that the boys ran it so well. I couldn't understand why my parents agreed to attend his wedding, because the whole exercise had too many undercurrents. Still, it was a wedding, the first I remember, so we felt a quiver of excitement. Any interest quickly faded when we learned that it would be held at Verna's mother's house in Shubenacadie, and that children would not be attending. For the big day, Mother made a bright red, crepe dress, and to complement it, she chose a red, cartwheel-brimmed summer hat from Mrs. Yorke's, all in all, making herself look red hot for the occasion.

Mr. Bishop was best man and drove down in a taxi rented for the trip. We all crowded around as he stepped out of the taxi, and when Mother emerged from the house, flashing into view, Mr. Bishop stopped in his tracks to enthusiastically declare, "Mary, you are brilliant." Mother, perhaps a little surprised by the effect said, "That's me!" She asked Dad how she looked, and he assured her that she looked like his wild Irish rose, the sweetest flower that grows (as the song goes). Mrs. McCormick was spending the day with us and said that Mother looked lovely, but I wasn't so sure. She seemed foot loose and fancy free, happy to be escaping us. Off she went that warm August morning to sing her heart out at the nuptials in her blazing red dress.

I think Mother had second thoughts about the dress after the wedding, because she never wore it again. Instead, she sent the dress, the hat, and a wedding dress off to Aunt Elsie, who was getting married against Grandmother's explicit orders. Dear Aunt Elsie who always powdered my nose. It seemed so romantic, almost dangerous that she was running away to get married and that Mother was conspiring with her. Mother made both dresses at the same time, and I thought Aunt Elsie's dress was exquisite and wished Mother would exchange them. Let Elsie get married in brilliant red. In the end Elsie got both. I watched as Mother carefully packed the delicate, pale pink georgette dress with cape collar, layering it in tissue, then wrapping the pale pink hat she bought at Mrs. Yorke's. She then packed the bright red dress and hat, and mailed them not to Montreal, but to St Andrews-By-The-Sea in New Brunswick, where Aunt Elsie's fiancé had built her a home.

Incidentally, Aunt Cathie and Aunt Nan quickly followed in Elsie's footsteps, running away to get married, leaving quiet Aunt Ellie alone with Grandmother. When the aunts were at the farm, they were all so eager; marriage seemed to be their prime requisite, their only requisite. It was a shame that the one thing they might have celebrated with Grandmother, they didn't, and for some time they celebrated her corrosiveness. With all the weddings that were going on, it almost seemed that marriage was a sneaky business. Only Uncle Peter's was out in the open, yet still far enough away to be vested in mystery. Obviously there were problems with getting married in the MacGregor household that were never revealed to me.

John McLeod collection

Written on the back: Aunt Elsie and Uncle Bill Johnstone on their wedding day. Aunt Elsie ran away to get married to outwit Grandmother, who didn't like Uncle Bill. He was nice.

After a brief honeymoon, Uncle Peter and Verna returned to their sparsely furnished, unfinished home and were supposedly still love birds in the off-season amid worries about their future. Our upstairs furniture filled their parlor, our couch sat in their porch, our old table and chairs sat in their kitchen, nothing was in their dining room, great empty spaces upstairs, et voila. But on their elevation half-way up McCormick's hill, Verna in her brand-new house could look down on our cluttered premises and down on Mother, which she most certainly did. The minute Verna took up residence, she invited Mother over, ostensibly for a cup of tea. No sooner had Mother sat down than she was asked by this enterprising chatelaine to show her the account books. Mother hesitated over her first sip at this surprising request, put down the cup and walked out the door without a word. No further words were necessary. Hardly ever.

Verna was a meticulous, industrious housekeeper, and she wasted no time preserving what was left of the summer fruit and vegetables. Mother rarely preserved vegetables except for pickles, but Verna's cellar shelves were filled with anything that she could fit into a jar. We all helped thrash peas and beans out of the dried stalks. Whatever was left in our gardens, we carried up to them: squash, turnips, potatoes, carrots, parsnips, horseradish. They dug clams and went out with friends to fish in the Bay.

They scurried about like squirrels gathering nuts; if they starved it would be a miracle. Hay had been deposited in their barn and the plowing had already been done in preparation for a strawberry patch the following year, which they eventually extended into a strawberry business for the rest of their lives. Realizing that currency was the best commodity, Uncle Peter became a budding entrepreneur. Everything that could be eaten and that we didn't need, he got busy peddling. He sold our extra milk and eggs to Verna's sister, Elsie Henshaw, and anyone else who would buy them. Nothing was wasted. The boys didn't dare smash eggs. In a way, they were as desperate as Mother and Dad were at the beginning. Their coolness indicated that life was punishing them, though they had everything but money. It must have been a terrible awakening for Uncle Peter. He was forced to rely on Dad's generosity, and that fact developed into an insult, explaining to me very aptly at that tender age the meaning of the saying, 'as cold as charity.' Dad left him with far more than he had started out with himself, including the fact that Uncle Peter was debt-free. But they always expected more. Grandmother's original assessment of Verna rang true, "She's an arrogant one." There was another quality she had, one that Uncle Peter lacked until his marriage, and that was ambition. Ambition has a boiling point.

John McLeod collection

CERTAIN YEARS STAND OUT as indelible because in so many ways they were traumatic. Traumas may be either forgotten entirely or painfully remembered, and because of their emphasis, by-pass lesser or happier events in the recall.

The dreary fall of 1931 arrived with the gardens and flowers dead, the leaves falling, and a terrible depression, not the one that spread over the country after the Wall Street crash, but a palpable depression that blew in from the Bay, chilling the sea of raw mud in the gardens that surrounded our dingy, white-washed home, where no one was happy. Along with the anticipation of another wretched winter of walking back and forth to school, there was a strange emptiness, a feeling of encroaching finality. I began to suffer terrible nightmares, disturbing the whole household: Uncle Peter beating the horses in a fury, Harry straining and rearing on his hind legs, a ripped and bloody arm.

That fall, Uncle Peter was surly and talked to no one. If he tended to the cows, he would put the milk in the separator in the back porch, take what he wanted, and leave the pails for Mother to wash. He ignored the boys when they spoke to him, so Mother forbad us from talking to either him or Verna. Coming home from school, we would call to Scotty sitting at Uncle Peter's back porch. He would excitedly run to accompany us down the hill, but Uncle Peter's shrill whistle would summon him back. The barn was relinquished for the coziness of a house; our dog had deserted us.

One day, we got home from school just as Uncle Peter drove the wagon in with two huge barrels holding a catch of cod. He rolled them down to the kitchen door and brusquely ordered Mother to salt them down right away. I can't imagine why she did it. I can still remember getting out of bed and going downstairs to see the horrible, ugly picture of Mother standing alone by the lantern light gutting the cod. She looked up and sharply told me to get back to bed. I knew she wasn't angry at me but I was afraid, and she looked spectral by the lantern light, scaling and slitting the cod. I lay in bed listening to the sharp bang of the knife cutting off the heads. The next morning when we rushed down to the outhouse, Uncle Peter had already milked the cows and taken the barrels of cod to his cellar. Mother remarked that he could have left her at least one. All that remained was a disgusting pile of entrails, gaping fish heads, and scales sparkling in the dew. Uncle Peter had moved the whole horrid mess into the path by Mother's rock garden, forcing us to detour around it. After school, Daniel and Mother shovelled it into a wheelbarrow and transported it down to the far end of the gardens, covering it between the rows. As I look back, it all became a graveyard, the gardens, the fields, everything, because the farm was never cultivated again.

Several days later, Uncle Peter stormed into the house and went straight upstairs, slamming a door behind him and shouting furiously at Mother. I heard a bang on the floor and Uncle Peter rushed down the stairs, slamming the front door loudly on his way out. When I called to Mother, she didn't answer, so I went upstairs and found her lying unconscious on the floor in a spreading pool of blood. I screamed for Daniel and we pulled at Mother screaming for her to wake up. I thought she was dead, but Daniel kept shaking her, saying no, she was still bleeding. Mother finally came to and crawled to the bed, her nose bleeding heavily. Daniel insisted on getting Dr. Campbell, but Mother said no and sent us away. We couldn't ask questions. Her face was black and blue for weeks, but Mother never said a word about it, not even to Dad when he returned. I cannot imagine what Dad would have done to Uncle Peter had he known. Later, I caught Mother in a lie when she excused her appearance to Mrs. McCormick by saying she had fallen off the dining room table while papering the walls. That must have been the day Uncle Peter found out that Dad was selling the farm.

A month later at the end of November, Dad returned from Camp Hill to finalize the dissolution of the farm. People came to buy the cows and machinery. One farmer carted away the sow and the boar, and they lumbered up McCormick's hill grunting and squealing. A steer and several pigs were killed for Mr. Dukeshire. I heard the pigs squealing in terror as they ran from being stuck. Mother kept us in the house so as not to witness the killing. Daniel was there and later explained in bed how a sledgehammer was aimed at the steer's head, right between its eyes, and how it was gutted and skinned. It was just another farm nightmare. I was sick. When the operation ended, we strayed over to the barn to see the dressed, red-raw steer hanging from the pulley like a splayed cut-out, high enough so the contingent of cats could only sniff in vain. Hanging about this spectre were splayed white piglets, hovering in the filthy barn like animal angels. Life was being drained from the farm, the dream was not only flawed, it was dead. Mother and Dad were calm, gentle individuals, but a destructive maelstrom swirled about them.

Mr. Dukeshire arrived to transport everything to his meat market. All the cows were sold except for Daisy and Buttercup, which Uncle Peter took up to his barn. But it was never enough, and Uncle Peter acted as though everything should fall into his hands. Dad's generosity seemed to scald like a burn. There was a furious shouting match when Dad sold off some of the machinery, and particularly when he gave Harry to Isabel Davis' father. Isabel was in my grade, and later on I would have twinges of wistful jealousy when she and her father trotted by. Mr. Davis lived in the village and owned a sleek, delicate little mare, beautifully groomed to a glossy varnish, looking as if her mane and tail were brushed a hundred strokes a day. She looked like a socialite and was used only for trips to the post office or to shop at the Trading Company; never as a work horse like Harry. Mr. Davis had a strange fixation about Harry, or maybe they had one for each other. Every time we met in the village, Mr. Davis would dismount his gig and pet Harry and remind Dad that if he ever wanted to sell Harry, he would pay his price. Dad said he would never sell Harry, but if he left the farm he would give Harry to him, knowing that he would be well cared for. Dad kept his word and when Harry left the farm, he left with his favourite belongings: the light wagon that Mother favoured when she drove into the village, his blankets, feed bag, Dad's saddle and other oddments. Mr. Davis was a happy man, and we were too, knowing that Harry would never have to fear Uncle Peter's cruelty, or associate with that insufferable, bad-tempered Jock, who kicked his stall if anyone so much as spoke to him. Instead, he could spend his days wooing Mr. Davis' sleek mare, and she would fall for his irresistible charm the same way I did.

When we moved from the farm, Harry's importance in our lives was suddenly forgotten, but it's strange about animals. Every time Mr. Davis would pass our house, Harry would whinny. We'd hear him and rush to the window for a glimpse. The next summer, the boys dashed into the house full of excitement, shouting that Mr. Davis was coming up the road with Harry. They scrambled for apples, hard bread and carrots and rushed out the door. I grabbed sugar cubes from the bowl on the dining room table and hurried to catch up. Mr. Davis dismounted while Isabel sat in the buggy, all but ignored. We crowded around Harry, repossessing him for a few moments. I enjoyed the remembered pleasure of his soft, velvety lower lip brushing the sugar cubes from the palm of my hand. Then, in the midst of all the excitement, Harry took an uncharacteristic nip at Jim's stomach, much to Jim's dismay and humiliation. Mr. Davis explained that it was too much excitement for Harry. That was the last time I saw Harry, except as I do now: his creamy, caramel coat, his chocolate mane and tail, his frosted fetlocks and melting eyes. Harry was a happy horse, far superior to Man o' War and Seabiscuit, who were raved about world-wide but only pieces of paper in my scrap book. Harry was a dream of a horse.

WHEN LITTLE CHILDREN START off to school they aren't entirely unschooled. They have been pupils of Mother Goose and been well-taught in the line of ditties, soon to be updated in the rowdy schoolyard. Daniel learned a ditty from Merton Yorke and boldly repeated it to Mother. It went: Beans, beans, the musical fruit, the more you eat the more you poop. Mother failed to see its merit and Daniel went to his room. I learned some ditties too, not so earthy. In kindergarten we sang "Twinkle, Twinkle Little Star," a simple song that didn't have the substance of the much more promising, 'Star light, star bright, first star I see tonight, I wish you may, I wish you might, grant the wish I wish tonight.' Alice Copeland told me I had to wish on the first star I saw at night and to never, ever tell what I wished for or it would not come true.

I wished a lot when I was a little girl. I knew nothing of religion and the power of prayer, but I believed implicitly in wishes. I wished on the brightest star in the sky, thinking it was the luckiest. I wished on Sirius. Then I wished on every other star that caught my eye. At 5, I was an inveterate star gazer. The stars were where heaven was and my pillow was my altar. After a few years, I had winnowed out a number of requests: a doll's buggy, a ring, a bed of my own, all of them dropped by the wayside like fallen petals, because I decided what I wanted most of all was to leave the farm. Daniel would catch me off guard in sober concentration and say, "You wished, I know you did." He would pester me to tell, tell, tell, but for a wish to come true, it can never be told. Daniel's wishes were always outrageous; he was going to conquer the world. Dad would watch Daniel flexing his biceps and say, "Sweetheart, the world is a big place." In bed at night, he would reveal his not-so-secret ambitions, but I never fell into his trap. I had to remain steadfast, true to myself and my stars. One night, in a fury because he had told me all of his bizarre wishes and I wouldn't reciprocate, not even after his deadly pinches, he said the stars were only balls of slush, "Dad said so." I thought it terrible that they might be slush and refused to believe him. The stars were diamonds, dispensers of wishes. Besides, I could never reveal my wish because it was as bizarre as any of Daniel's: I wanted to live in the Reade house.

On our forays back and forth to school, I was always aware of the empty houses along the way. They were nice homes with verandahs and porches, built of clapboard, not whitewashed shingles like ours. Some were stripped by age and weather, but the W.G. Clarke homes were prettily painted in various colours, as if standing by, waiting for new occupants. After school we would run across the verandahs and look through the windows and wonder which one we liked the best. We had a lot to chose from. The home of the outspoken, anti-George V, Ernie Baker stood forlornly at the edge of Mr. Clarke's orchards. Nearby was Truman Hamilton's, which had been empty for a while; there were no more King apples. Opposite was the secluded home once occupied by the ear-pulling teacher, the bushes and tall grasses getting taller in camouflage. Farther along was the grey spectre of the old Chute home. All that remained was the intangible memory of molasses taffy and the scent of dried apples and pears, a whiff of the old days. Opposite was the house that had withstood those few chaotic months of occupation by the Trimpers and their unruly tribe. It was empty once again and stayed that way. There were echoes everywhere in all the empty homes that rested by the side of the road like tombstones. It's strange that I bypassed them all and dropped my wishes on the neat front lawn of the Reade house. Other homes were more elegant, which made them seem beyond reach, but the ordinary Reade house pulled my imagination in past the polished windows and lace curtains to an atmosphere of contentment and comfort. Perhaps it was because Mr. and Mrs. Reade had been such a warm, genteel couple. Mr. Reade, the dignified, suavely dressed retired principal. Mrs. Reade, softly patrician, calling Mother in for tea or standing by the side of the road after school with a plate of cookies for passing children. The house had a warmth that the formality of the Clarke home next door never did with its maids, tennis court and summer teas on the verandah. There was something good interred in its bones. When Mother and I passed it on our way home from Barr's, I would say, "Wouldn't it be nice to live there." Mother would say that I shouldn't wish to live in someone else's home because I had one of my own. After Mr. Reade died, the house sat vacant, then a brief occupancy, and then vacancy again. In the meantime, Fred Reade kept his mother's house and grounds neat and orderly, while I gazed up to the heavens and appealed to Sirius.

Leaving the farm was one of the most unusual and one of the happiest days of my life. It was a lonely road coming home from school that dreary, late November day. The weather was cold and raw, and we were already wearing our winter coats and mittens. A freezing drizzle needled us as we ran, and we knew we'd be soaked to the skin by the time we got home. Passing the Reade house, we saw that the electric lights upstairs and downstairs were blazing away and a truck was backed up to the front door. Not even the Reade children knew who was moving in. My heart fell. It had stood so long inviting occupancy, and now the last of my wishes was gone. Daniel called for me to catch up, and we raced along to the sound of our boots scraping the muddy gravel. We hurried around Hamilton's Corner, passing darkened houses, then down the avenue of maples and finally to the top of McCormick's hill. As we scurried past Uncle Peter's, we called to Scotty, who barked in reply from the porch window. The rain had soaked us through, and I was anxious to slip behind the kitchen stove, but then as we ran through the maple grove, I looked ahead and noticed a kerosene lamp in the window, 'that's strange, what's it doing there?' We ran up the back steps and stopped short at the door, staring into an empty, dimly lit kitchen. Everything had been removed: the stove, the table, the couch, even the linoleum had been lifted. At the door were several barrels holding a jumble of brass work and pantry goods. We stepped inside and called for Mother, the kitchen echoing our shouts of alarm. Mother answered from an empty room at the other end of the house, her voice retreating and unreal. She rushed in to the kitchen with a bundle of blankets and the boys followed, shouting that we were moving. When I asked Mother where we were moving to, she said, "The Reade house." I could have burst with shock and happiness, but instead I just stood there in the middle of the empty kitchen stunned in disbelief, thinking I had willed it and the stars had listened.

Mother told us to hurry up and gather our possessions in sugar bags, because Dad was expected back with the truck. The boys scampered about, stuffing their bags with radio parts, sling shots and other valuables. I grabbed my scrap books, a *National Geographic* of my hero Charles Lindbergh, and a record with a one-inch crack interrupting the lovely voice of Luisa Tetrazzini singing "Cara Nome," my favourite record.

I was afraid I might never hear it again. Mother looked through my collection, saying I should get rid of those old scrap books and, "What's this, a broken record?" I was still speechless, but I couldn't give up my scrap books, my dream merchants. As Mother was taking them out I started to cry, so she looked at me and said, "Oh all right." The boys were irrepressible, racketing through the empty rooms and up and down the stairs, fascinated by the strange hollowness as they filled the house with sounds it would never hear again. When Mother heard the truck coming down the hill, she had us put on our coats and hats, and we slung our school bags over our shoulders. Dad arrived in a truck driven by young Mr. Wal Clarke, a teacher who briefly ran a village taxi service. They hurried to load the truck, but Mr. Clarke said that since it was almost dark, he would have to come back for the rest another day. The boys were running about taking a last swing under the maples, pushing the glide swing under the Bartlett pear tree and tearing about through the fallen leaves. With the truck loaded, Dad called out that it was time to go. Mother blew out the kerosene lamp, and in a cold, dark moment, I stood clutching my sugar bag in our haunted kitchen. Mother took my hand and led me through the hallway and out the front door, not once looking back. She got into the cab, while the rest of us clamoured into the back with the furniture and barrels. Dad sat in a chair and I sat on his lap, leaning in close to avoid the rain. The truck rumbled to life, we jolted forward, and as we passed through the maple grove, I watched our house merge into the darkness of that cold, drizzly night, fading like the last, final note of an opera.

John McLeod collection

The Reade house, 1944

*A*S WE SAILED ALONG the Chute road that night, crowded in the back of the truck and open to the wind and rain, I remember feeling a wonderful, relieved excitement that we had finally left the farm. By some alchemy of the stars, I had what I wanted most of all. There was an unreality to our leaving the farm. We were whisked away without explanation. There was shock and wonder, elusive echoes, and Sirius smiling down on me. It happened just like that.

The truck pulled up to the Reade house, and every room was ablaze with electric light, glowing like a magic lantern. We scampered down and were met at the door by Mrs. Johnson, who had attended Mother when Robert was born. That was another wonderful surprise, and from that moment, she became guardian angel of the family, our other mother for three years. There she stood haloed in light like a genie, smiling broadly with her one upper tooth, her hair gathered in a silvery top notch. She told us to remove our boots, place our bags by the stairway and go straight in to the dining room. We were tensed like springs and rushed inside to explore our new home. It could have been 100 years old, but it was new, brand new. Upstairs, Daniel went wild over the magnificent bathroom, but before I could run up to see, Mrs. Johnson levelled her authority, which sobered us and never wavered for years, "You'll eat yoor stoo the noo!" She was thoroughly Scotch with her Highland colloquialisms that we often misunderstood. She corralled us into the dining room and sat us down at the table. It was the only room in the house with furniture, leftovers from the former owner: a large dining table with chairs, and a cabinet filling the whole wall, still holding Mrs. Reade's intriguing collection of fancy dishes. As I sat staring in wonder, all I could say was, "Isn't this the best house?" And again "Eat yoor stoo noo."

I changed then. That's when the desperate longing left and my life became the dream I had always wished for. There was nothing more I wanted, not possessions, not anything else. I belonged in that house. While we ate, the men unloaded the truck, and we eagerly eyed their activity, commenting on what they were putting where. Dad went from room to room lighting all the pot-bellied stoves: in the den that looked out to the Chute Road, in the master bedroom opposite, in the large parlor under the stairs. I had hoped for hot air registers like the ones at school, and the floors had linoleum squares, but nothing could dim the excitement of being in that house. Upstairs, Mrs. Johnson had prepared all the bedrooms, where Donald, David and Robert were already asleep. At her insistence, Mother joined them. And with that, Mrs. Johnson took over Mother's job and gained control immediately, not only of the house but also of our hearts. It was such an easy transformation.

When I look back at all the wonderful people I've known in my long life, I always think of Mrs. Johnson, and not just because she was a childhood attachment. She was an unlettered but intelligent woman, and the most loving, cheerful person you could imagine. She spoke in dialect like a 'Rabbie' Burns poem, and whenever anyone looked glum she would say the silliest of Scotch tongue-waggers, "If ye can say it's a braw, bricht moonlicht nicht then yoor aw richt ye ken." We thought it great repeating that silly thing when we had nothing better on our minds. It always pleased her when we'd put on our best Scottish accent and say, "Dinny ya ken?" or any of the other expressions we picked up from her. She'd smile and say, "Aye, yoo'd make great Scotsman." I never once saw her angry, nor did I ever hear her complain, but at her advanced age, it must have been a challenge looking after nine children, all under twelve. She and her husband had a small farm out past the Waldec Line where they lived with a daughter Peggy, her husband Lemuel Blois, and their baby, wee Lemuel. The farm was unproductive, most farms were at the time, so this aged guardian angel took on our care as if she were our mother, working to support her family for $30.00 a month.

After we had eaten and the truck was unloaded, we were allowed to prowl from room to room and discover our new home. The magic carpet had landed. We climbed the back stairs leading up from the kitchen, padded across the upstairs hallway, looked in bedrooms to choose our space, and then ran down the front stairs, but not before stopping to marvel at the bathroom, the most glamorous room in the house. Nothing could equal the excitement of walking into my first real bathroom and surveying those magnificent white porcelain accoutrements: the wash basin with hot and cold water; the huge bathtub; and most impressively, a toilet with a pull chain. We babbled on and on, 'look at this, look at that!' The bathtub even had a shower, an unheard of revolution.

Dad came in, and seeing the excitement, he lined up the boys under the shower and they slapped about like a pack of seals. They were irrepressible and eventually had to be dragged out. After that, we never needed another reminder to clean up. The boys showered needlessly, and Mrs. Johnson would dismiss them with, "Oot, oot, yoor clean enough."

Turning on a light, flushing a toilet and turning a tap are such commonplace, mindless gestures, but that night we were fascinated by the luxury of having them right there in the home. We marched through the house turning lights on and off and dutifully washing up after flushing the toilet. Goodbye to smoking oil lamps that flickered and grew dim and had to be carried from room to room. Electric lights gave a patina of wonder. No more drawing water from the well or being exhausted exhorting it from the kitchen pump. No more dipping water from the tank at the side of the stove and pouring it into porcelain wash basins. No more baths in the copper wash tub, and best of all, no more chamber pots and no more outhouse. In the space of a day, they were ancient history. We had caught up with the Romans. Outhouses are forgettable, but not the chill of winter winds blowing up one's spine as you sit shivering, your bottom freezing in the sitting position. Nor can one forget the subsequent tingling of the mild thaw after running post haste into the house for the nearest warmth. People who live in glass houses can never know the earthiness of outhouses, the intensity of individual raindrops, the buzz of flies, and the mores of the boondocks.

By the time I tumbled into bed and my head touched the pillow, I knew the simple joys of luxury. That first night in the Reade house I was like Clara of the *Nutcracker Suite*, not dreaming of sugar plums, but of that heavenly bathroom. Thereafter, I hunkered down to the pleasures of indoor plumbing. I couldn't wait to flush the toilet. I revelled in a real bathtub, lounging in full-length euphoria. It was the most perfect sensual luxury of my life. I could be clean forever without the trauma of bathing in four inches of lukewarm water. Never again did I have to be asked if I had washed my neck. I could always be found wallowing in the tub, the water delicately perfumed by my favourite bath salts. I loved having my hair smell of coconut oil shampoo, and I dutifully brushed 100 strokes as I observed my mirrored image, not too pleased with what I saw, but happy to be clean.

I powdered my body the way Aunt Elsie powdered her face, and then I dabbed myself with Dad's Violette cologne. I once asked Dad after being dragged out of the bathroom, "Do I look nice?" He assured me, "Sweetlady, yew ah a mag-nol-ee-ah." With all this exquisite cleanliness, I aimed to be as dainty as the beautiful movie stars that cluttered my scrap books. I existed on the edge of a beautiful, dreamy life, replete with a bathroom.

Our new home had a Spartan lack of furnishings, since the clutter of the farm still had to be collected, so several days later when Mr. Clarke had finished his wood deliveries, he and Dad drove down to the farm. The truck returned empty. Amid whispers behind closed doors, it was obvious that Dad and Mother were upset, but once again, children were left to wonder. It was only later when Amanda Simon visited that I heard what had happened. I listened from the hallway as Dad told Amanda how he and Mr. Clarke had returned to the farm only to discover open doors and windows, and the house cleared out. Nothing was left, not even the curtains. Uncle Peter had taken everything: the dining room furniture, bureaus, tables, the gramophone, the hundreds of records, even the pot-bellied stoves. What I thought worst of all was that he had emptied the root cellar of the hundreds of jars of jam, preserves, and pickles that Mother had spent all summer preparing. Dad sounded beaten as he described the scene. Then Amanda's rasping, strident voice pitched in, echoing through our empty rooms as she explained the purpose of her visit. A day or two prior, as part of the Ladies Sewing Circle, she had been invited to Verna's, and after a lengthy preamble on the Marvins, Verna took the women down to the farm to show them just how we lived. There, a message had been stamped on the walls, unmistakably clear: every wall of every room had been smashed by a sledge hammer. Crumbled plaster crunched beneath the ladies' feet as Verna took them from room to room. Doors were torn off and windows broken; the house was a shambles. After their initial shock, Mother and Dad sat there with an air of complete resignation. Amanda got the information she came for, so the full story likely filtered through town, but I could never understand why Dad did nothing about it. I can only imagine that he deferred in consideration of Mother's family name.

Since Uncle Peter had taken our gramophone and all our records, it was Luisa Tetrazzini who became the mute representative of the old guard. I treasured that broken record, holding onto it like a gold nugget. For years, she lay in my bedroom cupboard, safe under my wrinkled scrap books. At times when I dusted, I would hear the faint recall of Luisa's heavenly voice, far away and getting farther. I would hum in vain, trying to reach the bell-like high notes to keep them alive. Eventually, when I left home for Ottawa at 19, I took it off my bedroom shelf and wondered whether it was worth keeping. I didn't think long; I put it in my trunk.

In a few days, Dad went to Halifax to order furniture for the den. It arrived in conflicting colours: pale Wedgwood blue for his easy chair, an autumnal chesterfield and chair, both patterned with yellow leaves and large Halloweeny flowers. The effect was rather jarring when combined with Mother's red, shaggy wool rug set down in the middle of it all. Despite the motley motif, the den was wonderfully cozy and soon became the family hub. A glance into the room would reveal Dad at his drafting board, Mother knitting in her chair, a studious child lying on the rug and one or two camouflaged on the couch. The best part of moving into the Reade house was that we could all indulge in the luxury of time. With school only five minutes away, Dad taking care of the house, and Mrs. Johnson taking care of the toddlers, my chores dwindled. We all dove into our hobbies, and mine was reading. Two walls of the den were lined with books, and everybody's favourite was the multi-volumed *Book of Knowledge*. Each volume had everything a child could ever wish to read: popular stories, plays and poems; articles on the arts, sciences, history and nature; projects and how-to's, all superbly written and illustrated. They comprised a well-rounded education for any child or young adult, which was the intention of the originator, Arthur Mee, an imaginative Englishman who understood so well how young people love to learn. Occasionally, I'll see a set in a used book store, the older, pre-war volumes, not the childish modern version. They're quite expensive now, so I can only browse. I'll flip pages to find the stories I loved to read and re-read, as frightening as they were: *The Snow Queen* and *The Red Shoes* by Hans Christian Andersen, *King of the Golden River* by John Ruskin. I suppose my love affair with the written word began with the *Book of Knowledge*. They really were books of wonder.

By the time we moved into the Reade house, Dad had given up his brass work, the farm was a bankrupt effort, and the plans for our new house had vanished, but there was one other continuing dream: the water turbine, Dad's last big dream. For years on the farm, the drawings for the turbine, so complicated and precise, lay stacked in large rolls on a shelf in the upstairs bedroom. On his return in the spring, Dad would tack the plans to the drafting board, but the demands of the farm never gave him more than fleeting moments at the end of the day. As soon as we moved into the Reade house, Dad positioned his drafting table at the den window and tacked the sheaves of creamy paper to the board. The water turbine became his life's work, and he pored over the plans daily with a sort of leisurely contentment. Some sheets were rolled up and placed beside the table, then plucked up for re-examination. He would scribble lengthy calculations on scrap paper and then pick up a ruler to carefully draw a line. As he worked, we would peer over his shoulders asking questions, and the little ones would toddle around with their arms up, wanting to be cuddled. Joan always stood off by the door holding her doll by its head. Dad would look around and say, "Come to your old Dad, Little Jo Otter, ah want to have a talk with yew." She would look at him saucily and roll around on the rug. Mother used to say, "That one is a little clip," a Scottish expression. One day as Dad worked intently, I lay on the couch complaining bitterly about being too tall, hating my straight hair, and just look at these freckles, can't anything be done about them? He took his T-square and gently whacked my bottom, mollifying me by saying that Mother had freckles and look how beautiful she is. I flipped through my movie star scrap book and showed him a lovely picture of Jeanette MacDonald, en point in a black velvet tutu edged with white fur. Her hair fell in waves and she looked innocently at a butterfly sitting on her arm. I asked him if he didn't think she was beautiful. He just looked. I asked him who his favourite movie star was and he answered offhandedly, "Oh, ah suppose Dolores del Rio." For a time, she was the most beautiful woman in the movies. Then Dad asked me not to disturb him because he had work to do. It's a wonder he got anything done. I never understood Dad's turbine, only that it was a new type of engine, but I often heard him discussing it with Mother. He seemed pleased with his progress as he mentioned a patent and prospective clients.

Opposite the den and looking out to the Chute Road was the master bedroom, more spacious than the upstairs bedrooms with their sloping ceilings, but for some reason it remained unused. An ornate mantelpiece framed a fireplace, a bed and chair completed the decor, while the echoes in the room called out for more furniture. I loved to sit on the cushioned window seat and tend to my scrapbooks as I watched the passing parade on the Chute Road. I would snip through piles of magazines and newspapers, alone and undisturbed with the door closed for as long as I wanted. When I was done, I could lift the seat for my very own storage space to put scrapbooks, clippings, and my first bottle of mucilage glue, which Mother had bought for me when we moved in. Never again would I have to mix messy, lumpy flour paste. Never again would my crackling pages turn into washboards, making my heroes look old and jaded. I decided to throw out my old scrapbooks and start over, but I couldn't let good information go to waste and wanted to keep my favourite pictures: Charles Lindbergh, Babe Ruth, Lou Gehrig, pug-ugly Al Capone and all the celluloid lovers that the aunts swooned over: Warner Baxter, John Boles, Ramon Navarro. I tried to rescue them, but they tore off the pages in shreds. I did save the picture I loved the most: Anna Pavlova, dead on the floorboards with her tutu fluffed around her body, head dangling over her knees, her poor, lifeless arms lying by her legs. She had finished her life with that last performance of *The Dying Swan*. I kept that sad, wonderful picture for a long time to mourn over, and I told all my friends that she had died then and there. In my grief and adoration, I took to hanging on to the end of my wrought iron bed and standing on my toes for as long as I could take the pain. Later, I was surprised to discover that Anna Pavlova was alive and well and still dying on the floorboards of Europe.

Once we moved into the Reade house, I attained nirvana. There was nothing more I could wish for. The house had an inherent warmth that I felt in the master bedroom as I glued my scrapbooks, or in the den as I lay on the couch reading. I felt it in the comfort of the cushioned window seats in the alcove above the front porch, practicing my violin or sitting with Mother doing her sewing. I even felt it in the unused parlor under the stairs, empty except for pictures on the wall. The farm house was open to all confusion, it was as if you had to get out to get away, but the Reade house had comfortable nooks everywhere. The back stairs led up from the kitchen to a small maid's room stuffed with boxes of old clothes, letters and pictures left by the Reades. I would go up to pore over letters and look at pictures, the hoi polloi of the village stiffly posed. Another small bedroom was stacked with old furniture, and on a bureau sat a number of pretty perfume bottles still holding their last drops of scent, much more vivid than Mother's lilac and lemon verbena. Even the back verandah was warm and cozy with its swinging hammock and wicker chairs and tables. Half was glassed-in and the other half screened-in, with fragrant clematis vines climbing out from the corners. As ordinary as the Reade house was, it sufficed for my dreams. Dreams do fade, once awake they are beyond recall, but the Reade house never faded. Many times over the years, I have gone back in reverie to all the comforting corners I loved, and they still feel as warm and cozy as they were when I was young. Despite tragedy, it is still, and always will be, the home I loved the best.

The upstairs alcove in the Reade house, now a B & B.

SEVERAL WEEKS AFTER THE furniture arrived, a truck pulled up one Saturday morning to deliver the last of the items Dad had ordered in Halifax: a Philco electric radio. We crowded around as Dad placed the elegant wooden cabinet on a table, plugged it into the wall and turned it on–just like that. At the turn of the dial we were listening to broadcasts from Halifax, Montreal and Boston right there in our den. It was a miracle! On the farm, we heard nothing but static on Dad's crystal sets, even Santa Claus sounded bad-tempered, but on the electric radio, voices came over the airwaves with a freshness and youth. Old records on the gramophone sounded faded and tired by comparison. Dad checked his watch, sat Mother down and turned that wonderful glowing dial. Suddenly we were at the Metropolitan in New York listening to Milton J Cross set the scene for the Saturday afternoon opera. Mother was ecstatic. So was I. After years of reading about the Met and hearing Mr. Bishop describe performances, it simply couldn't be true that we were about to hear an actual opera. But it did happen, and when the music began, it was as if we were sitting right there. It was simply unbelievable! The performance that day was *Die Walkure* with the great Lauritz Melchior, and though Wagner was never a favourite of mine, I savoured every note.

That day marked a turning point because from then on, Saturday afternoons were reserved for one thing and one thing only. Dad would be working at his drafting board, Mother would be knitting on the couch, and I would be lying on rug reading in front of the Franklin fireplace. At 2:00, the mellifluous voice of Milton J Cross would welcome opera lovers everywhere and set the stage for the drama about to unfold. His eloquent descriptions sat me in the audience as a hush fell and the lights lowered. With Maestro Gatti-Casazza watching from the orchestra pit, the conductor's baton would fall on the down-beat, and the magnificent curtain would open on the scene just described. As Milton J Cross marked the progress of the opera, Mother and I absorbed every dazzling detail, transfixed until the last note was silenced, the last bow taken, the last flower flung, and the last billowing gown swallowed the curtseying diva.

Young opera buffs today can't possibly imagine the cornucopia they have missed. It was a golden era that Pavarotti alone, as wonderful as he is, cannot revive. The list of artists seems endless, they came and went, and each shining new talent made the repetitious repertoire seem fresh: Rosa Ponselle in *Il Trovatore*, Lily Pons in *Lucia* and *Lakme*, Rise Stevens in *Carmen*, Lucrezia Bori in *La Boheme* and *La Traviata*, Gladys Swarthout, Edward Johnson, Lawrence Tibbett, Giovanni Martinelli, and so many other names that have slipped from memory, but not the magic of their wonderful performances. One lovely voice flashed like a shooting star and vanished just as quickly: the young and lovely voice of Marion Talley. Oh, the tut-tuts! Who was bad—Marion or the predator doctor? I loved Lauritz Melchior, and I tried to love Wagner in toto, but my blood was Latin in those young years, and I gave my heart over to Puccinni, Leoncavallo, Verdi, Donezzetti, Rossini and all their melodies you couldn't get out of your head—music for everyone. The chorus of voices rising out of the Met during those years has never been eclipsed or even rivalled. It was an era that passed like a charmed childhood.

So after years of isolation on the farm, we joined the multitude gathered around the radio. The 30s offered a feast of the most beautiful popular music ever, not heard since except by recall. The airwaves overflowed with hundreds of lovely voices: Jessica Dragonette, Felix Knight, Deanna Durbin and so many others. One epic night I fell in love with the ringing, mellifluous voice of Richard Crooks singing "Rio Rita." Oh, the abandon, the buoyancy, the clarity and exquisite love of this Rio Rita. It played on my heart strings and never left. There were the signature songs by the stars of their shows: Kate Smith's "When the Moon Comes over the Mountain," Bing Crosby's "In the Blue of the Night," The Street Singer's "Rambling Rose of the Wildwood," and so many other wonderful songs by endearing, enduring voices.

Often when I came home from school, Mother would be ironing and happily listening to *The Goldbergs* or *Ma Perkins*. You could see those shows as well as hear them. It was the golden age of radio, with programs everyone could listen to: *The Little Theatre Off Times Square*, the footsteps walking you to your seat; *Amos and Andy*, with Andy's widely discussed love affair with Madame Queen, an ample Harlem beautician; the ridiculous Burns and Allen; the utter silliness of Joe Penner—long gone and forgotten. Daniel, older and more privileged, was often allowed to stay up late and listen to *Death Valley Days*, *The Shadow* and other shifty radio dramas.

On the way to school, he would brief me on all the hapless murder victims who peopled the airwaves. One unfortunate woman was dispatched by a needle thrust behind her ear and into her brain. With that, I put murder right out of my mind, but I still can't seem to forget a long needle being deftly placed behind an ear. Why do I remember?

When the news came on, everyone would pause for the latest update on man's inhumanity. Never before had events been so close, too close for comfort. Newspapers arrived at the post office days or even weeks after the fact, but on the radio, everything was immediate and urgent, almost next door. I remember Daniel discussing with Dad the Japanese slaughtering the Chinese in Manchuria. Dad had seen much the same thing when he was in China, and in Mexico, where locals butchered their priests for some God-forsaken reason. He cautioned Daniel that the world was not about to change and that it would always be spinning away on its wobbly axis.

Dad with his biblical bent preferred all the diatribers expounding: Father Coughlan ranting and raving from his Church of the Little Flower; crazy, mad Billy Sunday, whom Mother said wasn't fit for a Sunday; Rabbi Wise, whom Dad seemed to think was wise; Aimee Semple McPherson, back at her Foursquare Church after her convoluted kidnapping; Judge Rutherford of the Jehovah's Witnesses, booming over the airwaves about heaven for the lucky few. All the doomsters predicting Armageddon and the end of it all had Daniel rattled. The countdown was on and they had tabled their final offer. Out of fear and fatigue, I tuned out the doomsayers, the Japanese, knitting needles, ice picks and various utensils. Then after one murder too many, Mother stepped in to regulate our radio time. World-weary detectives and fired-up bible pounders were sent packing, leaving a middle ground of music and not much more. Dad would be reading in his easy chair while Mother sewed, both of them listening to classical music on the *Firestone Hour* as Bach and Chopin shilled for the tire industry. And then on Saturday afternoon, Milton J Cross would offer greetings from box 44 and prime everybody for an afternoon of high-brow bloodshed, intrigue and forbidden love. Over the years, many institutions and icons have come and gone, spirited away by the thief of time, but the Met operas are still performed on Saturday afternoon, and I still listen and love them.

THAT FIRST CHRISTMAS AWAY from the farm, when I thought life was so ideal, an unfamiliar chill seeped into the house. For the first time, Dad and Mother openly quarrelled in hushed, brisk tones. Dad suddenly took over the downstairs bedroom, and rather than eat with us, he dined by himself on tinned food. It was the Christmas holidays, and all the children, observing the chill, went quietly around the house, afraid to break the silence. Dad would work at his drafting table and get up to do the housework. When I asked Mother to ask Dad to eat with us, she replied testily that he wouldn't starve, he could eat where he liked. Then she asked me a question that stunned me, "Who do you like best, your Father or me?"

I couldn't answer. There was no answer. My mind froze and I said, "I don't know, I like you both the same." It wasn't the answer she wanted.

When an order came from the Trading Company along with the monthly bill, so did the reason for the quarrel. Mother flew into hysterics, and her feelings surfaced to a higher decibel. The bedroom door was left open and everything became clear. Mother went down the grocery list, "Who got all these turkeys? Max Isles! Everyone knows Max Isles has always had spare ribs for Christmas!"

And Dad, "This Christmas he had turkey." Dad sometimes went moose hunting with him and Ned McCormick.

"And who got geese? And how many bags of grain does it take to feed that family—a dozen bags of grain? A dozen turkeys, geese and ducks!? Those people could kill their own chickens for Christmas!" It went on and on. The bill was over two hundred dollars.

Mother was shocked. "And who got so much grain!? Mr. Harrow!?" Mother despised Mr. Harrow. She couldn't stand fools, and she hadn't worked hard to survive only to feed Mr. Harrow!

Dad reminded her that it was a Depression. Mother shot back with her raised voice, "We've lived in a depression since we came to Canada."

Dad replied, "And we have survived." Then he said, "Dearie it will all come back to us."

Mother bristled and snapped. "Come back to us? Come back to us? What do you mean, Mr. Marvin? That Max Isles or the Reades will pay you for the order you sent? Or that all those 5 dollar loans will be repaid next week, even though a year has gone by? And what about all the orders for brass work not paid for? Have you bothered to ask Dr. Campbell or Major Simon? Come back to us? I assure you Mr. Marvin, it never will. I have worked for nothing."

In the back of my mind, when I was very young, before I started school and before Uncle Peter arrived, I recall Mother dressed in her navy-blue serge suit, the one she was married in, with buttons down one side of the skirt down to her ankles, and her broad-brimmed navy-blue hat she wore for years. She had a suitcase and seemed to be going somewhere. Dad was restraining her and they were seriously whispering while I watched. Dad drew Mother into the house and shut the door. That time she didn't go anywhere, but afterwards, whenever she left for the village it was a trauma to see her go. The picture stayed pigeonholed in my mind, and I was much too young to question. Looking back, it might have been her one and only attempt to get off the farm.

When Mother mentioned the order for Mr. Reade, I realized that I had been at the Trading Company with Dad when it happened. Ralph Purdy was giving Dad a rundown of who was suffering and in dire need. Fred Reade was begging for payment of his dairy products, and Mr. Harrow was destitute; he couldn't buy feed for his animals, they were starving and winter was coming. Dad asked Ralph to send out an order of food and grain to Mr. Harrow, and under no circumstances give out his name; he didn't want the embarrassment of gratitude. While Dad and Ralph were talking, Lois Reade came into the Trading Company and handed Ralph a list for delivery, to be charged on their account. Ralph told Lois to tell her mother that he couldn't fill the order. Dad immediately said he couldn't do that to Fred Reade with 10 children, "Just put it on my bill." Ralph resisted, saying no, the Trading Company couldn't do any more of that. Dad repeated, "Just put it on my bill."

Ralph objected, holding up the list, "Look at this, Dan—peanut butter! They can go without peanut butter."

Dad refused to look at the list and finally made his point by smacking his cane on the counter and saying, "Send the list and peanut butter too, or I'll take my business to Mr. Marshall." All the while, Lois and I stood glaring at each other. I could never forgive her for what she did to Dorothea. I remember that exchange because I always asked for peanut butter, but Mother and Dad would never buy it. Whenever I could, I traded sandwiches with Alice Copeland, on occasion getting sliced bananas in the bargain. I loved it.

I don't know why Dad helped so much. In later years Mother would say, "Your father was too generous." Perhaps he felt like one of the lucky few, having a pension while others were so desperate. The situation troubled me and I thought about it a lot. I remembered the Greek sage who said that charity was at the root of all evil, and that for every good deed you suffer.

It was a terrible holiday; the first and only quarrel I witnessed. I looked over my Christmas presents and they didn't excite me any more: a doll pyjama bag for my bed; a jar of scented bath salts; a manicure set with orange sticks, emery boards, scissors and a buffer to pamper my fingers; and *Little Women*, which I started and put aside.

Mrs. Johnson had gone home for Christmas, and when she returned, her starched presence stabilized the household. Immediately, everything returned to normal. She saw that Mother rested, and sent me upstairs with her tea saying, "Och, yoor puir wee Mither is no well. She musney let the wee ones play on her bed." I was glad to see Mother resting and would bring her little things that she asked for. Then I would sit on the bed as she showed me how to file and buff my nails to perfection. When Dad brought her tray up, I knew the quarrel was over.

Dad's bad habits never improved. Bruce Reade had grown up in the house we lived in, and though we didn't know him, several times he knocked at the door asking for a few dollars, which he promised to pay back. I was glad Dad didn't refuse him, because he was so handsome and the girl he was going to marry was so utterly beautiful. They would walk past our house, arms around each other's waist, desperately poor and desperately in love. He never did repay Dad, who finally told him no more.

One day that spring, we were playing on the front lawn when Verna passed by with a two-quart pail of milk. She called to Daniel, asking if Mother might buy it—for the elevated price of ten cents a quart. I don't know how much Fred Reade charged, but I do know that we later bought milk for eight cents a quart. Once again, Mother and Dad were at loggerheads, but this time, Dad was in no mood for charity. Mother argued, "Peter can't order his clothes from Davies of London on 20 cents." I remember realizing how people had blind spots: Mother with Uncle Peter, Dad with his brass, Grandmother with Alec and Jim. I wondered where mine was, and how would I ever see it.

Mother prevailed, so Verna or Uncle Peter would pass by, leaving a pail of milk and retrieving the empty one with payment. It was a frigid transaction. When I played with Ian, the new baby, on his blanket on the front lawn, they never once stopped to cast a glance. We watched them go by in silence like the strangers they had become. Dad rankled every time. Sometimes Mother would only have a quarter or a fifty-cent piece and she would plead that she couldn't let anyone starve. Dad said it might do them some good. That spring, Uncle Peter had been burning garden waste and the fire got out of control, destroying his tool shed and a year's worth of wood. They were desperate, and in those days, 20 cents made a difference. A furtive levelling was occurring, and everyone was blaming Prime Minister Bennett. He did it—that word—Depression. Dad discussed it at the Trading Company with Ralph Purdy and Will Brinton and whoever else walked in the door. There was anger and worry. Whatever Depression meant, it was on everyone's tongue, the connotation unmistakable, but exactly what was it? Not understanding a thing, I would wander over to look into the huge barrels of pickled salt pork or herring. What could I understand at 11 years of age—a knock at the door, a shabby young man pleading for a nickel or a sandwich for the price of tidying the lawn, asking if we had an old pair of shoes or if he could sleep in the barn. Where were they going? What would they do?

Courtesy of David Marvin

I SUPPOSE YOU COULD SAY we had moved to the good side of the tracks now that our neighbours were the village elite. Mr. W.G. Clarke lived next door in his lovely home enclosed by a wide, columned verandah. The Cunninghams were resident, the Frasers visited often, and the MacIntyres lived in their bungalow high across the road (*sans paterfamilias*). I often wondered what the Clarke women thought when the backcountry Marvins landed right next door with their nine children. Sometimes I would swing on the hammock and watch as the upper crust played their endless games of tennis. The thud of tennis balls would punctuate summer afternoons as talk and laughter filtered through our windows. Then they would repair to the verandah where uniformed maids busily served tea and sandwiches. One day as I sat on the lawn, Mrs. MacIntyre approached the fence and told me it was very rude to stare and I should go inside. I went in and told Mrs. Johnson, who said, "Well, I never. Such a nairve." She could hardly contain herself at the impudence, especially since Mr. MacIntyre had to flee the country after the pulp mill scandal.

I used to wonder why Mother always walked past the Clarke women in silence. Though Mother's life was confined to the farm, people she didn't know often stopped her to chat, but never the Clarke daughters.

**Donald, far left. Jim and Douglas, left. Mary, right.
In the front yard of the Reade house, 1932.**

I just assumed that rich ladies didn't speak to women like Mother, an immigrant who lived on an ancient farm and drove to town in a horse and buggy, while they were chauffeured about in a car. But Mother was well-spoken, her manners impeccable and she looked city-bred. She was more stylish than they were, so the Clarke woman could not have labelled her a farm drudge. Mother was fussy about her appearance and never once went in to the village but that she was turned out in as much style as Dad could bring home from the city. He loved seeing her in knitted bouclé three-piece suits: skirt, vest and long jacket, and he was always buying her pretty clothes and materials: special homespun from St. John, beautiful silks and serges from Montreal. Mother was always pleased with his choices and would stitch her suits together like a tailoress. When we moved next door to the Clarkes, the old rules still applied; there was never any neighbourliness. Mother would pass by in silence, realizing that they preferred their society, and by not speaking to them, she made it clear that she preferred hers. Even if they had made an overture or if Mother had acceded, I doubt she would have suffered their bridge clubs and formal teas, their favoured world of posturing and their studied indolence on the verandah.

I also wondered about attitudes trickling downwards. It seemed strange, but for some reason I realized that the same rules applied to me. One spring day when the mayflowers were out, we were passing through the woods behind the Clarke home. I treasured that lovely flower and was eagerly plundering the vines when Clarke and Mary-Ellen Fraser strolled down. They were visiting from Jamaica, where their father was Canadian Trade Commissioner. I was excited to see them and said hello, while Daniel and Clarke sat down on a log to talk. I envied Mary-Ellen her pretty dresses, barrettes and nice shoes, and was all set to chat when she superciliously reminded me that I was trespassing on their property, I had no right to be there, and I shouldn't be picking their flowers. I said, "But these are woods," not thinking they belonged to anyone. With a sweep of her hand she said that all the woods were theirs. And they were. I was hurt that Mary-Ellen would speak to me so high-handedly. Being my mother's daughter, I ended the exchange by dealing a snub and sitting down with Daniel. Mary-Ellen had to have the all-important last word, so she then informed me that her mother said I was always playing with boys. Another humiliation. Her mother had looked me up and down and dismissed me with a cheap shot. Ignoring Dad's good advice, I answered her insult, "What is wrong with playing with my brothers, you're here with yours?" The friendship ended there. Mary-Ellen declared war by turning her back on me. I shrugged my shoulders and sniffed my stolen mayflowers as we ignored each other from opposite ends of the log. Meanwhile, the boys chatted away, unaware of the undercurrent. No doubt Mary-Ellen would embellish the incident for her mother, and the Clarke women would nitpick away at me when I wheeled the baby. I passed by in silence, feeling very much the intruder. The Marvins were too close for comfort. And if I needed reminding, the Fraser and MacIntyre children often had their friends over for an afternoon of tennis, Dorothy Potter and Alice Copleand among them, but never the Marvins. I would see them lounging on the verandah as the maids served lemonade and sandwiches. I still aspired to studied indolence and longed for an invitation. Rubbing shoulders with the rich seemed like the thing to do, but I soon discovered that my status, now measured side-by-side, did not measure up. Even Jimmy Campbell and John Jefferson outranked me. After enough daily reminders, I saw Mother's point and retreated to my books.

The Jeffersons never visited us again after pilfering Dad's house plans, but they did put in appearances next door to play tennis. Mrs. Johnson once reminded Mother that her high-class friends were next door, to which Mother replied that high-class could be very low-class. Another day, John Jefferson and John Sutherland (Dr. Lovett's grandson) were playing tennis with Clarke and Mary-Ellen when the ball flew over our fence. I was on the lawn with my brothers and sisters, and I wouldn't let them throw the ball back. John Jefferson came to the fence and told me to throw the ball to him. I looked at him and didn't say a word. He called me stupid and started to jump over the picket fence, so I shouted as loud as I could, "Don't you dare jump into my mother's flower garden." If he wanted the ball, he would have to walk up to the road where I would give it to him. At the road, I was just waiting for him to put a foot on our lawn, and I told him if he wanted his ball he would have to ask politely. He was rude like his parents, and I still resented their treatment of Mother and Dad, so before he could call me stupid again, I got there first, "You're stupid, John Jefferson," for all the good it did me.

One cold, drizzly day shortly after we moved in, I was sitting at my bedroom window when I looked out through the stripped branches of the beech tree and saw a strange, solemn procession coming up the road. Black horses pulled a black carriage, while behind, the village Masons marched in formation wearing their top hats and white aprons. When the carriage turned in to the Clarke home, I recognized the village hearse and realized that Mr. W.G. Clarke had passed away. The news of his illness had spread through the village like an omen, as if the village itself had received a mortal blow. When the retinue went inside, I called down to Mother and Dad, neither of whom knew that Mr. Clarke had died. I sat watching and waiting, glued to the window with my elbows on the sill. I liked Mr. Clarke with his old-world charm, the handshakes and how-do-you-do's. Even though the firm became one of the wealthiest in the province, he never outgrew the village, chatting at the pot-bellied stove, vying with the other apple farmers at the fall fair. Often on our way to school, we would meet him coming out the door, and he would join us on his way to work, walking along like one of the gang.

In a little while, the mourners carried the casket out, and the carriage turned on to the Chute Road with the Masons slowly following, down the road towards Mount Hope. Several months later, Mr. W.W. Clarke died, bringing an end to the great firm of Clarke Brothers, begun so many years ago by two boys going fishing. The village of Bear River had served its time during the wooden ship building era and served it very well. The Clarke brothers had served just as well. Lesser tycoons came and went, leaving their names on roads and fields, but the wealthy Clarkes still remain geographically nameless. What is left? The orchards, lumber mill, pulp mill, packet, and schooners are all gone. Top verandahs of the lovely Clarke homes have been removed, marring their one-time elegance, though doors remain to be carelessly walked through into open space. Even that once-great emporium, the Bear River Trading Company, where childish dreams could be fulfilled, lost its name before degenerating into a shabby modern makeover. The pinions beneath the hindquarters are still anchored in the mud flats, the tides flow in and out twice a day, and most is washed away and forgotten. If the Clarke brothers did leave a statement, then it stands along the Chute Road in all the houses for their many hired hands; spacious homes, prettily painted with verandahs and tasteful trim. They are all that is left; testimonials to what seems like a lost civilization, not quite the toppled columns along the ancient roadways of Palmyra, but milestones in the passing of an era just the same.

Mount Hope, 2011

After the turmoil of fall and winter, spring arrived peacefully, infused with the delicate, tangy scent of apple blossoms from Mr. Clarke's orchards behind our house. Lilacs enclosed our front porch, clematis shaded the windows, and orange blossom crowded all around. Our lives took on an unusual and comforting calm that seemed to be part of the house. Almost in a blink, the burdens of the farm slipped away. No more never-ending chores. No more early morning to late evening care of the animals. No more aching backs and sore knees from constantly working the gardens. No more filth. Mother never had to milk another cow, shovel another stall, or pick another vegetable. She happily puttered in her flower garden. No more separating milk or churning butter; we had them delivered to the front door every morning without consideration of the labour entailed. I was in heaven having all the time I wanted to read or work on my scrapbooks in the downstairs bedroom. I would sit at the window seat clipping and pasting, the air perfumed by the heady scent of lilacs simmering in the sun.

That first summer in the Reade house is still sparkling clear. The boys spent hours on the ham radio Dad bought for them, or whole days roaming through the woods. Mother and Dad would be relaxing in the den, listening to the radio, Mother on the couch, constantly knitting, Dad reading in his Wedgwood blue easy chair, which he called 'colour blind brown.' From my window seat, I would hear them discussing books or the news on the radio, Mother deploring the state of humanity, Dad never disagreeing. In the evening, they would go out for casual strolls in the village. I remember Mother running in to the pantry, dipping her fingers in the flour barrel and dabbing her nose to take the shine off, then asking me, "Is that better?" Out she went, smiling and happy. Later, they would return in a taxi with boxes of ice cream from Mr. Darres'. It was all so leisurely. The normalcy bordered on luxury. At night as I lay in bed, the dewy air held the scent of apple blossom in a fragrant mist, mingling with orange blossom and clematis, straying in through my bedroom window like an intoxicating potion. I would get up and sit with my arms on the window sill, looking out into the night stillness and breathing deeply, trying never to forget something so evanescent.

Several times during that wonderful summer, Dad did something with the boys that he never had time for on the farm: he took them fishing. The boys were thrilled, even more so when Dad outfitted them at the Trading Company with their first fishing rods. On one trip, Dad brought along Jimmy Campbell to toughen him up, a hopeless concept that the boys objected to. Jimmy was Dr. Campbell's only child and an incurable thumb-sucker, evidenced by his distressing buck teeth. His mother hesitated about releasing little Jimmy into the wilds, but Dad persuaded her by hazarding a guess that Jimmy was, in fact, a born woodsman. On the day, they collected him in the taxi for the several-mile drive to a well-known stream. The boys threw off their sneakers, threw in their lines, and snapped the little trout on to the bank, smartly rapping their heads as they wiggled their last. This was a rude awakening for Jimmy. He watched as the boys, in a blood-thirsty way, cut up worms with sharp rocks and speared them onto hooks. He was traumatized by such rough stuff and wanted to go home. Dad told him no; the taxi wouldn't be back until the end of the day. To compound his woe, there were bugs and mosquitoes. The boys laughed that the cleaning of the fish almost put Jimmy in a coma. At lunchtime, Dad unpacked the frying pan, but when the fish were ready, Jimmy wouldn't nibble. Instead, he uncovered his own specially prepared picnic hamper, replete with linen napkins. Dad shook his head in dismay. Mrs. Campbell had sent Jimmy into the woods with devilled eggs, tiny tea sandwiches, chocolate cake and lemonade. Dad couldn't believe it. The next time they went, Dad sounded out Jimmy, who surprised everyone by pulling his thumb out of his mouth and eagerly accepting. Dad asked Mrs. Campbell to forget about the devilled eggs, just let him come and fry his own fish. The boys coached him, and Jimmy proved to be a quick study after all, later bragging to his parents about surgically slicing off a few heads.

Whenever Dad went away, he always came back with small gifts for everyone, and that summer when he returned from a week at Camp Hill, he gave me the most treasured possession of my young years. I can still see Daniel clutching his new football as Dad leaned towards me, playfully smiling as he hid something behind his back. He then presented me with a brand new violin. I was ecstatic. It was beautifully varnished, cushioned in a lightweight case lined with pearl-grey velvet. The small compartments held a mute, tuner, resin, and extra strings. Dad then gave me a large book filled with scores by Massenet, Schumann, Faure, Saint-Saens, all the pieces I knew and loved. Everything about the violin was perfect: the weight, the feel, the lovely tone, and it was mine, all mine. Daniel could no longer interrupt my practice by snatching away Grandmother's rasping antique. I practiced in peace, though the rest of the house suffered for my art. Soon, Daniel decided that I owed him compensation for sharing his violin. In payment, he began to use mine, but if I had learned anything during my years of doll desecration, it was that property must be defended. I showed Mother the resin he hadn't wipe off and the bow he hadn't loosened. Mother forbad Daniel from touching my violin without my permission, which I never gave because I never let it out of my hands. I knew I didn't have Daniel's talent, and I didn't mind when Mother called for me to close the door, but Dad encouraged me, and that was enough. I scraped away with a vengeance, as if I were destined for the world stage. I was convinced that my musical journey had just begun. Yehudi Menuhin and Ruggiero Ricci, both my age, were playing the concert halls of Europe. I would meet them along the way.

One day, Mr. Henderson, the pastor for the Jehovah's Witnesses (they were called something else at the time) was talking to Dad about hard times and mentioned that he couldn't afford the drive to Halifax for an important church meeting. Dad offered to pay for the gas if he could bring Daniel and me along, not to sit in with the Jehovah's Witnesses, but to see a movie.

That day, Mr. Henderson brought along his daughter, Marian, who seemed suddenly, exotically romantic, since she was going to marry one of the players on the Bear River baseball team. I had seen her sitting high on the steep hill behind Oakdene cheering on her boyfriend as he stepped up to the plate. She had the engagement ring on her finger and said they would be moving away to a home of their own. She was breathless with love and wanted to get married right away. It seemed like the right thing to do, don't waste a minute. Geraldine Purdy, Ralph Purdy's only pampered child, who had naturally curly hair and a slight lisp and whom everyone said was so cute as she walked the village in palazzo pyjamas, the latest style, married the Trading Company delivery boy without preamble. Neither the delivery boy nor the romantic Geraldine were seen again. It was excitement non-pareil the way love birds flew off together to see the world. I was captivated by Marian's engagement ring, and for the entire trip we chatted about love, marriage and a home fitted out for domestic bliss. At one point, Marian mentioned a nursery, and I said 'oh no, it was either bliss or babies but not both.' That much I knew.

In Halifax, Mr. Henderson let us off at the gaping columned entrance to train station. Next door stood the palatial Nova Scotian hotel, and behind it were docked several ocean liners. Daniel went wild. Dad had to chase him down before steering us into the hotel. The lobby was spectacular, with soaring marble columns and regal touches in brass and red velvet. Again, Dad had to contain Daniel as he led us in to a cafe for a sandwich. We sat on twirling stools and were unduly thrilled by the machinations of the busy lunch counter. Daniel was awed by the aluminum accoutrements and the large steel urns dispensing coffee at the turn of a spigot. He said it was like *Buck Rogers and the 20th Century*. We were bumpkins, alright. After our meal, Dad walked us down Barrington Street to the Capitol theatre, its marquee glittering in welcome. Back then, the glitter seemed appropriate to the movies. I sat in cushioned, velvety comfort and stared in awe at the huge screen, window to my dream world.

The Nova Scotian and train station in front of Pier 21, 'Gateway to Canada'

And what a revelation when the movie began and the actors not only talked out loud, but cutlery clinked, champagne corks popped, and violins quivered. No more rushing to read paragraphs of jittery text as old-timers mumbled and stumbled (What did that one say?) or misread entirely (*I want you, dear*, not *I want you dead*). Lively commentary often bounced around the room during silent films: 'she's in trouble now,' 'look out!' 'somebody save her!' and a wilting scream. At the talkies, the audience simmered down, and actors dropped the broad pantomime for whispers and sighs. The movie that day was *Merely Mary Ann* with Janet Gaynor and Charles Farrell. It was my kind of show. I could have watched it ten times over, and I could have been Mary Ann for the rest of my life. Oh! that last scene when she went up the back stairs holding Charles' shoes to her bosom and put them down at his bedroom door. The handsome scion opened the door, and oh my goodness, he took her in his arms and kissed her! I knew then all I needed to know about romance; it set me up for life. What a marvellous way to marry quickly, be a maid like Mary Ann. Later, I saw *The Perils of Pauline* and discovered another good way to be rescued—get tied up on railway tracks. It was a day of romantic crumbs, stowed in abeyance for my future, which I hoped wouldn't be too far away. After all the excitement of the day, on the long car trip home it had to happen—I was car sick. Poor Mr. Henderson and his frequent stops. I sat in disgrace by the open window and crawled up to bed, love sick.

The cafe of the Nova Scotian hotel

In all the years I knew the Simons, I never once suspected them of being parents. I had assumed they were childless because they just seemed the type. They were always so stern with us and ignored children except to briskly acknowledge our how-do-you-do's. Then one day towards the end of school, their grandchildren, Lawrence and Elizabeth, arrived from the States and joined our class. Elizabeth, a year younger than me, was shy and lonely, she didn't like Bear River, and she desperately wanted to go home to her mother. When we walked home from school, she would ask if I could visit to play dolls with her because Amanda forbad her from playing with the Reade children across the road. I had been doll-less for years, so I eagerly accepted. But Amanda hedged. Only after much consideration did I meet with her approval, squeaking in the door by the skin of my teeth. After removing my shoes, I padded across those polished hardwood floors and into the parlor. Elizabeth ended her piano practice and Amanda wiped the keys, closed the piano and cleaned residual fingerprints. I thought it might be nice to see Elizabeth's room, but instead we sat down in the parlor and started dressing and undressing her huge supply of paper dolls. Amanda sat on the couch, eyeing us as she knitted. The Major sat nearby in the sun porch, smoking his pipe and staring at the trees. Before long, Amanda had seen enough. She put down her knitting and hustled me out the door, closing it with a definitive thud before I could turn and say thank you. I was glad to be sent home early. Soon, Elizabeth went home as well, leaving her brother to lead a life of discipline with those two exacting people.

Lawrence was Daniel's age, a polite boy who loved to come in and join the boys as they worked the ham radio. He seemed like a model child, and Dad gave him open invitation to visit any time. Then one day while Dad sat at his drafting table and I read on the couch, we heard a man shouting at the top of his lungs and a boy crying loudly. Dad looked out the window and was appalled. Advancing past our house was Major Simon, his face red and livid as he lashed poor Lawrence with a heavy, knotted rope, driving him on like a terrified animal. Dad rushed out to confront the Major, pleading with him, "Surely, you can reason with the boy."

I watched from the doorway as the Major shouted back, "Damn you, Marvin, mind your own business!"

Dad said, "Major, how can you do that to a child? Nothing he did can be so serious as to be punished like that?"

There were more words, and then the Major shouted louder than ever, "If I want advice, Marvin, I'll take it from someone older than myself!"

In a flick of an eye Dad grabbed the rope from the Major's fist. The Major's ruddy face almost exploded as Dad raised his voice, "You won't hit that child again."

It was terrible to hear all the yelling. Lawrence stood off to the side crying in pain and shame. He was such a nice boy and I felt so sorry for him. It was a horrible cruelty, done in such a public way. Mercifully, Lawrence was shipped back to his parents, and that was the end of our friendship with the Simons. From that time on, the Major and Amanda passed by wordlessly, as if they never knew us. The only sound was Amanda's gargling tremolo or the tick, tick, tick of the Major's swagger stick against his leather puttees. One day the Major stomped past us, looking straight ahead as he refused to acknowledge Dad's greeting. Mother said, "Good riddance to bad rubbish. I never could stand the pair of them."

That was the end of Mother and Dad's friends in Bear River. There were no more picnics or busy parlors. Our excitement over the arrival of guests was replaced by interests and hobbies. Once or twice Mother saw Mrs. McCormick passing by and rushed out to chat on the sidewalk. The McCormicks had been injured that winter when their horse slipped and fell on the ice, throwing them from their sleigh.

Though our old friends were gone, Mrs. Johnson filled the void with all of her affection and care, and our lives began to revolve around her. She was as steady as the North Star. Even Mother seemed to cling. Tinglers were gone, left behind with the other farm implements, but we got away with nothing. For all her loving warmth, her voice had thorns and prickles in it. Her Scottish burr made an order an imperative. She was as unbending in decorum as Grandmother, decorum being patterned in those days, just escaping Victorianism, cut out and pasted in our minds. Imperceptibly, she became head of the household, giving Mother her first rest from babies and toddlers. The household ran like clockwork. No child doubted Mrs. Johnson's authority, and when the younger ones went to her with their cuts and complaints, the transition was complete.

One day Mrs. Alice Rice from Annapolis Royal, who had visited the farm once or twice, interrupted her tennis game next door to have tea and a chat with Mother. She was an elegant lady, a member of the Catholic Women's League, a true social worker. I tuned my ear to hear of the good deeds her parish of St. Thomas was performing at the little Catholic outpost on Indian Hill. They were teaching catechism, donating clothing and pointing the way to heaven. Best of all, Rosie Muise had stopped drinking, poor thing. Sadly, firewater remained the eternal flame on Indian Hill. But Mrs. Rice was encouraged by increments, much like the early Jesuits, who converted the natives not wholly into Christianity, but at least out of scalping. I wanted to hear more, but Mother dismissed me.

After the visit, Mother informed me that Mrs. Rice was, in fact, my godmother–that strange connotation, 'godmother,' another puzzling side to religion. Alice Copeland said her godparents gave her presents on her birthday; that's what they were there for. I always wanted a godmother and now it turned out I had one all along. Mother then added that my long-lost godmother had a special treat for me: on Sunday she would be stopping by with my godfather, her bachelor brother, Mr. Jack Flynn, and they would be taking me to mass at St. Anne's on Indian Hill. Religion had begun to nibble. I hesitated over giving up my Sunday morning, but Alice Copeland went every week, so I assumed that was the price we godchildren had to pay. Besides, I had never been to church; it might be fun. The auspices bode well when Mother made me a yellow dress and bought me a hat and gloves at the Trading Company, but then I learned that I had to wear my hat in church because we women lacked a soul, among other things. Well that was just too bad for us, but even then I knew we more than made up for it. Besides, any old excuse to dress up will do. But I would not be looking to the church for fashion tips; they were a little too quick to turn a good thing bad. So that Sunday after a twirl for approval from Dad, I stepped out the door feeling quite à la mode, an adequate proxy for the absentee Marvins, who were all busy that day.

Mr. Flynn politely held the car door for me as I scrambled onto the back seat. We mounted a steep hill and parked on a lookout with Bear River spread out below in a small-town vignette. Up a set of stairs, we crested a hill, on top of which stood the little church, a plain white clapboard building no bigger than a house, posed on its lofty perch. Faith, pure and simple would send these parishioners skyward. Personally, I was hoping for something a little more exalted, at least a steeple and some stained glass. I suspected I would need all the frills to bolster my belief.

We stood off to the side while Mrs. Rice nodded and exchanged pleasantries with the Indians as they quietly and respectfully filed into the church. Mr. Flynn then asked me to hold out my hand, and what did he do? He gave me a nickel—a wonderful start! But then on the next breath, he said I had to put it in the collection plate. Not really!! I had never given money away in my life. Once, I lost a penny and cried for days. A nickel was a lot of money to just throw away. Torn between God and mammon, deep into my first crisis of faith, I stepped into my first church. I was struck by the sterile white interior: the walls, the half-dozen pews on either side, everything crisply white and unadorned, like heaven's anteroom. We sat in the front pew, and when I looked around, the church was full of Indians, and we, the only palefaces. Mrs. Rice briefed me on the several artefacts adorning the church: the votive light, burning like a red eye; the statue of the Blessed Virgin, no explanation given; the exposed, bleeding heart of Jesus, which really wasn't necessary. Fine linen edged with gold draped over the altar, on top of which sat strange little cupboards, a book, napkins, a jug, an ornate cup, and candles—all set for a nice meal.

The formalities began when a side door opened and a man appeared— a man in a long linen dress trimmed with lace, his waist cinched with a tasselled rope. I didn't like men in kilts, and I certainly didn't like them in something that looked like Mother's nightdress. Mrs. Rice whispered that it was Father Mackay. I nodded. The same Father Mackay from the great baptismal skirmish. Mother still bristled at the thought of him gulping his tea and hotfooting it up McCormick's hill. So this was our Lord's henchman, diverting heathen to heaven. He strode up to the altar looking very holy, carrying knick-knacks that he began placing thusly. No good morning, no nothing. He then started to mumble and mime, clasp and unclasp his hands and perform other movements of minor theatrics: walking back and forth, hands up, hands down, chanting to himself a half-sung song, half forgotten. All the while, everyone seemed to know what they were doing: standing up, kneeling, bowing their heads on cue, and responding in a strange language that I thought was Gaelic. He took a little drink on the side, washed his hands, and only then did he realize he had an audience. He delivered a short sermon; finally a word of English. It was something I recognized from our Bible story days telling the Indians to be good children of God. It didn't apply to me. I watched Father Mackay's solo performance and it clarified nothing. Bells rang and he roamed about working his priestcraft, motioning with his hands and twirling around. I was bewildered. At one point, Mrs. Rice explained that Father Mackay was drinking the blood of Christ. Good Lord No!! I reluctantly dropped my hard-earned nickel into the basket, Father Mackay gathered up his curios and was gone in a flash, again. 'Did I like my first mass?' asked Mrs. Rice. I didn't know; it was total confusion. There was also the discomfort of being with strangers, and I don't recall having a thing to say except thank you. When I got out of the car, Mr. Flynn offered me his hand, and Mrs. Rice reminded me in her gentle way to say my prayers. We Marvins never prayed. The car sped off in a poof of dust and that was the last I saw of my once-upon-a-time godparents. No presents for me. Alice Copeland was Anglican, so I had to conclude that godparents in the high church of England were a little more forthcoming. For 11-year-old godchildren, belief in presents was a point of doctrine. And with that, I went back to being an orphan in the spiritual world. It was a one-day-only offer, and since my godparents abandoned me, I forgot about them, until now.

Not long after that eye-opener, I was out walking Ian in the pram when I ran into Evelyn Reade. Mrs. Johnson often made me take Ian or my younger brothers out for a walk, always with the warning, "And don't come back in five minutes." I would pace like a snail up to Fred Reade's and down to the River View Lodge, back and forth and then home at last. I often met Evelyn doing the same thing and would eagerly join her. She would be wheeling the latest baby and reading movie magazines sent by her sister Ethel, who had gone to the States to live with relatives and become a hairdresser. We would slowly walk along discussing movie stars and wondering who we liked best. One day Evelyn asked me to come along with her to the BYPU (Baptist Young Peoples Union). Grandmother had said some nasty things about Baptists, so I was prepared for more quirks and cabals, but instead, there were squeals of glee as we played musical chairs and received prizes for low-grade endeavours, happily doled out by Rev. McLeod. This was my kind of religion. I could have become a Baptist on the spot since Catholicism had so thoroughly disillusioned me. They had the right idea: scream and laugh and play games and gobble sandwiches with lemonade and go home sucking a lollipop. Why shouldn't religion feel better than a stranglehold?

A few weeks later on a peaceful Saturday afternoon, I was reading in the den with Dad, Mother was resting upstairs in bed, Mrs. Johnson had the young ones in the back verandah, and the boys had fled to the woods. There was a knock at the door, and I opened it to a rough-looking stranger. I thought he was a woodsman in his black and red check lumber jacket, heavy boots, and ruddy, sweaty face, not to mention a telling odour not found in the lilies of the field. His car was parked shy of the ditch at a cant angle, just missing Mother's begonias. He asked to see my parents, so I, in my formality, said, "Yes, and who may I say is calling?" He said, "Father Mackay." It didn't seem possible. Gone was the prissy austerity of his performance at the altar, all decked out in linen and lace, ready to sprout wings. He seemed to be in a very jovial mood and remarked that I was growing up to be quite a young lady. I seized up. Dad came to the door and greeted him in his pleasant, southern way. Father Mackay explained that he had been 'up on the hill' cleaning and polishing, putting St. Anne's in order for mass the next day. Dad loved visitors, even unsteady ones, so he ushered Father Mackay into the den while I ran upstairs to tell Mother about our distinguished guest. Mother put down her book and said, "Oh, is that so?" sputtering a lot of 'indeeds', 'well, I nevers', and "he needn't have bothered after all these years, treating us like the lost tribe." She made motions to dress, and I ran down to help Mrs. Johnson in the kitchen. Then, just as the tea and scones were ready, Mother burst into the kitchen, "Finally, he can spare a moment and he shows up drunk. And dressed like that, not even a clean shirt!" Mrs. Johnson rushed in to serve the tea and returned tut-tutting and mumbling the horrors of a good woman, "Och noo, the very nairve. And he, a man of the cloth. That man is sorely in need of a cuppa tea, right enough." Mother took the baby and returned to bed up the back stairs, saying that Dad had better get rid of him quickly. Dad wouldn't dream of it. He loved to chat, and it didn't matter to him whether Father Mackay was sober or sloshed. Considering Dad's drunken, bible-pounding relatives, the visit must have seemed like a breeze from the past. Father Mackay's loud voice and booming laughter resounded throughout the house, so I perked up my ears. He was admiring Dad's brass work and blurted out, "Marvin, you son of a gun. Maybe you could make something for my church?" Dad said he had once made a baptismal font, but he was emphatic, his brass making days were over. Then they settled into a long discussion about Father Mackay's opus, *The Rape and the Lock*. Grandmother and the aunts had discussed the book at length, but again I understood nothing and lost interest.

When I took Mother's tea up to her, she was fuming, "He's staying a little longer than the last time. It's just as well I baptized the children myself." Finally, Mother had enough and went downstairs to deliver the bum's rush. Father Mackay made another hasty exit, and we stood out front as he got into his car waving a jolly goodbye. Fortified by tea and scones, he narrowly avoided tipping into the ditch and sped off towards Annapolis Royal. Mother was disgusted. "Don't let that man into my house again. The nerve of him showing his nose around here."

Dad was mollifying, saying, "Ah believe he slipped."

Mother was just gearing up, "I'll not have riffraff like that showing up at my door."

Dad pleaded, "Dearie, Dearie, don't upset yourself."

But then she turned on him, "It's just as well you didn't give any more of my brass work away. Every bit of brass in this house is mine, you gave it to me and don't you forget it. It's a funny thing him showing up like that and wanting something for his church." Off she went upstairs, "Him and his *Rape and the Lock*. It doesn't sound very holy to me."

For good measure, Mother harped upon a recent theme by calling down the stairs, "And don't forget, Mr. Marvin, the same goes for Mrs. Campbell. I've worked harder for my brass than she ever did."

That summer, the Campbells went on holiday and left their home open for workmen to renovate. When they returned, every piece of brass work had been stolen. Mrs. Campbell had ordered the largest pieces, and her requests were a continuing source of irritation to Mother, who knew she had no intention of paying. After their loss, Mrs. Campbell was devastated and began angling about to have her brass replaced. Knowing Dad's bad habits, Mother warned him in no uncertain terms. Dad got the message and only gave away one last piece several years later.[1]

When the boys returned, I told Daniel all about Father Mackay's visit, and this revived a sort of sleeping dog from the epic baptismal episode. Daniel zeroed in on the title of Father Mackay's book and the one word he didn't understand: rape. Dad was reading in the parlor, so we went in and Daniel asked him what rape was. Dad didn't miss a beat and said what he always did when children found turning the pages of a dictionary too difficult, "Son, yew have a perfectly good dictionary in the den." Daniel and I flipped through the pages of a huge Webster's leaning on top of a table. We read all the explanations, but nothing made sense. Daniel thought it had something to do with war, but I, being a farmer's daughter, thought it was a type of turnip, the only recognizable definition. We were always told to do our best looking up words and if we didn't understand, to come back for an explanation, which we did. Dad told Daniel to read more carefully. We read and reread, and finally Daniel told Dad that it had something to do with turnips. Dad sat silent. He might have been re-evaluating his son and heir's genius. Daniel, always curious and argumentative, asked why would a priest write a book about turnips and a lock? Dad said, "Well, Sweetheart, yew can write about anything yew want." He asked Dad if Father Mackay's book was a good one, and Dad said he didn't think so. That was good enough for Daniel, who went upstairs to the ham radio. I wasn't satisfied. I loved mashed turnips, but a book written by a priest, even an occasionally drunk one, about a turnip and a door lock seemed silly. Back I went to Dad, who stopped the continual massaging of his forehead, looked up from his book, and said sharply that it was a book for grown-ups. That didn't quite settle the issue, so I went upstairs and asked Mother about the word in question, who looked up from her book and said, "What's all this?" I said I wanted to know about Father Mackay's book, so she outflanked me with a reprimand for listening in on grown-ups' conversations. And that closed the book on Father Mackay.

1 A cigar box given to the Hon. J.L. Ilsley, Minister of Finance

Mother with Ian

One day I was alone in the den reading when a car came speeding down the road and skidded to a stop in front of our house. Dr. Campbell jumped out, burst in the front door and ran straight up the stairs, where Dad and Mrs. Johnson ushered him into Mother's bedroom. Immediately, Mrs. Johnson came down and shuffled everyone outside, telling us to not come in until called. We stood in the front yard, alarmed and confused, thinking the worst, but unsure of what the worst could be. In a little while, Mrs. Johnson motioned us in, saying, "Whist the noo. Yoo musney make any noise." That afternoon, Ian Alexander Marvin, Mother's tenth child, unexpectedly came into our lives to stay for a few short months. We crowded around Mother's bed as she held him, all freshly pink and snugly wrapped in a lacy shawl. Ian was a beautiful baby, doted on by every member of the family. We would hang over his crib as he slept, wreathed in a cloud of angora, mouthing half-formed words and twitching his little fingers. The boys took turns holding him, and we all talked silly baby talk, especially Dad. He no longer had to hastily divide his attentions between each of us before rushing out to the chores of the farm. Mother took possession of Ian completely, as she never could have done on the farm. She became a different person that summer, more relaxed than she had ever been. A photograph Dad took shows her holding Ian, relaxed, young and happy. Even Dr. Campbell took a personal interest, stopping by regularly to bounce him on his knee. The birth had been difficult, so Ian's middle name was a courtesy to Dr. Campbell. Perhaps because of everyone's attentions, I took a second look at babies and didn't seem to mind them after all. Ian was a sunny baby, like David, but his happy, expansive nature extended in all directions. He was an early crawler, never content to just sit still, anxious to get on with things. The boys actively encouraged him and treated him like the newest member of the team as they played games and crawled about with him. When I played with Ian on a blanket out on the lawn, tourists passing by from the River View Lodge would stop to admire him and say how beautiful he was, that he was the most beautiful baby they had ever seen. I would hold him up with pride as Ian happily gurgled. When I told Mother what they had said, she said something strange: she wished they wouldn't say things like that, because it made her think that he was too beautiful to live.

One day, we were playing on the lawn when Dorothy Potter walked by on her way to Mary-Ellen Fraser's birthday party. I wished I could have been invited, but I saw very plainly that even though I lived next door to the Clarke's, their air was more rarefied—and I, gasping for breath. Needing to nurse my rancour with the rich, I dashed to the screened-in back porch where I could spy with sulphur in my soul. I watched the maid serve sandwiches and lemonade on the verandah, and when the candles on the cake were lit, I heard the laughter, indicating that Mary Ellen had blown them all out and would be married in a year. After the party, I sidled up to Dorothy on her way home, hating to hear the happy details.

Having developed the mind of a snob in those young years, I often wondered about the rich and even managed to look down my nose and sneer at them. But just when I had come to several conclusions, solid cement, things changed, and to show my fickle nature, I told myself that the rich were just like you and even me. Those last few weeks of the last summer in the Reade house were a vindication of sorts. I longed for status, and by summer's end, the upstart Marvins had risen high enough to become acceptable, and that was good enough for me. It was as if we joined the ranks of the 400.

Another day, Dad chased everyone out of the house to play on the front lawn and get the fog out of our brains, as he put it. Lorna, Joan, and I lay on the grass while the toddlers rolled about and the boys raced back and forth, from the stump of the recently cut oak on our front lawn to the fence on the back lawn, jumping over us along the way. Clarke and Mary Ellen Fraser saw us and strolled over, asking if they could visit. Daniel and Jim gregariously invited them over, and we all sat on the lawn by the tree stump getting reacquainted. They seemed so sophisticated, easily answering probing questions, thrown like darts. Lorna wanted to know where was Jamaica, why was it so hot, what about Christmas? What surprised me was how conversational my brothers and sisters were while I sat there tongue-tied. The talk turned to sports, particularly cricket, which they played in Jamaica. The boys were desperate to play baseball, and since cricket sounded close enough, Clark and Mary Ellen ran home to get their equipment. We rushed about preparing the field, scooping up toys and toddlers.

With the wicket in place, Daniel pitched the first ball, which Clarke smacked soundly. The ball arced toward the house and crashed through our den window, where it rolled past Dad before bouncing into a wall. We froze, waiting in silence. Clarke and Mary Ellen were horrified, but the boys suppressed sniggers, knowing that Dad would show his dismay in his usual way, shaking his head, eating his shirt, etc. He ambled around the corner of the house holding the ball and said, "Do yew know what yew littah bounders just did? Yew frightened ten years growth out of yewr old dad." The boys laughed and Clarke apologized, insisting he would have to tell his aunts. We were disappointed that the game was over, only just begun. Dad said it was just a window, and inquired about their parents. We were disappointed again to learn that they were leaving soon for Australia, where their father would be Canadian Trade Commissioner.

Several days later, Mrs. Fraser invited Daniel and me to spend the day deep sea fishing in the Bay of Fundy. I was still recuperating from my sailing debacle and my two near-drownings, but I had one compelling reason for going along: not because of John Sutherland or Jimmy Campbell, and certainly not because of John Jefferson, but secretly because of Clarke Fraser: darkly handsome with blue eyes and curly hair, intelligent and so polite, oh my! Early that sunny morning, I stepped onto Captain Seamone's powerboat an emotional wreck, convinced that my fate held more than fish. Mary-Ellen sat with the boys, but I was too shy to insert myself into the group. I couldn't sit with Mrs. MacIntyre, Mrs. Lovett, and Mrs. Campbell, so I chose a spot with plenty to hold on to, a railing nearby and coils of rope just in case. With my safety all but assured, I assumed my natural, ladylike composure and settled in to enjoy my first ride in a motorboat. We roared down the river, past the farm and Kniffen's Hollow. At Victoria Bridge, Capt. Seamone pointed out an old Micmac fishing camp, where they would set up for the summer and hunt porpoise. Several times on the farm, we saw them quietly canoeing past on their annual migration, done since the beginning of time, but now a fading relic. Strangely, those few canoes formed the totality of Bear River's fishing fleet. I don't know why, but while every village in Nova Scotia had fishing schooners and fishermen, Bear River had none. Digby, just down the road, had a huge fleet, and fish processing kept the whole town freshly scented.

In Bear River, people went into the backwoods for trout, or out onto the Bay for cod, but fishing was a sport, not a job. After motoring across the Basin and past the sheer slopes of Digby Gut, Captain Seamone decided that before fishing, we should stop for sandwiches on the beach. We scrambled ashore and were met by a strange sight: a swordfish that had lanced its snout through the bow of a fishing boat. It had rested on the shore for years as an exhibit, the flesh long gone, but the snout still razor sharp. The Captain then informed us that two men in a fishing boat just like ours had recently caught the largest Great White shark ever, just over there at White Head Island, but not before it had taken a bite out of their boat.[2] And not only that, sharks had even been seen in the Bear River! Goodness gracious me! My fear of water now ran deep and wide.

After lunch, we motored out to White Head Island, where we dropped anchor to fish the same waters as the Great White, the boat bobbing up and down like a sitting duck. The boys excitedly skewered tidbits of fish on their hooks and dropped their lines. I hung my head over the side of the boat, stared at the dark, rippling water and waited for the inevitable, which happened straight away. One of the ladies came over and held my head and sympathetically said I was a poor thing. She suggested that I might feel better if I tried fishing because it was an awful lot of fun and the Bay was teeming. No sooner were the boys dropping their lines in than they were pulling them out with a cod or haddock flipping acrobatically. I baited my hook and dropped my line over the edge of the boat, where it hung until we turned for home. I was the only one who didn't catch the merest of fish. John Jefferson revealed this fact to be nothing less than a character flaw. He was landing cod and expertly thwacking them over the head with a stick just like I wanted to thwack him.

Next was the customary stop at Bear Island, where the ladies would turn the day's catch into a delicious fish chowder. While they cleaned and chopped the fish, we explored the small island and gathered driftwood for the fire. But just as the chowder was ready and the ladies were calling for us, a sudden breeze blew in, followed by a squall that broke in a fury. Everyone scrambled to load the boat as the rain poured down in sheets, thoroughly soaking us. The day culminated in a terrifying run up the river.

2 1930, 37 feet, but it was unverified, so the claim is doubtful.

We bounced along lashed by torrents of rain and battered by ferocious crashes of thunder and lightning. I cringed in the bow waiting for the bayonet thrust of a swordfish. Mercifully, we docked without incident and I staggered onto the wharf somewhat the wiser after yet another disastrous day of fun. I said my thank you's and dragged myself home to bed, vowing to establish a few guidelines to love. Never again would I chase my heart's desire. They would have to come to me, and I would be on dry land. Australia was out.

Shortly after the fishing trip, the Clarke ladies invited Daniel, Jim and me to accompany them and the other boys for an afternoon at Deep Brook, where we would swim and picnic before observing the solar eclipse.[3] As we motored along, the adults kept up a steady flow of conversation about the miracle we were about to witness. Mrs. Campbell and Mrs. MacIntyre had broken pieces of green bottles and smoked them over a fire so that we could observe the eclipse safely. They warned us in stern tones of the terrible consequences of watching an eclipse unprotected.

At the beach, the boys splashed and swam, yelling and screaming to burn off their great quantities of restless energy. I dipped in and out of the water and sat on the warm rocks to dry off, eating sandwiches and testing my smoked glass, making sure not to smudge it. For a while, I chatted with the ladies about opera and our favourite arias. When the time came to prepare everybody for the eclipse, the ladies positioned us and checked our smoked glass, gently reminding us again of the dangers. Then slowly, inch by inch and passing in transit, the perfectly round moon fitted over the blazing sun, blanketing the earth in darkness. I felt a chill, and it became very quiet as all of nature stopped in its tracks. For a few brief moments, it was as if we caught a glimpse of the great watchmaker setting his clocks. Then, so soon, the moon pulled the clouds along, leaving the sun in its accustomed place. It was exciting witnessing such a phenomenon, something we didn't think possible. It was a wonderful day, a day full of wonder.

---

3 Eclipse was August 31, 1932.

Mary and Lorna in front of the Reade house, spring 1933

That fall, Mother spent most of her time in bed. It never occurred to me that she was sick. Before I left for school, I would go up to her bedroom when Mrs. Johnson served her breakfast, and it seemed right that she should live that way. Then I noticed a strange, pervading silence—Mother had stopped singing. I asked her why she didn't sing any more, and she used one of Dad's expressions, that she didn't have the gumption she was born with. She said she was tired. She lost interest in her favourite radio shows and the books and papers that fed her interests. It seemed like she was giving up, that the respite in the Reade house had been like a backlash leaching her last reserve of energy, that urgent, restless energy that had served her for so long on the farm. As winter approached, Mother rarely got out of bed, and I never saw her leave the house again.

It was about this time that Dad decided I should learn how to cook and clean, to establish the fact that I was growing up to be a lady, 'just like your mother.' This came as a rude shock, since I had dreams of becoming a lady of leisure, just like Madame Recamier. I would be reading in the den or working on my scrapbooks when Dad would haul me off to the kitchen, promising to teach me something interesting. I was a reluctant apprentice, scraping hundreds of carrots and peeling thousands of badly notched potatoes, not smoothly sculpted like Dad's. I stirred endless pots on the stove as he called me out of my reverie, "Sweetlady, now we ah going to make a stee-ooh," or steak and kidney pie (oh, those dreadful kidneys) or the entire menu. Dad loved to cook, and his enthusiasm eventually rubbed off on me, which was just as well, because shortly I would be cooking full-time. I learned to make soups and stews, rice and curry, Welsh rabbit, curried hash, and Dad's favourite lemon pie, all followed by the wretched clean-up. Eventually, I became quite happy working away in the kitchen, but oh, how I hated the boredom and triviality of housework. Dad would say on a weekend, "Sweetlady, yew and I ah going to get this house ship-shape." I'd follow him around with my dust rag as he told me how his captain wore white gloves to inspect portholes and ledges above doors, looking for dust left by sloppy sailors. Dad was fastidious and reminded me that, "A young lady must learn such things in order to run a home," as he heaped one chore after another upon me like the erstwhile Sisyphus.

He said the day was coming when I would, as he said, 'swab the decks.' I felt very insulted that day; I considered it quite unnecessary to be washing floors at my age. When I complained, Dad assured me that there would be many more floors to wash in my life, and it wasn't the worst thing in the world. That was true; worst of all was helping Mrs. Johnson with the washing, and diapers were complete degradation.

I used to feel that Dad expected too much from me. While the boys could listen to their ham radio or read and study uninterrupted, I was roped into endless chores. It was as though I was being singled out. Still, I had Dad all to myself, which rarely happened on the farm, and because of all the time we spent together, I liked to think I was his pet. As we prepared a meal, he would gently tutor me, offering praise for accomplishments and soft reprimands for carelessness, "If a job is worth doing, it's worth doing well." Many times during my long career in the kitchen, I've drifted back to those quiet afternoons we spent preparing meals. I can still hear Dad asking, "Did ah evah tell yew about..?" Yes, he had, but I liked listening to his ridiculous stories because they changed with every telling. I would reluctantly take his advice after he had patiently listened to my complaints, "Sweetlady, that's beneath yew," "Sweetlady, turn the otha cheek." I did a lot of complaining.

When I helped Mrs. Johnson in the kitchen, she would look at me and say silly things like, "Mony a mickle makes a muckle[1]."

I'd say, "Please don't make me laugh, I don't want to."

She would say, "Tak the bree wi the barm[2]," or some other silly thing until I giggled. I needed her perpetual cheerfulness. Sometimes she would send me away with a warning, "Don't let yoor puir Mother see that face on yoo. I can't say I want to see it myself. Och, noo, you musney greet (grieve)." I would pick up my violin and practice Schumann's *Traumerei* or Massenet's *O Doux Printemps*, sad, wistful songs, hardly seasonal.

Christmas that year was a subdued affair. Mother didn't do any shopping, but before Mrs. Johnson went home, they baked the pudding, cakes and cookies. Dad and I made Christmas dinner together, which included my first turkey, my first giblet gravy (liver included) and my first attempt

1 Many small amounts make a large amount
2 Take the rough with the smooth

at the exhausting drudgery of mashed potatoes, which Dad had to finish. When the table was set, Mother came down and took her usual spot opposite Dad, the first time in months. Throughout the dinner, the boys attended to Mother like a guest of honour, passing her things and directing the conversation her way. Everyone added to the excitement, even Ian, who sat in his high chair banging his bottle. Dad said we could eat only what we wanted, a present in itself and a Christmas privilege thereafter. For dessert, he flamed the pudding and let us all have a sip of his sherry, even Robert, who fell asleep in his high chair. That was such a wonderful Christmas dinner with all twelve Marvins at the table, everyone so happy. It is strange how routine, comfortable enough to be commonplace, can suddenly be swept away in the flick of an eye, never to return.

I can't remember that Ian was ever sick. What I do remember is the freezing cold, the terrible snowstorm and Mother awakening me late in the night, whispering not to make any noise and to come downstairs. At the bottom of the stairs, she held me and told me that Ian had died and that I mustn't cry to wake the others. The shock silenced me. She led me over to the chesterfield where Ian lay bundled in his white lace shawl as if he had just had a bath. The dim light gave his beautiful face a faintly bluish, marble-like tinge—so still. I knelt down and leaned over to hear him breathe and said, "I'm sure he's going to breathe again." I even imagined I could hear him and begged Mother to listen, saying, "I think I hear him breathing." Mother was sobbing softly and said that Ian was a little angel now and would never be sick again. I couldn't believe he was dead, but when I touched his cheek and his tiny fingers, they were cool and unresponding. I hugged him and cried to make him hear, but he just lay there like a porcelain doll. All the stoves had burned down, and my teeth began to chatter as I shivered uncontrollably. Mother held me and said to go quietly up to bed and to say nothing, that she would tell the others in the morning. It is only now, delving back, that I realize neither Dad nor Mrs. Johnson were awake.

The next morning after one last look at Ian, we stayed out of the den. The house was quiet except for the furious howling of the snowstorm. Dad went for Dr. Campbell and they returned in his car with a small, unpainted coffin.

I watched from the den as they carried the tiny coffin to the car, the snow swirling around them. Seeing Dad place the coffin in that back seat of the car was so wrenchingly sad. He rushed back and called through the door that if the storm was too severe, he would stay in Annapolis overnight. Ian Alexander Marvin died of meningitis and was laid to rest in the graveyard of the Church of St. Thomas in Annapolis Royal. He was eight months old. I never heard Mother or Dad mention him again, nor did I, nor did any of his brothers and sisters.

Everything changed after Ian's death and nothing was ever the same again. Dr. Campbell came often and there was a lot of whispering behind closed doors about contagion and x-rays. He had ordered Mother to stay in bed but didn't seem to know what was wrong with her. Mother was crying all the time, but I couldn't find out what it was all about.

One afternoon I answered a knock at the door and was surprised to see that it was Mrs. Cunningham and Mrs. MacIntyre. They had heard that Mother was very sick and had made her a snow pudding, would I tell her they hoped she would get well soon? I couldn't believe it. In all our years in Bear River they had never once spoken to Mother or even given her a nod in passing, and now this, their first recognition of her. Dr. Campbell had likely told them, but told them what? I took the snow pudding and thanked them politely, apologizing that Mother was too sick to come to the door and Dad was away. When I told Mother, all she could say was, "Oh, I wish they hadn't bothered. I dislike thanking snobs." She couldn't eat the snow pudding, so Mrs. Johnson meted out miniscule portions for our dessert.

When Dad returned, there were more worried discussions with Dr. Campbell, but children were left to wonder what was happening. I would take Mother her tea and sit on her bed, just sit, and if I tried to talk to her, she barely had the energy to answer me. It seemed as if her whole character was changing, she was so different, so distant, not there anymore. I retreated to the downstairs bedroom to be alone and work on my scrapbooks, but after a few days I fled the room in a terrible state of unease. I had the most overpowering feeling that both Mr. Reade and the previous tenant had died in that room and the incubus of death permeated the house.

Then Mother and Dad began packing for a trip. It seemed strange that Mother would agree to go away when she was so ill. The next day we called up the stairs with our usual goodbyes and ran off to school. When we came home, Mother was gone, to where and why, Dad didn't say, only that she was in the hospital and would be home soon. I didn't believe Dad and burst into tears, asking him if Mother had died. Mrs. Johnson shamed me, saying she couldn't believe I would think such a thing. Dad said nothing, and I went on the worst crying jag of my young life. Every day, Dad would leave on the early morning train and return at night, only saying that Mother would be coming home. I had never seen him so troubled and preoccupied, even unapproachable. I tried to question him, but Mrs. Johnson would shuffle me out of the den saying, "You musney disturb your puir Father." I retreated to the back porch and glumly sat in a slough of despair, an empty shell ready to crack. I was sure Mother was dying somewhere and I would never see her again. Why would she just go away, while we were at school, almost behind our backs, why didn't she tell me? I had never been so miserable in all my life. I cried and cried, unable to understand. My grades at school plummeted, and when Dad wrote on my report card, 'Mary has to be encouraged in order to do better,' I was humiliated. Dad had publicly exposed his opinion of my intelligence, there to be read by my teacher and principal. Why didn't he speak to me privately? At the half-year, Vera Heisler, my teacher, had decided that Daniel and I should be promoted, but Dad said only Daniel could advance. I was disappointed, but this note of Dad's was an unforgivable slur that made school seem unimportant. Shortly after, I developed severe pains that kept me in bed, and I was convinced I was going the way of all flesh. Dr. Campbell came and tapped my back and said there was nothing wrong with me except for growing pains. I would sit in the back porch like a miserable lump, watching the hired men next door roll the tennis court smooth and set up the net for another summer. The hot spring days made me listless and tired of so many things. In a few short days the apple blossoms fluttered to the ground like my wishes. When I couldn't sleep, I would lean on my window sill, looking through the clematis vines to the lights of the village and listening to night noises. The connecting door to Mother's bedroom stayed open, and I would look over my shoulder into her room, feeling a strange, empty presence. I used to wonder how Mother felt when Dad returned from Montreal telling her of the concerts he had attended, the movies he had seen, the people he had met. Did she wish she could have heard Rachmaninoff or Fritz Kreisler, or seen Janet Gaynor in *Seventh Heaven* and *Daddy Long Legs*. Dad was always meeting people of charm and wit like Sir Arthur Currie of McGill University, the rough-tongued Lady Byng, Lady Haig, and Camillian Houde, the ebullient Mayor of Montreal. Mother would have fit in beautifully, but the farm and the children were her lynch-pin, and she could only listen to Dad's recounting. Looking back, it would appear that Dad led a life of a certain fulfilment: the farm, his brass work, his travels, the people he met, and Mother, unfulfilled except for yearly babies. She reminisced about trips to London and Edinburgh, of dining with her parents in some palm court, of seeing plays and hearing great artists like Nellie Melba and Ivor Novello. All of that was lost in Bear River. What sociabilities did she have? To the village for shopping, with me to Barr's barber shop, chatting with people along the way, once to Digby for the circus, those sad trips to Halifax. She had never seen a movie. Her social life revolved around those two short months when the Kniffens and all our summer friends returned, and then winter set in. How much she had missed.

Mary's room, 2011

With Mother gone, the family structure fractured. As Dad left in the morning, he would give me my instructions: help Mrs. Johnson all you can; watch the little ones; give in to them, "Sweetlady, you must compromise." That spring, I was back to being a little mother. Donald, David and Robert would be waiting for me after school like lisping, tottering vultures. They wanted bread and jam, clamouring all over me, smothering me and strangling me with their needs, sticky little mouths covering my cheeks with slobbering kisses—demanding little birds. How strange what baggage is carried all one's life and can't be shaken. Destiny grabs one by the throat and almost chokes out life, all escape routes barred. Stray hopes and dreams snap back to reality like a rubber band, leaving a sting and a deep, inveterate resentment. Nothing was required of the boys; they fished, escaped to the woods and sat by the hour at the ham radio. Their only chores were splitting kindling and filling the wood boxes for the stoves. I wanted to be as favoured and as indulged as they were. I wanted no responsibilities. Last words ringing in my ears from Mrs. Johnson were to come straight home from school, "I'll need your help." Lorna and Joan, in their first years of school, could leisurely shuffle home with the lesser Reade children, all in a whispering clump. If I approached, they would dismiss me with the reminder that I had to hurry home. As I look back, I remember how I hated everything and with few exceptions, everyone. Mrs. Johnson, so loving and understanding, would ask if I had anything on my mind. I had nothing to say. There were no words I could give voice to. I was a mental criminal, ready to do justice to fate; I would cut its head off like a chicken. I was becoming, and I knew it, a nasty person, and as a last resort to save myself, I became a loner, holed up in the den with the *Book of Knowledge*. I brought home the second of many poor report cards, and Dad signed it with a shake of his head, a wordless affirmation of a faint echo, "Dearie, she just can't grasp." That awful spring. I hate to go back, but just as there was no escape, there is no forgetting.

Then one day towards the end of school, Dad came home in the evening and announced that we were going to see Mother, and, almost as an afterthought, that we were moving to Kentville. That was all the information we got, but it was all we needed. My pangs and fears disappeared as Dad spoke. Early the next day, we began a frenzy of packing, as if we couldn't get away soon enough. Mrs. Johnson wanted to wash the bedding, but Dad said, "Let it go." Daniel and I were wrapping dishes in newspaper, and when Daniel broke a cup. Dad said, "Forget it Sweetheart." Our job was happily haphazard, and Mrs. Johnson, hearing us giggling, cautioned us not to break anything else. All day long, the boys chattered like squirrels about their prospects in a new town: new friends, a new school, everything brand new. All I could think of was getting to Mother. We finished the packing and jumped into bed with the same delicious expectancy as on Christmas Eve. Early the next day, a truck backed up to the front door and was quickly loaded. Dad, Daniel, Jim and Douglas jumped aboard, and the truck drove off with our belongings piled high like a modern-day prairie schooner. Mrs. Johnson, wearing her best housedress and her little black straw hat, hurried us out the door to a waiting taxi. One last time we went down Oakdene Hill, past the school, the Trading Company and across the rattly bridge. Going up the River Road, I looked across to the farm, hidden behind Dad's stand of oak. High above in the bright sunlight was our hay field and the flat rock. Leaving Bear River was much like leaving the farm, quick and unexplained, a flight to nowhere. We shook off the dust of the little village and didn't look back. At Bear River station, I followed the tell-tale streamer rising above the tree line as the train approached from Digby, chugging rhythmically like Sibelius' "Intermezzo." As it thundered to a stop, Mrs. Johnson and I herded the toddlers on the platform. She was all politeness and gratitude as she handed them up to the conductor, who showed us to our seats in a conversational way, asking the boys their names and asking me, "And you, young lady, are you going to Kentville too?" I sat with Mrs. Johnson and the toddlers, while Lorna and Joan, always together, always separate, sat across the aisle. The whistle blew, the train pulled out, and a minute later Bear River was memory.

It is strange how when I was so worried, I sank to an impossible nadir, yet when my troubles were over and everything seemed right again, there was nothing left in my expended emotions. My excitement settled into a passive happiness lulled by the gentle rocking of the train. I watched as the toddlers stuck their noses to the window, and their animated little fingers tried to grasp the passing scene, punctuating each with a point and, "See! See!" before it was all gone and another one appeared.

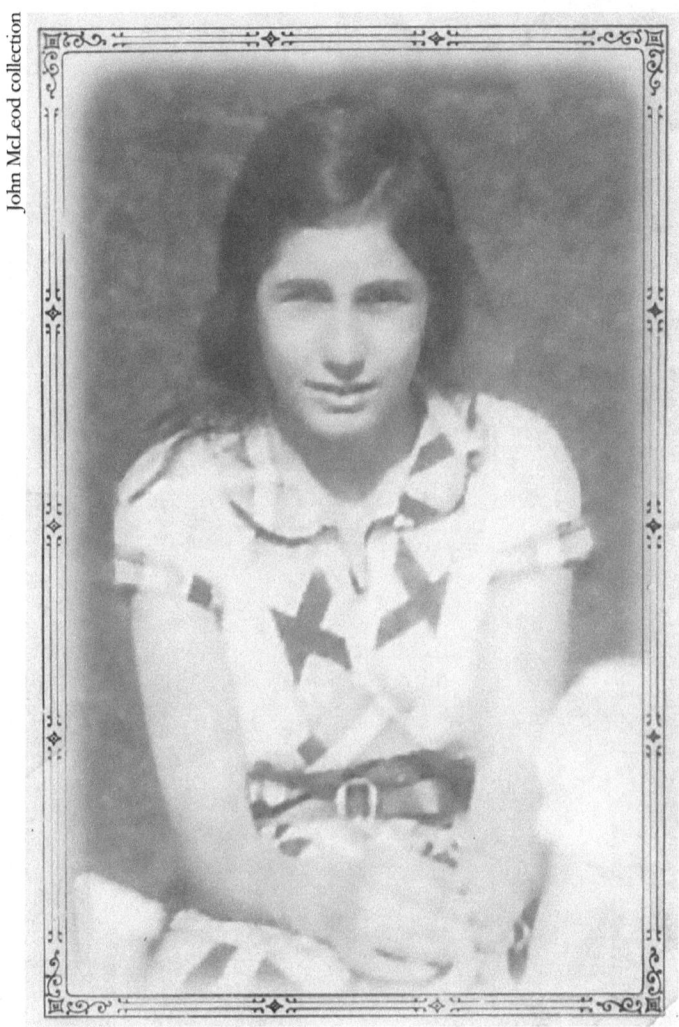

John McLeod collection

End of Book 1

John McLeod

The Skalings
The Marvins   The Leitchs   Oakdene Square
Nova Scotia Sanatorium
Joe Bell Hill (Gallows Hill)
St. Josephs
Kentville Station
Chisholm's
Kentville Advertiser
Main Street
Kings County Academy

John McLeod Collection

Excerpts from *A Far Away Place, Kentville*.1

Justifiably concerned about my lack of talent, Dad found a down and out drunken violin virtuoso, Professor Gordon, who had won his spurs of fame in various concert halls and had once taught at Acadia University. How did this stroke of luck happen? I can only suppose that while Dad was grocery shopping at Wade's, he spied the Professor with his violin case across the street at the liquor commission. Dad eagerly ushered him into the living room, showing him off like a prize catch. The Professor sat down, pulled out an empty Campbell's soup from his pocket, placed it on the floor and promptly demonstrated its usefulness as a spittoon. I reeled. He had left his violin case in the hall, so he twiddled his unclean fingers at me, indicating that he would play mine. He cradled it lovingly under his yellowed walrus moustache, drew the bow, and magic quivered. Truth be told, Professor Gordon played like a wizard, and once he got started on Saint-Saens he was unstoppable. Dad relaxed in his easy chair, oblivious to all but the music. For the price of my lesson, he was in a concert hall. So, while this teacher could play, I stood on the sidelines, my bow resined and ready, waiting for a lesson that I rarely got. The Professor would finish a piece, pause, expectorate into his Campbell's soup can, then pull a brown medicinal bottle from his frayed jacket pocket and take a draught. If Dad had been in perfect health, he might have recognized not only the Professor's illness, but also his cure.

I suppose Dad could be forgiven for holding me hostage. He wasn't well, but when the Professor played, he would relax in his chair as he seldom did, listening peacefully as the Professor's unclean fingernails touched each perfect note and his deft bow made those notes shimmer. Afterwards, they would chat while I helped Mrs. Johnson serve tea and scones. She would say, "The puir mon is nowt but skin and bone.

---

1 *Bear River* contains many musical references, ending with Sibelius' "Intermezzo" from his *Karealia Suite*, Op 11. The piece immediately following is "Ballade," which opens *Kentville*. I prefer the versions that emphasize the train-like rhythm.

What he needs is a good cuppa tea." What he really needed was the hair of the dog, which he surely got when he took his violin case home, heavy with rotgut instead of catgut. There was no liquor commission in Wolfville, so it must have been an inconvenience for the Professor to take the seven-minute train ride to Kentville and back to slake his thirst. It was obvious I was an inconvenience, even for what Dad paid him, but the Depression was an excuse for everything.

I don't think my brother Donald ever played with rattles and toys. I only remember him with the old radio parts that the boys tinkered with after Dad had given up making crystal sets. Donald was dit-dit-dat-ing in Morse Code as soon as he could walk, and when the Ham radio came into the house, he was right there with the rest of the boys, twiddling dials and listening on the earphones for hours on end. Dad enrolled Daniel in a radio correspondence course, and when the black-edged magazine arrived, a general excitement ensued because all the boys followed along. The third floor became a communications hub, with wires strung across the room, out the window and down to the ground. The boys were happy as clams listening intently on their earphones as they tuned the Ham radio or sent each other messages in Morse code from across the room. Donald certainly knew radios before he knew his ABC's, and he could read and write before he went to school.

That summer, Daniel began his career as a radio repairman at Delancey Newcombe's radio store, but for the two weeks he would be at Boy Scout camp, Cecil Corcoran, the other repairman was going on holidays. Delancey needed someone trained in that 'advanced technology' but couldn't find anyone, so Daniel recommended Donald, detailing his eight year history of radio destruction and repair from the cradle. Delancey was desperate and said that if he was as good as Daniel, "I'll take the kid." Daniel phoned with the news, and I ran up to get Donald at the San gravel pit, where he was playing with David and Robert. When I told Donald about his job opportunity, he bolted for home, washed his face, put on a clean pair of short pants and tore down Joe Bell Hill. As Daniel related, when Donald arrived, Delancey was yarning with his good friend, Mr. Wickwire, a florid-faced, white-haired, corpulent curmudgeon, a daily visitor, always well-fueled, and always fliply acerbic about the intelligentsia of Kentville. Delancey introduced Donald as his new repairman, and Mr. Wickwire observed that Kentville was going to "blue hell."

Delancey was such a prankster. That day he got a call from the wealthy Mrs. Smith, a widow who lived in a nice white house with columns and who liked Delancey, though he was already married. Delancey told Mrs. Smith that he would send his very best man, and Donald was sent off in his short pants and sneakers with a tool box. Delancey sat down tee-heeing and waiting for the telephone to ring, which it promptly did. Daniel said that Delancey was chuckling so hard that he was barely able to pick up the phone before sputtering, "I swear to God he's a full-grown midget…He's been doing repairs for eight years…Would I ruin my business by having a kid around here?" Delancey went out the door and jumped in his car, muttering, "I'm going to lay that woman out in satin," his way of saying he was going to put her in a satin-lined casket. That was one of his favourite expressions, "Boy, I's like to lay him (or her) out in satin." Delancey fixed Mrs. Smith's radio, asking Donald's advice while Mrs. Smith watched the performance, "Is this how it goes, what do I do next?" When Donald had first appeared at her door, she told him to go play somewhere else and that he was not going to play with her radio. Donald wouldn't budge. On the way out she asked him sweetly, "How old are you, dear?" Donald truthfully answered, "Eight." When they got in the car, Delancey said, "Hey kid, do you want to ruin my business? I told that old buzzard you're a full-grown midget. If anyone asks your age tell them you forget." There was a lot of laughing around town about that story, promoted by Delancey and Mr. Wickwire.

Aldershot Army camp was perhaps a mile up the road from Joe Bell Hill, and every soldier who came into town passed by our house. War seemed remote then, and the soldiers' presence was more like a new social order. Their marching feet in that steady two-step became the tempo by which we lived during those years. War was the culture of the times, and they were the song and dance men. On late-night treks back to camp, they sang the ballads of the 30s in loud, cheerful, marching tones, and those songs never seemed the same again. The outer edges of tender lyrics grew harsh, the fragility transformed by overtones into a reminder that love is not a dream, but a disaster. Those songs became regimental dirges, replaced, as the war aged, into the blasé jollity of rolling out the barrel; having the Hun on the run, run, run; hanging out their wash on the Siegfried Line; lyrically doing something I've forgotten to Hitler; and what a spree when the war would be over. I knew them, they were mostly boys just out of high school who hadn't the vaguest idea of love or war, but their heavy, marching tread, and those loud songs made it seem as if they had grown into men overnight. There was an awe about them, cut-outs as they were: all those black boots, all that khaki, patches of faces, swinging arms, and on and on they marched up and down the street, dun shadows accompanied by the rise and fall of their boots like drum beats. I heard it all from my pillow as it wafted in through my bedroom window, the pulse beat of their boots crunching the gravel and making you listen until the threatening rhythm had faded.

That first day, I went off to work at the Advertiser filled with all my romantic notions about books and newspapers and the printed word–Scott, Byron, Dickens, et al. I was in with the angels. Somehow, my love of literature and the refined words of poets included the local paper, despite the glaring fact that the Advertiser was held in utter disrepute in our household. I hadn't thought about family loyalty, or the hurt and humiliation the paper had caused in reporting Dad's death. It slipped to the back of my mind and almost dropped off. I was a young girl in the clutches of $12.50 a week.

It was a lovely spring morning the day I headed down Joe Bell Hill for the centre of town and into the warm embrace of the fourth estate. Snows were melting into puddles of slush, blue jays were calling noisily from the spruce trees in front of the Advertiser, and old tragedies and woes had no more substance than soap bubbles. I turned the door handle of the Advertiser as respectfully as I held my favourite books, and as I stepped inside, I was immediately carried away by a new kind of music–the rhythmic rolling and clicking of the press, the lively heartbeat of the news, the fount of all the deathless words of the world, at least in Kentville. The noisy clicking sounded like a giant sewing machine, stitching words onto huge rolls of paper as they threaded through the printer in a Chinese love knot. The press ran all day every day, and when it stopped, it was the death of all sound. Then a pause, a hesitant pulse, then the more insistent, steadily pounding heartbeat. The press was alive again, and would go on and on and never die a slow death as I would. After a week, I was praying to all the saints in heaven to deliver me from that purgatory.

The Bear River Weekly Courier

Home and Country   Edited by Woman's Institute Bear River

News of Bear River

We are glad to welcome to Bear River Mr and Mrs. D Marven, of Truro, who have recently purchased the J. L. Warren property.

Our Institute was requested by the Soldiers Settlement Board to meet and become acquainted with the new settlers wives. On July 5th we invited them to meet us in our rooms where we entertained them with music and served refreshments.

Miss Mary Kniffen and Mrs. Ruth Pratt arrived from Concord, New Hampshire last week and are the guests of Mrs. Stephen Kniffen and Mabel Kniffen.

Mrs. A. G. McIntyre entertained her Sunday School class and C.G.I.T. girls on Tuesday of last week by giving them a joint picnic at Kneffins Hollow. There were many phases of amusement for the girls and boys but probably nothing was more enjoyed than the swimming exercise when twenty were in the water at one time. The boys and girls were all unanimous in saying that it was the best time they had ever had and feel sure they are very fortunate in having a teacher who is willing to devote so much of her time for their enjoyment.

A Clam Bake at "Kniffens Hollow" was much enjoyed on Wednesday evening by the large number present This lovely gulch with it's smooth stretch of beach is an ideal spot for such an outing, and Mr Kniffen is an expert in preparing and cooking the chief articles of the menu.

Mr. Marvin arrived from Montreal on Saturday to spend a vacation with his family here.

Fred Schmidt
BEAR RIVER, N. S.
General Merchandise
Groceries,
   Canned Goods,
      Fruit,
         Confectionery,
            Etc., Etc.

STORE ON MAIN ST., NEAR BRIDGE

Steamer Bear River surpassed her record for trips last week, sailing on Monday, returning on Wednesday, taking the Masonic excursion to Annapolis on Thursday, again sailing for St. John on the same night, and returning to Bear River on Saturday afternoon. Heavy wind and fog forced her to put back into St. John on Friday night, or she would have been one day further ahead.

Last week a suspected case of smallpox was reported in town. Action was immediately taken by the united Boards of Health of Bear River, and all churches, schools, and societies were closed until further notice. No cases or symptoms have since developed and we expect the ban will soon be lifted as the Board of Health is meeting as we go to press. The Board of Health is to be congratulated for their prompt and efficient action, were all suspected epidemics treated in this manner, the burdens of our local physicians would be greatly lightened.

A Liberal Rally and Smoker was held in Oakdene Hall, on Saturday evening, when over 300 people were in attendance. The time passed pleasantly with speeches, music and songs by local talent, and later coffee and sandwiches were served.

A Conservative meeting was held in the Temperance Hall on Saturday evening, when A. L. Davidson, the Government candidate, spoke to the electorate of Bear River. The hall was decorated with flags and posters, and the room was filled to capacity.

The result of the election held on Tuesday, Dec. 6th, is as follows:—Dr. L. J. Lovett, the liberal candidate, won over his opponent A. L. Davidson, by the splendid majority of over 2,200 votes. His own home town gave the Doctor a majority of over 500; the electors turned out en masse in the evening, and after calling at his home, where smokes, coffee and cake were served, made a huge bonfire in the centre of town to celebrate the victory. Dr. Lovett then left by motor for Digby where an enthusiastic rally was held.

Dr. A. B. Campbell has opened his office in the Grand Central and will have charge of Dr. Lovett's practice during his absence in Ottawa.

The tern schooner "Rose Ann Belliveau," Capt. Comeau, was towed up the river on Monday by S. S. Bear River, Capt. Woodworth, and docked at the government wharf. The "Rose Ann" was partly loaded with lumber at Belliveau's cove and will complete her cargo here with another hundred thousand which is being shipped by Derby Jack. This cargo is being shipped to Barbados

Mr. Donaldson, of the Soldier's Settlement Board was in town on Thursday

Miss Alice Copeland, little daughter of Mr. and Mrs. A. Copeland, entertained twelve of her friends at a delightful birthday party on Saturday afternoon.

Lionel Roop has returned to Halifax to write his Dominion Board Exams, preparatory to settling down at his dental work in Bear River. Although his equipment has not yet arrived he has been doing some work at his father's residence.

Harry Benson has installed a radio receiver at his home and many Bear River citizens are having the pleasure of "listening in" every evening to the varied programs in the air as given in the Halifax Chronicle.

A RECORD

Henry M. Romans aged 9 1-2, son of W. M. Romans of the Royal Bank, Bear River, is one of our coming shots. His record is four partridge in four shots, and to wind off with, a wood cock on the wing, making five straight. Is this not a record for a boy of his years to be shooting on the wing? He used his fathers 20 gauge Ithaca which is still a little large for him to handle.

The heavy snowfall of Sunday filled all roads leading to and from town. On Monday there was very little traffic, and on Tuesday a heavy team and six men armed with shovels, started for Lake Jolly to make a passage through.

There is still plenty of snow in the outlying districts, as Dr. Campbell can testify, for one of his calls last week included an eight mile trip on snowshoes.

A baby son arrived on Saturday morning, February 11th at the home of Mr and Mrs Daniel Marvin.

BEAR RIVER
Drug Store
BEAR RIVER, NOVA SCOTIA

Drugs, Patent Medicines, Perfumes, Toilet Sundries, Lowney's Chocolates in Boxes

Prescriptions Carefully Dispensed

Kodaks and Kodak Supplies

Developing and Printing Orders given Careful and Prompt Attention.

An Up-to-date Stock of Post Cards

Souvenir, Fancy, Views and Comic. Panorama Views, size 8½ x 27 in., of Bear River, Annapolis Basin and Digby.

Only 10 Cents Each

Mailed to any address on receipt of 12 cents.

Mrs. S. Kniffen and daughter Mabel left on Friday to spend the winter in the United States.

Poppy Day

The seasons of the year have rolled around until it is now approaching "Poppy Day." This year a more extensive campaign then ever is to be carried out in the sale of "The Flower of Remembrance" and every effort will be put forward to make "Poppy Day" a day of real thanksgiving. Think of the many good things which have happened to you since that eventful day, Nov. 11, 1918, for which you should be thankful. Then think of those who gave their all and, today, lie in "Flanders Field" in order that you might enjoy all these things and live in peace. This is Their Day and must not be forgotten.

Then remember those who were a little more fortunate and have come back but not to their usual life of activity and usefulness as they are maimed and crippled for life. These are the men who left home and loved ones, perfect in their manhood and now have come back broken men, in body, but not in spirit, for they are working as best they may, to be, at least, practically self supporting The flower, which you will wear on Nov 11th is being made by their hands in Camp Hill Hospital Halifax.

When you buy your Poppy, remember you are honoring those who died and helping to make some man, not so fortunate as yourself, a self-supporting, self-respecting citizen. Boost Poppy Day.

Bear River, A Beauty Spot

To the Editor of the Courier,

Sir:—Joseph Howe, the poet, statesman, orator and prophet, had a great love for his native province, a profound and unbounded enthusiasm for its interests, its lovely beauty and its outstanding opportunities.

Could he but see the glories of the hills in and about the young Switzerland of America this day as I pen these words, resplendent with the touch of God's beauty, enshrined amongst the hills, cradled as it were in the hollow of His hand, he would realize as never before that which no pen can describe, no tongue can recite, and which no diction can indite, the sublime beauty of "A magnificent Country."

This short yet genuine tribute fro ma citizen of Weymouth passes in all its sincerety to our neighboring community Bear River.

Did people but know; ah! there's the rub, for they do not know, they do not realize their opportunities, otherwise there would be a Cherry Blossom Day that would commit Bear River to an outstanding place in the beautiful sight seeing places of this province that is unique in its magnificent splendour.

A recent winter visitor to Florida and the Southern States said to me but yesterday that she saw absolutely nothing in her ten thousand miles of journey throughout that section of the United States to compare with that which her eyes beheld as she gazed from the high hills across the valley to the steep rising slopes on the other side.

We need to get away from home often in order to appreciate fully the beauties that lie near at hand. How true.

Lloyd H. Potter.

LOCAL SHIPYARDS BUSY

When the schooner Leo LeBlanc arrived at Digby last week to load lumber the owners found that about thirty feet of false keel and a considerable length of shoe were missing, and they expected that it would be necessary to await her arrival at New York in order to have repairs made without delay. But after making enquires at Bear River they found that repairs could be undertaken at Clarke Brothers yard immediately. The necessary hardwood for both keel and shoeing were already in stock for just such an emergency. The Leo LeBlanc is a vessel of five hundred tons burden and went on the blocks on Monday, coming off on the following Thursday. The keel replaced was in one piece thirty feet long and eight by thirteen inches of best quality birch, the shoe one hundred and twenty feet in length of four by thirteen birch.

After the sinking of the Valinda at Granville Bridge last week temporary repairs were made which allowed her to be floated again. The holes were covered with canvas and she proceeded to Bear River under her own steam and docked at R. Benson's shipyard. An examination is now being made to determine the extent of the damage after which repairs will be undertaken immediately.

W. M. CHUTE
BEAR RIVER, NOVA SCOTIA
Watchmaker
And Jeweler
Repairing in all its branches Promptly Attended to.

STORE ON MAIN ST., NEAR POST OFFICE.

BRAVE ACT OF BOY SCOUT

One afternoon recently a number of small boys were enjoying themselves fishing from the wharves along the waterfront and one of them, Williard Peck, aged nine years fell from the wharf and was being carried up stream by the strong current. To the horror of the beholders, Peck was carried under the water and reappeared several times and it was feared that he had gone under for the last time.

Just then, Clayton Robbins, aged thirteen came along and saw the cause of the excitement and without any hesitation or loss of time to remove his clothing went over the side of the wharf and into the water and caught Peck, as he came to the surface again and brought him to the shore.

At the scout meeting last Thursday evening special mention was made of the heroic deed, by Scoutmaster Warren and also by Asst. Scoutmaster Mack, and at the conclusion, Clayton was heartily applauded by his fellow scouts.

On account of the extreme cold weather which has frozen up our river, the Steamer Bear River was unable to ply her way through the ice to her wharf and was obliged to remain at Victoria Bridge, where she is discharging her cargo and same is being hauled to Bear River on sleds.

NEW YORK CALLS BEAR RIVER ON LONG DISTANCE

On Friday the Bear River Central had a call from New York asking to be connected up with Clarke Brother's office. The connection was made through this Company's private exchange and the first "Hello" was heard as distinctly as though it had been a call from Digby. A conversation followed lasting several minutes and was carried on with perfect ease and with no line interruptions whatever. We understand that this is the first through call to New York from this part of the Maritime Telegraph and Telephone Company's territory and the Company is to be congratulated upon placing their lines and equipment in such a condition that conversation can take place over this distance.

So Nervous She Could Scream

These Hysterical Womenfolk

CRYING... sobbing... laughing. Nerves strung to the breaking point. What a state to be in! Constant headache, bearing down pains, dizzy spells are robbing her of health and beauty.

If she would only give Lydia E. Pinkham's Vegetable Compound a chance to help her. 98 out of every 100 report benefit. Watch your own troubles yield to its tonic action.

Try a bottle of either the liquid or the convenient new tablets. Let it help you as it has helped so many thousands of suffering women.

Lydia E. Pinkham's VEGETABLE COMPOUND

Corn Boil

Instead of the regular Tennis Tea last Thursday the Bear River Tennis Club enjoyed a corn boil in the moon light at Kniffins Hollow. Shortly after six o'clock, about forty members went by auto and were soon busy husking corn around two large bonfires: It isn't safe to state how many dozen of corn were boiled but it was certainly luscious corn, and at least one small boy in the party had a mortal gorge. Indeed every one present did full justice to the corn and the contents of the many picnic beskets, and then a "sing-song" brought to a close a very delightful outing.

SCOUT NOTES

Several weeks ago some of the boys decided that there must be a number of interesting places in the vicinity of Bear River, that they were not acquainted with, so they adopted as their slogan, "See Bear River First," and arranged for a series of "hikes" which would make them familiar with all the country within a five mile radius of their home town.

The first hike took them down the east bank of the river to "Kniffen's Hollow," and from there, they followed the Kniffen stream up to the point where it crosses the Waldeck road. Anyone who has not explored this route would be filled with surprise and wonder at the beautiful scenery to be found there, especially in the early Spring when there is a heavy flow of water. Waterfalls are very frequent and in places, this stream passes through narrow gorges with perpendicular sides. Over one of these, there is a particularly beautiful waterfall, which drops vertically to the bed of the stream, a distance of fully one hundred feet. This fall can only be seen during the early Spring or after a heavy freshet.

For Sore Throat Cold in the Chest, ec.

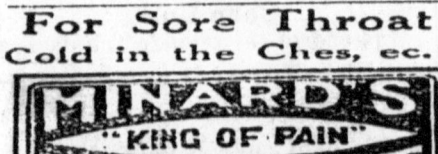

Mrs. Harold Hatheway was "At Home" on Friday afternoon, Nov. 23rd, for the first time since coming to Bear River to reside. The door was opened by little Miss Patricia Hatheway, dressed in a dainty white gown. Mrs. Reginald Goodday, wearing a gown of brown canton crepe conducted the guests to the reception and tea rooms. Mrs. Hatheway looked charming in a very pretty gown of georgette crepe over satin, and was assisted in receiving by Mrs. Harry Anthony, who was wearing brown velvet, fur trimmed. The soft light of candles in their sconces, and the glowing fire light, added to the attractiveness of the quaint living room in which Mrs. Hatheway received. The tea table in the dining room was a picture, with its centre bowl of yellow chrysanthemums, dainty plates of refreshments, and the beautiful antique silver tea and coffee service. Mrs. Ernest Mills of Annapolis Royal, wearing a black satin and lace dress and large black hat to match, and Mrs. Walter M. Romans in a gown of royal blue velette, presided at the tea table, and were assisted in serving by Miss Olive Saunders, who wore a pretty black velvet dress with hat, and Miss Edith Lovett in pink taffeta with black and silver hat. Though it was an unpleasant day, there were a large number of callers.

PROPERTY for SALE

House (7 Rooms), Barn, Hen House, about an acre of land, 15 apple and two cherry trees. $700.00 cash.
Mrs. Grace A. Wilson,
Bear River, N. S.

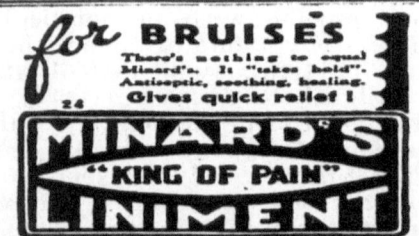

McRAYE'S LECTURE

Walter McRaye, well-known to Bear River audiences, will lecture in Academy Hall on Tuesday April 19th, under the auspices of the Women's Institute. His subject will be "Canada and the Empire" In addition to this, he will give a number of selections from Drummond and Service. Tickets may be secured from members of the Institute at the door. Home made candy will be sold before the lecture.

A special meeting of the Women's Institute was held in the Masonic kitchen on Monday afternoon, April 11th, at 3.30 p. m. to arrange for the lecture.

The following committees were appointed:—

Decorating Com:—Convener, Mrs. L. J. Lovett; Mrs. J. H. Cunningham; Mrs. Thelbert Rice; Mrs. J. Arthur Rice; Mrs. Harry Harris; Mrs. A B. Marshall; Mrs. Arthur Greggson

Advertising Com:—Convener, Mrs. L. V. Harris; Mrs. B. Alexander; Mrs. A. G. MacIntyre; Mrs. Percy Reed.

Candy Com:—Convener, Mrs. Howard Cress; Mrs. W. W. Wade; Mrs. Hubbard; Mrs. O'Keefe

Candy Selling Com:—Convener, Mrs. Fred Harris; Mrs W. J. Wright; Miss Harriet Rice; Mrs. Carl Miller.

Ushering Com: Convener, Mrs. Will Brenton; Mrs. Cebra Rice; Mrs. Brenton Rice; Mrs. R. A. Thurber.

Ticket Seller:—Miss Mabel Harris.

Ticket Taker:—Mrs. John Farquhar.

All Institute members are reminded of the pound of home made candy to be donated by each; and are requested to send this in to Mrs. L. J. Lovett's house on Tuesday morning, if possible.

HERRING IN THE RIVER

Citizens have been greatly interested in watching large shoals of herring, which have been seen every day during the past week, passing under the bridge during the incoming and outgoing tides. Why could not large quantities of these valuable fish be captured by some of our enterprising townspeople?

Schr. Valdare has been enjoying the Basin for three week's awaiting a favourable chance to sail.

Grades III and IV, Oakdene School "showered" little Roscoe Cress and Gerald Rice with letters on Friday last. Both these little boys have been ill—Gerald is somewhat better at time of writing and Roscoe is much improved.

Mrs. Jesse Harris and Mrs. Will Brinton, met with a serious accident on Saturday night, when they were run down by a sled in front of H. C. Anthony's store. Mrs. Brinton was badly shaken up, but Mrs. Harris is still confined to the house.

EMPIRE DAY IN OAKDENE

Empire Day was celebrated here by the Intermediate Department of Oakdene School in a manner suitable to the day. The following was the programme.

Composition on "The Early Jesuet" Effie Robilliard, Composition on "Champlain" Woodford Davis, Composition on "Wolfe" Alec Wentzell, Composition on "Isaac Brock" Estherde Long. Story, "Our Nation in War and Peace." Song, "The Maple Leaf." Study of the Canadian Coat of Arms. Song "Our Flag". Formation of "The Flag". Facts concerning Canada's Greatness. Recitation "Our Flag and Your Flag" Song, "Land of Our Birth" Address, Rev. R S. Cregg Song, O Canada. Flag Salute

Empire Day was fittingly observed by Miss Withrow's room, the second Primary of Oakdene. The room was tastefully decorated in accordance with significance of the day. The program consisted of songs, recitations and exercises. Two interesting features of the afternoon were an address on "Patriotism" by Mr. W. E. Read, and a pretty Flag Drill by the children. The children performed their parts in a most perfect manner, reflecting credit on themselves and their teacher.

The Crusade Club Reparatory Dept. Oakdene opened their regular meeting on Friday Afternoon with the singing of the "Maple Leaf", after the business of the Club an interesting and instructive program was given. It being Empire Day the members were mainly patriotic.

Song—O Canada!	School
Explanation of Coat of Arms	Nellie (Stevens)
Service to the Flag	Wendell Sullivan
Patriotic Story & Selections	Miss Henry
Paper — True Patriotism prepared by	(Florence Peck)
Canada, Our Homeland	Alda Benson
Exercise—The Canadian Flag by all the pupils through which was woven the resources of Canada and the debt we owe her.	
Men of Britain	Bernice MacDorman
Speech—Contrasting the American and Canadian Governments—Frederick Kempton	
The Native Born	Mildred Chuto
Paper—The Making of Our Flag prepared by Leland Robbins	
The Flag Goes By	Chester Snell
Country of Mine	Bertha Freeman

God Save The King.

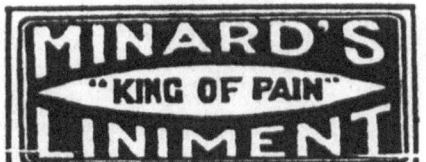

Those Having Sick Animals Should Use MINARD'S "KING OF PAIN" LINIMENT

Good for all throat and chest diseases Distemper, Garget, Sprains, Bruises, Colic Mange, Spavins, Running Sores, etc. etc. Should always be in the stable.—SOLD EVERYWHERE.

The teaching staff for Oakdene School is now complete. J. E. Steadman is to be principal, Miss Mayme Withrow, vice-principal, Miss Marion Marshall, intermediate, Miss Lexie Hatfield and Miss White, primary. A committee from the Women's Institute visit the schools each month and keep in touch with the work. Through their efforts they have secured about $80.00 to be distributed in prizes for the year.

Little Miss Paula Reade who has been the guest of her grand mother Mrs. Emmerson Reade, returned to her home in Post Washington, N.Y. on Wednesday.

"The Building of the Ship"

A pageant entitled "The Building of the Ship" will be given to-night, (Friday, Nov. 28th) in the auditorium of the Methodist church by the choir and young people of the congregation. During the presentation, which is founded on Longfellow's poem of that name, a complete ship is assembled in all its parts, from keel to topmast.

for DANDRUFF MINARD'S "KING OF PAIN" LINIMENT

JOHN H. YORK,
—MANUFACTURER OF—
Carriages, Horse Team Wagons and Ox Wagons

A large assortment of well-seasoned stock always on hand. Repairing a Specialty. Also AGENT FOR

McLaughlin Carriage Co.

FINANCIAL STATEMENT OF THE B. R. WOMEN'S INSTITUTE WAR MEMORIAL FUND

To all who have in any way assisted in the accumulation of the Women's Institute Memorial Fund, and to the Bear River Ministerial Association and others, for their valued co-operation at the dedication and unveiling of the Memorial, the Society wishes to express their most sincere thanks.

For the benefit of these, and all who are interested, the following financial statement is presented:—

RECEIPTS

Carnival Day Meals (1924) served by Women's In.....	$343.52
Transferred from Red Cross Fund	19.16
4 Gift Shop Sales (1925, 1926, 1927, 1928)	457.51
Local Talent Play (Carnival of 1925)	70.00
Benefit Lecture by Dr. W. J. Wright	41.20
Pantry Sales	58.10
Cash Donations	80.22
Bank Int.	242.94
	$1312.65

DISBURSEMENTS

Bronze Tablet	$350.00
Stonework	650.00
Bronze Torch and Wiring...	60.06
Foundation	30.00
Paid I. O. O. F. Toward cost of Curbing	25.00
Administration Exp.	14.85
Transportation for Professor Thomson	9.50
	$1139.41
Balance on Hand	$173.24

Respectfully submitted,
(Signed) Mary H. Marshall,
Con. Memorial Com.
(Signed) Jessie M. Romans,
Treasurer.
Audited and found correct,
(Signed) J. A. MacKenna.

Bear River, Dec. 3rd, 1932.

At a special executive meeting of the Women's Institute on Thursday, Jan. 19th, it was decided to provide hot cocoa at noon for the month of February for the children who bring their lunches. If this plan proves feasible and expenses can be met, the hot lunch will be continued during the winter months.

ANOTHER CASUALTY OF THE WAR

Fred Kennedy Passed Away as the Result of Shell Shock and Gas

On Sunday morning, April 17th, at the residence of his father, George Kennedy, Fred Grant Kennedy passed away to his eternal rest after a lingering illness of nearly three years, the result of shell wound and gas received while serving his country in France during the great World war. Private Fred Kennedy enlisted at Digby, February 1st, 1916, with the 112th, Batt., and later served in France with the Royal Canadian Regiment. He was discharged July 11th, 1918, as medically unfit for further active service overseas owing to shell wound in the left foot, on October 30th, 1917. This and the result of an gas attack so undermined his health that he was forced to return home, and has since been tenderly cared for by his mother and family in the little town of his birth and boyhood days.

The fact that this is the second bereavement in one week in Mr. Kennedy's family, has called forth the deepest sympathy of all classes in the community, which was evidenced by the large concourse who attended the funeral on Tuesday afternoon.

The funeral was held with semi-military honors under the direction of the G. W. V. A. of Bear River. The casket was gracefully draped with the old Union Jack, and 12 members of the 85th Batt., formed a body-guard, while six of the officers acted as pall bearers. Interment took the body to its last resting place in Mt. Hope cemetery. The service at the house and grave was conducted by Rev. W. J. Wright, and at the conclusion, while comrades and friends stood with bared heads Bugler John McGregor sounded The "Last Post", and another of Bear Rivers brave men was left to sleep his last long sleep till the dawn of the resurrection morn.

All the flags in town were at half mast out of respect to his memory, and Oakdene School pupils marched in a body.

There were many beautiful floral tributes from the G. W. V. A., Woman's Institute, and Methodist Church as well as from personal friends, but the later were delayed by the derailment of the Halifax train. They were placed on the grave on their arrival.

The collection of war pictures donated to Oakdene School by the Imperial Order of the Daughters of the Empire has been framed and is at present at the school. This fine collection consists of eighteen pictures and we should surely deem ourselves privileged to be the possessors of such an admirable collection. They were framed by our local photographer and the result is even beyond our expectations. There remains however a deficit of $13.00 on the framing of these pictures, and to meet this the school will hold a Tag Day Saturday, March 22nd. Pupils of the school will sell the tags and we ask your hearty co-operation in our last effort to meet this expense. Aided by the wholehearted efforts of the townspeople at our pantry sale of a few weeks ago we realized the sum of $34.00, this amount has since been raised to $42.00, leaving as stated before, a deficit of $13.00. If we may take your past support as any indication of what is to follow we feel sure these will be no difficulty in reaching our goal.

Knowing that everyone would wish to avail themselves of the opportunity of seeing this fine collection of pictures they will be on exhibition at Oakdene, Monday next, the twenty-fourth, from 3.30-5 p.m. An admission of five cents will be charged to help swell the general fund.

GRADE V—Class A
Clara Alice Copeland
Edith Muriel Harris
Eleanor Jean Morine
Lottie Alythe Coombs
Phyllis Margaret Harris

Class B
Mary Elizabeth Marvin
Dorothy Marie Potter
Eileen Margaret Banks
Daniel Peter Marvin
Allison Johnson Harris
Emma Alice Benson
Louise Evelyn McDormand
Hazel Mildred Henshaw
Ethel Louise Jack
Weldon Lyle Stevens
John Denton Langley
Jack Darrel Harris
Frances Elizabeth Parker
Gerald Archibald Buckler
Vivian Mae Freeman
Lawrence William Henshaw
Melvin Edward Rice
Alvin LeRoy Freeman
Aubrey Titus Darres
William Denzel Yorke
Phyllis Marie Rice
Arnold Gordon Rice

Class C
Douglas Lawrence Graham
Lawrence Sinclair Dukeshire
Phyllis Edith Thomas
Russel Garfield Gehue
Merton Edward Yorke

THE SCHOOL COMMITTEE

The School Visiting Committee visited the school on the afternoon of April 27th, and beg to report as follows:

Miss Morris', Miss Gibsons' and most of Miss Marshall's pupils had gone mayflowering. In Miss Rice's room we listened to a reading lesson. The room presented a very attractive appearance, having drawings of birds, animals, flowers, etc., on the walls. The children were learning a patriotic song for Empire Day, the words of which were on the blackboard. Upon inquiry we learned that only 9 out of the 33 pupils enrolled had been vaccinated. We next visited Mr Thurber's room where an algebra lesson was in progress. In this class about 75 per cent of the pupils had been vaccinated. We were shown a small patriotic play which the elder pupils are practising for Empire Day. Pictures of members of the Royal Family were noticed on the walls.

In Miss Morris' room we noticed one of the new Worlds Maps, also pictures of Currie, Borden and other prominent men.

Miss Cornwallis' pupils had been dismissed. The room was very bright and attractive and the words "Be Happy" were noticed on the blackboard.

Miss Marshall told us that 17 out of her 35 pupils had been vaccinated.

The School Lavatories were neat and clean, and the ventilation throughout the school was good. The basin in the hall was fairly clean, and the drinking fountain was working well. Mr Thurber drew attention to the fact that considerable annoyance was caused by the engine in the blacksmith shop, the fumes from the exhaust entering the rooms and the vibration being very noticeable. He stated that it was his intention to prepare a place on the school play ground for basket ball and he also told us that about 50 per cent of the whole school had been vaccinated.

Respectfully submitted,
MRS BENSON.
MRS. GOODDAY.

Is Your Harness In Condition for Snow Banks?

A lot of strain comes on the harness when your horse is working through a drift and the weak spots soon give way. Examine you harness carefully right away—today—and see if it needs repairs. It's a good time now before the rush commences. I also have New Sets, Collars, Blankets, Sweat Pads, Oils and Dressings.

J. W. FREEMAN
BEAR RIVER, N. S.

The New Pipe Line

The people of Bear River and vicinity are showing great interest in the construction of the new pipe line which will lead the water from the Little Salmon Hole on the East branch to the Pulp Mill at the mouth of the river. The work is being engineered by the MacDonald Construction Co., of Halifax, and steady progress is showing signs that the work will be completed according to contract, at present the road bed has been excavated and laid just beyond Canon Rock and the pipes are completed to the premises of L. V. Harris. The pipe has a bore of 24 inches, is made of Douglas Fir imported from British Columbia. The pipe comes in sections and is made up in its present form just prior to using. Every week-end the S. S. Bear River makes a special trip to St. John in order to bring back a cargo of the pipe.

The Bear River Pulp Co. is to be congratulated on their successful efforts in laying this pipe line for so great a distance since it means much to the people of Bear River industrially.

W. A. Chute well known as the Old Commodore and building mover, last week raised a large house and barn at Deep Brook for Avard Burrell. He also raised and put in new sills under a barn for Arthur Dunn at Bear River thus showing that he is still keeping up his old time record on the building moving business for which he is noted all over the Province.

The Strawberry Festival held under the auspices of the Methodist Church, proved to be a very successful event, the proceeds amounted to $35.

Some of the Bear River ladies started for Digby on Monday but spent such a long time at the Bar en route that they did not arrive until the next day.

Fred Reade has started a milk route, beginning Wednesday of this week.

Dr. L. B. ROOP
Dental Surgeon
Odfellows' Building
Bear River   -   N. S.
Phones: Office 44
426m   Residence 8-12

Developing & Printing
We guarantee to please those who look for the best from their films. Our Photo Cards are choice.
R. N. HARRIS,
Bear River

CLARKE BROTHERS PULP MILL REOPENS

After remaining closed for a period of several months on account of the serious water shortage Clarke Brothers' Pulp Mill has started operating again. All the old staff are back on the job and it is expected that both day and night shifts will be running by the end of the week. The extreme drought prevailing for the past few months has been detrimental not only to industrial work but it has made it difficult for many householders as well. In many cases the wells were as dry until the last rain came as they were at any time in the summer, and water even for ordinary uses had to be carried long distances in some cases.

LAKE JOLLY MEN HELP COMRADE

Last Tuesday Eldon Acker, head cook at Lake Jolly Cookhouse, was taken ill with appendicitis and it became apparent that an operation was necessary for him. When this became known among the Lake Jolly employees a collection was immediately started to help defray the expenses of their unfortunate comrade, and in a short time upwards of 50 dollars was raised and presented to him. The invalid was then put in a cot bed and transported comfortably to Bear River station a distance of fifteen miles where he was put on the train for Halifax. Robert Smith, Superintendent at Lake Jolly, says that the spirit of the men in the assistance they rendered to Acker cannot be too highly commended.

The latest report from the Victoria General Hospital states that the patient is being splendidly and should be around again within two or three weeks.

FIRE AT LAKE JOLLY

A disastrous fire broke out at Lake Jolly on Friday about midnight, when the entire mill, clothespin and dowel factory, and dowel stock were destroyed. Nothing could be done to stop the flames which soon had reduced all to a shapeless mass of ashes. All the cook houses, barns and dwellings were saved. There was no loss of life. The loss of this industry will be a great blow, not only to the company, but to the town as well—as for over twenty years this mill has given steady employment.

Pastime Players of Bear River Present "So This is London" to Crowded House

Oakdene Hall Bear River was crowded to its utmost capacity on Tuesday night to witness the presentation by the Pastime Players, of Bear River of "So This is London" and from the overture to the final curtain were all amply rewarded for the slight discomforts attending over crowding.

To write of the plot of the play the work of the different members of the cast or in fact to say much about it is almost superfluous, for every man, woman and child of Bear River who could get there was there, and everyone knows how good it was. The committee in charge and the director, Mrs. A. G. MacIntyre, as well as every member of the cast, who worked so faithfully to make of it a success, deserve the praise of the community and their reward was not only in the excellent patronage, swelling the box office receipts to nearly $150 00 but in the close attention paid to the acting and the instant praise in applause of every good point.

Before the opening of the performance Misses Thelma Morris and Hattie Marshall rendered a short programme of piano solos and duets, and this was greatly enjoyed.

The ladies' quartette, Mrs. E. J. Barrass, Mrs. L. E. Litchfield, Mrs. R. Benson and Mr. R. H. Purdy were heartily encored for their number between the first and second acts, and Mr. Walter Dukeshire, in blackface comedy, singing Travel On and the Coons Doxology, "brought down the house".

After the show the cast and committee were entertained at supper at the Grand Central, where the whole play was reacted over the dining tables.

When "So This is London" is repeated on Carnival Night, in the middle of the cherry season Oakdene Hall will need to be enlarged if the crowd is going to be accommodated.

Library For Oakdene School

Another decided improvement has been made in Oakdene School during Xmas vacation. The school had a fairly good supply of books, but no seperate room to be used as a library Now a 12 foot square has been partitioned off from the large chemical room, and fixed up nicely with bookcases and shelves, library tables, chaires etc. This room can also be used as a teacher's room and office, and will be a great convenience.

The sum of $53 was realized from the Xmas concert, and this money was to be expended on the library and equipment.

Mr. Reade, Secretary to School Board, has donated a fine set of books on "Historic and Scientific Progress of the 19th Century;" this set consists of about thirty volumes, and more books have been promised by other interested citizens.

The teachers are making a strenuous effort to build up and add to the library, and will welcome help from any citizen who can donate still more books.

Mr. Stewart Darres has secently purchased a Victor Electric Radio and has it installed in his ice cream parlor. We are sure his patrons will enjoy some of the good concerts received over the air.

Bear River local talent will present "His Uncle's Niece" at Lawrencetown Monday evening, June 29th and in Weymouth, July 3rd.

Mrs. John Yorke has received a large shipment of Easter hats which are now open for inspection.

**Dry Goods,
Groceries,
Boots & Shoes,
Crockery,
Etc., Etc., Etc.,**
at rock bottom prices.
Goods all Fresh and New.
Country produce taken in exchange.
Yours truly,

C. O. ANTHONY.

"Patty Makes Things Hum"
A Comedy in Three Acts
Oakdene Hall - Bear River
Tuesday, March 19th
at 8.15 p. m.

CAST OF CHARACTERS

CAPT. BRAITHWAITE, who wasn't so slow after all
    H. J. ANTHONY
CAPT. LITTLE, who had a little misunderstanding
    J. E. LANGLEY
MR. GREENE, who played the host   C. A. BURNS
MR. SMITH, a neighbor worth while   R. H. PURDY
MRS. SMITH, who proved herself a true friend VIOLA CRESS
MRS. GREENE, Captain Little's sister, who
  entertained under difficulties   JUNE S. L. SCHMIDT
PATIENCE LITTLE (PATTY) who managed
  to make things hum   GLADYS L. CURTIS
HELEN BRAITHWAITE, engaged to Captain Little
    FLORENCE I. HARRIS
HOPE DUNBAR, who is still hoping JENNIE B. HARRIS
HYACINTH, a loquacious colored maid CLARA W. HARRIS

Specialities between Acts
Homemade Candy for sale
PROCEEDS FOR THE UNITED CHURCH OF CANADA
This Play will be presented at
Bear River, Tuesday, March 19 Weymouth, Wed., March 20
Annapolis Royal, Thursday, March 21
Digby, Tuesday, April 2nd Bridgetown, Wednesday, April 3rd

Grand
Cherry Carnival
Under the auspices of the
I. O. O. F.
BEAR RIVER
TUES. - JULY 25th
1922

Biggest and Best Day Ever Held in Bear River
Band Music Throughout Entire Day
Calithumpian and Auto Parade at 9 a. m.
2 prizes will be offered of $15.00 and $10.00

10.00 a. m. Sack Race	2 prizes	11.45 a. m. Canoe Rescue Race	1 prize
10.15 a. m. 100 Yard Dash	2 prizes	12.00 n. Log Burling	
10.30 a. m. 220 Yard Dash	2 prizes	12.15 a. m. Canoe Tilting	1 prize
10.45 a. m. 3 Legged Race	2 prizes	12.30 a. m. Boys' Swimming Race	1 prize
11.00 a. m. Boys' Canoe Race	1 prize	Boys under 21 years of age.	
11.15 a. m. 440 Yard Dash	2 prizes	1.30 p. m. 1 Mile Race	2 prizes
11.30 a. m. Indian Canoe Race	1 prize	4.00 p. m. Base Ball Game, 2 league teams	

Grease Pole Contest open until prize is captured.

2.00 p. m. Grand I. O. O. F. Parade and Laying of Corner Stone
by Grand Master Wood.

PLAY 8.00 p.m. Play in Oakdene Hall Local Talent PLAY

Dinner served from 11. a. m. until 2 p. m. Supper served at 5. p. m.—in I. O. O. F. new hall.
Refreshments—Soft Drinks, Ice Cream, etc., at various booths
Proceeds from all sources for I. O. O. F. new hall.
All sport entries free Apply to F. A. CHALMERS, Chairm.

The social evening held under the auspices of the Bear River Women's Institute on April 26, in the Oddfellow's Hall, was very successful, both socially and financially. The decorations were simple and effective. The refreshment table, set at one side of the room, was especially attractive, centred with a beautifully decorated cake, flanked by antique Georgian silver candelabra each carrying three lighted candles; and with silver coffee services at each end. Mrs. A. B. Marshall and Mrs. W. M. Romans poured, assisted by other members. The attendance exceeded expectations, and an enjoyable evening was afforded to all. The officers and members of the Institute wish to thank those who assisted in making the evening a success, by their presence and in other ways. The net proceeds were $29.00. The programme was as follows:—

Choruses—Members of the Institute.
Short Address of Welcome—The President.
Vocal Solo—Mrs. Waldo Chute.
Piano Solo—Miss Harriet Marshall
Reading—Miss Vera Hiseler.
Violin Solo—Miss Marguerite Bain
Dances—Mrs. F. H. Hatheway, and Mrs. Waldo Chute, both in costume
Chorus—Institute members and guests
Impromptu Numbers—J. E. Steadman, Mr. and Mrs. John Harron Carl Miller.
Games and Contests—Small prizes awarded to the winners:
Potato Guessing—Bag of potatoes won by Mrs. J. E. Steadman.
Cake-Walk—Decorated Cake, won by Miss Florence Benson and Harry E. Harris.

---oOo---

A number of wee tots under the direction of Misses Hatfield and Rafuse, of Oakdene Academy Staff, gave a splendid demonstration in an amusing "playlet" of the modern manner of training children in health principles.

A recitation, Ode to Posture, was given by Master Ira Davis, in a very creditable manner.

Mrs MacGregor her four daughters and three sons arrived last week from Scotland and are visiting her daughter Mrs. Marvin, they expect to make their home permanently in Bear River.

Major A M. Simons is being congratulated on receiving two first prizes for his gladiola and one second for his dahlia at the Flower Show in Annapolis Royal last week.

RED AND RIPE CHERRY KING OF CARNIVAL

Bear River's Annual Celebration, in Honor of Luscious Fruit, Draws Throngs of Visitors.

Bear River's great annual event—the Cherry Carnival—took place Tuesday under ideal weather conditions. All day and all night auto parties were arriving, some from considerable distances. The Valley was well represented and there were several cars from the Capital City At an early hour the people from Annapolis and Digby, and the country near at hand, commenced to pour in from every direction by land and water until by the time the land sports started at 9.30 o'clock, fully five thousand people were there and this number was being constantly augmented.

The Cherry Carnival is a community affair in every sense of the word. Whether that has always been the case or not, it has been Bear River's annual event for two generations and over, but for many years it has been managed yearly by some society or association and the profits accruing from it go to swell the funds of the body conducting it.

Last year the Oddfellows who were building a new hall had it; the year before that the G. W. V. A. and so on. This year the Bear River Amateur Athletic Association which is in need of funds to finance the ball team, etc., managed the carnival, and at seven o'clock with several events yet to come off, it is said they had receipts of over $1,000. They have had a very efficient managing committee in J. H. Cunningham and M. B. Alexander, who have the happy faculty of selecting good workers for the various sub-committees with executive ability to carry anything they undertake to a successful conclusion. The land sports were the first events of the day and they were well contested working up a great amount of interest. The winners were:

Bicycle Obstacle Race—1st, Curtis Hinxman.
100 Yard Dash—Josiah Packard.
Quarter Mile Race—Josiah Packard.
One Mile Race—Shirley Eisner and Bruce Read.
Three Legged Race—James Harlow and Leslie Kennedy.

There was a heavy rain during the night and this discouraged many who proposed taking part in the parade, but the autos and floats which were out were exceptionally welldone. There were only two prizes offered in each class, but the floats were so good three were awarded, the first to Levi Brooks for his representation of a hunting scene; the second to Joseph Russell, whose float was entitled Vimy Ridge, and the third to the Bear River Trading Company as a general store. The prize for decorated autos was awarded to A. G. MacIntyre, whose auto was decorated in an original way, as it was entitled a "Poultry Farm—see them grow," and represented the growth of a hen from the egg to an adult fowl.

The school loaned their famous collection of copies of great war paintings, which had been presented them by the I. O. D. E., and this was visited by hundreds.

HARRY MORINE GOES TO DEATH NEAR PORTLAND

TRAGEDY OCCURS ABOARD SCHOONER EN ROUTE FROM N. Y. OFF PORTLAND, MAINE

Hurled into the dark sea from the bowsprit of the schooner, Dawn Wilkie, with the snapping of a jib halyard, Harry Morine, 16, of Bear River, lost his life somewhere off Portland, Me., early on the morning of Dec. 27, while the vessel was on passage to Saint John from New York. The Dawn Wilkie arrived at Saint John Friday. Morine was making his first extended voyage as ordinary seaman in company with his father, Walter Morine, cook on the vessel.

The youthful seaman was tying up the cap jib of the schooner in company with Harry Clorey and Charles Scott, two seamen, when the top lift parted. Clorey and Morine were thrown from their footing and precipitated over the side. Clorey became entangled with the jib sheet, dragging in the sea and managed to save his life by clinging to the starboard spring stay.

Morine was thrown clear of the stays and sheet and disappeared with a cry beneath the ship's charging bow. Frantic efforts on the part of the boy's father and ship's crew failed to locate him. It is presumed he was killed by the downward plunge of the ship through the wave and that he did not come to the surface.

In addition to his grief-stricken father, he is survived by his mother, and three sisters, all of Bear River.

First Voyage

"You might say it was the boy's first voyage," the father commented as he gazed toward the rolling bay. He made one short voyage lasting a month, some time ago, with me. He has always wanted to go to sea and while in Halifax recently, getting ready to sail for New York, I gave way to his pleadings, and a place was found for him in the Dawn Wilkie's crew.

"You know how boys are. He wanted to be a sailor and I guess he wanted to see New York, too. So he came along and now I've lost my only son. Harry was an eager lad,"

HALLOWE'EN ENTERTAINMENT

The "Jolly Juniors" of Grade 7 and 8 of Oakdene School held a very pleasant entertainment in the Preparatory Room on Tuesday afternoon at 2.30 o'clock. The room was very prettily decorated with various colored paper lanterns suspended from the four corners and black cats and Jack O'Lanterns added to the color scheme. The door was opened by a witch in black and orange, and the guests were ushered to seats around the room.

Pres.—Chester Snell
V. Pres.—Idellah Davis
Sec. Treas.—Catherine Hirtle.

The subjects of the club was:—
To promote better citizenship.
To have perfect order and perfect lessons in school.
To develop courtesy.
To have each committee perform their duties regularly and faithfully.
To have the club hold meetings every Tues. and Thurs. afternoon with a programme once every month and on special occasion.

On behalf of this club, Chester Snell the Pres welcomed the guests.

The minutes were then read by the Sec.
Song—by the School
Welcome—Bernice McDormand.
Recitation—Idellah Davis.
Reading—Louise Weir.
Recitation—Catherine Hirtle.
Song—The Maple Leaf
Recitation—Stellah Woodworth.
Recitation—Gladys Curtis.
Duet—Hattie Marshall and Idellah Davis.
Recitation—Mary Romans.
Exercise—8 ghosts.

After the ghostly visitors had departed, home made candy was passed to all in pretty Hallowe'en baskets, after which the meeting adjourned by singing 'God Save the King." Three cheers were then given for Miss Peck, the efficient teacher of the Prep. Dept as well as for the members of the club. Great credit should be given teacher and scholars for the excellent program. These occasions help to bring parents into closer touch with the school, and tend to promote a spirit of mutual helpfulness.

New Club Organizes

Through the courtesy of Mr. J. E. Steadman, Principal of Oakdene Academy, Bear River, a meeting of boys and girls interested in forming a "Jersey Calf Feeding Club" was held Wednesday afternoon, after school.

Twelve pupils were enrolled, and the following officers elected: Pres. James MacGregor, Vice Pres. Walter Reade, Sec. Treas. Willard MacIntyre.

Great things are expected from this club, as the members are very enthusiastic and are children from families interested in the raising of fine live stock.

Tamar Marshall

Particulars are given in the American papers of the loss of the barque Struan bound from Puget Sound to Melbourn with a cargo of timber. Three days afte clearing Puget Sound the Struan encoun tered heavy weather, with fogs, whic drove the ship out of her course, and th vessel was left under bare poles. Th rudder was also carried away, and she. be came unmanageable. She rapidly fille with water, and as a last resource Captain Skoglund gave orders to cut away the mast and rigging. This was done wit the utmost difficulty and danger, th vessel then floating a helpless hulk, an waves making clean breaches over her fron stem to stern. Provisions were rendered uneatable, and water casks were smashed Without food or water the 18 men com prising the crew had to subsist withou sustenance of any kind, the vessel sinkin lower and lower, and only prevented fron disappearing beneath the waves of he timber cargo. On the twelfth day, whe all on board were more dead than aliv from hunger, thirst, and exposure, a sa hove in sight, and noticing the signals o distress came to the relief of the Struan The vessel turned out to be the Tama Marshall, from Tacomba for England, he commander took off the starving people Under careful treatment the poor fellow recovered sufficiently to be removed to th tug, which landed them at San Francisco

TRAGIC DROWNING OF TW WELL KNOWN YOUNG MEN OF BEAR RIVER

The community of Bear River wa greatly shocked by the tragic drown ing of two of its well known youn men, Cyril Burne, a young English man, and George Langley, the 1 year old son of Mr. and Mrs. Josep Langley, which occurred supposedl late on Tuesday evening, April 14t

They were last seen on Tuesda evening, when they purchased sup plies of food in town, and returne down the River, en route to the fishing cabin, below the Creek.

Friends became anxious when the did not appear as customary, fo supplies on Saturday night, and large searching party, on Sunda afternoon located their bodies in th bed of the river channel, near Cros by's Point.

Both young men were fine swim mers, but evidently the darkness an chilly water, and the strong win which prevailed, were too much fo a handicap.

An inquest, with Dr. Lovett Coroner, and a jury of townsme was held on Monday morning, an a verdict of "accidental death b drowning" was returned. The wi nesses were those who assisted the search for the bodies of the un fortunate young men, and those wr had last seen them alive.

A double funeral for both wa held on Tuesday afternoon, from th United Church.

Much sympathy goes out to th parents, relatives, and intima friends of the youthful victims this sad accident.

SLEIGH DRIVE AND FRATERNAL VISIT TO BEAR RIVER

A team load of members of Home Division, of Smith's Cove, paid a fraternal visit to Royal Division, Bear River, on Monday night of this week, and to say that they had a good time is putting it mildly. Notwithstanding other special attractions which were on in the town, there were nearly sixty members of Royal and Home Divisions present. After the opening exercises an interesting program was presented consisting of music, speeches, readings, dialogues, contests and games, which were heartily enjoyed by all present. During the evening a very bountiful and tempting supply of refreshments was served. At a late hour the members departed felling that they had had a "Royal" good time.

SCHOOL TAXES
are past due.

$1500 needed to meet repair bills and salaries this month. Will you help us?
W. W. WADE,
Bear River, Feb. 24.   Sec.-Treas.

The male quarette of the Baptist church namely, Messrs. Anthony, Marshall, Cunningham and Alexander rendered very effectively the selection "Tell Some One," on Sunday evening, which was enjoyed by a large congregation.

The tides have been exceptionally high this week; overflowing the streets in various places, and even flowing into the cellar of the Royal Bank on Monday.

MASQUERADE CARNIVAL

The first carnival in Evangeline Rink for the past two years, was held on Tuesday evening, Jan. 17th, when the ice and gallery were filled with skaters and spectators. The Bear River Band furnished music for the occasion, and the ice was in good condition.

The costumes were as follows:

LADIES.

Bernice Power, Butterfly.
Marjorie McDormand, Xmas tree.
Elsie M. Withrow, Registered Nurse.
Kathryn Purdy, K-K-K-Katy.
Lillian Cornwall, Clown.
Lucie VanBuskirk, Navajo Princess.
Katherine Marshall, Gypsy.
Mary Romans, Pocahontas.
Ruth Purdy, Snowshoe girl.
Miriam Wade, Scotch lassie.
Isabelle Cossitt, Queen of Clubs.
Louise Cossaboom, Night.
Fern Cossaboom, Bluebell.
Edna Peck, College girl.
Winifred Sullivan, Sailor girl.
M. A. McGinty, Great Heart.
Mrs. F. W. Fraser, Huntress.
Mrs. J. H. Cunningham, College girl.
Mrs. A. G. MacIntyre, Winter girl.

GENTLEMEN.

Bruce Read, Ogilvie's Flour.
Kenneth Eisner, Indian.
Hal McDormand, School boy.
F. Courtney Purdy, Vamp.
Lewis Clarke, Cavalier.
R. E. Cossitt, Jack of Clubs.
Gordon B. Cossaboom, Joker.
Henry Romans, The Imp.
Shirley Eisner, Cowboy.
M. J. Lewis, Naval Engineer.
E. S. Cossaboom, Pierrot.

An Apology and A Warning!

The Courier last week was the victim of a practical joker whose "Smartness" has caused a great deal of embarrassment to innocent victims and has placed this newspaper in a most awkward predicament. In Tuesday's mail there came a report of a wedding said to have taken place at Bear River on March 6th. The report was complete as to detail, mentioning the name of the officiating clergyman and of the attendants.

Just here we wish to make it clear that the report was not sent to us by any member of the Publicity Committee of the Bear River Women's Institute. It came separate from their weekly budget, but was mailed in Bear River and appeared to be genuine. It was published in good faith.

On Saturday morning we were advised by a member of the committee, that the story was a hoax. False in every detail, and without any foundation.

We beg to tender to the young lady and to the young man mentioned in the report our sincere apologies for the embarrassment which the story has caused them and their friends. And at the same time wish to clear any responsibility in the matter the Publicity Committee of the Women's Institute. They did not know the report had been sent in. If they had done so it would never have appeared, and the Courier regrets more than any one else can possibly do so, the unfortunate mishap.

The matter has been referred to the authorities and the writer will find himself or herself in considerable hot water. Using the mails for an improper purpose is a serious offence. To cause to be printed an improper story is also an offence against all decency. No self respecting person would do such a thing and the prepetrator of this "joke" will not be permitted to escape without paying full penalty for the offence.

SCHOOL ORCHESTRA CONCERT

The concert presented by the Oakdene School Orchestra, under the direction of Mrs. Carrol Clarke, was thoroughly enjoyed by an appreciative audience. Great credit is due the leader and members of the orchestra for the splendid progress made during the year.

Violin Solo, "Reve Angelique," Rubenstein—Miss Marguerite Baird.

Musical Readings — "Just Plain Dog," Hazzard; "The Clown's Prayer," Grogan—Miss Vera Hiseler.

Vocal Solos—"Calling Me Home," "Love's Old Sweet Song"—Miss Bertha Dukeshire.

Cornet Duet—"Drink To Me Only With Thine Eyes," "There's Music In the Air" — Lenfest Ruggles, Billy Benson.

Following the solo given by Miss Baird, little Miss Emma Benson, in behalf of the orchestra, made a presentation to her as a small token of their appreciation of her deep interest and splendid help during the past three years. Miss Baird, in her usual delightful manner, thanked the orchestra.

Previous to the last number on the programme, Mrs. Clarke expressed the thanks of the entire orchestra to all who assisted in making the evening a success. Special mention was made of Walter Harris, who has so faithfully assisted in conducting the orchestra during the practice.

The Members of the orchestra are:

Pianist—Louise Harris

1st Violins—Marguerite Baird, Roy Gehue, Watson Peck.

2nd Violins — Aileen Seamone, Daniel Marvin.

Xylophone—Geraldine Purdy.

Trumpets — Lenfest Harris, Billy Benson.

Horn—Lewis Langley

Cymbals—John Harris.

Triangle—Emma Benson.

Drums — John Sullivan, Clayton Hirtle.

Conductor—Mrs. C. Clarke.

Major and Mrs. A. M. Simons entertained delightfully on Thursday evening, when guests numbering about sixty sat down at 7 o'clock to a corn supper spread on long tables on the verandah. The evening was spent at bridge and dancing. The novelty prizes were won by Dr. L. J. Lovett and Mr. Horace Moore; the prize for contract was won by Mrs. W. M. Romans.

The Bear River Meat Market has recently changed hands, having been taken over by Walter Dukeshire. We wish Mr. Dukeshire every success in his new venture.

OAKDENE SCHOOL CONCERT

Oakdene School held its Christmas Concert on Thursday evening, December 22nd, with a full house. The following program was given:—

Carols.
Orchestra.
Welcome—Wallace Clarke.
Motion Song — "Jingle Bells"—Grades III and IV.
"Confession"—Six boys of Grades I and II.
Recitation—"If I Were a Policeman"—Douglas Marvin.
"Guiding Star" — Six girls of Grades I and II.
Drill—Grades V and VI.
"Ten Little Indians"—Grades III and IV.
Play — "Christmas at Spectre's Corner"—Grades VII and VIII.
Drill—"Snow Ball Babies" — By Grade I.
Dialogue—"Going Home for the Holidays"—Jim Campbell and Lawrence Townsend.
"Christmas Wishes"—Grades III and IV.
Spelling Bee—Grades III and IV.
"A Real Santa"—Grades III and IV.
Song—"Three Old Maids From Lynn"—Alythe Coombs, Edith Harris and Dorothy Potter.
Play—"Squaring It With the Boss."—High School.
"Good Night"—H. McCormick.

Santa then arrived and stripped the tree. Walton Snell presented Mr. Brown with a gift and Eileen Seamone presented Mrs. C. Clarke with a gift from the orchestra.

MASQUERADE POVERTY PARTY

The Bear River Women's Institute is planning a novel form of entertainment for the members of the organization and their guests, at Oakdene Hall on Tuesday evening, Nov. 28th, at 8 o'clock.

All attending are required to mask themselves, and come arrayed in poverty stricken attire of cotton fabric alone. Any extra ornamentation or "frills and feathers" will subject the wearer to a fine.

A programme is being prepared, refreshmants will be served, and old fashioned games played.

While the social feature will be uppermost the financial will not be altogether ignored:—each person paying according to their height 2 cents per foot, up to five feet, and one cent per inch over or under that number.

The committee in charge promise many novel and fun-making features, their slogan being

"Hark! hark! the dogs do bark,
The beggars are coming to town,
Some in rags, some in bags,
But *none* in silken gown."

HIAWATHA TABLEAUX

Sixty Tableaux illustrating the most important parts of Longfellow's beautiful Indian Poem "Hiawatha" was given on Monday evening, March 27th in Oakdene Hall, Bear River, under the auspices of the choir of the Methodist Church. The Tableaux was explained by quotations from the poem, and accompanied by appropriate music.

Reader—Mrs. W. W. Wade.
Pianist—Mrs. C. M. Mack.

CAST OF CHARACTERS.

Hiawatha the Boy, Miss Mary Romans.
Hiawatha the Warrior, Harry Purdy.
Arrow-maker, George Tupper.
Iago, Douglas Wade.
Mondamin, Joseph Langley.
Nokomis, Mrs. Fred Harris.
Minnehaha, Miss Kathryn Purdy.
Fever, Miss L. VanBuskirk.
Famine, Miss Hardacre.

Set I—Hiawatha's Childhood—10 Tableaux. Hiawatha is cared for and taught by Nokomis. Presented with bow and arrows by Iago. Shoots a deer and brings it home.

Set II Hiawatha's Wooing—22 Tableaux. Hiawatha meets Minnehaha, a lovely Dacotah maiden and, disregarding the warning of Nokomis, woos and wins her.

Set III - The Famine—7 Tableaux. A long, cruel winter causes Famine and Fever; Hiawatha prays and hunts, but Minnehaha sickens and dies.

Set IV—Hiawatha's Fasting—15 Tableaux. Realizing the uncertainty of the food supply Hiawatha fasts, wrestles with Mondamin and finds the Indian corn

Set V—Hiawatha's Departure—6 Tableaux. Hiawatha blesses his people, gazes westward, enters his canoe and paddles into the setting sun.

The above programme was presented to a most appreciative audience on Monday evening, March 27th, when the auditorium of Oakdene Hall was filled to capacity. The tableaux presented were of a very high character, and evidenced very great care in preparation The scenery was most realistic, and proved a splendid background for the varying scenes portrayed.

All persons seemed admirably suited to their part, and the costumes were most attractive.

Particular credit should be given Mr. Mack who had complete charge of the posing and scenery, and threw himself whole heartedly into the play.

Mrs. Wade, who read the poem so admirably, was also responsible for the selection of a number of passages which were enacted in the tableaux.

The music which was rendered by Mrs. Mack gave added charm to the pictures, and the whole performance was one well worth witnessing. The net proceeds amounted to $95, which will go to swell the Methodist choir funds

Citizens of Bear River have been enjoying the freedom from dust and the renewing of all growing things which resulted from the beautiful rains sent last week by a kind Providence at a time when all nature was parched and every garden threatened with distruction because of the long drought of previous weeks, an unusual happening in this fertile Valley at this time of the year.

Two Cars Badly Damaged

On Sunday morning a serious accident occurred on the School House Hill, just opposite the United Church, in which a McLaughlin touring car and a Buick Sedan were very badly damaged. The Sedan, a new car belonging to Robert Yorke, was parked on the right side of the road, awaiting the conclusion of Church Service, and Alvin Yorke, twelve year old son of the owner, was sitting in the front seat, his brother having got out of the car only a few minutes previous to the accident. The touring car came down the Clementsvale Hill, driven by George Stevens, of Bridgetown, accompanied by a son of Chipman Brown, Clementsvale. Coming down the hill from Deep Brook was Dr. A. B. Campbells car, occupied by the Doctor and Mrs. Campbell, and little son Jim, who were unaware that there was any car behind them out of control, as no horn was blown as a warning. As Dr Campbell's car approached the parked Sedan, the runaway car gaining speed all the way down the hill, the space between the two cars was narrow, and the McLaughlin ran head on into the Buick, immediately turning over on its side, throwing the two occupants over the windshield, the top of the car being down. The parked car had the bumpers smashed, windshield broken, lights damaged, etc. and Alvin Yorke received severe shock and several bruises, the two men also escaping injury. As the brakes on the Stevens car would not function, the driver was unable to change his gears, and on such a steep hill the speed gained was terrific. Church service was interrupted as the men came out to do what they could to clear the road, and assist Mr. Yorke to get his car up into his garage, the other car also having to be left for repairs. This should be a warning to all owners of cars to make sure that their brakes are in good repair at all times, as if the runaway car had struck both cars, serious injury must surely have happened to some of the occupants.

Owing to the long period of rainy weather recently the farmers in this community have suffered severe loss by having large quantities of cut grain exposed to the elements.

MURRAY Y. HARRIS

The tragic death of Murray Young Harris, who was killed by being thrown from a truck on Wednesday morning, removes from the town of Bear River, one of its best known and most benevolent citizens.

"Murray" as he was familiarly known, had innumerable friends, not only in the town and vicinity, but all over Canada and the United States, as through his many years of Public service as proprietor of a livery, taxi, and mail line, he had come in contact with a host of tourist, commercial and local travellers.

Always courteous and affable, always ready to respond night or day, the late Mr. Harris leaves a record of unexcelled service to the travelling public.

BALL TEAMS PHENOMENAL SUCCESS

From a position of obscurity or non-existence two years ag the local team has emerged into the position of one of the leading teams of the Province at the present time.

This result has been brought about by hard and consistent training on the part of the boys against handicaps which are of a very discouraging nature.

Entertainment At Corn Supper

Major and Mrs. A. M. Simmons entertained on Thursday evening of last week at a very enjoyable corn supper; at which about thirty guests were present. Bridge was played at several tables and an informal dance was enjoyed by the younger members of the party. The supper tables were centered with boquets of gladioli; when the steaming platters of corn arrived flanked by delicious sandwiches and brown bread and coffee the moon looked down in amazement on the merry scene. After a last Paul Jones in the living room in which everyone joined, three hearty cheers were given for the hostess and host and the evening ended by singing "For They are Jolly Good Fellows".

A Fool-hardy Bear

On Tuesday afternoon as J. Steadman, Principal of Oakdene school was motoring up the River Road he overtook a large brown bear and as the bear made no attempt to leave the road, Mr. Steadman being unarmed was forced to back up and drove to Smith's Cove returning at once with men and guns but found a clear road to Bear River.

On Thursday the same bear made his appearance on one of the streets of this town and was seen for ten minutes walking along the street and through fields, but as it was only women and children who saw him he was perfectly safe, but later men went out to hunt him. He had followed the stream out and Bruin is probably safe in his native pastures.

PREVENTS SUMMER COLDS
The pleasant tasting food-tonic, rich in all cod-liver oil vitamins.
Scott's Emulsion
Scott & Bowne, Toronto, Ont.

Mrs. W. M. Romans held her monthly "At Home" day on Tuesday afternoon of this week.

Miss Lemma VanBuskirk of the staff of the Bear River Trading Co is enjoying a well earned vacation with her parents at Bear River East.

During the heavy storm which passed over Bear River on Wednesday night, the barn belonging to C. W. Jefferson was struck by lightning. Although a hole was torn in the roof, shingles scattered about and uprights splintered, the barn was not set on fire, nor were the animals injured

HALLOWE'EN PARTY

The ladies of Elta Rebekah Lodge, I. O. O. F., celebrated their first anniversary in a very unique and happy manner on Monday evening when they gave a Hallowe'en party in Oakdene Hall, the invited guests being the members of Friendship Lodge, I. O. O. F. and their wives, together with a number of the personal friends of the members of the Order. On entering the lower hall the guests were greeted by a committee of ladies very gorgeously attired in costumes "fearfully and wonderfully" designed in all the colors and emblems that go to make Hallowe'en celebration famous. The staircase leading to the upper hall was decorated on each side with large "pumpkin grinners" and the hall itself was a scene of festive gaiety and "spooky" forebodings with its elaborate decorations of yellow and black streamers, and the proverbial "black cat" everywhere in evidence.

The evening festivities were very ably conducted by Miss Mabel Harris, Noble Grand of Elta Lodge, who certainly left nothing undone for the pleasure of the guests.

In a few graceful words she welcomed the guests to the first anniversary celebration of Rebekah Lodge, and said the evening's program would be very informal. The first number was "The March of the Spooks" excellently carried out by twelve ladies in very realistic "spook" costume, followed by the inevitable and ever-present "black cat" in life (?) size, who persisted in toppling over during the march much to the merriment of the audience. Other numbers on the programme were a piano duett by Mr. and Mrs. J. O. Harris, cornet and violin duett, Messrs Harold Brinton and Karl Schmidt, Miss Gertrude Barr, pianist; and tamborine and piano selection by Carl Miller and Miss Barr, all of which were encored. These numbers were interspersed with fortune-telling by witches who stirred the old black pot and doled out to the anxious ones their future destinies. If these proved dissatisfying one had another chance for a better fate by applying to the "wheel of fortune" on the opposite wall, which was a very popular pastime. Even the old time "apple bobbing" was not forgotten nor the doughnut dangling temptingly before the eyes of the would-be happy contestant for ownership. Prizes were awarded to the first and second successful candidates in these feats of skill.

But the surprise of the evening still awaited the guests, for on descending to the dining-room a very beautiful sight was presented. A large table literally "groaned" beneath its load of dainties and decorations Sandwiches, pumpkin pies, doughnuts and sweet baked apples, nestled among the profusion of yellow and black streamers extending from the lights above to the corners of the table, with candles and electric lights throwing a soft yellow radiance over the room. The favors consisted of "Brown-eyed Susans" which the guests wore as a souvenir of the occasion.

After all had partaken of the delicious repast so beautifully provided and served by the ladies, L. V. Harris, in a few humorous remarks complimented the ladies on the success and pleasure of the evening's entertainment. Three cheers were then proposed and heartily given for the ladies of Elta Rebekah Lodge, and a very happy evening came to a close.

CAPT. JOSEPH RAWDING

The death of Capt. Joseph Rawding, at Bear River, on Tuesday, Nov. 27th, removed from that town, one of its oldest and best known citizens.

Born at Clementsport, Annapolis Co., on July 2nd, 1838, "Grandpa Rawding" as he was familiarly called by the many outside his immediate family, who knew and loved him, carried his ninety years lightly, until recently, and was always ready with a smile and pleasant greeting for those he met.

Living as he has, for the past twelve years, with his daughter, Mrs W. D. Chute, at the Grand Central Hotel, he made hosts of friends among its guests, and the genial Captain will be greatly missed by them.

Capt. Rawding belonged to the era of "Wooden ships and Iron men," and was one of those who captained ships in the days long past, when Nova Scotia's wooden trading fleet was at its best.

GRADE I	
Jimmie Campbell	89 9
James Marvin	89.
Dorothy Darres	84.
GRADE II	
Lawrence Henshaw	93
Denzel Yorke	81 1
Emma Benson	81.
GRADE III	
Alice Copeland	88.4
Dorothy Potter	88.4
Daniel Marvin	87.
GRADE IV	
Isabel Davis	94 3
Dorothy Morgan	89 6
Ronald Rice	88.9

The good old time sport of horse racing on ice is not altogether a thing of the past, as the two races on Monday last, and the pre-ceeding Monday show

The first race at Barne's Lake, in Digby County, near Bear River, drew a large crowd of spectators, who watched a spirited race of four horses, locally owned, down the gleaming lake ice, Reuben Alcorn's horse. African King, coming in 1st, followed by John Freeman's, Lucie, 2nd.

I beg to submit the following report:

The Ladies' Aid of the United Church of Canada has a membership of 72. Two removals by death during the past year, (called to higher service.) The average attendance is from 15 to 30 members at each meeting. On January 18th a pantry sale was held and proceeds amounted to $22.50. April 5th, pantry sale $20.21. A garden party on the lawn of F. R. Harris, August 6th brought $235.93. On December 11th, our chicken supper and sale proceeds were $81.75 Our Aid Picnic was held at the home of Mrs. Walter Payson on August 19th, with an attendance of 31 members. We have given the men of the church $114.26 to pay off a loan in the Bank; installed an electric pump in the parsonage at the cost of $124.70; We have also given the men of the church $65 towards a parsonage debt; paid a man $20 for the cleaning of the church; besides other bills. The sick and visiting committee have done a splendid work, making 675 calls during the year, 100 over last year. We need to speak of the Sunshine Bag, for it sure carries its rays of sunshine into the different homes. This year 50 different homes have been blessed by the Sunshine Bag, carying flowers, fruit and cards. We have raised in the Sunshine Bag $12.79; paid out $12.59, and have on hand a balance of 20 cents. Four little puffs and a pair of blankets have been sent to the wee new strangers coming to our town; also pieced and quilted two large quilts for sale. At Christmas nine cheer boxes were trimmed and packed with fruit, candy and nuts, and sent to the sick and shut-ins. Also 12 greeting cards were sent to our absent members. We had a balance of $275.01 on hand. Have raised $448.40; paid out, $507.03, and have a balance of $216.38 in the Bank. The officers and members have all worked to make 1930 a year of service for the Master.

Respectfully submitted
(Mrs.) Flo. J. Harris
Recording Secretary

Mrs. Bessie Parker, of Shubenacadie, Hants County, announces the engagement of her daughter, Verna Clare, to Peter Alexander MacGregor, son of the late Mr. and Mrs. P. MacGregor, of Helensburgh, Scotland, the marriage to take place in August.

On Sunday morning, December 27th, the congregation of the Hillsburg United Church, Bear River, presented a purse of money to their organist, Mr. Ralph Purdy.

This is Mr. Purdy's fiftieth year as organist of the Hillsburg United Church, and the congregation took this way of showing their appreciation of his loyalty and faithfulness.

Mrs. John Roop entertained at a dinner party, on Friday, in honor of Mrs. Lillian Hubley, a Bear River girl who has spent the past fourteen years in Manitoba, and has returned to remain indefinitely.

YE FRIENDLY TEA SHOPPE

will be opened for business on Wednesday, June 1st., at 2 p.m., under the management of Mrs. Lillian A. Hubley, a Bear River girl. Her aim is to give service and satisfaction.

A specialty is being made of waffles with maple syrup. Ice cream will also be served daily.

We cater to afternoon teas, also bridge and auto parties. If you want a lunch to take out try us, and see if we can please you.

THE MINSTREL SHOW

A large and appreciative audience, which filled Oakdene Hall to capacity, greeted the performance of the minstrel show, "Hello," put on by local talent of Weymouth, under the direction of Dr. D. J. Hill. The parts were all well taken, but special mention might be made of the step dancing of Miss Martin and to the ballet dancing by Miss Evelyn Melanson. The stage was attractively arranged by members of the Carnival Committee.

The annual business meeting of the Baptist Church was held in the church vestry on Wednesday, January 20th. A large number attended. Very encouraging reports were received from all church organizations. Each branch of the work reported a successful year, and all showed a small cash balance on hand. The Philathea and Progressive Bible Classes had sent out at Christmas time some 38 good cheer boxes which reached 54 members of the classes who were much cheered by the thoughtfulness of their fellow members. Many of those remembered have been unable through ill health to attend the meetings of the classes for some time. The Missionary Society had a good year reporting regular meetings well sustained and nearly as much money raised for Missions as last year in spite of the depression. The Church Treasurer reported a small balance on hand at the close of the year with outstanding indebtedness of about $100. The pastor reported 448 sick and pastoral calls made during the year. Other activities included work among the boys and girls, the Senior and Junior B. Y. P. U. and the Mission Band. All these are doing excellent work. More than 250 sermons, addresses and talks were prepared and delivered by the pastor during the year. The Church has served through its pastor, the community, Denomination at large, the Boy Scouts Association, and the Sons of Temperance during the year just closed. In spite of severe losses through death and removals to other places during the year just closed, the church faces the future with confidence.

Gerald Reginald Rice

Gerald Reginald Rice, son of Mr. and Mrs. Reginald Rice, passed away on Tuesday evening May 10th., after an illness of over three weeks. He was a bright, winsome little lad of 10 years of age, and will be greatly missed at home and at school. He is survived by his parents, three sisters and two brothers. The funeral was held on Friday afternoon from his late home, the service being conducted by Rev. A. A. MacLeod, assisted by Rev. P. C. Henderson. The Grades III, IV and V pupils of Oakdene School marched. The floral tributes were many and beautiful. Interment was made in Mount Hope cemetery.

The United Baptist church held its annual garden party on the grounds of Mrs. John Roop, on Wednesday afternoon of last week. Weather conditions were perfect, and the stately maples surrounding the lawn, made a fitting background for the bountifully laden tables, and booths where handwork and fancy articles were displayed. About 250 people were seated at the tables and did justice to the splendid fare provided.

FARMERS' MEETING HELD IN BEAR RIVER

Though the "depression" is very much in evidence in all classes of business, perhaps the Agricultural industry is not the hardest hit when everything is considered. But, however that may be, a not too despondent lot of farmers met Thursday evening in the Masonic Reading Room to hear addresses by County Representatives R. LeBlanc, of Digby County, and A. J. Steele, of Truro.

HAVE IT REPAIRED

Mr. Citizen, you who have a position and an income, don't forget that there are quite a number of men and women who are not so fortunate and consequently have empty larders and find it very hard to keep the wolf away. Look around and see if you haven't something to do to your home, or car, or boat, that will give some of these idle people a couple of days' work; then look them up if you need them because they consider that bumming a day's work is about the same as bumming a loaf of bread. Following is an approximate list of what one of those men could buy with two days' pay at two dollars a day:

4 loaves Bread	.40
1 lb. Dairy Butter	.25
2 doz. Eggs	.30
4 pts. Milk	.20
½ lb. Tea	.15
1 lb. Lard	.15
2 lbs. Beans	.06
1 qt. Molasses	.17
3 lbs. Sugar	.24
1 pkg. Cereal	.20
1 lb. Steak	.15
1 Fresh Fish	.15
1 peck Potatoes	.15
1 lb. Pork	.15
2 lbs. Prunes	.15
2 lbs. Onions	.10
Small Vegetables	.25
Seasoning	.25
2 pkgs. Tobacco	.30
1 box Matches	.10
	$3.87

The remaining 13 cents allows for a little leeway on the prices.

Our Long Service Employees

MISS AGNES E. LISKE
From the Monthly Bulletin of the Maritime Telephone Company.

Miss Liske was born at Port Medway, but early in life moved to Bear River, where she took a position with the Western Union Telegraph Company as Agent. Evidently, however, the science of transmitting the spoken word held a stronger attraction for her, for after a time severed her connection with the Western Union and took up Telephony. If Telephony was not her first love, it was, and evidently has continued, her greatest, for she has made it her life work.

Throughout the years that she has been in the employ of our Company, her work has always been characterized by an earnest concientious performance of it, and a deep appreciation of the watchward of Telephony, "Service."

Of Miss Liske's private life, interests and hobbies we have been able to learn but little. We hear that she almost forbade this write-up when approached by our correspondent in the "Valley" for material, and consequently, the information secured was somewhat meagre. However, of her personality we have learned that though she had a great aversion to being in any way forced into the limelight, she is noted for her kindliness and generosity. A worthy cause always finds in her a helping hand and a generous contributor, and the needy and indigent a kindly friend. Miss Liske's humane acts are always performed with the unobtrusiveness which invariably marks the truly generous spirit.

S.E Neville, our service salesman, has mentioned the fact that at one time Miss Liske taught him in Sunday School, at Port Medway. We must admit regretfully that S. E., to all appearances, has not profited as he should have and as one would expect him to from her precept and example.

Further "research" reveals the fact that Miss Liske in her younger days was an expert on skates. Report has it that she was both the pride and envy of the young folks around Bear River.

A charming little bungalow, in a beautiful situation on the hillside near to and commanding a beautiful view of the pretty village where she has spent the greater part of life, is Miss Liske's home. There, when the time comes for her to take a well-earned rest she will retire to a home of her own, the centre of such a circle of loving friends as can only be commanded by one gifted with a nature truly fine.

OSWALD O RICE
:: Mason ::
AND STONE CUTTER
Plaster of Paris Cement Mortar, Granite and Dynamite always on Hand
Blasting Done Satisfactorily

On Monday evening Jan.30th under the auspices of the B. R. W. Dr. W. J. Wright will give a lecture on Africa in "The Green Lantern Hall" illustrated by a large number of lantern slides. The proceeds to be given to the Memorial Fund.

As Dr. Wright has spent several years recently in Africa, and is fully conversant with his subject, this promises to be a most interesting evening. A detailed notice will appear later.

On Saturday night about nine o'clock when Edward Alcorn and little grand daughter were returning to their home from town, while crossing the bridge near Potters Mill the team was struck by a large car. Mr. Alcorn was thrown from the team and badly bruised, and one of the horses was considerably cut. The full extent of Mr. Alcorn's injuries is not yet determined.

BUILDING MOVER!

I am prepared to move and raise all classes of buildings by land or water. Also

Raising and Moving Vessels, Hoisting Boilers and Engines Out of Steamers.

Have had forty years experience in the business and am the only practical building mover in the lower provinces.

PRICES RIGHT.

W. A. CHUTE
BEAR RIVER, ANNAPOLIS CO

The Scouts are glad to learn that Don McDormand of the Beavers is able to be around again. Don had a shooting accident a short time ago and fortunately escaped from what might have been a serious accident.

On Tuesday evening Mr. and Mrs. Gilbert Hubley of Bear River were in their garden when a large cow moose came through their back yard, passed a few feet away, calmly surveyed them for several minutes, then crossed the front yard to the main road, again paused, and finally went away through the adjoining field of Harold Davis.

For several years the citizens of this town and vicinity have been trying to secure a continuous telephone service as our Sundays and holidays they were often greatly inconvenienced.

The new service came into operation on Sunday last, and will doubtless be greatly appreciated by telephone subscribers and by our summer tourists, many of whom considered the lack of continuous telephone communications with outside places a serious drawback to their interests while in Bear River.

CRASHES 30 FEET, BUT MISSES DEATH

Crashing through the bridge railing and a drop of about 30 feet to the river bed below and alive to tell the tale, was the thrilling experience Saturday of Benjamin Marshall, traveller for the Northern Electric Company, when he missed death in an auto accident. Mr. Marshall was enroute to Annapolis from Digby and was turning the treacherous corner on Victoria bridge when his car skidded on the planking slippery with heavy rains. It was impossible to stop headway and the car drove through the railing and fell to the river bed below, striking on the front end and turning over, to fetch up against a rock. The tide was out, but the car struck with sufficient shock to damage it extensively, the operator suffering cuts from flying glass. Assistance was not long in arriving and oxen hauled the damaged car to safety before the tide returned. Several cars have broken through the same bridge the past few years and it has been learned that only a little while before Marshall went through a truck preceding him had struck the railing of the bridge a glancing blow but recovered in time to avoid an accident.

At Bear River on Saturday afternoon, a new Whippet car with two out-of-town young men occupants, while going up the steep hill near Herman Harris' became unmanageable and plunged over a high bank, turning over five times, denting top of car, breaking three windows, crushing the running board, but not injuring the occupants.

SUNLIGHT SOAP

$5,000 REWARD will be paid to any person who proves that Sunlight Soap contains any injurious chemicals or any form of adulteration.

is equally good with hard or soft water.

If you use Sunlight Soap in the Sunlight way (follow directions) you need not boil nor rub your clothes, and yet you will get better results than with boiling and hard rubbing in the old-fashioned way.

WEDDINGS
Macgregor-Parker

A wedding of interest to Bear River friends was solemnized on August 26th, at the home of Mrs. Bessie A. Parker, North Salem, Hants County, when her daughter Verna Claire was united in marriage to Peter Alexander MacGregor of Bear River.

The bride looked very charming in a gown of white chiffon and lace with bridal veil and orange blossoms. Her arm boquet was of lillies of the valley and roses. The bridesmaid, Miss Marion Parker, R. N. of Salem, Mass. wore a dress of white chiffon and lace and carried a boquet of sweet peas and roses. Mr. Charles Bishop of New York was groomsman, Mrs. Lawrence Parker of North Salem, Mass. played the wedding march.

The ceremony was performed by Rev. A. I. Higgins of Middleton assisted by Rev. Mr. Vincent.

The home was beautifully decorated with cut flowers, the color scheme in the dining room being yellow and white, the gift room in blue and white, with the dining room in pink and white.

The ceremony was followed by a reception, and after receiving the best wishes of a host of friends, the bride and groom left on a trip through the province after which they will reside in Bear River. The bride's travelling suit was of blue and sand silk crepe with hat and accessories to match. The groom's gift to the bride was a wrist watch, and to the bridesmaid an amethyst pendant, and to the organist, a necklace. The wedding gifts of china, linen, cut glass, silver, etc., were very numerous, testifying to the popularity of both bride and groom.

On Wednesday afternoon a grass fire was set on the farm of Peter MacGregor, of which he lost control, and it caught in his woodshed, which with its contents, consisting of his year's firewood (about eight cords) and farming implements, were burned to the ground. There was no insurance.

W. W. Clarke

After a brief illness, W. W. Clarke passed away at his residence in Bear River, on Tuesday, aged 78 years. For many years associated with the late W. G. Clarke and B. C. Clarke, in the firm of Clarke Bros. Ltd., and later as President of the Bear River Trading Co. Ltd., his passing will be keenly felt by the community. He was a Commissioner of Schools and a member of the Board of Governors of Acadia University. As Deacon of the Bear River United Baptist Church, he was Superintendent of Sunday Schools for many years, and filled the office of Church Clerk for 35 years. In every walk of life he lived as a true Christian, and leaves behind him a community that mourns with his family. He is survived by his wife, three sons and one brother. The funeral service was conducted by Rev. A. A. MacLeod.

Charles Benjamin Bishop, of New York arrived here recently and is spending several weeks at the home of Mr. and Mrs. Jesse O. Harris.

Mr. and Mrs. Wm. McCormack had a fortunate escape from serious injury on Monday, when their horse stumbled and fell, throwing both occupants of the carriage to the frozen ground. Mrs. McCormack was unhurt, but Mr. McCormack received a nasty cut between the eyes and several quite severe bruises.

Little Joyce Townshend who has been spending the summer with her grandfather, Major A. M. Simons returned on Thursday to her home in Boston.

Rev. Father MacKey will hold services in the Catholic Church at Bear River on the first Sunday of every month until further notice.

Daniel Marvin who has been at Camp Hill hospital for some time, returned home on Monday.

Funeral of the Late W. G. Clarke

On Sunday afternoon, Dec. 6, after a short service at the residence for immediate relatives, the funeral service for the late W. G. Clarke was held in the United Baptist Church, of which Mr. Clarke was a member and was conducted by Rev. A. A. MacLeod, pastor of the church, assisted by Rev. C. L. Blanchard, of the United church of Canada.

The funeral was attended by many hundreds of people, including friends from Yarmouth Kentville and intervening towns in the Valley, and members of the Annapolis Municipal Council were present in a body.

Mr. Clarke was a member of one of the oldest Bear River families, and spent his entire life in this town, where he carried on business operations for a period of over fifty years, and his singular gifts of heart and mind early earned for him a prominent place in all phases of community life.

The late Mr. Clarke, who was a son of the late Richard Clarke and Ethlyn Rice Clarke, was predeceased a number of years ago by his wife, a daughter of the late Alpheus Marshall, of this town. He is survived by three daughters, Edith (Mrs. J. H. Cunningham), Josephine (Mrs A. G. MacIntyre) of Bear River; and Annie Louise (Mrs. F. W. Fraser), now residing in Kingston, Jamaica, where her husband occupies the post of Canadian Trade Commissioner; also two brothers, Wallace W., and Bernard C. Clarke, both of Bear River.

Interment with Masonic honors, took place in Mount Hope cemetery, conducted by The Keith Lodge, the pall bearers being R. H. Purdy, F. R. Harris, Boyd Rice, Harry E. Harris, Joseph Langley and Major A. M. Simons.

Mrs. F. W. Fraser and two children, Clarke and Mary Ellen, of Kingston, Jamaica, arrived in Bear River Tuesday and are the guests of Mr. and Mrs. J. H. Cunningham.

On Wednesday last Jim Campbell entertained a fishing party made up of a number of his young friends and their mothers. Unfortunately the threatening skies forced them to return to town before enjoying the traditional "fish chowder" on Bear Island. This portion of the refreshments was served at Jim's home. Fishing was not very brisk, but each family had at least one to carry home.

Mrs. Howard Cunningham entertained at a very enjoyable tennis tea on Friday afternoon at her home. After tennis the guests assembled on the veranda where tea was served, bringing to an end a very pleasant afternoon.

Blossom season in Bear River is fully three weeks ahead of the usual time. In a few days our apple orchards will be gloriously beautiful in their array of pink and white blossoms.

Mrs. William Johnson is nursing at the home of Daniel Marvin, Mrs. Marvin having been critically ill.

The worst storm of the season started on Thursday night last and continued Friday, Saturday and Sunday. Some roads are not passable.

Ian Alexander Marvin

The death of Ian Alexander, seven months old son of Mr. and Mrs. Daniel Marvin, occurred suddenly on Saturday morning last, after an illness of only a few days. Due to the severe snowstorm, the body was taken to Annapolis Royal by train on Monday, where with Father Leo Murphy officiating, interment was made in St. Luke's cemetery. Nine brothers and sisters survive.

Mr. and Mrs. Marven went to Kentville last Monday. Mr. Marven returned next day, but Mrs. Marven will remain there for medical treatment.

Mrs. Wm. Johnson, Waldeck, went to Kentville with Daniel Marven and family, to assist them in getting settled in their new home.

Cedar lined cigar box by Daniel Marvin, courtesy of Clarke Fraser.

Aunt Elsie's powder jar.
The dent from Grandmother is to the right along the rim.

Daniel Marvin's cigarette box, and if you open it up, you can still smell tobacco. He later used it to hold his war medals. Mary kept the remainder of his war medals inside along with a poppy, and they are still there. Mary only had two pieces of her father's brass work, but of all the pieces he made, this is without a doubt the most valuable, as she writes in *Kentville*.

Brass desk set made by Daniel Marvin and on display at the Bear River museum. Originally given to Mrs. McCormick.

/ 572

ATTESTATION PAPER.
205th BATT'N C E F
CANADIAN OVER-SEAS EXPEDITIONARY FORCE.

No. 240257

Folio.

QUESTIONS TO BE PUT BEFORE ATTESTATION.
(ANSWERS.)

1. What is your surname? .... Marvin.
1a. What are your Christian names? .... Daniel.
1b. What is your present address? .... 155 Hughson St. N. Hamilton, Ont.
2. In what Town, Township or Parish, and in what Country were you born? .... Newport, Virginia, U.S.A.
3. What is the name of your next-of-kin? .... Marvin, Victoria.
4. What is the address of your next-of-kin? ..... 119 34th St. Newport, Virginia. U.S
4a. What is the relationship of your next-of-kin? .. Mother.
5. What is the date of your birth? .... 10th August 1890
6. What is your Trade or Calling? .... Coppersmith.
7. Are you married? .... No.
8. Are you willing to be vaccinated or re-vaccinated and inoculated? .... Yes.
9. Do you now belong to the Active Militia? ...... No.
10. Have you ever served in any Military Force? .. Yes, United States Army. 4 years.
    If so, state particulars of former Service.
11. Do you understand the nature and terms of your engagement? .... Yes.
12. Are you willing to be attested to serve in the CANADIAN OVER-SEAS EXPEDITIONARY FORCE? .. Yes.

DECLARATION TO BE MADE BY MAN ON ATTESTATION.

I, ...Daniel Marvin........................., do solemnly declare that the above are answers made by me to the above questions and that they are true, and that I am willing to fulfil the engagements by me now made, and I hereby engage and agree to serve in the Canadian Over-Seas Expeditionary Force, and to be attached to any arm of the service therein, for the term of one year, or during the war now existing between Great Britain and Germany should that war last longer than one year, and for six months after the termination of that war provided His Majesty should so long require my services, or until legally discharged.

Daniel Marvin .... (Signature of Recruit)

Date ....27th March 191 6 .... W.R.C. English .... (Signature of Witness)

OATH TO BE TAKEN BY MAN ON ATTESTATION.

M-469   Available for one Month only from date of Discharge from Hospital.

NOTICE: This certificate is granted provisionally pending settlement of the Bearer's claim to Pension or Gratuity, for which purpose his Certificate of Service has been forwarded to the Admiralty.

This is to Certify that Daniel Marvin Official No. N.K. lately serving as ERA on board H.M. Ship Aquarius was invalided from the Royal Navy on 11th Dec. 18 and has this day been discharged from Hospital. 14.12.18.

His general character is VG   R.C.A.M.C.

Dated this 11th day of December, 1918

(Sgd) F. F. Mahon,
for Principal Medical Officer
Surgeon Commander

Lieutenant for
Commodore (on duty)

Marriages

MARVIN — MACGREGOR. — At St. Joseph's Church, on 25th January, Daniel Marvin, E.R.A., to Mary Agatha, eldest daughter of Mr and Mrs Peter MacGregor, 95 East Clyde Street.

MACGREGOR. — Suddenly, at 95 East Clyde Street, on 8th inst., Peter MacGregor, gardener, dearly beloved husband of Elizabeth M'Culloch, and third son of the late John MacGregor, Moss Moidart, Argyllshire — Funeral on Wednesday at 3 p.m. to Helensburgh Cemetery. — Friends please accept this (the only) intimation and invitation. R.I.P.

The Soldier Settlement Board

CANADA

Agreement for Sale of Land

Between

The Soldier Settlement Board

and

Daniel Marvin

Land _Joseph L Howe farm_
Shaw Rivers Campbell Co

Province _Nova Scotia_

Dated _Nov 11th_ 19_19_

```
                          H.M.S. NIOBE,
         A 7000          D. Marvin, E.R.A.,
                          4/4/19.
Sir:
         Am replying to your letter Ref.No.26-16-23
dated Feb.11th 1919 referring to my reinstatement
deferred pay as well as Separation Allowance which
neither my wife nor I received, the only payment
was from the Imperial Government which as you
know is very small.

         In my last request I distinctly stated my
case to which you responded as far as my knowing
is concerned you did all you possibly could.  The
fault is not with your Department nor the Authorities
at Whitehall, but the chief writer at Chateau he
simply disregarded orders from the Imperial and
Canadian Govt. and made orders that placed me in a
very disagreeable position by discharging me from
the R.N.C.V.R.. Not only that but disobeyed orders
when ordered by the Admiralty to have me reinstated.
The result is as you now see am back in Canada, family
in Scotland, pay stopped January 2nd, remained in
England from December 18th 1918 until March 2nd and
with a hard struggle had 5lbs. given to me only for
me and my family to live with and no other income.
On my return to Canada no one seems to know anything
about me. Invalided the little money that I possessed
is almost gone in fact pretty near an increase of the
family is expected. Can you imagine how I am situated.

         Sir, these are no sentiments but facts. All
I ask for is what is due to me. I do not want
actions from an outsider or anyone who is not with
the Admiralty. Have asked the Authorities at the
NIOBE to see me through. The result of is have been
waiting over a month and no reply . $50.00 is again
offered me as an advance considered sufficient for
my family to make preparations to come to Canada
to live on and for me to buy smoking with.

         As it were the AdmiralsySec is taking my case
up in the meantime am patiently waiting which is
almost beyond human endurance.
         I respectfully ask you again to see that
justice is given to me.
         At least to let the resettlement board know
that I am entitled to Vacational training so as to
at least get off the NIOBE.
                          Yours obediently,
                          /s/ D.MARVIN,ERA.
```

574

Dr. J. Hayes. D.S.C.O.

4-1-20

Dear Sir

Have been discharged from the S.C.R. about 6 Months ago, and according to what I read in the G.W.V. Magazine am entitled to Medical treatment

Have been paying for my own treatment up to date But am finding these quack remedies too costly

Am laid up about 2 or three days a week which is the busiest time of the year on a Farm, and is mighty discouraging

Have been discharged with the lowest catagory, and did not apply for pension so for one to carry on with limited capital still less limited health is a job

I therefore respectfully request transportation to enable me to visit you as soon as possible, as at present am badly in need of Medical attention

I Am Yours Obedient
D. Marvin

Ship or
V.R. 2550
DoRM12

P.S. Please make out Passage for Deep Brook — Anno County to Halifax —

REVIEW: P.N.I.   Halifax.   Dec. 8th, 1920.

The Board of Pension Commissioners for Canada

FORM FOR MEDICAL RE-EXAMINATION   B.P.C. 107978

The following is a definite description of the man appearing before me for re-examination:

Regimental No. V.R. 2550   Rank E.R.A.   Unit R.N.C.V.R.
Name Daniel Marvin.   Date of Discharge 11-4-1919.
Place of Discharge Halifax, N.S.
Age 30   Height 5' 7"   Build --   Weight 140 lbs.
Complexion Medium   Colour of eyes Brown   of hair Brown.
Marks of Identification Scar on back of right ear.
Nature of employment, former Engineer.
present Farmer.

Subjective Symptoms: Man complains of headache and weakness. Says that during the hot weather after two or three days work he would have to go to bed and rest for a few days.

Objective symptoms: Well developed and well nourished man, is nervous about himself and feels that he cannot do any work.

The man appears to be physically fit and no reason can be found why he cannot carry on at his occupation of farming.

Bear River, N.S.
22-10-20

Dr. Hayes, D.S.O.
Nurses Home
Jubilee Road,
Halifax, N.S.

Dear Sir:

Replying to your letter of recent date I may add to make myself better understood, as follows - My anxiety to get out of the service was so great thinking I would instantly be cured, that I was almost certain that my illness would leave no after effect although my category was as low as could be, which should entitle one to a pension without anymore ado. For you see Dear Sir the word "Demobilized" cuts me off no matter how low my health is which is to be judged by my Category. Being a farmer and having to be laid up now and again plays havoc with Farming in general. Regarding my hearing and sight, I may state that my sight nor hearing was never effected. Where my injury is effective is in the nerve system bodily (weakness where most of the time, to an extent where the everyday physical requirements in order to earn bread and butter do not respond in other words not strong enough to do my work in order to live.

Am sending you enclosed the usual Hospital Discharge which is given to every man who is entitled to a pension at being discharged from Imperial Hospitals Apparently due to me being in the Royal Navy and returned back to Canada through the H.M.C.S. "Niobe" on account of being one of the few or the only Royal Naval discharge case the wording of my discharge was not as essential as my exit from the Service, consequently my Category was low according my health as you can see in my Medical Sheets.

As it were as small as the pension may be it can be well spent towards things sorely needed whereas if my health had stayed with me I could have earned same and be more content.

I did not realize before as I do now nor did I care then as I do now all I wanted was to get out of uniform, but certainly Sir you will readily understand and see that no advantage is taken on account of my anxiety at being released from the Service at a time when physical and mental weakness both are only responsible for errors.

Please return my hospital discharge

I am yours obedient, (Sgd) D. Marvin

BOARD OF PENSION COMMISSIONERS FOR CANADA
RECOMMENDATION FOR AWARD OR CONTINUANCE OF PENSION

Halifax District Office.

Date 1-12-20

B.P.C. No. 107978

1. Regimental number V.R. 2550
2. Rank at discharge E.R.A.
3. Rank when disability was incurred E.R.A.
4. Full name Daniel Marvin
5. Address Bear River, Digby Co., N. S.
6. Unit R.N.C.V.R.
7. Date of discharge 11-4-1919.
8. Percentage of entire disability nil
9. Percentage of pensionable disability nil
10. Date for medical re-examination nil
11. Amount of additional Pension on account of helplessness
12. Amount of pension
13. Amount of additional Pension for wife
14. Amount of additional Pension for children
    Total Monthly Rate $
14A. Date of Marriage
15. Disability and Disabling condition

Disability negligable

576

To: Dr. John Rankine,
D.S.C.R., Camp Hill Hospital,
Halifax, N.S.

Bear River, N.S., June 17/

MAY - 3 2005

SUBJECT: Daniel Marvin,- V.R. 2550 E.R.A.

Dear Doctor Rankine:

I can appreciate the difficulty in making a decision regarding the disposal of this man. My contact with him began in 1922. At that time he was receiving no pension, and his condition was attributed to neurasthenia.

In Camp Hill it was discovered that he had a piece of shrapnel inside his skull imbedded in brain tissue, and he was sent to St. Anne de Bellevue. He remained therefor a number of years, with fairly

---

IN ACCOUNT WITH — **Marion & Marion**
ENGINEERS & PATENT ATTORNEYS

CABLE ADDRESS:
"MARION MONTREAL"

Offices
MONTREAL, CAN. & WASHINGTON, D.C. U.S.A.

ATTORNEYS and COUNSELLORS in PATENT CAUSES,
PATENTS and TRADE MARKS throughout the WORLD.
364 University St.
MONTREAL

Mr. Daniel Marvin.   April 29th, 1926.

	RE: Caveat "Still Water Pressure Turbine	
TO:	Preparing and filing the necessary papers for a Caveat including Government fee	$25.00
April 6	By Cash	10.00
	BALANCE	$15.00

DEPARTMENT OF SOLDIERS'
MEDICAL HIST

acc Ste Annes Hospital

(a) Regimental No. Vr 2550
(c) Surname Marvin

Age last birthday 33   Heigh

Personal History   Born in England   Had a fair education   Went to sea at 14 and was there till after discharge from the navy. Has called Nova Scotia his home for 15 years. Married 1916 has three children used to be a moderate drinker but now a teetotler; heavy cigarette smoker.

Cannot stand hard work. when he works too hard he is sleepless and nervous and irritable. Noises bother him. He cannot drive a mowing machine on his farm. 2 He is dizzy if he goes to any height. 3 Claims he has lost sense of small for 3 years

October 25/23.

He has shown remarkable improvement. He is constantly engaged in brass work at which he shows himself to be an expert. He is somewhat exalted and bound to have his own way. He speaks in quite a natural voice and often laughs during conversation.

March 26.. Is worried over the outlook as far as making a living is concerned. He does feel equal to returning to his farm and taking the management of it. The same difficulties will arrived as formerly. he realizes that most of the management of the farm will need to be left to his wife. The question of a change of occupation as arisen but for fina reason he does consider that feasible. We advising him to try to arrange matters so that he can have a man to help.

DEPARTMENT OF SOLDIERS' CIVIL RE-ESTABLISHMENT

Report for six months ending June 30th, 1927.
Name of Hospital or Clinic STE. ANNE'S HOSPITAL.

Name MARVIN. D.   Reg. No. VR.2550   Rank E.R.A.
Original Military Unit R.N.C.V.R.   Service: Canada - England - France
Present Condition (including notes on progress during past six months, occupation, therapy and prognosis.)

This man has been on extended leave at his home, which we hope may result in his remaining there permanently. He is an unusual character after the so-called genius make-up, better at invention than at business, and consequently infrequent mis-understandings with those with whom he does business. Occupation shows exceptional skill in brass work.

MEDICAL HISTORY OF AN INVALID
ON DISCHARGE FROM TREATMENT

1 REGIMENTAL PARTICULARS Place: STE. ANNE'S HOSPITAL. Date: May 3rd, 1928.

(a) Surname: MARVIN, (b) Christian Name in Full: Daniel.
(c) Service Unit: R.C.N.V.R. (d) Regimental No.: VR.2550 (e) Rank: E.R.A.
(f) Enlisted (date): Sept.1916. (g) Discharged (date): April 1919.
(h) If in receipt of Pension, state Pension Number: Nil.
(i) Name disabilities on account of which pension is being paid: DATE RELEASED

MAY - 3 2005

2 SERVICE

TO BE SECURED FROM DOCUMENTS ONLY	FROM	TRANSMIS TO
In Canada	With Royal Navy at Sea	
In England	Sept.1916.	April 1919.
In France		
In other parts		

What is the probable DURATION, in months, of the disability or of each of the disabling conditions, if there are more than one? Permanent.
Treatment now completed:
Where treated (Place and Institution): STE. ANNE'S HOSPITAL.
Duration of treatment: from March 14th, 1923 to date.

The Board of Pension Commissioners for Canada

AUTHORITY FOR PENSION PAYMENTS

Received at Receiver General for Canada,
"B" Dist., D.P. & N.H., Pension Section, for

THIS IS YOUR PENSION NUMBER
107978 T X
PLEASE QUOTE IN ALL CORRESPONDENCE.

MARVIN DANIEL
(Pensioner's Surname) (Pensioner's given name) (Relationship to member of forces)

Camp Hill Hospital, Halifax, N.S.
(Street) (Post Office)

MARVIN DANIEL
(Surname of member of forces) (Given name of member of forces)

V.R.2550 E.R.A. R.N.C.V.R.
(Regimental No.) (Rating or Rank) (Ship or Unit)

| ENTIRE DISABILITY | 100 % | CODE NO. | B |
| PENSIONABLE DISABILITY | 100 % | CLASS | 1 |

AWARD

For Pensioner	$ 75.00	a month
For Married Pensioner (additional Pension)	$	a month
For children or brothers or sisters (additional Pension)	$	a month
Additional Allowances for wear and tear of clothing	$	a month
Addition to Pension for helplessness	$	a month

S.O. 701-2

TOTAL 75.00

NEW MONTHLY RATE $

DETAILS OF AWARD

FIRST PAYMENT

Pension to be paid at class one from May 4, 1928.

Adjustment and pension to be credited to "B" District, D.P. & N.H. Trust Fund #3, for Administration.

Saint John, N.B.
August 5th, 1931.

Thomas Fenton, Esq.,
District Administrator,
Department of Pensions & National Health,
Camp Hill Hospital,
Halifax, N. S.

Dear Sir:

Re: #V.R.2550 - MARVIN, Daniel

This will acknowledge receipt of yours of July 20th and we have a long preamble from the settler under date of July 22nd, which boils down to a statement from him that he wants to quit the farm temporarily and return at a later date and take his children back to the place where they were born.

Replying to the second paragraph of your letter, I may say that I do not think that the fault is in the wife's management. The general public in and about Bear River are of the opinion that Mrs. Marvin is an exceptional woman and has good managing ability. As a matter of fact, when Mr. Marvin was in hospital at St. Anne de Bellevue, they considered Mrs. Marvin a good risk and gave her all the credit she asked for and she paid it, and they think that if Marvin would stay away from the farm entirely and give her the pension coming to herself and the children, that she could make a success of the farm and I concur in this viewpoint. The trouble is that when Marvin gets home he buys everything that is offered for sale. He built a very expensive house for , in which we assisted to the extent of $1500.00 and which was unnecessary, as the money put up by this Department would have built a house plenty good enough for the place and the settler. Marvin also spent considerable money in bringing his wife's family to Canada. He nominated them and wanted them to come out and live at his home and was going to give them all employment. We refused to allow them to come out under nomination and finally they came out under the 3000 Family Settlement Scheme. Marvin took them all to his home and it was not long until they got into a row and all left excepting one girl and the boy. who came out here some years before the rest of the family. When we refused nomination Marvin was very abusive of us in not allowing this family to come out and made all arrangements to take care of them and after he got into a quarrel with them he was very abusive of the family and of himself for allowing them to come out at all.

Personally, I do not think Marvin has any intention of quitting the farm.

C. . Curren,
Halifax, N.S.

Bear River,
Anna. Co., N.S.
7.8.31.

TRANSMIS

Dear Sir:

I had the D.S.C.R. representative, Col. Hayes, visiting me a few weeks ago. He asked if I was anxious to leave the farm while talking to him. He pointed out to me several advantages which I would gain if I were not living in Bear River, such as cheaper clothing for the children and cheaper foodstuffs. I was undecided and felt that perhaps I would be better off where I was even if it was isolated, but in my heart I would rather be somewhere nearer to the City, and I had expressed this desire to my husband a few times while he was at home. I told him I thought the children would benefit by it through higher grade schooling, also religiously, they have never been to church through living too far from a Roman Catholic church. However, I thought perhaps Dan. would be able to take up farming again and that's the reason why I kept on living here, but that is impossible now as he feels he is unable to continue working it, so what's the use of me working myself when I could live more comfortably somewhere else. It does not pay to keep a farm if the owner cannot look after it himself. It costs more than the farm is worth, taxes, hired help, feeding stock, with little returns for one's labour.

I have thought over what Col. Hay explained to me and this is the reason for this letter. Then again, I'll have more time to devote myself to my husband and would be able to have my little boy's feet straightened.

I trust you will understand and give my letter your consideration, I am,

Yours very truly,

Sgd. Mary Marvin.

Gentlemen: TRANSMIS

As you requested, the following is description of general conditions, namely, my home, family and myself, including the cause of present actions.

Owing to my condition I have reached a stage where to exhent myself either physically or mentally is not only vain and senseless but utterly impossible in addition a waste of money which my family miss.

My present home being a farm which is upkept to the descreation of Mrs. Marvin's budget convenience and children's general welfare, money spent without a remote hope of returns adding isolation, discomfort, in every way. Certainly all those ills would have been non-exhastent if I were able to carry on, but whereas my condition is such that my disability becomes more distinct every day it only menas that unless my family is quickly removed from the farm to a home where they will not have to rely upon me, and not have to waste money on a farm where the family budget cannot possible be managed economically, the disorganization will inevitably assume a more distinct aspect and heavens only can tell what may come.

It goes without saying that when I first left home, thw work done become undone, confusion increased, and at present the situation is that Mrs. Marvin cannot make ends meet owing to position and condition which is all confusion. Mrs. Marvin's ability is above question, I know and see the wrong and cannot help it. One ill reflects upon another, breeds,multiply, and no amount of resistance in order tp return to baric conditions can be advised unless it is the re-establishment suggested to me by a Medical Board at St.Anne's which I then could not agree to, and now regret.

Have been advised to get off the farm in order to be free from work and worry which then appeared to me as the end of the trail as a working unit on earth which was repulsive. Now I must submit to being expelled for the good of my family and myself. The farm did appear to me then as the only place where I could possibly find some creative occupation, but at present the reality is exactly the same as Dr. Porter's described it and suggested remedy. When I questioned as to means, I was made to understand that from the time of my return to Civil occupation until my disability was recognised, fully a period of about two years, during which I received no pension, nor pay and allowance, that period pension would be used towards my family re-establishment. Now if that could be done then, it is imperative that such course be taken now, as the only means out of present difficulty. Since my disability was pensionable before I returned from overseas, they told me that there will be no difficulty.

Sir, I reluctantly and regretfully take this course, but I see no other way out and considering that the house my family are in can hardly be lived in safely for health and comfort another winter, I respectfully request that this course be taken as soon as possible.

Yours sincerely,
Sgd. D. Marvin.   D. Marvin

farm being liability, and burden without any possibility of ever receiving any form of benifit out of, adding another uncalled for burden upon me in addition to the responsibility of caring for my nine children all small, besides the distance from town, school, church, Isolation. The house is unfit to live in, even if it were repaired, it would mean more money wasted, besides lacking all facilities other people have to make their work a possibility without wasting time and energy. Had Mr Marvin been able to continue doing some work, there would be some hope for a change for the better, but the condition he is in all responsibility and work falls to me and leaves me hopeless for any betterment besides such conditions inevitably has a very bad effect on Mr Marvin which makes matters worse. To conclude I again verify our verbal discussion and decision, that is to get off the farm as quickly as possible before cold weather sets in as the house is not fit to live in for another winter with the children
I remain sincerely,
(Mrs) Mary Marvin

Name: Marvin, Daniel.
Address: Bear River, Annapolis Co., N.S.
NATURE of REPORT:

DATE OF REPORT — Day 2, Month 12, Year 31

Mr. Marvin has taken a very nice ten-roomed bungalow at Bear River. Rented from a Mrs. Reid of Bear River three minutes from school. Rent is $12 per month. Electric light, good large kitchen with tubs and water supply, large dining room and five good b.drooms. Well heated by good stove. It is papered and painted and with the new furniture from Simpsons the home should be a happy one. Select neighbours. I called upon the bank manager who stated that he found both pensioner and Mrs. Marvin most trustworthy and reliable.

I trust that administration will not now be necessary. The expenditure monthly will amount to the following:

$12 per month - rent.
$10 "   "   - Fuel and light.
$35 "   "   - Educational Policies.
$80 "   "   - Groceries, clothing, etc.
$25 "   "   - Instalment Simpsons.
$35 "   "   - Incidentals, music lessons, etc.
$197 being the total pension.

So far as debts are concerned they owe the Bank $100 on the Educational Policies, the bank paying the full amount $174 each six months in full, the pensioner and his wife giving the bank the monthly pension cheque and the bank deducting therefrom their $30 and interest on any outstanding balances. $35 p.m. should fully cover this item and in course of time they should have caught up and wiped off the $100 outstanding.

DORM 571

However the least said the better, the deed was done, the Mother is well and the boy is a perfect human specimen which makes 7 sons 3 daughters, no sick ones. You and I for all you and I know probably one of them may do something out of the ordinary to make more wealth while living for one never knows. At least let us hope they will. As to ourselves, that's altogether out of question.

To conclude
My Best Wishes to you and all at Camp Hill.
Yours Sincerely
Dan

DORM 646

4. Regt. No. V.R.2550 / E.R.A. Name Daniel Marvin Date Oct 19 32
5. Diagnosis G.S. Wound skull retained schrapnel in brain
6. Treatment prescribed A.P.C. Tablets
Rest — Freedom from worry.

7. Brief progress report This man has had a good month. He complains a great deal of pain in his head but his mental condition is better.

(Gun shot wound skull retained schrapnel in brain
A.P.C. (Aspirin) tablets
Rest and freedom from worry.
This man has had a good month. He complains a great deal of pain in his head but his mental condition is better.)

DATE RELEASED
MAY - 3 2005
TRANSMIS

8. Disposal of case _Treatment of regd_ — DORM 639

(OVER)

Pensions Dept
Camp Hill Hospital
Halifax N.S.

D. Marvin.
Bear River,
Nova Scotia.

4-3-33

Dear Sir

Please be informed that my boy Van Alexander Marvin died today at 6:30 A.M.
Born 24th of July 1932

Yours Sincerely
D. Marvin

"Without preamble, she opened her mouth and sang out as if her voice belonged to the hills."

Above: At the top of the hay field near the flat rock

At the entrance to the hay field in front of the house, you can still see the wagon ruts.

Photos by John McLeod unless otherwise credited.

Below. At the end of the gardens towards where the Chute Road drops down to Kniffen's Hollow. The house is gone except for an indent where the root cellar was, and the gardens around the house are still evident, but greatly reduced by growth, even since I first saw them in 2003.

"The last time I saw Mr. Kniffen was when he walked up from the Hollow to visit Dad, who was hoeing the gardens row by row.."

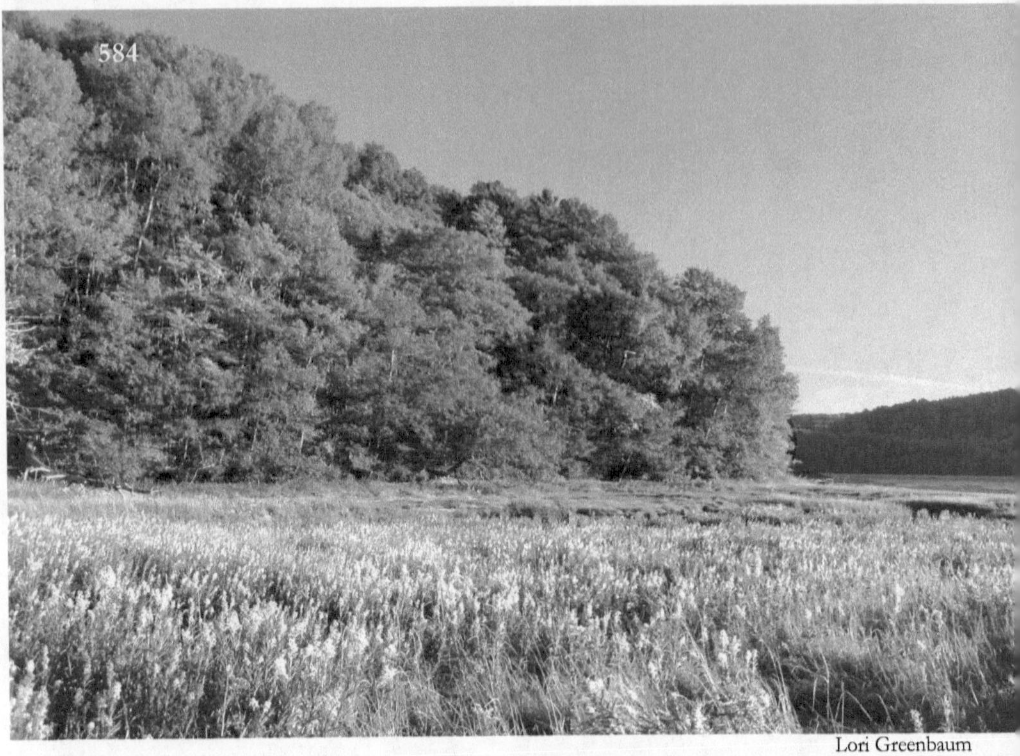

Lori Greenbaum

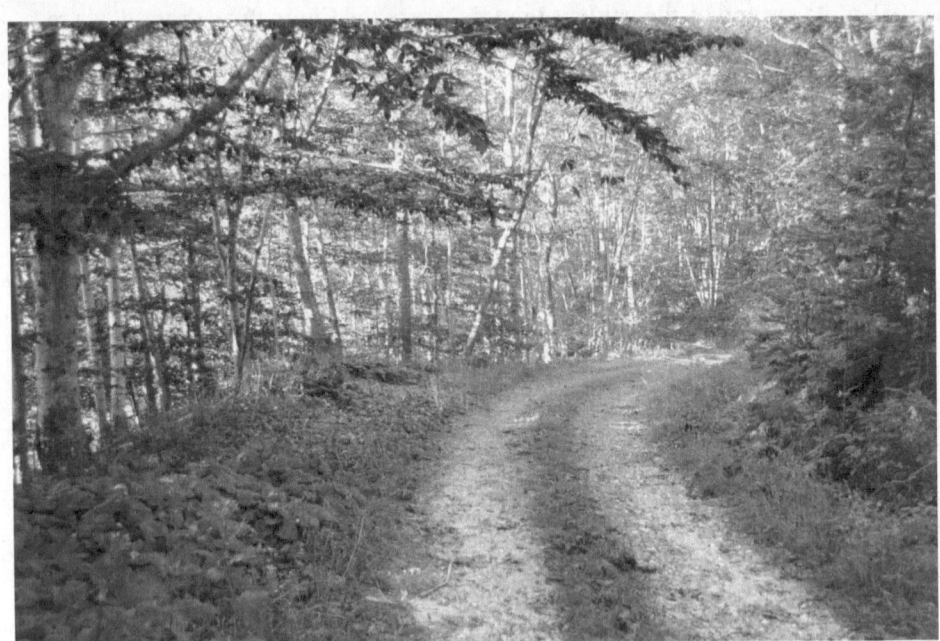

No longer with a colonnade of trees, but otherwise the same, the Chute Road leading down to Kniffen's Hollow is an S-shaped drop of about 100 feet. The foundation of the Kniffen's barn is still there, as is their well, but all the oaks are gone, the pasture and the lawn are overgrown, and the beach is now very grassy.

Kniffen's Hollow

"...I wish I could tell you about the magic of Kniffen's Hollow

The brook is not nearly as strong as it once was. The Chute Road crosses the Kniffen's bridge and turns up the hill (upper right) but ends before it reaches Mr. Bishop's, where the hill has been split (as if by a giant axe).

"Tooney sprung like the wicked witch and flailed away with her broom while Daniel cycled for his life. He saved himself by hightailing it through Jesse Harris' driveway..."

Lori Greenbaum

Uncle Peter's farm is the same and his house still stands.

The Chute Road

Except for the Kniffen's home, the Marvin's, and Mrs. Troop's, all of the homes on the Chute Road are still there. Above is Jesse and Stella Harris', now a B&B.

Although many untended apple trees dot the landscape, the Clarke orchards are gone, replaced in part by the Bear River Winery.

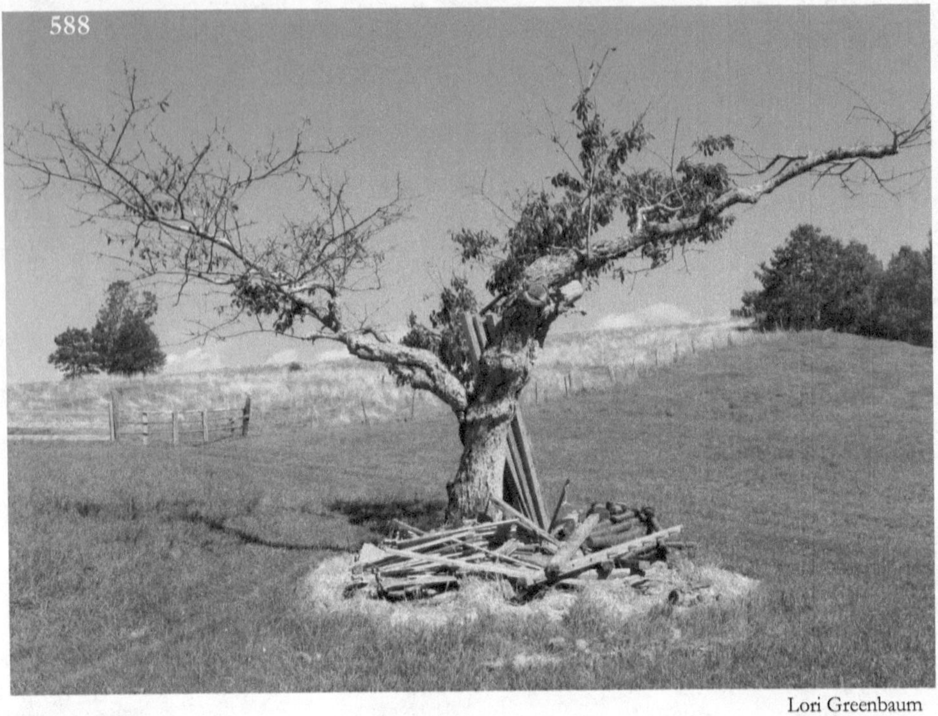

Lori Greenbaum

"...while on the other side, Fred Reade's expansive dairy farm swept up to the skyline."

'High on a hill opposite the Clarke home was the MacIntyre's bungalow with its lavish, well tended grounds, the nicest along the road.

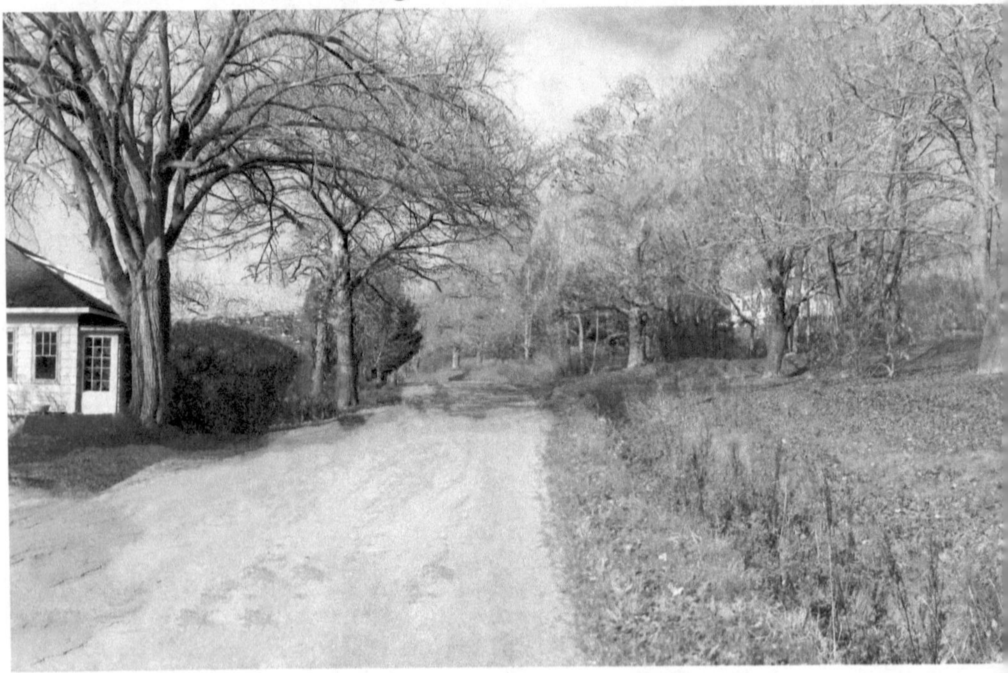

The W.G. Clarke house (left and out of frame) is still in the family, home of Clarke Fraser, world-famous geneticist (gifted with curly hair and blue eyes).

A reclining crescent moon hung like an ornament, while Harry clopped along through a shadowy canyon of trees."

W.W. Clarke's house on the Chute Road.
"we would detour onto the semi-circle driveway and run across the wide, wraparound verandah, peering through windows into elegant sitting rooms"

The Oakdene oak still stands thanks to a Principal who rushed out to stop a Department of Education work crew that had arrived to create a parking lot.

Lori Greenbaum

The Schmidt house

The lawn still spills down the embankment in front of the old Brinton house, and the stone wall is still there, though almost covered and difficult to walk on.

In the village

Lori Greenbaum

The Anglican Church

Lori Greenbaum

"that year I sat by a window that looked out the back of the school. There, I could watch the rise and fall of the tides, in and out, as if the ocean were taking long, deep breaths."

"Merton wanted to tell us a joke about a bitter end, which we didn't want to hear, not after Mr. Robinson. We stuck our fingers in our ears, and what followed was a bout of pulling and pushing and tearing about the tombstones to escape."

Lori Greenbaum

Many of the people in the book are buried in Mount Hope.

Inside the Changing Tides Diner, the Clarke Brother's safe is the last reminder of the old Trading Company

The cannon barrel is still in front of the Trading Company, which is now a book store and the Changing Tides Diner. Just up the street, the old Royal Bank space in the Oddfellows building houses an art store and a cafe.

Lori Greenbaum

Bear River has become something of an artist's community. Flight of Fancy in the old Clarke building and Oddacity in the Clarke warehouse behind it are both highly acclaimed in Nova Scotia.

It has been a long time since a ship docked at either the government wharf (above) or the Clarke wharf on the opposite bank.

Lori Greenbaum

The Trading Company and L.V. Harris' drugstore are still anchored in the mudflats, and high tide still laps at their undersides.

Across the street from Flight of Fancy (far left), L.V. Harris' (middle) is now a cafe. Mr. Anthony's store (right) sits in limbo with the original fixtures still in place. The old bridge is gone, as is the Packet wharf.

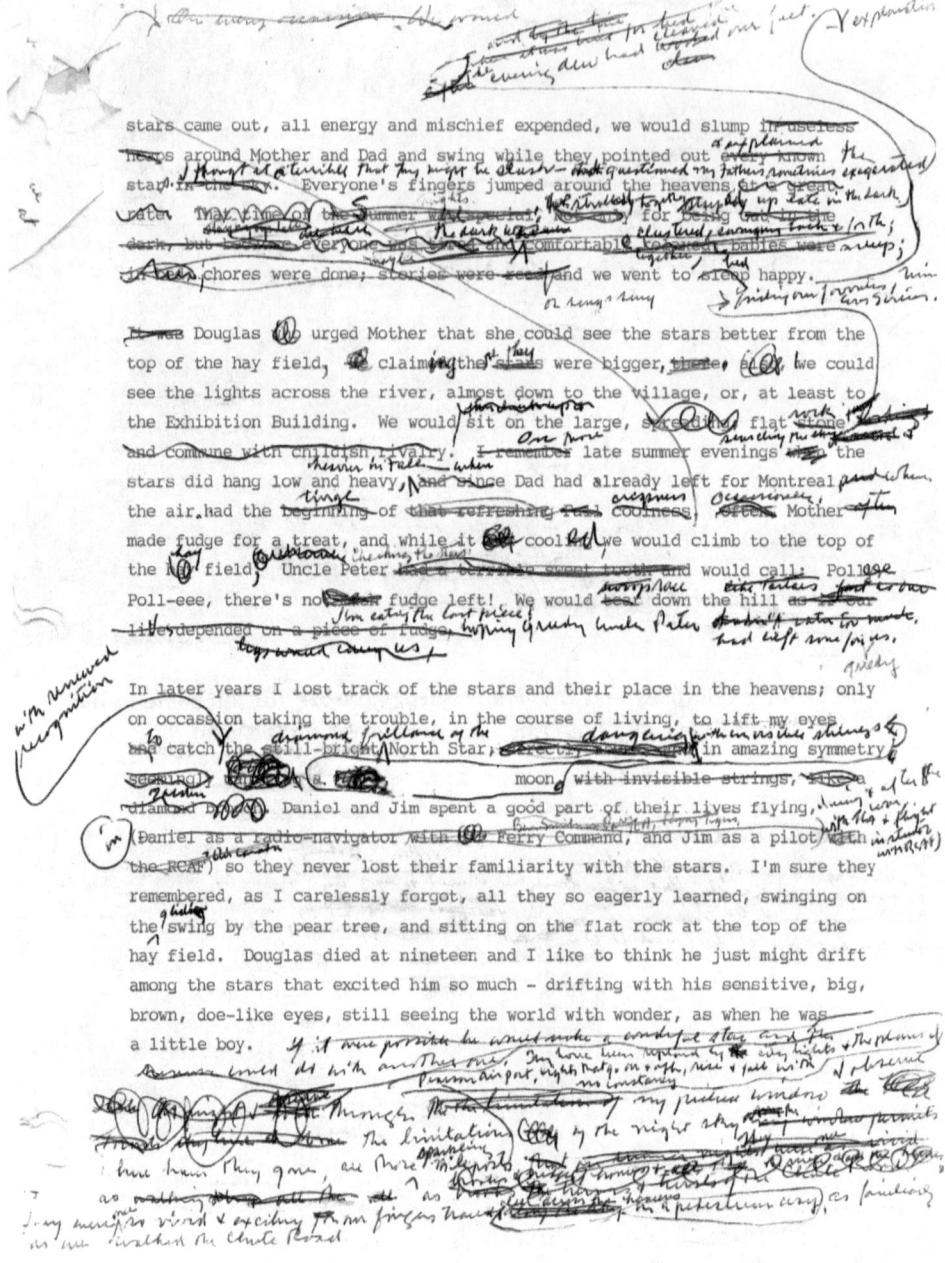

Most of *A Far Away Place* was hand-written, but perhaps half of *Bear River* was typed out and almost in a finished state (above). Many stories were written several times. I think Mr. Bishop was done six times. Some stories were written just once. Many pages were densely-packed scribble; to the right is one of the easier-to-read pages.

A span of many, many years has not completely dulled in me the ghost-like memory of Mother, then so young, confronted by all the chores demanded of a farm, and which, in effect, made me a proxy-mother to my siblings which established a life-long resentment of me. I faintly hear her admonishings to watch the baby and not let anyone near the stove. She was alone then and Uncle Peter had not arrived from Scotland, so I was three years old. Sometimes Daniel would go with her to help feed Harry & meticulously measure his oats, not too much or he would get frisky. I would look out the window and see Mother carrying buckets of water, buckets of slops for the pigs reconstituted with mash, and returning on the swirling snow with a bucket of milk. The milk would stand on the sink counter strained in cheese cloth, then until the cream rose to the top to be skimmed and put in the butter churn, a strange contraption standing on legs with a handle like a buggy which was pushed up & down to shake the butter out of the milk. Later on a milk separator simplified the skimming process in a matter of seconds, just as long as it took to pour the milk into the separator and see it stream and swirl into a large bowl-like receptacle, then go in the obvious ice directing it had to stand on a chair to satisfy my curiosity about the milking was done first thing in the morning, and the animals had to be nourished as carefully as children, the cows with hay, and Harry with hay & grain & oats. Then let to pasture (as per the weather). Stalls were shovelled clean of manure and heaved through the trap door to the manure pile, at the side of the barn, shovelled every spring & fall to nourish gardens. The manure pile, steaming away, was like an outdoor heating system for the cows' stalls. It seemed to steam away like an ugly brown slimy volcano. Inside the barn, the heat of the animals generated their odors. Harry almost purring contently as Daniel waited for Mother to finishing milking he munched. While Daniel waited for Mother to finishing milking he groomed his own took pride himself combing Harry's mane & tail more than he groomed his own. In the evening the animals were put to bed as we were. The cows were milked again, they for bed into stalls. The chickens got the same treatment. I once ran over to the chicken house (a euphemism if one considers the habitat and personal habits of those ornery birds) and there I found Mother sitting on the board clucking in front of the long row of nests with outraged chickens milling about & she was crying. A row of the chickens were clucking too. I asked her why she was crying & she said she didn't know what to do with all these eggs. I suggested we eat them and Mother laughed through her tears, but it was necessary to have the trouble of chickens for Sunday dinners. They had their heads chopped off.

Lori's portrait by Thelma Rock-Tipping

For Lori, who waited and waited.

Lori Greenbaum, my ex-wife and long-time best friend. Almost from their first meeting in 1980, Lori was encouraging my mother to write while the rest of us were encouraging her to cook. Shortly afterwards, Lori's quick thinking saved Mary; I saw it happen. From that point on, Lori, who was adopted, latched on to her 'other mother.' After Mary's death, Lori followed all three books every page of the way, offering moral and material support and never once doubting *A Far Away Place*. Lori was buried at Mount Hope in August, 2012.

John McLeod

Many thanks to:

The Bear River Historical Society. Joan Smith (Chair) and the ladies at the Historical Society were very helpful in making sure I had all the information and photos I needed. When in Bear River, you can visit the museum in the old Oakdene school. The Society is run by volunteers and is not on the best of financial grounds, so they do welcome donations, which are tax deductible. The Bear River Historical Society, Box 182, Bear River, Nova Scotia, B0F-1B0

Nova Scotia Archives and Records Management for their excellent resources online and in Halifax, for the generous use of their photographs, and to the staff who were so helpful.

The University of Toronto for the use of Robarts Library, and all the staff at Media Commons.

Sheryl Stanton and the efficient ladies who volunteer at the Admiral Digby Museum in Digby. Again, donations are tax deductible. www.admuseum.ns.ca

Uncle Jim. 50 missions without a scratch.

Bob Benson, of the shipbuilding Bensons. The Bear River runs through Bob's veins. He is a wonderful source of local history, photographs and Maritime hospitality.

Bear River residents: Zoe Onysko, Teresa Henshaw, Myrtle Selig, Father Adrian Potter, and Clarke Fraser, for their photographs and their help in other ways.

Donald Fullerton of the Helensburgh Heritage Trust, who took an immediate interest in the book and has been very helpful with every request.

Daniel's children: Douglas, David, John (and Susan) Marvin, who supplied me with photographs and continuous encouragement. All of them noted by Mary as being so much more polite than the McLeod children.

Douglas Marvin, Lucy Gabinet and Serge Suzin for proofreading.

Books on Bear River:

Heritage Remembered
E. Foster Hall, Bear River New Horizons Centre
ISBN-10: 096910460X ISBN-13: 9780969104605, 171 pages
A nicely written, well-illustrated history of Bear River to the 1920s.

Water Under the Bridge: Bear River, Nova Scotia, 1920-1980
Bear River Historical Society, Community Books
ISBN1896496288, 9781896496283, 230 pages
Anecdotes, newspaper clippings, photos and more.

Time and Tide: The Transformation of Bear River, Nova Scotia
Stephen J. Hornsby, Maine Folklife Center
ISBN 2009ISBN0943197236, 9780943197234, 79 pages
An interesting economic study of Bear River, from shipbuilding to the aftermath of the pulp mill. With many photos.

Oakdene Memories 1895-1993
100 pages approx.
In a wide variety of anecdotes, students and teachers recall Oakdene.

Echoes from the Past: Memories 1930 to 1950
Myrtle Selig, 100 pages approx.
Myrtle Selig is Billy and Janet McCormick's granddaughter, and in the 30s, she lived on the farm with them. A charming collection of childhood memories.
The Lynching of Peter Wheeler
Dr. Debra Komar (Publication in 2014)
A reexamination of the Annie Kempton murder, promising some startling results.
Also:
Nova Scotia historian Mike Parker is a Bear River native and often writes about the village in his entertaining and beautifully illustrated series of books.

Louis Comeau is the pre-eminent Kentville historian, and his book, *Images of our Past, Historic Kentville*, previews the setting for *A Far Away Place, Kentville*.

In Kentville, Mary's favorite bookstore was Chisholm's. They are still at the same location on Webster Street and they carry most of the above.

www.ingramcontent.com/pod-product-compliance
Lightning Source LLC
Chambersburg PA
CBHW031747220426
43662CB00007B/307